A Sci-Fi Swarm
and Horror Horde

OTHER WORKS BY TOM WEAVER AND FROM McFARLAND

The Creature Chronicles (2014; paperback 2018)

Universal Horrors, 2d ed. (2007; paperback 2017)

Universal Terrors, 1951–1955 (2017)

I Talked with a Zombie (2009; paperback 2014)

Earth vs. the Sci-Fi Filmmakers (2005; paperback 2014)

They Fought in the Creature Features (1995; paperback 2014)

Attack of the Monster Movie Makers (1994; paperback 2014)

I Was a Monster Movie Maker (2001; paperback 2011)

Science Fiction Confidential (2002; paperback 2010)

John Carradine (1999; paperback 2008)

Eye on Science Fiction (2003; paperback 2007)

Science Fiction Stars and Horror Heroes (1991; paperback 2006)

Interviews with B Science Fiction and Horror Movie Makers: (1988; paperback 2006)

Science Fiction and Fantasy Film Flashbacks (1998; paperback 2004)

It Came from Horrorwood (1996; paperback 2004)

Poverty Row HORRORS! (1993; paperback 1999)

Universal Horrors (and Michael Brunas and John Brunas; 2d ed., 2007)

A Sci-Fi Swarm and Horror Horde

Interviews with 62 Filmmakers

Tom Weaver

McFarland & Company, Inc., Publishers
Jefferson, North Carolina

The present work is a reprint of the illustrated case bound edition of A Sci-Fi Swarm and Horror Horde: Interviews with 62 Filmmakers, *first published in 2010 by McFarland.*

Library of Congress Cataloguing-in-Publication Data

A sci-fi swarm and horror horde : interviews
with 62 filmmakers / Tom Weaver.
p.   cm.
Includes index.

ISBN 978-1-4766-7828-3
softcover : acid free paper ∞

1. Science fiction films—United States—History and criticism. 2. Horror films—United States—History and criticism. 3. Science fiction television programs—United States—History and criticism. 4. Horror television programs—United States—History and criticism. 5. Motion picture producers and directors—Interviews. 6. Television producers and directors—Interviews. 7. Motion picture actors and actresses—United States—Interviews. I. Weaver, Tom, 1958–
PN1995.9.S26S267   2019   791.43'615—dc22   2009053833

British Library cataloguing data are available

© 2010 Tom Weaver. All rights reserved

No part of this book may be reproduced or transmitted in any form or by any means, electronic or mechanical, including photocopying or recording, or by any information storage and retrieval system, without permission in writing from the publisher.

On the cover: Bigger IS better. The atomically-enlarged ants in *Them!* (1954) are only part of the parade of monsters in this plus-sized smorgasbord of interviews with members of the Greatest Generations of fright filmmakers (Warner Bros./Photofest).

Printed in the United States of America

McFarland & Company, Inc., Publishers
Box 611, Jefferson, North Carolina 28640
www.mcfarlandpub.com

Table of Contents

Acknowledgments viii
Preface 1

1. Jimmy Lydon on Robert Armstrong 5
2. Joanne Fulton on John P. Fulton 15
3. Memories of Serials
   House Peters, Jr., on *Flash Gordon* (1936) 33
   Frankie Thomas on *Tim Tyler's Luck* (1937) 38
4. Jean Porter on *One Million B.C.* (1940) 44
5. Memories of Boris Karloff
   Jo Ann Sayers on *The Man with Nine Lives* (1940) 50
   Herbert Rudley on *On Borrowed Time* (1946) 54
   Tommy Ivo on *On Borrowed Time* (1946) 58
   Henry Corden on *The Secret Life of Walter Mitty* (1947) and *The Black Castle* (1952) . . . 63
   Fintan Meyler on *Thriller*'s "Well of Doom" (1961) 66
6. Michael A. Hoey on Dennis Hoey 70
7. Memories of Bela Lugosi
   Earl Bellamy on *The Return of the Vampire* (1943) 86
   Alex Gordon on *Bela Lugosi Meets a Brooklyn Gorilla* (1952) 88
   Herman Cohen on *Bela Lugosi Meets a Brooklyn Gorilla* (1952) . . . 92
8. Memories of Lon Chaney, Jr.
   Karolyn Grimes on *Albuquerque* (1948) 98
   Mickey Knox on *Of Mice and Men* (1948) 100
   Irving Brecher on *The Life of Riley* (1949) 102
   Barbara Knudson on *Born Yesterday* (1950) 103
9. Richard Kline on Sam Katzman 108
10. Sid Melton on *Lost Continent* (1951) 118
11. Memories of *Five* (1951)
    William Phipps 123
    Arthur L. Swerdloff 131
12. Marilyn Nash on *Unknown World* (1951) 136
13. Diana Gemora on *The War of the Worlds* (1953) 140
14. Fess Parker on *Them!* (1954) 148
15. Rosemarie Bowe on *The Golden Mistress* (1954) 152

16. Memories of Bel-Air Productions
    Paul Wurtzel 159
    John G. Stephens 172
17. Pamela Duncan on *The Undead* (1957) and *Attack of
    the Crab Monsters* (1957) 178
18. Marsha Hunt on *Back from the Dead* (1957) 184
19. Herbert L. Strock on *Blood of Dracula* (1957) 189
20. Peggy Webber on *The Screaming Skull* (1958) 191
21. Lisa Davis on *Queen of Outer Space* (1958) 196
22. Troy Donahue on *Monster on the Campus* (1958) 209
23. Nan Peterson on *The Hideous Sun Demon* (1959) 212
24. Richard Erdman on *Face of Fire* (1959) 222
25. The Calvin Beck–"Norman Bates" Connection 226
26. Roger Corman on *House of Usher* (1960) 235
27. Alan Young on Jack P. Pierce 240
28. David Whorf on *Thriller*'s "Pigeons from Hell" (1961) 243
29. Alex Gordon on *The Underwater City* (1962) 248
30. Arch Hall, Jr., on Ray Dennis Steckler 259
31. Arnold Drake on *50,000 B.C. (Before Clothing)* (1963) 264
32. Tony Randall on *7 Faces of Dr. Lao* (1964) 268
33. Frederick E. Smith on *Devil Doll* (1964) 272
34. Memories of *Tickle Me* (1965)
    Edward Bernds 276
    Merry Anders 278
35. Ib Melchior on *Lost in Space* (1965–1968) and *Lost in Space* (1998) 282
36. Memories of *The Wild Wild West* (1965–1969)
    Whitey Hughes 290
    Richard Kiel 307
    Kenneth Chase 314
37. Burt Topper on *Space Monster* (1965) 318
38. Peter Marshall on Edgar G. Ulmer 325
39. Tom Reese on *Murderers' Row* (1966) 331
40. Richard Gordon on Protelco Productions 335
41. Nick Webster on *Mission Mars* (1968) 347
42. Gary Conway on *Land of the Giants* (1968–1970) 350
43. Memories of *Nightmare in Wax* (1969)
    John "Bud" Cardos 366
    Martin Varno 369

44. Jan Merlin on *The Twilight People* (1973) 373
45. Robert Pine on *Empire of the Ants* (1977) 382
46. Ken Kolb on *Sinbad Goes to Mars* 386

Index 395

Acknowledgments

Abridged versions of the interviews featured in this book originally appeared in the following magazines:

Calvin T. Beck and Psycho: "Norman, Is That You?," *Monsters from the Vault* #8, 1999

Earl Bellamy: "I Remember Bela!," *VideoScope* #44, Fall 2002

Rosemarie Bowe: "Rosemarie Bowe and the Making of *The Golden Mistress*," *Classic Images* #406, April 2009

Irving Brecher: "The Life of Lon," *Cult Movies* #39, 2003

John "Bud" Cardos: "*Wax*ing Eloquent: John 'Bud' Cardos & Martin Varno on *Nightmare in Wax*," *VideoScope* #69, Winter 2009

Kenneth Chase: "Kenneth Chase on *Wild Wild West*," *Western Clippings* #85, September-October 2008

Herman Cohen: "Bela in Hell!," *VideoScope* #38, Spring 2001

Gary Conway: "Small Pleasures," *Starlog* #359, October 2007

Henry Corden: "Glad to Be Bad," *Starlog* #286, May 2001

Roger Corman: "*Usher*ed Into History," *Fangoria* website, January 11, 2006

Lisa Davis: "Sweetheart of Space, " *Starlog* #364, April 2008

Arnold Drake: "Arnold Drake (Reluctantly) Remembers *50,000 B.C.* (Before Clothing)," *VideoScope* #47, Summer 2003

Pamela Duncan: "Pamela Duncan," *Chiller Theatre* #13, 2000

Richard Erdman: "Richard Erdman on *Face of Fire*," *VideoScope* #64, Fall 2007

Joanne Fulton: "Special Effects Wizard John P. Fulton," *Monsters from the Vault* #24, 2008

Diana Gemora: "How to Make a Martian," *Starlog* #315, October 2003

Alex Gordon on *Bela Lugosi Meets a Brooklyn Gorilla*: "Alex Gordon on *Bela Lugosi Meets a Brooklyn Gorilla*," *Classic Images* #316, October 2001

Alex Gordon on *The Underwater City*: "Exploring *The Underwater City*," *Chiller Theatre* #19, 2003

Richard Gordon: "They Came from Protelco!," *Video Watchdog* #139, May 2008

Karolyn Grimes: "Karolyn Grimes Remembers Lon Chaney," *Monsters from the Vault* #14, Spring 2002

Arch Hall, Jr.: "RIP Ray Dennis Steckler," *Fangoria* website, January 9, 2009

Michael Hoey: "Dennis Hoey—A Son's Remembrance," *Films of the Golden Age* #45, 2006

Whitey Hughes: "Stunt Brothers," *Classic Images* #386, August 2007

Marsha Hunt: "Marsha Hunt on *Back from the Dead*," *Chiller Theatre* #18, 2003

Tommy Ivo: "*On Borrowed Time*—Herbert Rudley and Tommy Ivo on Working With Boris Karloff," *Classic Images* #329, November 2002

Richard Kiel: "Voltaire Talks," *Starlog* #353, March 2007

Richard Kline: "Katz-Mania," *Films of the Golden Age* #51, Winter 2007-08

Barbara Knudson: "Lon Chaney Goes Albu-quirky!," *Monsters from the Vault* #21, 2006

Ken Kolb: "The Lost Voyage of Sinbad," *Starlog* #362, January 2008

Jimmy Lydon: "Thrills of a Lifetime," *Starlog* #344, April 2006

Peter Marshall: "The Tortuous Tale of Edgar G. Ulmer's Final Film ... *The Cavern*," *Films of the Golden Age* #49, Summer 2007

Ib Melchior: "Justice ... Lost in Space?," *Monsters from the Vault* #20, 2005

Sid Melton: "Sid Melton Remembers the Making of *Lost Continent*," *Classic Images* #325, July 2002

Jan Merlin: "The Thrill of the Hunt," *Chiller Theatre* #20, 2004

Fintan Meyler: "The Life & Career of a Karloff Co-Star: Fintan Meyler," *Cult Movies* #35, 2001

Marilyn Nash: "Beauty at the Earth's Core," *Chiller Theatre* #20, 2004

Fess Parker: "King of the Wild Frontier," *Starlog* #321, April 2004

House Peters, Jr.: "*Flash Gordon*'s House Peters, Jr.—Last of the Shark Men," *VideoScope* #41, Winter 2002

Nan Peterson: "Beauty and the Sun Demon," *Monsters from the Vault* #13, 2001

William Phipps: "William Phipps: Surviving *Five*," *VideoScope* #68, Fall 2008, and "Four Remember *Five*," *Screem* #18, 2009

Robert Pine: "Acting With Ants," *Starlog* #285, April 2001

Jean Porter: "The Girl from *One Million B.C.*," *Starlog* #296, March 2002

Tony Randall: "The 7 Faces of Tony Randall," *Starlog* #325, August 2004

Herbert Rudley: "*On Borrowed Time*—Herbert Rudley and Tommy Ivo on Working With Boris Karloff," *Classic Images* #329, November 2002

Jo Ann Sayers: "Interview With a Karloff Co-Star: Jo Ann Sayers," *Cult Movies* #38, 2003

John G. Stephens: "Unearthing the *Pharaoh's Curse*," *Screem* #17, 2008

Herbert L. Strock: "Revisiting *Blood of Dracula* with Herbert L. Strock," *Monsters from the Vault* #21, 2006

Arthur Swerdloff: "Five Made *Five*," *Starlog* #290, September 2001

Frankie Thomas: "Frankie Thomas and *Tim Tyler's Luck*," *Films of the Golden Age* #41, Summer 2005

Burt Topper: "*Space Monster*," *Monster Bash* #9, 2009

Martin Varno: "*Wax*ing Eloquent: John 'Bud' Cardos & Martin Varno on *Nightmare in Wax*," *VideoScope* #69, Winter 2009

Peggy Webber: "Peggy Webber Talks About *The Screaming Skull*," *Chiller Theatre* #14, 2001

David Whorf: "David Whorf on *Thriller*'s 'Pigeons from Hell,'" *VideoScope* #68, Fall 2008

Paul Wurtzel: "The Black Prince of Bel-Air," *Fangoria* #269, January 2008

Alan Young: "Alan Young Remembers Jack P. Pierce," *Monsters from the Vault* #14, Spring 2002

Preface

It seems like only 20 years ago (when actually it was 21) that McFarland published my first book, *Interviews with B Science Fiction and Horror Movie Makers: Writers, Producers, Directors, Actors, Moguls and Makeup*. I remember thinking at the time that there were almost as many words on the cover as inside—this was my introduction to McFarland titles—but tickled pink that all of my chats with B- and Z-movie folks were actually between hard covers, even if they too were pink. This was in the long-ago era when many genre magazine and book publishers didn't give a fiddler's curse about oldtime monster movie-makers with less "name recognition" than, for example, the Ray Harryhausens and George Pals of the field; interviews with the likes of Reginald LeBorg, Gloria Talbott, John Ashley and Richard E. Cunha were wanted about as much as Custer wanted more Indians. I liked the idea of being one of the few trying to change that situation, and so with the help of Dave Everitt and Tony Timpone at *Fangoria* magazine, and then with McFarland's, I began getting into print my interviews with forgotten-but-not-gone filmmakers who were less "important" but no less interesting. In fact, often far *more* interesting. Soon my interviews were also appearing in *Starlog* (its editor Dave McDonnell became a de' Medici–like patron!), and then *Video Watchdog*, *VideoScope*, *Chiller Theatre*, *Monsters from the Vault*, *Cult Movies* and others. It's been a sometimes bumpy ride but, apart from the transcribing, I wouldn't change a minute of it, except the transcribing. Oh, and also all the transcribing.

For this book, I wanted something different—but above and beyond the "*Duh!*" notion of including *more* interviews, I didn't know what. Then, like the gym class nerd who wondered why the baseball kept getting bigger, it hit me.

Backstory: Circa 2000 I located Darlene Tompkins, the female lead in *Beyond the Time Barrier* (1960), and phoned to ask if she'd consent to a telephone interview. Charming Darlene hemmed and hawed a bit, wondered aloud whether she had enough anecdotes to make an interview interesting, and then asked if I'd write out my questions and mail them to her in advance, so that she could give them some thought. That's what I did, and when I called to do the interview, she had my letter in hand. In response to the first question, she told a story; then, looking ahead to the second question, she segued into *that*; and then into the third, and on and on. After about ten minutes, it occurred to me that, except for an occasional "uh-huh" or "Really?," I hadn't spoken once since she began. I had the feeling I could put down the receiver, quickly raid the fridge, perhaps even let the dog out, then come back and find her still talking; no previous interview had ever been *that* easy. When I transcribed the tape, it was one long monologue; then, because Q&A was the style I'd been using from the get-go of my interviewing "career," here and there I inserted questions and various comments I actually hadn't vocally made. But afterwards it occurred to me, "With her help, I could have fine-tuned the monologue a little, and presented it to a magazine as *an article by Darlene*, with 'As Told to Tom Weaver' slipped into the byline in small print. That might have been kinda cool...."

Like Jack Griffin's monocane, the idea seemed to light up my brain, and after a while I decided that from that point on, whenever I landed a real self-starter of a talker, I'd transcribe it as the monologue it practically was, deleting my questions. None of the magazine editors seemed to mind; in fact, I'd bet that some were quite happy to be running articles "by" people like Arch Hall, Jr., Richard Kiel, etc., even *with* that pesky "As Told to Tom Weaver" codicil inelegantly dangling from their bylines. So *that's* what sets this book apart: It's a collection of all my "As Told to" interviews, which read like a series of articles written by the moviemakers themselves.

Some of the interviews are rather brief—how long could, for instance, Troy Donahue be *expected* to be able to talk about his supporting role in *Monster on the Campus*?—but I'd like to think that's a good thing, because instead of the usual 20–25 interviews, this book features over 60. Just scratching the surface, the topics range from *One Million B.C.* to 1930s serials to *The Wild Wild West*, to a '60s sci-fi skinflick and a 1970s Filipino horror, and even an *unmade* movie (*Sinbad Goes to Mars*).

Another way in which this book is different: A few of the interviewees are people who worked with genre legends in non-genre productions (or never worked with them at *all*). I'm banking on readers having an interest in (say) Lon Chaney, Jr., beyond his monster movies, and being willing to read about Chaney Jr. the stage actor in productions of *Of Mice and Men* and *Born Yesterday*; an interest in how director Edgar G. Ulmer fared on his final feature, the war drama *The Cavern*; what it was like to have Robert (*King Kong*) Armstrong as a lifelong friend, and to have Dennis Hoey (the Sherlock Holmes' series Inspector Lestrade) or special effects legend John P. Fulton as a father.

Also dropped into this kitchen sink of reminiscences are a few interviews written in editorial style: Pamela Duncan, Nan Peterson, Roger Corman, Ib J. Melchior and Ken Kolb, plus a special article on the secret inspiration for the character of Norman Bates in the Robert Bloch novel *Psycho*. I'll never write enough interviews in editorial style to fill a book so I figured that, McFarland compilation-wise, it was now-or-never for these six.

I can't abandon my habit of dedicating each new book to interviewees who have recently joined the Invisible Choir; this time the 16 dead-icatees are all interviewed *within* this book: Earl Bellamy, Edward Bernds, Irving Brecher, Herman Cohen, Henry Corden, Troy Donahue, Arnold Drake, Pamela Duncan, Alex Gordon, Whitey Hughes, Fintan Meyler, House Peters, Jr., Tony Randall, Herbert Rudley, Herbert L. Strock, Arthur L. Swerdloff, Frankie Thomas, Burt Topper and Nick Webster. But if I *could* forego that custom, this book would be dedicated to Joe Indusi, not only a longtime pal but also a techno-whiz kid who never met the crashed computer he couldn't un-crash, a damaged photo he couldn't Photoshop back to life, etc. He knows this because I tell it to him all the time, but now I'm telling *you* that I'd be sunk without his help; our computercentric society bores the bleep out of me, I don't know a pixel from a Pixar pixie, and trying to *teach* me is like trying to teach the difference between Tuesday and Thursday to a donkey. But with a Joe Indusi in my "support group," I don't *need* to learn. Hee-haw! Hee-haw!!

Biggum thanks and shout-outs to the Astounding B Monster Marty Baumann (who co-wrote the Pamela Duncan interview), Ron Adams, John Antosiewicz, Rudy Behlmer, Michael F. Blake, Ted Bohus, John and Michael Brunas, Bob Burns, the late Robert Clarke, all the great guys and gals at the Classic Horror Film Board (www.monsterkid.com), Jim Clatterbaugh (*Monsters from the Vault*), John Cocchi, Dave Conover, Joe Dante, the late Michael Fitzgerald, Frank Griffin, Brett Halsey, Richard Heft, Dotti Hughes, Paul Jensen, Joe Kane (*VideoScope*), Sue Kesler, Bob King (*Classic Images* and *Films of the Golden Age*), Robert Kiss, Jim Knusch, Tim Lucas and Donna Lucas (*Video Watchdog*), Scott MacQueen, Boyd Magers, Laurie Marshall, Mark Martucci, Darryl Mayeski (*Screem*), Dave McDonnell (*Starlog*), King of Proofreaders Barry Murphy, the late Tim C. Murphy, Ray Nielsen, Mark Phillips, the Photofest gang, Paul Picerni, Jeanne and Oconee Provost, Fred Rappaport, Alan Rode, Robert Rotter of the incomparable Glamour Girls of the Silver Screen website, Mary Runser, Dan Scapperotti, Rich Scrivani, Tigger, Tony Timpone (*Fangoria*), Jennifer Topper, Laura Wagner, Edric Weaver, the late Jon Weaver, Lucy Chase Williams, Mark Wingfield and Francine York.

1

Jimmy Lydon on Robert Armstrong

In recent years there's been no shortage of literature about the classic horrors of the 1930s, and yet little has been written about the life of the star of the decade's most enduring monster movie ... perhaps its most enduring movie. In the 1933 King Kong, *Robert Armstrong played Carl Denham, the fearless, fast-talking adventurer-filmmaker who leads an expedition to fog-shrouded Skull Island, discovers the mighty ape Kong and, against all odds, brings him back alive. No one now living knew the actor better than Jimmy Lydon, a teenage stage and screen actor when he first met Armstrong in the early 1940s; the two remained close friends right up to (and including) Armstrong's dying day.*

A child actor on Broadway, the New York–raised Lydon came to Hollywood in the late 1930s, appearing as juveniles in films ranging from 1940's Tom Brown's School Days *(Lydon played the title role) to the Henry Aldrich series of B-comedies, with Lydon as the likable, blundering small-town teen. He acted right through the 1980s, including a co-starring berth on the pioneering 1950s SF series* Rocky Jones, Space Ranger, *and has also directed (*Hawaii Five-O, The Six Million Dollar Man, Simon and Simon*), written and produced.*

Robert Armstrong was my semi-adopted father, my adviser, my pal and my mentor. Always gentle and understanding. My rock to lean on in times of trouble and unemployment. I have met and worked with some incredible people in my 82 years (62 as a professional actor, producer, director and writer), and Bob was a giant who towered over all the rest.

I think it was 1941 when I met Bob for the first time. It was at Republic, one of the "B studios" in those days—Bob and I called it Repulsive. I was about 18, and Bob was 33 years older. He at that time was the president of Hollywood's Masquers Club, which was like the Lambs Club in New York—a club for actors with a full theater, a restaurant, bar, pool rooms and card rooms. Bob and I got along fine, and so he asked me to join the Masquers Club, which I did. I was the first young member of the club.

Bob and I also began to play golf together. Another thing we'd do, just to "get out of town," was hop in the car, his or mine, drive up the coast and stop somewhere for lunch. We grew to be such good friends that one time when we were having lunch, I asked, "Bob, you never had any kids, did you?" He said, "No, I never did, Jimmy."

"Well," I said, "*I* never had a father." (My father was a violent alcoholic and a terrible man.) I told Bob, "Since I never had a father ... do you mind if I adopt *you* as my father?" Bob laughed and said, "Sure, it's fine with *me*, kid." And from that time on, he *was* literally my father, a wonderful man to talk to when I had problems. He was a great listener: He wouldn't fill you full of advice or anything, he'd just hear you out and then *gently* advise. It was that kind of a relationship.

Over the years, of course, I got to know a lot about Bob, some of which probably isn't in his bios. Born in Saginaw, Michigan, in 1890, he was originally a stage actor, like most of us were. He played stock in all sorts of places throughout the country, and he was in year-round stock in North Carolina for a while. Finally he made it to New York. Jimmy Gleason, in addition to being an actor in the 1920s, also wrote three or four Broadway plays, and one of them, a play about boxing, was called *Is Zat So?* Jimmy not only wrote it, he directed and produced it; he begged, borrowed and stole enough money to present it on Broadway and it ran for over a year [1925–1926] and was a smash. In it, Jim played a small-time fight promoter and Bob was a pugilist. After its Broadway run, Jim and Bob went to England with it, and it played for a year over there. From that time on, Bob and Jimmy were great buddies, and they talked on the phone almost daily for the rest of Jimmy's life.

Bob started acting in the movies in the silent days, starting with a Pathé picture called *The Main Event* [1927] which was directed by the brilliant William K. Howard. Bob, again playing a pugilist, was just marvelous in it, and that was one of the reasons he got a contract at Pathé, where he transitioned from silents to sound movies. By 1933, Bob was making *$4000 a week* at Pathé—and those were the days before heavy taxes. At that time, taxes were just a little nuisance. Bob lived very well but not ostentatiously. In Coldwater Canyon in Beverly Hills he built an authentic Mexican hacienda which has been featured many times in *Architectural Digest*. It last sold for about two million dollars.

In the early 1930s, RKO came along and absorbed Pathé, and also inherited its contract list, which included Carole Lombard—to whom Bob was once *engaged*, by the way. David O. Selznick, the man in charge of production at RKO-Pathé, would call actors into his office one at a time and tell them, "You're a terrible actor and you're gettin' paid all this money. You oughta be ashamed of yourself." The actors would get mad and say, "All right, I don't want to work for you any more," and rip up the contract—which is what Selznick was hoping they'd do! Selznick didn't have any work for Bob but had to pay him $4000 a week anyway, so Bob knew *his* time was coming very soon.

In *Is Zat So?*, Robert Armstrong punched his way to stardom. The Broadway hit was written by his actor pal James Gleason (left); real-life boxing great Jack Dempsey joins them in this gag shot.

Future screen goddess Carole Lombard not only shared the screen with Armstrong (right) in 1929's *The Racketeer*, she was briefly his real-life fiancée. Shown in the center is Kit Guard.

But before it did, a guy on the lot announced that he was going to make a picture about a 40-foot-tall monkey, and everybody thought he was crazy. That guy was Ernest B. Schoedsack—people called him Monty. Monty Schoedsack was a very tall, thin, gangling, angular man whose wife [Ruth Rose] wrote most of the screenplay of *King Kong*. Monty was wondering how he was going to cast the lead in the picture, because no actor on the lot wanted to fool around with this guy Schoedsack who was crazy about the idea of a movie with a 40-foot monkey. One day Monty was going to lunch, walking across the lot toward the commissary with Selznick, and he said, "I don't know what I'm gonna *do*, David. I can't get a leading man for the picture." Suddenly the light bulb went on over Selznick's head and he saw a way to make money off of Bob until Bob's contract ran out. Selznick said, "Listen, Monty, I could do ya a favor. How would you like Robert Armstrong?" Schoedsack exclaimed [*excitedly*], "Oh my *God*, could we get Armstrong?" and Selznick said, "Yeah, I think I can arrange it...." When Selznick lent Bob to Monty Schoedsack for *King Kong*, Selznick made a bundle on Bob by charging Schoedsack maybe *twice* Bob's regular weekly salary. *King Kong* took months to make, and all that time Selznick was making big money on Bob's contract!

King Kong has been showing *some* place in the world ever since it was first released; it's never been out of circulation for all those years. It eventually became like an albatross around Bob's neck, because Bob made more than 120 features in his lifetime, he was a wonderful, wonderful actor, and he got stuck with being known for just that *one*. I'll say more about that later...

I also knew a lot about Bob's family and his personal life. His uncle Paul was a well-known playwright, and another uncle, Rolf Armstrong, was a very famous artist for Brown & Bigelow Corp. Back then, in every service station in the country, there was a Brown & Bigelow calendar, and all the calendar girls—who weren't naked, but darn *near* it—were done in pastels by Rolf Armstrong. They were very tastefully done, like the Vargas girls in a later era. Rolf also pasteled the portraits of movie stars like Jimmy Cagney and Hank Fonda. I have four of his works.

Rolf, who was only three or four years older than Bob, was married to a woman named Louise. But Rolf was always falling in love with his models. It got to be pretty messy, and finally Rolf went to his wife and said, "Louise, I love you very much, but you shouldn't be married to me. I can't *help* this sort of thing!" So they had a *very* friendly divorce. Meanwhile, Bob, who had been married and divorced a couple of times, was then *un*married, and of course *he* knew his aunt, who was a couple years younger than *Bob* even ... and so he and Louise got together, and they finally married! Louise didn't even have to change the initials on the silver, she married a Rolf Armstrong and then a Robert Armstrong! Every time I ever met Rolf Armstrong, it was at Bob's house. Rolf was a charming, charming rascal and a marvelous artist, and Bob and Louise loved him very much.

There was a group in Hollywood that people called "The Irish Mafia," which was just a fun title—there were no criminals involved! The Irish Mafia was Jimmy Gleason, Jimmy Cagney, Frank McHugh, Pat O'Brien, Spencer Tracy, Allen Jenkins and Bob. Bob was Scottish, not Irish, but he was a Gael and they speak the same language, Erse. Through Bob, I

Armstrong (right) and Gleason were paired in eight movies, among them *Suicide Fleet* (1931) in which they vied for the attention of Coney Island taffy stand owner Ginger Rogers (Photofest).

became a member of that illustrious group of actors—once again, the *youngest* member. They were a great bunch of fellows: As I've already mentioned, Jimmy Gleason, the wonderful character man, was Bob's oldest friend in Hollywood. Frank McHugh was one of the greatest storytellers you've ever heard in your life. Jimmy Cagney was a very quiet member of the group. With *us* he was okay, but he didn't mix with the public or anything like that. Spencer Tracy very rarely ever came to our get-togethers because he was a tortured man—he was an alcoholic, he didn't sleep well and so on. We didn't see too much of him although everybody certainly admired him as a great artist.

Meanwhile, Bob and I were also still occasionally working together. One time when we were starting a film, we walked on the set the first morning and George Blair the director came to us and said, "Fellows, come here, I got trouble." This was a picture we had 12 days to make, so we couldn't afford trouble! He said, "Jim, Bob ... your leading lady just got out of an asylum the day before yesterday. I don't know what's gonna happen." I won't tell you the actress' name even though she's been dead a long time; I'll call her Helen. The very first scene involved Helen and Bob and myself, on a living room set. George said, "Okay, let's rehearse this thing," and we started in on the lines ... and Helen just sat there. She never said a word, she was just staring.

George came to us and said, "Fellas, tell ya what we're gonna do. Helen is going to sit in

The live soap opera *The First Hundred Years* was a career interlude which Lydon laughingly brands "garbage." Left to right in this cast shot are regulars Nana Bryant, Armstrong, Lydon, Olive Stacey, unidentified, Dan Tobin and Valerie Cossart.

that chair and you two are going to stand in front of it, and I want you to play the whole scene. It doesn't look like she's gonna say anything at all, so you just leave me holes for the cutter to put in her closeups for those lines. Whenever you get to one of her lines, just leave me a pause and then go on with the scene as if she *had* said her line." We said fine, and we shot the scene like that. Then after we did the master shot, he got the cameraman to come in closer on her and he told her, "Helen, say so-and-so." She said so-and-so. Then he said, "All right, now say such-and-such." She said such-and-such. In other words, he read her lines to her and she said them back to him, and that's the way we shot the whole picture—which, as it turned out, we *did* finish in 12 days! It was quite an experience.

In 1950, Bob and I went to New York to do the very first daytime TV soap opera that was ever done. It was a CBS soap called *The First Hundred Years*, sponsored by Procter & Gamble, and there were only six of us in the cast—a young husband-and-wife, her mother and father and *his* mother and father. I played the husband and Bob played my wife's father, and we relied on each other tremendously because, at that time, nobody knew if it was even *possible* for actors to memorize and *do* that amount of dialogue on live television every day of the week. In fact, Bob got the part because another actor felt that he could *not* do it: They originally cast as the girl's father Bill Frawley, who you'll remember as Fred Mertz the neighbor on *I Love Lucy*, but he dropped out at the last minute, before we left for New York, because he didn't want to memorize that much stuff every day. That was the point at which Bob came in.

The studio was an old Bund hall on East 58th between Park and Lexington, Liederkranz Hall. There we did 26 pages of garbage every day, Monday through Friday, 52 weeks a year. It was a big, very old building, about three stories high. In the show were three guys and three women; we three guys had one dressing room and they had the other, and those were the only dressing rooms in the whole place! We had one big soundstage, and Frank Sinatra would also come in there to rehearse his live once-a-week TV show. So we'd have to tear down our set every day and move it across town, and then build it back the next morning again! We did 400-and-some-odd shows in a year and a half, late 1950, all of 1951 and half of 1952. It got to be a tremendous strain. Once a month Bob and I went up to the head office at Benton & Bowles, the advertising agency and producer, and announced, "We quit!" They'd laugh at us, "*You* can't quit, read your contract. Now go back and behave yourselves!" And we'd laugh and we'd go back and do some more shows! Working day in and day out on that series was another reason I got to know Bob very, very well, not only as a person and "my father" but as a fellow actor, because in those days, and in a situation like that, we were depending on each other for our *lives*.

In New York, Bob and Louise had an apartment on East 86th Street and I had one on West 74th. I was a bachelor when I got to New York but not when I left. Bob and Louise were at the wedding, and Bob was my best man. I'm still married to Betty Lou 53 years later.

As I mentioned, Bob hated *King Kong* because it became so identified with him. For instance, after we'd finish a *First Hundred Years* we'd go and have a quick lunch somewhere, before going back in to start staging the *next* day's show. We'd be walking down the street together and some other pedestrian would spot Bob and say, "King Kong! King Kong!"—and Bob would growl under his breath, "Oh my God, there it is again...!" Another thing he hated about *King Kong* was the last line in the picture, as Kong was lying in the street in front of the Empire State Building after having been shot *off* of it by the airplanes: "It was Beauty killed the Beast." He told me, "Jim, *no* actor could say that line. I *begged* Monty Schoedsack to change that line, I told him, 'I'll do *any*thing, Monty, but don't make me say that line!'" But Bob finally

King Kong made stars Armstrong (pointing), Bruce Cabot and Fay Wray immortals of the monster movie screen.

had to deliver the line. All his pals, especially the Irish Mafia, used to kid him about that so often. Bob *hated* the notoriety that he got from *King Kong*. He loved Monty Schoedsack and the work on the film and everything else, but he just hated the notoriety of it as *I* hate the Henry Aldrich series, which was the dead bird around *my* neck. I made 10 or 12 features before I became Henry Aldrich and I made 60 or 70 afterwards, but I got stuck in nine Aldrich pictures, and wherever *I'd* go, somebody would say, "Hen-*reee*! *Henry* Aldrich!" And I would want to dive under a table!

Here's a cute story, a "theatrical story," really, about Bob, and what actors are all about. Before Bob and Frank McHugh hit it big, they were starving to death in New York, living in a cold water flat in the Village somewhere. It was costing them $11 a month and they were both broke. The only person they knew who was working was Luis Alberni, a character man.

Luis at that moment was in Detroit, in a play with John Barrymore—and both of them were very great drinkers, by the way, Barrymore and Luis. Since Luis Alberni was the only guy Bob and Frank knew who was working, they went to the nearest Western Union and sent him a collect wire: DESPERATELY NEED FIFTY DOLLARS. BOB AND FRANK. Then they sat there in the Western Union office waiting for two hours, and finally a wire came back with a money order for $100, and all the message said was, THE REST IS FOR VINO. LOVE, LUIS.

Bob made *lots* of money in his lifetime, and Frank did very, very well too. But in the meantime, Luis went on his butt and he was a danger to himself and to society—he was a great ladies' man and he was now in his sixties and he was drunk and carousing all the time. When he was drunk, he was impossible. Bob was paying him $100 a month, *all* the time—and Luis at this point was really a despicable person! I'd say to Bob, "Why do you want to go *on* with this?" and he'd look at me and say, "Jim ... the rest is for vino." That's all he would say on the subject. Eventually we had to put Luis in the Motion Picture Country House, where he'd go chasing the nurses up and down, trying to grab one of 'em. The Country House would throw him out but, since Bob and I had some pull there, we'd get him back *in* again. And every time I would start to object, Bob would say, "The rest is for vino, Jim." 'Til the day he died, Luis got $100 a month from Bob. "The rest is for vino...."

One time Bob and I hopped in the car and headed up the coast for lunch. Bob had a manila envelope with him. Over lunch up near Oxnard, I finally asked, "What's in the envelope, Bob?" He said, "That's for you when I die." He was then about 70, so this would be in the late 1950s or early '60s. I started to object and he said, "Don't be Irish, for God's sake, Jim. Everybody's got to die some time, and when *I* die, this is for you. All the clippings for the press are in there, all about my background, and there's a phone number in there."

"Oh? What's the phone number for?"

"When I die," Bob said, "all you do is open this envelope. Give the press the clippings, and then you dial this number."

"Yeah. And *then* what?"

He said, "Then, when somebody answers, you say, 'Mr. Robert Armstrong has just passed away at such-and-such a time' and you hang up." I realized that what he was saying was that he had arranged for some organization to immediately come pick up his body and dispose of it.

I said, "What?? No funeral, no bunch of the guys gettin' together to lift a glass?" No, no, he said. I asked, "Don't you want *anything*, Bob?"

There was a pause, and then he answered: "Yeah, I do. I want my friends—my *real* friends—and you can count your real friends on the fingers of one hand. I want my *real* friends to remember me kindly once in a while."

It was in the early or mid-60s, I guess, when Bob finally retired from acting. By then, he also had a few health problems. For one thing, he had a bad hip, which frustrated him because he owned a wonderful new white T-bird and he just loved that car, and with the hip giving him trouble, he couldn't get in and out of it any more. It also frustrated him that he could no longer play golf, because he *had* been a fine golfer—a seven or eight handicap most of his life. So Bob just lived very comfortably with Louise in their beautiful home in the Will Rogers Estates in Pacific Palisades area of L.A.—a house I'd helped them find in 1952, when we came back from New York after *The First Hundred Years*. Bob had his lifelong friends always around and I was there at least once a week unless I was working. He was still interested in the goings-on in the business and, since I was now a producer-director, he would query me about how

TV was growing. Yet he wanted no part of it any more. He felt that even if he got eight acting jobs a year (which would be a lot), not one of them would require him to stretch his muscles as an actor, not one would be fulfilling for an actor. They would all be routine roles—and he'd done zillions of those. It would be just a matter of going in and making money. And he didn't need any money, particularly. He wasn't wealthy, but he was certainly not poor.

Bob and I were going to go out for lunch one afternoon in 1973. When I got to his house, I went in and said hello to Louise as Bob was in putting on a jacket or something. Louise said, "Jim, watch him at lunch today, will you? I don't think he's had anything to eat in the last two or three days and I'm worried about him." We went to a place somewhere up the coast, and he ordered the same lunch he always did—bacon and eggs (sunny side up), coffee and wheat toast. And it just sat there. We talked, as always, and he

Lydon was a teenager when he first met Armstrong (seen here in a 1955 photo) and was his friend until the day Armstrong died.

never touched the lunch, but I didn't say anything. Then we paid the check and away we went, back to Louise. When Bob went in to take the jacket off, I said, "You were right, Louise, he didn't have a thing to eat. What are we going to do?" I suggested calling his doctor and asking him to come over, which we did.

The doctor came right to the house and he took Bob in the bedroom and gave him an examination. When the doctor came out, he said, "I can't find anything wrong. But Bob did admit that he's just not hungry, that he doesn't want to eat. Do you think we can talk him into going to the hospital and having an exploratory guy look at him?" Bob came out, and Louise and I both tackled him—I said, "What about it, Bob? Louise is worried about you." Bob said, "Yeah, all right. Don't get excited, okay, fine...." We put him in the St. John's Hospital in Santa Monica that day, and the next day they did an exploratory operation on him. I was there when the doctor came out and said to Louise, "I've just gone through two and a half feet of your husband's colon. There's no stoppage, there's not a thing wrong. I can't find *any*thing wrong with the man. I've put him back together and he's in recovery. He'll be out for four or five hours, so why don't you go home? Maybe see him tonight or tomorrow morning."

I drove Louise home, and when we got to the driveway I could hear the phone inside ringing. I always had a key to their house, just in case, so I rushed and opened the door and answered the phone. The man on the other end of the line said, "Mr. Robert Armstrong has just passed away."

After breaking the news to Louise, I opened up the manila envelope and dialed the number, which connected me with an organization called the Neptune Society. In accordance with Bob's wishes, they came, got the body, took care of the cremation and everything. Bob wanted his ashes scattered somewhere where nobody would have to come and mourn, and the Neptune Society also took care of that. I still to this day don't know where his ashes are.

Incidentally, there was one very odd thing about Bob's final days: From the time he agreed to go to the hospital for more extensive tests, Bob never said another word. The only exception was not long before they did the exploratory operation. Louise and I were in his room when a nurse came in and said, "I'd like to move Mr. Armstrong, I don't want him to get any bedsores. Would you help me, Mr. Lydon?" Bob was a chunky, solid man, so she didn't want to have to do it by herself. I said, "Bob, put your arms around my shoulder. The nurse and I are going to help you turn over." Bob and I got a-hold of each other and I said, "Okay, *go*," and as I turned him, he cried out, "Oh, God *almighty*!"—it must have hurt terribly. Those were the only words he spoke for the rest of his time on this earth; he never spoke again. And they never did find anything wrong with him. Bob was 82 when he died.

Louise lived on for a number of years, and I was her "guardian" because of a promise I had made to Bob years before. The same afternoon that we had lunch in the Oxnard area and he sprang that manila envelope on me, the *other* thing he said to me, which I'll never forget, was, "Oh, and by the way, when I die, you're Louise's guardian." I said, "*What?*," and he repeated, "Yeah. You become Louise's guardian."

"Bob, Louise doesn't need a guardian."

"I know that. Louise knows that. And you know that. But one day she *might*, and you're *it*." I said okay. Well, Louise lived 18 years after Bob, she died when she was 97, and the last two years of her life she really *did* need me as her guardian. How *wise* that man was ... how very, very wise. So he left me his wife in his will!

Oh, Bob was just a wonderful, wonderful man, and I have the greatest respect and the deepest love for him. He really *was* my "father" for all those years. And *my* children also kind of became his surrogate children: Cathy was baptized in 1954 with Bob as her godfather and Julie in 1956 with Louise as her godmother. It was a marvelous experience to know him. I never forgot the wish that he expressed to me: "When I die, I want my *real* friends to remember me kindly once in a while"—and, believe me, I *have* remembered him. Every day of my life.

2

Joanne Fulton on John P. Fulton

In a perfect Monster Kid world there would be a Mount Rushmore dedicated to the men most responsible for the classic Universal Horrors, and one of the 60-foot faces would be that of John P. Fulton, supreme alchemist of movie magic. His special effects were among the highlights of these never-to-be-forgotten thrillers—man-into-wolf transformations, glow-in-the-dark monsters, exploding miniatures, invisible men (and a woman), much more—and yet just a fraction of what he achieved in his long behind-the-camera career.

The ups and downs of his professional and personal life are remembered on the following pages by his daughter Joanne.

Looking back on the life and career of my dad John P. Fulton, one of the most interesting things, and one of the *saddest* things, is that I believe he felt that the only way to really express yourself in film is to be a director. Most of my recollections of my time with Dad, 25 years, are of Dad wanting to be a director. And it was so pathetic, because my dad did not have any empathy for the human condition! My dad could not feel for you. He just didn't have it. And of course, as we all know, that's the thing that directors *have* to have! They have to understand human suffering, how people feel.

Another interesting/sad thing is that Dad felt that directing the special effects of a movie was somehow really low on the scale. I do *not* think this opinion was shared by the other men who were good in that field, Gordon Jennings and others of the time. But to Dad the really important thing was the directing of the movie, and all the stuff *he* did, the effects, were not important. So he kept trying to get into this other area, kept *trying* to be a director, which he wasn't suited for. Here he was, this genius director of special effects, and he just didn't *get it*! I'm sure people like Cecil B. DeMille, the great producer-director, tried to talk to him about it; at some point someone *had* to have said to him, "John, you're one of the best in your line. Why do you want to be a director? You do fabulous things!" And, knowing my dad, I'm sure he just pooh-poohed it.

John Phipps Fulton was born in Beatrice, Nebraska, in 1902. Our ancestor Sarah Phipps came over to America on a ship in the 1600s; the Phipps name was very big in old New England, and I'm eligible for the Daughters of the American Revolution. One of Dad's first jobs after graduating from high school was as a surveyor, I think for the Department of Water and Power. Being quite bright, he found it not very challenging at all—in fact, quite boring. After a year or so, one day when he was working in Hollywood he happened to come upon D.W. Griffith and his crew shooting scenes for some motion picture. Dad wandered over and started talking to some of the different guys about film work, and it sounded very interesting to him. I guess at some point Griffith asked him if he had any training in doing this kind of thing, and of course Dad said no. But Dad liked math and he *could* do stuff like that, and I think it was Griffith who suggested that he go to work for the Frank Williams Studio. At this time, 1924, '25, the Frank Williams Studio was I believe the only show in town, and all the movie companies were using it to do their special effects. Dad went there and became an apprentice, and for the next two, three years learned the trade. Well, he learned *what they knew at the time*—which wasn't a whole lot! I'm sure what they were able to accomplish was pretty rudimentary, because the *pictures* were pretty rudimentary [*laughs*]!

Then, long around 1930, he went to Universal. Carl Laemmle, head of the studio, must have quickly become aware that Dad had some special talent above and beyond the average, so they agreed to set up a department of special photographic effects and make Dad the head of it. The first really major movie that people today remember that he made there was *The Invisible Man* [1933], for which he certainly would have been nominated for an Oscar if special photographic effects men were *getting* Oscars in those days. Which of course they were not. The first Oscars were awarded for the films of 1927–1928, but the first Oscars for my dad's area was in 1939–1940, a dozen years later. The reason for that was, basically, that the studio heads did not want the public to know that they were being fooled. But the American Society of Cinematographers went to bat for the special effects men, and managed to convince the Academy that the work of these men was the reason why certain movies, *The Invisible Man* for example, were so wonderful. It was a long battle, but eventually the Carl Laemmles and Adolph Zukors and Jack Warners were overrode, and finally the first Academy Awards were given to special effects guys. Much to the disgust of the studio heads who did not want the public to know there even *was* such a thing as special effects!

I believe my dad and mom Bernice Brenner knew each other on and off from the time they were kids, because their two families were close. They were married on December 25, Christmas Day, 1926, and lived at first in a couple of rentals—the typical "young couple" thing. Then in 1933, after Dad had been at Universal a couple years, they built a great big home above Sunset Boulevard, on a street called Kings Road. This was during the Depression, needless to say, but Dad was making tons of money—*every*body in the picture business was. My mom and dad were just rolling in money and had *no clue* about the Depression. I think Dad was makin' a thousand a week or something crazy like that, at a time when there were no taxes, so they built this huge Kings Road home, a 17th-century Spanish-style place on the side of the mountain above the Sunset Strip. My mom told me that at that moment in 1933, the depths of the Depression, there were only two houses being built in L.A., ours and someone else's. Builders, framing guys, painters and so on were coming up and *begging* to work on this house, because there just wasn't any work, *period*, for them. Mom said it was really sad, because they desperately wanted to be employed and Dad could only put so-many people to work. The tiles on the roof of this 5500-square-foot house were all handmade on

John Phipps ("Hard Way") Fulton.

the spot, because that was one of the make-work projects Dad came up with to help them out.

When my mother got pregnant with my brother Johnny in 1936, it very quickly became apparent to her that this house was just not going to work out as a place to raise children. Incidentally, I don't think my dad ever really *wanted* to have children ... I really don't. I think it was just "a happening" for him. Because in his "infinite wisdom" he had built a 5500-square-foot home but it had only one bedroom [*laughs*]—don't you love it? So when Johnny was born, the playroom became his room. This playroom was like 30 × 40 feet, it was enormous. Well, *every* room in the house was enormous, as you can imagine.

From that time on, Mom was badgering Dad to move off the mountain but of course Dad, who had just built this gorgeous dream house for himself, wasn't really all that anxious to do that. Then I was born in '39, and now there was no denying that they didn't have enough space—now they had *two* kids in a house with one bedroom.

One day during this time when Mom was always reminding him to be on the lookout for a new house, Dad was playing golf, which he always did on the weekends. Right next to the Lakeside Golf Club was the home of the late Amelia Earhart—who, incidentally, had been a very good friend of Dad's. Back in the days when Lockheed was *nothing*, when it was a Quonset hut and a bunch of oil drums in the middle of an airfield over in Burbank, Dad and Amelia Earhart and Paul Mantz would sit around on the oil drums and chew the rag. Paul, with a little help from Amelia, taught Dad to fly—Dad's California flying license number was 28 or some ridiculously low number like that. My dad's love of flying went way back to his very early days, even before people *were* flying.

Anyway, Amelia built that house in 1937, the same year she attempted an around-the-world flight but vanished somewhere in the Pacific. The books were kept open on her for sev-

The desert airport miniature for Universal's 1932 *Airmail*.

Fulton riding on the front of a Universal truck, with human colleagues; and working with a furry friend as his camera operator.

eral years, but finally she was declared dead and her husband George P. Putnam the publisher put the house on the market. In October 1941, one "FOR SALE" sign was put up in front of the house and another put up in the back, in order to catch the golfers who were walking right by that house all day long. (Right out in Amelia's house's "backyard" were the Lakeside Golf Course's clubhouse and the first tee.) Well, Dad happened to be one of the golfers walking by on the very day the signs went up, and he grabbed it. That's how we came to live there. I lived at 10042 Valley Spring Lane, Toluca Lake, for 23 years, from the time I was two years old 'til I got married and moved at the age of 25.

For Dad, one nice thing about this new house was that Universal was now very close to where he lived. From the back of our house, there was the golf course and then the L.A. River, and on the other side was Universal. I can remember many nights of going to bed at 8, 8:30 when I was a kid and, man, they were going full-tilt on the back lot over at the studio. You could see the lights blazing and you could even *hear* the director on his megaphone, barking out the directions. And they sometimes shot *all* night. In fact, they worked whenever they *had* to. If they needed to shoot something on a Saturday or Sunday, they came in and did it. Nights, weekends—these things meant nothing to them in those days. Dad would go to work at eight, nine o'clock in the morning and he wouldn't come home 'til midnight. The studio moguls did whatever they damn well pleased.

Of course, that was before the big Hollywood union strikes in the mid–1940s. When they started, the horrors began. Dad had a friend who was an artist at Universal, and when he tried to cross the picket line, the union guys put his hand on the curb, pounded it with a hammer and broke every one of his fingers. As young as I was at the time, I still remember the nightmarish tales Dad came home with, that one in particular—it made quite an impression on this little girl. And my dad was reeeally upset about it. My dad didn't display emotion very often, but *that* got to him. It was a very ugly part of Hollywood history, and not much information has gotten out about how vicious it was and how many people were injured.

Deanna Durbin loved riding with Fulton on his Harley. Universal, fearful that one of its biggest stars might be injured, decreed that they could ride on, but never off, the lot.

Another one of my earliest memories is of Dad and Mom talking about his past battles with the Universal front office for more money to do the tricks they wanted him to do. When Carl Laemmle ran the studio, he and Dad were forever fighting, because Laemmle wanted Dad to create miracles—but he didn't want to pay for it! Ongoing battles like those really colored my Dad's *whole view* of the movie business. In the '50s, around the time my brother was

Joanne was once shocked to discover in a store a greeting card with this image of her father and a miniature plane.

graduating from high school, he very badly wanted to be a cinematographer, but Dad boycotted him from the ASC. Dad said, "I do not want my kids to be in the movie business. It's *horrible*." He fixed it so that Johnny couldn't *do* it—and, as you can imagine, *that* caused some problems! But Dad had had too many battles with the higher-ups through the years over the budgets he was given to do his effects. He wasn't free to do his work in that he was *always* shackled by this money thing. Always. Always. Always.

I myself started building miniatures, putting together little funky things, when I was still quite young. I started working out in Dad's garage workshop about as much as he did [*laughs*]! As a result, Dad would take me over to Universal and show me some of the miniatures there. Then, around 1945, when I was about six, Dad left Universal and went to work for Sam Goldwyn, who had promised him his own stage and his own little company *within* the company if he, Dad, would come to work at the Goldwyn studio. One of his first Goldwyn movies was *Wonder Man* [1945] with Danny Kaye, and for that he received an Academy Award nomination. It was his fifth—he'd already been nominated for *The Boys from Syracuse*, *The Invisible Man Returns*, *The Invisible Woman* [all 1940] and *Invisible Agent* [1942]—but he hadn't attended the Oscar ceremonies those years and he didn't go the year of *Wonder Man* either, even though Mom really wanted him to go. He didn't think he stood a chance of winning and was happy to be spending the night in his garage workshop. "John! You'll probably *win*," she said, but he just growled, "Ohhh, no, no, *no*...."

Fulton was M.I.A. on Oscar night 1946 when his *Wonder Man* special effects took the prize. Shortly afterward, he posed for this photo with the movie's star Danny Kaye.

The night of the Oscars [March 7, 1946], I was six years old so I wasn't paying a whole lot of attention, but Mom was in the kitchen, listening to it on the radio, and Dad was in his workshop, completely unmindful of the whole thing. All of a sudden there was Mom running out to the garage saying, "John! *John*! You won the Oscar!" She was so excited, she was just about turned inside-out, but Dad was like, "Oh? Okay ... well ... *that's* nice...." It was ... weird. Most men would have come unglued, but Dad was so casual. My mother could never get over the fact that they didn't attend. In my mind's ear, I can still hear her voice saying [*with amazement*]: "He ... wasn't ... *there*...!"

Dad didn't usually bring his work home, but I recall one time that he did. For the Goldwyn movie *The Best Years of Our Lives* [1946] they needed some footage shot from the nose of a plane. Paul Mantz had a B-25 bomber that he dearly loved and Dad asked if he could use it, and Paul said sure. What Dad did blows my mind: He decided to build a clear plastic nosecone for the B-25—*in his workshop in the garage*. I kid you not! And these were the early days of plastics. To this day, I cannot tell you how he was able to mold, in three or four sections, this total nosecone, but he did it all by himself. I can remember him working on it for a long time, and when it was assembled, the thing was like seven feet across—huge! I went out to the garage the night he was starting to glue together the sections and—it's funny how smells stay with you—the smell of the glue was the worst thing I'd ever experienced in my life [*laughs*]. We even made the comment to each other, "This stuff smells absolutely god-awful!" But the glue held the sections together, and the nosecone was fitted on the front of the B-25 and he went off and shot the footage. You can't fly and photograph at the same time so Dad must have had a cameraman in the nosecone operating the camera and I presume that Dad was doing the flying, because that flight was in his flying log that I recently found.

Dad went on location from time to time, and sometimes my mother, Johnny and I went with him. I remember being in New York with him one whole, horribly hot summer, but I can't remember what he was filming—it might have been *The Secret Life of Walter Mitty* [1947]. I just recall living in a hotel during the summer months while Dad was making *some*thing. I did *not* go with him to Minneapolis when he went there to work on a movie, because that was during the school year, but I know the whole company went to Minneapolis in the winter to shoot some scenes of snow falling, and it never snowed. They had a company sitting there in the dead of winter for seven weeks, and it was *cold*, but there wasn't a single flake!

One set I remember well was the ice skating rink for *The Bishop's Wife* [1947], which in the movie was supposed to be outdoors but was actually built on Dad's Goldwyn soundstage. Johnny and I were both doing a little ice skating at the time, he was ten and I was seven, and I was just utterly fascinated with the set because here was this gorgeous outdoor rink, built *indoors*, with bushes and trees and a bridge across it. Two or three Saturdays in a row, Dad let Johnny and me come over and skate, just for fun. One Saturday a couple of trainers were trying to teach Loretta Young just enough so that she'd be able to skate once or twice around. Well, she was terrified [*laughs*]! The trainers never got more than six inches away from her because they didn't want her to fall and injure herself, because that would delay production and be a disaster. Johnny and I were skating all around, having a good time, and she was lookin' at us with a face that said, "How do they *do* that?"

The first time Dad went to the Academy Awards was when he was nominated for *Tulsa* [1949]; he'd already won for *Wonder Man* so I guess my mother had a little more leverage at that point. *Tulsa* was a story of wildcatting days in oil-rich Oklahoma in the early 1920s, partly shot *in* Tulsa. For that movie, Dad built an entire oil field outside, on the outskirts of Tulsa: oil derricks, buildings, etc., all in $\frac{1}{12}$th scale. When you see it on the screen, you'll think it's the real thing, but the derricks were actually 10 or 12 feet tall, and the buildings were like dollhouses. The oil drums were coffee cans!

Dad's being nominated for *Tulsa* that year created an intra-family problem, because the special effects guys who had done *Mighty Joe Young* [1949], including Grandpa [matte painter Fitch Fulton], were up for an Oscar also. *Mighty Joe Young* was I believe the only movie with my grandfather's name listed in the screen credits and the two pictures were up against each other, *Mighty Joe Young* vs. *Tulsa*, father vs. son. Not good! Apparently RKO loaded on the publicity for *Mighty Joe Young*—in those days, publicity did have some effect. RKO went hog wild publicizing it and making sure Academy members went to see it and all that business, whereas [Eagle-Lion] didn't do much with *Tulsa* in terms of the Academy Awards. *Mighty Joe Young* won and Dad didn't. *Not* a good event in the Fulton family! There was a little bit of a "family thing" over that, but it didn't last long. Well, Dad felt—and I think rightly so—that the trick work in *Tulsa* was much better than in *Mighty Joe Young*.

It was so strange: In 1946 Dad couldn't be bothered to go to the Oscars, he just wasn't interested, but then in 1950 he was put-out about his own father winning. To put it mildly, Dad was an extremely complicated person—I think every man and woman who ever worked with him would tell you that. Charlie Baker, Dad's forever right-hand man, was one of the few who did understand Dad and his genius, and the complicated personality that came with it. But my mother was forever baffled by my father. She was a very simple, down-to-earth lady in terms of lifestyle. She was *smart*—she graduated from UCLA and taught second and third grade for ten years when they were first married—but not in terms of figuring out difficult personalities. And Dad was certainly a difficult personality. My brother and I never really unraveled it either. Although our relationship certainly was children-and-Dad and all that business, I never got really close to the man. Because you really couldn't do that.

When I think of Dad, of having him around the house through the years, I think first of how he loved to read. His favorite magazine was *Scientific American* and I still can picture him sitting in his big chair in the living room, reading his *Scientific American* as soon as it came. As for his other hobbies, I can sum it up in three words: Golf, golf and golf. My dad had a three handicap on Lakeside, one of the toughest courses in L.A., and he won innumerable studio tournaments. That was another "problem" with his personality: He was *extraordinarily* competitive. Before he learned how to play golf, he played tennis—*killer* tennis. And then he played killer golf. My dad never understood the concept that you can go out on a golf course and play for the sheer enjoyment of it, the fun of it, the comradeship of it. Noooo way. And he wasn't out there to make a business deal, like many of the men. My dad went out there to challenge himself and to beat *you* [*laughs*]. Period! Flat out! That's *it*! And he did! After a while it was hard for him to get up a game, because people knew his attitude and they knew what they were in for.

For me as a child—and maybe even for adults, come to think of it [*laughs*]—he wasn't real approachable. I never would, in my wildest nightmare, like sit on his lap and hug him, because he wasn't a warm'n'fuzzy person. I know he loved Johnny and me dearly, and he cared about us dearly, but he didn't know how to show it. I don't think Dad really understood children. It wasn't that he didn't *like* them, I don't think he knew what to *do* with 'em [*laughs*]! Some people can *really* relate to little kids and get right down on their level, but Dad ... no way could he get on the level of a child.

Something else that made things hard for me was the fact that Dad bragged about my accomplishments to anybody and everybody who would listen. But never once did he ever say to *me*, "You did a really good job" or "I'm proud of you." I was a straight-A kid and I don't recall him ever complimenting me on that. I did strive to *get* his approval but it never really happened, and yet people would tell me, "Your dad, my God, he goes on and on about you." Never once to *me*! Same thing with my brother. But, boy, everybody *else* heard about us.

A for-instance: The Christmas [1954] that he was in Egypt working on *The Ten Commandments* [1956], there was a competition in Toluca Lake to see who could make the best outdoor Christmas decoration for their house. I was then only 15, but I decided that for the top of our house I'd make five reindeer and Santa and his sleigh. I cut the different shapes out of plywood, put 'em together, painted 'em, the whole bit, all by myself. Wellll, a neighbor-friend named Ben Richey, a carpenter at Disney, helped me build the sleigh, because at 15 that *was* a little beyond my capabilities. Then I had Ben help me put it on the roof. I had learned a lot from watching Dad, and I did it the same way he did the planes in *The Bridges at Toko-Ri* [1954]: I got some wire that would be hard to see at a distance, wire that had been dulled so that it would not shine, and I rigged it from the chimney of a one-story part of the house up to a two-story part of the house, and I had the five reindeer attached to that wire. When I was done, the full-size sleigh was sitting on the roof and the reindeer looked like they were in flight. Then Ben gave me some big lights that I could clamp onto the gutters and shine at the reindeer and sleigh; they came from the Disney Studios, we kinda borrowed them permanently [*laughs*]. Well, I won first place for best house decoration. By the time Dad came home from Egypt, it was all down and put away, but he heard about it big-time and saw the pictures, and he bragged to everybody. But never once said to me, "Gee, it's really incredible what you did." Never.

He *had* helped me on an earlier project, though. When I was 12 or 13, I was in junior high and we were learning about the Netherlands in history class and, since by this time I was getting pretty good at miniatures, I decided to do a project for extra credit—I was very big on extra credit! I wanted to build a fully working windmill. Dad was like, "Okaaaay...," and he helped me. That was probably the closest time that Dad and I ever had together, because we worked and worked on it. I have to say, he probably built the miniature windmill seen at the end of *Frankenstein* [1931], because when we were building ours, he seemed to know what he was doing [*laughs*]—he kinda knew his way around windmills, that's for sure! In fact, while helping me, he used diagrams from real windmills. Our finished windmill (with the sails) was three and a half or four feet tall, the sides came off and everything inside was authentic; we even made the cement grinder things (which turned) and the whole bit. I put it on a base and made thousands of little tulips out of crepe paper, and put a boy and a girl doll in it. When he put it outside to take pictures of it, the sails of the windmill actually turned when the wind blew. We brought it out onto one of the golf course fairways to take the pictures, with Mount Hollywood behind it. It was beautiful. When the history class teacher saw it, she couldn't believe it. She couldn't get half the class to even write the report on the Netherlands, and then into the class comes this working windmill on a base that was like two by three feet! I can still remember the funny expression on her face! That windmill was on display at the L.A. Library for quite some time, in a case that they built for it. Then, believe it or not, I ended up selling it to the Van de Kamp Bakery Company, who would put it in the window when they opened a new shop.

With that windmill project, Dad had gotten into it and the two of us had worked mightily for a *long* time on it, and I think he enjoyed it. That was one of the first times that he could sort of relate to me and make an attachment with me, and I think for the first time he realized, "Hey, she really *can* do this stuff." So it was a neat time for the both of us, because Dad's best way of relating *to* me was to be doing something that *he* understood and *I* understood and we were workin' together toward a common goal. That really stands out in my mind as the best time I ever had with my dad.

My brother Johnny and I are both fairly artistic and right-brained and math was just horrendous for both of us, so Dad set it upon himself to try to tutor us. He was *such* an incredible mathematician he could just do it all in his head, and I don't think he could believe that he had two kids who were so *awful* at math [*laughs*]! Johnny being older, it was him and Dad first. In those sessions, Johnny wasn't getting it, he struggled and they fought and so on. Then I came along three years later and I didn't do any better! I finally got good grades in math but I really never understood what I was doing, I just finally learned how to get the right answers. It frustrated Dad terribly that we didn't get it, because it was so easy for him. When something is so easy for you, sometimes you just cannot understand why someone else has to struggle with it; it's like, "*What* is your *problem*?" Dad didn't have any patience with kids anyway, so ... it was kinda gruesome! Hard for him, hard for us, hard for *every*body. That's about the only time my dad ever tried to help me with homework!

Dad's boss Sam Goldwyn was a very irascible man and he could change his mind instantly, and Dad had a very hard time with that. Finally Goldwyn pulled the rug out from under Dad by saying, "Oh, our deal's off," and Dad was out of there! Therefore in the early '50s, he didn't have a job. Maybe that was partly because he had a reputation of being very difficult to work with—and he *was*. He was difficult to *live* with! He was a difficult *man*. My dad did not spend any time being Mr. Social Wonderful [*laughs*], he was *not* good at that. When he was working, he was working, and there was *no* funny business, *no* being Mr. Nice Guy. It was just, "Get the work done!" His nickname was "Hard Way" and that was because Dad wanted to do it *right*, and very often, the right way is the hard way. And sometimes the expensive way. That was his ongoing battle from the time I can remember.

Dad was also nothing if not a proud man, which is another story. During the time when he was out of work, Dad had a chance to perhaps work for Otto Preminger, who was planning to do a movie in Hawaii. Preminger asked Dad to come to Hawaii and talk with him about the job. Well, Dad flew to Hawaii and he expected to go out and interview with Preminger—and Otto Preminger being the "sweetheart" that he was [*laughs*], he made

Fulton with wife Bernice in October 1953.

Dad sit around for maybe two days, without even contacting him. Preminger just ignored him, had him sit there. Dad was so good in his field—he should sit tight for days and wait days for the Great Mr. Preminger to deign to see him, to have an audience with him? I mean, Otto Preminger was an asshole on a *good* day [*laughs*]. Dad had too much pride for that. He flew home and said, "To *hell* with him," and that was the end of *that* deal!

One dramatic day [January 11] in 1953, when I was 13, I was out in the backyard when I suddenly heard the sirens of an ambulance and a fire truck. I hurried into the house and I said, "Mom, somebody's been hurt on the golf course!" and then I went running out towards where everything was happening. Of course the thought that crossed my mind was that it might be Dad. There at the fourteenth or fifteenth hole, all of the gawkers were being kept back, you couldn't get real close, but still I could see that the fellow on the ground to whom they were giving CPR (or whatever passed for CPR in those days) was not Dad; Dad was nowhere to be seen. I did not know who the man was, but I watched as they tried unsuccessfully to revive him and as he died and as they took the body away. Turned out the man was Gordon Jennings, the head of the Paramount special effects department. He'd died right out in our backyard, practically, and I *saw* it happen.

So here was Paramount with no Gordon Jennings, and pretty soon Dad, who was still out of work, got a call from them. They were up a creek because they had movies to finish effects-wise, and *The Ten Commandments* was looming on the horizon. Dad went to work there, and one of his first big jobs was the World War II movie *The Bridges at Toko-Ri*. Jennings had started it but I don't think that he had gotten very far. So now Dad was trying to do work for *both* movies, *Toko-Ri* and *The Ten Commandments*. First he had no job, and now he had *too much* job [*laughs*]!

They got *The Bridges at Toko-Ri* done in pretty much jig time, I recall. I was still fascinated with miniatures, so when they began building the set up in Mint Canyon, slightly northeast of L.A., I must have gone out there ten times, including the day they were sculpturing the quote-unquote gorge in which they were going to put the massive bridges. The bridges were eight feet tall and, being 14 years old and skinny as a rail, I could turn sideways and *just* get through between the concrete support pillars. Also there at Mint Canyon were the little houses, etc., of Toko-Ri, all 1/12th scale. They'd built 'em at the studio and then they brought them out to Mint Canyon and proceeded to fit them in the landscaping. Charlie Baker knew that I was "into" miniatures, so he let me help a little bit with the landscaping. The railroad was O scale, and I was really interested in watching them build it around and through the miniature Toko-Ri.

Then, getting *that* put to bed, they launched into *The Ten Commandments big*-time. Mr. DeMille had already been working on it for about a year at this point; the whole deal took about two and a half years, and there was a hard deadline because Paramount had already scheduled the theaters. Because so much of the shooting was done over in Egypt, Dad was there for six months, from September of 1954 to February of '55 or something like that. They used the Egyptian army—re-costumed, of course [*laughs*]! Dad said they also had at least 5000 animals. I have slides that Dad took of what was going on, and there were camels, geese, chickens, ducks, lambs, you name it. *And*, said Dad, there were like 3000 extras. They hired entire Egyptian families to show up and get into costume every day. ... and every day they all went home with the costumes on their backs. Then they came back the next day in twentieth century clothes and the costume people would ask 'em, "Where are your costumes?" The extras would say [*she spews out something incomprehensible to represent an Egyptian-language answer*], and the costume people would have to re-costume them. The extras were collecting the costumes! Over and over again, Paramount had to re-costume thousands of people! It was incredible.

According to Dad, Mr. DeMille at this point was really having some serious heart problems. He'd already had a couple of heart attacks at home, and nobody was really sure if this man was going to survive the making of *The Ten Commandments*. In the movie there was a big wall, 50 feet tall and, I dunno, 100 feet long. Because Mr. DeMille wanted to look at the camera angles and so on, he insisted on climbing up a ladder to get up on the top to look out and see what was going on. Well, nobody thought it was a good idea for him to do that, and it was *hot*, but before they'd know it, he'd be halfway up the ladder. Well, he had two heart attacks, *up on top*. They had to keep pulling him down after his little heart attacks, all the time! It was very, very dicey.

Getting *The Ten Commandments* done on time got to be such a problem, Mr. DeMille was getting so frantic to get this movie in the can, that on December 31, 1955, New Year's Eve, Charlton Heston and Dad and a handful of crew members were called away from their celebrations to film, at the studio, the famous scene where Heston is up on the rock and he says, "Behold!" and spreads his arms. So there they were on New Year's Eve, 'til God knows what time (late!), with Heston standing on a crate in the middle of this set, with a blue screen behind him, and with huge fans blowing on him. That was just one of *countless* times that things like this happened on that crazy movie!

Mr. DeMille, probably more than any other higher-up in the movie business, understood Dad *perfectly*. Implicitly. A very wise and canny man, he knew "how to play" my dad! And one of the things he learned very quickly about Dad was, you get the best work from him if you're not all over him about the budget. Mr. DeMille kept all of that crap away from Dad and let him be the creative person that he was. *The Ten Commandments* was the result. It was nominated for seven Academy Awards [Best Picture, Cinematography, Art Direction, Editing, Costumes, Sound, Special Effects], and Dad was the only one who won. Now, you have to keep in mind that I was just a teenager and not paying a *whole* lot of attention at this point to the politics of Hollywood, but I remember Dad or Mom or *some*body saying that for some reason Hollywood had turned against DeMille and they were going to punish him. I don't have a clue why, nobody was going to explain all this to some teenage kid, but I was told that Hollywood wanted to punish him and they *did*. But they did give Dad the Special Effects Academy Award; there was no competition [except MGM's *Forbidden Planet*], so they *had* to do it. They really wanted to completely shut DeMille out Oscar-wise, and they did except for Dad's. Hollywood can be very cruel when it wants to be. *The Ten Commandments* was the last movie he directed. It wasn't very long after that DeMille had a massive heart attack and died.

Mr. DeMille kept all of his storyboards at his home on Copa de Oro in Beverly Hills. In 1961, when I was a registered nurse at UCLA, there was a horrible Beverly Hills fire. We all went up to the hospital roof and we could see the fire swoosh down the crest of the ridge where DeMille had lived, and where I presume Mrs. DeMille *still* lived, and wipe out everything. It burned the house to the ground and all of the storyboards were lost. *But*, as a gift, DeMille had given Dad the storyboard of the opening of the Red Sea, the one where Moses is standing on the rock and the Israelites are coming along. It's now hanging in my family room and I suppose it's quite a treasure since not a lot of others exist because the rest were there in DeMille's house, being "carefully protected" [*laughs*]. It's a good thing Mr. DeMille was already dead when that happened, 'cause it probably would have killed him anyway!*

---

*Tragic irony: On Friday June 13, 2008, nearly all of John P. Fulton's surviving photos, scrapbooks, slides, etc. (including all of this chapter's illustrations), were destroyed when her Joanne's Butte Valley home burned to the ground in the Humboldt Fire. "It is way beyond devastating to lose everything you love, I can't even begin to describe it to anyone," she e-mailed me. "My husband Ralph and I have decided that we are survivors and need to get on with what's left of our lives."

Right to left, Fulton, Joanne, Bernice and John Fulton, Jr., at Hollywood's RKO Pantages Theatre during one of their regular treks to the Oscar ceremonies.

Now Dad had *three* Academy Awards, for *Wonder Man*, *The Bridges at Toko-Ri* and *The Ten Commandments*, and still he longed to be a director. It was a sort of a theme throughout his life, and he didn't understand himself that he didn't have what it takes, so to speak. What Dad wanted to direct, however, were not pictures that involved a lot of human feelings. There *was* a movie he wanted to make, and he had a script for it, and it just sort of sat there and burned in his soul for many years. It was a script about Paricutin, a big volcano in Mexico that erupted in the 1940s and wiped out two nearby villages. Dad wanted to make a movie called *Paricutin* about this tragedy and what resulted with the villagers; of course, it would have involved a huge amount of special effects. Dad kept trying to push this with the studio guys, trying to sell them on it so that he could become a director. I remember *hours* of him talking to Mom about *Paricutin* and how he wanted to do it because he could be a director and blah blah blah. And she would say to him—this was back in the good years, before things started falling apart in their relationship—she would say to him, "John, you're the best at what you do. *Why* do you want to do that? There's only a handful of men who can do what you do." He never *got* it. And he died without ever realizing his dream. If he had any tragedy to his life, *that* would be it, that he never got to be a director. As I mentioned earlier, directors have to understand how people feel, and Dad could not do that. Not for my mom, not for Johnny, not for me, not for anybody. He just didn't have that particular aspect of the personality. And I think that people in the movie business *knew* that. You only had to work with the man once to realize that he did not have a lot of empathy for people!

Although my brother Johnny had the same problems that I did with Dad (the unapproachability), I have to say this: When Johnny was grown and married and had a couple little kids, Dad did spend quite a bit of time with him at his home. Dad enjoyed, once in a while, going over there and staying with them, and I think he and Johnny finally *had* a relationship. I unfortunately did not get that opportunity because by this time there were a lot of problems between Dad and Mom, and since I was close to Mom and aligned myself with Mom, Dad sort of threw me in the same pot with her and didn't want much to do with *both* of us.

Dad felt freer to be with Johnny—because Johnny was having a few problems with Mom, too! My mom was a very rigid person. She, in her own way, had a really difficult personality. The two of them, Mom and Dad ... it was kind of a sad thing, because I think each one of them *married to someone else* would have had a much happier life. There was not anything terribly wrong with either one of 'em, they just didn't belong *together* [*laughs*]. They just should not have been married *to each other*, they each needed someone different. My mother would have been the *absolute* perfect wife of a cattleman or rancher or farmer, because the way my mother showed love and care and attention was how she *fed* you. We had wonderful breakfasts. I never saw cereal growing up; we had bacon and eggs, or waffles, or pancakes, or French toast, or whatever. And right after breakfast, she'd already be busily planning the dinner menu. Her love poured out through her food. Well, the problem with that was that my dad, *forever*, was watching his weight. He was 6' 2" and had a fabulous figure for his age, and he never wanted to put a pound on. So of course here my mother would put out these meals and my dad would sit there and pick, and eat very little of it. He didn't mean it this way, but to my mother, that was like a criticism. She was showing that she loved him by preparing these wonderful meals, and he, always trying to stay thin, wasn't very accepting of it. If he had eaten everything that my mother fixed, he would have weighed 300 pounds *easy* [*laughs*]!

When it finally just all collapsed, it was neither one of their faults. So my brother did have Dad there at his home quite a bit, and in the years since Johnny has said, "That was the first time I really knew Dad." Dad softened in terms of family, he started loosening up, and a little bit of himself started coming out, and they had a relationship that they'd never had before.

Fulton with his Academy Award statuettes.

After he left Paramount in 1963, Dad was out of a job again. So he got together with Pinewood Studios in London and he worked there for the last years of his life. By this time he'd divorced my mom and he was now remarried and living in a suburb of London, Iver Heath, with the woman he had been seeing for ... *many* years. Dad had met Gladys some time in the mid-1940s, in the dining room of the Papillon Hotel in Mexico City when he went down there to check on the deLee Company, a ceramic company that he had invested in. [See Joanne's 1997 book *deLee Art: The Pictorial Story of a California Artist and Her Company*.] Gladys, as I understand it, was a very "international"-type woman who had been married a couple of times and had lived all over the world. I never met her but I was told by my Auntie Bernice, Dad's sister, that on some level Gladys seemed to really understand Dad and knew how to handle him.

Dad was making some movie on the outskirts of Madrid when he got what they thought was the flu and became quite ill. (Dad was a highly allergic person and had a lot of nasal problems and what have you, and he came down with colds very easily.) They took him to a hospital, hopefully the best one they had in Madrid, God only knows, and they gave him chloromycetin. At that time, the mid-60s, Europe thought chloromycetin was going to be the cure for everything up to and including ... world hunger [*laughs*]! But what it *is*, is a very dangerous antibiotic, and if you have an allergic nature, it gives you aplastic anemia. That's what it did to my dad. It gave him full-blown aplastic anemia and from that time until the day he died, about a year and a half later, he never made another red blood cell.

Once the doctors found out they'd screwed up big-time by giving him concentrated chloromycetin for several days, Gladys had him flown to a very fine clinic in London, one of the best hematology clinics in the world. That's when they diagnosed it as aplastic anemia, and in those days there was absolutely nothing they could do for it. At this time, I was newly wed and we were a struggling young couple that didn't have a lot of money, so hopping on a plane to go to London just wasn't in the financial cards. And Johnny didn't go for a similar reason—he had a new baby. In the hospital, they gave Dad concentrated blood transfusions to keep his blood level up, but he never really got any better. Nowadays there would be a possibility my brother or I might have been a bone marrow match for him, but they weren't doing that in 1965–1966 and aplastic anemia was 100 percent fatal in those days. They kept giving him transfusions, and he was able to work in between transfusions. After a transfusion, he'd get better and he could work for a while, but because he wasn't producing any red blood cells of his own, he would soon go downhill and have to go back into the hospital and get *another* transfusion that would help him to be okay for a while. This went on until he couldn't take any more transfusions—his body couldn't handle one more foreign thing. He'd finally become allergic to *all* blood after getting blood from so many different people, and they couldn't give him any more blood because his allergic reaction would have been fatal anyway. At that point he became extremely ill and, on July 1, 1966, at age 63, he died of aplastic anemia—and all that from chloromycetin. In Madrid he'd probably had a virus and an antibiotic wasn't going to do him any good. But they gave him one, chloromycetin, and here's what they caused. Nowadays, as a result of Dad and *many* others dying of aplastic anemia caused by chloromycetin, they use it very little, almost never. It's so very dangerous.

There was a memorial in England, but I couldn't afford to go over there for it. I think his new wife Gladys didn't quite know what to do about all of this; they'd only been married two years. And of course my mom was not having anything to do with it. So my Auntie Bernice, his sister, took charge and made all the arrangements. Gladys had him cremated in London and then she brought his ashes to Auntie Bernice in Santa Barbara. The urn is in a mausoleum there in Montecito; I just visited this weekend.

Since 1974 I've belonged to an organization called NAME, which is the National Association of Miniature Enthusiasts, for all of us who are crazy enough to be building small things [*laughs*]. They had a convention coming up, and somebody who was involved knew that I had this background and asked me to do a program on miniatures in the movies. Well, I knew that I had two albums of things Dad had done—neat pictures of some of his work. (The only reason there are albums is because Mom put 'em together; Dad wasn't interested whatsoever in saving *any*thing.) With slide film I photographed those pictures; and then I remembered that somewhere in our vast slide collection there were pictures that Dad had taken in Egypt while doing *The Ten Commandments*, and also slides of doing *Tulsa*. I pulled together all the stuff and ended up with a nice 45-minute program I call "Movie Magic." I first did it at that miniature convention, and now it's a very popular show. I've presented it maybe ten times to various groups, and *men* love it. The Rotary, SIRs [Seniors in Retirement], the Masons, Native Sons of the Golden West, all these places call and ask me if I will give the program for 'em. My *big* splash, they're still talkin' about it, was three or four years ago at the United Federation of Doll Clubs national convention. They never had talks on anything except dolls until I came along with my miniature program, and the men who were there just flocked to it 'cause finally it was something that didn't involve *dolls* [*laughs*]! That was a biggie—I had like 500 people at that one!

In closing, I have to stress that, back in the days when I was a youth, being a dad was different than it is nowadays. Most of the fathers on my street were entertainment industry people and titans of business. They were very busy men and had little time to devote to their children. But they did share one "fathering" concept: Their idea of being a good husband and

Forty years married in 2005, Joanne and W. Ralph Schaefer celebrated their "ruby anniversary" with family at Disneyland's Napa Rose Restaurant.

father was to earn good money with hard work, and provide their family with a lovely home, nice clothes, good food, medical attention, entertainment and, for their children, toys. The idea that you should actually spend *time* with your family was not really big in the equation. None of these men understood children.

I know without question that I grew up in a very privileged, well-to-do world where there were fascinating people in my life; there were interesting things to do; and everything was possible. This wonderful "storybook" childhood was provided by my parents who, in their own way, dearly loved my brother and me. My mom always provided whatever tools and supplies I needed to carry out my grand building schemes and I am very grateful for that. She thought my talents were amazing and never hesitated to tell me so. My dad would have been proud of my continuing work with miniatures, and I have no doubt that he would have sung my praises to everyone. Well [*laughs*], everyone but me!

3

Memories of Serials

House Peters, Jr., on *Flash Gordon* (1936)

With news of the growing shark population and shark attacks so often prevalent in the media, it only makes sense (stretching the definition of the word "sense" here) to turn our attention to one of the few actors ever to play a Shark Man: House Peters, Jr., a member of the cast of Flash Gordon. *In that science fiction adventure serial, teenager Peters was seen as one of the swimsuited minions of King Kala (Duke York) of the Shark Men, sharing the screen with Flash (Buster Crabbe) in scenes set on land, water and in the air.*

The son of House Peters, a stage actor turned early silent film star, Peters, Jr., made his screen debut a year earlier (1935) and went on to forge a long co-starring career in low-budget Westerns and serials (and small parts in A-pictures). Peters wrote of life with his famous father and his own movie and TV days in his 2000 autobiography Another Side of Hollywood.

My first serial was Universal's *The Adventures of Frank Merriwell* [1936], and here's how I landed that job: One morning while looking over the trade papers, I came across an article mentioning that Universal was looking to cast the children of famous Hollywood personalities as featured players in an upcoming serial [*Frank Merriwell*]. I immediately phoned my agent Jack Pomeroy and informed him as to what I'd read. A day or so later, he called to say he couldn't get anywhere with Universal's casting office. However, he did come up with a bit of encouraging news: He'd heard the studio had tried to get Tyrone Power, Jr., for one of the roles, but that Power's agent had turned them down. So I decided to take matters into my own hands.

I knew that Henry MacRae was going to produce the serial, and since he had been the production manager on many of the projects my father did at Universal in 1925 and 1926, I decided to drop in on him. Going over to the main gate, I had the intention of walking through, but the guard on duty had other ideas. Despite my persuasiveness and name-dropping, he refused to let me pass inside. Having worked at Universal only a few months earlier in *Yellowstone* [1936], I was aware that MacRae's office was situated on the back lot. What I did next would be impossible today due to the hi-tech security system undoubtedly now in place there: I drove to the east side of Cahuenga Boulevard and came upon a small dirt road near a hill on the side of the studio. I parked my car, got out and started walking. The hill was the only thing separating me from the studio's back lot, and the chain link fence there posed no problem. The whole thing only took a few minutes. Once I was on the lot, nobody bothered me. I strolled up to MacRae's office, walked in and introduced myself as the son of House Peters. Mr. MacRae was pleased that I dropped in to see him. After some small talk about my father, I asked about a part in *Merriwell*, and he gave me the role of the hero's adversary. They used my real name, House Peters, Jr., as the name of the character.

MacRae produced quite a number of serials at Universal, and *Flash Gordon* was the most famous. I played one of the Shark Men. I wore a leather thing around my waist; the hair was shaved off my chest and legs; and a skullcap was put on over my hair. (I still had a pretty good head of hair in those days but it was receding badly in the front.) The rest of me was covered with body makeup, which in those days was greasepaint. Makeup consumed, oh, an hour in the morning, if not longer, and then I was ready to play a Shark Man.

We worked long hours on the serials—there was no union in the early days. Sometimes we quit at 11 o'clock at night, or at *midnight* for that matter, and get a six o'clock or seven o'clock A.M. call. All the [serial] directors that I worked for, they were well-liked by the producers because they could bring the pictures in on budget and on time, and that meant a lot to the producers.

I got to know Buster Crabbe real well. He was an extremely nice guy but rather quiet, a guy who kept to himself quite a bit. I remember that he hated his hair being dyed [blond] like it had to be for the show! When he'd go to the commissary, he'd wear his hat—he didn't like the color of his hair, he thought it made him look unnatural. I also got to know Jean Rogers [Dale Arden]. Duke York was in it, too [as King Kala of the Shark Men]; he unfortunately later committed suicide. And Charles Middleton, who played Ming. Middleton was a Broadway actor, and pretty damn good at what he did back there. He came out here and played Ming and he did a terrific job. Very few people could play Ming.

One funny incident: Henry MacRae's car was a '34 Ford, and it was a beauty—black, suicide doors on it. Wish I had it today, it'd be worth quite a bit! But the very first day I drove it onto the Universal lot, there was a heavy wind that blew over a flat, and the flat landed on the roof of the car! MacRae was the first to notice what had happened and, forgetting I guess that he was no longer the owner, he came over to us and began shouting, "Who the hell parked my car where a flat could fall on it?!" I told him that it was now *my* car, that I'd bought it after he traded it in, but he didn't give a damn about that, he said that I should be taking better care of it.

Well, a little later on, when he was still upset at me about the damn flat landing on his car, we were working on a spaceship set. I was at the controls of the spaceship, and Buster and Jean were standing alongside of me. And guess who had all the dialogue! Well, I just had a terrible time. Hell, I went into, oh, I don't know, 28 takes or something, and that's *forbidden* when you do a serial. Twenty-eight takes is just too many, the budget won't stand it. Well, MacRae was directing that day. He was a very dapper sort of a person, stickpin with a diamond on his tie and all that—and he always wore a hat. To hide the fact that he was bald, he did with his hair what I think General Douglas MacArthur did when *he* started to lose *his* hair: He would let it grow long on one side and then he would comb that long hair up over the top. Well, this particular scene, he was really frustrated over *me* and my dialogue and he took his hat off and hit his knee with it. But when he put his hat back on, the hair had flopped down over his ear, almost to his shoulder! He was completely unaware how silly he looked. The set got very quiet as Buster and Jean and I—*everybody*—stared at poor Henry! MacRae's sister, and I've forgotten what her name was, bless her heart, she was the script girl, *she* finally noticed what had happened. She reached over, kind of nudged him a little bit—here he was with his hair hanging out of the side of his hat—and he told her to mind her own damn business and be quiet! We were *all* watching this! She finally got his attention and whispered in his ear, and very gingerly he got up and walked off the set, and when he came back, his hair was back in place under the hat [*laughs*]! [*You mention that MacRae was directing that day. But the director listed in the screen credits is Frederick Stephani.*] I'll be honest with you, I don't recall him too well.

Flash Gordon soared at the kiddie matinee box office, which was a good thing for Universal since its production costs had soared as well (a reported $350,000).

The reason I went 28 takes that day was that, as usual, they changed dialogue just before we went into that scene: "We gotta change this because it doesn't fit" and so on. So often you'd come onto a set all prepared for your scenes, and then somebody would say, "Hey, House, we got a little *change* here...." And you just had to wing it, that's all, because if you couldn't, you'd never come back [you wouldn't be re-hired]. In those days, they wouldn't put up with fluffing your lines *too* much, so you were always under that tension. For me, I think it was a throwback to my grammar school days when I was always the last one out of class because I took the longest memorizing a poem, or some bloody thing. From my seat by the window, I'd watch the kids outside, see them playing baseball or football out there. Memorizing was *not* easy for me, I could *not* wing a script like Broderick Crawford could, for instance. When I was doing [the TV series] *Highway Patrol*, Crawford would come in and—sometimes it kind of griped me—he'd say, "What are the *jokes* today?" That was his way of asking, "What are the lines today?" He'd get the script and start flipping through it: "What are we gonna do? Oh, page 27? Yeah ... let's see ... oh, yeah ... hmmm ... okay, let's shoot it." [*Laughs*] Then he'd do the scene—but he'd never give you the right cue! You were always on edge, 'cause he never gave you the right cue!

Buster Crabbe and I, and several stuntmen, have an underwater fight scene in *Flash Gordon*. We shot that in a big old steel tank that had been constructed years earlier on the Universal back lot. It was probably 11 or 12 feet deep and it held thousands of gallons of water. Up on the top was a platform for the big floodlights that they aimed down at the water. The tank was round and it had four big windows for the cameras outside to film in through. But, I'll never forget, one of the windows was cracked, and somebody had reinforced it with carpet-covered planks that were propped up against it with two-by-fours and one four-by-four. So they just used the other three windows. The glass in those damn windows had to be about an inch thick, or thicker.

Peters in 1948. In addition to *Flash Gordon*, other serial assignments included *Adventures of Frank and Jesse James* (1948), *Batman and Robin* and *King of the Rocket Men* (both 1949).

We'd fight underwater, at the window level, down at the bottom of the tank. I didn't have a stuntman help *me* at all, hell, no, I had to do my own. Buster and I, *we* had to fight because we had closeups. But I was pretty agile at 19 years of age, I knew how to swim and all that. We could fight underwater for 20 seconds, 30 seconds, and that was about it. They'd be outside filming in through the window. And, oh, that water was cold—it was colder than heck. In fact, I remember there was snow on the ground outside. It was the first time in a *long* time that you saw snow in San Fernando Valley. Man, when we got out of there, what with the wind and the snow from the night before, it was cold. Between takes we would get out and put blankets around ourselves, and the prop men *really* looked after us—blankets and hot coffee and so forth. I was so blue, one guy brought a glass and he said, "Here. Drink this, House. It'll help ya." It was straight whiskey. It's the only time I really drank straight whiskey on a set.

The punchline, not to extend this *too* long: The next morning, I come on the set and Buster's there, and he gets up out of his chair and he says, "Come with me, House." We get in his station wagon and I notice that there seems to be more water on the ground as we proceed across the back lot—mud and so forth. We come down to where the tank is and get out of the car, and he takes me over and he says, "Take a look at *that*. Take a look at where we worked yesterday." Well, the shored-up window had blown out, and thousands of gallons of water had flowed all over the lot. And there were thick, jagged shards of glass still in the window frame. Buster said, "Can you imagine if we'd have been on the bottom—if *any* of the boys had been on the bottom—when this happened?" We'd have been cut to ribbons. Buster and I drove back to the set rather mute, thinking about it!

When I did *Flash Gordon*, I was on a stock contract of, I think, 75 bucks a week, something like that. Which was a lot of money in those days for a young fella. [*Was your dad glad to see you getting into the business?*] At that time, my dad and I were no longer speaking. One day I walked out of our house, 148 Lapeer, and that was the end of it for ten years. I never spoke to him, I never saw him—well, I take that back, I did see my dad one day walking up above Flintridge. But, no, I got absolutely no help [from him] whatsoever.

I didn't go to the movies to see myself in serials, because we saw the dailies. Which we shouldn't have. That's a thing you really shouldn't do, you shouldn't watch the dailies. But we did, the young people there—all of us did. At the end of the day, we'd see yesterday's rushes. But when you see yourself in rushes, then you start correcting yourself. It's rather a bad thing to do, especially when you're young. [*As you were beginning your movie career, and getting jobs in one serial after another—did you think that was the right "first step"?*] Not particularly. But because of some difficulties that I had getting started, I went that route.

Years later, after the war, I was

A great late-in-life shot of Peters and wife Lucy. When the 92-year-old actor died in 2008, obits played up his 1950s–1960s TV commercial stint as Mr. Clean, the egg-bald grime buster with the hoop earring; "Mr. Clean has gone to the big utility closet in the sky," quipped the *New York Daily News*.

also in some Sam Katzman and Republic serials. Katzman was a character. He was always on the set, smoking a cigar—he was a great one for visiting and sitting around the set and chewing the fat. And he had a walking stick with an electric battery in it, and he got a great kick out of using that on people, especially girls. He would approach them with it and jab their knee or their leg in the back! And, needless to say, he was a producer who worked on slim budgets. One time when my agent Jack Pomeroy was in Katzman's office trying to get me $75 a day for a role rather than the $55 that Sam was offering. I was standing outside the office door smoking my pipe and overhearing everything that was going on. Katzman would not budge, he insisted he didn't have any more. Then he picked up the phone and dialed his bookie and put a thousand dollars on a horse! And he couldn't afford giving *me* a lousy $20 raise?!

I'm preparing right now to move into the Motion Picture Home. The time has come, I'm 85, for goodness sake! (I hope I don't *sound* like it!) My wife Lucy is 80, and my concern is for her too. Sure, we have children and grandchildren and so forth, but after all, they've got their own lives to lead. We paid into it and, really, we'll be so lucky to live in such a wonderful place. There is no actor, nobody connected prominently with the motion picture business, who should end up in a hovel of a hotel somewhere with nothing but old newspaper clippings. It is just ridiculous, because [the industry is] loaded! We went up there last week to look over the premises. We're going to have a double cottage with a nice patio and a work shed and you name it. You're looked after entirely. We're looking forward to going to the Home.

[*Whose idea was it for you to write your autobiography?*] It was the fans, and also people who were in the industry. One night, I'm at a friend's house in Sherman Oaks, a fellow who played on *Matlock*, did 40 *Matlock*s as the judge. Richard Newton. He gives me a glass of wine, and then I had a second glass [*laughs*], and I start telling a story. A story of my life, in a sort of haphazard way, for about an hour. When I get through, he says, "My God, House. You had another *Sunset Blvd.*, except there's no murder involved." He was very sincere about it. Then, from time to time, when I went to the festivals, the fans would say, "When are you gonna write a book? When are you gonna write a book?"

I'll be honest with you, I'm glad I did it, but when you come right down to it, I really never should have, because I wasn't big enough in the business. But I wrote a book that is clean and that is honest—I'm not too kind to my*self* in places. I think I wrote a good book, *Another Side of Hollywood*.

Frankie Thomas on *Tim Tyler's Luck* (1937)

Talk about a recipe for a successful Saturday matinee serial: Darkest Africa, lions, gorillas, a panther, an elephant, quicksand, an ivory-poaching villain named Spider Webb, a futuristic-looking armored tank—and, perhaps best of all, a hero not much older than the kids in the audience! In 1937, all these ingredients were whipped up together as the 12-chapter Tim Tyler's Luck *with Frankie Thomas as Tim, a resourceful lad who arrives on the Dark Continent in search of his missing scientist-father and finds himself on the adventure of a lifetime. Thomas was only in his mid-teens during production, but nevertheless a seasoned pro; the son of actors Frank M. Thomas and Mona Bruns, he had already made his mark on the New York stage and starred in two Hollywood features, RKO's* Wednesday's Child *[1934] and* A Dog of Flanders *[1935]. (Amazingly, more than a dozen years after* Tim Tyler's Luck*, the then-thirtyish Thomas would begin playing another juvenile hero: the title character in network TV's first-ever outer space series,* Tom Corbett, Space Cadet.*)*

3. Memories of Serials

In this interview, Thomas (1921–2006) enthusiastically reminisces about his one stab at serial stardom and his real-life exploits in Universal's back lot and soundstage jungles.

Henry MacRae was the producer of the serials at Universal—as a matter of fact, he was practically the king of the serials at that time. He did *Flash Gordon* [1936] with Buster Crabbe and a bunch of others. When MacRae was looking around for an actor to play Tim Tyler, my agent heard about it and went to Universal *with*, of all things, a print of *Wednesday's Child*. Now, the character I played in *Wednesday's Child* is about as far away from *Tim Tyler* as you could get! But MacRae, very conscientious, looked at the film and he said, "Well, of course, physically Frankie's not the type for the part at all, but then again he's grown since then. Anybody that can act like *that* can do Tim Tyler"—at any rate, that's what I heard somebody say that he had said. I never had any problems, never had to go out to Universal to talk to anybody, that was *it*. Off we went!

[*Did the idea of being in an action picture with horses, animals, etc., appeal to you?*] Oh, yes! My early childhood had been on a farm—my father and grandfather owned a farm in New Jersey, about five miles outside of Summit. We had 3000 white leghorn chickens. We also had nine horses on the place, and I was riding when I was knee-high to a grasshopper. As a matter of fact, my father was brought up in St. Joe, Missouri, and in the mornings he would ride a horse down the street of St. Joe with saddlebags on both sides full of newspapers. He'd be riding bareback, and he'd pull out the newspapers and throw them at each house where they were supposed to go. So if he could do *that*, I guess he could teach me how to ride! On the farm, they had a Shetland pony for me. So *Tim Tyler's Luck* was right up my alley.

I drove to Universal every morning—I was 15 or 16 by then. At that time, my parents and I were living in California. For a while we had been going back and forth between New York and California—we would do a picture [in Hollywood] and then go back and do a play back in the East. Things were very good then. Then around ... let's say '36 ... we moved our permanent headquarters to the [West] Coast. We kept the farm, but we were based out here. Our house was on Addison Street out in the Toluca Lake area. It doesn't exist any more, the freeway came along and wiped it out.

Anna the elephant [Tim's elephant in the serial] was the love affair of my life. I don't know why, but for some reason she took a liking to me. This was my introduction to Anna: I was lying on a jungle trail, having supposedly been grazed by a native spear, and I was "unconscious," and she was to come on the scene and pick me up with her trunk and put me up on her shoulder. Elephants are very quiet so I didn't hear her coming ... but the earth seemed to be moving as this elephant approached! I said to myself, "My God, if one of those great big feet of hers comes down on me, there won't be anything *left*!" I arched my back so that she could reach under me with her trunk ... I felt this thing coming underneath me, a tapered trunk which was fairly small ... and I thought, "Jeez, she can't lift me with *that*." But, no, it was like riding an elevator—up I went!

Anna had a few little tricks. I'd be talking to somebody, and all of a sudden I'd feel that trunk around me, and Anna would lift me up onto her head and she would walk away from whoever I'd been talking to. Because, you see, she was *jealous* [*laughs*].

The monkey was a different matter. I have a couple of pictures of me with the monkey [Tim Tyler's "sidekick" Ju Ju], and in the pictures it looks like the monkey is laughing—all his teeth are bared. But that was not the case: They bare their teeth when they're *mad*. They did

Tim Tyler's Luck-y if he doesn't get chomped: Thomas pretends to enjoy the company of the belligerent monkey that kept trying to bite him throughout production.

the sequences on the riverboat and surroundings first, and for the first two days of shooting I was not *in* the stuff. During that period, they needed a shot of the monkey in a cage, and they wanted the monkey to look mad and shake the bars. So they got a-hold of the chap who was doubling for me, a guy who had my costume on, and *he* started wrestling with the monkey's trainer, who was a woman. That made the monkey *very* mad. And after that, why, the monkey thought I was the fellow who grabbed and wrestled with his trainer. There are a *lot* of shots of me walking, holding the monkey by the paw. Well, every time, he wanted to bite my wrist. So we put an Ace bandage on my left wrist—my costumes were long-sleeved so the bandage was concealed. Fortunately, an Ace bandage is pretty durable; the monkey kept biting away and biting away and getting nowhere. Then after a few weeks of biting the wrist and nothing happening, he realized he was wasting his time, and the next thing I knew, there were a couple of monkey hands around my throat! They pulled him off, quickly, but he left some gashes on the back of my neck. We had a property man who had been around, and he grabbed a bottle of Absorbine Junior and poured it on these open wounds. It burned—I thought I would go up in smoke [*laughs*]! But thank God he did it, because monkeys are pretty dirty, and I'm sure what he did helped prevent infection. The next day, my neck was swollen up quite a bit, and I bet it would have been worse if the property man hadn't put that Absorbine Junior on there. And ... so much for the monkey! From then on, we did not walk down the jungle path holding hands!

We had another thing happen that I won't forget: The horses were on a tethering line, standing there waiting to get into a shot, and Anna the elephant moved around so that the wind was at her back. When those horses smelled her, they took off—horses are afraid of elephants! *Every*thing is afraid of an elephant [*laughs*]! We spent the rest of the day trying to locate our horses! One whiff of that elephant and, man, they didn't want to *be* there!

If our producer Henry MacRae said something, I believed him, because he never missed. I had this scene where I had to go up to Fang the panther and bandage his paw. I wasn't too worried about it, because I figured they'd have *some*thing figured out to insure my safety. When they were ready to shoot this scene, on an indoor jungle set, I saw that the leopard was in a cage, a *big* one, and there were two guys sitting on top of it, one guy on one corner, the other guy on another, and they each had a high-powered rifle. I said, "W-w-what about *that*?"—I knew those guys wouldn't *be* there if there wasn't some big potential problem! MacRae said, "No, no, we've got it all figured out how we're going to shoot this scene. But we have to do this [have armed men around] because of certain rules and regulations." Well, when I went into the cage, I saw that the camera crew was inside a cage of their own. [*A cage within the* big *cage?*] Yes! I thought, "Gee, there are an awful lot of cages around here!" But they had the panther sedated, and when I picked up his paw and did all that stuff, he was practically asleep. So we didn't have any trouble with him. No, the monkey was our only problem. Then there was "the pet lion" that they had at Universal. His trainer worked, I think, at the studio, and they had this lion around like it was a *cat*—I was told that he was *very* tame. I wouldn't have wanted to *test* that [*laughs*]! The trainer could put his head in the lion's mouth.

Frances Robinson [the female lead] was delightful. Wonderful gal. She rode horseback with me quite a bit. We had Australian cavalry saddles and I would be *up* on the irons, on the stirrups, almost standing, so that she could sit behind me. She never complained about anything, she was a doll. Without makeup, she was attractive. But there was a difference in her looks with and without makeup. One day I was standing off to one side as they were shooting something, and this nice lady came up to me and said, "Hello, Frank!" And I said, "Hi there." Then, after about a minute or so, I realized it was Frances. She wasn't shooting that day, she had no makeup on, and her regular clothes, and I didn't recognize her [*laughs*]! She was a very nice gal who died much too young.

I've been lucky in my career, working with awfully nice people. She was very, very nice; Jack Mulhall, who played the head of the Ivory Patrol, was great. He had been a big star in silents, and Universal made a practice of taking some of these people who really made it in silent days and keeping 'em busy. Frank Mayo, who was also in *Tim Tyler's Luck*, had been a *big* name in silents, and he was another one of those chaps that Universal sort of "took care of." I saw some other Universal films done in that period and I spotted Frank a couple of times. They kept him working all right.

The two heavies, Norman Willis and Tony Warde ... well, to *me*, they were the proof of a show business adage: "You want to find a nice person, find somebody playing a heavy." The actors who play heavies, somehow or another they're just *wonderful* off-screen. *These* boys certainly were, they were awfully nice. Well, *every*body on that show was nice. At that time, there was something that I don't think exists nowadays, a *unity* of thought. Everybody was rooting for the show. It was exhilarating. And *all* of our pictures, pretty much, were that way.

[*I look at the scenes of you and your father, played by Al Shean, in* Tim Tyler's Luck *and I think, "Either Al Shean was terribly miscast, or Frankie was!"*] Gallagher and Shean were a *very* big vaudeville act. [*Thomas sings*:] "Oh, Mr. Gal-la-gher ... oh, Mr. Gal-la-gher...." Our producer Henry MacRae must have said, "Oh, give him a job!" He didn't realize that we were complete opposites. I was not in too many shots with Shean and I really never got to know him. He, in my mind and memory, was nowhere near as important as the heavies, Jack and Francie.

We shot a great deal of *Tim Tyler's Luck* at Vasquez Rocks, which as you know was almost a *must* in those days. But I don't think we used any other locations other than Vasquez Rocks. At that time, Universal had an amazing "cliff and jungle" area on their back lot. It went as high as four stories. It was really very impressive! All of the scenes set in Gorilla Canyon, with the "apes" [men in ape suits] throwing rocks at us, were shot right back there. I wish that was still there—gosh, it was impressive. When we did those scenes, I met a man who, I was told, was the best gorilla in Hollywood, and he did look like the real thing. He took off his mask and showed me where he'd worked it so the "muscles" in the face would move. It was interesting to see what he had done. He was a little fellow, very nice.

The scenes with the riverboat and the Ivory Patrol's fort was also at Universal. On the set, when I wasn't working, I had a teacher, a nice woman. Actually, she helped teach me how to play bridge. At the same time I was doing *Tim Tyler's Luck*, there were three girls making a picture on the lot who also had to go to school, and they had a school on the lot. One of those three little gals *loved* this jungle idea and all of the horses and everything, and she would come out maybe two, three times a week. Called Deanna Durbin [*laughs*]. That's where I knew her from. Deanna Durbin, Nan Grey and Barbara Read—they were making a picture called *Three Smart Girls* [1936] which turned out to be a big hit and "bailed out" Universal, and made Deanna a star. The other two girls weren't particularly interested, I think they were interested in *boys*, but Deanna came out all the time. *Very* nice. I sound repetitious when I keep saying "very nice," "very nice," but that's the way it was.

There was a funny thing about Earl Douglas, who had really a very important part in the show as a baddie who turned around and became a goodie. He had a brother, Frank Yaconelli, who was quite well-known, and MacRae, through some mistake or other, thought that he had hired the brother [*laughs*]. So MacRae was "put out" with Earl! But after the second week, MacRae came to Earl and told him that he, MacRae, was quite satisfied. MacRae said, "If I had to cast it all over again, I would ask for you, not your brother."

In *Tim Tyler's Luck*, the villains travel around the jungle in their armored "Jungle Cruiser." That was a Ford truck, and they put this plywood shell around it so that it looked like a tank. *Tim Tyler's Luck* has a reputation of having cliffhangers that are a bit more realistic than other serials, and of just being very realistic in general, and in this case it wasn't, because when they shot interiors of the Jungle Cruiser, they were shooting on a set, of course. And the interior looked *very* large! Then you'd look at the Jungle Cruiser again from the outside and you'd say to yourself, "Hey, wait a minute ... where *is* all that space inside?" [*Laughs*].

[*Stunt-wise, do you wish you had been asked to do more or less?*] As I mentioned, I had a lot of faith in Henry MacRae. There was one scene where Tim was pushed off the top of the riverboat and he falls a long ways, down into the water. There's a lake at Universal, or there *was* at that time. When they told me what I had to do, I said, "Wait a minute ... this lake is kind of shallow, isn't it?" Henry said, "When you look down at the surface of the water, you'll see that one part looks darker than the rest. That's where we've dug a ten-foot hole. So when you go down, make sure and hit that spot!" I was a little worried about hitting that spot, but it worked out!

We had two directors [Ford Beebe and Wyndham Gittens]—one would direct one day and then the next day it would be the other guy. "Windy" Gittens was actually a writer, and he had also co-written the screenplay. He was a little ... fussy. The first scene that I had where

I worked with him, he was, "Now, look, Frank, so and so and so and so and so...." MacRae, who was on the set because this was the beginning of the show, called Gittens over. I found out later that he said, "*Leave* that boy alone. Don't tell him anything. He'll do fine." And "Windy" did leave me alone. He didn't *like* it, but he did!

We had a cliffhanger in which Tim falls from the Gorilla Canyon cliff. It was quite a drop, so they didn't want me to do it. I was at the base of the cliff, hiding behind a big rock that was between me and the camera. The stunt double dropped and landed next to me behind the rock. I took a pause which I thought was reasonable—after a fall like that, a guy *would* have to pull himself together. Then I got up and became apparent to the camera. *That* way, it would look on film like I had taken the fall. But the director, Gittens, didn't like that pause, he told me, "No, no, no! I want you to get up right away. I don't want people to think that this is a phony"—which it *was*, of course. So we did it a second time, and the poor stuntman broke his leg that time! [*Frank Coghlan, Jr., acted in a serial directed by Gittens, and he told me that Gittens didn't mind putting people in danger.*] Evidently not. Well, he was a writer, and he probably thought to himself, "I want everything just the way I imagined it." The other director, Ford Beebe, was a nice guy. Never had any problems with him. I didn't even know he was there [*laughs*]. There are two kinds of directors: One, they hire actors that they *know*, and they know what they can *do*, and they let them do it. And then there's the other kind, who are always fussy and trying to change this and change that. They're not so much fun to work with.

When we finished the show, Francie and I decided to have a party on the back lot. Earl Douglas got together with Francie and me, and we put up the money. The boys on the set [the crew] put up a tent and a stove and seats and everything we needed—they really "got with it." Earl Douglas was Italian, and he had his mother and two sisters cooking, and we had a whale of a party, it lasted until midnight. And we decided one thing: We'd had so much fun, we wished we were doing *another* serial!

When *Tim Tyler's Luck* came out, I didn't have the opportunity to see it. I was workin' pretty steady then. I think I saw it for the first time on TV [in the early 1950s]. When *Tom Corbett, Space Cadet* was a big winner ratings-wise, the Dumont Network got a-hold of *Tim Tyler's Luck* and every week they showed an episode. And when they were finished, they started all over again [*laughs*]! What did I think of it? It's hard to say. When you're watching a show that you've done, you're thinking about the people and the little things that happened. And *Tim* was a happy cast. I *liked* it, but if I sound a little wishy-washy about that, here's why: I believe any actor who sees something that he did notices things that he would have done differently, if he had a chance to do it again. There are always those little things, you say, "Oh, Jesus, I should have done this or that." I thought that one of the better cliffhangers was that drop from the mountain ledge in Gorilla Canyon. Also the one where Anna the elephant picked me up, I liked that one. As I mentioned, *Tim Tyler's Luck* got the reputation for having the most realistic cliffhangers.

Everybody who knows my career usually asks about *Tim Tyler's Luck* sooner or later. I would have loved to do a sequel. I was envious of Buster Crabbe, who played Flash Gordon, and then played the role twice more in two more Flash Gordon serials. But, for me and Tim Tyler, the opportunity never arose. Maybe in another world [*laughs*]!

4

Jean Porter on One Million B.C. *(1940)*

Man and dinosaur may never have co-existed in real life but they frequently collide in fantasy films, most spectacularly in the stop-motion animation masterpieces The Lost World *(1925) and* King Kong *(1933) but also in films of the "photographically enlarged lizard" variety. One of the granddaddies of the latter genre,* One Million B.C. *was a fanciful depiction of the trials and tribulations of a pair of inter-tribal lovers (Victor Mature, Carole Landis) in prehistoric times, directed by Hal Roach, Sr., and Jr., and—some say—the legendary D.W. Griffith. Enacting the role of Landis' young sister: teenage actress Jean Porter.*

Born in Cisco, Texas, Porter began her career as a child entertainer there. In 1935, when her parents brought her to California in order for her to take dancing classes and learn some new routines, Porter unexpectedly landed a minuscule role in a Fox musical and put her tap shoe on the first rung of the Hollywood ladder. She rose from extra to supporting player to B-movie lead in the 1940s— and became the wife of director Edward Dmytryk—before making her final film in 1955 (Dmytryk's The Left Hand of God*). She looked back 1,002,002 years at some of her most unusual soundstage exploits in this interview.*

My parents and I came out here to California for a two-week vacation [in 1935], and my dad had saved up enough for me to stay an extra four weeks and take some dancing lessons. I began taking my dancing lessons at Fanchon and Marco, a very famous school at the time, on the corner of Western and Sunset. Fanchon took an interest in me and she told my mother, yes, definitely, I could train there if my mother played the piano for the classes. My mother was a good pianist, she taught piano in Texas, and her playing piano for the various classes at Fanchon and Marco paid for my dance classes. They taught mainly dancing there—and Rita Hayworth was the one of the teachers. She was Rita Cansino then, and she taught Spanish dancing and castanets. Her father also taught there. They were great.

My first movie was *Song and Dance Man* [1936] but I did practically nothing in it. It was a fluke getting that part. I was at Fanchon and Marco when a director walked in and saw me practicing in front of a mirror and acting silly; my mother was playing the piano and my tap teacher Arthur Dreifuss was also in the room. This director asked, "Would you like to come around the corner to Fox Studio, down here on Western Avenue, and do a little song-and-dance scene?" My mother's jaw dropped and so did Arthur Dreifuss'. He was just in ecstasy, he said, "This is marvelous! What a break! Yes, do it!" I was 12 years old at the time, and I looked ten. For the picture, they put me in a little white rabbit coat and white rabbit hat and I was out in front of a drug store with snow falling down—the snow was white corn flakes. That's all I did, just one little dance scene with Paul Kelly, and yet within that period of two or three days that I spent playing that little tiny part in an unimportant film, I was paid more than my dad made in a month—he worked for the Texas and Pacific Railroad, he was the chief clerk of the freight department between Fort Worth and El Paso. My mother thought I'd just be workin' all the time and my dad said, "*Stay* there [in Hollywood]! You got it made!"—but this was fool's gold. Doing *Song and Dance Man* was wonderful but it didn't mean a thing, I certainly wasn't "discovered." I didn't get another job for a *long* time; getting that first job was just kind of an accident! *But* ... 12 years old, and I had done a film! [*The movie reference books say that you were born in 1925.*] Oh, they are so *good* to me. I was born December the 8th, 1922. I'll tell you the truth on everything, and I don't care *who* knows it!

Fanchon had some new pictures made of me, new photographs with a résumé on the back, and she changed my name: My name was Bennie Jean Porter but she dropped the Bennie and I became Jean Porter. I was 12 but she put my age as ten. (She said, "You don't look 12 so you're *not* going to interviews for 12.") She registered me with Central Casting and I started getting calls for extra work, which was so good for me. I was on the sets and got to watch how they did everything. I did some extra work which kept my mother and me living, I did some bits, and on *The Adventures of Tom Sawyer* [1938] I was lucky enough to get a run-of-the-film contract, where you sign on that you'll *be* there every day. I was one of the kids in that whole picture—they knew they'd need a bunch of kids in school, a bunch of kids on the hayride, all those things. And Mr. [Norman] Taurog, the director, gave me the name of Pauline and he would throw me a line once in a while. That gave me a credit—I wasn't just an extra any more, because every time they needed somebody to say something, he gave it to me. I'd say, "Hey, Becky! Goin' on the hayride?," and that was more money that week. He liked it that I was so interested—I stayed by the camera most of the time.

That run-of-the-film contract gave me quite a bit of money to stay [in Hollywood] longer, which I did. I never went back to Texas to live. My dad, of course, went back to his job, but I stayed, and my mother stayed with me. We had an apartment not far from Western and Hollywood Boulevard and I stayed in the Fanchon and Marco classes, and I did Fanchon and Marco's stage shows at the Paramount Theater every holiday. Lon McCallister was my best friend there, and he and I worked in all the big stage extravaganza numbers. We'd stand on

Jean Porter says that, contrary to Hollywood legend, the film's producer D.W. Griffith did no uncredited directing that she was aware of.

balls and roll 'em all over the place and bump into each other, that kind of thing.

It was suggested that I take classical singing and they sent me to Doc Humphrey, and there is where I met Carole Landis [future star of *One Million B.C.*] and there is where I met Mary Martin—I became Mary Martin's protégé, she loved my coloratura. I took classical singing, and Doc Humphrey thought I would have a wonderful classical voice. *But,* I clowned around too much. I'd hit a high note and cross my eyes—I couldn't stand it! I eventually talked him into letting me do comedy songs. Carole Landis was also taking singing lessons because she *wanted* to sing. But she wasn't very good. She could play ping pong, though—she was the greatest ping pong player! Every weekend we had a party at Doc Humphrey's place, we all had to sing, and we all got to have barbecue and play ping pong. She was the champ, she was marvelous. And she had the greatest looking boyfriends—she always had good-looking guys with her. And she was crazy about me. I have an autographed photo from her, it says, "To the sweetest girl in this whole wide world." It's framed, up on my wall.

Carole Landis and I became *very* good friends at the singing school, and then when they were going to do *One Million B.C.*, it just so happened that my agent knew they needed a teenager my age. I think I was about 17 when I did that and I looked younger. (When I was 12, I looked 10, when I was 14, I looked 12, and so on.) So I played Carole Landis' little sister. I don't know whether she had anything to do with it or not, but I'd like to think she did, because we were together every day. I was really and truly *like* her little sister. Her hairdresser became *my* hairdresser, her makeup person *my* makeup person, and we were together every day, all day. I think "Shotgun" Britton was the makeup man. And the hairdresser, Loretta, was Carole Lombard's hairdresser and one of Carole Lombard's best friends. Carole Landis loved knowing that, because we all *loved* Carole Lombard.

All of my scenes in *One Million B.C.* were shot on a set, it was all inside. We didn't go outside for anything. They built the whole forest, the caves, the pools, the pot that we had our food in ... everything was on a stage. No, actually, it was on *two* stages. What they did was take two stages and make it into one greeeat big one, almost like an MGM Esther Williams set.

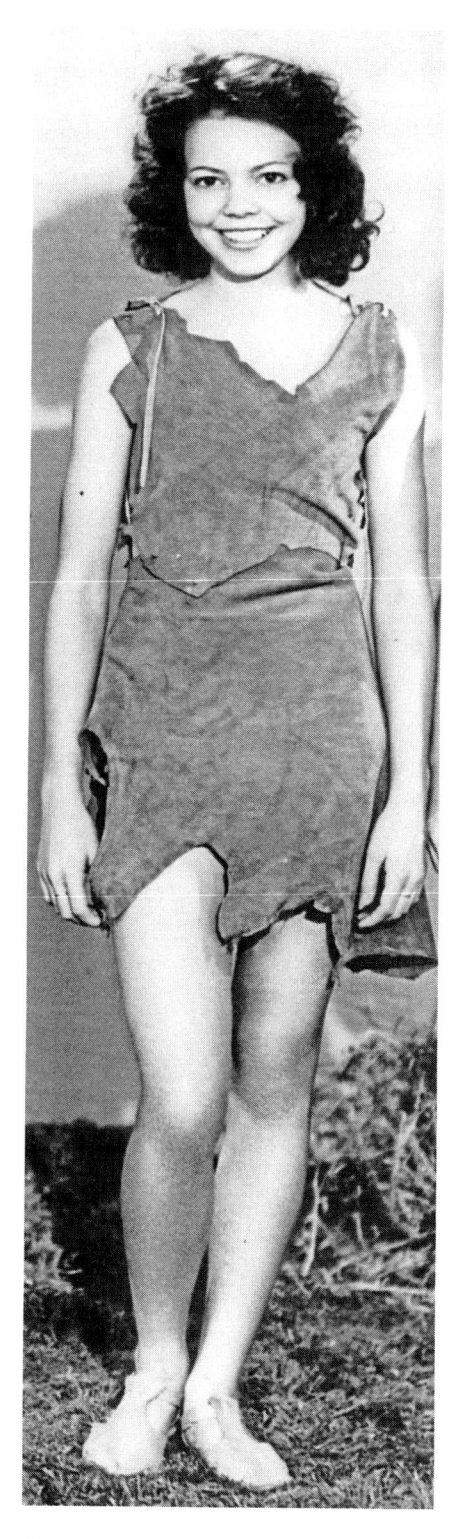

"No makeup" and "Don't comb your hair," cave girl Porter was told by *One Million B.C.*'s producers.

They knocked out a wall and they did this, that and the other thing. I had been on larger sets with *Tom Sawyer*; for *Tom Sawyer*, they also had to build a cave, so they built some big sets over at the Selznick Studio. But the sets for *One Million B.C.* were very impressive too.

You know that D. W. Griffith was the producer ... and this was his last producing credit. It was kind of an honor to even *talk* to that man, Griffith having done so many beautiful and wonderful films. On *One Million B.C.* he didn't *do* much except sort of "oversee" everything. He sat over by the soundstage door, the great big sliding door on wheels. I'm talking about the big door which they brought set walls in through, that they brought the trees in through, the door that all the trucks came through. That's the door he always sat by ... I'd hate to think it was an easy getaway [*laughs*]! But he liked that door open about a foot, and his chair was near that open door. All of us remarked about that. I don't know if he had asthma or something and he needed it for breathing, but he just liked to be right near the door. We all knew where to find him! He kept sitting in that chair, and we knew that was Mr. Griffith, and he was there for a reason. He was there every day, I think. But he didn't direct.

[*What was he like personality-wise? Serious?*] Not *too* serious ... he spoke very nicely. But very quiet. And he was all wrapped up. We [the actors] were mostly unclothed, we were running around in skins, and *he* had an overcoat and a felt hat that was kinda pulled down. He looked like he was chilly all the time. I just remember he was nice to talk with, and we were so respectful that he was even *there*. He and I didn't carry on conversations that I can remember, just "How are ya?" and things like that.

[*So who did direct the scenes you were in?*] I'd say it was Hal Roach, Jr., but don't go by *my* word because *both* of 'em were on set [Sr. and Jr.]. It seems to me Hal Roach, Jr., did most of the directing, but Hal Roach, Sr., was on the set, and it would be hard for me to be absolutely sure which one was doing what. Years later I did a picture called *Cry Danger* [1951] directed by Dick Powell, and he wasn't given director credit. Dick gave Robert Parrish the director's credit, but Dick did all the directing.

[*Was anybody self-conscious in those skimpy, daring—for 1940—costumes?*] No, because we all wore dance pants underneath, which was just like a bathing suit. I think every one of us had been on stage—certainly Carole and I—and we all wore dance pants with *every*thing. You could stand on your head and people wouldn't be able to see anything they shouldn't see. They were the same color as the animal skins we wore.

The cast of *One Million B.C.*, everybody was so nice. Vic Mature was nice, and there was another guy on there, John Hubbard, *he* was very nice too. Of course, they all treated me like a child. Well, I *was* a child! And, as I say, Carole and I just spent every spare moment together. [*How much older than you was Carole Landis?*] Old enough to go out with guys [*laughs*]. She had really nice boyfriends. In the movie, she was in love with Vic, but in real life, she didn't date him at all—well, not as far as I knew. She was going with someone else at the time, I don't remember now who it was. But she did like Vic a lot. Vic was *very* friendly, he was very well-liked everywhere. In the movies, he played all kinds of tough-guy parts, bandits and gangsters and so on, but he was actually really ... *mellow* would be a good word to describe him. He wanted everybody to know that he wasn't this big, rough, tough guy that he was supposed to be. He was a real sweetheart. And he *talked* with you, he asked you questions like he was really interested in you. He wanted to know what I was studying at school and he wanted to see what I was reading. He paid attention to other people. Sometimes stars just go off into their dressing rooms and prepare for the next scene, or whatever, but he was on the set a lot of the time, which *every*one appreciates.

I also think Carole Landis liked John Hubbard a lot. And *every*one loved Carole. Later on, she became so *absolutely, devastatingly* in love with Rex Harrison, it just was almost pitiful how much she loved him ... because he was married. I hope she *knew* he was married, because I too fell in love with *my* husband [Edward Dmytryk] when *he* was married, but I didn't know it. Eddie didn't tell me he was married when we started going together because he and his wife were separated and planning a divorce. I marked that off as okay later, because I *had* to; I had already fallen in love with him, and he had already fallen in love with me. We were already planning our life together when I found out from an RKO hairdresser that he was married. So I know what it is to fall in love with a man who's *married*...

In *One Million B.C.*, the monster that trapped me in the tree—they never let me see it until they shot that scene. And the reason they never let me see it was so that I would actually get scared [on-camera] when I did see it for the first time. And I did. Oh, gosh, it scared me to death! I mean, *it really scared me to death*. I never saw them building it ... I saw a few drawings [before shooting the scene], but to me they were just drawings. But I didn't know what it would really look like. They said for me to run and climb up the tree, and that when I got up there I was gonna *see* something and I was to scream for help. The word for "help" was "Neecha! Neecha!" (I'll never forget my dialogue [*laughs*]!) They sent this mechanized monster thing after me—great big jaws! And it was as big as the tree! I think they did an awwwfully good job on it, because it looked *real*. I had been told that there'd be somebody inside it, and I guess there *was*, but I couldn't *see* that there was anyone inside it and it just looked like a real monster coming for me. I was *so* scared, I was shaking and yelling and screaming. And then Victor Mature ran in and he saved me, he got the monster away from me. Even later, I never did even ask to see inside it, 'cause I didn't want any part of it! Good-bye, mon-ster! Ugh!!

At the same Hal Roach Studios where Porter appeared in *One Million B.C.*, she later played the leads in low-budget musical comedies.

Shooting went from the end of 1939 into the early part of '40, I believe. It took quite a while, and I loved every minute of it. I went to school on the set while I was on that picture, me and the other kids—there was one little girl younger than I was, and two boys. We had our school sessions over in one corner of the set, so that we would be right there whenever they needed us. I was attending Mrs. Lawler's School for Professional Children at the time, and so they kept in touch with my teacher there. So that's just to tell you that *every*thing was on the set, including our little "school area." My mother was on the set as well, she came with me. She didn't *have* to be there when a welfare worker was there, so any day she didn't want to come, she didn't have to. But she kinda liked going with me at that time. And I didn't mind. But after a while, I didn't want "Mommy" there by my side. So by the time I was 17, I said, "Mommmm....!" [*Did she mind being dis-invited?*] No, by that time she was kind of bored with it all. Also, she was so beautiful that men would come up to her and try to talk with her, but she was *very*, very shy and sedate and proper. That became a bother for her; and the men would be a little upset that she didn't respond. So it was better all the way around if she just didn't come on the set with me any more.

I saw *One Million B.C.* when it was finished, and I thought it was marvelous. When they first ran it at the studio, Carole and I saw it in a projection room, and she was pleased with it too. [*A screening for just the two of you?*] No, not just the two of us, but we saw it together, and we both liked it and we both laughed a lot through it. *I* thought it was better than the Raquel Welch one [the 1966 remake *One Million Years B.C.*]. I've had a lot of fan letters come in saying that they liked the first one best.

[*Did you ever again play a role in a movie that was quite that far-out?*] In *Hellzapoppin'* [1941] with Olsen and Johnson, I was thrown around by devils. They picked me to do it because I was the smallest, the most lightweight girl there—I only weighed 98 pounds. I had to go and rehearse with all these great big musclemen down at Muscle Beach. And I loved it! When they shot the thing, I guess we were supposed to be in Hell, I was in orange and red and the musclemen were dressed as devils—just bathing trunks, horns on their heads, and tails coming out the back. They threw me from one to the other, and I looked so *relaxed* ... and I was, because I knew they'd catch me. They threw me waaay across the room—up in the air and awaaay she went, across the flames and into the arms of these muscle guys. That was more far-out for me than *One Million B.C.*, because in *One Million B.C.* I'm just running around and picking up fruit and eating out of the pot and climbing the tree. *Hellzapoppin'* was chaotic!

I just watched *One Million B.C.* again and I *loved* it. I remembered feelings that I had while I was doing it, and I remembered all those kids who were around. And there was Carole ... oh, we were so close. It was such a good feeling. I don't remember any problems on the set, and I truthfully still don't remember who directed it. I know Hal Roach was there all the time and Hal Roach, Jr., was there all the time, and either one of 'em could have directed it and I don't remember who did. But ... *some*body did [*laughs*]!

5

Memories of Boris Karloff

Jo Ann Sayers on *The Man with Nine Lives* (1940)

Boris Karloff's five-film "Mad Doctor" series at Columbia began with the exciting The Man They Could Not Hang *(1939) and ended quite ignobly with the failed comedy* The Boogie Man Will Get You *(1942). Falling somewhere in the middle, both chronologically and quality-wise, the somber* The Man with Nine Lives *stars Karloff as Dr. Kravall, a researcher in frozen suspended animation. Most of this B-movie is set in the claustrophobic confines of the icy cellars of Karloff's island home, where the single-minded medico intends to use uninvited guests as guinea pigs in fantastic deep-freeze experiments.*

The prettiest of Karloff's prisoners, leading lady Jo Ann Sayers (real name: Miriam Lucille Lilygren) was born in Seattle, Washington. Named after Moses' dancer-sister Miriam, she danced as a child, took violin and piano lessons and acted in school plays. She attended the University of Washington with hopes of becoming a lawyer, but was drawn to the drama department instead. Agent Andy Lawlor "spotted" her and offered her a chance to make a screen test, which in turn led to Sayers' brief but busy run in Hollywood features and shorts. While under contract at MGM, Sayers was among the multitudes to test for the part of Scarlett O'Hara in 1939's Gone with the Wind.

Widowed and residing in Princeton, New Jersey, Sayers, now in her eighties, continues to indulge in her first love—dancing.

After Andy Lawlor saw me and offered to arrange for a screen test, my mother and my uncle and my grandfather and I drove down to Hollywood. When we got there, Warner Brothers put us up at a hotel and sent us cars to get around. I went in to Warner Brothers for my screen test and, after makeup and clothes and so forth, I walked on the set. It was the first time I had been on a soundstage ... and I had real *déjà vu*. *Déjà vu* is when you do something you have never done before, but you have a feeling you *have* done it. Well, that was my feeling. I just suddenly felt at home, like this was where I belonged. Mother was sitting on the set and they made a test, and they all thought it was great. But then Max Arnow, the talent scout at Warner Brothers, got canned because he was a relative of Warner's and he [Arnow] had put himself somehow in a bad position or something. So he was put out! And his replacement, of course, wanted to do his own choosing and thinking and whatnot, so nothing happened to the test.

I wanted to go home—all my friends were there, and I wanted to go back to school. But I was urged to stay, and I did. Mother had to go home, so she put me with some family friends out in the Valley and I stayed there. The agents communicated with me once in a while, and then finally said they had arranged another test for me, this time at RKO. So I made a test at RKO and then waited, waited, waited, waited. Then finally they got back to me, and evidently they had decided that they wanted somebody who could sing. I thought, "Oh, the heck with

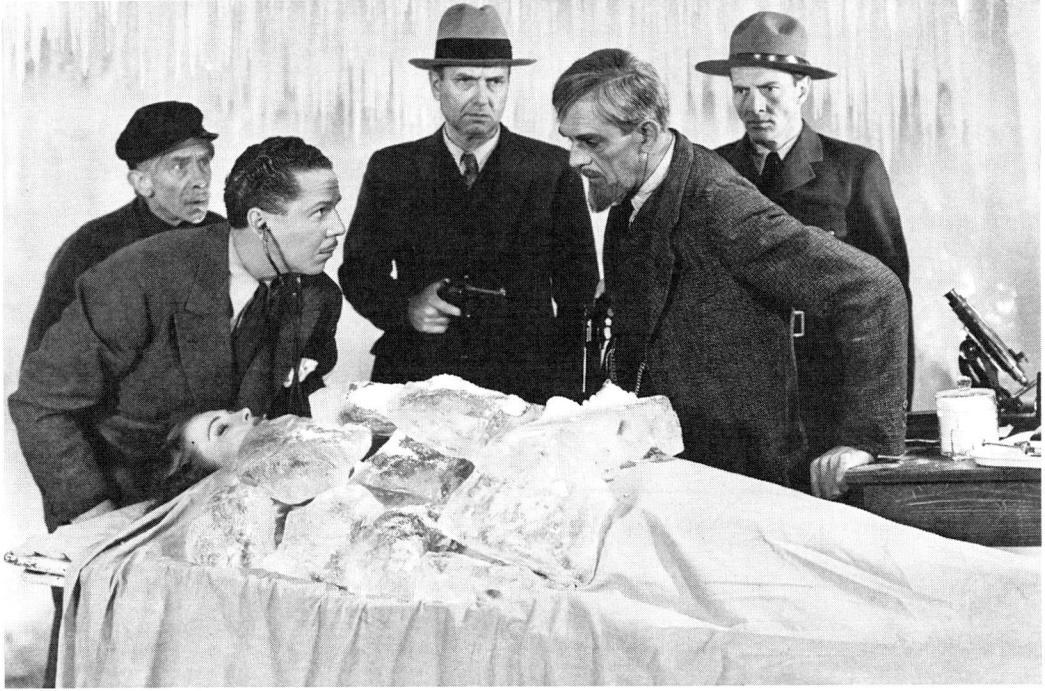

Top: Boris Karloff may have raised goosebumps *on*-screen but his *The Man with Nine Lives* co-star Jo Ann Sayers says that *off*-screen he was a sweet man who raised roses. *Above*: Sayers had a few goosebumps herself when packed in ice in *Nine Lives*. (Sayers is on table with, left to right, Ernie Adams, Roger Pryor, Ivan Miller, Karloff, Bruce Bennett.)

this! I want to go home!" But I stayed on. Finally an agent called up and said, "Guess what? Mervyn LeRoy [an MGM producer-director] has your RKO test locked in his desk drawer. You've got to come over and sign." And that's what happened: Mother came down and we got me a new outfit and went over to the studio and signed. MGM's Dr. Kildare series was about to begin with *Young Dr. Kildare* [1938] with Lionel Barrymore and Lew Ayres, so that was my first movie.

I did quite a few things at Metro, then my contract had to be renewed. And [studio boss] Louis B. Mayer called me into his office and started chasing me around the desk! He didn't catch me [*laughs*], so my contract was terminated! It didn't make any difference to me because I did several other things after that with other studios, including the Columbia *Man with Nine Lives* with Boris Karloff.

[*Any reluctance to do a horror picture?*] I had no idea what exactly it was going to be. Of course, Karloff didn't wear a gruesome mask or anything like that, he was just himself. He was such a sweet man. He raised roses, and that's really what he cared about. He mentioned that to me, and we talked about it. Then at one point in the picture, during the part where we were all captives in his secret cellars, there was a "kitchen scene" where I offered to make some tea. So I started, I poured hot water into a teapot. Well, Karloff stopped the whole thing—the cameras, the action, *every*thing, he stopped it. And then he gave me a lesson on how to make proper tea [*laughs*]! First you pour boiling water into the cold teapot. Then after a minute or two, when the teapot is good and hot, you pour that water out. *Then* you put your tea in and pour boiling water immediately on top of it and let it steep. But you have to heat the teapot first—"hot the pot," as they say! If you use a cold pot, the tea will cool off too quickly. So I learned something from him. And I do it to this day!

Karloff was very pleasant, very cooperative. He wasn't *social*-social, exactly, but he was very amiable and we didn't have any problems or confrontations or anything. *Man with Nine Lives* was partly filmed in a huge warehouse, an ice house somewhere in L.A. where I guess meat and stuff was frozen and stored. Just the scenes where we were in Karloff's ice room were shot there; everything else was shot on soundstages at Columbia. It really *was* cold, and so we were told to wear heavy underwear and whatnot. We only filmed for about 15 minutes at a time, then we'd come out to a little warm room. We weren't allowed to get *terribly* cold—but it *was cold*! You could see your breath in there. The crew, obviously, could dress more warmly than the actors. And they *did*!

There's a scene in the movie where I'm lying on a gurney in the ice room with ice packed all around me. There was a blanket over me, and then a big heavy rubber sheet, and then piles of ice—the real stuff—on top of me. I was supposed to be almost dead, but my breath was showing, my warm breath in this cold air. So they tucked a little rubber tube in my mouth, the off-camera side of my face, which was my left side, and the tube hung out of the left side of my mouth and I could breathe through that. Then it was perfect, because I could look almost dead. Of course I had to hold whatever breath I had anyway, so that the ice that was piled on top of me wouldn't shift. I had to be very careful about that! There were lots of fun little, interesting things like that.

My love interest in the movie was Roger Pryor. I guess he couldn't make me out: One day when my mother was hanging around on the set some place, I was inside my little trailer alone and he entered, grabbed me and kissed me [*laughs*]! It sort of startled me! When I looked at him in a kind of a surprised way, he kind of stood back and looked at *me* in a surprised way. Then he turned and left, and that was *it*! [*How old were you in 1940 when you made that movie?*] I have no idea. I don't put things in terms of years, I don't pin things down in years. People ask me how old I am and I don't know. And when people ask me how old my children are, I say, "I really don't know. That's *their* problem!" Who am *I* to go around spouting all these things [*laughs*]? I've got other things to think about!

The Man with Nine Lives was, I think, my biggest role in a movie, that and *The Light of Western Stars* [a 1940 Western]. After *Man with Nine Lives* I was signed to do a movie at RKO called *Sunny* [1941], but I had a little time off in between and I wanted to go back to Seattle 'cause I hadn't been home for ages. I went, and of course had a great time, with all my friends and whatnot. And when I found out that my aunt was going to New York, I thought, "Oh, what fun. I'd love to go too." I had time, so I went to New York with her ... and absolutely fell in love with New York. In fact, after she went home, I stayed, because I had a little time before *Sunny* started. MGM looked after me there, by the way [even though she was no longer working for MGM]. Billy Grady was the head of talent at MGM in Hollywood and he had always championed me and was very sweet. So somebody from MGM's New York office was assigned to me and he was on my tail all the time, which was really nice because I didn't know anybody or anything.

While I was in New York, I was put in touch with people, including Marc Connolly the playwright. Marc Connolly asked me to dinner, and then he called [Broadway producer] Max Gordon and set up an appointment for me to go over to Max's office and meet him—Max was about to do a new play. I had another, oh, two or three weeks before I had to go back to Hollywood and so, not knowing exactly what I was doing, I went. There was Max Gordon, and

Behind-the-scenes shot of *Man with Nine Lives* director Nick Grinde rehearsing Karloff's resuscitation scene with Pryor and Sayers.

[writers] Jerome Chodorov and Joe Fields, and George Kaufman, and they were in the process of casting this new play. They kind of looked at me—I didn't know what they were looking for—and somebody said, "Well, how 'bout the Eileen part?" They talked awhile, and they asked me what I'd done before on stage. (That was important—they kind of looked down on people who'd been in movies as having not very much know-how on the stage. I'd *had* quite a bit, and of course I made up a few things too [*laughs*]!) Finally they said "thank you" and so forth and I left.

It was getting on toward Christmas, and I reeeally wanted to go home to Seattle for Christmas, I had never in my life been away from home at Christmastime. Finally I got a call to come to the theater, and every ingenue in the countryside was there! I went out onto the stage and there I was, under this work light, with all these voices out there in the black. I didn't know whose voice was whose, but we chatted and whatnot. And that was that. I sat around again for a while, finally got called back and there were *ten* girls there. We read scenes and so forth. In a week or so I was called back again and there were *two* of us, and we read *again*. (I'll never forget, there was this darling old guy on the curtain, he'd been there who knows how long, and he would say, "Now, don't be noivous!") I was staying at the Barbizon Plaza on 58th Street, and a short time later, when I came into my room, there was a telegram tucked under the door that said REPORT FOR REHEARSAL MONDAY MORNING. And that's how I knew I got the part of Eileen in *My Sister Eileen* with Shirley Booth [one of the big Broadway smash hits of the 1940s].

I immediately made some calls and said, "You've got to cancel my movie contract [for *Sunny*]. I don't really want to do it, I want to stay here. Cancel it before they know what I'm up to!" Somehow they were able to do that for me. And then I just had a wonderful time in *My Sister Eileen*. We opened in New York on the 26th of December 1940. Shortly before opening night, Max Gordon came up to me: "You had better be good," he said, "or I'll *annihilate* you!" [*Laughs*] That was exactly what he said! I guess that was his way of telling me that he had really put in a strong word for me or something. He had been my champion, and he was very sweet.

I left the play after a year and a half to get married. The play sort of dwindled on, and then Shirley Booth wanted to do something else. Also, there were so many young men in it who were being drafted constantly, and the producers had already gotten their money out of it anyway, so it finally closed. I only acted a little after I married—a little radio, TV, summer theater.

I have a happy life today. I ballroom dance, which I love; I've competed a couple of times and I showcase twice a year. I have a very busy, happy life. And I still get fan letters every now and then, and I can't believe it. I even got a telephone call from a fan in Wales ... amazing! So many of these people say what big fans of the old movies they are. Which I can understand. When *I* look at old movies on television, I *must* say, the dialogue is so much better, the directing is better, there's no hi-tech action junk that is just distracting. I enjoy some of the old movies myself.

Herbert Rudley on *On Borrowed Time* (1946)

A native of Philadelphia, actor Herbert Rudley made his first stage appearance in 1928 and enjoyed a long career in theater, motion pictures and television. In the mid–1940s, Rudley and Keenan Wynn began their own Los Angeles theater group with the ambitious goal of presenting play revivals, and the third of their four productions was a Rudley-directed revival of On Borrowed Time *with Boris Karloff.*

Let me start by explaining how I started the Players Production group. At that time, there were very few "little theaters" in L.A., the little theater movement hadn't started yet. My idea was that, in order to get a theater to *go*, to draw the public, you had to have at least one star performer—that is, from motion pictures. But that wasn't sufficient reason to start a theater, from my point of view. So the premise of *our* theater was that it would allow stars to break the mold that they were cast in, in motion pictures. Each play would feature one of those actors, desiring to get away from typecasting, *plus* a newcomer or relative newcomer who hadn't made it yet. I got Equity to give us permission to rehearse for three weeks instead of the two-week period [usually permitted] for stock companies, and each show was to play four weeks. Keenan Wynn and I started that theater together. I had directed him in a play out at Laguna Beach the summer before—*The Petrified Forest*, with Keenan as the gangster.

I got permission from MGM and 20th Century–Fox to start the series with Tyrone Power in *The Petrified Forest* and Judy Garland in *Stage Door*. On the basis of those two announcements, we had for the first time in the history of L.A. an advance sale of 60-some thousand dollars. Unfortunately, though we had permission from the studios to use these two stars, we could not have a written contract with them because they were under contract to the studios. We announced that we were opening with Tyrone Power in *The Petrified Forest*—Power would have played the role that Leslie Howard played in the [1936] film. But our *first* setback was, there was an actors' strike at that time and all of a sudden 20th Century–Fox sent Power down to Mexico to do the picture *Captain from Castile* [1947] and avoid the strike. So we lost him. I called Judy Garland and asked her if she could step it up, re-arrange *her* schedule, and she said yeah, sure, she could. We announced that we had to postpone Tyrone Power in *The Petrified Forest* and that now we were opening with Judy Garland in *Stage Door*. So that didn't affect the advance sale. *Except* that Metro then pulled Judy Garland and put her in a new musical! So we lost *both* of them. And our box office was reduced to zero!

We put on our productions at the El Patio Theatre on Hollywood and LaBrea, an 800-seat theater that has since been torn down. The first play we did was a revival of *The Desperate Hours*, the first of the psycho-

Horror movie fans may remember Herbert Rudley (1910–2006) best as Dr. Ramsay, mad medico Basil Rathbone's unwilling assistant in the all-star chiller *The Black Sleep* (1956).

logical thrillers in the theater. George Coulouris had played the father in the original New York production, and I cast him in *our* production. He told me during rehearsals that, although he had played the part for over a year in New York, he never really understood what the play was about until *we* did *ours* [*laughs*]. That was a pretty nice compliment! Next we did *Twentieth Century* with Keenan Wynn in "the Barrymore part," and then we did *On Borrowed Time*.

On Borrowed Time was a play that I always loved—a very touching play. I'd be directing it, and I thought of using Boris Karloff in it. I got the idea that Karloff would [under ordinary circumstances] be cast as Death, and so I decided to use him as "Gramps," which was a reversal, a complete turnaround. We had a great cast—Beulah Bondi as "Granny," Margaret Hamilton as Demetria and Ralph Morgan as Death, the role that would "normally" have been played by Karloff. And then we had a young newcomer, Tommy Ivo, play the kid, "Pud," and he was marvelous in it.

I had not met Karloff before that. He was a wonderfully intelligent man, totally contrary to the kind of roles he played. He was quite brilliant, a marvelous linguist—I don't remember how many languages he spoke, but quite a few. *Very*, very modest ... very erudite ... and a very hard-working actor. He was always the first one there at rehearsals and the last one to leave. He had a zest about him still, and he enjoyed the whole idea of playing a role that he would normally not be cast in. So we had a great time together.

The cast of the Rudley-staged *On Borrowed Time*, which ran at the El Patio Theatre from November 5–24, 1946. (Left to right, standing: Ann Tobin, Mort Werner, Richard Irving, Frank Cady, Tim Whelan. Sitting: Boris Karloff, Tommy Ivo, Beulah Bondi, Ralph Morgan, Keenan Wynn, Margaret Hamilton, Edward Clark, Richard Reeves.)

The public, unfortunately, shied away from *On Borrowed Time*. People came to see Boris Karloff in *On Borrowed Time* thinking they were going to see him like they saw him in the horror films, they expected to see him playing Death. So when they saw him as the kindly grandpa, they were completely bewildered! He got good reviews, but the public shied away because they expected horror from Boris Karloff. However, the reaction was good once they adjusted to the new idea. And the reviews were excellent.

It was a wonderful production. And, consequently, the Theater Guild in Manhattan, the foremost theater of drama in the '30s and '40s, started negotiations to bring it in as a revival—they had done the original play. But it never materialized for some reason, I don't really know why.

All the stars we used, even Karloff, got $55 a week, regardless of what their motion picture salaries were. They were being paid actors' minimum, which at that time was $55 a week, and yet they came to each production with such zest and interest and vitality because it was a chance for them to get back on the *stage*. All of them had been involved in films for many, many years and had gotten away from the theater, so they really loved the venture. And we had wonderful reviews for all the plays.

Our fourth production was *Macbeth*. I as an actor had already appeared on Broadway in the Maurice Evans–Judith Anderson *Macbeth*, I played Macduff in the original version. And I couldn't stand Maurice's performance as Macbeth—he was so bad in it. He was *terrible*! Judy Anderson should have played Macbeth and *he* should have played the queen [*laughs*], because

Rudley opted to give Karloff the change-of-pace role of the kindly "Gramps," no doubt surprising audience members who expected the customarily creepy actor to play the part of Death. The critics raved.

she was so much more powerful than he was. So we decided on doing a young production of *Macbeth* in which I did the Macbeth role. It was an interesting production ... and our last production.

The reason we failed was that the woman who put up the backing for us [gave us problems]. I had said to her, "Now, look—we'll accept your money, but you have to understand that you have nothing whatever to do with the creative end. You don't 'buy' *that*, you just give us the money and you're a sponsor of the theater. That's all." She said, oh, yes, yes, yes, yes, yes. And of course she tried to do *everything*. For example, *our* idea was a modest-priced theater, a $3.50 top ticket, so that we could draw on the popular audience instead of the chi-chi group. And of course *she* wanted only the chi-chi group, because of her friends—"It would be demeaning to tell them that they were going to a theater which only cost $3.50." We said, "You don't like that idea? Okay, here's your money back," and we gave her all her money back. And then of course *we* were strapped, because we were dependent then only on our income from the productions. At the end of four plays, we had to give up the ghost. Unfortunately, I lost all of the data about that venture in the Bel-Air fire in 1961. My home burned to the ground, so all of my memorabilia of the theater and motion pictures and television was burned up. I don't have any of the records.

My memory of Boris Karloff is that he was a very, very dedicated actor and that he had a real depth about him, contrary to the superficial things [the horror movies] that we saw him in.

Tommy Ivo on *On Borrowed Time* (1946)

In the long stage career of Boris Karloff, one assignment stood out as a particular personal favorite of his: When he was cast against type as "Gramps" Northrup, the wheelchair-bound oldtimer who manages to trap Death up an apple tree in On Borrowed Time. *He first played the role in a 1946 Hollywood production of the fantasy play, directed by Herbert Rudley and co-starring ten-year-old Tommy Ivo as his beloved grandson Pud.*

Already a veteran of several movies, Ivo went on to appear in hundreds of films and TV episodes in the late '40s and '50s, then turned his full attention to what had been a sideline hobby—hot rod racing. Nicknamed "TV Tom" and renowned in racing circles for his showmanship and driving skill, he was for 30 years a popular race track attraction. Retired since 1982 and now preparing to write a book on his soundstage and speedway exploits, Ivo recently borrowed some time from his schedule to reflect back on that important credit in his early acting career, and his friend Boris Karloff.

I started tap dancing and singing in Denver when I was about three years old, and everybody said, "Boy, he is *so* cute!" And they told my parents, "You oughta take him to Hollywood or New York." My mother had arthritis, and every winter she was all but crippled. So we picked Hollywood because my mother figured, "If that helps my arthritis, it would be a double hit." We came out here for the winter first, to see if it helped her arthritis.

The first movie I ever did was a Republic picture called *Earl Carroll Vanities* [1945] with Constance Moore and Dennis O'Keefe. They wanted a certain-looking kid for the thing, a blond, curly-headed little kid. The Republic casting people were canvassing all the tap dance schools in town, like they used to *do* in those days, and when they came to the bottom of the barrel, there I was! I went out on the interview with my two front teeth gone ... and I got the part. In fact, Constance Moore thought I was gonna be a male Shirley Temple or something, and she wanted to sign me up as her protégé! But all my mother's Swedish buddies told her, "Oh, no, he's gonna make a lot of money and she's gonna take it all," and so she turned Constance Moore down.

I made several movies before I did *Carnival in Costa Rica* [1947] with Cesar Romero and Vera-Ellen, a pretty big picture ... Technicolor. Then I got this play, *On Borrowed Time*, which was about the fifth or sixth thing down the line.

On Borrowed Time was quite a deal. That was what started me, that was the thing that really got my foot into the movie business. They were doing it in Hollywood, at the El Patio Theatre, which is no longer there. It was being put on by a bunch of stars who had gotten together because they wanted to bring legitimate theater to Hollywood—there wasn't much of it being done out here. They did several [four] plays. On one play, one of 'em would be the director, then on the next play he'd be the star, then on the *next* play he'd do something else ... they'd alternate. In fact, on our particular play, Keenan Wynn was moving stage stuff around, if *that* tells you anything! The stars would all do different stuff, directing and acting and what have you. But [having a kid in one of the plays] was a one-time deal, so they had to go to an outside source.

I went down and read for it—I read for it with Keenan Wynn, who was a great guy. And I *got* the thing. [*Did you have much competition for the role?*] Oh, I'm sure I did. I'll bet they checked ... well, not *every* kid in town, but ... a lot! When I used to go out on interviews, I'd always see Billy Gray or Gary Gray or Bobby Driscoll or ... there were about six of us in that age group who did the work in town at the time. Something I had in my favor was the fact that I always looked really young for my age, so people would think I was a wower [a sensation]. I was ten years old when I did *On Borrowed Time* but I looked to be about seven. People seeing me wouldn't think that I was a good ten-year-old, they would think I was a *genius seven*-year-old!

When they said, "Boris Karloff is gonna be your grandpa in this," I thought, "Boris Karloff—how can that *be*?," because my image of Boris Karloff was of a guy with a square head and pegs sticking out of the sides of his neck. Back in Denver, I'd been on the stage a bunch, singing and dancing—we'd go around to all these little kiddie revues and what have you. I'd entertain all over town, that's how my name got kinda known a little bit there. At some movie theater, I was going to be in a show with some of the other kids from my dancing school, we were gonna do it in between pictures. They had a rehearsal in the afternoon before the theater opened, and when we got done, they said, "If you want to stay and see the movie for free, you can do that." It was a Frankenstein movie. My mother didn't want to see it but her sister, my Aunt Becky, did, and I was going to stay with her. "Are you *sure* you want to see this?" Aunt Becky asked me. "Oh, yeah, yeah, I wanna see Frankenstein!" Well, the first time the Monster came on the screen, I was tugging on my aunt's sleeve and saying, "I think we better *leave* now!" [*Laughs*] She was crushed, she wanted to see the rest of it, but I didn't want to hear any more about it—Boris Karloff had scared the hell out of me!

It was with that in mind that I was sitting on the end of the El Patio Theatre stage, staring up the aisle, waiting for this guy with a square head and pegs sticking out of the sides of his neck to come walkin' down [*laughs*]. And, of course, Boris could *not* have been a nicer guy. He was really a sweetheart. It was just like he *was* my kindly old grandfather on the deal.

People ask me if I was nervous, a ten-year-old starring in a play like that. The truth is, I didn't even have butterflies in my stomach the first time the curtain went up. I couldn't *wait* 'til there was a crowd out there. That first night, I was there looking out through the curtains and eager to get started, "Oh, boy ... here we go!"—they couldn't pry me away from the place. I don't know if that's a bad feature or a good feature. I wasn't that way because I thought that I was *good*, it was because ... I'm perennially looking for the "Attaboy!" I go out of my way to do a lot of things for people, *just* to get an "Attaboy!" out of 'em.

Another thing that was *very* helpful for me: I had a photographic memory. Later on, when I was doing television shows and they'd do last-minute rewrites, I'd read it through once and throw it off to one side and say, "Okay, let's go." They used to call me One-Take Tommy, because I *was* pretty good. And my photographic memory was really a help when I did *On Borrowed Time* too. Boris used to call me "my living script" because he'd "go up" on stage and I'd whisper his lines to him. [*He'd "go up" during rehearsals?*] No, no—this was when we were actually doing the show! He used to do that frequently. No, not frequently, but ... periodically. I'd ask him, "Where should we go *today*, 'Gramps'?"—and *nothin'* would come back [*laughs*]! Finally I'd whisper, "To the playground...." Then he'd start right back up: "Well, let's go off to the playground...!" And, being the quintessential actor, he'd start up again in such a way that the audience would never know he'd "gone up" at *all*. Normally when an actor "goes up," someone has to whisper the next line to him from the wings, and the audience can hear *that* coming across. But the audience wouldn't know what was going on if *two of the actors* whispered to each other. I was reasonably savvy for being ten years old—I knew to whisper very quietly, and to turn my head to the back before I'd whisper to him, so that no one in the audience would hear me or see my mouth moving. He told my mother, "I don't know what I'd do without my living script here."

It wasn't a bad cast. They had Margaret Hamilton as Demetria the wicked aunt, and Ralph Morgan was Death, and Beulah Bondi played Granny. Not a bad cast at *all*! There was also another kid in the cast, and this kid, I think, was a bad influence on me—he'd lie and I'd swear to it! They also had a schoolteacher for us there, so one time me and this kid, we took a bucket full of water and set it up on the top of a door, a door that was ajar. The teacher came in, swung the door open, and down came the water bucket. But we missed her—thank God! Also, I have to tell you, there's a scene in the play where I attack this other kid. He's messin' around, stealing apples, and that's why "Gramps" says, "I wish anyone who climbs that tree couldn't come down until I let him"—the line that starts the whole thing going. Well, me and this kid had been round and round about *some*thing that day, he had rubbed me the wrong way, and when I was supposed to jump on him, I took a jump at him from about six feet away and hit him like a ton of bricks! And *down* we went! (I remember, when I hit him, hearing out in the audience a couple of people in the front row go, "*Oooooo!*") And he went limp on me! He was supposed to roll us over and get on top of me and beat me, but he didn't, he was limp. I had to *drag* him over and around on top of me. Then "Gramps" came along and grabbed him by the scruff of the neck and ran him off. I was up in the tree a little later on in the play, and I could hear Keenan Wynn backstage talking to the kid: "Are you all right? Are you all right?" I thought, "Oh, dear!"—I was up there shakin' in that tree, 'cause I knew I had it comin' from Keenan Wynn when the play was over! And, yeah, he did come over and talk to me afterwards. He said, "*Listen*. I don't want to ever see anything like that happen again!" Actually, he took it pretty easy on me—I thought I was gonna be read the riot act, but he just told me, "Hey ... no more of *that*." So I calmed down a little bit after that, I began minding my ps and qs.

I got so I knew where the laughs would come. In one scene, I'm admiring a girl [Ann Tobin] and her sweater, and I said, "Gee, I wish Granny would sew bumps on the front of *my*

Two photos of Ivo in *On Borrowed Time*: with Ralph Morgan and Beulah Bondi; with Ann Tobin and Boris Karloff.

sweater like Marcia has on hers...," and that would bring the house down! I knew it was comin' every night. This was my first and, really, *only* big-time play, and I loved it. *Loved* it. *On Borrowed Time* was really quite a big deal, and Pud's a pretty good role in that thing. I *almost* wish that my parents had turned toward New York instead of Hollywood, because I *loved* live audiences so much. Then there was the excitement of all the people coming backstage afterwards—I remember Jack Benny came back there, I was floored by that. Directors, producers, stars, casting directors ... we had quite an audience. And, as I say, Boris got to be just like my kindly old grandfather, we spent *so* much time together. I was a likable kid, and we really got along good together—except for when I tackled that kid that one time [*laughs*]. We did the play right around Thanksgiving time, when they used to have a big parade down Hollywood Boulevard. It had floats and everything, it was quite a parade. The theater was right on the corner of Hollywood Boulevard where the parade turned left, so everybody went up on the roof of the theater, Boris and me included, and we stood up there and watched the parade go on. We still put on the show that night but, instead of having an eight o'clock start-up, we had a ten o'clock start-up, after the parade was over with. And they packed the theater.

Boris Karloff and I seemed to form an attachment with each other, primarily because of his personality. Beulah Bondi was just a nice old lady that I was acting with at the time, she didn't leave much of an impression, and neither did Ralph Morgan. The only other one who made any kind of an impression on me at all was Margaret Hamilton, because she was the Wicked Witch of the West [in *The Wizard of Oz*, 1939]—I knew her from that. And even the Witch didn't have the impact on me that Frankenstein did. She was only green! No pegs out the sides of her neck, no square head. (Thinking back on it, that play's cast was a kid's worst nightmare! All I needed was Bela Lugosi and I wouldn't have slept for the whole time we did the show!) No, I can't tell you much about the other people in the cast. Boris Karloff and Keenan Wynn were the two people I drifted to.

It just *killed* me when the show was over. I remember crying, and Boris Karloff saying,

"Tommy, don't *worry*, you'll do a *lot* more. You're *good*, you're good," as the tears were running down my face. So I got all excited when it started to look like we were going to do it all over again: They were going to do it down in Mexico City, they called me up and said, "You're gonna get to go down there and do another three weeks of it." But everybody started getting sick going down there, from the bacteria in the food. So they scrubbed it at the last minute, which of course just killed me again!

On Borrowed Time really kick-started my career. In fact, about 11, 12 years after I did that, when I was in my young manhood, I got a role on an episode of the *Mike Hammer* TV show, and the director said, "I saw you in *On Borrowed Time*. Damn, were you good in that thing!" It was amazing to me, the fact that it carried on that long.

It's kind of a disappointing thing to know that I will never be able to see myself in *On Borrowed Time*. I've got a satellite dish and I've "captured" a lot of my own stuff, taped it off *The Late Late Late Show*. But I'll never "capture" *On Borrowed Time*. Of course, I *had* to see the MGM movie version with Bobs Watson [1939], and I've got *that* recorded and saved, and that's as close as I'll get to owning a tape of the one with me and Boris Karloff. The only other guy that I was *as* close to as Boris was William Powell—I did a couple of pictures with him, and he was another just-nicer-than-nice guy. A funny thing about Powell: When we did *The Treasure of Lost Canyon* [1951], at that time he had a colostomy bag on his side and they were all worried about him. For a scene where he had to run across a room, they got a guy who looked pretty much like him and, just to run across the room, they threw the double in there. They were *that* worried about him. Then he went on to live into his 90s [*laughs*]!

On Borrowed Time was probably one of the most memorable things I did, that and *I Remember Mama* [1948] and a TV series called *Margie* [1961–1962], which was the last [acting] thing that I did. I enjoyed *Margie* because, all through my younger life, I was always playing either an orphan or a cripple—a little sad-eyed kid. Then as I grew up, I began playing the ten-thumbed, bumbling boyfriend who couldn't walk and chew gum at the same time. I played that type of character on *The Donna Reed Show* and other shows that I did, and then on *Margie*. Then, after playing these bumblers all week, I'd go out and drive my 200-mile-an-hour race cars on the weekend [*laughs*]!

I did the picture deal for a looong time—19 years. I was a

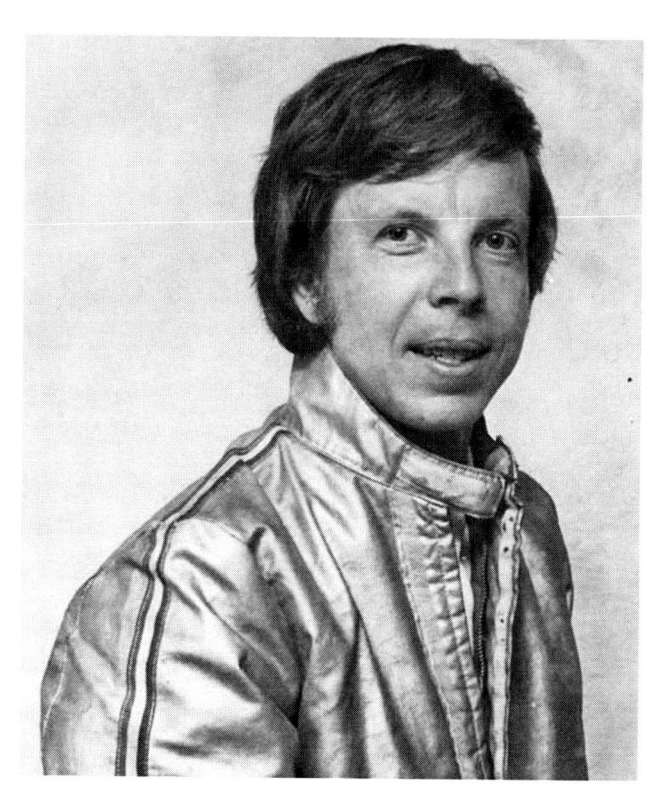

Time marches on, and Ivo grew up to become drag racing's master showman. Before his track career ended, he turned speeds over 300 MPH and raced 36 different cars in 12 classes; one of the proudest moments of his life was his 2005 induction into the Motorsports Hall of Fame of America.

working actor, I made about 100 movies and a couple of hundred television films in that time. In fact, when I started, like with the *On Borrowed Time*, they didn't even *have* television, if *that* tells you anything [*laughs*]! But then I got all wrapped up in the hot rods, and that turned into quite a deal. And in 1964 I was doing a picture called *Bikini Beach* with Annette Funicello and Frankie Avalon, driving all the cars in the thing—and at the very end of it, Boris Karloff had a cameo. Well, Boris found out that I was in the deal and he wanted to see me again. They called me in one day when I wasn't supposed to be there, because they said Boris wanted to see me. I don't know *what* happened, but he *didn't* come in that day, and then they never called me back again. It would have been fun to see him again...

All these [acting] experiences, I remember them all pretty vividly. And I remember them fondly. The bad parts I forget. It's the same thing with racing, it's *all* good. That kind of attitude [is not the norm] with kid actors, though. Look at Rusty Hamer—he *did himself in*, he couldn't take the falls. Then I turn on A&E and I see Paul Petersen and a bunch of other [former kid actors] sitting in a circle, all saying how traumatic and how terrible it was that they lost their childhood. I just shake my head. That kid acting thing, it was like a trip to the wishing well, it was *magnificent*, it *couldn't have been better*. Chasing guys on horses in Westerns, swinging through the trees on a vine with a loincloth on, with Bomba at my side—my God, how much better does it get?! I had three trips to the wishing well. The first one was to be in the movie business, the second one was to be a race car driver, and the third one has turned out to be that I lived long enough to find out that I've stood the test of time. That's kind of nice.

I've done everything from walk-ons to starring roles, hundreds of 'em, and there's a handful of assignments that stand out. *On Borrowed Time* is right at the top of the list. I'm so glad you've stirred my memories of this great time so many years ago. Boris was probably my "most favorite person" I ever acted with. Being a live show and my first big part could have something to do with it as well. But it's one of those memories that give you peace of mind in your older age. It's pretty nice to know you didn't waste your youth.

Henry Corden on *The Secret Life of Walter Mitty* (1947) and *The Black Castle* (1952)

Throughout his 1950s–1960s Hollywood heyday, character actor Henry Corden was often seen in decidedly unsympathetic parts. Downright nasty, in fact. There was something about that grim face and sepulchral voice that made casting directors think of Corden when cold-blooded creeps cropped up in a script. Corden fell into a routine of playing baddies on the big and small screen—but behind that icy countenance was a man who was grateful for every opportunity he had to ply his craft. "Oh, I was happy to be working. I was a working actor," *Corden gladly reveals.* "I was married, had two kids, had to support them. The result: I took anything. My agent said, 'I got you a part. You're gonna work for x-number of dollars. Go!' And so I did it—I had to!"

Born in Canada and raised in New York, Corden acted on the stage and in radio before migrating west in the mid–1940s; it was a sign of things to come when his first movie role turned out to that of a baddie in the 1947 comedy The Secret Life of Walter Mitty, *with Danny Kaye as the milquetoast proofreader prone to sensational (and self-aggrandizing) daydreams. Corden worked in his debut film with one of the baddest movie badmen of all time, Boris Karloff. Five years later they shared the screen a second time in Universal's* The Black Castle, *a chilling costume adventure with an eighteenth century Black Forest setting, Karloff as a cagey court physician and Corden as the abused servant of a tyrannical count (Stephen McNally).*

Boris Karloff was the sweetest, most wonderful man I'd ever met in show business.

On my first picture *The Secret Life of Walter Mitty*, the assistant director came over to me with Karloff, to introduce me to him. The a.d. said, "Boris, this is Henry Corden. Would you please watch out for him and try to give him some tips? This is his first picture." And the first thing Boris said was, "Well, I'm sure Mr. Corden could give *me* far more than I could give *him*." I mean, of *course* it was horrendously untrue [*laughs*]. But the kind of person who could say a thing like that has got to be a wonderful guy. Of course I did a lot of sitting next to him during the making of the film, and he talked quite a bit about himself. Having loved movies since I was a kid, I remembered seeing him in *Scarface* [1932] as the bad guy and a couple of

The gruesome twosome of Karloff and Henry Corden, international spy ring members, gangs up on Virginia Mayo in the whimsical comedy-adventure *The Secret Life of Walter Mitty*.

other things—I think even in *silents*. I loved him because he was willing to talk to me ... willing to talk to somebody who was *no*body, so to speak. He wasn't seeking out Danny Kaye to talk to all the time; he just sat there, and if you came over to talk to him, there he was for you. You know of course that his name was William Henry Pratt. "In *this* career, how could I be William Henry Pratt? Who would be frightened of *me*?"—that was one of the things he said to me.

Were you aware that he was one of the early starters of Screen Actors Guild? His card number was number 9 and he was one of the beginners with James Cagney and Ralph Morgan and a few others. Karloff told me, "We used to have to park three and four blocks away from where we were going to meet, because the word was already out [that they were trying to form a Guild] and the producers were already *following* us." They had to park blocks away and walk to their destination! He was on our side—the *actors'* side. It was so easy to be on the *other* side—you didn't want to risk the anger of the producers, so a lot of actors were *afraid* and didn't get involved until much, much later.

Corden did a great deal of voice work in the cartoons of Hanna-Barbera, from *Jonny Quest* villains to Fred Flintstone. He died at age 85 in May 2005.

There was another story that Karloff told that I thought was terribly interesting: At the time of *Frankenstein* [1931], Universal came to him and said, "We have this thing we want you to do, it should only take four or five days. It's the part of a monster," blah blah blah. In those days, according to what Karloff told me, you made a deal for the picture, 'cause there was no union. It was like, "For this picture you'll get x-number of dollars," "For that picture you get *this* amount of money" and so on. Well, what happened according to him in *Frankenstein* was, Universal was not aware that the Monster would come off as well as he did. Universal was gonna put [the emphasis] on Frankenstein, the scientist [played by Colin Clive]. The deal Karloff made, it was gonna be like a week's work for $400, which for then wasn't bad. But when Universal saw the dailies, they began to open their eyes and realize that [the Monster] was where the story was. So they changed it, and Karloff became *the* guy. I think he said he worked 12 weeks on it—and still only got $400! That was Universal for you! He said, "I'd get to the studio at 4:30 every day, because it took all that time to get the makeup on. And then we worked 'til ... when*ever*. I didn't get much sleep and I didn't get much money, but we got the picture done!" And it made him a star, of course.

I really enjoyed sitting and hearing his stories. What a lovely man.

Fintan Meyler on *Thriller*'s "Well of Doom" (1961)

In one of Thriller's *eeriest first-season episodes, "Well of Doom," a wealthy Englishman (Ronald Howard) en route to his bachelor party is abducted by a creepy pair of netherworld characters (Henry Daniell, Richard Kiel) with seemingly supernatural powers ... but a very Earthly interest in their prisoner's moneys and estate. Cast as Howard's fiancée, another captive of the unholy duo, was actress Fintan Meyler.*

A dark-haired, brown-eyed daughter of Ireland, Meyler (one of seven children) knew from girlhood that she wanted to be an actress, and yet as a kid she never revealed her secret ambition. But after completing her early years of schooling at a Dublin convent, she began studying at the Gate Theatre. Meyler next entered a beauty contest on a whim—and won. (Her mother had to hide the newspapers from her father.) A two-week vacation in New York was part of the teenager's prize, as Meyler picks up her own story from here...

When I arrived in America, I knew that I'd "come home," that I'd found my place in life. I *loved* the American people and I didn't want to leave the American people, because they were *wonderful*. I lost my heart to this country. I wouldn't go home, so my mother and father got on a plane—my mother had never flown before!—and came over to get me. They stayed a little while in New York, and then we got on a plane to go back to Ireland. I was *so* unhappy getting on that plane to leave America. I was on the plane with my parents but, just before they shut the door, I said, "Goodbye, Mommy. Goodbye, Daddy," and I jumped plane, with 35 cents in my pocket and my little overnight bag. Everything else, all my luggage, went back to Ireland. I did what my heart and soul told me to do: stay in America.

I got 200 jobs, one after the other—I didn't know how to do *anything*. Then I came out to Los Angeles and I got a job downtown in a diamond firm, as a receptionist. I also went to school at night, in the Drama Department at Los Angeles City College. I'd go from work to school on a bus at night. I did summer stock, four plays in Santa Fe, New Mexico, then came home to Los Angeles and got a job as an usherette at Cinerama Theater at night. That way I had my days free to go on interviews. I was totally miserable, nobody would give me *any*thing.

I got my first job on *Matinee Theater*, a live television show. They gave me the script the day before and they said, "Read that part there"—but the guy pointed to the wrong part! I studied that part that night and went back the next day. I began reading the part, and the casting director said, "Wait, wait, wait, wait! *That's* not the part. *Your* part is on the very last page—the two lines there, where the little English maid says, 'Tea is served.'" *I* had read the juvenile lead! Well, the director Lamont Johnson said, "Let her alone, she's *great*!"—and gave me the job! They liked me so much in that, they later gave me a lead—not just a juvenile lead, but a lead in one with Nico Minardos, the Greek actor. I went on from there. Once I began getting some good roles, MCA [the talent agency] came after me and they put me under contract.

I didn't see Boris Karloff when I did my *Thriller* because he only hosted it. But I'd worked with him before, on a *Playhouse 90* called "Heart of Darkness" with Roddy McDowall and Eartha Kitt. They promised me the female lead in that, but then they gave it to Inga Swenson and gave me a small part instead. I cried and everything about that. Karloff was in "Heart of Darkness" too, and I loved him. He was the gentlest, sweeeeetest man, with a little Indian-English accent. His skin was ... not saffron, but it had a yellow tinge to it. He was part East Indian—did you know that? I was very tired on the set one day and he said, "I go to this little, quiet spa on Santa Monica Boulevard near La Cienega. It's a private spa, run by a family, and they're wonderful. You ought to go there if you're tired." He said he went there at night when he left the studio, he said, "It *helps* me"—he had the most dreadful arthritis in his legs. I think that's why he walked the way he did—his legs were almost bowed from it. My sister and I went, and it *was* a lovely Swedish spa. It had a steam room, and a massage table in another room—it was *that* small. My sister and I went into the steam room and sat down, and the lady came in and poured some water on the coals and closed the door. Well, my sister and I almost fainted from the heat! We couldn't breathe, and we were young girls! We couldn't get out of there fast enough! But I did tell Boris the next day that we had been there—I said, "It was a little *hot*, but..." [*laughs*]. And he was delighted. He was lovely, so gentle to everyone, and very quiet. A very charming man.

At the time I did *Thriller*, my first baby was six weeks old. I didn't want to do that part because I had a *very* bad birth. Oh, horrible—I could barely move. But MCA pleaded with me to do it, because I think MCA handled Ronald Howard too—MCA liked to "package" the talent. They said, "It's not a big part, but they *talk* about you all the way through!" [*Laughs*] They said it wouldn't be tiring for me, so I did it.

The director, John Brahm, I remember only vaguely. Before we started shooting, I went in to see him and I was talking to him about the part—I didn't really want to do it, I just told you why. Well, I spilled something on his desk and I said, "Oh, I'm so embarrassed!" And he said, "That's the *very* thing, that's just what I want in this part! That characteristic!"

I also remember the boy, the *big* boy [Richard Kiel]. He was *so* big! And I was scared to death of him because he was so *evil*-looking! Actually, he was a *nice* boy, so sweet and kind on the set, and yet I couldn't help being a little frightened because he was just so big! I have a picture here somewhere of me in his arms, and I look like a doll.

Torin Thatcher was in that, too, and I liked him, he was darling to me. Ronald Howard was the son of Leslie Howard, the actor, and Ronald was kind of aloof. American actors are different, American actors are friendly and they're warm and we'd kid and laugh. Ronald Howard was very nice, he was charming, but he was aloof. I don't think he was comfortable in the part.

There's a scene where Ronald Howard is climbing up out of the water at the bottom of a well. He wore a wetsuit under his clothes when they shot that. The water was cold, and I guess he didn't want to be wet all through. I wasn't there when that scene was shot, I was only there for *my* scenes. But the night I saw the show on TV, I said, "Oh, my God, you can *see* the wetsuit!" The front of his shirt was open a bit and you could see the wetsuit shining right through the wet shirt! That show was an old piece, set *years* in the past, and they didn't *have* wetsuits in those days. And even if they did have wetsuits then, Ronald Howard's character wouldn't have been wearing one that night, under his tuxedo! I got the biggest kick out of that. I don't know why they didn't cut that out.

I saw "Well of Doom" again recently, and I couldn't believe how thin I was! My baby was almost eight pounds, and this was six weeks after the baby was born. Look at my little waist, isn't that amazing? And did you notice in the last part that there was a diamond ring on my finger? That was real. I was married to an oil man. You know [dancer-director] Gower Champion? I married his young brother Bob. Bob had bought me this gorgeous diamond ring—it was almost a six-karat, brilliant cut, and beautiful color. And I would never take it off [*laughs*]! They begged me at Universal when I was doing that damn show, "Pleeease take the ring off," but I said, "No, I'm gonna wear it." They had a prop man follow me around the set because of the ring, it was *that* valuable. They were scared to death. Isn't that funny?

I stopped acting after my second baby was born. Once I had my babies, I just lost the interest. Even though we had a lot of wealth, and I had a nanny and everything, I wanted to be with my children myself. I wanted to rear them, not somebody else. I wanted to teach them and be with them. Also, once MCA closed down, it wasn't easy any more. They were so good to me, absolutely wonderful—I'll always remember them.

I was twice married and twice divorced, and I have two daughters and five grandchildren. The older daughter, Darcy, is a lawyer, and the younger daughter, Rory, is a writer who lives in Ireland. There's an old expression, "If you take a daughter or son from Ireland, it'll take one back."

Meyler with Richard Kiel in her *Thriller* episode "Well of Doom." She lost interest in acting after the birth of her daughters, but in later years appeared in commercials (and worked as a literary agent). She died in July 2005.

And, you know what?, Rory went there on a holiday and fell in love with it, and that's where she lives.

I appreciate your sending the *Thriller* to me, but ... I didn't really like it, to tell you the truth. I did it, but I was sorry afterwards, because I didn't like the script. It was too dark and dreary. *Very* dreary. I don't like scary movies or TV shows. I love beautiful things. I *really* love beautiful things. I love the ocean. I love flowers. I go out every night and look to see where the Moon is and say hello to it. That's the truth!

6

Michael A. Hoey on Dennis Hoey

Film fanatic Leonard Maltin always called them Hollywood's "Real Stars": The great supporting players of the 1930s and '40s, many of whom became so well-known and well-liked that moviegoers knew what sort of character they would be playing the instant they appeared on screen. Well-known and well-liked, but not nearly as predictable, was the versatile Dennis Hoey (1893–1960), the English-born character man whose range enabled him to tackle everything from Nazty Germans to men of the West ... and Middle East ... and as far south as the Australian Outback! For many film fans, his claim to fame was playing Scotland Yard's Inspector Lestrade, forever two long steps behind "Mr. 'Olmes" (Basil Rathbone) in Universal's enduring Sherlock Holmes series.

His son Michael A. Hoey is also multi-talented, but behind *the camera. In his 50-year career, he has worn many hats on an assortment of projects, from documentaries to teen comedy and from sci-fi to Elvis; five years on the critically acclaimed* Fame *(as writer-producer-director) is just the tip of his TV iceberg, with other credits on* McCloud, Murder She Wrote, Dallas *et al. His half-century career has been crowned with several awards and many more award nominations, and now his tales from the movieland trenches have come together in the pages of his book* Elvis, Sherlock & Me: How I Survived Growing Up in Hollywood. *In this interview, he provides a preview by reminiscing about the life and times of his famous father.*

My father was what was known in the movie business as a character actor. Which meant that he was part of that extraordinary group of men and women whose faces you recognize, but whose names you seldom recall. He is undoubtedly best remembered for having created the role of the slightly inept but affable Inspector Lestrade in six of the 12 Sherlock Holmes films featuring Basil Rathbone and Nigel Bruce that Universal Pictures produced during the early to mid–1940s. This role has made him somewhat of a celebrity over the years; recently his name was even part of a *Los Angeles Times* crossword puzzle. He also appeared in a number of British films during the '30s, as well as on the London and Broadway stage and in many Hollywood films of the '40s and '50s. All in all, he made 70 films in the United States and Britain.

He was a true Victorian, having been born in London in 1893, the son of a hotelkeeper who ran a small "bed and breakfast" in Brighton, one of the beach resorts close to London. He originally intended to enter the teaching profession after he graduated from Brighton College, although he actually began a career as a stockbroker before discovering his singing talents performing for the troops during World War I.

When he returned from the war, he became actively interested in acting and was soon appearing on the London stage in musicals and as a concert singer. He made his first stage appearance in 1919 at London's Drury Lane Theatre in *Shanghai* and quickly followed that up by portraying Arif Bey in the musical *Katinka* at the Shaftsbury. He initiated the role of Ali

Ben Ali in the London production of *The Desert Song*, which ran for 432 performances at the Drury Lane in the late '20s. Wanting to make his name as a legitimate actor, he studied Shakespeare and for several seasons was a member of Sydney W. Carroll's Shakespearean troupe in the Open-Air Theatre in Regents Park. He also toured with Godfrey Tearle's Shakespearean repertory company. In 1931 during a special production of *Hamlet* at the Haymarket Theatre in London, the actor portraying Hamlet became ill, forcing Tearle to take over the role, and my father to take Tearle's place as Horatio. He also toured in a production of *Treasure Island*, in which he starred as Long John Silver.

According to my father, somewhere back in the family history, probably in the early to mid–1800s, we had some relatives who escaped Russia during one of the pogroms and came to England. Hoey was not the real family name, it's actually Hyams. We're related, in fact, to Peter Hyams, the director, and his sister Nessa, who was both a casting executive and a producer. They're my second cousins, and they in turn are the grandchildren of Sol Hurok. So, the family has a show business background [*laughs*]! I have a theory as to why he chose the name Hoey: There was an actress who was somewhat older than he, Iris Hoey, a musical comedy star around the turn of the century who was still performing in the '20s. Hers was a name that many people associated with show business, and I think that may be why he chose it.

In an English stage production of *Treasure Island*, Dennis Hoey was the one-legged Long John Silver, "as delightful a pirate as ever shivered his timbers" (*Evening Express*).

In the mid–1920s, my father traveled to America to co-star on Broadway in two more musical operettas, *Hassan*, in which he had the dubious distinction of appearing in blackface, and, during the fall season of 1926, in *Katja*, in which he had a more prominent role and enjoyed a very respectable run of 112 performances at the 44th Street Theatre. I only know of one silent film in which he appeared, *Tiptoes*, which was directed by Herbert Wilcox and starred Dorothy Gish and Will Rogers. It was made in England in 1927, and shortly after that, talkies came along and all of the rest of his films were with sound.

He married my mother, Josephine (known as Jo), in 1933. She was somewhat younger than my father when they married, and a very, very beautiful woman all through her life. I think she might have briefly worked as a photo model but, according to her sister (my aunt), she never appeared in any films or plays.

Also in 1933, my father was signed to play the title role in a film called *McCluskey the Sea*

Rover and left for Tripoli, where it was to be filmed on location. At that time, the Italians controlled Tripoli. Before filming could begin, however, there was a disagreement between the moviemakers and the Italian government regarding the firearms that were to be given to the Bedouin tribesmen appearing as extras. The government got nervous about the Bedouins getting their hands on guns and perhaps causing some sort of an insurrection, so they said, "No, you can't do that," and the film was cancelled. A movie like *McCluskey the Sea Rover* could have been a big break for my father; that was one of a number of disappointments that he had in his lifetime.

He came back to England and within weeks he was signed for a featured role as a Foreign Legion captain in *Baroud* [1933], a film by Rex Ingram, who was famous for having directed Rudolph Valentino in the silent *The Four Horsemen of the Apocalypse* [1921], a film that was a big break for *both* of them. Ingram and his wife Alice Terry filmed *Baroud* on location in Morocco, then shot their interiors in the south of France at the Victorine Studio, the same small studio where, many years later, Francois Truffaut filmed *Day for Night* [1973]. *Baroud* is famous as Ingram's only talkie; he not only wrote, produced and directed, he also played a role in it. As it turned out, it was Ingram's last film.

Baroud was just one of many films my father made in the '30s. That was the time of "the quota quickies": American movie companies had to finance x-number of British pictures before [Hollywood's] films were allowed to come into the country and play in theaters, so there was a big run of English films and my father appeared in about a dozen of them. He did *Chu-Chin-Chow* [1934] with Anna May Wong, *The Wandering*

Hoey and his wife Jo (1907–1974) on their wedding day in 1933.

Jew [1933] with Conrad Veidt and the marvelous *The Good Companions* [1933], directed by Victor Saville and starring Jessie Matthews, Edmund Gwenn and John Gielgud. He worked with many fine actors in the films of that era, Cedric Hardwicke, Dame Peggy Ashcroft, Francis L. Sullivan, Stanley Holloway and Jack Hawkins, to name just a few. *Tell England* [1931], in which he co-starred as a padre, was the same story as the much more recent Mel Gibson film *Gallipoli* [1981], about that famous World War I battle. He was even in pictures like *The Mystery of the Mary Celeste* [1935] with Bela Lugosi and *The Murder in the Red Barn* [1935] with Tod Slaughter.

Then there was a whole series of films that he did with Stanley Lupino and his [Stanley's] cousin, Lupino Lane. Stanley was Ida Lupino's father and Lupino, who was also my godfather, was what they called a knockabout comedian. He used to do physical comedy on the stage, and then he directed and starred in a series of comedy films. My father was in four of them: *Never Trouble Trouble* and *Love Lies* [both 1931], *The Maid of the Mountains* [1932] and *My Old Duchess* [1933].

The British pictures that he was most proud of were *The Good Companions* and *Baroud*—and probably the films in that Lupino Lane series. I don't know if he sang in any of the Lane films, but I do know that he sang in *The Good Companions* and in *Facing the Music* [1933], which also starred Stanley Lupino; in that one, my father performed an aria from Gounod's *Faust*. My father did more singing in his career while he was in England than after he came to the United States; here he *briefly* became a leading man, and then the character actor that he continued to be throughout the rest of his career.

As a lecherous ship's mate forcing himself on the captain's wife (Shirley Grey), Hoey appeared in the early Hammer film *The Mystery of the Mary Celeste*.

At the time of my birth, 1934, he was appearing at London's Princess Theatre in a revival of Sir Edward German's light opera *Merrie England*. Later that summer, he appeared again in repertory at the Open Air Theatre in Regents Park in several Shakespearean plays, including *Romeo and Juliet* and *The Comedy of Errors*. Interestingly enough, his namesake Iris Hoey was in the same company, and I've often wondered how she might have reacted to learning what he'd done!

In the mid–30s, when I was still an infant, he went to Queensland, Australia, to star in the film *Uncivilised* [1936], in which he played the part of Mara, the white leader of an aboriginal tribe. The plot is hard to describe, but it includes a white authoress, looking for a story in the Outback, who is kidnapped by an Afghan slaver, betrothed to a white jungle man (my father) and menaced by a hostile witch doctor and opium smugglers. On top of all this, my father breaks into song on several occasions. I finally saw *Uncivilised* for the first time about seven years ago, and it was a marvelous screening. I received a tape of it at a very propitious time: My mother's sister Yola, her son Lawrence and his wife Sharon had come from England and were visiting with my wife Katie and me, and none of us had ever seen the film. We all sat down to watch it, and it was quite an experience. It was interesting as a piece of family history and to see my father as a young man, but it was so heavy-handed that it was hard not to laugh at it. In fact, I don't think we've ever laughed so hard in our lives! It astounds me that the Australian actor Paul Hogan [*Crocodile Dundee*] once told an interviewer that *Uncivilised* was one of the films that he based *his* films on; I don't know *what* he could have been looking at! Several times my father just slightly missed having some great moments in his career: Charles Chauvel, who directed *Uncivilised*, was known for also directing *In the Wake of the Bounty* [1933], which starred an unknown by the name of Errol Flynn. Flynn had a lot more success with *that* film than my father did with *his*; *In the Wake of the Bounty* was one of Flynn's "steps to stardom." But I can't imagine that *In the Wake of the Bounty* was that much better a film, based on what I saw as an example of Chauvel's directing and writing on *Uncivilised*!

After he came back from doing *Uncivilised*, he appeared in another stage musical, a revival of John Gay's *The Beggar's Opera*, opposite Isabel Jeans. The following month, signed to appear in a new Broadway play produced by the Shuberts, he sailed off to America for the first time since 1926. The play, *Green Waters*, opened and closed in five days [in November 1936]—and almost closed the theater as well! But while he was in New York City, he met an agent who said he could get him plenty of work on the radio, which was very hot at that time. My father remained in New York to find out what the new agent could do for him. Well, he was immediately working on radio's *The Theater Guild on the Air*, and then co-starring in a 15-minute, five-times-a-week radio serial called *Pretty Kitty Kelly* and playing a recurring role on *The Adventures of Ellery Queen*.

In December of 1936, my father was signed to play Edward Rochester opposite Katharine Hepburn in a Theater Guild production of *Jane Eyre* that would tour the country and then come to Broadway. At that point, Hepburn's film career was in the toilet—she was box office poison. I think my father and Hepburn were on the road for something like six months, and for part of that time my mother came over to travel with him, while I of course stayed in London with my nanny at my mother's parents' home. It was when *Jane Eyre* was in Chicago that suddenly Hepburn had a new suitor, a tall man who wore Stetson hats pulled down over his eyes. It was Howard Hughes. He and Hepburn would run off together after each show and have dinner in a quiet corner of a restaurant. My mother and father also frequently dined there, and quite often would see them huddled together.

Jane Eyre was doing quite well, and I think my father had high hopes that it would go into Broadway; obviously, playing the romantic lead opposite Katharine Hepburn on Broadway could have done his career a great deal of good. What no one knew at the time was that Hepburn was only doing *Jane Eyre* as she bided her time waiting while playwright Philip Barry was writing *The Philadelphia Story* as a vehicle for her. By the time *Jane Eyre* reached Washington D.C., *Philadelphia Story* was completed, and Hepburn decided that *that* was the play

Jo, Michael and Dennis Hoey in New York's Central Park, 1939.

she wanted to open on Broadway. For her it was the right choice, there's no question about it, but it didn't help my father's career!

Amidst all this work, the war clouds were beginning to build in England, so my father decided to move my mother, me, and our nanny, Violet Miller, to the U.S., to be with him. That's when we came over, somewhere around mid–1937. He rented a lovely two-story flat in a brownstone at 175 East 71st Street.

On September the 2nd, 1937, just before my third birthday, my father was part of the enormous cast in the opening performance of the new Broadway production *Virginia*. The book was written by Laurence Stallings, who had written *What Price Glory?*, and Owen Davis, who had *Jezebel* and *Whoopee!* to his credit, and the music was by Arthur Schwartz, who co-wrote the songs for the movie *The Band Wagon* [1953]—and yet *Virginia* enjoyed only a run of about eight weeks. Which is unfortunate, because by all reports it was a marvelous spectacle. My father played Sir Guy Carleton, one of the wealthy landowners in the Virginia colony, and another member of the cast, portraying the governor of the colony, was Nigel Bruce, which is rather interesting considering what happened later on. As a special birthday treat, my mother took me to the theater to see a matinee. I don't personally remember doing this, because I was just three years old at the time, but years later I was told that when my father first appeared on the stage, I grew very excited and announced to the entire audience that there stood "my daddy" [*laughs*]! Of course, the poor actors had to wait for the laughter to die down before they could continue with the performance, but I'm sure my father secretly enjoyed being singled out in that enormous cast. He might not have appreciated my upstaging him, though—probably the only time in my life that I ever did!

In 1939, the New York World's Fair opened, and one of the big things that was introduced by RCA there was television. Later that same year, my father starred in a live television production of Noël Coward's *Hay Fever*. Appearing opposite him in the small cast were his very close friend, actress Isobel Elsom, and a 19-year-old Montgomery Clift, in one of his first professional appearances.

My father went on tour again, this time playing Col. Pickering opposite Ruth Chatterton and Barry Thomson in a revival of Shaw's *Pygmalion*; the plan was for the play to finish its run in Los Angeles and for us to join him there. The war in Europe had started by that point, and my father felt that Hollywood would soon need British character actors who could also be called upon to play rather nasty Germans. So that's when he decided to move the family to California. We came out in the spring of 1940 and lived at first in a very lovely little apartment on Charleville Drive in Beverly Hills. Then, about a year and a half later, we moved into a house on North Crescent Drive that he had bought. I can tell you the exact date—December the 7th, 1941—because I still vividly remember standing for the first time in the driveway at 167 North Crescent Drive, listening to the radio in our car announce the bombing of Pearl Harbor.

My father made his first Hollywood picture in 1941, a small scene in *A Yank in the R.A.F.* He had a good run in Hollywood, as many as seven pictures a year. That was terrific in those days, and nowadays it would be *impossible* for an actor to get that many films a year. He was very well-known at 20th Century–Fox and did a number of films there in the early to mid–40s: In addition to *A Yank in the R.A.F.*, he was in two other Tyrone Power films, *Son of Fury* and *This Above All* [both 1942]. In *Bomber's Moon* and *They Came to Blow Up America* [both 1943] he played German officers. Fox director Henry King liked him a lot, and so did John Cromwell, who directed him in *Son of Fury* and *Anna and the King of Siam* [1946].

It's always been a mystery to me why my father's name is listed in the credits for *How*

Green Was My Valley [1941], but he doesn't appear in the film. I remember once seeing a production still from the film, showing him standing in young Hew's (Roddy McDowall) classroom with Rhys Williams and Barry Fitzgerald looking threateningly at him. In trying to fill in the gaps, I visualized a scenario where director John Ford cast my father as the sadistic teacher who takes a cane to Hew's back and is then in turn beaten by Fitzgerald and Williams in retaliation. In my version, when Ford saw how small the two men looked beside my father he decided to recast and reshoot the sequence with another, more diminutive actor. I would have liked to have questioned Mr. Ford personally about this while I was working as his assistant editor on *Sergeant Rutledge* [1960], but I never found the appropriate moment. As it turned out, the answer was much simpler. Ford filmed Philip Dunne's screenplay exactly as he had written it, with Morton Lowry playing Mr. Jonas, the sadistic teacher who gets his comeuppance from Williams and Fitzgerald; however, the scene then continued with my father [playing Mr. Motshill, the school's headmaster] entering and angrily confronting the two men. What takes place next is definitely anticlimactic and it's my guess that it was appropriately cut from the final print after one of the previews.

In several '40s war films, Hoey's character played on the wrong team. Here he is as German Col. Von Grunow in 20th Century–Fox's *Bomber's Moon* (1943).

In those days, 20th Century–Fox had a magnificent back lot filled with all kinds of wonderful sets and set pieces and props. The back lot backed up to a fence near the Beverly Hills High School football field—and there was a hole in that fence. One Sunday afternoon, my buddies Neville Jason, Ed White and I decided to crawl through that hole and go exploring. So these three little ten-year-olds went scrabbling through the hole in the fence, and through a lot of tall grass, and then began walking toward a group of Naval aircraft that were probably being used for Fox's movie *Wing and a Prayer* [1944]. But before we got to them, I saw a rooster tail of dust in the distance and realized that there was a car speeding out towards us. We'd hardly gotten through the fence and we'd already been spotted! We hid in the tall grass and the car pulled up and stopped, literally inches from my head. The driver, one of the Fox security guys, climbed out and said, gruffly, "All right, kids, come on, get *up*!" Eddie and Neville stood up, and I did not. But I thought to myself, "I've *got* to get up, because if I don't, when this car moves again, it'll roll right over me," and so I also got to my feet. The three of us were put in the back of this guy's car and, as he drove us down to the studio police office, he gave us a line about, "Don't you kids know that there's a war on, and we've got machine-guns on the top of every stage? You could have been killed!" Of course, all of this was just to scare the heck out of us. But what scared me even *more* was, I ended up having to give them *my* father's name and phone number—and he was working at Fox at the time in *The Keys of the Kingdom* [1944], playing Gregory Peck's father. "Oh-oh," I thought to myself, "this is going to go over like a lead balloon!" So on this Sunday afternoon, my father had to get in his car and come over and pick us up, and he *was* pretty furious. But by the time he dropped Ed off, and he dropped Neville off, and we got home, his anger had subsided enough that I didn't get the belt—just the lecture!

This, incidentally, was just one of the *several* times in our lives when Neville and I tried to get away with something, and always we would get caught before we ever got three steps into it. One particularly boring summer afternoon, we sneaked up onto the roof of the California Bank Building and discovered that we could work our way from building to building up the entire block of Beverly Drive from Wilshire Boulevard to Dayton Way. We were happily playing cops and robbers on the roofs when suddenly it turned into the real thing, as two Beverly Hills policemen showed up with drawn weapons and escorted us back down. Somebody had reported two suspects with guns up on the roof and there we were, busted again.

In the spring of 1942, my father returned to New York to appear in the Broadway production of *Heart of a City*. It was based on the true story of the Windmill Theatre, a small London playhouse that was famous for its musical revues and for the fact that it refused to close its doors during the London Blitz. My father played Leo Saddle, a character based on the Windmill's impresario, Vivian Van Damm—the role recently portrayed by Bob Hoskins in the film *Mrs. Henderson Presents* [2005]. In spite of a *New York Sun* review that called the play "funny and moving and full of unobvious excitements," it managed to go dark in less than a month and my father was on his way back to Hollywood and the beginning of a new chapter in his career.

In 1942, my father was hired by Universal to play the Scotland Yard Inspector Lestrade in *Sherlock Holmes and the Secret Weapon*, the second in the Basil Rathbone–Nigel Bruce "Sherlock Holmes" series, and the first in which Lestrade appears. My father eventually did six of the 12 Holmeses. He *could* have done seven: There was one other film, *Dressed to Kill* [1946], that called for Insp. Lestrade, but unfortunately my father was committed to doing another film at the time, *Anna and the King of Siam*, and was not available. So Universal went back to the script and gave the Scotland Yard man a new name, Inspector Hopkins, and hired an actor who was one of my father's best friends, Carl Harbord, to play the part. I noticed when I saw *Dressed to Kill* that they also cut down the importance of the character.

One day he decided to take me onto the set of the Holmes film he was then working in, and I asked if my friend Neville Jason could come along. (Neville was also English; he, his mother and his brother had been evacuated from London during the blitz.) My dad was agreeable to that, and so the two of us went with him over to Universal and watched the shooting of the museum scene in *The Pearl of Death* [1944] where the villain steals the pearl, runs across the room and up some stairs, crashes out through a stained-glass window and escapes. In the movie, the villain was played by Miles Mander, but it was a stunt double, naturally, who went out through the window. At the time I thought, "My *God*, it's real glass!," but of course in those days it was actually candy glass—plates of "glass" which could be broken without injury. After the scene was shot, the director Roy William Neill gave Neville and me, as a souvenir, a fairly large piece of this broken "glass." Of course, when Neville and I went home, we began to turn my garage into a "soundstage" and put together a "camera" out of cardboard boxes and

Hoey (right) as Scotland Yard Insp. Lestrade in *The Pearl of Death*, one of the Sherlock Holmes movies he made with Basil Rathbone (standing) as Holmes and Nigel Bruce (seated) as Dr. Watson.

immediately began to "re-film" the whole sequence with our imagination. That was how I first began to really become fascinated with film, by watching the making of films with my father. And maybe Neville was inspired, too, because *he* went on to become a successful actor.

My father's hair was light red, a "blondish" red color—what there was *of* it. He lost his hair fairly early, so in most of his films he's wearing this marvelous toupee that he owned. *Except* when he plays Lestrade. In real life, he grew his hair long on one side and combed it over the bald spot on top, and so as Lestrade you see him as he actually looked, with his own hair. Only in one Holmes film, *The Pearl of Death*, does he wear his toupee.

He was very good friends with Nigel Bruce—"Willie" Bruce—a lovely, lovely man. I visited the Holmes sets on a couple of occasions, and one time Basil Rathbone and Nigel Bruce signed 8 × 10 photographs for me. Nigel Bruce signed a photograph of himself, "To Michael, who is a nice boy in spite of his father." [*Laughs*] I had that picture pinned to my bedroom wall for some time, and then one day it "mysteriously" disappeared. I think my father must have gotten tired of seeing that particular comment up there! As for Rathbone, I found him to be somewhat of an aloof person, and I didn't really warm up to him. Rathbone and my father probably respected one another, I don't think they *dis*liked one another, but they were never close.

One day in 1965, while I was working at Producers Studio on an American International film called *Sergeant Dead Head*, I wandered over to the soundstage next door where they were filming *The Ghost in the Invisible Bikini*, another of the AIP teenage specials. I had heard that

Mr. Rathbone was working that day and I wanted to pay my respects. It had been 21 years since I had sat with him on the set of *The Pearl of Death* at Universal and, although I had watched him perform in numerous films over those years, I was nonetheless shocked to see the frail old man seated in a director's chair, away from all of the activity, quietly drinking a cup of tea. It saddened me to think that this once-great actor was now reduced to playing a supporting role to a cast of callow teenagers in a low-budget exploitation film. I introduced myself, reminding Mr. Rathbone of my father, and of our meeting in 1944 on the set of the Holmes film. He seemed to vaguely remember my father and politely asked about his health. When I informed him that my father had died several years earlier, he nodded silently, as if acknowledging the inevitability of what he knew would soon be his own fate. I couldn't help feeling that I was intruding, as he seemed to drift off into his own thoughts, so I made some self-conscious comment about the continuing popularity of the old Sherlock Holmes films, to which he smiled in gratitude, and I excused myself.

My dad was under a non-exclusive contract to Universal, playing Lestrade. They only used him in two or three other [non–Holmes] pictures—but they seemed to see him playing only one role, Lestrade, even though they might have called his character by another name! In *Frankenstein Meets the Wolf Man* [1943], he plays a Scotland Yard inspector and even wore the same bloody wardrobe—Lestrade's bowler hat and the raincoat! Then he did a film called *She-Wolf of London* [1946] and it was the same thing, a Scotland Yard inspector, only at least he was not wearing the same clothes in *that* one. So my father was very typecast at Universal.

He also kept busy doing radio. There was also a *Sherlock Holmes* radio series with Rathbone and Bruce, and my dad played Lestrade on that for about a year of its run. One evening he took me to watch a live broadcast of *The Whistler*, a very popular CBS mystery program that he was appearing on. The Whistler, you'll recall, was the host-narrator whose opening speech went, "I am the Whistler, and I know many things, for I walk by night. I know many strange tales, many secrets hidden in the hearts of men and women..." and so on—and of course he also whistled. The thing that absolutely amazed me the night of that broadcast was that the whistling was actually done by a *woman*—a woman who, I learned years later from one of the Old-Time Radio

Lestrade (Hoey) comforts a shaken Holmes (Rathbone) in a scene from 1946's *Terror by Night*. In real life, the two actors were not close.

websites, worked at a local defense plant. Apparently she was a very accomplished whistler, so she would come in once a week on the night they did the program and she would do the [*Hoey whistles the* Whistler *theme*]!

Another mystery program on which my father appeared quite frequently was *Suspense*, and there's one episode I particularly liked. It was based on "August Heat" by W.F. Harvey, a marvelous short story that takes place during—if you can imagine—a heat wave in London. The first time it was done for *Suspense* [May 31, 1945], Ronald Colman and my dad were the stars, and it was so very successful that it was re-done for radio about three times. For each remake they brought my father back, but the role that Ronald Colman played was now done by somewhat lesser actors. I don't think it was re-done as many times as *Suspense*'s other big success "Sorry, Wrong Number," but "August Heat" was performed at least four times over the years and it was a wonderful story.

Rex Harrison, whose first film role when he came to this country was as the king in *Anna and the King of Siam*, was a friend of my father's from London. My father was cast in *Anna* as the British ambassador to Siam and there's an interesting story about that: In the film, there's a sequence where the king has invited the ambassadors from various governments, England, France, Germany and so on, to a dinner at the palace to show them that he is an educated man. For entertainment, the wives in the king's harem are going to present a production of *Uncle Tom's Cabin*. Anna, played by Irene Dunne, is supervising the wives as they get into their costumes and she expresses her concern that the women aren't wearing any underwear under their hoopskirts. In the film as it was released, there's all this buildup to presenting the play, but no pay-off, as the play is never seen. Well, I remember my father telling me that there *was* a pay-off gag, and that he was the one who reacted to it: When the wives took their bows at the end of the play, all their hoopskirts went up in back. Of course, in 1946 they couldn't show what was revealed—the reaction was played off my father's face, as he saw their nude bottoms smiling at him. But that was enough for the Breen Office to say, "No, no, you can't do that, it's too risqué," and Fox had to cut the whole sequence. After this cut was made, my father, who was *on* the film for weeks as I recall, now had only one brief closeup and I think maybe one line of dialogue. This, coming after *How Green Was My Valley*, was the second time he'd been cut out of a film at 20th Century–Fox.

Naturally, I would go to the movies to see the films my father was in. I *loved* movies—I wouldn't miss any movie that came along. My buddies and I loved my dad's Sherlock Holmes films and also the war movies he was in. I'm sure that I saw just about every new film of his, with the exception of a couple of the "women's films" that he made during the latter part of his career. One of my favorites, I think *the* favorite, was *A Thousand and One Nights* [1945], the only film he made at Columbia, a wonderful "play" on Aladdin and the magic lamp. The reason I liked it so much was that my father had a dual role: He played the caliph and the caliph's evil brother, who at one point sneaks up behind the caliph and hits him on the head. As in *The Prisoner of Zenda*, the real caliph ends up imprisoned somewhere while the evil brother pretends to be the caliph and does all these dastardly deeds. Evelyn Keyes played a genie, Cornel Wilde was Aladdin, Phil Silvers was Aladdin's pickpocket sidekick (and played it very anachronistically, as if it was 1945), and "the *other* Rex Ingram," the African-American actor, played a giant, recreating his role from the 1940 *The Thief of Bagdad*. *A Thousand and One Nights* was fun and had a lot of sharp dialogue, and I really enjoyed seeing *two* of my father in some scenes, via a split screen. Years later I edited the sound effects on a film that Cornel Wilde directed, *Beach Red* [1967], and when we reminisced about *A Thousand and One Nights* he agreed it was one of his favorites as well.

Being the son of an actor, and growing up in Hollywood, naturally I had ambitions to become an actor myself, and all through high school I was appearing in plays. The first production in which I appeared was an original musical at Beverly Hills High School in which James Drury [from TV's *The Virginian*] and I were members of the chorus. (The student directing was Jay Sandrich, who went on to become one of the top television directors. Everybody went to Jay to do their pilots.) In addition to acting, I also started a vocal group called the Harmonaires with two other singers and two musicians—one of whom was Robert Blake, who played guitar! Shortly after graduation, I went to the Laguna Summer Theater, spending one season there as an apprentice (I appeared in two plays that year), and then came back a second year only as an actor and appeared in *Black Chiffon* with Selena Royle. I also did a couple of plays in Los Angeles—"little theater"-type stuff. But I didn't make any headway in films because I wasn't "the right type." I wasn't the blond, good-looking boy next door, I was *tall*, which was also a problem for my father, who lost several roles because of it. He had a terrific chance to play a ruthless sea captain opposite Alan Ladd in *Two Years Before the Mast* [1946], but since my dad was 6' 3", Ladd didn't want to work with him. The *Two Years Before the Mast* role went to Howard da Silva, who was much shorter.

Another near-miss: He was actually signed to play Paulus the Centurion in *The Robe*. Not the 1953 20th Century–Fox *The Robe* with Richard Burton, but an earlier [never-produced] attempt to film that story. Several years before the Burton *Robe* was made, Mervyn LeRoy, who was going to direct, and the producer Frank Ross hired my father's good friend Herb Meadow to write the screenplay. But unfortunately, for budgetary reasons, they never got the film off the ground, and then Fox got a-hold of the project and of course they hired an entirely new cast. Jeff Morrow, who played the Centurion, became a character star out of that film. My dad, poor guy—again, *close*, but didn't get the brass ring.

But despite the parts he did *not* get, he made a *very* comfortable living. He did very well throughout his career, and we enjoyed living in good surroundings at all times. We had a baby grand piano in the living room of the house on North Crescent, and for years, *long* after he last performed professionally as a singer, he would vocalize and do some singing every morning, as part of his routine. My father had a marvelous voice and I

Hoey had a comic part in Fox's *Anna and the King of Siam* until the Production Code folks saw it and had it excised from the film. As if his *Anna* appearance was cursed, even this rare portrait shot is negative-damaged.

really enjoyed hearing him sing. Two of the songs he'd sing, I really loved: "Danny Boy," which to this day when I hear it brings me to tears, and "Old Man River." He was a bass baritone, but his lower range was very, very solid. He would sit at the piano and do chords [*singing*]: "AH AH AH AAAH AAAAH AH AH ... AH AH AH AAAH AAAAH AH AH!" To some extent, I inherited his voice, but I was more of a lyric baritone, I had a higher range than he did.

My father was still interested in writing and directing, and in fact came up with a story about the famous Drury Lane Ghost, which supposedly haunts that London theater. He wrote a treatment that he thought he could sell to Universal for the Sherlock Holmes series. It would have been a natural but, unfortunately, his timing was off; by the time he did this, they were winding down the series. I still have a copy of the treatment and it would have made a wonderful episode for Holmes, Watson and Lestrade. Then in 1946 he optioned a book by Anthony Gilbert, adapted it into a play, took it back to New York, and actually got some producers interested in it. The play, which he called *The Haven*, was a "drawing room mystery": one set, five or six characters. He didn't direct it, he hired someone else to do that, but he *did* play the lead, and he had in the cast Melville Cooper, Dennis King, Valerie Cossart and Queenie Leonard. Marvelous actors, right? It should have been a hit. It was a ... well, it was a bomb [*laughs*]. It lasted about five performances, and then it closed. He was trying to do kind-of an "Agatha Christie mystery," but it *wasn't* Agatha Christie and I guess that's what went wrong. Ironically, only a year later, there was an *enormous* success on Broadway called *An Inspector Calls* by J.B. Priestley, which was in effect the same idea. But there was a much more philosophical bent to the story, it wasn't just a straight murder mystery.

Shortly after my father returned from New York, he and my mother were divorced. A short time later, he married the younger sister of foreign correspondent Charles Collingwood. I barely got to know her because I was away in boarding school in Canada for several years, and by the time I returned, the marriage had also ended in divorce. I remember that I spent an interesting week with my father while he appeared at the La Jolla Playhouse with Sylvia Sidney in Edward Chodorov's play *Kind Lady*. Gregory Peck, who was born in La Jolla, Dorothy McGuire and Mel Ferrer had formed the Playhouse that year, and my father's play was the second one of the inaugural season. My mother remarried in 1949 and my father moved back to New York the following year. His last film before he left Hollywood was a Universal Western called *The Kid from Texas* [1950], starring Audie Murphy as Billy the Kid. I didn't see much of my father for the next few years, although he did return a couple of times to perform in films. The first time he came out in 1952, I met his newest wife, a wealthy widow who, under the pen name of Bayka Russell, wrote poetry and published it herself. I have to admit that she and I didn't hit it off.

One of the three films he made after his move to New York was *Plymouth Adventure* [1952], in which he had a rather small role. It was a large-scale film with an all-star cast and my father "opened" the film, playing the constable who sends the Pilgrims off on the *Mayflower* at the very beginning. Another was *Caribbean* [1952], sort of a B-grade pirate movie made at Paramount by Bill Pine and Bill Thomas—"The Two Dollar Bills," as they were called. It had a good cast, including John Payne and Arlene Dahl, with my dad playing the first mate of a notorious pirate captain [Sir Cedric Hardwicke]. Once again I visited him on the set and met Payne and Hardwicke. I was also *re*introduced to the director Edward Ludwig, who was directing my father for the fourth time. I had originally met him on the set of the John Wayne movie *Wake of the Red Witch* at Republic in 1948; of course, at *that* time I was far more impressed with meeting Wayne. *This* time around, however, my interest lay with the job of the director. In fact, I had decided that a director was what I wanted to become.

Following these two films, my father returned to New York and I wouldn't see him again for almost eight years. He did do some more TV work there, including one show that was very interesting: an episode of *Omnibus* in which some of the world's most famous detective story writers attempt to solve a murder. The irony was that, although my father was playing Sir Arthur Conan Doyle, he was dressed like Sherlock Holmes, with the pipe and deerstalker hat!

He and Bayka had an apartment on Park Avenue, a co-op, and she also had a nice home in Tampa, Florida. Tampa, unfortunately, was definitely where my father should *not* have been living, because he suffered from emphysema, and the humidity must have caused serious problems for him. In 1959, when my second child was born—my son Dennis, who of course was named after him—my father immediately flew out to spend a week or two with us. It was the first time he'd been out here since doing those last two movies, and it was sort of a reconciliation, because for a few years we had been somewhat estranged. It was kind of a wonderful time, as we were able to rekindle our relationship. I was then working at Disney Studios as an assistant film editor, and I took him to the studio to meet an old friend of his from England, Albert Whitlock, the matte artist. I had written a screenplay called *The Guilty*, which I gave him to read, and he was very impressed with it. *So* impressed, in fact, that he gave it to our very successful writer-friend Herb Meadow to read, saying, "Look what the kid has done," but with great pride, Herb later told me.

In the midsummer of 1960, I was working at Warner Brothers as an assistant editor on the movie *Sunrise at Campobello*. One morning my then-wife Barbara told me across the breakfast table that she'd just had "the most awful dream": She was standing in a room ... there were rows of chairs on either side, and an aisle that led down the center ... and there at the other end of the room was an open casket. She couldn't see who was in it, but somehow she knew that the head was on the left side of the casket and the feet were on the right. I went to work and, about an hour and a half later, Barbara phoned to tell me that *she* had just received a call notifying us that my father had passed away. My father's wife ... I suppose I could call her my stepmother, but we didn't get along ... had never called to tell me that he was in hospital. Dore Schary, the writer-producer of *Sunrise at Campobello*, knew my father because he [Dennis] had appeared in a number of MGM films both before and

Michael Hoey has worn many hats in Hollywood, including executive producer of the Academy of Television Arts & Sciences' Creative Arts Emmy Awards. He's a two-time Emmy nominee himself.

during Schary's tenure as head of the studio. Schary told me, "Go to Florida, we'll find someone to take over your job while you're gone. Take as much time as you need."

My flight to Tampa was quite a hair-raising experience, actually: From L.A. to Dallas I flew in my first jet, which was quite wonderful, and in Dallas I transferred to another airplane, a four-engine DC-4. About four minutes after it left Dallas' Love Field, we passengers all suddenly noticed black smoke coming out of the side of one of the engines. Black smoke meant fire—and that wasn't good! I had recently worked on a film called *The Crowded Sky* [1960], which was all about a midair collision [*laughs*], so I was *full* of information I didn't need to have at that particular moment about what the pilot should be doing! I was sitting there saying, "The pilot should be pulling the lever that activates the fire extinguishers so that it will extinguish the flames and the black smoke will turn white. That's what he *should* do." But he didn't; instead, the plane suddenly went into this very steep dive, which was the pilot's attempt to snuff out the fire before it burned through the firewall into the fuel tank. He succeeded in putting the fire out, but by this point the passengers were in hysterics. Then, of course, that wonderful, quiet voice that pilots have came over the loudspeaker saying, "You may have noticed that there was a slight problem..." [*Laughs*]. The pilot turned us around and returned to Love Field, and in the landing he blew a tire and almost ground-looped the plane. I was able to book myself on another plane, and during *that* flight it was struck by lightning! I thought, "My father is definitely trying to *tell* me something!"

I finally arrived in Tampa at about 6:30 A.M. of the day of the funeral. My "stepbrother"— again, that's only a technical term, I hardly knew the man—was kind enough to come out at that time of the morning and pick me up and take me to the hotel that they had arranged for me to stay at. (I wasn't invited by Bayka to stay at their house, even though it was a large mansion on one of the canals in Tampa.) I slept for about an hour, and then my stepbrother picked me up and we went to the funeral home. When I walked in, it was the exact replica of my wife Barbara's description of the scene that she had dreamt. I walked down the aisle between the rows of chairs to the open casket, and there he was, lying in state, his head on the left side and his feet on the right. That was the last time that I saw him. After the funeral, I did have a brief opportunity to come to the house, where my "stepmother" said, "You can go in your father's study and spend an hour in there if you'd like, and take whatever you can." That's why, today, I have some of his pictures—he had retained a few of his movie stills—and his scrapbook.

In spite of our sometimes fractious relationship, I loved my father, and his loss was a terrible blow. I had no brothers or sisters and had never known my grandparents on either side of the family. Years later I would learn that I did indeed have a family in England, that I would come to know and love, but at the time, apart from my wife and my children, the loss of my father carved out an enormous portion of my immediate family. I still keep the photos of him in his various film roles, and I enjoy watching his films on television. Although he seems to have become forever associated with his portrayal of Inspector Lestrade, I personally think that some of his best work was in other films such as *Kitty* [1945], *Wake of the Red Witch* and, of course, *A Thousand and One Nights*.

My one regret has always been that my father's death, two years before Jack Warner promoted me to producer at Warner Studios, denied me the opportunity of ever working with him, or of knowing if my later career as a writer-director would have made him proud of me.

7

Memories of Bela Lugosi

Earl Bellamy on *The Return of the Vampire* (1943)

In the 1940s, Universal was ahead of the pack in the production of fright films, and other studios were following their lead. In 1943, in the wake of Universal's Frankenstein Meets the Wolf Man, *Columbia decided on a two-in-one monster mash of their own: Bela Lugosi (Universal's Dracula) played a vampire and Matt Willis (a dead ringer for Lon Chaney, Jr., Universal's Wolf Man) played his werewolf-flunky in the company's kitschy* The Return of the Vampire.

The film's assistant director Earl Bellamy (1917–2003) was a Minnesotan who attended college in L.A., began working at Columbia as a messenger in 1935 and then worked there as an a.d. for over a dozen years. He is best-known for his subsequent TV directing work, including scores of episodes of most of the top "baby boomer" series: Leave It to Beaver, My Three Sons, The Andy Griffith Show, Get Smart *and more. (He even went back to directing vampires and werewolves on* The Munsters *and in the big-screen* Munster, Go Home!, *1966.) Here he reminisces about his initial soundstage encounter with the supernatural…*

I remember Bela Lugosi, the star of *Return of the Vampire*, very well. Bela was a funny guy, you never knew what he was gonna do. He would come in in the mornings with that cape on, and flourish it around, and then go get the makeup. The makeup was mainly white, to give you that feeling of … well, I don't know *what* [*laughs*], but he wanted it white! And a bit of red on the lips. Let me tell you a very funny situation with him: When he worked, he *believed* that [character] was who *he* was. When playing a monster or vampire or what*ever*, he was *it*. He didn't talk much to anybody, he was kind of "within himself," but nice to work with. Between takes, *you* could go up to him and talk. But you could tell he really felt he was a vampire, *off* stage or *on* stage. He was a real character!

Frieda Inescort [playing a vampire hunter in the film] was a doll, and a wonderful actress. Very dedicated to her craft, I'll tell you that. She knew at all times what she was doing, and worked very hard. She was just a first-rate lady. I also thought the guy who played the werewolf [Matt Willis] did a darn good job. The makeup was superb.

Sam White was a good producer. He knew what he was after, and he worked with director Lew Landers very well. Sam was a nice person; I enjoyed working with Sam *and* with Lew. Lew was fine, and he was fun. He worked very fast, and he did a good job with what he had to work with.

A very funny thing happened: Bela gave out tickets to everybody to come up and see him in *Arsenic and Old Lace*, the play that he was starring in, at a theater [the Music Box Theater] on Hollywood Boulevard. We all went, and the funny thing was that he gave us all seats right down front—we had the first and second row of seats 'cause it involved all the crew. And if you moved, why, he would look down and see you, and watch what you were doing, whether you were leaving the theater or *what*. When the intermission time came, we all wanted to go, it was so terrible [*laughs*], but we *couldn't*, he'd stiffed us by putting us in the first two rows. We had to sit through the whole play—he really *got* us all with those first and second row seats! He kept us "under lock and key"! [*Do you remember why you thought* Arsenic and Old Lace *was bad?*] Well, the cast for one thing. And Bela for another—he was just so *bad*. He was better in [*Return of the Vampire*].

As a horror picture, *The Return of the Vampire* wasn't bad at all. Lugosi and the werewolf guy were both good—very good. As I say, Bela got to the point where he really and truly believed himself to be the character, the vampire, and when he would go into scenes out in the cemetery and all like that, boy, he was the real thing.

Author's note: I mentioned Bellamy's eye-opening comments about Lugosi acting like he "truly believed himself to be" a vampire to Richard Kline, a *Return of the Vampire* assistant cameraman. "I would agree with that," Kline said without hesitation. "Well, he would sleep in the coffin at lunchtime! I don't know why; it was almost like a gag. When he wanted to take a nap, he'd use the coffin on the set. And he really did appear to

Top: Vampire Bela Lugosi gets a wake-up call from his werewolf henchman (Matt Willis) in *The Return of the Vampire*. Reportedly the actor slept in that coffin during lunch breaks. Well, it had to be more comfortable than the crypt staircase (*above*)!

sleep. If I'd come back early from lunch, there he'd be, sound asleep. Finally when the lunch hour was over, the assistant director, Earl I guess it was, would yell, 'Okay, we're baaack!' and Bela would get up! He was the consummate vampire.

"We shot that picture at a place Columbia didn't own but which they used a lot, Darmour Studios on Santa Monica Boulevard, not far from Columbia proper. I saw *Return of the Vampire* on Turner Classic Movies just the other day. It really *is* a bad picture, isn't it? Just terrible!"

Alex Gordon on *Bela Lugosi Meets a Brooklyn Gorilla* (1952)

No one should judge a book by its cover, or a movie by its title. But any misgivings one might have about Bela Lugosi Meets a Brooklyn Gorilla, *based on that undignified (and unwieldy) moniker, would likely be confirmed by a viewing of this schlock comedy. Martin and Lewis imitators Duke Mitchell and Sammy Petrillo star as castaways on a South Seas island where mad scientist Lugosi (in one of his final speaking roles) is conducting revolutionary evolutionary experiments—and transforms Mitchell into a gorilla.*

A daily visitor to the set was Lugosi's English-born friend and fan Alex Gordon (1922–2003), a young writer-producer then collaborating on various film projects with Edward D. Wood, Jr. Lugosi's self-appointed chauffeur and Man Friday during Brooklyn Gorilla *production, Gordon reports here on the making of the notorious no-budget horror spoof, and its young stars' efforts to make a monkey out of Lugosi.*

In 1952, I was seeing Bela Lugosi, trying to set up pictures with him and accompanying him to various places. One day Lugosi mentioned to me that he had an offer to appear in *Bela Lugosi Meets a Brooklyn Gorilla* with two actors he had never heard of. It was going to be a Jack Broder production, and he wondered if I had ever heard of Jack Broder. I told him that I had rather an unfortunate experience with Broder, and that was with the script *The Atomic Monster* [later filmed as *Bride of the Monster*, 1956] which I had written in New York. After I'd come out to Hollywood and produced *The Lawless Rider* [in 1952], I tried to set up *The Atomic Monster*. I went with Sam Arkoff to see Jack Broder and pitched it to him. Broder's exact words were, "What are you trying to do?" I said, "Well, I'd like to produce this picture *The Atomic Monster*." He asked, "Have you produced anything before?" I said, "Only *The Lawless Rider*."

"Well," he said, "you don't really have a record as a producer here. I would be the producer, or somebody I would appoint, and you could be, like, associate producer or something like that." I said, no, that wouldn't be satisfactory. Then he said, "Well, leave the script and let me read it." To make a long story short, what happened was that he put the title *The Atomic Monster* on his reissue of *Man Made Monster* [1941], the Universal picture with Lon Chaney, Jr. When Arkoff and I threatened to sue him, he paid off $2000, of which Arkoff took half and I took half.

So when Lugosi told me he'd be working for Broder, and asked me if I would accompany him to the set and sort of act like his valet, I wasn't *too* happy about it because of the experience with Broder. I felt that he would probably resent my being on the set. But then Lugosi told me that Herman Cohen would be the producer, and that sort of made it all right. I said, like Claudette Colbert said to Clark Gable in *It Happened One Night* [1934] when he hung up "the Walls of Jericho," "I suppose that makes everything all right." [*Laughs*] I felt that the mention of Herman Cohen "made everything all right," so I agreed to do it.

On the first day of production [May 15, 1952], I picked Lugosi up at his apartment. I didn't drive before I came out to Hollywood at the beginning of '52, but once I got out here I bought my first car, a used little Pontiac. That was the car that I used to drive Lugosi. *He* didn't care what kind of transportation it was, because he didn't drive himself and for some reason, I forget why now, Lillian Lugosi his wife couldn't drive him to the set. I think she was then working as secretary to Brian Donlevy and she couldn't take the time off every day to drive him back and forth.

When we arrived at General Service Studios, Herman Cohen greeted us very nicely. I've always been friendly with Herman, I've known him for umpteen years and I thought he was a nice person and a good producer, someone who knew what he was doing. He had no objection to my being Lugosi's "butler," which is what I was there for. To act like Lugosi's valet, which I had done before at functions—hold his cigar and all that. Herman said that as long as I didn't get in the way of the shooting, I could just wander around and do whatever I wanted.

I already knew William Beaudine, the director. First of all, I knew his reputation, I knew that he had directed *Sparrows* [1926] with Mary Pickford and many other fine pictures in the silent days, and also some very interesting pictures in the talkie era. But the same thing had happened to him that had happened with so many old-time directors: Producers or the bigger production companies somehow think they're passé or old-fashioned. Beaudine had directed Lugosi in *The Ape Man* [1943] and in *Ghosts on the Loose* [1943] with the East Side Kids, both of them Sam Katzman pictures for Monogram, so Beaudine and Lugosi knew each other already and Lugosi felt comfortable having him as a director. He was still an all-around acceptable director in those days, for B-type pictures and horror pictures and so on. He was very friendly and said I would certainly not be in the way, and I could help look after Lugosi and so on. So it was fine with everybody.

Now as far as these two would-be Martin and Lewis "actors," so-called, are concerned...

I'd never heard of Sammy Petrillo and Duke Mitchell before. Mitchell was certainly not an actor. I understood that he was sort of a nightclub singer, but on a very small scale, one who appeared in some small places around town. Not many people I talked to seemed to have heard of him. He was very *vague* about everything, and haphazard. He sort of went through the motions of everything, probably thinking he was another Dean Martin. But he certainly was not. He didn't *look* anything like him and he didn't have that kind of a voice and he had no personality whatsoever.

Petrillo was even more obnoxious than Jerry Lewis in person, and that's really saying something if you knew Jerry Lewis [*laughs*]. Years later, when I was at Paramount, there would be times when I would be walking through the lot and Lewis would be standing outside there. And when he saw an executive he wanted to talk to—one of the lesser executives (because he didn't *dare* do this with the higher-ups)—he would *scream* across the whole parking area: "*You! Come* over here!" He would, in a very rude way, *shout* to them to come over to where *he* was, and then he'd dress 'em up and down. He was a terror with anybody who had anything to do with him. This was in the 1960s and I encountered him several times like that.

Petrillo did look like Jerry Lewis, but he was no Jerry Lewis. To paraphrase Lloyd Bentsen in his debate with Dan Quayle, "I knew Jerry Lewis, I was a friend of Jerry Lewis, and *you're* no Jerry Lewis!" Petrillo was a wild man around the lot, and what he was trying to do was to behave in every way like he *was* in fact Jerry Lewis. He played "the *biiiiig* man," as though

Alex Gordon says that Jerry Lewis imitator (and *Bela Lugosi Meets a Brooklyn Gorilla* star) Sammy Petrillo was one of the most obnoxious people he'd ever encountered. Well, except for Jerry Lewis! (Left to right: Lugosi, Petrillo, Charlita.)

he was a superstar on the show. He was never ready when they called him, never on the set—he was always doing something else or in his dressing room or whatever, and they had to drag him out. Then he would improvise on his lines, because he always thought that he could do better than the lines that were written for him. He didn't tell anyone ahead of time—no one would know until they were actually shooting. He'd say [about the script], "This is *rubbish* that you got here." This annoyed Bill Beaudine *very* much. Petrillo was in all respects really trying to *do* a Jerry Lewis. Everybody hated Lewis at Paramount ... and Petrillo was hated by everybody at Jack Broder Productions! I have seldom encountered people like this, people who are *that* obnoxious and *so* egomaniacal—except, of course, the original [Jerry Lewis]!

Lugosi, as usual, knew his lines perfectly, but there was a problem because of all the ad libbing that was going on. Lugosi was completely at a loss when people like Red Skelton [on TV's *The Red Skelton Show*] would ad lib all around him and wouldn't give him his cues so that he could speak his lines. When there was a pause, Lugosi would speak his lines anyway, but they would make absolutely no sense in view of what Skelton or other comedians had *done* to him in ad libbing. Mitchell and Petrillo never spoke their proper lines, they were all over the place and making fun of Lugosi and so on. But he stoically spoke his lines and did his stuff.

One of the scenes that stands out in my mind is the scene where they were all squatting on the ground eating papayas. Lugosi apparently was unfamiliar with papayas, but when he first tried it, he ab-so-lute-ly *loved* the papaya. In fact, he became such an addict that he deliberately fluffed his lines several times so that they would do another take and bring fresh new plates of papaya! There must have been something about them that appealed to Lugosi ... maybe they were unknown in Hungary! Lugosi was not now in Hungary but he *was* hun-gry [*laughs*], so he kept eating 'em and eating 'em and eating 'em, which was very funny!

Between takes, Lugosi would either stand around and smoke a cigar, or he would go to his dressing room and lie down, or have a little something to eat. Sometimes he'd have some visitors and he'd talk to them, but mostly he would go to his dressing room and rest. Lugosi never held the picture up or anything like that, he was always on time and he was in pretty good shape. And his performance in the movie was very good.

I had no idea that Lugosi was on any drugs at the time. I never saw him with a needle in his hand or anything like that, and I was at his house *so* many times, Ed Wood and I, or I alone. We'd sit there for hours when he was talking and I never had the slightest inkling. We knew he had a liquor problem; he was never drunk in our presence, but we knew he liked to knock 'em back. But I had absolutely no knowledge of [Lugosi's morphine addiction] until much later, when I saw the headline in the *Herald Examiner* that he had entered a hospital for drug treatment.

Herman Cohen was on the set all the time. Very conscientious, very good, never lost his cool no matter what happened with these two guys [Mitchell and Petrillo]. As far as I'm concerned, he was a very good producer. He is of course responsible for many of the American

In the mid–1960s, Gordon left the "monster world" to produce two cowboy star-studded Westerns. Here on the set of one of them, *The Bounty Killer* (1965), is the amazing lineup of (left to right) Alex Gordon, Buster Crabbe, Richard Arlen, Bronco Billy Anderson (in chair), Dan Duryea, Alex's brother Richard Gordon, Fuzzy Knight and co-producer Pat Rooney.

International pictures that Sam Arkoff takes credit for, *I Was a Teenage Werewolf* [1957] and quite a few others. He helped put AIP on the map. As for William Beaudine, he was a very fast director and was always thoroughly prepared. He knew every line of the script and every camera angle that he wanted—he knew exactly what he wanted to shoot. But he was one of those directors who acted out the scene for the player, a director who would actually crouch down or move around and act out the scenes. He acted it out for Petrillo and Mitchell. With Lugosi, less so—he had a lot of respect for Lugosi. But he indicated to him in exact detail what he wanted.

I saw the movie and I thought it was pretty awful, but I'm not really one to talk considering the kind of pictures that *I* was doing at that time! But I thought that, as we low-budget producers so often say, considering the limited time and the limited budget and everything, it was a very competent job. I think Herman (as usual) did a very nice job, and certainly William Beaudine should take a lot of the credit for directing it so well despite the difficulties with Petrillo and Mitchell. He brought the picture in on time and budget, as he usually did, and was very, very efficient.

I thought the movie would be a success because of the novelty aspects of it, but I really couldn't see that Mitchell and Petrillo could do anything *else*. And in the case of Mitchell, not even *that* [*laughs*]! I thought they were too limited in what they could do—certainly as far as Petrillo was concerned, unless he was going to make a living just imitating Jerry Lewis.

Herman Cohen on *Bela Lugosi Meets a Brooklyn Gorilla* (1952)

There have been other, more notable get-togethers in horror movie annals—the historic confab of Frankenstein and the Wolf Man, the memorable "Meet"ings of various monsters with Abbott and Costello, etc. But for offbeat behind-the-scenes monkey shines, few rival Bela Lugosi Meets a Brooklyn Gorilla *(1952).*

In the early 1950s, there was no hotter team in show business than Dean Martin and Jerry Lewis, stars of stage, screen and TV. Imitators were inevitable, and Jerry Lewis' was uncanny: A teenage Bronx comic named Sammy Petrillo who once appeared opposite Lewis (as his baby son) on TV. Petrillo subsequently teamed with singer-actor Dominick "Duke" Mitchell, a Dean Martin type who cut his hair to look more like "Dino." Mitchell and Petrillo began making appearances in small Los Angeles clubs while their personal manager Maurice Duke pitched them to various movie producers. Duke finally found a willing partner in Jack Broder, the head of Realart Pictures—but Broder's assistant Herman Cohen had misgivings making a movie with Mitchell and Petrillo. In fact, says Cohen, "I thought they stunk."

When I got out of the Marine Corps in 1949, I started working for Columbia Pictures, as sales manager in their Detroit branch. I didn't want to stay there, but my mother wasn't too well at the time. When my mother passed away, then there was nothing holding me in Detroit, and that's when I came out to California. I got a job in the Columbia publicity department.

Jack Broder owned theaters in Detroit, but I had never met him. But now that I was out in Hollywood, I was told by many people, "You ought to look Jack up," because he was an ex–Detroiter. He was the head of Realart Pictures, the company that had bought the Universal library. Jack was about to go into production [of his own low-budget pictures] and he was looking for an assistant, someone who would work very cheap. I went to his offices in Beverly Hills, in the Bank of America Building, and had an interview with him, and he hired me. When we started the production company, our first offices were at Hal Roach Studios in Culver City. From Hal Roach, we moved to Sam Goldwyn Studios in Hollywood, where we did *Bride of the Gorilla* [1951]. Then we moved to General Service Studios, 1040 North Las Palmas Avenue. Our offices were next to Desilu, who were getting ready to shoot their first *I Love Lucy* there. We were the only picture company on the lot, it was basically at that time a TV studio.

Jack Broder was a wonderful, wonderful guy and I owe a lot to him. He wasn't too good with [paying me] the bucks but he certainly gave me all the titles, up to and including vice-president. Oh, he gave me a *lot* of titles! I was over his sales manager, Budd Rogers, in New York! I was a little *pisher* [squirt], and I was Budd's boss! I was just out of the service, and at first the job was too big for me. But if I didn't know something, I'd go to the Cinema Department library at UCLA to know what the hell they were talking about. Our first picture was *Two Dollar Bettor* [1951], then *The Basketball Fix* [1951] and *Bride of the Gorilla* and so on.

The way *Bela Lugosi Meets a Brooklyn Gorilla* came about is this: Maurice Duke brought these two guys, Duke Mitchell and Sammy Petrillo, in to see Jack and me. Mitchell and Petrillo were a junior Martin and Lewis, and Maurice had them under personal contract. Maurice was a personal manager for very cheap acts, acts you'd see in small clubs. Maurice was crippled, he'd had infantile paralysis, and so he had braces on his feet and he had to walk with canes. (And he walked pretty damn good!) He'd have a big cigar in his mouth, and he had a *wild* tongue. He would say *any*thing, he didn't give a shit about any*body* or any*thing* because of the fact that he had these medical problems.

Maurice sold Jack Broder on the idea to do a picture with these two boys, Mitchell and Petrillo. They had a cockamamie nightclub act imitating Martin and Lewis, and Maurice took Jack to some little club someplace, Culver City maybe, to see these guys. Jack thought they were hilarious. I thought they *stunk*. I didn't go with Jack and Maurice, I went to see 'em with some friends. Oh, God, they were terrible! But, hey, I was just working for Jack Broder, you know. I was very unhappy on that film because it was such a piece of shit, at the time we made it. But Jack Broder thought these two guys were funny.

Who had the idea of adding Bela Lugosi to the picture, and *why*, I don't recall. I can't take credit for it because I can't remember, and I don't think it was Jack who brought Bela Lugosi's name in either. It *could* have been Maurice Duke. But I can't recall.

At first, the title of the picture was *White Woman of the Lost Jungle*—Jack came in one day and said, "We're gonna call the picture *White Woman of the Lost Jungle*." "*Jack*! That'd be *ridiculous*! We got Bela Lugosi, you gotta use his name!" I remember we had a *big* argument about that! Actually, I think Bobby, one of Jack's *kids*, came up with that title. And Bobby at the time was about ten! Jack consulted Bobby all the time. Anything that was submitted to the office, Jack would say, "Let me give it to Bobby," and he'd take it home for Bobby to read. Then Jack would come back in the next day and say, "Turn it down. Bobby doesn't like it." [*Laughs*] And that ended that! I became very friendly to Bobby to keep him on my *side*—Bobby could talk his dad into *any*thing, his dad loved him so much. I had no trouble with Bobby, because I won him over with ice cream! Bobby was the pride of Jack because he was the first and the oldest son. He was a good-looking young kid, smart as a whip, and he actually was the "king" behind the scenes of his dad; his dad would discuss everything with Bobby. And I think Bobby was ten at the time! (But *I* was only *12*, so there you are! We had a very young company!) His name now is Robert Broder, of Broder-Kurland-Webb-Uffner, a top Hollywood talent agency, especially for TV. Bob Broder's turned out to be one of the top agents here.

Jack Broder was a millionaire and he was a member of the Friars Club and he knew [producer] Hal Wallis at Paramount, who had Martin and Lewis under contract. Now, there's a funny story that very few people know: The rumor got around that we were gonna do a movie with these two guys Mitchell and Petrillo. My office was right next to Jack's, you had to go through my office before you got to Jack Broder. Anyway, one day at the office, this guy came dashing in and he said [*in an angry voice*], "Where's Jack Broder?!" I said, "Well, he's in his office, right there—" It was Jerry Lewis. He came in because he knew Jack Broder through the Friars Club and he was *furious* about this [the Mitchell-Petrillo movie]. And Jerry Lewis and Jack had a screaming session. I didn't go into the office, I stayed out. I didn't want any part of it. Then when Jerry Lewis walked out, they were still calling each other names: "You fuckin' asshole," "You this," "You that" and what have you. Maurice Duke had an office on the other side of the lot, but I don't know whether Lewis saw Maurice or not.

On the set, Mitchell and Petrillo were funny guys. Duke Mitchell was much more classy than Sammy, but Sammy was the Jerry Lewis character and Duke thought he was Dean Martin. They were easy to get along with ... we told 'em what the *fuck* to do, they *did* it. Duke Mitchell had a pretty good voice; in fact, after he

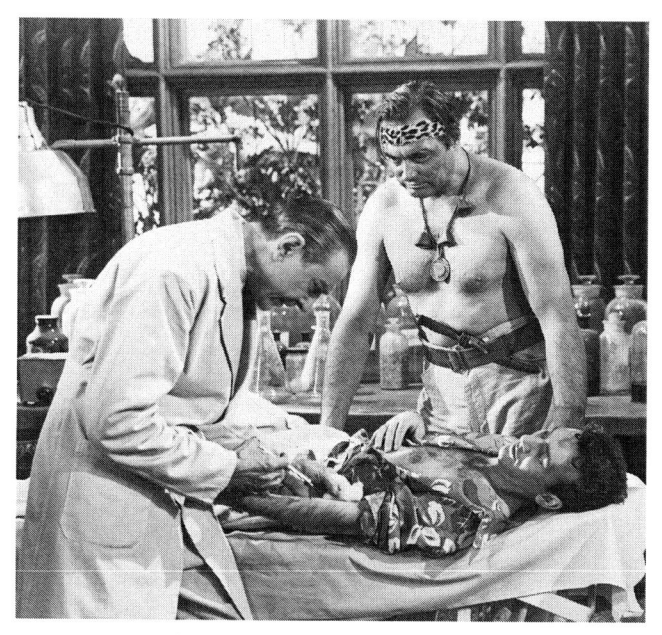

Top: Petrillo and Duke Mitchell tried to make a monkey of Lugosi off-screen, and he returned the favor *on*-screen: With the help of native servant Mickey Simpson, Bela transforms Mitchell into a gorilla that confronts Petrillo (*above*). Hilarity ensues ... *not*.

and Sammy split, I saw Duke in a small club in Palm Springs where he was singing. Petrillo was a nutty kid. Duke Mitchell was much more serious. Petrillo, as they say in Yiddish, was *meshugah*, he was crazy. And he was funny. But he was insecure.

I signed William Beaudine to direct—I got him to direct the picture because he did the Leo Gorcey-Huntz Hall Bowery Boys movies at Monogram. We needed somebody who was *fast* ... who was not too bright and intelligent, but who knew *film*. I went over to Monogram and I watched him work on several things, and I said, "Jack, this is the director for this movie. He knows comedy, he knows *crap*"—and we got William Beaudine. And he was wonderful. I mean, no prima donna in him at *all*. You could tell Bill Beaudine to do *this*, do *that*, blah blah blah, and it'd get done. I loved that old guy. He just loved the business, he was unbelievable. And the photographer was Charles Van Enger, who I used in about seven pictures. This guy was terrific, and we were lucky to get him. There was nothing he didn't know about lighting—*nothing*. And he was so fast—God, was he fast! We used him in picture after picture. I loved him too. We hired all these oldtimers, and they taught *me* a great deal 'cause I'd sit and talk to them about the industry and about what they were doing and this and that and what have you. Now I look at some of these prima donnas today ... they don't know what *day* it is!

I would say we made the picture for about $100,000, including Bela Lugosi—he didn't get paid that much. Bela only worked, I think, four days. Bela was not too well, he looked sick all the time. And I had a tough time getting him on the stage, because I didn't realize, young *pisher* that *I* was, that he was taking morphine. Whenever he had to dash back to his

Associate producer Herman Cohen thought the *Brooklyn Gorilla* set was a fun workplace—but that the movie itself was "such a piece of shit." (Pictured: Mitchell, Ramona the Chimp, Petrillo.)

dressing room, I thought that he was going to the bathroom or something, and he was getting his morphine shots. But he was a nice man—oh, golly! I used to break up talking to him, because he *always* was playing Dracula. "Herrrman! Herrrman, I vant to talk vith yyyooouuu...!" I used to break up! But he was difficult to get into a conversation with. (And if you mentioned Boris Karloff, he got pissed off. "Boris Karloff cannot act like *meeeee*!") He did have some trouble with lines, but ... we made the bloody thing in seven days, he couldn't give us *too* much difficulty!

We also had this little fat broad named Muriel Landers—*she* was funny. In the picture, she was in love with Sammy Petrillo and was chasing him all around. I remember Bela Lugosi laughing at her, he also thought she was funny. Muriel Landers was very talented, a funny Jewish girl from New York. Ramona the Chimp we got from a company in Saugus that had chimps and apes and what have you. He was smart. The gorilla in the picture was Steve Calvert—what a nice guy. You know where I met Steve? He was the head bartender at Ciro's—I got free booze whenever I came into Ciro's. He was also the gorilla in *Bride of the Gorilla*.

Jack Broder would come onto the set a few times during the day. Jack was a very short guy and he had a habit of putting his right hand in his belt—he'd walk like Napoleon. He'd say, "Herman. You tell dem if dey're behind schedule, I pool the shwitch. I pool the shwitch!" (Jack had a foreign accent, he was born in Europe.) Then when Jack would leave the soundstage, Maurice Duke would get up and repeat Broder: "Herman! If dey're behind schedule, pool the shwitch! *Pool the shwitch!*" That used to be our running gag every night! Oh, Maurice Duke had a grrreat sense of humor. Did you ever hear of Borrah Minevitch and His Harmonica Rascals? Maurice was one of the Harmonica Rascals as a kid—he played beautiful harmonica! I liked him and his wife, because he was a bundle of laughs, and *he* took to me. The night that James Dean, who was a friend of mine, was killed, I was at Maurice Duke's house for dinner. All during the years, I stayed in touch with Maurice.

Maurice had a strident voice. He'd arrive on the lot, wherever I happened to be, if he wanted to see me. No appointment or anything, he'd just come on the lot. I could be in my office and I'd hear [*shouting*], "Hoiman! Hoiman! It's Maurice! It's *Duke*!" And I would take him to lunch, 'cause he wanted me to take him to lunch [*laughs*]. And Maurice had this wonderful guy, Tony Roberts, who *loved* him. Maurice couldn't drive, and Tony Roberts was his driver and right hand man and he ran Maurice's errands for him. This guy did everything for Maurice; in fact, his name is in the credits of *Brooklyn Gorilla*, as "Assistant to the Producer." Maurice treated him like shit but deep down he loved him, they loved each *other*, and this big, big, *nice* guy stuck with Maurice for *years*. Maurice Duke was quite a character. I really enjoyed this man, I really liked him.

Brooklyn Gorilla was a fun set. There were lots of set visitors, because they wanted to see Bela Lugosi. Not Mitchell and Petrillo—Bela Lugosi. General Service was like a family in those days, so we had Lucy and Desi drop in—in fact, *I* would bring 'em on the stage. Ozzie and Harriet and their two little sons [David and Ricky Nelson] came on, and, oh God, this one gal I *loved*, Joan Davis, who then was doing her TV series *I Married Joan*. She would come on and we would yock with laughs. In those days, everything was fun. General Service is now Hollywood Center Studios—they just built two new, *beautiful* soundstages there. It's now owned by this multi-millionaire from Canada.

People have speculated that Jack Broder made the picture planning *not* to release it, that he made it figuring that Hal Wallis would pay him off not to release it. That's not true. *However...* Jack did have a meeting with Hal Wallis, to see if Wallis wanted to buy the film. Wallis knew Jack Broder, and was pissed off at Jack [for producing it]. Jack figured, "Hey, if he wants to buy the negative, I'll make a lot of money!" Wallis wanted to buy the negative and

From humble beginnings at Jack Broder Productions, Cohen (1925–2002) graduated to bigger, better horror productions. He's seen here with Judy Geeson in a gag shot from his 1967 Joan Crawford starrer *Berserk*.

burn it. I was in on that meeting, but I don't remember how much money they were talking. (We *made* the picture for three cents!) But Jack couldn't get what he wanted from Wallis, and he decided he was going to release it. [*Did Wallis go away mad?*] He never talked to Jack Broder again at the Friars Club. *That* should tell you something!

[*Did you think the team of Mitchell and Petrillo was "going" anywhere?*] Yeah, they were goin' to Schwab's and see if they could pick up a free meal [*laughs*]! This was their first movie and their *last* movie. And I didn't think the picture would be a success ... never in a million years. I thought it was *so* bad, I didn't even want my name on it. I told Maurice Duke, "Look, *you* take all the credit," and he said, "But *you* did all the work!" Maurice got the producer credit, but he didn't do anything but bring in Duke and Sammy, because he was their personal manager.

The picture didn't have to do too much to make its money back, we only spent about 100,000 on it. It didn't break any records any place, but it did well. Then it became a cult thing because of Bela Lugosi. I've had a lot of calls on it because of Bela Lugosi. *Not* because of Mitchell and Petrillo. Because of Bela Lugosi.

8

Memories of Lon Chaney, Jr.

Karolyn Grimes on *Albuquerque* (1948)

Famous as Zuzu, the rose petal–dispensing daughter of James Stewart's George Bailey in the Christmas classic It's a Wonderful Life *(1946), child actress Karolyn Grimes also includes among her film credits the 1948 Western* Albuquerque *with Randolph Scott, "Gabby" Hayes and, in one of his characteristically brutish "heavy" roles, Lon Chaney. Grimes, eight years old at the time, still has vivid recollections of her first Western and of her "villainous" co-star.*

The thing that I liked about *Albuquerque* was the fact that we got to go on location. That was cool, being out there in the open, out on the studio ranch. A car picked me and my mother up at five o'clock in the morning and drove us out there. It'd be dark, and kind of cold up in the mountains, so we'd all hover around the wood stove in this building that they used for wardrobe, hair, makeup and all that sort of thing. That was the first time I ever saw Lon Chaney. He was a fearsome feller! *The Wolf Man* [1941] had been one of my favorites as a kid, and when I looked at him and my mother pointed out that that's who he was, the Wolf Man, well, I was fascinated from then on. He always had a cigarette hanging out of his mouth, he had real red eyes, and his face was kind of red. And he was intimidating, because he was so big. I was scared to death of him. And I think he knew it, because I probably stared at him a lot. So one day when we were around the stove, he came over to me and he started talking to me. He said, "You know, Karolyn, I think you're ugly." I asked, "You *do*? Why? Why am I ugly?" And he said, "Because you have *freckles*." Of course, immediately I liked him because I *hated* my freckles, I thought they *were* ugly. From then on, we were sort-of kind-of buddies.

In the movie, there was a huge fight scene. Lon Chaney and Randolph Scott got into it—and Lon was the bad guy. Everybody was standing around watching this fight, and I was really entranced because they were knocking each other around. They didn't use stuntmen, they did it themselves. At one point, blood came pouring out of Lon's mouth. I thought it was real, and so I was scared. Afterwards, he came over to show me the capsule that he put in his mouth and busted at the right time. But he came over to me with this intimidating look, and blood running down his face [*laughs*]! I thought it was nice that he took time to show me that he wasn't hurt and that it was all pretend. My eyes must have been as big as saucers! [*Telling you that you were ugly, and glaring at you with blood on his face—that was his way of trying to be friendly?*] Yeah, it really was.

I also remember that he ate a lot. He ate ... ferociously [*laughs*]! They had lots of food out there and we'd pick whatever we wanted, and he'd eat a lot. (I always thought it was funny that "Gabby" Hayes had the same thing for lunch every day, cornbread and buttermilk. That's what he had every day, every single day. Alllll this good food prepared for us, and he'd be sittin' there gummin' that crap down. I thought, "Oh, my Lord!") As for Lon's drinking, I wasn't

Top: As a stock Western baddie in the Pine-Thomas production *Albuquerque*, Lon Chaney, Jr., was never without a cigarette: Here, atop a stagecoach, he puffs away as he snares off-camera hero Randolph Scott with his whip. *Above*: Scott pulls Chaney off the stagecoach and the two go fist to fist — Chaney *still* retaining the cigarette, and blowing out a cloud of smoke every time he's punched!

old enough to notice. I never really saw any of that ... until I got around John Wayne [on *Rio Grande*, 1950]! *That's* when I started seeing that [*laughs*]! Lon could have been tossing it down—in fact, I'm sure he was and that's why he was so red and his eyes were red, I'm sure he was hung over every day and hideously in misery.

I had another scene where I had to pull a burro around. They're stubborn little boogers, and I was having trouble. Lon told me, "You know, all you have to do is just swat it on the butt. It'll move." He gave me a little stick. So I carried the stick around with me in every one of those scenes, and when I wanted it to move and it wouldn't, I'd just swat it. And it worked—it worked real good!

Lon Chaney was fascinating to me because I was scared to death ... and entranced ... by the Wolf Man. Just the fact that he had *been* that creature, played that part—I still saw him as the Wolf Man, I really did. It was hard for me to see him with guns on and all that sort of thing.

So I thought he was a nice guy ... and the scariest person ever...

Mickey Knox on *Of Mice and Men* (1948)

Fans of Lon Chaney, Jr., know that in the late 1930s, after years of struggle, he achieved acting fame via his career-best performance as the powerful but pea-brained migrant worker Lennie Small in stage and screen adaptations of Of Mice and Men. *In later years he would play a number of Lennie-like oafs in movies and on TV, sometimes spoofing the character, but he also legitimately reprised Lennie in little theater productions, once in Santa Barbara, California, in the summer of 1948.*

*That production's George was 26-year-old Mickey Knox, a recent Hollywood arrival whose movie career was off to a good start (*I Walk Alone *and* Jungle Patrol, *1948,* The Accused *and* Knock on Any Door, *1949, et al.) before he was tainted by the blacklist. Relocating to Italy, he worked as a screenwriter (including a rewrite on 1968's* Once Upon a Time in the West*) and dialogue coach, and became known as "the mayor of Rome" where his apartment was the place to be for American artists spending time in Italy. Knox made a living acting, writing and coaching in motion pictures for five decades.*

I arrived in Hollywood around Christmastime of '46 and "legally" became a member of the Screen Actors Guild in January of '47. Hal Wallis brought me here and I was in his picture *I Walk Alone* with Burt Lancaster and Kirk Douglas, which did very well. The year that picture came out [1948], I was hired to play George on stage in *Of Mice and Men* with Lon Chaney, Jr., as Lennie. *Of Mice and Men* was done at the Lobero Theater, which still functions after all these years—that was 60 years ago. They do pretty good stuff. Or, they *did*.

At that point I wasn't familiar with Lon, but he turned out to be a very sweet guy. He disliked dirty language and was opposed to it for the most part, especially in plays. He was a very delicate kind of guy. He was big and husky and all of that, but there was a kind of "niceness" about him. A very decent man. [*How did you find out that he didn't like rough language?*] We talked about it, and I said, "Well, to each his own." In the play, there were a coupla spots that I guess disturbed him, they were too literal.

Here's the funny thing about him: Before going on, both of us would be off in the wings, ready to make an entrance, and he would begin sweating and become very nervous—every night [*laughs*]! I patted him on the back and I said, "Come on. You're a big boy!" [*Laughs*] He was really sweating and nervous, you could just *see* it. [*How funny that* you, *a comparative newcomer, had to be the one to reassure* him*!*] Well, I had done a lot of theater work earlier, in New York. I was a member of Actors Equity when I was quite young, and every summer I did a lot of summer theater, and then my first play on Broadway was *Jason* [1942]. So I'd been around.

There was one *Of Mice and Men* review that was very good for me, that made me feel good to see it. Let me just read a coupla lines, if you'll bear with me: A critic called Ronald D. Scofield gave it a long review, and when he got to me, he said, "Mickey Knox does very well by George, the little guy who mothers Lennie and finally has to shoot him to save him from the lynch mob. Knox does exceptionally well up to the final scene, and then one senses a lack of conviction or intensity of feeling." Well [*laughs*], I'll tell ya what happened there. At the end of the play, there's the scene where Lon would sit in a chair facing the audience, stage center, and I would be talking to him, soothing him—and as he'd sit there supposedly engrossed in what I was telling him, I'd be preparing to shoot him so that he would not be picked up by the police. When I'd gotten the gun, I said to the assistant director, "Make sure you got another gun or two handy, to back me up in case this one misfires." The gun was loaded with blanks, obviously, and blanks tend to misfire, so I was "protecting" myself by having two other guns backstage; the assistant director could fire one of those if mine didn't fire. So there were three guns for that scene, mine and, backstage, the two others. Well, at the very end of the scene, when I went around in back of Lon, my gun didn't fire. So I waited to hear the sound of a shot from backstage, and what I could hear was "click." And then *another* "click." [*Laughs*] Two more guns gone—*they* had *also* failed to fire! *Three* guns failed to fire! What do I do?

Lon also knew that something was wrong, of course, but there was nothing *he* could do about it; he had to sit and wait for me to come up with a solution. So I turned the gun around so that the handle was like a club and I pretended to club Lon and I went *bang* [for the sound of impact] and I whispered to him, "Fall over." [*Laughs*] And he fell out of the chair, "dead"! Man, I sweated through that one! So that reviewer Scofield, naturally, thought I wasn't very good in the last scene! That was supposed to be my best moment in the play, and it didn't turn out very well for me that night. And as I said, Lon couldn't help me, all he could do was sit there. He *fell* very well [*laughs*]! Things like that *happen* in the theater. That happened on the second or third night, and after that we made sure we got proper guns.

I also remember that, in one of the stories that somebody wrote about the play, they interviewed him and he said he was 6' 3". I don't think he was because he wore extra-high

Lon's *Of Mice and Men* co-star Mickey Knox in a shot taken the following year (1949) during the making of the movie *Outside the Wall*. Knox shared with cineastes the story of his long career in his 2004 book *The Good, the Bad, and the Dolce Vita: The Adventures of an Actor in Hollywood, Paris, and Rome*.

heels in his shoes, to get the height. If he had been 6' 3" and added another three inches with the heels, I'd have noticed; it didn't seem to me he was *that* tall.

I thought Lon's performance was brilliant. His father left enough talent for *six* guys like Lon, I guess. His father was an incredibly talented man who dominated the whole silent era, in his genre. Lon, Jr., was a very sweet fellow and we got along very well.

Irving Brecher on *The Life of Riley* (1949)

Lon Chaney, Jr.—TV sitcom star? It's difficult, almost impossible to picture, but shortly after Chaney completed his run of Universal monster characters (the Wolf Man, the Frankenstein Monster, the Mummy, Dracula), he was briefly considered for the role of the bumbling family man Chester A. Riley in the early television series The Life of Riley. *The notion to cast Chaney as the lovable lug was short-lived, and this "revoltin' development" was soon forgotten—but now, after more than 50 years, the Riley character's creator Irving Brecher checks in with a few sketchy but amusing memories of Chaney.*

Brecher (pronounced Breck-er) *not only created Riley for radio (Lionel Stander and William Bendix played the role over the airwaves) and brought the character to the big and small screens (played by Jackie Gleason and Bendix), he has directed a few features and written a number of screenplays, from* Bye Bye Birdie *and* Meet Me in St. Louis *(garnering an Oscar nomination) to a pair of Marx Brothers free-for-alls. (He is also a distant relation of actor Egon Brecher, Boris Karloff's sinister "Majordomo" in the 1934 horror classic* The Black Cat!*) After suffering a series of heart attacks, Brecher died in November 2008.*

There isn't a hell of a lot that I can tell you. I'm generally pretty good, my memory is pretty good for someone my age, but in this instance I cannot recall much in terms of detail. I know I was in New York and I was auditioning for someone to play Riley in the TV series—I couldn't get William Bendix, who was on the radio for me. Agents were rounding up all kinds of people, men, for the possibility of casting one. When they brought the name Lon Chaney to me, I said, "I don't think so. I saw him in *Of Mice and Men* [1939], he was great, but he's a huge man. I'm looking for someone who has a comic streak in him." But they *prevailed* on me to give him a try.

I think I met Lon Chaney in New York but my memory, my *feeling* is that the little bit of footage we shot with him as Riley was shot here, California. The only thing that I recall about him, aside from the fact that he was nice and sweet, a *very* nice person, was that one day when we were working, I guess on the set, he opened a bottle of beer with his *teeth*. He wasn't trying to show off, he just took the beer, put the cap in his mouth, closed his mouth and opened the beer. That was a nice piece of work, but I wasn't about to hire him!

I ran the footage for the sponsor, Pabst Beer, and it was obvious that he was not right for the part. He was a *huuuge* guy, and I had the feeling that he would be totally wrong playing a family man. If you're familiar with the Riley character, you know we were looking for somebody who would be helpless. He didn't *look* helpless. We eventually went with Jackie Gleason. *The Life of Riley* helped start Gleason in TV.

I thought Lon Chaney was a good actor. But [his performance as Riley] didn't ring a bell. He was not right for that character. I don't know where that footage is now.

Barbara Knudson on *Born Yesterday* (1950)

For Lon Chaney, Jr., a stage performance provided the springboard to success in the acting world: In 1939, at the same time that he was playing small supporting parts and uncredited bits in movies, Chaney gave a towering co-starring performance as the gentle giant Lennie in West Coast stage productions of John Steinbeck's Of Mice and Men; *this made him a natural choice for the role in the subsequent (1939) film version, and monster movie immortality soon followed. But from that point on, the Wolf Man of the movies concentrated on that medium (and, later, on TV work), and largely forsook the branch of show biz that made him a star.*

But there were a few additional stage interludes, one of them a late–1940s road company of Garson Kanin's hit comedy Born Yesterday. *In this touring production, spun-off from the Judy Holliday–Paul Douglas–starring Broadway hit, Chaney was Harry, the crude, pushy millionaire junk dealer who wants to crash Washington D.C. social circles, and Jean Parker played his mistress Billie, the Brooklyn showgirl. Following that engagement, Chaney tackled* Born Yesterday *at New Mexico's Albuquerque Little Theatre (May 23–27, 1950); here, however, instead of Parker it was Paramount contractee Barbara Knudson in the showy central role of the brassy Billie.*

In 1950, Chaney was 44 years old and a seasoned veteran, and Knudson, half his age at 22, just a newcomer—but beautiful Barbara had not *been "born yesterday," and she quickly figured out how to contend with Lon and his scene-stealing antics. More than a half-century after her ordeal, she raises the curtain to reveal this little-known side of the Lonster...*

From the day we are born, be it yesterday or today or tomorrow, we learn valuable lessons in life. Potty train ... tie our shoes ... achieve ... love ... etc. Well, in the early years of my adult life, at the beginning of my professional career, I learned a valuable lesson from Lon Chaney, Jr.

At the time when I did *Born Yesterday*, I was under contract to Paramount Pictures and I was either going with or engaged to William Henry, a well-known actor who did hundreds of films and TV shows. He and I had met in summer stock; that was my background before Paramount picked me up, summer stock in Las Vegas. Bill and I had already done a play, *Dream Girl*, at the Albuquerque Little Theatre in Albuquerque, New Mexico, and Jim O'Connor and his wife Kathryn, the directors of this little theater, were very happy with my performance in that. And when they got ready to do *Born Yesterday*, they decided that I would be the one they would ask to come and play the part of Billie in it. Because *I* was doing it, Bill took the part of the

Beautiful Barbara Knudson.

reporter, the second male lead. So Bill and I went down to do *Born Yesterday* with Lon Chaney, Jr.—they already had him as their big headliner in it. The theater was a local, community theater, not prestigious in the *world* or anything like that, but prestigious in that area. Like any really good little theater, they wanted to bring in guest actors [with recognizable names], like Lon Chaney, Jr. I thought, "Oh, Lon Chaney, Jr., great!"

I met Lon Chaney, and [*laughs*] ... he was Lon Chaney, all right! I mean, he didn't look much different with or without makeup, he had cultivated a face that possibly he was born with; then, with his horror films and all, it had kind of become a natural look for him! I mean, it got to be where it didn't require a lot of makeup, you looked at him and you thought, "Oh, dear me! A mean man!"

We started the first day's rehearsals, a walk-through rehearsal, and I was polite as you would be to a person [Chaney] who's recognizable as a star. We went through this rehearsal, and I already knew what the script said, I could read where it suggested the positioning of the actors. Like, for instance, the Billie character should be center stage when she says *this* line, and she should be exiting as she says *that* line. You go pretty much by what the writer has outlined. It didn't take five minutes for me to see, every time that I had some lines, that Lon Chaney was speaking up to the directors, Jim and Kathryn, making suggestions. And not only was he changing the positioning, but changing who-had-what-*lines*—and *that* was a no-no, you just didn't *do* that. And of course the O'Connors were babying him because he was Lon Chaney, Jr. He'd say to them, "Well, you know, I've done this before, and at this point, she should be over *here*." And later: "For *that* line, she should be over *there*." Well, he was doing

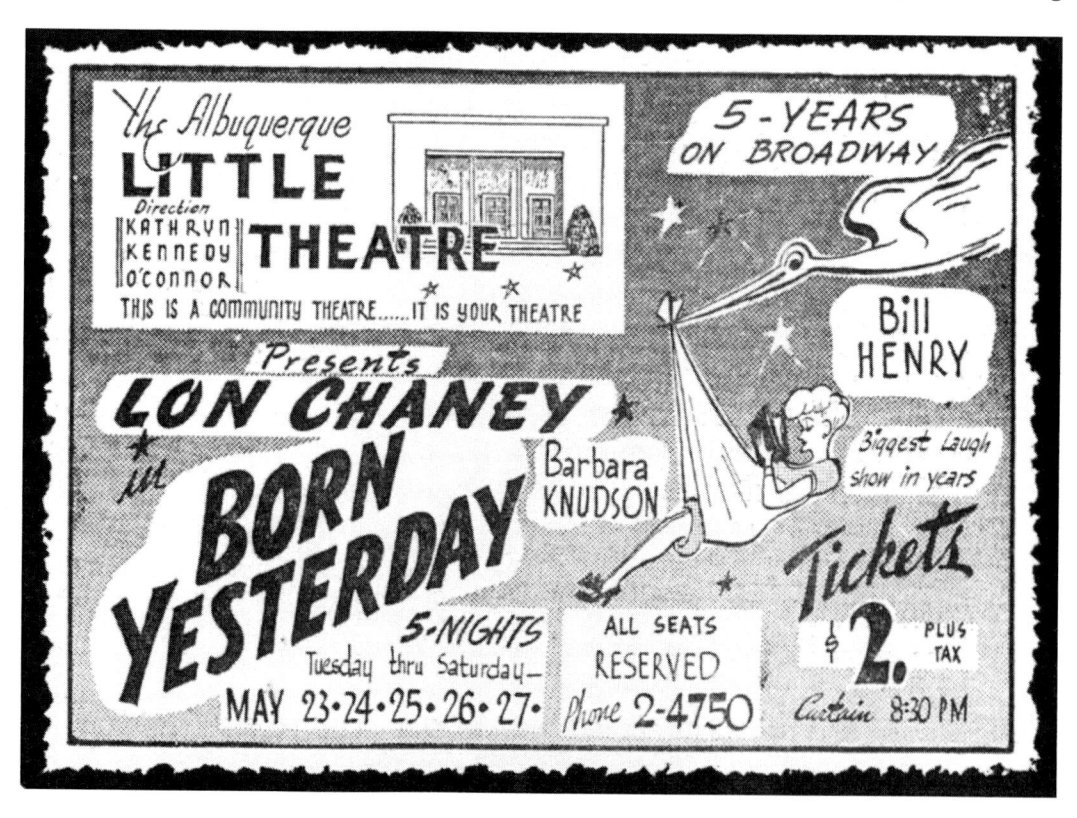

Chaney Jr., got all Albu-*quirky* during the run of their play, but Knudson was a match for the scene-stealing actor.

everything but putting me behind a curtain! He'd want me over on the left side of the stage, behind a sofa. Then it was on the other side, behind a lamp. Every time he went to direct something, it was taking Billie, the star role, and sticking her in the weirdest places for her lines! Well, I wasn't stupid, I knew where the script said I should be, it doesn't take too many brains, and I began thinking, "This is ridiculous." But I was polite for a certain length of time. In the meantime, of course, Bill was watching too, and being a seasoned actor, he was thinking, "My goodness...!"

Came time for lunch break, I asked Kathryn and Jim O'Connor if I could speak to them. After Lon went off by himself, I had a little talk with them right there at the theater: "I just don't understand why you're letting him block this scene this way. I don't mind being here or there, but I really don't think I should be standing at the back of the stage behind a lamp or behind a tall chest of drawers or something!" So they said to me, very politely, 'cause they were star-struck ... very good people, but star-struck ... they said, "Well, Barbara, the thing is, *he's* done this play before, and he really has a right to suggest and direct because ... *he's* Lon Chaney, Jr. He is the star." Fortunately for me, I had my youth, the tell-the-truth–type attitude of youth, and I thought it over and I said, "You know, I am under contract to a major studio. I can't afford to do a bad job. They are going to expect me to do a decent job. *He's* already a star, he can afford to do a bad job if he wants to or happens to do so. But I'm starting and I can't *afford* to be bad in this." So of course they thought that was a little bit uppity and they must have thought, "Well! We've got a prima donna *here*." But I did it nicely and I was sincere. I probably even had tears in my eyes, 'cause I thought, "This is ridiculous."

After lunch, we went back to work, and of course I went ahead and let Lon Chaney direct it the way *he* wanted it. Kathryn and Jim tried every once in a while to correct a little bit, but nevertheless it was being directed by him. *Born Yesterday* was written for whoever played Billie to be the *star* in the production. But not with Lon Chaney directing the production!

A very famous part of the play was a scene in which Billie and Harry had a gin rummy game, and it was hysterically funny. It was written hysterically funny ... the artist who wrote the book had done a perfect job. And so, why change it? That was the art of this writer. But of course Lon Chaney changed it around, and all of a sudden some of the good lines were his that shouldn't have been, and etc., etc. There again, I had to stand back and be polite about it. At that point I thought, "Oh, well ... big deal. I will just do the best job that I can possibly do, and that's gonna be *it*." I was disappointed but not devastated. I had to adopt an attitude of, "We're here, we're havin' fun, let's do it."

Incidentally, Lon Chaney had quite a reputation for alcohol. Now, I'm not saying that he fell down on the job. He was a very good actor, he certainly came on stage and was able to deliver his lines. I don't remember him ever forgetting his lines—in fact [*laughs*], he was very clever to make sure that he got all of his lines *in*! But it was obnoxious to be close to him, because of the reeking of the alcohol, his breath in particular. You know if you've seen *Born Yesterday* that when Billie and Harry would get into an argument, he would get right up in her face and he would *holler* at her, and *scream* at her. Every time Lon would come up to me, I would cringe [because of the odor]. But I just held my face up to him. Probably the biggest acting I did was to *not* look like, "Goodness sakes, your breath's gonna knock me over!" I was able to stand toe to toe with him and keep a straight face!

Opening night came, and we started in. Well, the audience accepted me. They liked me. Of course, it was the way my part was written, *and* the fact that I was doing it well. So I was very, very well-accepted. The reviews came out in all the local Albuquerque newspapers the next day, and I got all the attention, how marvelous I was, outstanding, blah blah blah blah

blah. Well, I guess that must have just really done him in—he couldn't stand it. That day when Bill and I showed up for makeup, Lon didn't even say hello to us. Bill said to me, "Oops. You're in trouble!" These reviewers went overboard, highlighting how I stole the show. I was tickled by it, but also embarrassed, in a way. And, as I say, Lon wouldn't even speak to us when we showed up. Oh, well, what are you gonna do? I was happy happy happy.

We got ready, and we started to do the play. Well, Lon had decided to pull a trick, probably a trick that he used for years, I'm sure he didn't think it up that day: The trick was, to do anything he could to distract the other actor that he was dealing with. He would come up close to me to deliver a line, but under his breath he would mumble something. Which was either calling me a kind of a dirty name, a *dumb* name, or just mumble or growl at me. Of course, the audience couldn't hear it, but I *could*. But he was playing opposite a young actress who was very, very good on dialogue, and he couldn't distract me with that. The first time he did it, I thought, "Well, what is *this*?" He did it two or three more times, and then I got a few seconds off-stage to think about it, and I realized what he was doing, and I thought, "*No*, he is not going to do this to me." I got back on stage and he came up to me, and he quietly mumbled, "You so-and-so, you blah blah blah," and then in a loud voice he started to deliver his line. But I didn't give him the chance to deliver his line, I looked at him, *in* character, and I said to him with a big, wide face [*in a loud, Brooklyn-accented voice*], "What didja say, Harry?" He looked at me in shock, and then started to say his line, and I interrupted, "No, what did you *say*, Harry?" He didn't know what to say! Later, he tried the mumbling bit a couple of times again, but every time I'd just look at him and say, "*What?* What didja say? You're just *mumbling*, what are you saying to me, Harry?" [*Laughs*] So now, he had to stop *that*. He thought, "Oh my goodness, I'm on stage with a girl who's gonna say to me, 'What didja say?' every time I do my trick." It didn't take too long for him to stop that!

So now I'm really upset myself, and I thought, "The card game scene was written a certain way and I'm gonna do it that certain way. I'll fix *him*." So we got into the card game, and I just played it to the hilt. Remember I told you that, in rehearsals, he had decided that he wanted *that* line of Billie's 'cause it was funny, and he wanted the *next* line 'cause *it* was funny. Well, I went back and read the lines that belonged to me in the first place, and completely threw him! Now he was at that point where I'm sure he'd have liked to *kill* me, but we were on stage and there was really nothing he could do about it!

There's a scene in the show where Harry slaps Billie, but I don't remember him taking advantage of that. By that time, I think he was dumbfounded. There *was* a slapping scene, but, no, he was not a violent person. He was just conniving. And he probably thought it was beneath his stature to be starring in Albuquerque, you know what I mean? I don't know, that's just a guess. But I also don't know why he felt he had to try and make himself look good at the expense of others. The part he was playing was not a role that was written for the actor to steal the show. In the movie *Born Yesterday* [1950], Broderick Crawford was very good as Harry. Broderick Crawford had an appeal. He could play as mean as he wanted to, but he also had a soft appeal. You felt sorry for him. Lon Chaney didn't have that. But, "soft appeal" or no, nobody could steal the show from the girl playing Billie if she was halfway decent, because *Born Yesterday* was basically written for the girl, it was a female vehicle. It was pathetic that Lon Chaney, a big star, felt that he had to do that, to try and wreck a play and a young actress.

Well, then out of the blue came this one opportunity. There's a scene where Billie comes down a staircase in her little negligee and she's really into herself, and she descends the stairs singing "Anything Goes." I started down the staircase and, so help me God, I did not do it

Knudson flanked by her *Born Yesterday* co-stars Chaney and (her future husband) William Henry; presumably they're about to do (or just *did*) a radio interview with the men on the left (unidentified).

on purpose, it was just sent from Heaven, something to fix him up good: I'm not the greatest singer in the world but I had a *decent* voice, but I got halfway down the stairway and all of a sudden I was off-key. I was off-key to where it was just obnoxious *to me* [*laughs*]! I realized how awful it was, and I just stopped and I [*Knudson makes a disbelieving-type noise*], like anybody might do in their own home. And I went back up to the top of the stairs and started over! Well, it just happened to "hit" the audience right, and they went *wild*. They laughed and laughed, probably one of the biggest laughs of the play, as big as the laughs we got in the gin rummy game scene. A lot of laughter, and some applause. As I say, it was an accidental thing, sent from Heaven.

Well, *that* did it for Lon Chaney. I mean, at the end of the play, he went into his dressing room—by that time, I think he'd taken about ten more nips than he normally would have—and he was a goner! I won my battle that night, and of course I'd gotten the good reviews, so he was dead in the water. But we still had the play to do for maybe three more days. He went back to doing the best that he could do, and every night from then on, I took back a little bit more stage. I thought, "No, I'm not gonna be behind that sofa or that lamp any more!" But I didn't overdo it.

I will never forget *Born Yesterday* because I learned the biggest professional lesson. I learned what people can do to an innocent young person trying to do their job. I learned about the things that they can do to you on stage if they want to. That was a lesson I learned from him. Throughout my years in the business, I didn't have to use what I learned too often, because most people are nice and even helpful to beginners. But that was the lesson I learned from Lon Chaney.

9

Richard Kline on Sam Katzman

In 2006, Richard Kline received a Lifetime Achievement Award from his peers at the American Society of Cinematographers, a fitting tribute to a man who earned Oscar nominations for his work on Camelot *(1967) and* King Kong *(1976), and also lensed such popular pictures as* The Boston Strangler, Hang 'em High *(both 1968),* The Andromeda Strain *(1971),* Star Trek: The Motion Picture *(1979),* Body Heat *(1981) and scores more. But these plum assignments came at the end of years of uncredited work as assistant cameraman and camera operator on pictures both major and minor: The son of cinematographer Benjamin H. Kline, Richard began at Columbia in 1943 as a 16-year-old, and then spent the better part of the 1950s stomping out B pictures in the low-budget vineyards of Sam Katzman, maverick moviemaker extraordinaire. From cut-rate swashbucklers, Biblical "epics" and Jungle Jim jamborees to* It Came from Beneath the Sea *(1955) and* Rock Around the Clock *(1956), Kline saw it all through his viewfinder during that era, and formed some very definite opinions about exploitation filmmaking's most prolific purveyor.*

At the beginning of my career, I spent eight years [at Columbia] as an assistant cameraman, minus a few years in the service, and then ten years as a camera operator. And they kept you busy. If you finished one project and there was an extra camera on another film that was already going, they'd put you on that. You'd go from one to another. It just so happened that once I became a camera operator, for a six-year period I worked for Sam Katzman. I'd worked for Sam prior to that, too, off and on, different projects, but from about 1951 to '56 I did practically nothing else *but* work steadily for him.

Sam had his own unit at Columbia Sunset on Lyman Place. It had been the Tiffany-Stahl studio [and before that, the Fine Arts Studio, where movies like 1915's *The Birth of a Nation* were shot]. Columbia bought that place and made it Sam's unit. There was another unit there, too, the Irving Briskin unit, doing B pictures the same as Sam Katzman. The place had perhaps four stages; it was a very small studio, it was not luxury. For instance, there was no commissary, and I don't think they even had a hot dog stand! So you'd have to go off the lot and eat somewhere in the area.

Sam was a likable guy, and such a character. Have you ever seen a picture of Sam Katzman? He looks just like you would think a Sam Katzman *would* look like. He was the *perfect* Sam Katzman [*laughs*]! He had the big cigar ... he was a clotheshorse, with the plaids, a really flashy dresser ... he had one of the first gullwing sports cars, the year they came out. He looked so wrong in it [*laughs*], but he could afford it and so he *had* it. He had money and he spent it well. But not pompous at all. He was soft-spoken, very "controlled," always a nice smile, a nice demeanor. He really was a lovely man. He was always very nice to me and I liked him a lot.

As a producer—well, you wouldn't want to work with a better producer. He was always available. He wasn't on the sets a lot but he *would* come on, like 10, 2 and 4 Dr. Pepper [at

At the start of his career, Richard Kline was the youngest camera assistant and camera operator in the industry; he became a d.p. at 35 at a time when the average age for that category was closer to 60. In this backstage shot from *It Had to Be You* (1947), star Cornel Wilde (center) helps 20-year-old Kline (behind the camera) with a tape-measurement.

intervals], to see that everything was okay. He was friendly with everybody, and he had a great sense of humor. He didn't need a cane, he was in good health, but he had different canes, a *lot* of different ones, including one with a handle in the shape of a fist with one finger extended. That was his goosing cane, and he was always goosing people! He was a jokester, really a perfect guy to work with. Katzman was just one of a kind, without a doubt.

As I said, he didn't spend a lot of time on the sets, he'd spend it in his office on the lot, prepping his *next* pictures. If we got a little bit ahead and finished a movie early, we'd start the next one that same *day*. He didn't waste a moment. He could zig and zag like nobody's business. When we were doing some Biblical thing, somebody called a discrepancy to Sam's attention: "Sam, on the call sheet here, you only have ten disciples. There were 12 in the Bible." Sam said, "There might've been 12 in the Bible, but there's only ten in my budget!" [*Laughs*] And that ended that! That was typical Sam. "I know I've never made a great film," he said to me once, "but I never made one that went over budget." You could never produce another Sam today. And if you were to make a picture about the making of one of these Katzman films, nobody'd believe it [*laughs*]!

Katzman had the most proficient and fastest screenwriter ever, Robert E. Kent; as fast as he could type, that's how the script came out. I'd walk by his little office, the door would be open, and he'd say, "Oh, hi, Richard!" and we'd talk about (say) a ballgame from the night before, and he'd still keep typing while we were talkin' about the ballgame! A lovely man and [*laughs*], even though I never really *read* one of his scripts, I know he was a very competent writer; he really knew the technique of writing. Sam would throw him an idea or show him a newspaper item and say, "Here, make a story out of this," and Kent would knock out a completed script in no time at all. I can't imagine there were many screenwriters who wrote more scripts than *he* did!

Everything was shot on that lot, except when we'd go on locations here and there. We went to New Orleans [*New Orleans Uncensored*, 1955], to San Francisco [*It Came from Beneath the Sea*], to San Quentin [*Escape from San Quentin*, 1957], we went several different places. To show you how resourceful Sam Katzman was, there was one time when two chartered prop planes took us up to Columbia, California, in the morning, we did our day's work, and we were due to come home that night. We worked right up until sunset, finally got the work done, we rushed to the small airport—and the two running lights on one of the planes were malfunctioning. By regulations, it couldn't take off. But Sam was *so* very clever: Since we were into penalty time and this was costing him time and money, he went up to the tower and he went through the regulation books with somebody, and nosed around until he found out that a plane *was* allowed to take off with *one* running light. So it was Sam who requested that they take a good running light from the plane that had two, and put it into the plane that had none. Now both planes had one, and both could take off! What producer could do that today? Today, producers aren't even around, they're out having lunch! But that's the kind of guy Sam was.

Sam had pretty much the same crew all the time. In fact, that's the reason I know that we did 108 features in six years: After I stopped working for Sam, a sound mixer named Josh Westmoreland and I were working on another project at Columbia, and we started talking about having worked for Sam. Josh was Sam's mixer, he worked on practically everything Sam did, and one of us said, "God, how many pictures did we *do*?" Josh and I came up with 108 titles! They were all "companion features" running 78 or 80 minutes, and they would play in your neighborhood theater *with* the A-film. (I can't remember ever going to see one, to be truthful!)

While I was there, Sam used maybe a half a dozen different cinematographers. Ira Morgan worked [as d.p.] on some of them. Fayte Browne didn't work on many but he *was* a d.p. there for a short period, and then died at an early

Low-budget legend Sam Katzman (1901–1973) looked "just like you would think a Sam Katzman *would* look like," says Kline. Here's a photo of "Jungle Sam" (taken by Kline) to prove it. Kline calls him "one of the most amazing moviemakers of his time."

age. Bill Whitley and Henry Freulich were the "major" ones. Gene Anderson was his production manager, and he *really* was good, very efficient. Well, that was the whole thing: Sam had efficient people, good craftsmen, good grips, good electricians. We were a team that liked Sam, Sam liked *us*, and we all worked hard for him. We enjoyed our work a lot, we had a lot of fun, a lot of gags and things like that. On-the-set, fun things. You *need* that, in order to keep that pace. We'd do between 60 and 100 set-ups a day, and that was with two cameras, sometimes three. My dad was on quite a few of them [as d.p.]; right around the time I left Sam's was when my father started there. The only time I ever worked with my father was for one or two days on Sam's *Rock Around the Clock*. He was the cinematographer and I was an extra camera.

[*How much time did a d.p. have to prepare for a Katzman picture?*] *Very* little. We were going from one movie to another, and didn't really have much time to prep. I would say zip. Maybe if there was a location to look at, [the d.p.] might be taken to that location. But the production people selected the locations, with the director. You had to be careful, though [about the locations selected by production people]. I remember, when I was a d.p. in the early days, we went to look at one location, and the production manager said, "This is great!," and *I* didn't think it was a good location at *all*. I said, "What's so great about it?" He said, "Well, I can park the trucks over *there*, and we can serve the lunch over *there*..." [*Laughs*]. He was looking at it from [the standpoint of the job he had to do], it was convenient for *him*. I had

Occasionally the Katzman crew got to go on a location; *It Came from Beneath the Sea* took them to San Francisco.

to say, "No, no, this is not the right location," and he said, "Oh? Okay, we'll look for something else." Everybody had, like, an agenda. But on these B pictures, they'd just *grind* 'em out. It was amazing how skilled the crews were. You wouldn't have as much equipment on the Bs. There'd be half a dozen different types of lights, there were like six lenses, there was no crab dolly, it was just simplicity. But we made it work. The industry was ... I hate to say "prehistoric" [*laughs*]! Today there's so much equipment, and that's a plus. But back then, it was just basics. The lighting was kinda the same, everybody was lit the same way, and practically everything was done on the sets. It made it much simpler to function.

Also, in those days almost every director had a system where it was a long shot, a medium shot, two over-the-shoulder shots, two close-ups. That was the coverage. While you're doing an over-the-shoulder, you'd have the second camera doing the single. Or, while you're doing the long shot, the second camera would be doing the medium shot. Because you were lit for everything, you were able to do it that way. There really was a routine that was kind of ... *standard*, let's put it that way. And there was no such word as "organic." No actor would say, "I have to be organic," "I have to process the moment," and no actor would say he refused to *do* this or that. I don't want to mention names, but I remember one actor who did Westerns—*not* for Sam. He was the number six cowboy in Hollywood, a real nice guy, but he never knew his lines. And one day, one of his lines was, "Remember to forget what I told you." Preparing to do the scene, he said, "How can I remember to forget? Either I *remember*, or I *forget*..."—he started analyzing the line! The director said, "Just do it any way you want," and the cowboy said okay. So he tried it one way: "Remember what I told you." But he didn't like that, and said, "Let me try it another way," and the second time he said, "*Forget* what I told you." And, *again*, he said, "No, no, no, that's not right. Oh, *I* know," and the way he finally said the line was, "Remember to forget what I told you"! [*Laughs*] Right back to the original!

Sam's appreciation was for the below-the-line crew. Actors ... well, he was kind to them and all, but he really believed in crew and he put them first and he treated them extremely well. As a camera operator in the Katzman unit, I had to have been making 180 or 200 dollars a week, which was very good money. We worked six days a week in that period of the industry, and on a football weekend when SC was playing, Sam would show up in the morning and say, "Guys, if you finish at noon, there'll be a bus outside, lunch will be served on the bus, and I've got tickets for you on the 40-yard line." Well [*laughs*], sure enough, we'd finish, and that afternoon we'd be at the Coliseum. And after almost every quickie show, there was always a wrap party on the set, with *hors d'oeuvres* and drinks. Sam threw all kinds of "appreciation parties," he was very good about that. At these parties, his wife Hortense would show up. Sam called her Hortie, she was a flaming redhead—dyed, of course—and she wore mink coats so long, it was just unbelievable. A very nice lady.

When people talk about Sam today, they often talk about how cheap he was, but Sam was actually a very generous person. You want to hear about a cheap producer? Again, I won't mention any names, but there was one picture where we were going to photograph a flotilla of Navy ships from the deck of a submarine. We boarded the submarine in the harbor at Long Beach and went out to sea, and the minute we got into rough sea, the producer got seasick. While sick bay attended to him all day long, we photographed the flotilla, and then we went back into the harbor where it was calm water and the producer was his old self again. He called a meeting while we were still on the deck and he asked, "How'd it go today?" and Ray Gosnell the assistant director said, "We got the day's work." The producer asked, "What did you guys do for lunch?" and Ray said, "The crew served us lunch, and I gave them a dollar per man to put into their ship's fund." The producer said, "Oh, good.... But don't give 'em a dollar for *me*, I didn't eat." [*Laughs*] I tell that to people, when they talk about people being cheap, because that one tops *every*thing. *Nobody* could beat that!

As for the directors who worked for Sam ... well, Lew Landers was probably the most prolific of *all* directors. I don't think anybody directed much more than he did, between features and TV. He was a great character. I was the operator on one of his pictures and he said, "Roll 'em, speed, action," the actors started the scene, and there was a whisper in my ear: Lew said, "I have to go to the phone. When they stop talking, just cut the camera" [*Laughs*]. I could go on and on about Lew Landers, he really was fun, a terrific guy to be around. Rarely would he do a scene twice, he'd just pick it up: "Okay, we'll pick it up from the point where...." He knew all the [low-budget moviemaking techniques]; performances took a back seat. One time he was kinda moaning, "*Damn* it," he said, "everybody else gets 30, 40, 50 days to do a picture, and I only get six, eight, ten days." Somebody asked, "What would happen if you *got* 30 days to do a picture?" Lew thought a moment, and then he said, "I'd probably shoot it twice...!" [*Laughs*] Oh, Lew Landers was unbelievable. We were good friends for years, because he was a great, wonderful character.

Lew was always into different hobbies: He had hopped-up cars, the Ford AVs and things like that; he had a miniature train hobby that earned him the nickname "Choo-Choo" Landers, because when his wife divorced him, she claimed that he would fall asleep on his little choo-choo track [*laughs*]! That was actually in the papers! And he had a hobby of photography. I'll never forget one day when he invited me over to his place. He lived in one of the better areas of L.A., in Beverly Hills. I think his home was on Beverly Drive, near Sunset. Very, very expensive homes today; nowadays that home would be probably worth ten million. As I mentioned, he'd picked up a photographic hobby and he had a darkroom, a little separate unit, built in his yard. Well, this one day he invited me to come over because he wanted me to see it. We were in his darkroom and he was showing me these things he had bought: "Here's the enlarger, it cost me blah blah blah," "This is the dryer, it cost me blah blah blah"—he was pointing at each piece of equipment. And one time when he pointed at something and his arm was extended, his watch was uncovered, and he saw it and said, "Oh my God, I'm due at unemployment! Come with me...." Here he was in his gorgeous house, one of the great mansions in Beverly Hills, showing me all of this extremely expensive equipment, and he was worried about missing his unemployment, which was then like $35 a week. So we drove to the unemployment together and he got his $35. It could only happen in Hollywood!

I believe I *can* tell you another Lew Landers story, because he's dead now. As I said, he had all kinds of hobbies, and another one of them was boating. He'd gotten into yachting and he bought a small boat, and he tried to join the Balboa Bay Club—but they didn't allow Jews. So on a Saturday when we were working [making a Katzman movie] out at a ranch, he collected all the catering garbage and took it home in a sack, because he was going to take it to his boat and go out in front of the Balboa Bay Club and dump it there [*laughs*]! Oh, he was one of a kind, there has never been anybody quite like Lew Landers! He was one of my favorite people of all time.

[Director] Fred Sears came to Columbia from Broadway. In the theater, he'd been kind of a combination actor-promising director, and when Harry Cohn brought in to Columbia five promising "potentials" as dialogue directors, Fred Sears was one of them, along with Henry Levin, William Castle, Mel Ferrer and Bobby Gordon. Fred was from New England, he had a New England accent, and he was a very bright, intelligent man. He developed into a very good craftsman, but I don't think he really cared to do better pictures, I really don't. I think the best thing he ever did was *Cell 2455, Death Row* [1955], which was above the B level. He died fairly young, right in his office at Columbia, which was a shock.

Bobby Gordon was already out here, he was a product of L.A. and had started out as a child actor. He and I were personal friends for years; he was a lovely guy, and we were beach bums together and that type of thing. Bobby did a lot of writing, and he always tried to do *better*, and he never quite achieved it. For years he thought he had a project with Brando, and it was always put off, or Brando would put him off, and he just never really achieved what he wanted. He was, *I* think, a talent, but just never got the break.

Prior to my going to work for Katzman, William Castle was down in Acapulco with us as a dialogue director on *The Lady from Shanghai* [1948]. I'd worked as assistant camera on some of the very first pictures he directed, like *Klondike Kate* [1943] and some of the Whistlers. I did a lot of things with him. He was a competent director but he was caught in the rush of quickie films, and he could never get out of that type of filmmaking. But he had a real Hitchcock complex, he *loved* Hitchcock. Hitchcock was the Master of Shock, and Bill was the Master of Schlock [*laughs*]—that's the nickname they gave him. And, some way or another, he tried to get a picture of himself in each movie. It was usually like a picture on a piano, or whatever it might be. It was just something he had to do, and he did it. He was a lovely guy and just a little more colorful [than the other directors], and he made more out of what he did than any of the others. It was like a job with some of the other directors, boom boom boom; Bill did garner some publicity so, as far as publicity goes, he did better than a lot of the other B

Former Tarzan Johnny Weissmuller took the money and ran (or swam) as the star of Katzman's *Jungle Jim* series. Here he battles a cannibal disguised in a crocodile hide in 1954's *Cannibal Attack*.

directors. But I don't think he was any better, to be truthful. When he was first getting started, he used to use the crew to judge a scene: After he'd yell "Cut!" he'd look around at us and ask, "What do you think? How was it?" We [in the crew] got together behind his back and said, "Let's agree on the fourth take"—we'd shake our heads "no" on takes one to three, and on the fourth, good or bad, we'd nod to indicate that we liked it. And he'd *go* for it [*laughs*]. But Bill was a very nice person. In fact, they *all* were, they all were really great characters.

[*On Katzman's Jungle Jim series:*] The Jungle Jims were by-the-numbers again. They took six or seven days to shoot, and the direction was always the same when it came to Johnny Weissmuller [Jungle Jim]: As he walked through the jungle, the direction was, "Okay, roll 'em ... speed ... *action*. Come ahead, Johnny ... you see something ... you stop ... you react ... and now you *go*." That was all the direction! He'd be walking along, and then all of a sudden he'd stop ... a blank stare when he'd see something ... and then he'd react with a puzzled look ... and then on he would go. Somebody once said that Johnny could go on a one-man theater tour, and call it "An Evening of Blank Stares and Double-Takes" [*laughs*]!

Johnny did a couple Jungle Jims a year and he was the nicest guy. A marvelous person, very cooperative, really good. And, God, could he swim. He must have had webbed feet or something, 'cause he amazed everybody. We worked out at a couple of lakes around L.A., most of which don't exist any more. The water could be cold but he'd go in, he didn't care. No fuss at all. Johnny would arrive each morning asking, "What are we doin' today?" He would always joke about it: Because he had very little to say in these movies, nobody expected him to [read

If Jungle Jim and Tamba can do it, maybe the work of a camera operator *isn't* all that tricky!

and learn the dialogue in advance]. And he didn't! They knew that the few lines he had, he could memorize when the time came, and that was it. We worked with a chimpanzee quite a bit, too, and Johnny was very good with the chimp. The chimp liked him a lot.

I also worked on a couple of the serials that Sam made. As I recall, they each took about 30 days. They were the same [as working on features]. The weather was taken into consideration: If there were going to be a lot of exteriors, we would shoot it when the days were longer, not in the winter. But as I say, it was the same (shall we say) *pattern* of work—the long shot, the medium shot, the over-the-shoulders and singles. And rain or shine. I was an operator on a Gene Autry Western [*Cow Town*, 1950] where he sang a song called "Powder Your Face with Sunshine"—and when we shot it, it was raining! It was raining all around him but not *on* him, because we put protection over him, a huge gobo. It looked like he was out in the sunshine because it was lit well, and in reality it was raining. But we had to get the shot!

By the way, we had a very clever publicist whose name was Robert Yeager. He could get things planted *so* well. He was working for Sam as a publicist for a while, and he got a two-page spread on Sam into *Life* magazine called "Meet Jungle Sam" [March 23, 1953]. Well, Sam *hated* it. Sam was featured in various photos with an elephant and a chimp [plus a pirate, a man in a gorilla suit, midget Billy Curtis, giant Max Palmer, etc.] and the piece made him appear to be a real character. In my opinion there was nothing negative about it, I thought it was a great spread. But Sam hated it and I think he fired Bobby Yeager.

Working in Katzman pictures might have been a downgrade for actors, Paul Henreid [star of four Katzman movies] who'd done pictures like *Casablanca* [1942] and others like that, but now it was kinda getting toward the end of their careers. I can understand that attitude from actors; their egos are different than ours. Sam would get promising actors on the way up and tired ones on the way down, and get them for a price. I just marvel at the number of actors I saw go through there in that six-year period where we did 108 features. Sam was clever in casting, he was clever in whatever he did. I remember on *The Magic Carpet* [1951] that Lucille Ball was very cooperative, just as nice as could be. I worked with her again later: At one point when some of the oldtimers [older camera operators] weren't working as much, a seniority program was worked out—"rigged up," I should say!—and we [younger camera operators] couldn't work until the *older* ones were all working. So there was a period when the union wouldn't let me work any more, but Lucille Ball had started her *I Love Lucy* series and I was able to work over there on about a dozen *Lucy*s. I could work in television, because at that time television was a stepchild and nobody really thought anything about it, and so the union had no control in television. That's when Lucy and I renewed our friendship. [Karl] "Pappy" Freund, the d.p. on *I Love Lucy*, was a wonderful, very colorful, loving man—*really* a good man.

Anyway, getting back to Katzman, I enjoyed working there. [*Was there any type of Katzman movie you especially enjoyed making?*] I didn't have any preference at all, it really *was* a job. It was almost like being a doctor, a surgeon; does he prefer doing appendectomies vs. who-knows-what? No, it's all the same thing, it's all part of the job and you do it. You just work in different locations, or the sets look different, or whatever. It all kinda ran together. We *did* work hard, but not a "complaining hard." We enjoyed it. But there was a lot of drinking then, too. I think the families of the behind-the-camera workers suffered quite a bit. A lot of neglect, 'cause it's a long, long day. You leave early in the morning and sometimes don't get home 'til late. [*Were you married at the time?*] I've been married twice and, yes, I *was* married during the early Sam Katzman period. I'd gone to college in France and met a French girl and brought her back; she didn't speak very much English. And I knew that marriage was in trouble right

Two-time Oscar nominee Kline getting his Lifetime Achievement Award from the American Society of Cinematographers in 2006.

off the bat: She didn't realize what the business was like, and my first day going to work, she asked me what time I'd be home for lunch [*laughs*]!

So it was hard work, but nothing could be more colorful than being around all those people. And nobody was ever serious. No one would *dare* be serious! It really was a great period in my life, I'll tell ya. I've been very lucky, I've enjoyed every bit of my life, but that one especially. With *that* much film going through a camera over a six-year period, I learned a lot. It was very good experience. And I'd see Katzman again afterwards; for instance, shortly after my spending six years with him, I was operating on *Pal Joey* [1957] and there on the stage were the partial deck of a luxury yacht and several posh yacht interiors. Sam came on the set, saw these built portions and asked me, "When are you finishing with this set?" I told him, "In three days." He said, "I want to use this set. I'm gonna write a story around it." He'd keep his eyes peeled all the time!

So Sam Katzman was a B picture maker, and probably the best. I mean that sincerely, I'm very high on him. Sam was a sensational person, really, just a marvelous man. I wish we had more production people like him. If today's executives had his moxie, we wouldn't be in the trouble we are now. I don't think pictures would cost that much, there'd be no playing around. And there'd be no actors or directors who could ever use the word "organic"!

10

Sid Melton on Lost Continent *(1951)*

Brooklyn's own Sid Melton (real name: Sid Meltzer) inherited his comedic talent from his father, a well-known comic who appeared on stage with many of the greats of his era. (Melton: "When my father was playing in London, Charles Chaplin came backstage and wanted to meet him. To tell him how much he enjoyed his performance.") Sid made his stage debut in the road company of the Broadway play See My Lawyer *in 1939 and then, with an assist from his screenwriter-brother, broke into motion pictures two years later. TV fans are apt to associate him with some of the popular series (*Make Room for Daddy, Green Acres, *etc.) he worked on as a regular, while B movie fans will remember him as the "house nebbish" for Lippert Pictures, the low-budget outfit that churned out scores of late 1940s–early 1950s pictures—and, it seemed, tried to "make room for Melton" in nearly all of them! Here he talks about one of his favorite movie roles: the comic relief Air Force crew chief in the dinosaur "epic"* Lost Continent.

My brother, who's gone, was Lewis Meltzer, a wonderful screenplay writer who wrote I-don't-know-*how*-many movies. His first movie was *Golden Boy* [1939]—he adapted the Clifford Odets play for the screen. He also wrote Rita Hayworth's *The Lady in Question* [1940] with Brian Aherne. It was a great movie. And he put in it a part for a guy called Glenn Ford, and that started *him* on the road. My brother wrote for Cary Grant, Charles Laughton ... wonderful pictures.

My brother had friends in the industry, and one of them was an agent who got me an interview at MGM. And I got the part: In 1941, I did a little one-scene thing with William Powell and Myrna Loy, who were giant stars. *Shadow of the Thin Man*. It was just a couple of days, but I loved working in front of the camera with people like Powell. William Powell was a wonderful actor. I was 20 or 21.

I remember exactly how Robert Lippert and I met. I met him because of a friend who's gone, Harry Berman. Harry was an actor—he was talented, and a wonderful guy. Six-five! And you're talkin' to a fella five-four. Five-three-and-a-*half* or four. Harry was with us when we went over to entertain the troops, toward the end of World War II. After the War, he suggested that I call this Englishman we knew, an English writer, wonderful fella. Aubrey Wisberg [a Hollywood screenwriter]. Harry said to call Aubrey, 'cause we both had met him and knew him. When I called Aubrey, Aubrey said, "You'd be good for one of the little parts in *Treasure of Monte Cristo*" [a 1949 crime drama Wisberg co-wrote and co-produced]. We went to San Francisco and did it. It was a Lippert picture and Lippert, having seen me in that, I guess became *slightly* interested. Not excited.

Then I did a nightclub revue, wonderful revue, called *Smart Set*, at the most famous club in Hollywood *ever*, Ciro's on the Sunset Strip. I guess Lippert saw that too, and one of his associates, Murray Lerner, called me in to do a part in another Lippert picture. Lerner was a nice guy—he knew pictures, the making of 'em, the marketing, the distribution, everything. This new picture they put me in was called *Tough Assignment* [1949] with Don Barry and Marjorie Steele. After *Tough Assignment*, I went back to New York on a bus—the All American Bus, I'll never forget it. Forty dollars with meals, and the meals were always chili [*laughs*]. In New York I did a couple of shows, including one I did on Broadway and I got wonderful notices, wonderful reviews. Called *The Magic Touch*. I was staying at the Capitol Hotel near Madison Square Garden, on Eighth Avenue and 50th or 51st Street, and one day I got a message that I was to call Murray Lerner in Hollywood. When I got him on the phone, he said, "You want to come back? Bob Lippert wants to sign you to a contract." I went back by train—three days. The bus was five days.

When I got back to Hollywood, they talked to me about signing with Lippert. Which I did. Terrible, terrible pay, but that didn't matter, I was thrilled. I will *always* be thrilled, because I learned to use my talents before the camera. That was the thing I loved about it, the fact that I learned to work before the camera and got to know the "tricks." I always, always loved the movies, ever since I can remember.

My favorite director then, and will *be* one of my favorites forever, was Sam Newfield, who did *Lost Continent* and many other great pictures. His *Lost Continent* is an epic that was waaay ahead of its time. He could do anything, Sammy Newfield, he was one of the most wonderful directors. He used to let me re-write my own scenes in the various pictures, which I did. [*Do you remember re-writing any of your* Lost Continent *scenes?*] No, on *Lost Continent* I don't think I did. Maybe I put in a line or two ... I don't remember.

Sammy Newfield's brother was Sig Neufeld, a producer. (Sammy had changed his name to Newfield.) It was a strange thing: Sammy and his brother Sig Neufeld, they both had one short arm. I don't know what the reach is for most people, 31 inches maybe. Well, both Sammy and Sigmund, I would say there was almost a foot's difference between the two arms. About 10, 12 inches—*very* noticeable. Each had an arm that was *really* crippled at birth, *both* sons. It was an amazing thing.

Newfield knew what he was doin'. I think that guy has gone down on record as being the fastest B picture director, and he was (I think) superb at what he did. Sammy Newfield was an ace behind the camera, knew what he wanted. He was one of the most wonderful directors and one of the most *underrated*. He was never given his "big break," the chance to do big A-budget pictures. We did *Lost Continent* in 11 days, Nowadays, for the same type of picture, if not the *same* picture, they would take five to six months. Eleven days, we did it in. Most of the features I did for Lippert were done in *five* days! Would you believe that? I thought so much of Newfield, he was that easygoing and that tremendously gifted. He was the sweetest guy in the world, and I was so sorry when he went [died]. He and Sidney Furie [who directed Melton in *Lady Sings the Blues*, 1972] were my two favorite directors. Sammy was very inventive and very, very kind, he was the nicest director I ever worked with. I never worked with anyone as kind and as understanding and as inventive ... such a great director.

[*What was your reaction to being offered a starring role in a sci-fi movie?*] It was a very good one, it was a *happy* one, a happy reaction. I hadn't read the script yet, but I liked the *idea* as soon as I was told, "You guys are assigned to go and look for a missing rocket." You know who is in your camp, who really thinks as [highly of *Lost Continent* as] you do? Frank Sinatra, Jr. *Lost Continent* is one of Frank Sinatra, Jr.'s, favorite movies of all time. He never stops talking about it. He got me for Christmas a case of about 10 or 15 VHSs he wanted me to watch, and one of them is *Lost Continent*.

We shot *Lost Continent* at Sam Goldwyn Studios. The thing that really stunned me was that set that they built for the climbing-the-mountain scenes, a wonderful, wonderful set. It was about 60 feet high, and they didn't have a net—that really threw me! I'll never forget the fact that I was *that* frightened and worried. And a few others were, too. There were no nets under us, and you really had to dig into that material that the special effects men and set designers and carpenters built it out of. It was at least 60 feet high—*big*!—and there was nothing under us to catch us. But no one fell, thank God. No one except for the stunt double for Whit Bissell. The stuntman fell into a mattress or an air bag or something. It was a pretty good fall—and he had to fall backwards. It was not less than 30 feet.

Everyone in the cast was wonderful. And I don't just say that. The cast was wonderful to work with—Cesar Romero and Whit Bissell and Hugh Beaumont and Chick Chandler. Cesar Romero I got along with fine. He was a good actor. Whit Bissell—excellent, excellent actor. And John Hoyt, oh my God, he was a wonderful actor. You know his real name? Hoysradt. German name. I remember my brother the writer taking me to see John Hoyt (when he was John Hoysradt) in a club. A little club, like café society. I was about 16 or 17. My brother said, "This man is very funny and very wonderful." I never drank then, I never drink now, I never will, but I sat and had my root beer, and Hoysradt did his stand-up act. Very, very intelligent, very intellectual, you know. He'd talk about this friend of his who was [*imitating Hoyt*] "veddy, veddy, veddy much into gardening. He'd have a lovely garden outside his window. A bed of roses ... a bed of marijuana ... a bed of roses..." [*Laughs*]. In *Lost Continent*, he was excellent, playing the guy everybody *thinks* is the heavy. Wonderful actor and nice man. He was really a gentleman.

Scientists and military men (from left: Sid Melton, Whit Bissell, Hugh Beaumont, John Hoyt, Cesar Romero, Chick Chandler) witness a battle of the giants on the *Lost Continent*.

I shouldn't even say this, because I have so much respect for the late, wonderful Sammy Newfield, but for the scene where I'm killed by the triceratops, I said, "Sam, you know what'd be a good idea? When the triceratops comes toward me, let's cut out a cardboard with horns and shadow it over me." I'm terribly immodest to say that that was my thought.

Robert Lippert liked me very much. Why *shouldn't* he [*laughs*]? If I may be immodest, aside from working cheap, I think there are very few who can do what I do. I got [good] notices, writeups from critics—I throw 'em away, I don't even save 'em any more. And I still get fan mail, quite a bit. You know how Lippert started? He owned theaters in and around San Francisco, and he was supposedly [the theater owner] who started free dish night. And he *loved* making movies once he got into it. I will never stop being appreciative, appreciating what he did for me. Because I learned to work before the camera and do these things with the looks and the reactions and the delivery. You pick these things up. [*Do you mind if I ask how terrible your Lippert salary was?*] I don't mind, because it was *that* terrible! It was 140 a week. And he did a terribly sneaky thing, Lippert, may he rest in peace. I was on a loan-out from him, because Bob Hope wanted me for a part in *The Lemon Drop Kid* [1951] at Paramount. I had Bob laughin' for nine weeks, talkin' and ad libbing. Anyway, Paramount [paid Lippert] either six or seven hundred a week [for Melton's services], and Lippert was givin' me my 140 a week. Lippert just gave me my salary and *took* the rest. Then, come tax time, he was gonna have me pay the tax [on the full amount]! An attorney, Eddie Rose, said, "How *dare* he do that! We'll go to the IRS!" Eddie Rose was wonderful, he called Lippert and told him, "You think you're gonna have Sid Melton pay the tax on what *you* made on that deal?" And Lippert immediately backed out, he said, "No, no, no!" [*Laughs*] But he never gave me the difference!

[*Which of your movies do you hope are still being watched a hundred years from now?*] Well, I think *Lost Continent* ... *The Steel Helmet* [1951] ... and *Lady Sings the Blues*. I was very, very proud of Diana Ross' performance in that, and *she* was wild about *my* performance. And *Knock on Any Door* [1949], because of Humphrey Bogart. I had a wonderful scene where Bogart questions me on the witness stand. Oh, he was wonderful—and apologetic! He said to me, off-camera, "Sid, do you mind me wearing glasses?," "Sid, do you mind me holding the script?" I mean, *no* one ever did that but Bogart. I am still, at this moment, sad about his going [dying] that early. I used to call him at home, and he'd get right on the phone with me. Oh, he was wonderful.

Funnyman Melton, in his TV heyday, strikes an urbane pose. In the introduction to Melton's autobiography *The Rise and Fall of Absolutely Nothing*, Bob Hope says of the book, "Be kind to [Melton] and buy a copy. I'll sell you mine" (Photofest).

I remember so much about *Lost Continent* for the simple reason that I thought it was that wonderful a picture. And the amazing thing is that no one—*no one* I ever speak to—fails to bring up that picture when they're talking to me about my career. And I've been in the business over 50 years. In fact, make it 60 years [*laughs*]! There's a very, very successful, very big, big star, *very* successful, his name is Billy Crystal. You know ... the Academy Awards. He had them call me in [for an interview] when he was producing a TV thing and also a feature called *Mr. Saturday Night* [1992]. And he gave me neither [*laughs*]! But when I walked in the first time, he looked at me and he said, "You—you—you kept me up four nights! What you did to me!" Talking about *Lost Continent*, where the triceratops had me for lunch! He said had nightmares for four nights over the scene where the triceratops got me. I couldn't get over that!

11

Memories of Five *(1951)*

William Phipps

An embittered young man (William Phipps), a pregnant woman (Susan Douglas), an elderly bank cashier (Earl Lee), a black janitor (Charles Lampkin) and an arrogant, bigoted European mountain climber (James Anderson) ... on the Day After Tomorrow, these are a post-apocalyptic world's last living souls in writer-producer-director Arch Oboler's Five. *Set in a mountain lodge where the quintet has congregated (and shot in and around a Frank Lloyd Wright–designed guesthouse on Oboler's own 360-acre Malibu ranch), the offbeat, low-key sci-fi tale dramatizes how Life After the Bomb brings out the best and worst in the lucky(?) survivors.*

Making the low-budget movie also brought out the best and worst in some of the participants, according to star Phipps, who was so dismayed by the on-set shenanigans that he's seen the movie just twice, at its 1951 premiere and in May 2008, when it played for the first time on Turner Classic Movies. Here, in an interview conducted just hours after that second screening, he reappraises the movie and relives some of these unusual experiences...

When I heard that *Five* would be running on Turner Classic Movies, I thought I would watch the opening, and then go on to other things. But once it started, I found myself sticking with it right through to the end. After so many years, it was like seeing it for the first time. I haven't seen it in, what?, 50 years? I saw it when it came out and haven't watched it since, so ... almost 60 years. Surreal! I was 28 years old when I did it.

In 1950, I was on stage in Chekhov's *Cherry Orchard* with Charles Laughton, Eugenie Leontovich, Margaret Field and Vic Perrin, at a theater called The Stage on La Cienega Boulevard. It was a little place, 90 seats, something like that. Oboler, who was about to do *Five*, saw me in *Cherry Orchard* and wanted to test me for the part of the mountaineer. He'd already signed Leo Penn, Sean's father, to play the lead character, Michael.

I went up to Oboler's ranch in the hills above Malibu—I had a horrible time finding it the first time. There in his house, sitting in front of the fireplace, I tested as the mountaineer. Oboler was there, and Lou Stoumen the cinematographer, and Gerry K. [Geraldine Klancke], a silly broad who was the script girl. She had big tits and toothpick legs—a bad combination [*laughs*]—and a squeaky, irritating voice. And *in* that high-pitched voice, she always called him "Mr. *Ohhhhhhh*!" Not Arch or Mr. Oboler, it was never anything but [*in a squeaky voice*] "Mr. *Ohhhhhhh*." Just fawning all over him, dripping with drool...!

When I tested for the part of the mountaineer, it was half-assed; I really wasn't that interested because I knew I was wrong for the part and I didn't really *want* it, I didn't give a goddamn. But apparently Oboler found me very interesting, and he'd already seen me on stage as Trofimov, "the perpetual student," in *Cherry Orchard*, and he liked the beard I'd grown for *Cherry Orchard*, and he liked my voice, and after I tested as the mountaineer, he said, "*Now* I want you to test for Michael." That really threw me a curve, it was so totally unexpected. I said, "You've already cast somebody in that," and Oboler said, "Well, nothing's in *concrete*." Of course, I was completely unprepared because I'd gone there to test for the mountaineer; I hadn't learned any of *Michael's* dialogue. So when I tested for Michael, Oboler did an extreme close-up and I had a script [down out of camera range], on my lap. I would look down at the script and read two lines ahead, look up and deliver the two lines, look *down* and read two *more* lines and then look up and deliver *them*, and so on and so on.

I really thought nothing of all this, I didn't expect to get *either* part, because I was more wrapped up in doing *Cherry Orchard*. When your head's in one place, it's hard to get off into another place, so I didn't really much care one way or the other whether I got a part in *Five*. Well, the guys on the crew were very instrumental in swaying Oboler to get me to play the lead. They all liked me very much, and Lou Stoumen in particular was very high on me and really wanted me to play Michael.

Oboler liked my test and he cast me as Michael, and he paid off Leo Penn. Incidentally, years later, Leo Penn directed me in a [TV] episode of either *Boone* or *Sara*, and before one take he said, "You replaced me once in a movie, you know." And I said, "Really? I didn't know that"—but of course I *did* know it. Fortunately, that was the end of the discussion. Because ... what do you say to the other actor in a situation like that? [*With British accent*] "I say! Really? Oh, that's tough! That's tough, old boy!" [*Laughs*] What do you *say*?

When Oboler called me up and told me I had the part of *Michael*, he next said, "We start shooting tomorrow. Be here." I said, "*What*?" He said, "Be here tomorrow morning, bright and early." I said, "Okay, but ... what do I wear? I don't have any wardrobe." He said, "Just come as you are, and we'll think of somethin' when you get here." So when I got there, they found me a pair of shoes, they got me that T-shirt and so on. None of that was my stuff, it was stuff that they found, and I don't know whether it was from the crew or from Oboler's own wardrobe or *what*. We improvised it on the spot.

I already had the beard and I would trim it about once a week so that the length wouldn't change much throughout the movie. I'd also grown my hair long for *Cherry Orchard*. All the actors lived at Oboler's while we were making *Five*, and I was still doing *Cherry Orchard* at night. After working on *Five* every day, I would drive all the way from Malibu to La Cienega Boulevard in Hollywood and do the play, and after the play at night drive back out to Malibu. It was over an hour's drive—it's a long distance from the hills of Malibu to La Cienega in Hollywood, and a lot of traffic, etc. That's a tough schedule: a three-act play at night, Chekhov, and

A shot of RKO contractee William Phipps from a portrait sitting in 1947, the year he debuted in the studio's multi–Oscar-nominated crime drama *Crossfire*.

then come all the way to Malibu. We shot most of it on Oboler's ranch, some of it on a beach, and some of it in a country store somewhere up there in the hills in Malibu, not too far from Oboler's place. Thirty years later, back at that same country store, I did an episode of a TV series called *Darkroom* with Gloria DeHaven [the Robert Bloch–scripted "The Bogeyman Will Get You," 1981].

The house that you see in *Five* is *not* the house where Oboler and his wife Eleanor lived. The house where we shot was their little guesthouse that Eleanor used as a sort of a retreat—she'd go up there and be alone and do her paperwork, etc., etc. The Obolers lived, and *we* stayed, in another house on the property. It was bigger than the guesthouse; it had several bedrooms, swimming pool and so on. Oboler had a cook, a matronly, heavyset woman who was very nice and a great cook, so we had great food all the time. We'd eat outside at a long picnic table, with the benches on each side.

My biggest problem, when I started the movie, was trying to figure out, "How the hell do you *act* if you're the last man on Earth? What do you *do*?" There were no indications in the script how Michael was to behave. I thought, "Well, I'll just try to be natural and believable. What else *can* I do?" Think about it: If you were faced with that situation of being the last man on Earth, what would you *do*? If everyone in the world died except you, you might go around hysterical and lose your mind. You'd be manic, you'd be all over the place because of the shock and the grief. Well, you can't do that for a whole movie [*laughs*]! Without discussing it with Oboler, I came to the conclusion myself that the best way would be to simply try to be natural, and that the most important thing was for the people watching the movie to *believe* me.

Susan Douglas was very, very difficult, a real prima donna, and the biggest reason was this: Oboler had the hots for her. When a woman knows that, she's got the guy by the nose. She's got a ring in his nose and she can lead him around and she can make all kinds of demands, because she's got that edge, that advantage of knowing that the guy has got the hots for her. Like, she wanted to change things and alter things, and she wanted her way, and she wanted to come in to do the scenes in her own time, and she stalled and piddled and fucked around as only women can do, and blah blah blah blah blah. (I don't want to be a chauvinist: Male prima donnas do the same thing.)

During the run-up to *Five* (Phipps' first and only starring movie role), he appeared in over a dozen films—including a gangster in drag, robbing wealthy women in a Broadway theater powder room in *No Questions Asked* (1951)!

Oh, remember the scene where she suddenly falls on the floor because she's about to give birth? Well, lying on the floor, pretending to be going into labor, she farted [*laughs*]. And of course, that broke me up; I mean, you can't take that with a straight face. I was leaning over her when here came this fart, so I starting laughin', straightened up, moved away from the smell. And the *crew* broke up, *every*body did. But she never cracked; from her, there was no reaction at all, like it never happened. If she was any kind of a trouper, she would have laughed *with* us and said, "Oh my God!" or "Sorry about that, it slipped out!" or something. A Lucille Ball would have made a whole *skit* out of it! Everybody would have applauded and laughed *with* her and she could have turned it to her advantage and really endeared herself, because farts *happen*—like the president [George H.W. Bush] puking on the Japanese prime minister [*laughs*]. But the way she handled the situation, it was like, "I'm the queen of England, I don't let on that I did that." Why in the hell couldn't she have laughed *with* us?, why couldn't she make a joke about it?, instead of being a stick in the mud!

Because I was also doing *Cherry Orchard*, toward the end of every day of *Five* shooting, we always had to watch the clock, to make sure I would get to the theater in time for the curtain. Late one afternoon, we were doing an outdoor scene and Oboler wanted to catch the sunset. Waiting for the sunset would make me late for the play, but I think Oboler had a right to ask that. I mean, he had a crew there and it was costing him a lot of money and the shot would be just right if the sun was sinking in the west, and he said, "No, you can't go, I gotta get this shot." I give Oboler points there. Also, I had a SAG contract with him, I couldn't just walk off. So Gerry K., the ubiquitous, big-titted script girl, called the theater and said I'd be a little late.

Since I was going to be late, Laughton got out in front of the curtain and talked to the audience and read some poetry and blah blah blah, which was a big treat for them. When I got to the theater, about a half an hour late, he was still talking to the audience. He was notified that I was there, and he came backstage and he tore into me: "If you were in New York, Equity would *r-r-ruin* you!" and on and on. He was vehement! And everybody [the rest of the cast] heard it. He was publicly dressing me down, which I could not take. And that's why I said what I did: I said, "I couldn't leave the ranch 'til the director told me to leave. You should understand. Have you ever made a movie?" Which was kind of a low blow, and I'll tell you why: This was at a time when [movie-wise] Laughton couldn't get arrested, he was in the midst of a period where he was labeled box office poison by people in the industry. Happens to everybody. This was why he was able to put on a play, which is very difficult—there were rehearsals, he acted in the play, he directed it, etc., etc. He wouldn't be doing that if he had a big movie with Charles Boyer or something! Also, there was a little jealousy there: Here I was doing a movie, starring in it, and he's fucking around in this little theater [*laughs*]! But that's what I said to him, "Have you ever made a movie?," because I had *my* pride too.

That same night, I gave my notice: I told the producer of the play, Paul Gregory, "I can't do this any more, it's killin' me" [simultaneously doing a play and starring in a movie], and he said, "I don't blame you. I don't see how you've been able to do it." I *would* have stuck it out, doing the play at night and the picture in the daytime and not getting enough sleep, which was asking too much of me, but I would have continued doing it if it hadn't been for Laughton turning on me. I told Gregory that I would continue doing the play until he got someone sufficiently rehearsed to take over the part. Laughton and I didn't speak, we completely ignored each other for the next two weeks as Vic Perrin prepared to take over, and then I was gone. And I thought that was the finish of my relationship with Laughton. I mean, I burned the bridge, I walked away from it, and as far as I was concerned, that was the end. But a few weeks or a few months later, Paul Gregory and Laughton were driving up onto Sunset Boulevard from a street called Havenhurst, and I happened to drive up right by the side of them, and they said hello to me and they invited me to dinner that night at Laughton's house, which was just north of Hollywood Boulevard, pretty high up, on Curson Avenue. There at the house, I said, "I want to tell you what happened that night, Charles," and he said, "I don't want to hear it, I don't want to hear it..." I said, "Well, you're *gonna* hear it or I'm going to leave." Honest to God. "If you don't want to hear my explanation of what happened, let's forget the dinner and everything," and I was getting ready to leave the house. He said, "I was told you were sitting around [on the set of *Five*] having drinks." I told him what happened, about the sunset, and he said, "Well, that's not the way I heard it. I heard you were sitting around having drinks, and that's what made you late." Now, *that* was a lie; nobody told him that. And if he *assumed* that, that's *his* problem. You know why I think he made that up? Guilty conscience. He had to justify what he'd done. That was just shitty of him not to want to hear my explanation— but he did hear it. I *made* him. "You're gonna hear it or I'm gonna leave." He wasn't gonna make *me* eat shit!

Getting back to *Five*: One thing happened that I thought was incredible. We were *way* up in the mountains, and every time that I went there, I had a hell of a time finding the place. Winding roads and one-lane roads and up hills and down through gullies and so on and so forth—*very*, very hard to find, even if you knew where you were going, which I did. But I'd mentioned to Robert Mitchum that I was doing a movie at Oboler's ranch, and one day here comes Mitchum, he showed up at Oboler's with his neighbor, [actor] Tony Caruso! He'd *found* me! He showed up early in the morning when we hadn't started work yet; we were still down at Oboler's house, just milling around and getting ready. Mitchum showing up there, it stunned everybody, as you can imagine; Oboler was just nonplussed. And I'll tell you the reason I know that everyone was stunned: None of the others ever talked about it, and silence sometimes is more eloquent than words! By not mentioning it, it was like, "Oh, we're gonna be nonchalant about this, and jaded, and blasé. People like Bob Mitchum show up here every day!" I had some weed—I did smoke some marijuana while I was shooting—and Mitchum wanted some of it [*laughs*]. So I gave him some and he stayed for a little while and then he left!

I'm very naïve and very slow on these things: Mitchum didn't come up to see me to get pot, he could find pot in a dozen different places. I never thought of that at the time, but in retrospect, we figure out a lot of things, don't we? He could have found pot in a dozen, no, a *hundred* places; being Mitchum, he could walk into any situation and be offered anything he wanted. That visit from Mitchum was his endorsing me and wishing me luck [on Phipps' first—and, ultimately, *only*—starring movie role]. Being Mitchum, he wouldn't come out and say that. Most people would say, "I wish ya luck with your movie" and blah blah blah, but he never said any of those things. Just by *being* there, it was giving me that bon voyage, and I didn't realize it at the time.

In addition to all the actors living there at Oboler's, the crew was there too—five men who had been students of [Slavko] Vorkapich at USC. They didn't live in Oboler's house, I vaguely remember that they lived outside, in a tent or *some* kind of temporary shelter. So it was the actors and the crew and Oboler, and Oboler's wife Eleanor, and our script girl Gerry K., who also was Oboler's mistress. Oboler and Eleanor and Gerry were a *ménage à trois*, by the way. Eleanor and Gerry took me out to lunch once, and the two of them were like buddy-buddies. Just the three of us had lunch together in the Valley somewhere, at some very nice restaurant, they'd made a point of inviting me: "Eleanor and I want to take you to lunch, Bill!" They got along fine, these two gals in Oboler's little "harem." And Oboler was a *weird*-looking guy. He was a *gnome*. He was like 5'1", 5' 2", short arms, bald-headed, Coke bottle glasses kind of like Dr. Cyclops. No, *not* like Dr. Cyclops; Dr. Cyclops was kinda interesting-looking, and Oboler was just a creep [*laughs*]!

Eleanor, by the way, was someone I really liked. She was the mother of his children—I think there were two boys living there at the time, their sons, and they were very nice—and she was a doting, very attentive mother, very attractive, and a wonderful disposition. I truly liked her.

There comes a point in *Five* in which my character, Michael, is thoroughly fed up with Eric the mountaineer [played by James Anderson] and tells him to get out. After I did that scene, Lou Stoumen, the cinematographer, came up to me and said, "My God, I forgot that you were an actor. I completely believed that you were really mad and gonna jump that guy and throw him out!" I never forgot that. What a great compliment! Stoumen was a nice guy and an unflappable, steadying influence during the making of that picture.

Now, as to the directing of *Five*. Did you ever hear of Rudy Maté? For many years he was a cameraman with a first-rate reputation, and then he became a director. He directed *The Violent Men* [1955] and *The Far Horizons* [1955], both of which I was in, and so I got to know this very sweet, wonderful guy. One day he said to me, "As a cameraman, I tried every angle known to man, I tried *all* the tricks, and it all boils down to *simplicity*. The viewer should never be aware of the camera, he should only be aware of the story and the people." The point I'm getting at is this: On *Five*, I don't think you were ever aware of the camera. Any [critical] recognition of any quality in that movie came because of the camerawork. For that, I thank those brilliant kids from Vorkapich's class at USC. *They* were responsible for that movie, *they* gave it whatever quality it had. They brought their knowledge of the camera to that set and they selected where to put the camera, and then [in post-production] where to cut, etc., etc., etc. The flaws in the script—and there are many!—would have been exaggerated if the camerawork and the editing had also been flawed. There was sometimes conflict and friction between Oboler and the guys, and it may have existed partly because they were *kids* and yet they had worked hard and they were star pupils of Vorkapich, and I think Oboler was very jealous of them! Oboler was a radio man and, on *Five*, he was filming what was in essence a radio script; in fact, after the rehearsal of each scene, Oboler would then put on the headphones and he would not watch the filming of the actual take, he would just listen! It took those USC kids to make it plausible as a movie by taking care of everything else, they're responsible for whatever credibility there is in that movie. I have no memory of Oboler ever telling the guys where the camera should go; he probably kept up his cloak of being the boss by saying, "You say you think the camera should go here? Well, all right, let's put it here," but the decisions were theirs, really. That's why *Five* "plays" very natural, and that's so important. How many times have we seen movies where there are jarring angles and the camera circling people and all that shit? That draws attention to them [the directors], and Rudy Maté said that was a no-no. The camera should tell the story, which is the purpose of making a film—you want to tell somebody a story. Those USC kids understood that.

The premiere of *Five* was at the Four Star Theatre in the heart of Hollywood. It was the very first premiere that was televised, so it was a big deal. I was there, and after the movie was over, a man came up to me in the aisle and stuck out his hand, shook my hand, said one word, "Congratulations," very warm and very nice, and walked away. He didn't say my name, didn't say who *he* was, I'd never met him before. It was Huntz Hall! Years after that, I got to know him, because he was dating a woman that I knew. We smoked a lot of pot together [*laughs*]!

Years after *Five*, Oboler called me in to play a part in "The Chicken Heart" for his album

11. Memories of Five (1951) 129

Phipps (center) is surrounded by a passel of female pulchritude at the Hollywood premiere of the macabre social drama *Five*. (Others are unidentified.)

"Drop Dead!" and at that time, when I met Gerry K. again, she was pregnant—and *big*. She said something about being pregnant by a captain in the army who was overseas. Of course, it had to be Oboler's baby. Gerry was a very *silly* gal, and she had the big boobs. One time on *Five*, James Anderson was looking at them, sort of leering at them, ogling, lasciviously drooling [*laughs*], and Oboler noticed and cautioned him about it, he said "That's *my* girl" or something. And Anderson said [*apologetically*], "Ooh! Just lookin'!" [*Laughs*] I knew Anderson very well, we were at the Actors Lab together; and he owed me money, by the way! Every once in a while when I'd run into him here or there, he would remind me that he owed me ... but he never paid me [*laughs*]! He was a very sick man: He was a raging alcoholic and died very young [in 1969]. He didn't drink when we were making *Five*, though.

Watching *Five* again on Turner the other day, I liked it more than I thought I would. I don't think that I've ever *dis*liked it, my dislike was more for all the things that went on during the shoot: It was a tough shoot for me, doing the movie and *Cherry Orchard* at the same time ... there was a lot of friction between Oboler and Susan Douglas, and the rest of us were "catching the vibes" ... it was hot and dirty ... there was worry that Anderson was going to get drunk while we were doing the thing ... there was my falling-out with Laughton ... there was Oboler, who was creepy ... there was his "harem" ... and there was the day that Oboler got mad at [crew member] Art Swerdloff and punched the hell out of him, caught him by complete surprise. Broke his glasses and cut him all up. Oboler was a little guy but stocky, and he'd been a boxer at one time. I don't know whether it was amateur or professional, but he had athletic boxing training, which made it even worse. I'd love to know what happened with the lawsuit that Swerdloff brought against Oboler over that. [*Swerdloff dropped it.*] If I had been Swerdloff ... you can never be in another man's shoes, but if *I'd* been working in the crew and Oboler did that to me, I would never drop the lawsuit, absolutely not. In moviemaking, that kind of physical violence is very, very rare, and I don't think Oboler would have done it if he'd been shooting on, say, the MGM lot, or Universal, or Warner Brothers. But he was on *his ranch*. That's no justification—it might have been in *his* mind—but we're supposed to be professionals. *He* was supposed to be a professional. It was almost a playground incident, like something a six-year-old would do. A six-year-old bully. The fact that Swerdloff was wearing glasses *compounds* it. I think Oboler should have paid dearly for that. In my mind, he was a felon.

Also, there was a lot of silliness between Gerry K. and Oboler. I *love* silliness on a set, but the silliness between her and Oboler was of the inane, cutesy, childish kind; and when they indulged, they were oblivious, like three-year-olds are, to everything around them. It was like, "Fuck the crew and fuck the actors, we're having our little silly sandbox potty humor here." It was painful to watch, it was disgusting to me. So the atmosphere on the set of *Five* was dysfunctional, if you follow me. Between everything that was happening on *Five*, and doing *Cherry Orchard*, Chekhov's melodrama, a heavy, somber, Russian tragedy, *every*thing was depressing around me [*laughs*]!

But after looking at *Five* freshly the other day, I like it much more than I did in the past. I thought that Susan Douglas was very believable in the thing, very effective. I liked her in it. She plays it a little shell-shocked, but if that was a real situation, you *would* be a little shell-shocked, wouldn't you? Having a dead husband and a dead baby and all that shit [*laughs*]? And then I would say Charles Lampkin [was next-best in the movie]; then Earl Lee; and then Anderson last. He was too stagey ... he was posing too much ... it was too affected. Also, he would carry a small mirror in his shirt pocket, and before every take he would take it out and look at himself and fix his hair. And, if you'll notice, he painted on a little widow's peak. A vain man, *very* vain ... and for what? I mean, he wasn't that gifted, and he wasn't handsome!

That said, I think that if I'd been testing for that part [the mountain climber] and that part alone, I don't think I would have gotten it. I was just wrong for it. I was 28 years old and I still *looked* young and innocent, and with me in that part, I don't think an audience could look at me and believe this guy would have climbed a mountain. You yourself know if you can't do something, if it won't work, and I knew it would not have worked, I would have embarrassed myself! In fact, if I'd been offered the part of the mountaineer, I would not have *taken* it. Anderson, even though he was affected and a bit pompous, he still was kind of a stereotype that worked okay; he was just offbeat enough that he was not *un*believable.

Watching the movie again, I was reminded that there was absolutely no humor in the movie. Oboler could have put some gallows humor in there, or *some* kind of humor, *somewhere*, just *once*. Well, there was no humor on that *set*. Oboler did not have a sense of humor. The only time that I really had any fun, any good-natured, give-and-take, sittin'-around-talking, was with Charles Lampkin, the black man. He and I got along just fine. For instance, remember, after his character is killed, the scene where I bury him? I was pretending to piss on the grave [*laughs*], and Charles and I got a big laugh out of that ... while Oboler and the other people just ignored it.

For me, the biggest "surprise," seeing *Five* again, was the scene where Michael [Phipps] tries to rape Roseanne [Douglas]—I'd kinda forgotten about it. That jarred the hell out of me, that was misplaced, that was so unnecessary. If Oboler was gonna put a scene like that in the movie at all, it should have been after Michael and Roseanne got to know each other better. Coming so early in the picture, it made Michael very unsympathetic, the way he tries to jump right in and rape this girl. It was just so *wrong*. As I mentioned earlier, I think that the most important thing that *Five* had to have in its favor, if you accepted the premise and watched it, is that the characters had to be believable ... and I think they were.

Today I live in Malibu, not very far from the Oboler place. But, y'know what?, I could never ever find it. I have no idea where it is. It's up there in the hills somewhere. I'm told it's in disrepair now and they're trying to raise the money to fix it up. Well, rotsa ruck [*laughs*]. Who gives a shit?

Turner Classic Movies host Robert Osborne capped a recent showing of *Five* by saying that Phipps retired in 2000. "Not true!" exclaims the rarin'-to-go octogenarian.

Arthur L. Swerdloff

Five people made Five, *says Arthur L. Swerdloff: writer-producer-director Arch Oboler; Swerdloff, a recent USC graduate with a master's degree in cinema; and Swerdloff's fellow students Sidney Lubow, Ed Spiegel and Louis Clyde Stoumen. Right out of school, the four USC alumni had formed a company called Montage Films to produce a short called* The Earth Sings, *and next found themselves making the acquaintance of Oboler and working as photographers, editors and production assistants on his offbeat drama.*

Making a movie about the end of the world was just the beginning for the Baltimore-born Swerdloff (1921–2008), a documentary filmmaker of note; The Earth Sings *won awards at the Venice and Edinburgh Film Festivals, and his later works* Out of Darkness, Heart Behind the Whip, Conquest, To Sleep ... Perchance to Dream, The Big Dig *and others were prize winners as well. Over his long career, he wrote, directed and produced more than 120 documentary and educational films.*

I met Arch Oboler in 1950, when we were editing *The Earth Sings*. We were editing at CFI and Arch Oboler, who had a cutting room next door, heard us working on it and came in and saw us editing. He began coming in quite frequently and he was wondering, gee, what were we *doing*? I told him that we had been taught by Slavko Vorkapich; Vorkapich, who was famous for his montages, also was the head of the film department at SC. Vorkapich taught the four of us, and many more people, his theories about filmmaking, which were really just the choreographing of motion picture images.

Vorkapich was an artist, he wasn't interested in story or any of *that* stuff. He gave filmmakers the "tools" with which to control the movement on the screen. For example, you could analyze an action: A man sitting at a bar orders a beer and the bartender, down at the other end, fills a glass with beer, then shoots it down to him along the bar. You could get that covered in one shot, *or* you could have a shot of the bartender, have him pull the lever, have the glass filling up, have the glass hit the bar, have the glass start down the bar after he throws it, have the customer slap his hand down in front of the glass and stop it. You could analyze that movement in such a way that it would make the sequence more vital, it would make it come alive. That was one aspect that you could control, the intensity. We had to explain all this to Arch Oboler, just like I'm doing to you [*laughs*]! 'Cause he thought, the first time he came in, "Oh, I see. You make shorter and shorter cuts and it gets more exciting." We said no, there is a geometry of the movement and you have to consider the geometry of the move, not just shorten the cuts.

We explained some of these principles to him, and he said, "Can you guys edit a movie I shot in Africa?" He showed us the footage that he shot there, but we couldn't edit the film because we weren't in the union. But an editor named Chet [Chester W.] Schaeffer said, "You guys just tell me where to cut, and I'll do it." [*Laughs*] So we edited the picture that way. While we were working on that, Arch said, "Do you think you guys can make a feature?" There were only four of us, but we were kind of brazen; when you're young, you're very confident. *Over*confident! So we told him, "Why, sure! No problem!"

Arch gave me the script, called *The Last Woman*, to read; that was *Five*'s original title, *The Last Woman*. I read it, and I said, "Well, I think there're some changes we can make," and we worked on it together. I was a writer as well—I had done the first private eye series on TV, *The Cases of Eddie Drake*. We made some changes in the script, and then the four of us (plus Arch Oboler was five) went to work on the picture.

Five was shot at Arch Oboler's ranch in Malibu. He had a beautiful Frank Lloyd Wright guesthouse that overlooked the whole area. He also had another Frank Lloyd Wright house down below, and that was the house he lived in, he and his wife Eleanor and his secretary Gerry. I don't know whether you know the relationship between Arch and Gerry and Mrs. O., but ... we saw the three of 'em in one bed! It didn't bother *us*, we were too young to worry about it [*laughs*]! Arch had mentioned it already, he'd set it up, he'd told us what the story was, that he had a wife *and* a secretary and that they all had a great relationship. A *ménage à trois*. It was really interesting.

Five was about the last five people alive after the world has been subject to nuclear fallout. The story was about fallout ... and this was made in 1950. The first H-Bomb with fallout didn't occur until 1952, at Bikini Atoll—that's when the United States exploded the first H-bomb. So one of the great things about Arch was the fact that he was up on research and he was aware of the potential of fallout. That was the fundamental premise of the story of *Five*, that this could *happen*. It was science fiction then but, like a lot of science fiction, it was proved to be correct.

There were, of course, five people in the movie, and five people made it.* I directed the

---

Swerdloff isn't counting William Jenkins Locy (sound) and Mel Shapiro (boom operator).

camera. Arch directed the actors. Sid Lubow operated the camera (he had never operated a Mitchell before!). Ed Spiegel edited the picture. And I think one of the most significant contributions was made by Louis Clyde Stoumen. Lou was the director of photography, and he gave the picture a *quality* that I thought was just unique. I thought it was brilliant at the time, and I *still* do. He used a heavy red filter so the world all looked gray, like it had been radiated. And indoors, everything was shot with reflected sunlight, since there was no electric light. Those were all Lou Stoumen's concepts; he had been a still photographer before, so he really knew his stuff. We had all these big silver reflectors around to shoot the sunlight into the rooms. Finally the characters in the movie discover an electric generator, and [from that point on] we lit the interior scenes differently, we no longer used indirect sunlight reflected into the rooms with reflectors. That gave it *another* quality. After making Five, Lou won Academy Awards for two documentaries [*The True Story of the Civil War*, 1956, and *Black Fox: The True Story of Adolf Hitler*, 1962].

In order to circumvent the unions, Arch made us [the Montage Films guys] all producers, and producers can do *any*thing on a movie. The IATSE, the motion picture union, came up to the house in a truck one time, and Arch told 'em that these were all producers and we were *all* making this movie, five of us. And to go home!

Whenever we shot, by the way, Arch would put headphones on and he would only listen to the sound. Because he was such a great radio person, he could tell if the acting [was what he wanted] by listening. He wanted the sound quality to be right, he was more interested in the sound. He knew what the set-ups were 'cause we rehearsed them before we shot 'em, and then he would just listen through the headphones.

There was a very unusual incident that involved me, which I don't know whether I should mention but I *will*, because it was part of the history of the making of that movie. I was taking care of the camera, picking the angles and all that, and Arch was directing the actors. We were on the balcony of the guesthouse and we shot a scene. We were in a hurry and, in the confusion, Sid Lubow, who was operating the camera, hadn't loaded it. Arch said to Sid, "Since when, Mr. Lubow, do we make motion pictures without film in the camera?" And Sid, who was very thick-skinned and doesn't accept any responsibility for anything [*laughs*] ... Sid came right back, without battin' an eye, and said, "Well, since when does Arch Oboler never make a mistake?"

I should add that, earlier on, while we were rehearsing that scene, Sid made another remark that upset Arch: "You know, Arch, this picture's gonna win the Peabody Award for radio!" That's what provoked Arch. *Then*, Sid shot without film in the camera!

Well, when Sid came back at him with "Since when does Arch Oboler never make a mistake?," Arch got *reeeally* pissed. There were about ten steps down off the balcony, and Arch said, "I'm goin' off the set. And if I hear another word from anybody, I'm gonna punch him in the nose!" So he went down the steps ... got himself together (he was only down there for ten seconds!) ... he came back up, and I said, "Look, Arch, nobody's gonna hit anybody. Let's get the next shot—" And, *boom*, he popped me! Right in the eye. My glasses were on, and they broke.

I was an all–American athlete, a lacrosse player and so on, and I didn't want to hit him. I knew he had been a boxer, but I still didn't want to hit him. I did hit him back, but just once, I think—I didn't want to hurt him. But he wanted to hurt *me*! I kept saying, "Look, I don't want to fight, Arch!" He was screaming, and Susan Douglas was goin' wild because of what was going on. Finally, Mel Shapiro, the boom man, came up with a Jeep and he took me away. And Arch kept runnin' after the Jeep, he wanted to fight some more [*laughs*]! He was really

In 1938, Arch Oboler wrote for Bette Davis "The Word," a radio show about a couple alone on Earth; he later turned it into the movie *Five* (and chatted with Davis and her husband Gary Merrill, right, at *Five*'s Hollywood premiere).

mad! I came back the next day and we went on to finish the picture, but I *did* bring a lawsuit later.

When it came time for the editing, that was Ed Spiegel's job, Spiegel and John Hoffman, who was Vorkapich's protégé and sidekick. Hoffman was not on the shooting, but in the editing room he was there. When the picture was ready, in order to get a [distributor] Arch premiered it in two theaters, one in New York and one in California, and he invited all his star friends and so on. He subsequently got an offer from Columbia, and they made a deal. After Columbia released it, it got some good reviews. It got one *bad* review that really got Arch upset—that was from *The New York Times*. But [the *Times* reviewers] were all theater people, and horror movies and stuff like that very seldom got critical acclaim.* *Five* really had some substance to it, *I* thought, but it was talky, so they mentioned that a little bit. But other reviews were very good. On a scale of one to four stars, I'd say that it got about a three-star average.

---

*The Times' Bosley Crowther wrote of Five, "[A]n idea which bears some imaginative thought is reduced to the level of banality and somewhat 'arty' pretense.... [The Five] are such a wretched crew that the skeptic is well provoked to wonder whether it wouldn't be better if everyone were killed."

Five began grossing very well, we'd read in *Variety* that all the grosses were good—but we weren't seeing any money! So Arch again got really mad, and he hired a producer's rep to watch the grosses in all the theaters. Finally he had all the evidence to show how well the picture was doing, and he went into Columbia and he said, "Look, if you guys don't want to pay me, just *buy me out*." So they bought him out, 'cause they knew the picture was doin' well. It was a flat deal, and we [the Montage guys] got about 15 percent of it. We four split it up, and it was quite a hunk. Just out of college, I got a room with daily maid service and a Buick convertible [*laughs*].

[*And what about the lawsuit you mentioned?*] There was a lawsuit—I had an attorney, I gave a deposition of what happened and so on. But the day before it went to court, I said, "All I want's an apology, Arch...." And when I got one, I dropped the suit. Even though this happened, I want you to know, I loved Arch Oboler. I'd listened to his radio show *Lights Out* when I was a kid, and the thought of working with him was just so great. I really loved the concept of *Five* and I loved him. I thought he was really a terrific guy. He thought I was talented, and he respected me, and he knew I loved him, really.

12

Marilyn Nash on Unknown World *(1951)*

Marilyn Nash appeared in just two films. The first was Monsieur Verdoux *with screen legend Charlie Chaplin as a French bank clerk who makes a business of marrying and murdering women for their money; the 1947 black comedy was also written, produced, directed and scored by Chaplin. The other was the somewhat less auspicious but nonetheless ambitious science fiction film* Unknown World, *which was heralded in ads as "An Adventure Into the Unknown! A Journey to the Center of the Earth!"*

Produced by special effects men Jack Rabin and Irving Block, Unknown World *offered an Atom Age variation on a certain Jules Verne tale. In it the Detroit-born Nash portrays an award-winning biochemist (and "ardent feminist"), part of a scientific expedition that descends to the Earth's core in search of a safe haven for humanity in the event of atomic annihilation. The film, fourth in the early 1950s sci-fi cycle that began with* Destination Moon, Rocketship X-M *and* Five, *was produced in secrecy, and all involved were asked not to divulge its plot to the press prior to release. Now, Marilyn Nash reveals a few details for the first time.*

I never planned on acting as a career. No. No, no, no! I was going to be a doctor. I made quite a change [*laughs*]! I was "discovered" on a tennis court. From school in Tucson, I went to L.A. for Christmas—we took a train up there, a gang of us, students from the University of Arizona. They were going home for the holidays, and I was just going up to meet my mother. Mother was still a Michigander, but she didn't like to spend the winters there. I stayed at the Beverly Hills Hotel; Mother wasn't going to be arriving for a couple days and I had nothing to do, so I went down to the tennis courts. I always traveled with my tennis racket, and Alice Marble, a famous tennis player in my era, was my idol.

When you wanted to get a game up, whoever was around, you just asked. So I was at the Beverly Hills Hotel, playing tennis for a couple days with this one fellow, Carl. Well, it turned out that Carl was a tennis friend of Charlie Chaplin, and after a couple days I was invited by Carl to play in a foursome up at Chaplin's that Sunday. I said okay. We went up on Sunday and played. There was a fellow there named Tim Durant, who was married to a Whitney ... it turned out *he* was my partner, and Carl was Chaplin's partner. We had tea afterwards, in the teahouse above the tennis court, and then I went up to the pool to shower and change. Later, in the car on the way back down to the hotel, Carl said, "Chaplin's very interested in you for his new movie." I said [*cautiously*], "Oh...?" I'd heard of his reputation. It was all over the United States, the news story about Joan Barry [an aspiring actress who had recently brought a paternity suit against Chaplin]. She claimed the child was his, and there was a to-do. In those days, it was really big.

When Carl told me Chaplin was interested in me for his next movie, I said, "Oh, I'd have to ask my mother." Later Chaplin's butler phoned me and he said, "Mr. and Mrs. Chaplin would like to invite you for dinner." Chaplin's wife Oona was my age, maybe a few months older, and we got along super-duper. And that's how it happened. I went up to Chaplin's and [I did a reading from] *King Lear* for him, had dinner with Oona and Charlie, and he wanted to put me under contract. I told him, "I have to go back to school and take my exams." That's what I did, and I came back *after* my exams and did a screen test. He put me under contract and I was in *Monsieur Verdoux*.

I learned a lot from Chaplin. He was very, very tough, but he taught me the essence of being an actress, and got me started into doing comedy. And I studied hard—Chaplin had sent me to Nina Moise, so I really studied. Nina Moise was Eugene O'Neill's [Oona's father] first director back East, so naturally Oona thought she was wonderful. I was under contract to Chaplin at $50 a week. I started out with $50 a week and I got up to $200—that's what they paid in those days. I was under contract to him for about three years.

Marilyn Nash went from tennis racquet to the movie racket while a University of Arizona student in the mid-1940s.

Soon after *Monsieur Verdoux*, I married [playwright-screenwriter] Philip Yordan. That was around the time of McCarthyism, and a lot of Philip's friends were out of work. So what he did was, he had to put *his* name on their scripts, but he paid the fellows who actually *had* written them but who couldn't take the credit because they were blacklisted. Those fellows had families, and they'd have all starved to death [if *some*body didn't "front" for them].

Everything was so new to me. It was great fun. It all just seemed to fall into my lap. Philip and I built a home next to Chaplin's; it just happened that we bought five acres right next to him. On the other side was Ronald Colman's home. Fred Astaire was up the street, and next door to *him* was Pickfair. It was a very close neighborhood. [*Author's note: At the urging of her friends, and with the support of her husband, Nash finally severed her ties to Chaplin.*] People were telling me, "Oh, Chaplin makes a picture every ten years, you don't want to stay under contract with *him*!" I shouldn't have listened to people, but I was young, what did I know? So I got out of my contract. Then I did a picture called *Unknown World*. *To the Center of the Earth* was the shooting title. It wasn't a part I *really* wanted, but I thought, "I gotta do *some*thing." At the time, films like that [were still scarce] unless they were serials.

I hope [Jack Rabin and Irving Block] are not alive to read this, but I felt they didn't have any talent [*laughs*]. I couldn't imagine how they became producers. I just thought that they didn't know what they were doing. You know, compared to Chaplin, who had to rehearse *every* scene. And if Chaplin wanted to change it, he would change it right then and there. But *these* fellows ... [*laughs*]. They were really nice fellows, but, oh, my God...! And they didn't show

Nash, just 24, played the top role (receiving special "and" billing) opposite Bruce Kellogg (left) and Jim Bannon in *Unknown World*, one of the '50s' first sci-fi films.

us drawings of the Cyclotram, or the caves, or *any*thing. It was all special effects, added later. I never could really visualize what it was supposed to be.

The director, Terry Morse, was very nice, but *he* had no talent either! I felt like a stupid, ridiculous person, because the director didn't give any directions! I had learned a lot from Chaplin. In a comedy situation, always deliver your lines straight—don't try to make 'em funny. *He* taught me that. And he was *so* particular about where your hands were and how they looked and how *you* looked. With Chaplin, there was constant direction, which I *needed* at the time. Well, on *Unknown World*, *no*body got any direction from Terry Morse...!

Millard Kaufman wrote *Unknown World*. Oh, Millard, God love him. He was such a nice man. I've met so many ... idiots [*laughs*], and I was too shy to tell the idiots what I *really* thought! But Millard was a gentleman through and through. [Leading man] Bruce Kellogg was also a very nice man. Jim Bannon started out as a stuntman. They were *all* very nice. [*Did you notice that the star of the picture, Victor Kilian, gets no screen credit?*] Oh, my God! They sure goofed, didn't they? [*Do you think he had blacklist problems?*] I don't remember *any*body having blacklist problems on that shoot.

Phil Yordan and I saw it at a theater, opening night. To Phil, it was just another picture. *I* was ... horrified. Because nobody got any direction. What do I think of my performance? Like I said—no direction! As for the movie itself, it drags at the beginning. Then it finally

Kellogg, Nash, Otto Waldis and Victor Kilian stand at the center of the Earth—described in the movie as "a vast and radiant cavern," but more closely resembling a sunlit Los Angeles canyon. In the 1970s, Nash worked as a location casting director; more recently, she authored the book *Secrets of Hollywood Heydays*.

picks up a little; about halfway through it, when the action starts, *then* it becomes interesting. But before then, it's *nothing*—the beginning is a bloody bore! Today it seems old-fashioned, and yet a lot of the things that were said in the film would be right up-to-date today. I don't know whether *Unknown World* was successful or not. It was in [theaters] and then it was out. It came and went very quickly.

13

Diana Gemora on The War of the Worlds *(1953)*

One of the artists involved in the creation of the It Came from Outer Space *(1953) Xenomorph and the* Creature from the Black Lagoon *(1954) Gill Man costume, Milicent Patrick, is usually regarded as the first gal to break into the all-boys club of 1950s monster costume creators. But she was actually preceded by Diana Gemora, the daughter of Paramount makeup wizard Charles Gemora. In fact, Diana had already crashed not only the all-boys club but also the all-adults club: When she helped her father fabricate the Martian costume he wore in the farmhouse scene in* The War of the Worlds, *she was just 12 years old!*

True, Diana was mostly just an extra pair of hands in the all-night emergency session, but she was a contributor nonetheless, and in this interview, she recalls her talented dad (and his sideline of playing movie monkeys) and all the messy details of How to Make a Martian.

"Hey, who's the gorilla in this flick?"

A question asked for decades by fans of such legendary films as *The Unholy Three* [1930], *Murders in the Rue Morgue* [1932], *The Monster and the Girl* [1941]—even classic comedies with the Marx Brothers and Laurel and Hardy.

Well, my father was the gorilla, and he was a great deal more. My father was awesome in his capacity to do *everything*, from makeup to monster-making to portrait-painting. Starting as soon as I was old enough, I *helped* him do everything: Building his gorilla suits (crocheting the yak hairs on, three at a time), mixing and baking latex, keeping clay moist for his incredible sculptures, cleaning brushes, sweeping and cleaning the makeup lab *ad absurdum*. I was the original studio brat, raised on the Paramount lot every free day from the age of three 'til I became a stunt double for children at 18—and during that time, I was also the original "sorcerer's apprentice" to my wonderfully multi-talented father, Charles Gemora.

What many people have lost sight of is Charlie's influence on the makeup industry and his many achievements. "Studio blood" that didn't stain. Lipstick in a tube. The first Kleenex box. Falsies. "Whipped" latex that felt spongy, like skin. Having been Lon Chaney's apprentice, his credits wrap around the whole foundation of the movie industry. His generosity of spirit reached beyond his ego and allowed him to give just about all his ideas away. He wasn't a businessman, he only wanted to do his art, and he couldn't care less who got the credit as long as everything came out all right. He knew what he was responsible for and had no problem sharing information. He was a true "mad scientist" and inventor and at home we had a special effects lab that wrapped around the swimming pool on a cliff that overlooked Hollywood and Vine. It was too unreal even for Hollywood.

Charlie was still working at his "home studio" Paramount in 1952, when I was 12 years old. As the head of the makeup lab there, his newest assignment was to make the Martian for producer George Pal's *The War of the Worlds*. At the time, we lived virtually in a straight line to Paramount. It was Hollywood all the way: Our home was up in the Hollywood Hills, under the HOLLYWOOD sign, Durand Drive, Hollywood, California 92808, HOllywood-7-0228. And, as so often happened in Hollywood homes, dinnertime at our place meant, "The pot's on the stove. Help yourself!"

One afternoon in 1952, right about "pot time," I've just put my hair up in curlers, the big wire curlers that were still being worn back in the early '50s. Little do I know what adventures await me that night. As soon as I finish (I'd just learned how to do it—and I was so proud of myself!), my father, the great Charlie, comes rushing in, dives into his usual (rice and pickled fish out of a jar)—and then tells me we are on a "mission" and it will take all night. He gulps down his food, grabs me by the arm and out we go, curlers and all. I never protested, no matter how weird or bizarre his flights of fancy, because I loved being his mad apprentice.

On the ride to the studio in Charlie's 1951 Cadillac convertible, he explains to me that he had already made a Martian for *The War of the Worlds* but now, at practically the last moment, the art director has decided that the Martian is too big to work on the set (a devastated farmhouse). Gee, I thought, the *monster* should be the main attraction—not the set. But in those days, even though the story might revolve around the monster or effects, the technicians (i.e.,

Separated by a quarter century, two views of Charles Gemora: as a 17-year-old sculptor, standing next to one of his creations at Universal Studios circa 1920, and as a makeup man in 1946, clowning with an unidentified actor on the set of Paramount's *The Emperor Waltz*.

props and makeup) were at the beck and call of the art directors. Charlie has to rebuild the entire monster, using some of the same mechanisms, in time for an eight A.M. shoot the next morning. It's already seven at night. The thought "Good *luck!*" comes to my mind.

At Paramount, Charlie's lab was specially built for him in the upper corner of a soundstage, just about mid-lot, making easy access to every set. It was a suite of rooms, one containing hundreds of life masks (some dating back to the '20s), used as reference for every star he had ever worked on. There was the latex room, the special effects makeup room, the storage areas and lots of nooks and crannies. I still remember the "smell of the studio," that odor that says it all, and dust, lots of plaster dust, that gave a certain eeriness to the place. Everything looked like it had been sprinkled with talcum powder.

We arrive to more than the usual chaos—limbs, masks, plaster dust, wet stuff all over the place. Charlie throws me what looks like an automobile headlight. It's actually the salvaged eye from the original, "too-big" Martian. I have serious doubts about making this thing look realistic. I become even more dubious after seeing some of the sketches for the arms and body. It seems to me that our Martian is going to look like a mushroom.

The latex sheeting from the original Martian has already been "compromised," so Charlie must start from square one. The new wood armature for the small replacement Martian has already been constructed (he had started at four o'clock, just before coming home for dinner). Standing about three and a half feet tall, its top is bulging with the beginning of the chicken wire form for the head. Besides the headlight eye, the only parts of the "old" Martian we will be able to use for our "new" one are the arms, which now seem too long for the shorter body.

Charlie, a master at working under pressure, dives right in. He is always one step ahead of himself; his eye sees the process steps ahead, and he goes at it so feverishly, you'd think he was working from a blueprint. He loved to push against a deadline; in fact, I think he worked *better* when he didn't have to stop to think for too long! He worked on sheer artistic instinct. His style never ceased to amaze me, it held me in awe *always*, from my first thinking day. Once the process starts, there is no stopping, no time-outs, no breaks. I am *in* for it!

Charlie tears the rest of the other monster apart for whatever pieces we can re-use. That's it, mold the chicken wire around the new armature like a capped mushroom. I hold up the "old" Martian's arms, up and into the wire, and he sculpts it like the expert he is. Always using the flowing curve, the graceful line. The old Martian arms have been made around wood two-by-twos, hinged at the elbow. By now the tape on them is starting to unwind and fall away. Oh, no! Another added layer of work, but not unexpected.

On goes more of the chicken wire, but leaving the "back" of the Martian open so that Charlie can just kneel into it—Charlie, of course, is going to be the one *inside* the Martian, too, when it comes time to shoot. Charlie works quickly, speaking to me the whole time: "Get this," "Do that," "Turn that on," "Hand me that," "Quicker! Quicker!"

Around the armature-and-chicken-wire framework, we begin gluing rubber sheeting. Then 'round and 'round with plaster bandages—wet bandages with plaster dust in them, around the head and torso. They'll harden as they dry and give it some structure and strength.

The rubber sheeting for the Martian head was pre-made. He had gotten down a technique for gooey globs of rubbery stuff. He could make it translucent with veins showing distinctly, or opaque with clusters of cloudy veins like a hemorrhage, or dye or paint it any way he wanted.

Now the real fun begins as Charlie, the envy of any Dr. Frankenstein, starts what I call his "process": On go the machines. He had a giant latex mixer (converted from a drill press) and he put it to work on a huge vat of what looked very much like thick whipped cream. (Charlie came up with the technique of beating foam latex and at the same time aerating it via an air hose in the vat.) Then he throws in the catalyst, waits five minutes and—*voila!*—the foam latex gets painted and spatula-ed onto the Martian, like frosting a cake.

The fact that he conceived these innovations is even more incredible when you know the background of the man. The youngest of 18 children, Carlos Cruz "Charlie" Gemora was born on June 15, 1903, on the island of Negros, one of the biggest islands in the Philippines. His father died when he was very young, and at this point, the story begins to read like a swashbuckler novel: Each of the 18 children were willed a million acres on Negros. But the eldest brother took over the assets, forcing even his own mother to relinquish her rights. Charlie ran away to the capital city of Manila and, along with other native youths, dove for pennies thrown from ships. He was later found by the eldest brother and sequestered in a monastery where, according to the brother's scheme, he would stay until he was old enough to sign his land away (Charlie was then nine). But at 15, he was in the monastery on a death watch with a body that suddenly rose straight up into the sitting position (an effect of rigor mortis). That was it! Charlie got up and walked out, never looking back. He returned to Manila, drawing sailors and begging to be stowed away on a ship bound for the U.S. of A. Finally he charmed some sailors who took him on board their ship and hid him. Halfway through the journey, a pressure valve got stuck and it was necessary for a very small person to wrench it open. Charlie to the rescue! As a reward, he was given the freedom of the ship and was smuggled past Customs at the port of Long Beach.

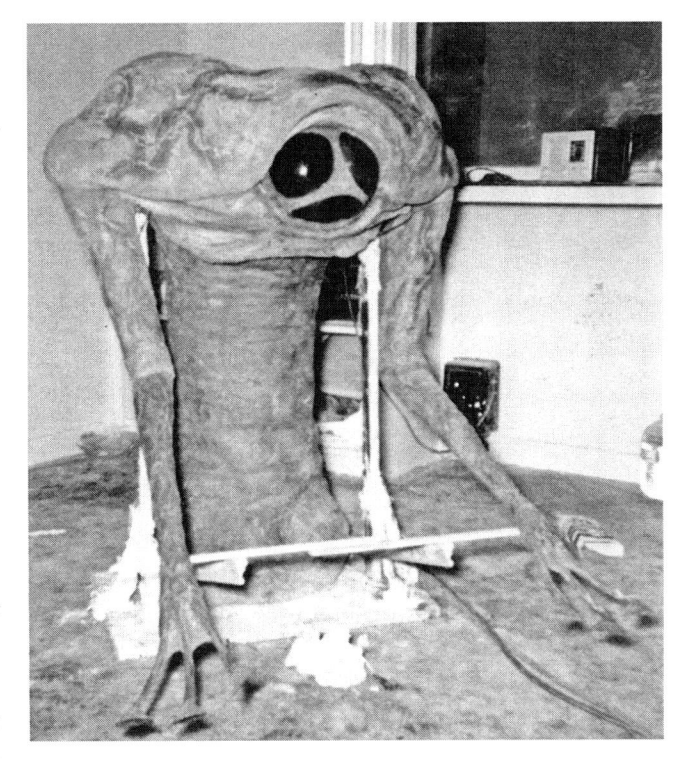

A rush job but an impressive final result: the Martian costume worn by Charles Gemora in *The War of the Worlds*.

Charlie began earning a living by washing bottles for a dairy, and somehow he ended up renting a room at the Westmore Boarding House. Soon he and the Westmore boys were camping out in a gully across from Universal Studios, hoping to be used as extras on "cattle call" jobs. (People camped out there by the hundreds, men and women alike, and then every morning they were literally herded into a corral to be picked out for extra work. John Wayne got his start this way.) When Charlie began drawing people as they exited the studio, he was immediately snatched up by the art department. The Westmores, who were also brought in around that same time, all ended up in makeup, but Charlie started with sets. He did most of the sculptures on the façade of the Cathedral for *The Hunchback of Notre Dame* [1923] and he designed and was in charge of building the soundstage for *The Phantom of the Opera* [1925].

Charlie is said to have made and lost a million dollars seven times before the Depression. He was first and foremost a gambler (his gambling stories could fill up a book by themselves!) and secondly an inventor. I was seeing a good bit of both that night in the makeup lab as he brought all of his ingenuity to bear during this last-minute, overnight rush to make a Martian—and gambled that it'd be completed in time for its eight o'clock "call"!

The head still needs lots of work and I have to hold the headlight-eye up as Charlie wires around it. It's quite a precarious operation. He has to make more sheeting as we go, so the kiln is cranking. He realizes that, since he's going to be on his knees inside the Martian when they shoot the scene, the electric wiring powering the eye needs to be strung up out of the way, across the top of the Martian head. To camouflage them, he decides to add veins like the ones he made for the arms. "Impromptu" should have been his middle name!

Even though this is a big job with a hard-and-fast deadline of eight the next morning, it's just me and my father—that's all there is. Nobody worked with him, he always worked alone. He was a one-man show. If he *really* needed help with something, like he did with the Martian that night, he'd bring in my brother Pat or me. In those days, the unions wouldn't raise a fuss about a man's kids coming on set and being there helping.

Time is beginning to run short; we have to move fast, no time to think! Charlie uses lots of gauze to get the Martian's "curves" nice and graceful. Seems funny to have a graceful monster. He has very thin sheets of latex baking, then puts them on over the metal of the eye and chuckles as he adds the lid. Suddenly this headlight is starting to actually look like it is staring back at me. Cool!

I get no opportunity to nap during the long night—too much to do. My father's sleeping habits were unusual, to say the least. Being from the Philippines, he very much thought in Eastern-style ways: Charlie felt that you never needed to sleep, that you could just sleep in five-minute segments, and that's pretty much what he did! Which I'm sure didn't help him live any longer. On top of that, he got work as a movie gorilla fairly regularly, and that gorilla suit weighed 60 pounds. He was only five three and weighed 130 at the most. No wonder he got worn out!

As we begin putting the finishing touches on the Martian, it's like we are in a time warp: Time and we are moving, but it feels as though everything around us has frozen still. Charlie runs air tubing (as the veins) along the arms and head and "frosts" and colors it as we go. What stands out in my mind is the sheer joy he got when it came time to get artistic. The hard part was now behind him and he is able to "loosen up" artistically. We paint the Martian with studio blood and glycerin, to make it keep that wet look, which was a great asset (the wetter, the better!). Charlie starts having fun with the coloring, making it darker around the veins. I was suddenly realizing that the old skin was showing through and giving a deeply translucent and realistic effect. The throbbing of the veins is going to be accomplished by what is called the Venturi suction effect: The air tubing in the arms and head will run to both the pressure and vacuum sides of an air compressor. Operating the compressor with a "hand clicker" will make the tubes pulse like veins. Pure genius! And it's going to be *my* job to control the air!

It's getting close to dawn. Our Martian monster is barely together when Charlie has me start cleaning up. Pretty soon there's going to be someone coming to approve the Martian, and Charlie wants all the mess cleared. I think it strange that we should take valuable time to do this, but part of "the studio thing" is impressing the higher-ups. Sure enough, just as the sun starts coming up, somebody does stop in to check the Martian out, to be certain that it's going to be ready on time. It might have been George Pal, but I can't say for sure. Whoever

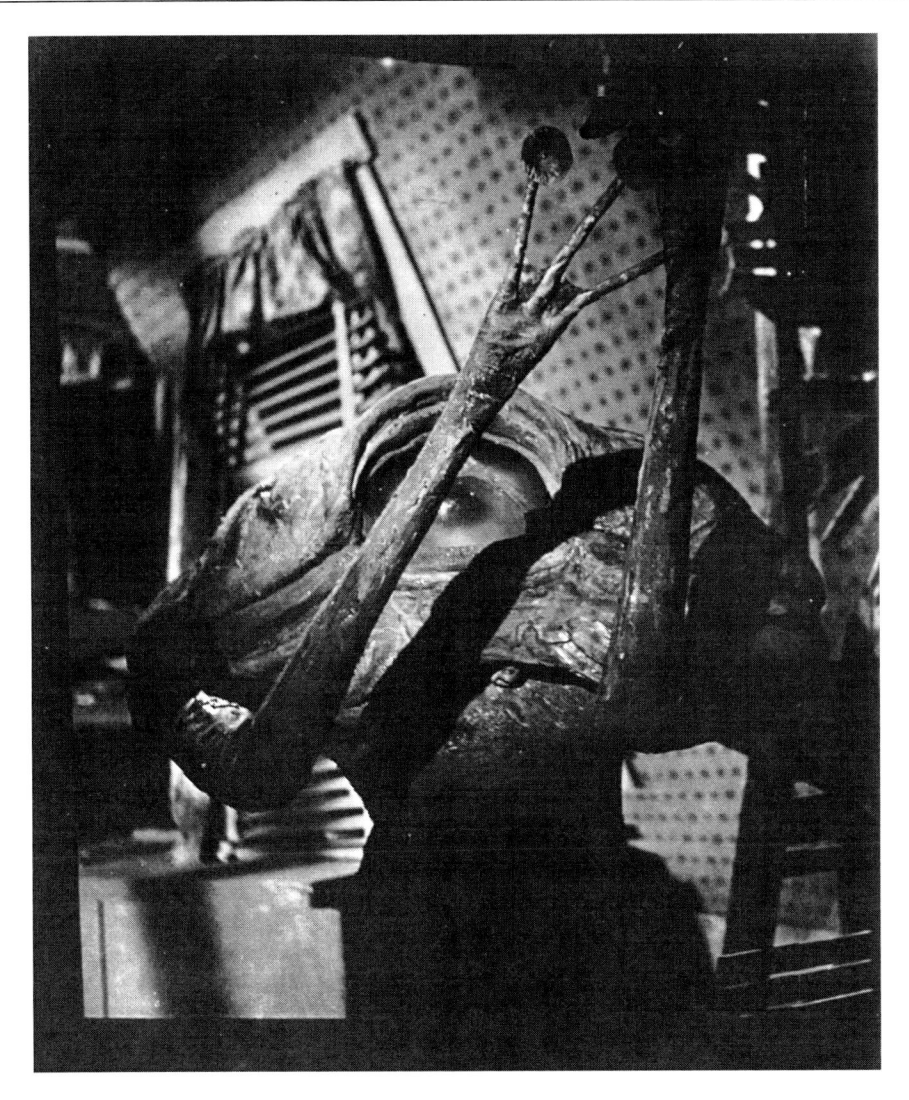

Charles Gemora invades the farmhouse as the Martian in the suit he and Diana fabricated overnight.

it is, he says it looks good to him. A project that should have taken days, we've done in several hours.

The Martian is now together, standing on a wooden pallet. The next major challenge will be getting it onto a furniture mover (with casters) and transporting to the set. Charlie grabs wet sheets and the biggest rags we can find, *any*thing to cover it and hold it together as we roll it out. We will have the help of two prop men in moving it. The lab has a long ramp down to the ground floor for just such times. I'm now very nervous.

Up goes the Martian onto the mover. The vibration of movement makes some of the tape start to come loose. Unsure whether to laugh or cry, I begin laughing. Our Martian is like a big mound of taped-up Jell-O. The two prop men do the actual moving while Charlie and I try to hold it together, holding the sheets and rags around it. Here and there the tape starts to come loose, so we have to hold the sheet against those areas to prevent further unraveling. The head is wound and cradled without pressing too hard. Wrapped up in sheets, the Martian looks like E.T. in the Halloween scene. We push the monster to the set, barely able to keep it together, treating it like the delicate thing that it is.

The wrecked farmhouse set is spectacular in its profound dark scariness. It is Klieg-backlit, with shafts of light streaming up through Venetian blinds. Surrounded by heavy darkness, and with those beams of light shining out like beacons, it is a living charcoal drawing. I now understand what the art director had in mind and I know he has done the right thing in making such a night of wonderful madness for us.

First things first. We take the rags off the Martian, mash, mush and push, repaint, pull out the sprayer for the final "wet" look. Glycerin and studio blood here, some Vaseline there, a dab more purple on the veins. Yup! Looking good!

By now I am as profoundly tired as the set is scary, but I realize Charlie's day has just begun and I'm the young one. I pull myself together for the "real" work. The Martian is so small that Charlie has to be on his knees inside of it—and now he realizes that he cannot move around in the Martian on his own by pushing his feet. The whole thing has to be on a dolly with casters and will have to be pulled by wires. Now he has to figure out how to work around the electric cord, air hose and guide wires. The really funny thing is watching as Charlie tries to coach the prop men working the pull wires. As they pull, he goes off one way and then another and awkwardly teeters back and forth. It will be a disaster if the Martian falls over!

Charlie also has to "work" the Martian arms in the scene. Of course, they're the arms made for the first, larger Martian, and so long that Charlie can't reach into them far enough to move the three suction-cup-tipped fingers. To solve that problem, he has attached to the inside of each of the three fingers a wire with a small ring on the far end. The three wires come up the arm to where he can reach them and the small rings, which go over just the tips of his fingers. Every time he pulls on those rings, the Martian fingers pull in; when he lets them go, the Martian fingers flex out. Very realistic movement for its day. So realistic, even *I* get scared—even though I'd just helped *make* it!

Since I'll be working the clicker to make the veins throb, I have to be wedged under the set floorboards. (The floor of the farmhouse set is about two feet up off the soundstage floor, so they can get low-angle shots.) Down underneath I go, all balled up and crunched, my curlers catching on snags. I am told to respond to "Pump! Pump!" Of course it really should be "Click! Click!" but I guess that's too hard to say in the heat of the shot.

Charlie gets on his knees and gets inside the Martian, putting *his* arms into *its* arms. I'm adjusting myself into position under the floorboards, a clicker in each hand. Lights! Camera! Action! At the appropriate cues, it's "Pump! Pump! Pump! Pump!" as he is pulled across the scene. I'll never forget the absolute comedy of this poor monster barely holding together and my dad inside of it, teetering, trying to breathe life into his creation, while at the same time remembering marks and yelling, "Pump! Pump!" The suit is almost melting from being still wet—the foam rubber hasn't even "cured" yet. It is seriously funny to me. But, sure enough, the reverse-suction pump blows air into the veins, making them full, and then sucks the air out, making them collapse. My click-click-clicking makes them look like they are pulsating.

I don't remember the reaction of the people on the set to the scene after it's finished; I was so tired, I just wanted to go to sleep. I hazily remember falling asleep in the lab until Charlie drove me home at lunchtime. What I remember distinctly is the wonderful relief of taking out those darn curlers. It was a night (and morning) not to be forgotten.

The great surprise came months later, when we went to see the movie—and it looked so real. The wet, unfinished look gave it a slimy, living appearance. Watching the scene, you see

13. Diana Gemora on The War of the Worlds (1953)

Artist Diana Gemora at Glacier National Park in a recent photograph.

how the body movement is kind of "teetery." I still can't watch the end of that scene (the Martian running away from Gene Barry and Ann Robinson) without remembering those funny off-camera prop guys giving Charlie such a yank that he almost fell backward! My only letdown is that the Martian is only on-camera about 15 seconds, and it's difficult to see the great vein action on the head created by my feverish pumping—or, I should say, clicking.

But what really struck me, seeing it for the first time in a movie theater in 1953, was that I was actually scared to death. Believe it or not, even though I knew the entire process involved in *making* that Martian, the effect was so incredible and so intense that to this day I still get the same feeling that I got when I was a child.

14

Fess Parker on Them! *(1954)*

A native of Fort Worth, Texas, the son of a tax assessor, Fess Parker was a 6'5", 26-year-old Navy veteran when he went out to California in 1950 and studied at USC's School of Theater. He soon landed a role in a West Coast touring production of Mister Roberts *and then began his motion picture career with supporting parts. Parker had a small but choice comic role in* Them! *as an agitated, pajama-clad Texas ranch foreman-pilot, confined to a Brownsville psychopathic ward because of his impossible-to-believe claims that he was forced to ditch his plane in order to avoid a midair collision with giant flying ants.*

Them! *led directly to Parker's casting in the star-making title role in the ABC-TV anthology series* Disneyland's *"Davy Crockett" trilogy. Also seen on TV as Daniel Boone (in NBC's same-name series), Parker has blazed a trail of success in other fields as well: The courtly, silver-haired actor has gone from Hollywood to vines, now running a winery and an inn and developing other real estate in the Los Olivos, California, area.*

[*For the first time in my interviewing career, I'm going to begin with a one-word question: "Fess"?!*] It's a surname. The gentleman who inspired my grandmother to name my father Fess was Dr. Simeon Fess, the president of Antioch College ... later a United States Senator ... a close friend of Will Rogers. Mentioned as a possible presidential candidate of 1932. His granddaughter Margaret Fess I met when she was a reporter for the *Detroit Free Press*—that tells you how long ago *that* was [*laughs*]. And then another of the Fesses was a judge in Indiana, I believe.

When my dad, who was born in 1900, got to his 20s, the cool thing in America was to have initials. He didn't like "Fess" because people always wanted to know where that came from, so he adopted the initial E. and became known as F.E. Parker. About the time I got to high school, I asked him, "What is my name?" "F.E. Parker Jr." I asked, "Well ... what is *your* name?" "*Fess* E. Parker." I said, "Well, there's an inconsistency here, Dad...!" [*Laughs*] And I told him, "I'm gonna be Fess." Then I didn't have a name for E., so I looked up all the E's and I found that Fess *Elisha* Parker Jr. was rather rhythmic. *My* son is named Fess Elisha Parker III, and then *he* has a son named Fess Clayton. So there's a *few* more years of "Fess" to be put up with...!

In 1953 I was working in a film for the United States Navy, playing a classic case of battle fatigue. I've never seen it and I don't know what it's called, but it was interesting! At the end of the day I got a phone call from a casting director at Warner Brothers, Hoyt Bowers, who said, "Fess, when you get through with your shoot down there, come by to see me. I have something I think you should do. It's only a day's work and I know you don't like to do day work, but ... I think it'd be good." I said, "I'll *be* there." I came in, and they interviewed me—Gordon Douglas the director and David Weisbart the producer of *Them!* I met them and they

With the assurance that he'll neither be laughed at or clucked over, *Them!*'s Fess Parker (center) describes his close encounter of the ant kind to Joan Weldon and James Arness.

gave me the part, and then very shortly we did the scene. When *Them!* was reviewed, many of the players in the film were singled out by the *New York Times* critic. Probably the only time I ever got a legitimate review as an actor [*laughs*]!* The film became a cult film. Jack Warner didn't like it and wouldn't spend any money on publicizing it, but in Great Britain it became the number one science fiction picture. It's *still* a cult film over there.

 Them! led to "Davy Crockett" because Jim Arness was one of the people they were lookin' at to play Davy Crockett, and that's why Walt Disney ended up watching [*Them!*]. And I've always said to myself, "Walt probably asked, 'How much would Arness cost?' and then '*This* fellow [Parker] we ought to be able to get real economical!'" [*Laughs*] After *Them!*, I was ... not what they call "hot," but I was getting noticed. I was up for a role in *Gunsmoke*. While I was doing the "Crockett" thing, they started *Gunsmoke* and Jim Arness took that, and that was a marvelous career, 20 years. [*You were up for the part of* Gunsmoke*'s Marshal Dillon, or a different part?*] I never knew for sure, but they were going to interview me. Probably I was up for the Chester part, I guess.

 [*According to old articles about you, at the beginning of your career you gave yourself 36 months to figure out if you could make a go of it in the picture business.*] In the summer of 1951 I was 26 and I thought, "I'll take three years and see what happens. If I can't do *this* [make it as an

---

*The New York Times' *A.H. Weiler wrote in his June 17, 1954, review that Parker added "a few necessary comic touches" and that he was among the players who were "natural in their roles."

Post–Davy Crockett stardom (but *pre*–9/11 airport security!), a costumed, loaded-for-b'ar Parker makes one of his many public appearances.

actor], I'll find something else." That period of 36 months began on Labor Day 1951. In the first year, I moved refrigerators and stoves with a friend of mine, an actor named John Wiley. We made like a dollar an hour. I did inventories for department stores and ... whatever I could do. It was typical actor's scramble.

When the 36 months began in September 1951, I had no agent. So I got the list of agents in Hollywood and I started with the A's, and no one would talk to me until I got to the R's [*laughs*]. Wynn Rockamora was a successful agent who wasn't able to handle me, but he said one of his associates might. I was sent down the hall and I met a guy named Bill Barnes, a retired postal worker who had become a Hollywood agent. He asked me if I could find Warner Brothers and I said sure, so I went in there. [Casting director] Bill Tinsman asked me if I ever played baseball. I said yeah. He asked, "Hardball?" and I said, "Well, is there any other kind?" [*Laughs*] Brynie Foy was a Warner Brothers producer, and when I walked in his office and he said, "My God, you look the part. Can you act?" I said, "Oh, yes *sir!*" They wanted to do a screen test and they gave me the script [for *The Winning Team*, 1952], but three days later they called me and said they *weren't* going to do the screen test, they were going to use an actor they had under contract. I said, "If you don't mind tellin' me, who are you going to use?" They said, "Ronald Reagan." I lost my first film opportunity to Ronald Reagan!

Incidentally, without those three years of playing little parts, and becoming a little more comfortable on sets, I would have been a disaster.

[*No other actors were up for the part in* Them!, *correct? Someone thought of you and brought you in and you did it?*] That's right. And my scene in *Them!* was set up so I couldn't lose. I like that my character asks the investigators, "You're gonna help me get out of here, aren't ya?," and they say, "Yeah, we're gonna help ya." And then they walk out into the hall and tell my doctor, "Keep him locked up!" [*Laughs*]

15

Rosemarie Bowe on The Golden Mistress *(1954)*

For a grim tale of voodoo vengeance, The Golden Mistress *featured a lot of lovely sights, and none lovelier than its breathtaking leading lady Rosemarie Bowe. Born in Butte, Montana, and raised in Tacoma, Washington, the 21-year-old former fashion model traveled to Haiti to appear in the Technicolor production, playing a New York model (typecasting!) partnered with a down-and-out boat captain (John Agar) in a search for "The Golden Mistress"—a lost treasure protected by a voodoo high priest.*

In the storyline, there was a trace of the supernatural; behind the scenes, in true life, there was much more *than just a trace in the way that Bowe became involved in the movie, as the actress explains...*

At school in Tacoma, I did a lot of light opera things. My sister Claire, the whole *family* was very musical, so we did a lot of those shows. We went to a school called Stadium, which looked like a castle because it was originally a luxury hotel. In that beautiful place, they had a big stage where we used to do light operas. I loved to dance, I took dance most of my life, and so I did a lot of the choreography and I also did parts. Really, we all started performing when we were quite young.

How I got into [movie-TV] acting was, my mother and I came down here to L.A. to see my brother Sidney off to Korea. I had already done fashion [modeling] in Seattle, and so when we got here, I checked into the fashion agencies. Washington is very much like London, kinda gloomy, dark skies, unless it's summertime. Summertime in Washington State is beautiful from June to September, but after that it's overcast, every day practically. The minute my mother and I saw California palm trees and the sun, we really liked it and we decided we would stay here a while. The fashion agency started sending me on jobs, and I ended up being very lucky and appeared on the cover of *Life* [June 23, 1952]. I also got sent to interview for a movie, *Lovely to Look At* [1952] at MGM with Ann Miller, Red Skelton, Marge and Gower Champion. It was a film version of *Roberta*, a Broadway show with Bob Hope. The fashion office said, "There's an interview at MGM. Bring a bathing suit." (Of course they were one-piece bathing suits—no bikinis!) It was what they used to call a cattle call so there were about 200 girls there, all in bathing suits. I was like 19 years old and it was so embarrassing, I thought, "Oh, no, what am I *doing* here?" You had Mervyn LeRoy the director of the movie, and Vincente Minnelli, who directed the fashion show sequence, and it was the last movie of Adrian, that great clothes designer. They were all sitting together at a long table on the soundstage, facing the length of the stage, and girls had to walk five abreast toward them. Also, all the Stage Door Johnnys in town heard about this, like for instance Greg Bautzer the well-known

In this promo shot, *Golden Mistress* star Rosemarie Bowe takes time out from contending with Haitian spiders, sea urchins and crabs to strike a knockout pose. *Harrison's Reports* called her "physical charms" one of the picture's definite assets.

lawyer, and they were standing there, too, gawking at these pretty girls. And then people on the lot who were doing other movies came hanging around too. I had no idea there were going to be so many people there!

When it was my turn to be in a group of five that approached them, I was in the middle, two girls on each side of me. Someone called out, "You!," and I was so shy, I thought he was talking to the girl on my right, so I said to her, "Somebody's talking to you." Then somebody, either Adrian or Mervyn LeRoy I think, said, "No, *you*. Step out!" I just didn't believe that I was being chosen! They chose only 16 or 18 women out of 200, and I was one of the ones chosen. Musicals like that used to have big schedules, like three months, but this was the early '50s when they were clamping down on overspending. That fashion sequence was shot in one day but it took three months to build the set!

Charles Feldman, who produced *A Streetcar Named Desire* [1951], signed me when I was at MGM and I was under personal contract to him. But at a time when he happened to be in Europe, his lawyer made a mistake and was one day late picking up my contract, and [Columbia president] Harry Cohn saw my *Life* cover and he wanted me to do *From Here to Eternity* [1953] and he signed me under Charlie's nose. Charlie was *not* happy that that happened while he was in Europe! I didn't end up doing *From Here to Eternity*, Donna Reed did it, because [director] Fred Zinnemann wanted somebody who had already done some movies. If I had done *From Here to Eternity*, my whole life would have been different, so it just wasn't meant to *be*. But Columbia loaned me out to do *The Golden Mistress*, which was my first lead.

Before I tell you about *The Golden Mistress*, I must tell you about George Darios, who was amazing. He was a well-known astrologer-psychic whose family was quite well-to-do; they owned, like, the corner of Broadway and Ninth or something, downtown. So he was very, very wealthy, *and* he was gifted with this psychic thing. His house was not far from MGM, and because astrology was then very much in vogue, a lot of the producers and actresses would go to see him. A girlfriend of mine, an actress ... I can't remember who it was ... but one day her car was in the shop or something, and she asked me if I would take her somewhere. I didn't ask where, I said, "Oh, sure." Well, it was to the house of this reader, George Darios. I was nervous because I'd never been to anything like that!

As I mentioned, his house was near MGM and there was a lot of green foliage around it, and we were there during the day. He was going to give her this reading on his porch, and I was sitting on a little patio waiting for her. But at one point he walked past me to go look up her astrological chart, and he said, "After I finish with her, I have to talk to you. I have things to tell you." I was kinda shocked, 'cause I really wasn't interested in that type of thing—readers and astrology. My mother always was, but I just didn't care about it. But I was always taught to respect my elders, and he was an older man. So, after he finished with my girlfriend, he talked to me and he said that I was going to meet a man who looked like Robert Stack. Then he said, "No no *no* no no, it *is* Robert Stack. There's going to be a romance..." I thought to myself, "Well, I'm under contract to Columbia. He could do a movie there. Or I could meet him at a premiere. It's logical that I could *meet* him." And then he said I'd be going on a long journey to the West Indies, which I thought was *so* strange.

After I left, I totally forgot about the prediction about the West Indies, all I remembered were the predictions about Robert Stack. Then a short time later, maybe a week and a half later, Columbia called and said, "We're loaning you out for a movie [*The Golden Mistress*], and it's all location shooting in Haiti." The only problem was that I had to go for wardrobe fittings immediately, because I'd be leaving in a week or so, and I'd be gone for several weeks. Well, I didn't think of George Darios in connection with the trip until I got to Haiti. I got over there and one day I realized, "My God, that man *said* I was going to be here"—and I got the chills.

When I was there [the fall of 1953], it was beautiful weather, sunshiny. I noticed that on weekends, American women from Florida—secretaries, or whatever they were—would come there to the hotels and date the black guys. You could see them in the bars and so on. And there was gambling—Lucky Luciano, or somebody *like* that, had a gambling place. Everybody spoke French but at that time, I didn't speak it. We stayed at the Port-au-Prince Hotel, which was a nice hotel down near the water. There was another hotel up on the mountainside that was probably nicer, but this place was nice enough. And the food was wonderful, lobsters and so on—that hotel had very good food. So the hotel was fine except for the first night I was there. I was lying in bed and I was looking up at the ceiling and I saw this great big black spider. [*Groan*] The first night I was there! So I got dressed, I went down to the desk and I took the desk clerk up there to look at this spider. And he was like [*shrugs*]—he didn't care, and he

15. Rosemarie Bowe on The Golden Mistress (1954)

Bowe at the mercy of Haitian savages in *The Golden Mistress*. "Haiti becomes synonymous with hokey in this treasure hunt story," sniffed *The Hollywood Reporter*.

left me with the spider! I kept my eyes wide open all night, watching this spider, wondering what it was going to do. [*You weren't tempted to kill it?*] I couldn't, the ceilings were so high. And it was *big*. Yuck! It was horrible.

A company in L.A. provided my clothes for *Golden Mistress*. In the movie, they had me changing clothes all the time, and one reviewer said he couldn't figure how I had so many clothes on that little boat [*laughs*]! The producers got all the okays to film here and there, at the Citadel and places like that. In the scene where John Agar is in jail, that was a real Haitian jail. I'm surprised he got out!

Abner Biberman was in it, playing my father, and he also wrote and directed it. He didn't look anything like me but he played my father [*laughs*]. But he was a good director. The little boy who played Agar's cabin boy Ti Flute [Jacques Molant] was adorable! He wasn't an actor but he was so cute and he did a real good job. And Agar was *so* nice, really a nice guy. He kept his nose clean while he was there; well, of course, his lovely wife was there with him, which was good. In one scene, Agar and I were in the jungle and we ended up under a tree, lying in these leaves, and it turned into a love scene on the ground there, Agar kissing me. Well, Biberman said "Cut!" but neither of us heard it, so John *kept* kissing me, the kiss went on forever! Then finally we heard "Cut!" and we found out that he'd already said "Cut!" a *couple* of times! And Agar's wife was sitting right off-camera, so I was a little embarrassed about that!

I was told I'd be taught how to use an Aqualung in the swimming pool at the Port-au-

Prince Hotel, but they never did teach me. So when it came time to shoot the underwater scenes, I just had to *use* it. And Abner Biberman announced to me that they didn't know how much air was in the lung [*laughs*], and to be careful when I breathed! Well, come on, you can't do that to somebody! Can you believe what I went through? It's a good thing I was a good swimmer. In a scene toward the end, I wore an Aqualung, a real one, on my back as Agar and I were fighting the rapids [wading upstream through rushing water] coming down from the mountain. The phony lung didn't look good on camera, so I had to wear a real one, a pretty heavy Aqualung, as I was fighting these rapids. It was like *The Perils of Pauline*. We had as our cameraman Hal Mohr, who was an Academy Award winner, and he said to me, "I don't care *how* many movies you do in this business, you'll never ever have to work this hard again." I was never in better shape in my entire life! And they wanted me to take my bathing suit off, like Hedy Lamarr in *Ecstasy* [1933], and I wouldn't do it. So they dyed my bathing suit flesh color—they put it in some tea, I think. But, watching the movie, you can still see that I had on a bathing suit. I wasn't gonna take my clothes off for them...!

I did my own stunts because the double they hired didn't look like me—she was black [*laughs*]! Remember the scene where Agar and I are swimming, with a rock wall behind us? The water was not deep there, it was very shallow water to be doing a crawl, but the director liked the look of the rock wall. That's when a sea urchin jumped at me! You don't have to touch a sea urchin, they *jump* at you if you get near. When it stung me, I thought, "My God, the arm is gone," because the movie company guys were trying to catch a shark in the same waters and I didn't know if it was a shark that had my arm or *what*. Back on the boat, they soaked my arm in fresh water—I think it was my left arm. What happens is, those sea urchin spines break off in your arm, and it took about six months for the last of them to grow out. For a long time, every time I turned over at night in bed, I'd get "stuck" by one of those spines. You have to wait for each spine to grow out of your arm a little, and then yank it with tweezers. One at a time over a period of months, I pulled 30 or 40 of these things out.

At another point, we were about to do a scene where Agar and I were running, trying to hide from some natives, and we come around a corner and I was supposed to fall face down into a mud puddle. Behind my back, Biberman told Agar that when I fell, he [Biberman] was going to throw crabs at me. *Real* crabs. Agar said, "You can't *do* that to her unless you tell her. You can't surprise her like that!" Well, it was almost the last day of shooting, and I had been through so much with the sea urchin and everything else that, when Biberman asked me if it

After playing her first lead in *The Golden Mistress*, Bowe went on to prominent roles in other features, among them *The Big Bluff* (1955) and *The Peacemaker* (1956).

was okay to throw the crabs at me, my attitude was, "At this point, I just want to get home. So do whatever you have to do." I came around the corner and I fell in the mud and he threw this bucket of crabs at me. My God! Most of them scattered but some started crawling on me and, I'll tell you, I got hysterical, I started to cry. *And*, it turned out, it was so repulsive, they couldn't show it in the movie. Well, poor Hal Mohr, one time when we were riding to location, he was in the front seat of the car and the window was open and his arm was out the window. And a donkey that we were passing turned its head and broke Hal's elbow! It was horrible! [*Mohr may have photographed the movie but he didn't get a screen credit; a guy named William C. Thompson did.*] Well, *that's* weird!

I can't tell you what the [Haitian jungle] natives were like; they were there as extras and you just didn't get involved. The real Haitians would have serious voodoo ceremonies of their own, and in the evenings, sometimes we would watch them. It was really quite fascinating. These people really did believe in the voodoo.

When the producers came back with that movie, Warner Brothers showed an interest in taking it and rewriting and redoing it, but the producers wouldn't agree to it. That was too bad, 'cause I think Warner Brothers would have made it a really interesting movie. But the producers wouldn't do it. So that was another one of those "wasn't meant to be" things. I can't remember where I saw *The Golden Mistress* for the first time, but when I did, I thought it was okay. I get a lot of fan mail on that movie ... and I still would like to know what Warners would have done with it. Meanwhile, I came home with a golden suntan that you only got from being in the sun every day. In those days, we weren't afraid of the sun. It sure felt good to get home.

At that time, you were able to bounce into your agent's office, talk shop, find out about an upcoming interview, or what*ever*. (It was a friendlier time than it is today. Today you hear from agents when they've got something, and that's about it.) One day I was in my agent Bill Shiffrin's outer office and, once I was there, the secretary wouldn't let me leave; every time I said I had to get going, she said, "No no no, you have to stay...." And then in the door walked Robert Stack. I was kind of stunned, because George Darios' prediction came to my mind. He was ushered right into Bill's office. I waited another 20 minutes or so, it got to be around five o'clock and I really *had* to leave, and that's when Bill came out of his office and he introduced me to Bob. So there I was, meeting Robert Stack, just as George Darios had predicted! I found out

True to the psychic's prediction, Bowe did meet Robert Stack and there *was* a romance, and eventually wedding bells: Bowe was 23 and Stack 36 when they wed in January 1956. Here's the happy couple several years later, at Hollywood Race Track.

later that, when I first got there, Bill phoned Bob and said, "You gotta get over here"—Bill wanted Bob to meet me. I had just returned from the West Indies with my tan, and I had on a yellow shoestring-strap dress. Bob said there was a cute little French restaurant downstairs in the same building, the Harlequin, and, "Why don't the three of us have a drink together?" I wasn't about to say no, right? We all went down there, and then Bill "conveniently" got a call from his secretary saying he had a long distance phone call. He said, "I'll be right back," and then of course he never came back [*laughs*]. He left us alone. So that was how I met my husband.

This was in '53, around Christmas. Bob was doing *The High and the Mighty* [1954] with John Wayne and I was about to do *The Adventures of Hajji Baba* [1954] so right off the bat, neither one of us had time to see each other that much. We got together when we could; like, for two years, we were both working. Then he proposed on the 8th of January, '56, while he was doing *Written on the Wind* [1956], and we married January 23.

He didn't want to have a Hollywood wedding like Jayne Mansfield or Elizabeth Taylor, so it was just immediate family. I wanted to be married in a Lutheran church because I was raised Lutheran, baptized and confirmed, and I didn't want to be married by a justice of the peace. Oh, and this is a funny story, wait 'til you hear this one: One Saturday, Bob drove me to a Lutheran church in Beverly Hills and I popped in there and I asked if I could talk to the minister. Bob and I had to keep this top secret, we were hiding from [gossip columnists] Louella Parsons and Hedda Hopper! I asked the minister, "Are you available for a wedding on Saturday, January 23?" He looked at his book and he said, "Yes, I'm free." He wrote down my name, and then he asked, "And what's the groom's name?" And I said, "I can't *tell* you." [*Laughs*] Now, imagine telling a minister you can't tell him the groom's name! I said, "He's very well-known and this marriage is top secret. It cannot leak out." But on the Thursday night before the wedding on Saturday, he insisted on meeting the groom, and so I invited him over to the apartment on Wilshire Boulevard where I lived with my mother. Here was a man I didn't know, he wasn't like the minister from my home, and ... he wasn't that warm. In fact, for a minister, he was the *strangest* man! He had a list of weird questions, and then he started saying that he didn't have a happy marriage himself: "My marriage isn't good. The only thing my wife and I have in common is religion." Yeah?, who cares [*laughs*]? I was so proud of Bob: He got so teed off, he said, "I don't care about *your* marriage. We [Stack and Bowe] are gonna have *fun*." If I could have changed ministers at the last minute, I would have, but there was no way because it was like this secret thing goin' on. Oh, and I couldn't even go get a wedding gown, because if I went into the places that had wedding gowns, Louella and Hedda would have heard about it in one minute. Fortunately my mother was in the couture department of MGM, so she made my wedding dress. Bob and I were married 47 years [until Stack's death in 2003].

So George Darios predicted *every*thing, he predicted my meeting Bob and he predicted my romance with Bob and he predicted *The Golden Mistress*. Incidentally, he got in trouble one time, poor George, when an undercover policewoman went to him. Somebody once explained to me that [psychics like Darios] are allowed to read the past to people, but they can't read the future; that's when they get into trouble, if they read the future. Of course, if he was so psychic, I don't know why he didn't realize that she was a policewoman!

16

Memories of Bel-Air Productions

Paul Wurtzel

In the early days of independent horror filmmaking, the chillers made by Bel-Air Productions bridged the gap between the 1930s–1940s breed of horror film and the more graphic shockers that began appearing on the scene in the mid–1950s. At first glance Bel-Air's The Black Sleep *(1956),* Pharaoh's Curse *and* Voodoo Island *(1957) may have resembled traditional fare (black-and-white photography, old-school stars Karloff, Lugosi, Rathbone, Chaney Jr., Carradine, etc.), but their then-strong scenes of violence and ahead-of-their-time horror effects set them apart from other Hollywood fright flicks.*

The son of legendary Fox producer Sol M. Wurtzel, Paul Wurtzel worked on and off throughout the '50s as a Bel-Air assistant director, on their horror films and movies in other genres (Westerns, dramas, etc.). To commemorate the ghoul-den anniversary of Bel-Air's run of horror hits, he reminisces here about the productions, their stars, company founders Aubrey Schenck and Howard W. Koch, and some of the pleasures and perils of hurry-up moviemaking.

I graduated high school in 1939, and that summer my father Sol M. Wurtzel gave me a job in the publicity department at 20th Century–Fox. In those days, Darryl Zanuck was the head of production and he produced the high-budget pictures, of which they made 26 a year, and my father produced the lower-budget pictures, of which they made 26 a year. Between the two of them, they made 52 pictures a year. There were two publicity departments, although they were under one head man, Harry Brand: The high-budget Zanuck pictures had their publicity department and the B-pictures as they were called, under my father, had *their* own. I went to work in the publicity department for the summer of 1939. Eighteen years old, and I was writing publicity blurbs about what was going on in the pictures they were making, and they were sent out to the various magazines and newspaper columnists of the time. I got to go on one location, which was up in Utah, Bryce Canyon, where my dad was producing a picture called *20,000 Men a Year* [1939]. Randolph Scott was the star, and one of the stories I put in was that he was in an airplane on the field and he leaned forward and unintentionally hit the throttle, and the plane started taxi-ing down the field. Well, the story got by, and I later got the hell bawled out of me 'cause it wasn't true. In fact, Randolph Scott's mother called up the studio wanting to know how her son almost got killed in an airplane and what the hell was going on!

After the summer, I went to UCLA. I was only there a couple of years before the war came along, and I went to work at Fox as a second assistant director in 1941. Fox was where I met Howard Koch. Howard had started working at 20th Century–Fox in 1936. He began as a messenger, worked in the camera department, worked for the film editors, and then *he* became a second assistant director. Oh, he was the most friendly man you'd ever want to meet. He was very sharp; in fact, he probably had the best memory I've ever seen in *any*one, which really served him well. He could meet someone casually, and then if he saw that person again eight months later, he'd remember his name and what they'd discussed and *every*thing. Which is a big asset when you're in the picture business—well, in *any* business, in *any*thing.

My father started in 1914 at Fox, in the distribution office in New York. As the prints went out to theaters all over the country, he was in charge of keeping track of the comings and goings of the various prints. It was a bookkeeping job. William Fox's secretary died and Fox needed a new secretary, so somebody recommended my father, who could take shorthand. Well, Fox hired him as his personal secretary. Then, eventually, in 1917, Fox sent my father out to Los Angeles to run the Fox West Coast studio. Which my father knew *nothing* about; his previous job had been working as a bookkeeper in the Fulton Fish Market [*laughs*]! But he stayed with Fox until 1945, and then he left and he formed his own company, Sol M. Wurtzel Productions, to produce the same type of picture *for* Fox, under his own name, which he did for three years. I left Fox and went with him in 1946. Then after the three years he got ill and retired because of his illness, and that was the end of that.

After he folded up in '49, I went out on my own. I worked some at Fox, and I also did some really small independent pictures, like one called *Not Wanted* [1949], directed by Ida Lupino, that became a big hit. I also worked on one of the first anthology TV series, *Fireside Theatre*, produced by a fellow named Frank Wisbar. Then I got a TV show that Peter Lawford was starring in, *and* he owned the production company. *Dear Phoebe* was the name of that series; it only ran one season.

After *Dear Phoebe*, in '53 or '54, I got in a serious car accident and was really busted up. Finally I got well enough to go back to work, but I couldn't really walk well, I had to use crutches. That's when Howard Koch brought me into his company, Bel-Air Productions. He gave me a job as a location manager so I didn't have to do the amount of walking an assistant does. That was the first job I got after I had my accident, and Howard gave it to me just to give me a *job*. I don't remember what my first picture for Bel-Air was; we did a lot of Westerns, so it might have been a Western. We used to go to Kanab, Utah, and do Westerns. At Kanab, we'd usually do two of 'em back to back. Once we did the same thing in Hawaii: We went over and did *Voodoo Island*, which was the low-budget picture, and then we stayed and did a bigger-budget picture with Lex Barker, *Jungle Heat* [1957]. Doing two on location at the same time made more sense.

At Bel-Air, Aubrey Schenck was the dealmaker and Howard was the one who got everything together for the money and made the pictures. Aubrey would go out and then come back with these deals he had made, and Howard would say, "There's no way we can make those pictures for the amount that you've promised we can make 'em for. We can't *do* it, Aubrey, you're *crazy*." But somehow we did 'em! Some were a little over 100,000 apiece, some were a little under. Nowadays you can't do one day of a television episode for 100,000—and that's leaving out the actors, because some actors get a million dollars for a TV episode, like Jerry Seinfeld.

Aubrey was a real character, very gregarious. He was an attorney but you would never think of him as an attorney. He was very funny, had a great sense of humor, and a very sharp mind. Everybody could kid him and rib him, and he laughed a lot. And he thought he was Alfred Hitchcock, he'd always want to be in the movies [as an extra]. "Get *outta* there, Aubrey!," "No, I wanna be in the picture!" [*Laughs*] He was crazy like that. He married his secretary Florie, who's still alive.

The director of *The Black Sleep* was Reginald LeBorg, who'd been brought over to Hollywood from Europe in the '30s. Howard and Aubrey used to have him direct a lot of the back-to-back Westerns. He was a kind of a suave, dapper type, and could be very serious. But he was a good person, and we got along fine. He was a character also! Do you know his real name? Grobel. Then he spelled it backwards so it became LeBorg. It didn't sound too good, Grobel, LeBorg sounded better, and he became Reggie LeBorg for the rest of his life.

With *The Black Sleep*, Bel-Air was trying to do something a little bigger than their usual pictures; in fact, it was one of their biggest ones. Basil Rathbone and Akim Tamiroff were pretty well-known names at that time. Rathbone was the most professional individual I ever worked with. He was on the set, made-up, dressed, ready, never took the wardrobe off or anything, sat right behind the camera whether he was in the scene or not in the scene, watched everything, knew exactly what was going on. In my book, he was like the perfect actor. He was *so* professional it was frightening [*laughs*]—really! He was a gentleman, he never scoffed at anything or looked down on anything. Karloff was exactly the same way on *Voodoo Island*. These actors came up the hard way, came up out of the school of hard knocks, and learned the business. Not like some of the "stars" we have today...

Basil Rathbone, star of *The Black Sleep*, "was the most professional individual I ever worked with," says Paul Wurtzel. "He was so professional it was frightening—really!"

Akim Tamiroff, who played the gypsy tattoo artist, was another very professional actor who came in and did his work. I always loved him, he was a great character, too. These actors were really substantial people. [*Bel-Air initially wanted Peter Lorre to play the gypsy, but he asked for too much money.*] I never worked with Lorre but my father made movies with him, the Mr. Motos at 20th Century–Fox in the '30s.

Lon Chaney, Jr., would come to work in his pick-up truck, which had a little camper shell on it, and in this camper he'd cook chili in a big pot for everybody. When it was ready, we'd go out to the camper and he'd give some to us on paper plates, and it was terrific chili. He did that for us a *couple* of times at least. I also remember that he used to perspire so much that the makeup man had to carry a bucket with ice in it, and a shammy, to mop him down. I think Lon probably imbibed a little too much! He was a very nice man. I only worked on that one picture with Chaney but he was great.

John Carradine? To be honest, I forgot he was in the picture. I'm surprised he *did* it! Carradine was a real pro also, and a fantastic fellow.

Watching *Black Sleep* the other day, I didn't remember Bela Lugosi doing so little in it. He didn't say one word in the picture! Tor Johnson, the huge wrestler, was Bela's "keeper." We hired Tor to play a part in *Black Sleep* because he was the only one who could get Bela Lugosi to work in the morning and then take him home at night. I think Bela was on medication or something, he was sort of "out of it," and we saw very little of him. Tor would have to practically pick Bela up and carry him around because he could barely walk. Tor would put Bela in the scene, and then after it was over, he'd take Bela out and put him in a chair. Bela was just *there*. It was a *body*! In the scenes, we didn't know if he was gonna fall over or *what*. [*Isn't it tough for a little production company to get insurance on an actor like that? Is it a good idea to put somebody who's in that kind of shape into a movie?*] Sometimes it is, sometimes it isn't. I did a pilot with Melvyn Douglas after he'd had seven heart attacks. He got through the pilot; we thought he might die in the middle of it, but he got through it. And it never sold anyway [*laughs*]! As for Bela Lugosi, if he'd died on the set, they'd have just written him out and you wouldn't have seen that character again. That would have been easy to do, because his character did *nothing*, actually. Bel-Air just wanted to get Bela's *name* in; they were going to try and sell the picture on the names.

Black Sleep was shot at American National, which was right next to what *was* Goldwyn Studio. I worked there again after that, when it was Ziv. They did a lot of TV series there like *Superman, Treasury Men in Action, TV Reader's Digest, Highway Patrol* with Broderick Crawford and so on. It's been torn down, and there's nothing there now but little stores—a Trader Joe's market, a couple of small Chinese restaurants and so on.

For *Pharaoh's Curse*, we had to fly up to Death Valley to shoot the scenes in the desert. We chartered a DC-3, a plane that carried 47 passengers, and we made arrangements to fly out of Burbank Airport, which is now called Bob Hope Airport. We had to be at the airport at like four in the morning. Everybody showed up at the airport, the actors and the crew—but not the plane [*laughs*]. The place was so fogged in, the plane hadn't yet arrived. And we had to shoot that very *day*. I think this was a six- or seven-day picture and we only had three days to get all the work done in Death Valley. I ran to the phone and I called Howard at home, I woke him up, and I said, "Howard, the plane isn't here, and we gotta get goin'. Can you call and find out what we can do, and where it is, and what's goin' on?" He did, and in the meantime, right in the lobby of the airport, we made-up all the actors and got 'em dressed in their wardrobe so that as soon as we arrived in Death Valley, they'd be ready [*laughs*]! Then we sent 'em to have breakfast. "Meal penalties" are imposed on a production company if the people aren't fed every five and a half or six hours, and we knew that if we didn't feed them then and there at the airport, we'd have to feed them as soon as we landed in the desert instead of putting them right to work. So as long as we were sitting there in the airport anyway, we sent

Playing non-speaking roles in *The Black Sleep* were (right) Lon Chaney, Jr. ("I think Lon probably imbibed a little too much!") and an out-of-it Bela Lugosi ("Bela was just *there*. It was a *body*!").

For use in country-wide exploitation *for The Black Sleep*, life-size figures of (left to right) Rathbone, Chaney, John Carradine, Lugosi, Akim Tamiroff and (not pictured) Louanna Gardner were made by makeup man George Bau (top) at a reported cost of $20,000. Their first stop was New York—where they were shipped in individual coffins!

'em to breakfast in the cafeteria. Finally the fog lifted enough and the plane arrived and we got on it, all the actors in wardrobe, and left. When we got to Death Valley, we could go to work.

We'd sent the equipment up to Death Valley the day before, the trucks and the stand-by cars that'd be used to run us around. One thing that happened, I'll never forget: Aubrey was there with us and we had two cars but only one union driver, so Aubrey drove one of the station wagons. The other car, with the union driver in it, we kept by the set, out in the middle of the desert, for emergencies or for whatever. At one point, the two of 'em were on the road at the same time, one coming up from the location and the other going the other way, with Aubrey driving. The desert is flat, it's wide-open out there, one two-lane road, a million square miles of nothin'—and Aubrey ran head-on into the other car, and wrecked *both* of them [*laughs*]! It was unbelievable! But that's the kind of man he was—a character!

We had to bring enough food to provide breakfasts, lunches and dinners for the entire cast and crew, 'cause nothing was open up there. On our first day in Death Valley, the day when we'd had breakfast at the airport, the caterers from Los Angeles came out to the location to bring us lunch, and they had forgotten all of the utensils. As I mentioned earlier, the production company has to pay penalties if you don't feed the people on time, and so there we were, and the meals were there, but no forks and knives for anybody. So everybody was eating with their hands! Then I got sunstroke because it was so hot; it was like 115 every day, and I didn't have a hat. So they pushed me under a truck in the shade. The more I talk about this movie, the more it sounds like we were all idiots running around loose. Well, in a way maybe we *were* [*laughs*], but we did have a plan and we did carry it out. But I remember that show for *that* stuff, I remember it because *every*thing went wrong.

Our location was maybe a half-hour ride from where we were staying. I can't remember the name of the place, it was like Poison Water Wells or something. Every place out there has Death in its name, or Dying, or Fire, or Furnace. Stovepipe Wells, I *think* that was the name of the place, and we stayed at some kind of a broken-down campground. The enclosures we stayed in, you couldn't even call 'em cabins, these were just like wooden things with canvas roofs, almost like tents. There were maybe 20 of 'em. And we didn't each get our *own* shack, it'd be like four people to a shack. In those days, you always had a minimum of two people. (Today everybody gets their own hotel room—which is fine with me!) So there we were, out in the middle of the desert, in the middle of nowhere, in these shacks, and I don't even remember where we got the water from. Everybody complained and screamed and squawked, but we had told 'em what the conditions would be like ahead of time, so now we'd tell 'em, "You took the job, so … shut up and *do* it." [*Laughs*] Then they were okay. Luckily, we were only there three days. Everything was out of sync, everything was just wild on that *Pharaoh's Curse*.

At American National, we shot on sets representing the pharaoh's caves and so on. I liked the director, Lee Sholem. They called him "Roll 'Em" Sholem. No matter *what*, he'd shoot it: "Shoot it! Shoot it! Roll 'em! Get it!" Nobody would be ready, but he'd shoot it [*laughs*]! In one of the shows we did, *Crime Against Joe* [1956] with John Bromfield, we shot in Tucson, Arizona. Patricia Blake, who played the girl in *The Black Sleep*, was also the lead in this, we were shooting on a downtown street in Tucson and, whenever anybody had to [relieve themselves], we used the rest room in one of the stores. This girl Pat had on a

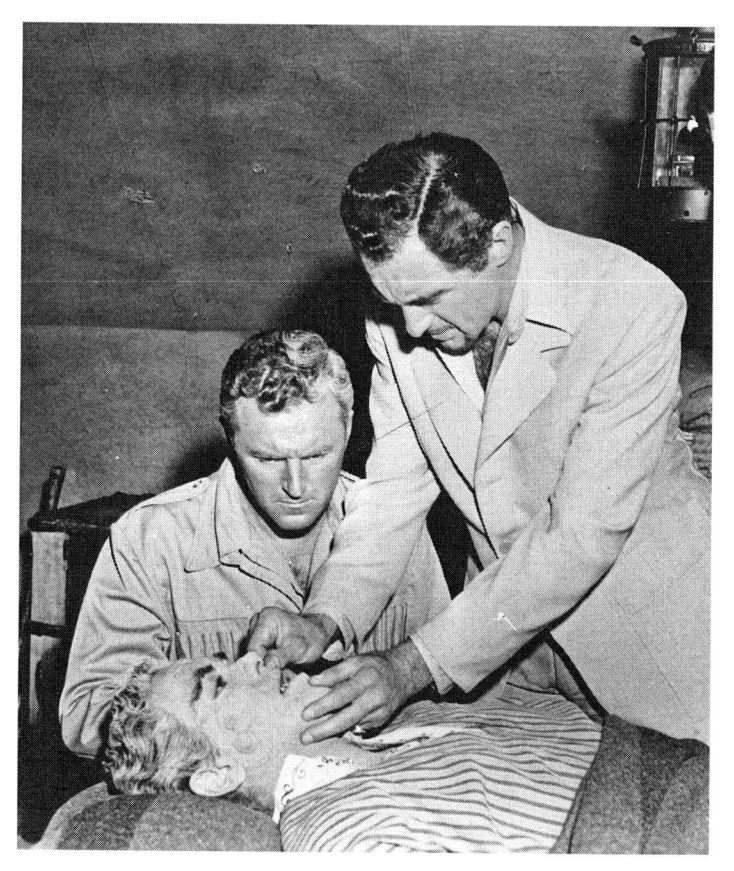

From bad to Wurtzel: George Neise (seated) and Guy Prescott examine a mummy in the making (Alvaro Guillot) in *Pharaoh's Curse*, a movie the assistant director remembers well "because *every*thing went wrong."

From the English movie trade paper *Kinematograph Weekly*'s review: "The characters are taken from stock but not even dusted.... [I]f this is how the British behaved in Egypt, no wonder we were slung out!"

Western dress, and at one point she had to go to the rest room. She ran into the store, into the rest room, and while she was in there, the director Sholem overheard the cameraman Bill Margulies tell me we were ready. So Sholem said, "Okay, let's go, let's go, let's go. Where's Pat? Where's Pat?" I said, "She just went into the bathroom." Well, he *ran* into the store, into the rest room and pulled her off the commode [*laughs*]—I'm not kidding! She came out pulling her clothes up! Sholem actually took her off the commode to put her in the scene. I told the cameraman, "For Christ's sake, never yell to me, 'We're ready.' Always come up to me and whisper, or signal me, or something!" It was crazy, but we had *fun* because things so often were crazy. It's a crazy business!

Incidentally, my father didn't want me to go into the picture business. He wanted me to become a farmer [*laughs*]—he pictured me, like, up in the Central Valley of California, being a farmer! He was under tremendous pressure his whole life, and I guess he felt that it wouldn't be good for me! [*His* Variety *obituary says there was a seven-year stretch where he made 190 movies.*] Well, actually, someone years ago made a count, and it turned out that he had produced about 1500. Yes, that included lots of 10- and 20-minute comedies that he oversaw, but there *were* like 1500 titles, so they said he had produced more pictures than anyone else in that era.

Voodoo Island ... that one was kinda blanked out in my mind. I think I was drinking then—luckily [*laughs*]! Reggie LeBorg was the director again, and we made that in Kauai, Hawaii, in six days. Bel-Air Productions went over ahead of time and picked all the locations. The airport you see in the picture was at Lihue, and that's also where the port for the ships is. We shipped all the equipment over from L.A. on a freighter, and when it got to Lihue, the local union wouldn't let the stevedores come on board and unload it. On that freighter was a huge trailer we'd rented, the kind of trailer you'd see on the back of an 18-wheeler, and in it we'd loaded everything we'd need in Hawaii, the arc lights and the camera equipment and the wardrobe and the props and the grip equipment, *every*thing—that trailer was bulging. And now in Hawaii, they wouldn't unload it from the freighter! But Howard was a terrific talker, and smart, and he made some arrangement, and everything got unloaded finally so we could start working.

The weather was typical Hawaiian weather, it would rain two or three times a day for like ten minutes, and it was hot and humid. We had a fishing boat we'd rented for a scene in the picture, and one day on that boat, Reggie LeBorg, who was always trying to get something "special," was spending too much time [getting the shots]. The captain of the boat kept saying, "I gotta get the boat out of here, the tide's going out and I'm gonna get stuck." But Reggie was Reggie—"One more shot! One more shot!" Well, the tide went out, the boat touched bottom, and here was this big fishing boat stuck out there. We had to somehow get the crew and the cast off the boat, row 'em back to shore, and wait until the next day when the tide came in and freed the boat. This is all on a six-day movie. Howard would yell at Reggie, he'd get so mad at him. "Reggie, why don't you *listen*? Paul told you to move the boat!," "Yeah, but I needed another shot...." It was almost like a comedy! The best part about these pictures was the *making* of them, because it was such an adventure.

We also had trouble with the man-eating plants. A top special effects man, Milt Rice, built 'em, but he had very little money to work with. We wanted plants with eight tentacles, to grab the people, and he didn't have enough money, so they wound up with *three* tentacles [*laughs*], stuff like that. To make the plants "attack," we used compressed air, wires, springs, Milt Rice's *arm* stuck in a tentacle [*laughs*], whatever we had to do in order to make the plants work "for cheap."

We stayed at the Coco Palms, which was one of Hawaii's great hotels, except for one night when a group of people on a tour, tourists who had booked rooms there a *year* in advance, came in. We knew we'd have to move out of the Coco Palms that one night while that tour group came in and took *our* rooms, and then we could come back the next day after they left. So that night we had to move to another hotel, a place up on a mountain that was nearby—a hotel that was closed, but was being opened up again just for us. This hotel had been closed for a couple of years because of superstition: Nobody would work there because they thought it was haunted by the Menehune. The Menehune is a Hawaiian superstition, they're like pixies, like the Irish "little people." Some of the help from the Coco Palms Hotel had to go try and clean up this other hotel so we could move up there, and a lot of *them* didn't want to go up because they were superstitious. We had to try to get non–Hawaiians to do it. We didn't even want to tell anybody in our own company why this hotel was closed because some of them, the actors especially, might not want to move in; we didn't want some of 'em saying, "I'm not gonna stay in that hotel. If the Hawaiians are *that* scared, there must be *some*thing goin' on up there!" Things like that [the hotel switch] disrupt everything. By the way, Howard and I talked about *buying* that second hotel; we said, "We can buy it and really make something out of it," but we never did. And years later, somebody bought it, and now it's a bigger place than the Coco Palms was! It became a big destination point. Howard and I said, "God, we shoulda bought it, we coulda had it for *nothing*." Incidentally, just as a sidebar, about 15 years ago they had a big hurricane in Hawaii, Hurricane Iniki, and the Coco Palms was so demolished, it still has not reopened.

The place where we shot all the jungle stuff was a plantation that was owned by a couple of Chinese men who also owned Aloha Airlines and some nightclubs in Honolulu and God knows what else they had. I met 'em, the Tong brothers, and got to know them pretty well because they were interesting people. They were very wealthy and they'd bought this big plantation, and so we used it for the jungles.

Boris Karloff was like Rathbone, the consummate pro. He never would indicate that the script was not quite [on the level of] *Frankenstein*; he just came in and happily did the job. He had to do some physical things, and he was no spring chicken then, but he went through the jungle and climbed up rocks and did *every*thing, and was always very pleasant and just a perfect man. It's *sad*, when you think of what happens to these people [former stars now making minor movies], what it must do to their egos.

[*Who thought Boris Karloff in a baseball cap was a good idea?*] Who knows? It might've been *Karloff's* idea, to keep his head out of the sun! Or, there's another possibility: Howard Koch was always wearing a baseball cap, or a Directors Guild cap with their logo on it, or *some* kind of cap. And if somebody seemed to be eyeing his cap, he'd say, "Oh, you *like* this?," and he'd give them his cap. He used to give *me* caps, and he might have given that very cap to Karloff— "Here, Boris, wear this!" That's just the way Howard was, he'd give you the hat off his head if he thought you'd like it. I still have a couple of them.

Also in the movie was Murvyn Vye, a good character actor. And Elisha Cook was great. "Cookie" was another character, a little bit of an off-center type in real life. I worked with him a lot. He lived in Bishop, California, which is way up in the snow country. He lived there all the time, and came down [to Hollywood] to work. "Cookie" was a good guy.

On *Voodoo Island*, the big thing was, at the end of the picture, Elisha Cook's character was going to fall off a bridge, fall into a big wide stream. Of course, that wasn't "Cookie" who fell off the bridge; we hired a local native, because those guys are all good swimmers. I don't know what we paid him to double "Cookie," probably a coconut or something [*laughs*]. Anyway, Reggie LeBorg insisted that he wanted a shot of the fish that were in the stream coming to eat the body. I know how Reggie got that idea: The Coco Palms had a huge outdoor patio, with tables and umbrellas, overlooking a lagoon, and people would eat out there and they loved to throw bread into the lagoon and watch the fish jump up and eat the bread.

When Reggie said he wanted a shot of fish attacking the body, Howard said, "Reggie, we don't have time," because we had to start the next feature, the "big" feature [*Jungle Heat*], on such-and-such a day. Well, Reggie figured, "Well, all right, I want the fish to attack his *head*," and he had the prop man Arden Cripe go out and get a real human skull [*laughs*]. Everybody thought Reggie was crazy—which he was! *Some*where on the island of Kauai, Cripe got a skull, and then he went back to the Coco Palms Hotel and into the kitchen and told the chef, "If we take bread dough and put it around this skull and make a face, would you bake it?" That was Reggie's idea; according to Reggie, the fish in the stream would attack the head because of the bread dough. Of course the chef said, "I can't put a skull in my oven!"—number one, the Hawaiians are very superstitious, and number two, he thought he'd be fired. I don't know what Cripe did, maybe he went and found some restaurant where they'd do it. *Someone*, I don't know who, put bread dough all over the skull and made a face, and the thing was baked, and then our makeup man Ted Coodley painted it up to look as close to Elisha Cook as possible. We called it Bread Head. Then we got a dummy for the body and put Bread Head on that.

Howard told Reggie that he could take the little Arriflex and a camera operator and shoot this Bread Head scene while the rest of the crew went off to start the new show, *Jungle Heat*. Well, they had a different assistant director on *Jungle Heat*,

From a stranded fishing boat to a night in a haunted hotel, *Voodoo Island* was another moviemaking experience Wurtzel categorizes as "an adventure." (Pictured: Beverly Tyler, Boris Karloff.)

so I was with Reggie the next day when he tried to shoot this. We put the body in the stream and it floated, and we had to throw some chum in so the fish would come around. But the bread was baked so hard, it never dissolved, and the fish couldn't eat it. Once we put the body in, we couldn't get it *out*, and now the slow-moving current started taking it downstream. Reggie, the camera operator and I ran along the bank after it, and the prop man Arden Cripe followed in a rowboat. Well, this was the stream that came down and formed the lagoon right outside the Coco Palms Hotel dining area, and sure enough, this weird-looking thing floated down to where the tourists were eating their lunches. They got to see me and Reggie and a guy with a camera running along the bank and, floating in the lagoon, a body with a bread head and the face of Elisha Cook [*laughs*]! They couldn't figure out what the hell was going on!

Just the other day when I watched the picture, I looked to see if a shot of Bread Head was cut in. It wasn't, I guess it was never in the picture. So Howard couldn't get Reggie off the island fast enough [*laughs*]. That's one thing I'll always remember about that picture, the stupid Bread Head. Arden Cripe probably got that body fished out of the lagoon eventually and gave the skull back to whoever he got it from. Probably some cemetery [*laughs*]!

[*Did you get to have any fun at all on this trip to Hawaii, or was it just work work work?*] Work work work. At night, you go out and have dinner, but you've gotta be up at five and you get out there as soon as it gets light. Whatever fun you'd have was when things were ridicu-

Right to left, Paul Wurtzel, actress Mari Blanchard, Howard W. Koch and his wife Ruth on a Kauai beach near the Coco Palms Hotel during the *Voodoo Island–Jungle Heat* location trek. Koch later went on to become head of production at Paramount.

lous and you'd just have to laugh, it was so crazy. Like Reggie with the Bread Head. Because there are things you're not allowed to take through customs, when we were about to come back from Hawaii, a lot of the guys hid coconuts in the arc lights which were going back on the freighter [*laughs*]!

The last horror movie I did for Howard was William Castle's picture *Macabre* [1958], which was *not* a Bel-Air. Bill Castle was a boyhood friend of Howard's, they lived across the street from one another when they were kids in New York, and now Castle wanted to make this picture *Macabre* [Castle's first picture as an independent producer]. Castle came to Howard and he asked, "How do I go about putting a company together?" Howard said, "Rent *mine*. I've got all the guys, and I've got the stage here at American National that we can get. We'll do all the bookkeeping, we'll do *every*thing, so that you can just walk in like you're doing a picture for a studio. And we'll charge you the cost plus..."—I don't know, 10 or 20 percent or whatever Howard charged him. So it was Howard's company that did the show, but they had no control over the script, no control over anything that Bill Castle wanted to do. They didn't have any creative say about it, they just supplied the tools to make it.

Bill Castle promised me that if we came in on schedule and budget, he'd give me a big bonus. Well, we came in on schedule and *under* budget, but I never saw a bonus. But you hear that kind of thing a lot. On *Macabre*, he was very, very nervous, because this was his big chance. He probably died of a heart attack—he was very high-strung, nervous. [*Some of* Macabre's *stars were actors brought out from New York.*] Maybe they were old friends of his from New York. I worked on a picture called *Viva Zapata!* [1952] that Elia Kazan did, and he brought all these actors from the Actors Studio out. All these New York actors, and he had 'em all playing Mexicans [*laughs*]. It was unreal. They were nice guys but they were New York actors and they didn't know what a Mexican looked like or acted like!

One guy who was good in *Macabre* was Jim Backus as the sheriff. When I ran it the other day, there was no castlist at the beginning, and when the sheriff came on, I kept looking and looking, and I thought to myself, "Is that Jim Backus? I'll be damned!" I didn't remember him being in it. He was a nice guy and he was darn good in *Macabre*, he was *terrific*. It was very interesting to see him playing that.

Macabre was shot at American National and in a town called Chino, where I later worked again on a TV series called *Twelve O'Clock High*. We also shot at a private house the scene where the girl [Christine White] gets into the swimming pool into the living room and swims underwater through an opening in the exterior wall to the part of the pool that's outdoors. That home belonged to Lance Reventlow, Barbara Hutton's son, a very wealthy kid. That stupid swimming pool scene was all we *did* there at that house, as far as I remember, and it seemed to me a lot of money and time to *do* that. But I was kind of impressed looking around that house. Reventlow later got killed in a plane crash.

Bill Castle made a fortune out of *Macabre*, that was the picture that got him going [as a horror movie producer-director]. A lot of his pictures had a gimmick; with *Macabre*, it was the insurance policy [insuring audience members against death by fright]. Then he did another one, *The Tingler* [1959], where buzzers were put under the theater seats.

After Bel-Air, I was at MGM 'til 1960, then I went with Quinn Martin, QM Productions. I was with Quinn Martin 17 years. Then I wound up at Universal and at Disney and at Warner Brothers, and I retired in '88.

Making those cheap pictures at Bel-Air was a great experience. I'll tell you one last, quick, interesting story. Aubrey Schenck died first [in 1999] and was cremated, and then when Howard passed away two years later, *he* was cremated. And Howard's wish was to have his

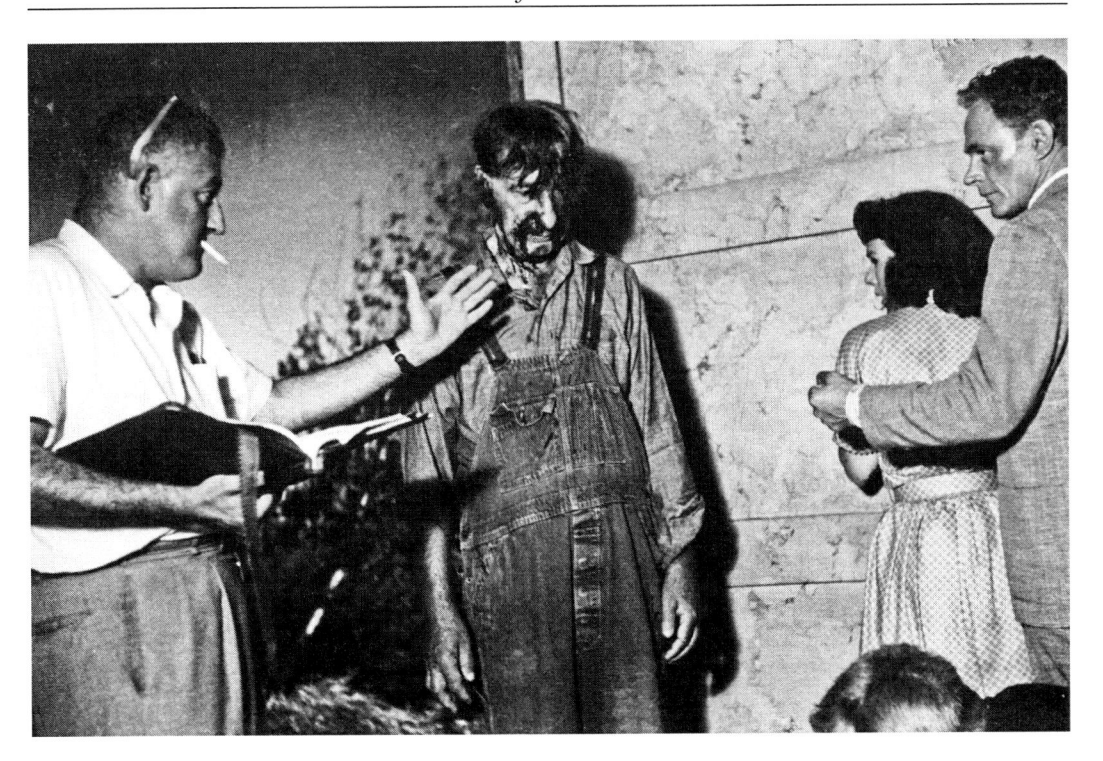

Wurtzel recalls *Macabre* **producer-director William Castle (left, with players Howard Hoffman, Jacqueline Scott and William Prince) as a "very high-strung, nervous" man who "probably died of a heart attack." (He did!)**

ashes scattered over Kanab, Utah. He loved Kanab and they loved him: By making these cheap pictures there at a time when Kanab was not doing too well financially, Howard gave a lot of employment to the local people. So they thought Howard was a great guy—which he *was*. Anyway, nobody could believe that Howard wanted to have his ashes scattered over Kanab, they thought he'd want to be buried out here, but no, he wanted his ashes scattered over a fort set [originally built for a major-studio Western] outside of Kanab that Bel-Air had used.

When Aubrey's widow Florie heard about this, she said, "I've got Aubrey's ashes. Why don't we send him up and scatter *both* of their ashes out at the same time over Kanab?" So their two sons went there, Howard's son Hawk and Aubrey's son, writer-producer George Schenck, and they approached Mickey Whiting, a fellow we used to work with when we were on location there. Mickey, who owned a lumber company and also had his own plane, said, "Oh, sure, I'll fly you up and we'll go over the fort and you can scatter the ashes"—and that's what they did.

Well, after the plane landed, along came a flock of geese from Canada, flying south for the winter. This huge flock of geese came over and they circled the fort where the ashes had just been scattered, and then they continued on their way. The natives up there said, "We've never seen anything like that. We see the geese all the time at this time of year, flying south—but never before have they ever stopped to circle the fort." I know the story because I talk to both of the women [Mrs. Koch and Mrs. Schenck] and the sons, and they told me about it. It's kind of an interesting story. It's almost like one of those miraculous things.

John G. Stephens

Like the Egyptian cliff tomb where its story takes place, Schenck-Koch's Pharaoh's Curse *(1957) has also been buried by the sands of time, with TV airings infrequent and a home video release non-existent. Set in the Valley of the Kings at the turn of the 20th century, the chiller finds members of an Anglo-American archaeological expedition and several British soldiers stalked through the torch-lit tomb corridors and secret chambers by a blood-drinking, corpse-like figure, the reincarnation of the ancient king whose burial place has been invaded. Despite the low budget, it's eerier and more effective than the better-known Schenck-Koch horrors (*The Black Sleep, Voodoo Island, Frankenstein 1970*); in fact, in its day, it may have been the most atmospheric movie of this type since Boris Karloff's 1932* The Mummy.

John G. Stephens, who cast Pharaoh's Curse *and other Schenck-Koch flicks, soon went on to bigger and better projects. He remembered many of the highlights (and "lowlights") of his long career with great humor in his 2004 autobiography* From My Three Sons *to* Major Dad: My Life as a TV Producer.

I never wanted to get into the movie business. I majored in poli-sci [political science] in college, and never intended to work in the movies. But when the opportunity came along, and the salary was good, I *did* get into it. My father William Stephens produced the *Dr. Christian* movies [between 1939 and 1941], plus a number of other B-movies, a lot of six-day wonders, ones you never heard of, like *Thunder in the Pines* [1948] and *Jungle Goddess* [1948]. He also ran a studio: It originally was Eagle-Lion, and when a couple fellows called Bernie Tabakin and Eliot Hyman bought it, my father and his partner Eddie Conne ran it. The name of the place was changed from Eagle-Lion to American National. Ziv was there, Hall Bartlett was there, Schenck-Koch were there, a whole bunch of shows were done out of there.

Schenck-Koch knew about me and asked me to work for them, and I did a number of their shows. We did two great films, one called *Shield for Murder* [1954] with Edmond O'Brien, a sensational movie, and then we did a tremendous movie called *Big House, U.S.A.* [1955] with Brod Crawford, Ralph Meeker, Charlie Bronson and Lon Chaney. I worked with a lot of gentlemen who were "alcoholically challenged" in those days but Lon Chaney was the only person that I ever had to load onto an airplane who was drunk at six in the morning [*laughs*]. I was absolutely stunned! It was at Burbank Airport, I was loading the charter plane to go on location, and he came in there at 6:00 drunk. No one else showed up drunk; even Brod wasn't drunk. But Chaney was drunk 24 hours a day! He was very pleasant, very nice, never got out of hand. He just ... [*laughs*] didn't know where he *was*! What happened to him, happened to a lot of other actors. When he was starting in, he was so great in *Of Mice and Men* [1939]—he was the best Lennie there ever was. Then, I think, being the son of [silent movie star] Lon Chaney hurt him a lot, he could never live up to his father. All of a sudden he got involved in all these horror movies, and he just sunk and sunk and sunk. And drank and drank and drank. But he was a nice, sweet man. There were so many alcoholics in *Big House*...! When we walked into the Canon City Prison in Colorado, believe me, the *prisoners* were scared [*laughs*]! It was a tough bunch with Brod Crawford, the nicest drunk in the world, Bill Talman who was a mean drunk, Ralph Meeker, who had just lost the starring part in the movie version of *Picnic* after doing it on Broadway and wasn't in a good mood, and all the rest.

When you worked for Schenck-Koch, you had to go on location, work as an extra, work as a stunt driver, what*ever*. There's no way you ever worked for Schenck-Koch that you didn't have something to do. In *Shield for Murder*, they wanted a bunch of extras to crowd around after there was a murder, and you had to say the usual line, "Hubba hubba hubba hubba"—you couldn't use dialogue. Then once you were established in the master shot, you had to stay around 'til sometimes three or four in the morning. For no extra money, of course! But it was fun. [*Needless to say, all of this isn't in the line of duty for the average casting guy.*]

John G. Stephens in 2006.

Oh, no, no. Just Schenck-Koch casting guys [*laughs*]!

The casting of the Schenck-Koch pictures took place at American National, in Aubrey Schenck's office. Seldom would the director sit in, because it was entirely up to Howard and Aubrey. Mark Dana [starring in *Pharaoh's Curse* as a British army officer] was the only person that I didn't cast in that picture; normally what [Schenck and Koch] would do was have one or two people that they had pre-cast. I cast the rest of that show from top to bottom. I loved Terence deMarney [playing one of Dana's troopers], who was a tremendous actor. George Neise [playing the caddish head of the expedition] was a guy I worked with a *lot*. The director Lee Sholem held him down, I must say, 'cause George had a tendency to go over the top quite a bit [*laughs*]. Ben Wright was a sensational actor and I worked with him a lot too.

Also in that movie was Ziva Rodann [as the enigmatic Simira, ostensibly a native girl but actually a cat goddess]. Originally her name was Ziva Shapiro, Aubrey and Howard changed it to Ziva Shapir, and *she* changed it later to Ziva Rodann. She was not the most pleasant person to work with, but she was very good in the picture, you really believed her in that part. She had served in the Israeli army; *all* the Jewish girls in Israel at that time had to serve in the Israeli army. She had a tough attitude, but probably all the girls who went through what she did [army life] had a tough attitude. She was always feeling that she was being put-upon, and she pretty much stayed to herself. We also had in that movie a guy who claimed he was a prince [Alvaro Guillot, who plays the boyish Egyptian guide who transforms into the monster]. An agent brought him in and said he was a prince in Egypt, and Aubrey and Howard looked at me as if I would know who he was. I said, "Uh-huh ... yeah...." I never believed any of those people, and I have my doubts whether he was a prince. Ziva, whom I did mention this to, said that he was no prince. All I know is that he went through a heck of a deal with that mummy makeup. Which was very, very good, incidentally. The poor guy was dying from the heat, but [*laughs*] the makeup was good!

For the role of Neise's wife in *Pharaoh's Curse*, we had a number of girls come in and read, and Diane Brewster by far gave the best reading. After she left the room, everybody said, "Boy, she was great!"—but then added, "But she weighs so much...!" I remember calling her and saying, "Look, I think you can get this part when you come in for the next reading, but you've *got* to lose weight." By the time she came in again, she must have lost 30, 35 pounds and she looked great. She got the part.

What Aubrey and Howard did was, if they *liked* people, they would want to sign them for two shows. So I signed Diane for two shows, *Pharaoh's Curse* and a Western. But then after seeing her in the dailies, they didn't care for her that much and so they said, "Get us out of it" [break the promise of a second picture]. I said, "What??" and, again, "Get us *out* of it." I had to call her up and make up a bunch of stories, I told her that doing the Western wasn't going to be good for her career and so on, and I talked her out of it! She wound up being the lead lady in [TV's] *Maverick* and she had a good career and she was a very, very nice person. She passed away, unfortunately, much too young.

That's the way it was with Schenck and Koch. If I may diverge for one second, when we made *Shield for Murder* they wanted Carolyn Jones, who was an up-and-coming actress at that time. She would get $500 a day for one day, the deal was all set, Schenck-Koch were very happy and Carolyn was very happy. Now, the night before she was going to come to work, Howard called me at home and said, "John, about Carolyn Jones...." "Yeah?" "She's working tomorrow." "Yeah." "Well, what I want you to do is make sure she throws in a day of free dubbing." I said, "What??" and he said, "John, John ... do it, do it." I called her up, I went through all this rigmarole, and she did it. But they operated that way. If we had extras on a set, the extras had to do everything, including dialogue, and if one ever complained, they'd never work for Schenck-Koch again!

According to Stephens, a hitch in the Israeli army gave *Pharaoh's Curse* star Ziva Rodann "a tough attitude."

You were given a cast budget for every part, and no one could go over that amount of money. After Paul Newman did *The Silver Chalice* [1954] and *that* bombed, we offered him $20,000 to play the lead in *Desert Sands* [1955]. But I think his agent wanted 35,000 or 40,000 so, no, he didn't get the part. *That's* the way [Schenck and Koch] were. They made money because a fellow they were kinda in partnership with, Eddie Zabel, had some connection with the United Artists theaters, so every movie Schenck-Koch made had guaranteed playdates. Their movies each had a budget, and every movie came in *on* that budget. They didn't come in one penny over, 'cause Howard was in charge of *every*thing. We had no production managers; Howard was the producer and production manager, and that was *it*.

[And Mr. Schenck?] [Long

pause] [*Longer pause*] Who? [*Laughs*] In the first draft of my book, I was kind of mean to him; when I was doing the second draft, I said to myself, "I don't really like to knock anybody," so I [toned it down]. Aubrey was a Hollywood producer, and he was very enthusiastic about everything. But Howard just ran the whole company. Aubrey had a say in everything except the production part, that was entirely Howard.

Every show we did opened the same way, with a person in charge telling the hero what he had to do, and who he had to take along, and so did *Pharaoh's Curse*. We shot it on location up in Death Valley, and it was pretty awful there, but we had no choice. *Pharaoh's Curse* was filmed in Death Valley 'cause it was the cheapest place to film. I learned more from Howard Koch than I did from any other man or woman that I ever worked *with* or *for* in my life. He knew *everything*. When he said we were going to Death Valley, we went to Death Valley, we didn't even question that. It was very difficult there but, hell, a lot of shows are difficult. I did the TV series *How the West Was Won* for three years and that was a tough show ... they're *all* tough. But it was fun working for Howard, it was really great.

Here's how Howard did his location work: He would never ever land at an airport and then have to bus the crew 30 miles, or whatever, to the place where we'd be shooting. He would pick out exactly where the locations would be, as close to where the plane could land as possible. We'd land, and within 30 minutes we'd be filming. No one had ever done that before. Instead of getting one and a half pages on the location the first day, we'd get about six or seven. He was just brilliant. We got the *Pharaoh's Curse* cast members into their costumes and makeup in the lobby of Burbank Airport, and then they got on the plane and sweated [*laughs*]. We took off from Burbank and we landed in Death Valley and we went right to work. On location with a Schenck-Koch picture, usually we'd stay in a dinky hotel. I never stayed in a nice place, ever, when I was on locations with Schenck-Koch, never! The place where we stayed on *Pharaoh's Curse* kinda looked like an old Kampgrounds of America campground. That was not the only time we stayed in shacks on a Schenck-Koch location. But that's what we expected. No one was shocked when we got there, they weren't expecting to stay at the Hilton.

All of the locations were Death Valley. We did the trek shots in the daytime, and the night stuff was mostly night-for-night, which was not done that often in those days. When we were on location, the cave and tomb sets were being built on the soundstages at American National. The production on that, for what it cost, was just unbelievable. Those sets were impressive, they actually looked like cave chambers and a tomb.

After we did the picture, Aubrey Schenck called me into the office on a Friday, about 11 o'clock, and said, "*Pharaoh's Curse*, boy, we're really happy with it, it's great. We're previewing it tonight, and you're gonna be there." I said, "Oh? Okay." Then he said the preview would be at the Fox Beverly Theater. I said, "What??"—I thought it was a joke! In Beverly Hills? All those high school kids? Aubrey said, "Here's what I want you to do: You know a lot of girls. I want you to bring four girls, and we'll pay their way into the theater. Remember *The Uninvited* [1944]? The way, when the door slammed shut, everybody [in the audience] screamed? In the spot in *Pharaoh's Curse* where we first show the mummy, I want all four girls to scream on cue. It'll get the whole audience in hysteria. It'll really 'make' this movie. You got that?" I said [*hesitantly*], "...Yeah."

I went and I called about 30 girls, and found this one girl I knew from college, Maxine Griffith, who agreed to come, and said she'd get three girlfriends to come with her. I met them outside the Fox Beverly Theater and showed them the script, explaining when they had to scream. Then I gave them the money for their tickets. They were all happy and went in and got seated and all that. I didn't sit with them.

Even though the mummy makeup on Alvaro Guillot (applied by George Bau, right, and unidentified makeup man, left) was effective, his first on-screen appearance was greeted with audience laughter at a Beverly Hills preview.

I forget what picture was showing that night at the theater, but they were also advertising a MAJOR STUDIO PREVIEW, and so the place was crowded and the people were expecting to see a movie with Clark Gable or Lana Turner or somebody like that. Our movie, the "major studio preview," comes on, it says on the screen BEL-AIR PRODUCTIONS ... and the audience starts to hoot. And they continue to hoot at everything as the movie played. You could barely hear the movie, they were laughing so much and making so much fun of everything. Then the laughter died down for a few minutes, and I thought to myself, "Thank goodness...."

Now came the part where the mummy was about to show himself. The audience was quiet, the mummy appeared and the girls *screamed*—and the audience started to laugh hysterically! By the time the movie was over, there couldn't have been more than 20 people left in that theater, and that includes the crew, the girls and myself. As I was leaving, Aubrey Schenck got a-hold of me and he chewed me out: "Why didn't you stop them? You saw how the audience was reacting, you shoulda stopped those girls, you shoulda stopped them! That's your *job*, you shoulda stopped them!" "Yes, you're right, Aubrey, you're right...." According to Aubrey, the girls "ruined" the whole movie! That was quite a moment. I have a lot of stories about Schenck-Koch, but that was one of my favorites. I always will remember what happened at the theater that night even more so than the movie [*laughs*]!

When I got the tape of *Pharaoh's Curse* in the mail from you, I thought, "Oh my gosh, I don't wanna see this again, I was embarrassed by that movie...." But I watched it and I actually liked it. For what it was, it was *good*. We had very good production in that; Howard Koch was absolutely a genius. And the acting was tremendous, I was really impressed by the acting. It was a good movie. I couldn't believe it!

17

Pamela Duncan on The Undead *(1957) and* Attack of the Crab Monsters *(1957)*

Pamela Duncan will always be remembered by cult-film aficionados for the two Roger Corman horror movies in which she starred. *The Undead* and *Attack of the Crab Monsters* are today regarded by many fans as two of his very best early efforts, and Duncan recalls working for the maverick filmmaker fondly. "He treated me as though I was something fragile," she remembers.

Duncan was conceived in Brooklyn, born at her maternal grandparents' New Jersey home and raised in Brooklyn. When still in school, she married a serviceman; while attending New York's Hunter College, she juggled school and work, making the theater and TV rounds. "I would bring my high heels and a little jacket and put them in a subway locker," she laughs. "When I would cut school, I'd go and put on the high heels and go on interviews for acting jobs. And I found that by going on these interviews, I was *getting* jobs. I was making my living out of the theatrical profession, *while* I was still finishing school. One thing led to another."

It was on a trip to the West Coast to greet her husband's ship that Duncan learned that he wanted the marriage dissolved "because he didn't like being married and wanted to stay in the service. I was in Hollywood working at that time and I didn't know what to do with myself. One day, I stopped to get my hair done at a place called Helen Hunt's Salon, and Helen happened to be there. She was Columbia Pictures' hairdresser-stylist, and she brought me in to meet the casting people at Columbia. I had gone west to meet my husband's ship and instead I met Helen Hunt and the casting director of a studio!" The meeting led to appearances in the screen tests of many Hollywood hopefuls. "One time, when Columbia was asking me to do a screen test with a man they had in mind, it was a rough scene. He grabbed me around the waist and *lifted* me. And he grabbed too tight, and I had fractured vertebrae tips. But they healed by themselves. Whenever they had a male potential contract player, I would always be asked to do the scenes with him. And I would do them, hoping that [the Columbia brass] would notice *me*, too. The notice didn't happen, but the paychecks did. And you could always have a [copy] of the film, although your face wasn't in it. It *might* be as you moved around each other, but it wasn't shot for my advantage."

Duncan landed her first co-starring film role opposite Whip Wilson in a low-budget Western called *Lawless Cowboys* (1951). As she was learning first-hand the rigors of B-moviemaking, she furthered her acting education (on both coasts) via the fast-paced creative frenzy that was early TV. "I enjoyed live TV very much—even though you had to wonder whether you were going to get through the show or not [*laughs*]!" She also learned a bit about the acting temperament in the bargain. "I remember Jack Palance was on a series called *Martin Kane*. He was the guest star, the heavy, the gangster. After we changed costumes between scenes, he was waiting in the wings for his cue to go in. The stage manager tapped him on the shoulder to go and Palance turned around to him and said [*through gritted teeth*], '*Don't cue me.* I'll go when it's time to go.' And he went out and he did his usual good job. But it was a startling thing, to have the stage director [told off] by an actor! Palance was 'in character' all the time! I also did four or five shows with Frank Wisbar. He was a good director, and he gave you a free hand to do what you wanted. He was well-liked and well-known. He picked five girls who would be 'stars of tomorrow,' and I was one of them. He was just a lovely person."

At age 31, Pamela Duncan received top billing for the first and only time playing a dual role in the reincarnation melodrama *The Undead*.

Duncan's list of New York credits also includes a slew of Army Signal Corps films. "Al Oaks was the agent who used to book the extras and the bit players for these Army films, which were done out in Astoria. The Army Signal Corps films would tell the sailors and soldiers not to forget their sanitary kits, and things like that [*laughs*]!" She also acted in a pair of pioneering science fiction television programs. "I was on *Captain Video*," she says, "and another 'space cadet' show called *Rocky Jones, Space Ranger*. On one episode, I don't recall if this was *Rocky Jones* or *Captain Video*, the script called for the bad guys to put me in a closet. Then they went on and finished the show, and nobody remembered to get me *out* of the closet!" Duncan has happy memories of the programs, despite the relatively primitive conditions. "*Captain Video* was shot in New York at Wanamaker's Department Store, in the piano section. We would rehearse in the ladies' room! There were chairs and mirrors in there. The studio was booked solid, so we would rehearse in the ladies' room." Actors *and* actresses? "Yes. The studio was right off the piano department section."

Though she had made numerous television and movie appearances, the actress was nevertheless amazed when Corman called her out of the blue concerning the lead in his upcoming *The Undead*. The whirlwind, six-day shoot went smoothly, and the film has since earned a reputation for its delivery of moody thrills on a modest budget. "I think that film was underrated," she says. "The title made you think there were zombies in it. Actually, it was the Bridey Murphy story."

Capitalizing on the public's interest in reincarnation (Duncan: "I don't think I believe in reincarnation!"), Corman needed a leading lady who could deliver credible performances as both a streetwise prostitute *and* a medieval maiden. "He called me and offered me the role," Duncan recalls. "I don't know what made him think of me, except that he must have seen me in something; I worked a lot and I was on TV a lot. Things like that just *happened* in my career. Somebody sees something and likes you, and then he hires you."

Informed that *The Undead* was the first movie Corman produced using money out of his own pocket, Duncan responds, "That makes me feel proud that he picked *me* out, without auditioning or anything. He just said, 'I want you for this film.'" Duncan was cast as Diana Love, the hooker who, regressed by a half-mad hypnotist (Val Dufour), relives her existence as the doomed Helene. The Devil (Richard Devon), a buxom witch (Allison Hayes) and a mischievous imp (Billy Barty) also populate the foggily atmospheric scenario. *Variety* called *The Undead* "one of the most mixed-up movies in a long time," but some Corman fans consider it one of his most satisfying efforts.

As shooting began under the title *The Trance of Diana Love* (which Duncan preferred to *The Undead*), the actress realized that her live TV experience had been excellent training. "Roger Corman's movies were six-day wonders. He shot the Crusades on a 60-foot soundstage, with horses and the knights with their maces and the rest of the weaponry! He was a good director—business-like. He directed according to what he felt. And since he was also the producer, that was what he shot."

Many of his actors remember Corman as a difficult director, unsympathetic to their needs. Duncan had a different experience. "He accepted what you brought him," she states. "The end of *The Undead* was very reminiscent of Hamlet's 'to be or not to be' soliloquy: Should I go to the guillotine and give [my future incarnations] their lives? I remember he was sitting with his head down, *listening* as I worked. And when I finished, he said [*quietly*], 'Cut and print.' He didn't want to redo anything." Told of actor Richard Devon's claim that Corman displayed a ferocious temper when things went awry, she seems taken aback. "I think Richard was [overstating it]—unless he had some discrepancy with Roger; in which case, that's *any* director's prerogative. Roger didn't directly guide you: He would go for the shot, and if it didn't please him, we'd do it again. But I don't remember his scolding anybody. In six days, I don't think there'd be time! In fact, we very rarely saw second takes! He was that precise about what he wanted." She was also impressed by what Corman could accomplish on such a minuscule budget. "It was a soundstage, with beehive smoker pots. It was the Crusades, shot in six days! We shot some of it at the Witch's Cottage in Beverly Hills. It's a cottage covered with vines and plants. It looks like it's in a forest. An old-type building. That was [actress] Dorothy Neumann's home in the film."

Duncan maintains that she barely had a chance to strike up an acquaintance with her costars. "Everybody kept pretty much to themselves. Richard Garland was a quiet person. He was going through a divorce at that time from Beverly Garland. He did his work well. Dorothy Neumann was a very nice lady. Allison Hayes played the 'cat woman'—the witch who turns herself into a cat. She was engaged to a director at that time. Later she did *Attack of the 50 Foot Woman* [1958]. And Billy Barty is unique. I don't think there are many actors that give him competition for the roles he plays!"

Corman always said that filming *The Undead* was great fun. Duncan is quick to agree—with certain reservations. She didn't like playing a scene inside a coffin, and "I had a rather skeptical moment or two which had to do with the ax man [in the climactic execution scene]. He kept lifting this ax up over his head, getting ready for the blow, and the blood was running down the handle. His hand could have slipped off. It was a real ax."

But Duncan had no qualms about working with Corman a second time, on *Attack of the Crab Monsters* ("I would have liked to have kept *on* doing films for him," she declares). *Crab Monsters,* which features Duncan as a scientist on a small Pacific island overrun with giant, super-intelligent crabs, required more of its cast than just acting ability. "Corman had me taken to a swimming pool to try on the underwater gear. I couldn't handle it, even

According to Duncan (left), the "six-day wonder" *The Undead* was shot on a small (60-foot) soundstage. Notice the sky backdrop.

in a swimming pool!" She also stopped short of swimming in a tank filled with live sharks. "They said, 'Don't worry about it. The sharks [won't attack you].' I said, 'You tell that to the sharks! I'm not about to go swimming with sharks!'"

In a scene of scuba-equipped Duncan popping up out of the ocean, the hefty gear proved more than she could handle. "It was men's equipment—too big for me—and they had forgotten to turn the air valve on. And I couldn't reach the valve. So I went shooting back up to the surface. Roger said, 'Go down! Go down! I need the shot!' And I had the courage to say, 'You just got it!' One of the boys who had a part as a Navy crewman was about my height and weight—and he had good legs! So he was 'padded out,' and he did all the doubling for me underwater." At another point, she balked at the idea of climbing a cliff face by rope. "They said, 'On action, you shimmy up the rope to the top of the cliff.' 'Roger,' I said, 'you're kidding. I can hold onto the rope with my feet on the ground, and that's about it!' So they brought in the trusty extra again, and shot *him*."

Though she rarely screens her own movies, Duncan retains good memories of her genre film appearances. "When I saw *The Undead* recently, I thought it was well done. In fact, I enjoyed seeing both of them, *Crab Monsters* and *The Undead*. I can see where *The Undead* would become a cult film."

Following the completion of these low-budget shock classics, Duncan worked sporadi-

Duncan and Richard Garland contend with the flailing claw of one of the attacking Crab Monsters. In the mid–1990s, a hip-breaking fall landed Duncan in Englewood, New Jersey's, Lillian Booth Actors' Fund of America Home; in 2000 she appeared in *Curtain Call*, an Oscar-nominated short subject about the Home, and in 2005 she died there.

cally, popping up in small roles in larger-budgeted films—*Career, Don't Give Up the Ship* (both 1959) and *Summer and Smoke* (1961) among them. "Now you're talking about production moneys in the millions," she says. "There's a big jump between *Crab Monsters* and a major movie! [In the bigger pictures] I was mingling with the top directors and the top producers, and a break could come out of that. *That's* your compensation for taking a smaller role. But they would always give you billing and they would always pay you your salary. I got a thousand a week when I worked.

"George Cukor called me to come and be the other [female] lead in a Gina Lollobrigida movie. I went out and he had me test with the wardrobe people, and they used me and paid me my full salary while I was on duty. He remarked to people while they were making me up, 'Look at her wonderful cheekbones' and all these comments that gave *me* a lot of courage. But unfortunately that movie [*Lady L*, 1965] was postponed, and Sophia Loren was substituted for Gina Lollobrigida. Then they went and cut my character out of the script. And a new director [Peter Ustinov] was chosen, too. But it was a tribute to me, because George Cukor was known for 'making' female stars. And a thousand a week was nice, too, in the days when that *meant* something!"

Duncan's West Hollywood home was badly damaged in a mudslide (with Duncan inside at the time), and the consequent legal action left her little time to pursue an acting career. In 1969, back in New York, she appeared in commercials and also returned to stage work, including *Open 24 Hours* (off-Broadway) and *A Teaspoon Every Four Hours* (97 previews, *one* Broadway performance!). In the latter, co-written by its star Jackie Mason, Duncan understudied two actresses, "the yenta [Marilyn Cooper], the gossipy woman across the hall who was trying to snare Jackie Mason, and his sexy maid, Lee Meredith. Lee was six feet tall and built like you wouldn't believe [*laughs*]! She did a *very* good job. I was covering both those women, if they hadn't been able to go on. And they were making changes [to the play] every day. It was *hard*!"

The one lucky break that might have secured lasting success for Duncan never came her way, and she slipped quietly from the show business scene. Though she lives peacefully with many happy memories of her filmmaking days, she doesn't appear to be yearning to get back in the game; she prefers the good old "studio system" days when actors were carefully prepared for stardom. "The reason there are so many [present-day] actors whose names are *not* familiar is because they're not grooming actors now. They're grinding out films—and they're using computers to do it! And ... I don't know ... they call things [in modern movies] funny, but it escapes me. There are certain male actors who make grotesque faces, and then they're *also* the leading romantic man in the movie at the same time! It doesn't *sit* well."

The impression Pamela Duncan gives is that she doesn't much care for modern films and the direction they've taken. "I wouldn't say I don't like them," she corrects. "I struggle to *understand* them!"

18

Marsha Hunt on Back from the Dead *(1957)*

In the mid–1950s, an intense public interest in reincarnation was sparked by the widely publicized story of Virginia Tighe, a Colorado housewife who claimed (after "hypnotic regression") to be a nineteenth-century Irishwoman named Bridey Murphy. One of the many movies made in an attempt to cash in on the craze was Regal Films' Back from the Dead, *a chiller set on the Carmel, California, coast, with Arthur Franz as the husband of a woman (Peggie Castle) who is now suddenly possessed by the malevolent spirit of Franz's deceased first wife. The film was actually based on a novel that predated the fad, Catherine Turney's* The Other One *(1952), a weird tale told in the first person by one of its characters, the possessed woman's sister Katy. Turney's novel was "resurrected" for the movies at the height of Bridey-mania, and the key role of Katy assigned to Marsha Hunt.*

Born in Chicago and raised in New York, Hunt was a fashion model before landing a Paramount contract in the mid–1930s. She was later under contract to MGM ("My happiest years!"), playing such a variety of roles that she came to be called "Hollywood's Youngest Character Actress." But in the late 1940s, Hunt was one of a number of stars who protested the House Un-American Activities Committee's probe of Communist activity in movieland—and promptly became "unemployable," a casualty of the Hollywood Blacklist era. One of her few movies in the half-century since: Back from the Dead.

When *Back from the Dead* came along, I was so grateful to be offered a chance to act again. I was in the midst of being blacklisted. Without ever having any interest in Communism, I was blacklisted nonetheless for speaking out *against* blacklists. As a protestor against what was happening at that time of Cold War paranoia, I just stopped getting offers of work. I was as thoroughly blacklisted as if I had *been* a Red. So, to get an offer of something [*Back from the Dead*] that was at least an interesting assignment was just fine. It was not deathless drama, it was not something I yearned to do as a vehicle, but—never mind! I was being allowed to *function* again.

[*The people who made* Back from the Dead—*were they not aware of your status, or were they defying the blacklisters?*] I have no way of knowing. Before I did the film, I didn't know the names of anyone connected with it, with the casting or the production or direction or writing of it. Perhaps they didn't know I was blacklisted. I was never a publicized figure in that plight, because I was never subpoenaed, never called before a committee in Washington or Sacramento. I just quietly stopped working. It may be they didn't even know that I had a "problem." Or, it may be that they *did* know, but it didn't matter to them because they were independent filmmakers and not part of that "major studio" conspiracy that had agreed to just blacklist anyone who was even controversial.

18. Marsha Hunt on Back from the Dead (1957)

Actress Marsha Hunt came back from "the Blacklisted Dead" for this horror flick which was no doubt inspired by the 1950s' "reincarnation fad" even though it's about possession by the dead.

The Bridey Murphy story—I didn't give that a whole lot of credence. But I don't really condemn anyone for liking to believe in the occult or in reincarnation or whatever. I think it brings comfort, and I think that's fine—unless in some way it hurts someone else. I don't form judgments about that. I found it an interesting phenomenon, the fact that [the topic of reincarnation] caught on with the public as much as it did. I think it was probably mostly a media thing, wasn't it? But it very likely did inspire them to make the movie.

About Arthur Franz, there was ... nothing memorable. I do seem to recall that he was not a particularly jolly fellow. I didn't get to know him. We worked comfortably together, but there was no exchange of the kind that might start a friendship. That is often the case when you work in a film, particularly in a film that was ... not leisurely. *Back from the Dead* had a tight schedule, and you were kept *at* the job of rehearsing the scene or shooting it. Quite often in those circumstances, your fellow actor ... well, he's sort of just like a fellow worker in an office. You get along, you do your work, and then you go to your separate lives at the end of the day. I think it's rare when a friendship begins in a production. It's not the same as the theater. In a play, you're much more intimately associated with fellow actors. You have a long rehearsal period, and the fate of the show determines whether you keep *eating* or not. If the critics don't like it, and you close right after you open, you're all out there looking for the *next* job. So you have a common fate in it, and there's a camaraderie and a chance to get to know and like each other, more than in filmmaking.

Don Haggerty was much more personable and light-hearted and pleasant to work with [than Franz]. That was a great pleasure. Peggie Castle ... I had not known her, or even her *name*, prior to that. But she was professional and very *good* in it, I thought. And certainly very pretty. Nice person. I didn't get to know her well, because we were all working pretty hard ... I didn't come away with any strong impression about her. I was startled to learn that she died not terribly long after [1973, at age 47]. It's a shock, of course, when someone that young leaves us.

There was one person in the cast who I may have met her for the first time on that, someone who later become a good friend. That was Evelyn Scott [playing Molly, a friend of the family]. And there was someone else I liked, Marianne Stewart [playing a cultist]. She had been married to that very distinguished Broadway actor Louis Calhern. We rode together to the location and had one of those nice, intense conversations between old

In *Back from the Dead*, Hunt seeks to free Peggie Castle (right) from the dominating influence of her (Castle's) husband's late *first* wife.

Broadway actors who meet in California and find how many friends in common they have from New York.

Back from the Dead was shot at an independent studio, one of the smaller ones, I think it was on Melrose Avenue in Hollywood. I remember a couple of encounters that had nothing to do with the film. I ran into George Montgomery, who was such a beautifully handsome and very dear man. He was a fine actor, but never had the starring career I think he might well have deserved. He was married then to Dinah Shore; my husband [screenwriter Robert Presnell] and I had them over to the house a few times, and we went to theirs. That was the first time I'd seen George in some years, and we had a great reunion there on the studio street. And I saw Sophia Loren in person for the first and only time, in the little commissary on the lot where people went for a little bite of lunch. I couldn't resist introducing myself to her, because she had *just* completed a film my husband had written, *Legend of the Lost* [1957] with John Wayne. I spoke to her about that and asked about her experiences shooting in the desert. She was very cordial, very nice, but I remember she looked just a little baffled when I mentioned Robert's name. Later, when the film came out and I saw it, I understood why she didn't respond to my husband's name: Ben Hecht, who was a very famous writer and newspaperman and a colorful person, had done some rewrites because John Wayne wanted it a little more "butch"—more one-syllable words, less educated-sounding than my Robert's script. So Sophia Loren was apparently more aware of Ben Hecht. Anyway, I remember *those* encounters more than the actual shooting of *Back from the Dead*!

It was Laguna Beach where we did all of the exteriors. That is down the coast from L.A., a goodly drive—I think it's an hour and a half to two hours. Laguna Beach is a particularly beautiful community. It's tasteful and colorful and utterly charming. Everything out of doors was shot in and around Laguna. I remember that location because where they put us up was a hotel, motel, whatever, right up a cliff above the beach. You just looked out your window at the whole Pacific Ocean. And wwwonderful flowers, which bloomed particularly well with the ocean spray watering them all the time. The flowers that you plant along a beach bloom like crazy! I loved this place and I remembered it so fondly that some years later, when my mother was very ill with cancer, and still *just* able to get around, I wanted to give her a treat, and so I took her to that same place. The festival was on, the annual, wonderful Art Festival at Laguna, which is quite famous. They do "living paintings"—live people replicate classic paintings—and we went to that. And Mother had some great meals—a friend

Hunt in a more recent pose. Today, in her nineties, she's still on the go, attending film festivals and reminiscing for fans about career highlights.

of mine was running a very good restaurant there. Mother had one treat after another, packed into several days, all working out of that same Laguna hotel. It was a joy. And I was grateful to the location for *Back from the Dead* that gave the idea of giving my mother "time out" from being ill. She remembered it fondly the rest of her days.

The director was Charles Marquis Warren. (The pronunciation of his middle name had been Americanized for some reason, it was **mar**-kwis rather than mar-**kee**.) I remember him more vividly than I remember anyone in the cast. Charles was a very charismatic, personable man, a delightful presence, good director, fun to talk with, a stimulating conversationalist. I remember he and his wife had my husband Robert and me to dinner a time or two. And that was all, I never did see him again. But after Robert died [1986], I was startled to have a phone call from Charles—I was surprised that he even still had my number. He talked for, I don't know, maybe 20 minutes about my Robert, about his respect and near-awe for my husband's writing talent and accomplishments, and how it was a thrill for *him* to be around my husband. I had no *idea* until Robert died that Charles had this extreme interest in Robert's work, and in him as a man. I was so touched that Charles called to give that lengthy tribute, as I was getting over the shock of losing a man who was *not* ill—Robert died without warning. I was terribly touched that Charles did that.

[Back from the Dead*'s shooting title was reportedly* The Other One—*does that ring a bell?*] Yes, I think that *was* on the script when it was sent to me. I do remember that title, and finding it intriguing. [*Were you disappointed at the change to the more lurid title?*] Oh, well—that's movies for you! I know I saw *Back from the Dead* when it was finished; I don't know where, I suppose in a theater. It was not a horror film, it didn't send chills up the spine, there was nothing grotesque in it. The horror movies of today, of course, are drastically different from the ones made back then. Today it's a festival of special effects and what I call "shock and schlock." It has *very* little to do with the kind of drama that I grew up watching, the kind of drama that we were making when I was active in the field. Our stories were about people's relations with each other, and they were biographies of people of great achievement, and they were adventure dramas, and the heroes were heroic—they weren't flawed, they weren't "warts and all" as they are today. It was an entirely different approach to storytelling and as to what stories to *tell*. I'm in a state of dismay about today's films, I really am. There *are* exceptions, of course, but in general, I think they're trashy, I think they're overly revved-up. I don't like the jump cuts that give you a different image every second. You don't have time to see one image before it's replaced by another. And finally you wind up not caring. It takes continuity, it takes a flow of continuum to get involved with a character and care about him or her. But that's not the approach to films today.

Back from the Dead ... it's certainly not a fine film, I don't think that I could even say it's a *good* film. But it's such an interesting premise—an ex-wife, deceased, inhabiting the second wife's body—that you stay tuned. It's something that is intriguing and holds the interest and it's professionally done. It just doesn't have a quality to make it memorable. And *I* certainly was not memorable in it; my role was *mostly* hand-wringing. But my character was a *little* spunky. She certainly does more than the poor husband's role. He is barely *there*! And *he's* the one that both those wives chose to marry! But it's my character, the sister, who does all the detecting and standing up to evil.

No, *Back from the Dead* is not going to make history as a film. But it's not a disgrace either. Somewhere between the two, I think. And it was a break in the [period of blacklisting] I had in my career, and I was just happy to be back at work.

19

Herbert L. Strock on Blood of Dracula *(1957)*

In 1957–1958, Herbert L. Strock directed three of producer Herman Cohen's notorious "teenage monster" movies: I Was a Teenage Frankenstein, How to Make a Monster *and, on the distaff side,* Blood of Dracula, *with Sandra Harrison as a troubled teen, terrifyingly transformed into a female bloodsucker and now on the prowl in the halls and on the grounds of a private girls' school. In 2005, Strock re-watched the movie for the first time in many years, and shared his honest reactions:*

It is difficult to remember details of a movie shot so long ago, but I'll try. As I ran the tape you sent me, I couldn't even remember directing the shots as I watched them.

I didn't think that the box office potential was very good with this script, which I felt talked itself to death, and I hated the vampire makeup transitions which were used over and over again. We had no money to really develop a technically perfect transition and therefore used the cheap dissolve method, holding Sandra Harrison as still as we could while the makeup man added makeup to her. Monroe Askins—"Monk"—was a wonderful guy and a great cameraman. We did many Ziv TV shows together, and I found him easy to work with and always ready to come up with suggestions. "Monk" was quiet and fast. When I first met him, he was a camera operator.

Everyone in *Blood of Dracula* was a pro—many I had used before in TV shows or features. But as I recall, the set was always tense with actors striving to outdo one another, especially with the girls.

Blood of Dracula producer Herman Cohen and star Sandra Harrison, all smiles in a behind-the-scenes shot.

189

I thought the performances of Thomas B. Henry, Malcolm Atterbury, Carlyle Mitchell and Paul Maxwell were pretty good and they held up for me. Gail Ganley was, to me, the weak link. I knew little about Jerry Blaine; Herman Cohen cast him. He wasn't much of an actor, but Herman got his way. I always thought Herman liked boys and thus enjoyed casting males in films, but this might just have been an impression he gave when he asked males to strip down to their skivvies.

Herman didn't like Sandra Harrison as she had a mouth and spoke up for her rights as the lead in the show and wanted to be treated as such. I got along with her fine, and I thought she was the best actress who read for the part. I think Herman always resented her as *he* didn't find her, and I *did*. He always wanted the last word in everything on a film, and when he didn't get it, he pouted. She was extremely easy to work with, and I think did a fairly good job. I wondered why she never got any other parts. She called me [circa 1999] when she came to L.A. from New York, and we had lunch and talked. I couldn't believe it ... she'd become dumpy. Fat. She and her sister were doing a singing act in nightclubs. I have not heard from her since. She was an oddball to start with and that's why I thought she'd be good for the picture.

The plot—well, phooey. I really didn't like the script and didn't really enjoy making this film that much.

I was shocked and amazed that Herman came to me after *Teenage Frankenstein* and asked me to direct the other two films [*Blood of Dracula* and *How to Make a Monster*] as we had a terrible argument one night while shooting on location, and I almost quit. I never really had any trouble with Herman except for that outburst, and I would have been glad to work with him again with a few minor adjustments: I wanted more say in script revisions. He was stubborn in this area, and only with the help of the script supervisor Mary Whitlock Gibson could he be persuaded to plug up story holes I came across. I also feel that a director should be able to choose his camera personnel, which was difficult with him. I did not want Maury Gertsman on *How to Make a Monster*, and I had trouble getting set-ups I wanted. On *Blood of Dracula*, Herman gave in on "Monk" Askins as he had seen "Monk" and me working together well on many TV shows. Herman never really interfered with shooting and rarely came on the set. He did trust me and let me go my own way.

In November 2005, just weeks after doing this interview, Strock and his wife Geraldine were on a highway (with Herb behind the wheel) when a bale of hay fell off the back of a truck ahead of them; swerving to avoid it, the Strocks' car hit the center divider and flipped. Passersby pulled them from the totaled car, covered them with blankets and prayed over them as emergency vehicles raced to the scene. Their injuries were minor but four days later, the hospitalized Strock died of a heart attack at age 87.

I don't think *Blood of Dracula* holds up at all. It was a boring exercise in talk with nothing much to make it last over the years. *Teenage Frankenstein* and *How to Make a Monster* are more interesting films. I think *Teenage Frankenstein* is the best of the three.

20

Peggy Webber on The Screaming Skull *(1958)*

A large, unfurnished house on an isolated country estate; screeching peacocks; a half-mad gardener; and, at the center of the story, the unusual romantic triangle of a husband, his timid new bride and the living skull of the man's first *wife.*

Between this far-out plot and a bare-bones budget, The Screaming Skull *would seem doomed to failure, but director-co-star Alex Nicol didn't let these hurdles deter him from the serious business of raising goose bumps. Against all odds, the chiller delivers the icy goods, enhanced by Floyd Crosby's ominous black-and-white photography and an eerie score by future Oscar winner Ernest Gold (*Exodus, Inherit the Wind, It's a Mad Mad Mad Mad World*). The cast was also a capable bunch, headed by John Hudson as the husband and radio-television veteran Peggy Webber as his victimized young wife.*

The daughter of a wildcat oil driller, Webber commenced her career at age two and a half, performing during intermissions in silent movie theaters. She started working in radio at age 11; by 18, she was writing, producing and directing early television shows; at 21, she won the award that was later known as the Emmy for her drama anthology series Treasures of Literature. *Among her many thousands of radio credits, workhorse Webber appeared in over 100* Dragnet *programs and there became acquainted with "New York actor" Richard Boone, brought in by* Dragnet *star Jack Webb to play several small roles on the airwave series. With help from Webber, Boone subsequently began an "acting workshop" which brought her together with stage and film leading man Alex Nicol, director of* The Screaming Skull.

Richard Boone came out here from New York, brought out to do the movie *Halls of Montezuma* [1950]. At that time, I was a regular on the *Dragnet* radio show, playing Ma Friday and a lot of other characters on a regular basis. All of a sudden, Jack Webb brought in Richard Boone; they were both working on *Halls of Montezuma* and I guess Boone thought it would be a lark to come in and play these small parts on a radio show with Jack. I remember Richard Boone wandering around in the studio like he was a lost soul—he'd never done radio, and so he latched onto me and said he wanted to find out from me different things that he had to do. He came back for maybe six or eight shows, and at one point he asked me if I would help him set up a workshop. There was no Actors Studio on the West Coast at that time, and he wanted to get actors who worked with some kind of "method" to do a workshop.

We were together for seven or eight years with the workshop. During that time, Alex Nicol became a part of our workshop and he liked my work. I would do scenes with Richard Boone, *Man With the Golden Arm* and things like that, and Alex was very complimentary. So when Alex [began work on *The Screaming Skull*], he told me that he had a remake of *Rebecca*

Silent skull meets screaming star: Peggy Webber with the title "character" in *The Screaming Skull*.

[1940] that he wanted to do [*laughs*]! I was interested—I thought, "Gee, if it's a remake of *Rebecca*, that'll be wonderful." Alex wasn't *lying* when he told me that; what he was trying to say was that the storyline was similar. And I remember him saying that *he* was playing "the Judith Anderson part"! In *Rebecca*, the housekeeper [Anderson] was jealous of the new bride [Joan Fontaine] and was still attached to the dead woman who had been the first mistress of the place; Alex was going to play the gardener who was still devoted to John Hudson's first wife. Alex grew a beard to play that part.

Alex came to my house in Rustic Canyon, a suburb of L.A., and brought me the script. The screenwriter was somebody I knew, John Kneubuhl; I had done a couple of live television shows that he had written for CBS. Alex told me that he had cinematographer Floyd Crosby, who had won an Oscar [for *Tabu*, 1931] and a Golden Globe [for *High Noon*, 1952], and he went on and on. He said, "We're going to rehearse for a week and *then* we'll shoot it. We feel we'll cut a lot of our shooting time by having this rehearsal for a week." So we all had to know our parts and be "up" to do the rehearsal. But they still hadn't told us the title. I think *that* would have turned me off! At that point, they didn't yet *have* a title for it.

The Huntington Hartford Estates was where we rehearsed and that's where we filmed. Huntington Hartford was a multi-millionaire who'd married some actress [Marjorie Steele], and I guess she didn't like living in Hollywood, so they weren't using this estate; in fact, the house was unfurnished. It was in Hollywood, right off of Hollywood Boulevard. There were other houses around, but not right up close. It was a huge city block that this estate took up, and it was on a kind of a hillside, slightly sloping uphill. From where we were, the neighbor-

The promise of free burial for any audience member who died of fright was one of the movie's come-ons. In this publicity shot, John Hudson and Webber are confronted by the vengeance-seeking ghost of Hudson's first wife.

ing houses couldn't be seen—except those that were up on hills above us. It could have been maybe three or four acres of land that this estate was on. It was a beautiful place. Alex utilized every bit of that estate.

[Production] went rather smoothly, except that I found out that I was three months pregnant with my son. The script called for my character to fall down stairs and other things, so I went up to Alex and explained the situation and said, "Alex, I don't think I better do some of this...." He was a dear friend...

Each day I had to drive in from the Palisades, so I had to get up really early to get there. A little trailer would pull up to the Huntington Hartford Estates in the morning, the trailer where they'd cook our breakfasts. Well, when a woman is in her first trimester, she usually has a lot of morning sickness. They would give us our breakfast about seven o'clock, and it would be greasy fried eggs with greasy bacon—on greasy buns! I was so nauseous through most of the picture, it was just terrible! Normally I probably wouldn't have cared, it wouldn't have bothered me, but I was in this first trimester, and it was giving me trouble.

We tried our best. I felt there were weaknesses all the way around. It was a first directorial job for Alex, and his playing the part of the gardener and also trying to direct ... *may* have been a little bit of a weakness there. I felt that they let things go, things that they should have corrected in filming. Not to take away from Floyd Crosby, but there's one scene where Hudson and I embrace and my hair went under Hudson's nose and made like a mustache. He looked like he was doing a Charlie Chaplin! I noticed this the first time I saw the movie and I thought, "This looks so stupid. Why wouldn't they have stopped and re-shot that when they saw that he was doing a love scene with this black hair under his nose?!" But nobody had said anything. I don't think we had a regular script girl on this film, so nobody was watching these things! There was a crew of maybe eight or ten—not a lot.

Alex, I thought, did a credible job of acting. He had worked in a number of Broadway productions, and then in films. He was an "elitist," you know, and really was quite dedicated to Method acting. And I must say that *I* utilized a lot of that Method in acting—which I didn't feel really *helped* me [*laughs*]. I think that my *own* method was probably better! But because I had worked with Alex in Richard Boone's workshop, which was primarily Method, I felt that I had to be "true" to what Alex expected from me. So I didn't break down and do probably what I *would* have done had that not been the case. [My performance] was understated. I received a copy of the film several years ago and I looked at it on TV—and I couldn't understand a word I said [*laughs*]. I couldn't understand *any* of the dialogue!

John Hudson was fine. And I thought that Tony Johnson, who played the minister's wife, was very good. She was an actress in New York and the wife of [actor-director] Lamont Johnson. I thought everybody tried their best. I wish somebody had been there to look after my hair [*laughs*], which was a terrible mess throughout the whole thing! Also, I was *not* supposed to be seen through the flimsy negligee. They back-lit that scene [so that the negligee became

Webber first saw the movie in "a terribly tacky theater" and, by the time it was over, "wanted to throw up"!

see-through] and they didn't tell me what they were doing. I was so dumb and naïve, I didn't know that I was getting this kind of treatment until I saw the preview. Then I was rather shocked [*laughs*]!

We were paid a minimal salary, like a thousand a week, and I think we were involved for two weeks. My agent frowned upon this because I was pretty busy at that time, doing a lot of television. We were also given a percentage deal, we were *supposed* to get so-much percentage of what the ultimate box office was. My agent wasn't crazy about my doing this on a percentage basis, and he was *right*! But there was no other way that Alex could have *done* it at that particular time, and he *needed* the credit because he wanted to become a director. We were all put on a percentage basis—and many lawsuits followed! I didn't keep involved in the lawsuits, they went on and on. I was told that, "one of these days," I was going to get something out of my percentage, but as it turned out, I never got anything out of the film except my salary. Alex was not responsible, it had something to do with the distributor.

Peggy Webber in a recent shot.

I first saw the film in Hollywood, in what I think was a theater where they only ran X-rated films. I had never been to this theater before—it was on Western near Sunset Boulevard. A terribly tacky theater [*laughs*]! I went with my physician-surgeon husband, and I think both of us wanted to throw up when we came out! It didn't impress me. But of course I hate to see myself on film, so that could have been my own personal reaction. I felt that it should have been a lot better—that was my main feeling about it. But I *liked* Alex, and I really felt that he was an artist, and I felt that he as an actor (when I did other work with him) was really excellent, and had a very dedicated attitude about his work. Alex had really good taste; I think we were all just kind of goin' up a slippery slope there [with *The Screaming Skull*]! Alex was a very talented fellow and he had a really good intent. John Kneubuhl basically was a very good writer, he really was, and of course the cameraman [Crosby] should have been excellent, his having received an Academy Award and all.

So the *basics* were there, and it should have turned out, in *my* estimation, to be a better picture. *But*—it was made on a shoestring, so I suppose that was part of it. *Mystery Science Theater* has since gotten a-hold of it, and I've had all kinds of people call me and tell me that they had a ball making fun of this picture.

It's amazing to me, but there *are* people who say that *The Screaming Skull* is a favorite of theirs.

21

Lisa Davis on Queen of Outer Space *(1958)*

*Say all the bad things you want about the 1950s' low-rent "planet of women" movies—*Cat Women of the Moon, Abbott and Costello Go to Mars, Missile to the Moon, *more—and chances are, they'll all be true. But beyond criticism are the producers' casting choices: Whether on Mars, Venus, our Moon or one of Jupiter's, the panorama of pulchritude, sometimes dominated by national and international beauty contest entrants, brought new meaning to the expression "heavenly bodies."*

A 21-year-old English rose, Lisa Davis was no stranger to the silver screen or the LA social scene when she landed a top role in the Technicolor Queen of Outer Space. *As the beautiful Motiya, a Venusian girl anxious to help free her people from tyranny, she was victimized on-camera by her planet's masked, despotic ruler (Laurie Mitchell), and off-camera by the movie's star, the high-camp, high-maintenance celebutant Zsa Zsa Gabor. Davis recently reminisced about all the bad, good and great things that resulted from her notorious voyage to Venus...*

In 2005, *Queen of Outer Space* was honored at the very famous Castro Theatre in San Francisco, and I went up there for that event. I'm just blown away by that movie's continuing popularity, because when we made it, it was so minor. I mean, it was definitely nothing that I was *proud* of at the time [*laughs*]. That was a time when Hollywood *wasn't* making really wonderful movies; those were the days of Roger Corman and quick movies, and it was rare that you did something that was of quality. For instance, working for Disney on *One Hundred and One Dalmatians* [the 1961 animated feature, with Davis in the voice cast] was definitely quality. But *Queen of Outer Space* was shot very quickly at Allied Artists Studio over near Vermont Avenue in the Los Angeles area, and there was hardly any preparation for it; it was really just a starring vehicle for Zsa Zsa. In fact, I do believe that the budget was higher for her wardrobe than it was for the rest of the movie [*laughs*]! Everything Zsa Zsa wore in it was brand new, custom-made for her, and ours were all retreads, used stuff from Western Costume that was made for another science fiction movie, *Forbidden Planet* [1956]. My clothes were Anne Francis' clothes, and the outfits the astronauts wore were also from that. The *Queen of Outer Space* set was, like, made of cardboard [*laughs*]—I mean, it was *nothing* that you would tell anybody that you were doing with any great pride! It's only in latter years that it's become such a bad movie that it's a *good* movie. When I showed up at the Castro, there was a line of people around the block! The Castro screens vintage movies and they like to bring in somebody who worked in each movie and interview them on stage. *Queen of Outer Space* was shown all day and the "major" screening was at seven o'clock that night, with my interview before that. I was amazed at the turnout, and they were crazy about this picture!

[*Was* Queen of Outer Space *your first encounter with Gabor?*] No. In those days, there was

21. Lisa Davis on Queen of Outer Space (1958)

Promotional *Queen of Outer Space* photograph of Lisa Davis as Motiya (provocatively garbed in Anne Francis' gold micro-skirt from *Forbidden Planet*). Her real name is Cherry Davis; her father gave her that name because he thought her eyes "were as big as two huge cherries."

a very popular disc jockey named Peter Potter, who was married to my sister, [singer] Beryl Davis. Peter had a [television] show called *Peter Potter's Platter Parade*, where he played records back in that glorious day of Sinatra, Tony Bennett, Peggy Lee, Kay Starr, Patti Page, Teresa Brewer, Frankie Laine—the *best* music, there's never been music better than that. He also developed a show called *Juke Box Jury* which was both on radio and TV. Sitting with Peter would be four panel members, two men and two women. He would play a record and they would all make a comment on whether they thought the record would be a hit or a miss. If it was a "hit," Peter would hit a gavel and it would make a really nice, pretty sound, and if it was a "miss," it would make like the sound of a dud. The four panelists were always very well-known within the business; on a panel, for instance, you might have Dean Martin, Jerry Lewis, Donald O'Connor ... popular stars of the day. They would talk about the merits or demerits of the record, and sometimes, which was quite funny, the person who actually recorded it was hidden behind a screen and the panelists did not know that the person was within about 15 feet of where they were sitting. Somebody like Mickey Rooney, who was often on the panel and very funny, would say, "This is the worst piece of junk I've ever heard in my life! This is a *dud*, this is never gonna go anywhere!" and they'd cut to the person sitting behind the screen, making a face [*laughs*]!

Juke Box Jury was a hugely popular show and we had an orange juice sponsor, and part of the deal was that everybody would drink orange juice during the show, Peter Potter and all the panelists, and they'd say, "I'm really enjoying my Cal-fame Orange Juice." I was Miss Juke Box Jury and I'd wear a cute little, short, stupid outfit and I would pick up their ballots at the end of each record and give them to Peter, and I would serve them orange juice. And occasionally as a song which had a storyline was played, the show's team of dancers would "act out" the record, do things that matched the lyrics. I participated in that too, many times.

Zsa Zsa, being who she was at the time, was one of the "outrageous-type" guests that they would have on *Juke Box Jury*: "Dahlingk, that vuz the vurst thing I've ever heard in my life, that vuz *horrible*, sveetheart!" And when she guested on *Juke Box Jury*, she was a handful. Zsa Zsa would always want her own, very specific dressing room, and other things, in order to do the show; she'd decide she wanted to shave under her arms [*laughs*] and somebody would have to run out and get her a razor; she would want tea, and when she was served the tea, she might not like the *cup* it was in. She'd want a particular fine china, for instance Wedgwood or Spode or something that was really a good piece of china, because she wouldn't drink from just any cup, it had to be in the *right* cup. I saw that happen on *Juke Box Jury*. So whatever problems she *could* create, she *would* create. [Celebrities] didn't *do* that at that time, this was just television. But she looked beautiful and she'd always dress and always have the furs and the jewelry and ... you know ... she'd "do" Zsa Zsa, which was schtick. I suppose she was the Paris Hilton of her day.* She lived for publicity, and she'd always sweep in with a boyfriend and a retinue of people.

Also, in addition to seeing her on *Juke Box Jury*, I was one of the "glamorous young women" out about town, and Zsa Zsa was too—much older, of course, I was a youngster. So *Queen of Outer Space* was definitely not my first encounter with her, we were "aware" of each other and we'd seen each other around a *lot*. Zsa Zsa dated anybody who was wealthy, and *I* dated a lot of the same people that Zsa Zsa dated, so *that* caused a lot of problems too. She was always very worried that I would become involved with [international playboy Porfirio] Rubirosa, whom she was crazy about. So, yes, I knew her from other times, working with her and socializing with her.

She was just a *bitch* on *Queen of Outer Space*. She was a horror. She did *not* like women at all, and here she was in this picture with all these women! She just didn't like women, and especially blonde women, and I was a blonde, and she made my life hell on that picture. Oh, yes! In fact, I never change my costume in the movie, because she wouldn't let me. *You* know what our characters go through in that movie, running through the Venusian jungle and the explosions and the fight with the giant spider and all that stuff, and everybody's sort of in a mess. We wore the same costumes through all this action. Well, once the vicked kveen has

---

Gabor was once married to Paris Hilton's great-grandfather, famed hotelier Conrad Hilton of the Hilton Hotels.

Davis (left) with other denizens of "Venus—the Female Planet!": Barbara Darrow, Zsa Zsa Gabor, Mary Ford and Coleen Drake. Notice the *Forbidden Planet* ray guns.

been overcome and the movie is coming to its end, there's a sequence where we're celebrating that victory, and we find out that the Earthmen will be staying with us on Venus until their spaceship is repaired, and everything is glorious. Well, you'll notice in that scene that everybody [the actresses playing the other insurgents] has changed into something more glamorous, changed into "jubilant costumes," except for *me*; *I'm* in the same outfit I wore throughout the entire movie! I'll tell you what happened: I came onto the set in my "jubilant costume," a beautiful silver lamé pantsuit which was *also* from *Forbidden Planet*, and we were all waiting for Zsa Zsa to make *her* appearance in her most glamorous costume, which they'd saved for the last sequence. Well, she took one look at me in that pantsuit and turned around and shut herself up in her dressing room and wouldn't come *out*. One of the assistant directors, I think it was Harry Sherman, came to me and said, "I'm terribly sorry, Lisa, but Zsa Zsa says she will not finish the picture with you in that outfit. You *look* too good, and she won't stand near you if you're wearing that. You're gonna have to go back to your original costume." I thought, for the sake of the picture, it was not very professional, it didn't really make much sense plot-wise [for Motiya to continue to wear the same outfit], but then again *Zsa Zsa* was not very professional. She was grossly *un*professional! But I said, "Oh, to heck with it, that's fine," and I changed back into the original costume. Many, many years later, the director Ed Bernds phoned me to apologize, he said, "Oh, can you ever forgive me for doing that to you?" and I said, "Of course, of course...!" Oh, sweet Ed Bernds!

I'd gotten [hired for *Queen*] through my agents Irving Kumin and Julian Olenick of the Kumin-Olenick Agency. The casting call went out for "lots of attractive women" for *Queen of Outer Space*, I think they were seeing all the attractive young women about town, and I was one of them. It was a standard audition over at Allied Artists where I met the producer Ben Schwalb and Ed Bernds and read for it. Incidentally, I was always good doing my own hair and makeup, and for *Queen* I swept it back up in that very long ponytail. When, many many *many* many years later Madonna did her world concert tour Blond Ambition, that was exactly the hair style that she used, she wore a very long blond ponytail. And when she was asked in an interview where she got the idea for that hair style, she said, "From a '50s science fiction movie." She didn't say which movie it was, but I *know* it was my hair style from *Queen*.

Zsa Zsa got on well with Barbara Darrow [the insurgent Kaeel] because Barbara was a brunette, and Zsa Zsa didn't mind if Barbara stood next to her, while I was always delegated out of the shot. Barbara was beautiful, one of a very famous family of beautiful girls. Marilyn Buferd [an insurgent guard killed by the queen] was a former Miss USA, a beautiful blonde. Marya Stevens [another guard] was lovely. She was a bit of a serious actress caught up in this mess. Tania Velia was, like Zsa Zsa, Hungarian or something. She's masked in the movie, playing one of the councilors, but she was very beautiful. Marjorie Durant [an angry guard] was an heiress, she was related in some way to the Post cereal family. She was very, very wealthy and doing the whole thing as a lark.

Eric Fleming, who had the lead, was a sweet man. At that time I had become very religious, and on the set I used to read the Bible. (I was so embarrassed that I was doing that, that I had the Bible cover covered with aluminum foil so nobody could see what it was.) We filmed that movie at Allied Artists, and a church that I used to go to, the Monastery of the Angels, was near that studio. It was a convent, it had a chapel where you could sit and meditate, and then another part of the chapel had cloistered nuns who were singing all of the time. It was a very peaceful and beautiful place to go, and I remember taking Eric Fleming there, a *lot*. He loved going with me.

Dave Willock [another Earth astronaut] was very nice, very funny. Laurie Mitchell, who played the queen, was also sweet, and she suffered dreadfully in that "radiation burn" makeup. It was very hard on her, terribly uncomfortable, and terribly ugly. And once they put it on her, she had it on all day. When she'd walk around with the makeup between takes, she'd wear a beige piece of fabric, like a heavy veil, totally over her head, down to her shoulders, so nobody would see her, because it was frightening.

[*Another one of the heroes was played by Patrick Waltz, whom you met on that movie and later married. How many days before you realized how much you liked him?*] It was immediate. When you watch our love scenes in the movie ... they're real. We were definitely not acting, that was the real thing. Now, Paul Birch, who played the professor, was a little difficult, a little bit disgruntled, because all the other actors playing Earth astronauts got to kiss the girls. Eric had Zsa Zsa as a girlfriend in the movie, Dave Willock had Barbara Darrow, Pat had me, and Paul didn't have anybody. So he was pinching every girl's bottom, every opportunity he had! He wanted to get in on the action. Everybody else got to smooch with a girl and Paul didn't, so he was making up for it on the sidelines. There's one scene where several of us run and hide in a cabinet in Zsa Zsa's laboratory, we were all jammed together in there and I was standing very close to him, and we almost came to blows. [*Because he was touching you?*] Yes. He was very lascivious.

Of course, that was a very common thing during that time. When I think back to the sexual intimidation that would occur on sets in those days ... [*sighs*]. That's another story alto-

Davis and co-star Patrick Waltz met and fell for each other on the *Queen* set and later married. The movie's campy end credits dubbed them "The Lovers."

gether. In the early '50s when I was 14½, I was under contract at MGM, and I was later under contract to Columbia and Fox, and you'd find yourself running away from all of these very famous men [studio bigwigs] who had their girlfriends in the studio system. There were a lot of girls somewhat in that position on *Queen of Outer Space*, girls who were there I think because they were willing and able to "give a little" in order to "get a little." [*And even actors down on the level of Paul Birch thought they were entitled to a free grope?*] Yes. As I say, I'd come to Hollywood at age 14 in the midst of the era of the casting couch, which was definitely a reality. By the time I was 21 and doing *Queen of Outer Space*, I was at the stage where I was really, totally fed up with it all, and not at all interested in romance, or *sex*, so to speak, because every time I turned around, somebody was pinching my butt, or tweaking my breast, or doing *something*. I was always "escaping" and running from people who wanted to offer me a role if I would "cooperate." I managed to come through that unscathed—I don't know how I did it but I managed it, it was very, very important to me. It was only because Patrick Waltz was such a nice person, that I was even interested in him, because I'd sort of "had it" with all of the sexual innuendo that was part of every attractive young woman's life in show business. So Paul Birch carrying on and doing *his* number was something I was *definitely* not interested in. And Paul was very upset with me, and quite insulting.

On *Queen of Outer Space*, Ben Schwalb the producer was *so* nervous! He used to come on set and he would be in such a state—he'd be perspiring and wringing his hands, because of Zsa Zsa's shenanigans. She was so difficult and so temperamental, and he was trying to keep her happy. He was a nervous guy trying to get the picture done in a certain amount of time. Zsa Zsa never learned the lines. She was so busy with her makeup and her hair that she didn't know the lines or the scenes. Finally [the moviemakers] gave up on her and put her lines on cue cards, and then they put the lines on a monitor for her. If you look at the scene in her laboratory, you can see that she's reading off the monitor. And she could *never* remember my character name. She would say to me, "Dahlingk, vot is your name in this dreadful movie? Vot is your name, sweetheart?" I'd say, "Motiya," and she'd say, "Oh, this is terrible, dahlingk, I can never remember your name...." She was ill-prepared every day. *Queen of Outer Space* was really an opportunity for her to pose around in beautiful dresses, beautiful makeup and hair, and she didn't respect the fact that she was acting in a movie; to her, it was like a lark. But I must tell you, she *was* a very, very beautiful woman. *And* a tremendous courtesan. I mean, she was *trained* for that, that's what the mother [Jolie] trained her daughters to *be*, courtesans. Zsa Zsa certainly knew how to flirt and deal with men.

[*According to Bernds, Patrick Waltz actually cut his head during the fight with the giant spider, and Zsa Zsa, when she saw the blood, started laughing.*] Well, she was just a bitch. Really, she was not a nice person, and I definitely did not enjoy working with her. But she did say a wonderful thing to Pat, a great line: When we did that cave sequence where the giant spider jumps on him, he was very diligent and he did the huge fight with it, and then the spider is shot by a ray gun and blows up and catches on fire. At one point when the giant spider was lying on him, we were all standing in the cave looking down at him between takes, and Zsa Zsa's line to him was, "Dahlingk, if I vere you, I'd get myself a new agent!"

[*I look and I look for you in the big fight scene at the end, and I don't see you.*] I wouldn't *do* it, because they [the actresses playing Amazon guards] were all so rough! They had that big girl, Marjorie Durant, who was ready to bash everybody [*laughs*], and Lynn Cartwright—huge! She looked like a female wrestler and she was going to be in the midst of all of that fighting. I wasn't going to go in there for that! Since they didn't need to use *every*body in the fight scene, I wasn't standing in the front row of girls saying, "*I'll* do it, *I'll* do it." No, I was sorta hang-

Davis' other camp movie was the 1957 B-Western *The Dalton Girls*, in which she played "sort of a female Jack Palance"; "That was a riot, too."

ing back, and making myself scarce, and doing a lot of going to the bathroom [*laughs*]. I did *not* want to be part of that melee and be pummeled, I really didn't, and somehow or other I escaped doing it.

[Queen of Outer Space *is neither fish nor fowl—it goes back and forth between being semi-straight sci-fi and being campy.*] Oh, *very* campy. I think that's why it's so popular. *That*, and Zsa Zsa, and the fact that everybody can imitate her and "do" her line "I hate that kveen!" It's the world's best line, "I hate that kveen!"; when she says that, the audience falls apart! Did you know that they play *Queen of Outer Space* in gay bars? When she comes to that line, every guy in the place says, "I hate that kveen!" [*Laughs*]

That picture was done in January 1958 and in February I went to Palm Beach, Florida, to do a beautiful play at the Royal Poinciana Playhouse with Bob Cummings, Ann B. Davis, Olive Sturgess, Lyle Talbot and Dwayne Hickman, *Holiday for Lovers*. And Zsa Zsa was there, chasing after Rubirosa! Palm Beach was where Rubirosa hung out, I was staying at the hotel *she* was staying at, she knew I was there and she called me on the phone in my room: "Dahlingk, have you seen Ruby yet?" And I said, "Yes, Zsa Zsa, as a matter of fact, I was with him last night!"—I'd been out to a club and he hung out there. Oh, she was mad about Rubirosa. Wasn't that the time when she went around for a while with a patch on her eye? I think Rubirosa popped her in the eye, because she did have that black patch for a while.* Oh, God...! I saw Zsa Zsa many times after *Queen of Outer Space* and she was more friendly to me after the fact than she was *on* the movie, because I was no longer in scenes with her. Just today I bought the new edition of *Vanity Fair* [October 2007] and there's a picture of Zsa Zsa, one of the first that they've taken of her in quite a very long time. She's a very old lady now and she's had a devastating stroke, and she doesn't like to be seen.

[*How did you get into the business?*] I was born to a show business family in England. My mother and father were in vaudeville, my sister Beryl Davis was a singer, and we were all in show biz in England. I went to a professional school in England called Arts Educational, which still exists, still trains children for show business. It was just a natural progression for me, following my family. I played Jean Simmons as a child in a movie called *The Woman in the Hall* [1947], and Walt Disney saw me in that and he thought that I would make a good Alice in Wonderland in his upcoming movie. He brought me to America to audition to play Alice, because his original concept for the movie was to have a live Alice and animated characters around her. Back in the '20s when he first started, some of his earliest movies [*Alice Comedies*] had animated characters around a young girl playing a live-action Alice; and now he was going to have a movie with a live Alice in Wonderland and animate around her. I looked just like Alice when I was a little girl: Alice wears her hair long with a hair band, and I had long hair and always used to wear a hair band. However, he changed his mind because it was phenomenally expensive to do it that way, and sent me back to England a very, very disappointed 12-year-old. But I got back to America when I was 14. My very first agent was a man called Peter Shaw, who was Angela Lansbury's young husband, and he got me a contract at MGM. Then I went on to be at Columbia where I did a picture called *The Long Gray Line* [1955], and 20th Century–Fox where I did a picture called *The Virgin Queen* [1955].

[*All the sexual intimidation you mentioned earlier ... did you have any of that in England before you came over, or were you too young then?*] I started working when I was six and I left England when I was 14, so, no, I didn't really have any problem with that in England. But I definitely had it here. My mother and father were not in show business here, we had basically come to America to further my career, so I felt a huge responsibility. My family was sort of struggling [in the U.S.] in the beginning, because at that time when you immigrated to America, each family was allowed £500; that was about $2000, maybe even a little bit more than that, but it still wasn't very much. So I was trying to please everybody and yet remain a good girl, and keep working, and keep paying the bills, and trying to go to school, and I had all of these big, big people, heads of studios and what have you, coming after me. Every time I was approached by one of these dreadful people who scared the daylights out of me—I was only 14½, 15—I would say, "I'm very encouraged and I'm very flattered that you find me attractive, sir, but ... if you touch me, you will go to jail, because I am San Quentin quail." They were the heads of the studios, and they used to say to me, "Well, if you want to stay here, you know that this is

---

*Unless Rubirosa popped her twice, Davis may be "off" a bit here. The Hollywood Reporter's "Rambling Reporter" Mike Connolly wrote in his November 29, 1953, column, "Zsa Zsa Gabor carried a big blockbuster of a black-&-blue bump on her forehead the size of an ostrich egg onto the floor for her opening at the Last Frontier in Vegas last night. Zsa Zsa says she fell in the bathtub; onlookers claim she ran into Porfirio Rubirosa's fist in a knockdown-dragout brawl they had in Vegas, after she had spurned him."

what you have to do," and I'd say, "No, that's not what I'm gonna do...." It was a dangerous world out there. Even some of the actors I worked with were nightmares. *Some* were very well-behaved: John Forsythe was a gentleman on *Bachelor Father*. Bob Cummings was wonderful when I did *The Bob Cummings Show*. Efrem Zimbalist on *77 Sunset Strip*—a joy to work with. But there were other ones who would take terrible advantage of the fact that they had a lovely young girl, and they would make no bones about it, that if you wanted to be at work the next day, you'd better cooperate. I walked a tightrope to keep my role in the studio but not succumb to the likes of Dore Schary and Eddie Mannix and all the rest. I even had an encounter with Howard Hughes, who wanted me at his studio RKO, but I knew that that would be really bad, because he had a whole stable of women who never did anything except wait for his call in the middle of the night! Every studio had this crew of people [men] who were havin' a wonderful time: Here were all of these gorgeous young girls who wanted to be in the movies, and these men could turn the key in the lock.

I would say that, *to this day*, it colors the way I look at relationships, because it was so much a part of my very young years. My mother and father *needed* me to be a success, because we were here and we were living on my salary. If somebody made an overt pass, you couldn't smack their face and say, "God damn it, leave me alone"; you would have to say, "Well, *thank you*, I do appreciate that you're interested in me, but it's nothing that I can do, I'm only 14 and this is not good...." You wound up trying to be a politician to keep these people from getting angry with you, to keep them from getting upset with you, to keep from sounding like you were putting them down for being sexually interested in you. It was a hard role for a 14-year-old to play. When I look at a 14-year-old today, I don't have the slightest idea how I did it! I must have been incredibly mature, to be able to handle it. As a *lot* of the girls were. But some of the girls *did* [succumb]—I remember so many of them who were on their backs three-quarters of the time, and that's how they got the roles. The terrible thing was, they started with the men at the top, and they wound up doing it with the guard at the studio gate, to even get on the lot, because there was no level of respect. So by the time I encountered Paul Birch on *Queen of Outer Space* at age 21½, I'd *had* it, and I got quite nasty with him and he got

Maybe it was Davis' English breeding that equipped her to pass safely through Hollywood's horndog-dominated 1950s minefields.

nasty with *me*. When I met Pat, who was so decent, on that picture, I married him because I wanted to be *safe*. I was 21½ and fed up with it, and I was looking for safety. He was so nice and so different, basically a straight, corny small-town boy from Akron, Ohio, who happened to be an actor and very attractive. I said, "Oh, this is for me. He's a nice guy and I'll be safe." If it hadn't been for Pat, I don't know *where* I might have wound up, I really don't. He was so nice and so gentle and so unusual in a sea of people who were so ... *lecherous*.

Incidentally, I started dating Pat during the making of *Queen of Outer Space*, then I left to go to Florida to do the play, and when I returned we started dating seriously; after I came back, our very first date was to Disneyland. We got married on June 28, 1958, and, as time progressed, *Queen of Outer Space* came out. Well, when we saw the poster and he saw that my billing was over his, he was quite upset! Pat wanted to be a star very badly, it was part of his "small town boy makes good" dream, and one of the first major fights of our young marriage was because I got better billing than *he* did [*laughs*]. He couldn't stand it!

Here's something *else* good that came out of *Queen of Outer Space*: I learned, because of that picture, to imitate Zsa Zsa, I can do a very good Zsa Zsa Gabor imitation. And when Walt Disney first started the casting of *One Hundred and One Dalmatians*, he envisioned Cruella De Vil as rather Zsa Zsa–like, because Zsa Zsa at that time was always out at premieres draped in very expensive mink and chinchilla. She loved furs, and of course that was the character of Cruella; *you* remember Cruella's line, "Darling, I love furs, I worship fur, I live for fur." So when he first thought about Cruella, he wanted her with a Zsa Zsa Gabor accent. I had imitated Zsa Zsa quite a bit, just larking around, and he heard that I could do that, so he called me in to interview for Cruella De Vil.

I was reading with Walt Disney in a small, private casting room, he was reading the role of Anita in *Dalmatians* and I was doing Cruella like Zsa Zsa. But as we read, I was struggling with it because Cruella really wasn't who I *was* at all. I was 21 or 22, I was *not* this evil character, and I thought, "How do I tell the great Walt Disney that he's wrong? That he's brought me in for the wrong role?" But I got brave enough and I said, "Excuse me, sir, but as we read this, I realize that I'm much more Anita than I am Cruella." And he said, "Would you rather be Anita?" and I said, "Oh, I'd *much* rather, sir." "Well," he said, "let's try that." That's how I got to play Anita, but originally he brought me in because I was so good at imitating Zsa Zsa. So that *Queen of Outer Space* association with Zsa Zsa actually did get me the role in *One Hundred and One Dalmatians*.

I drifted away from acting, purely for economic reasons. My husband died very young [on August 13, 1972], and I had our three children to support, and I had to do something that would bring in some steady, regular money. I worked for 20 years as a consultant for a plastic surgeon—I *still* work for him. [*May I ask what your husband died of?*] Yes, he had his third heart attack. This business killed him. I was much more casual about [acting as a career]: I was very lucky in that I had a natural, easy access into show business because I had grown up in a show biz family, and for me it was second nature, show business was all I knew. Pat, the son of a policeman walking around Firestone Tire and Rubber in Akron, Ohio, was far away from the type of [show biz environment] that I had grown up in. He was [*sighs*] ... oh, star-struck. That's why he was so upset when my *Queen of Outer Space* billing was over his. It meant more to him. I couldn't have cared less whether I *had* any billing! I've always been incredibly professional; him, he was a cornball. He was very corny and it all meant a great deal, and he wanted more than anything to be a star. He never made it the way he *wanted* to make it, and it literally broke his heart. Now, he did work under another name [Philip Shawn] for a while and he did a really dreadful movie called *The Sun Sets at Dawn* [1950]. That was as close as he came. He was supposed to be a big star from that, but it never happened. And he was just very hurt by the business; the business drove him nuts and he never really made it. He did that classic thing that people do: He did all sorts of minor [non-show biz] jobs, earning *no* money whatsoever, to keep his days open for show business. [*He didn't want to get a steadier, more responsible job, because then he wouldn't be able to take time off for interviews?*] Exactly. And in the meantime, life goes away while you do nothing, trying to keep your schedule open for lesser and lesser and lesser roles. That was a very common thing then, and still today. You have people who want to be major stars and they're still servers at Hamburger Hamlet, and they never go further in life than being a server, waiting to become a star and it never happens. I know so many people who work a job that allows them to run off on an interview, and in return for that freedom, they earn nothing, and they never go anywhere, and all of a sudden they turn around and they're in their mid-forties and they *have* nothing and they've *done* nothing. That's what happened to him, and he was heartbroken over it.

I still do a lot of things that are show business–related. For instance, I lecture on board Holland America cruise ships—I'm what's called "an exploration speaker." With an audience of maybe six or seven hundred people at a time, I do four presentations: One is called "London, the Early Years" and it deals with my life in England and growing up as a child in show business and in vaudeville in England. The second one is called "Lights, Camera, Action—The Golden Years of the Silver Screen" and it involves my starting off at age 15 in the studio system, and a *lot* about *Queen of Outer Space*. The third lecture "Remembering Walt—Memories of *One Hundred and One Dalmatians*" deals with the making of that movie and some of the history of Disney, and my personal involvement with Walt Disney. Then the fourth presentation is a Q&A on the three previous lectures. I do that a lot on board ships going to Hawaii, to the Caribbean, wherever the ship is going. People just love it when I talk about *Queen of Outer Space*, *every*body "knows" this movie. Not at the time [of its original release] they didn't; at the time, it was just nothing. But now it has a following, especially the gay community; the gay community *adores* it. I'm thinking about actually booking it and going onto a gay all-male cruise [*laughs*]! I'm suggesting that they do a *Queen of Outer Space* party, and they can do a drag show, and I can judge who is the best queen of outer space [*laughs*].

I also do a lot of work for Disney, doing lectures, both to the Collectors Clubs at Disneyland, *and* to the current people working

Davis with Digby, "the love of my life."

at the studio who want to know what it was like to actually have worked with Walt Disney. *One Hundred and One Dalmatians* is *so* revered by the current crop of people who are working there, it's inspirational to them, and they're just so thrilled to meet with me and hear about how we made it. And everybody wants to hear me say one line from the movie, and that is, "Roger, dear! Teatime! Teatime!" So I do quite a bit of in-front-of-an-audience–type work, which I'm extremely comfortable with, and enjoy very, very much.

Queen of Outer Space is a good memory now, and it did bring me my husband and we had three children together, and I now have three *grand*children. So that picture brought me a lot of gifts, and now enables me to work on cruise ships. As I started out this interview by telling you, it was done in a very fast manner, Zsa Zsa was acting up and ill-behaved, and it was nothing that you were proud to say you were doing. When I did *Dalmatians*, that was entirely different because there were *years* devoted to that and it was very prestigious to be working for Disney, the cream of the crop, the Rolls-Royce of the studios, and I was aware that it was a quality product. Of course I wasn't aware at the time of the longevity it would have; it just knocks me out, the way it just keeps on going. Now, the same thing is true of *Queen of Outer Space* but for a different reason, and that's because it is so darn camp and so funny. *Queen* is *infamous,* as opposed to *famous* [*Dalmatians*]. These days I'm delighted that I was a part of *Queen of Outer Space* because it's given me such a ride.

22

Troy Donahue on Monster on the Campus *(1958)*

In Warner Brothers' heavy-breathing sex drama A Summer Place *(1959), Troy Donahue co-starred (opposite Sandra Dee) as a romantically inclined teenager—and, soon after its release, began getting more fan mail than any other actor on the lot. Prior to that unexpected leap to teen-idol stardom, however, the blond-haired, blue-eyed Donahue learned his craft at a contract player at Universal, in parts both prominent (*Man Afraid, *1957) and paltry (*Man of a Thousand Faces *and* The Monolith Monsters, *1957). Falling somewhere in the middle was his role as college student Jimmy Flanders in* Monster on the Campus *(1958), a Jekyll-and-Hyde–style horror yarn with Arthur Franz as a professor who unknowingly transforms into the title terror. Unusual movies demand unusual action, Donahue learned, as the Jack Arnold–directed fright flick had the young actor wrestling with a prehistoric dog and, aided by his on-screen girlfriend (Nancy Walters), attempting to capture a giant prehistoric dragonfly!*

Several months after guesting at the 2000 Memphis Film Festival where Monster on the Campus *was shown and this interview took place, Donahue suffered a major heart attack and died at age 65.*

[*On his screen test for Universal:*] Universal had me in what they called a "personality interview" test where you walk around a room—a little set. There was a bookshelf, and as I walked around I'd take a couple books down and look at 'em and put 'em back. Then I'd come back down in front of camera and get on a swivel chair and I'd do a 360 and face the camera again. That's when they'd start interviewing you, asking you about your life. I began talking, and I could feel my face starting to twitch. I knew this was the beginning of the end. But when it was over, as I was walking off the soundstage, somebody said, "Wait a minute. We gotta shoot it again." Seems they hadn't checked the footage in the camera, and it had run out of film. And I knew that I could go back and do it again and *relax*, maybe, this time. I went back and knocked it off, and they signed me.

By the time I got there, Sophie Rosenstein's school [for training young actors] wasn't there any more. The building where the old school *was*, was still there, and all the scripts and all material that they had used in the school were still there, but there was really nothing going on. Since there was nobody running that school, and since I'd lied about all the studying I'd done in New York [*laughs*], I was put in charge of teaching three Miss Universe girls how to act. And if you don't think I pulled down every love scene I could find out of all of those scripts they had there, you're *crazy!*

My first picture was *Man Afraid* with George Nader, in which I had a lot bigger part than I did in some of the Universal movies that followed. You'd think that it would go the other way, wouldn't you? Later, at Warner Brothers, I did *The Crowded Sky* [1960], a little part, after *A Summer Place*. At Universal, my first decent part was in *Voice in the Mirror* [1958].

I saw a little of *Monster on the Campus* the other night, with an audience [at the Memphis Film Festival], but I got too frightened to stay. Frightened that the audience was going to rise up! I think Arthur Franz was a wonderful guy, but you had the feeling that every time they wanted a professor for a monster movie, they took him out of the box and let him go. Nancy Walters was [*big, suggestive grin*] o-kay! I spoke to her just a couple of years ago on the phone. She's fine and she's well and she's happy and living a wonderful life. Jack Arnold, the director, was a little dour. Boy, Jack took his work seriously, and he took that *movie* seriously. That's not easy. You're gonna have a hard life if you take a movie like *Monster on the Campus* and you think it's *A Streetcar Named Desire*!

My fight scene with the dog—some of it was me and some of it was a stuntman. And that scene with the giant dragonfly was the funniest freakin' scene *I've* ever seen! God, I thought it was a beaut. The dragonfly bangs on the classroom window and what do they do? They *open* the window?? I mean, is *that* logical? "Oh, let's open the window and let it in!"

The funny thing about *Monster on the Campus* was that it was about a prehistoric fish called a coelacanth, which they said was extinct—and then later, [in real life] they found out that the coelacanth wasn't extinct at *all*! They hadn't done their research very well, had they? Off

Above and opposite top: Dunsfield University student Donahue earns extra credit, helping professor Arthur Franz subdue a prehistoric dog (wrapped in blanket), before hearing Franz's discourse on a past-its-freshness-date coelacanth. "After *Monster on the Campus*, I never ate fish again!" the actor joshes. The actress is Joanna Moore.

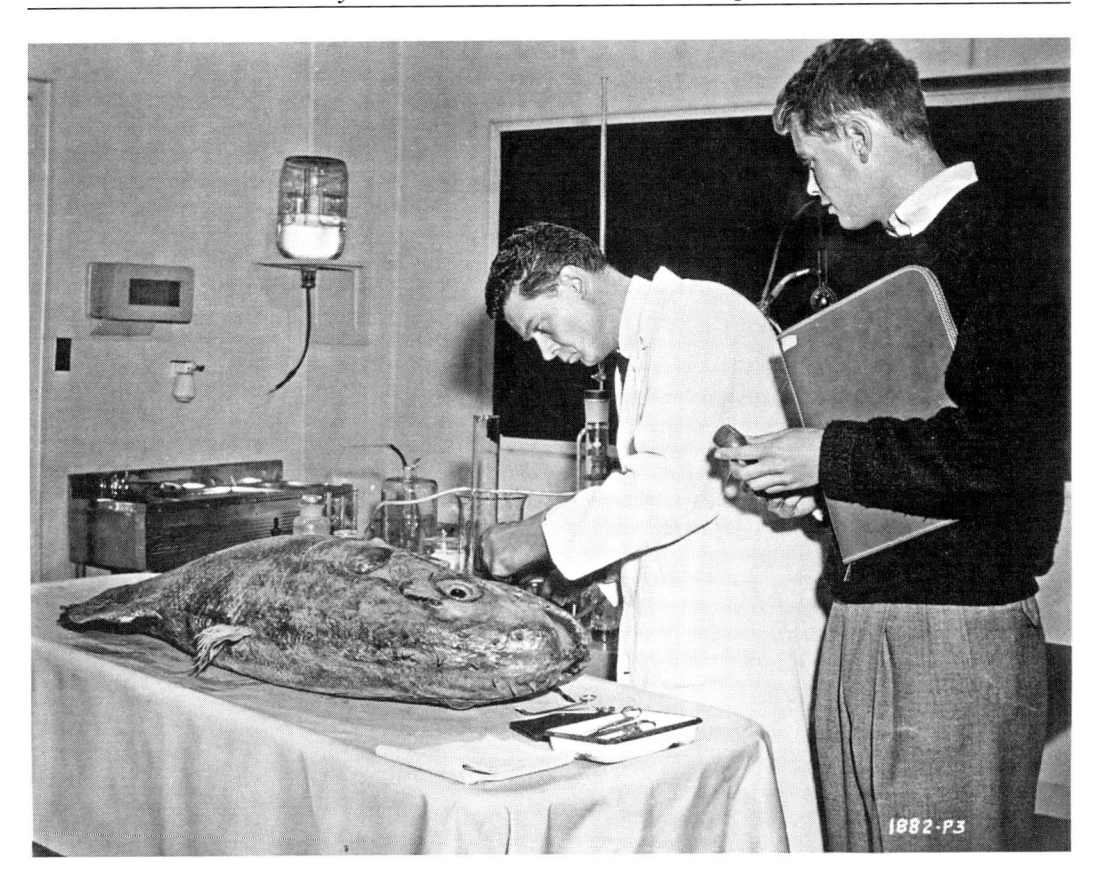

the coast of Madagascar, some fishermen had caught one 20 years earlier. Of course, they all turned into crazy animals, these Madagascar fishermen! After *Monster on the Campus*, I never ate fish again [*laughs*]!

I didn't have any scenes with the monster, but I saw him, sure. Just because we weren't in a scene with it doesn't mean we weren't sitting on the set waiting to work in the *next* scene. I thought the [monster makeup] was appropriate to the rest of the movie; it was just schlocky enough to fit in. But, look, in one way it was *better* than [today's monsters]. Today they can do *any*thing, and so—so what? They do [computer effects] just because they *can* do 'em. I don't care *what* I see on the screen, it doesn't surprise me or throw me because it's "magic." Everybody's gotten so crazy with all that stuff that there are no stories any more, there's no more romance, there's no payoff, there's no *any*thing. That's okay *some*times, but ... *all* the time? But that's what makes the money. If you want to appeal to the lowest denominator in a culture, you *can*, and it's going to be very effective because you can really inbreed people's moviegoing tastes. You make a lot of money, but you've reduced the brain capacity of the moviegoing public to about a nine-year-old. That's what's going on. I hope this is just a passing thing.

I was there at Universal for awhile and then that was it, because MCA came in and *every*body was let go, everybody except the people who had "picture deals"—Rock Hudson and Tony Curtis and Jeff Chandler and all of those guys. Picture deals were different from stock contracts. But during the time I was there, I learned *so* much about making movies, from looping and dubbing to walk-ons, where to stand, where to go, what to do. It was wonderful.

23

Nan Peterson on The Hideous Sun Demon *(1959)*

Like flies to honey, young beauties have been trekking to Hollywood for as long as there's *been* a Hollywood. Some never get past the gates of a single studio; a few become great stars; most probably fall somewhere in the middle.

Nan Peterson's career was comparatively brief, but at least she attained a small measure of lasting fame—with 1950s sci-fi fans, anyway—as the busty blonde girlfriend of Robert Clarke in her debut film *The Hideous Sun Demon*. Six years later, newly married, she played her final feature film role (unbilled) in 1964's *Looking for Love* with Connie Francis. In the decades since, she has written for magazines, had her own interior decorating business, done charity work and sold real estate—and yet she still hasn't quite gotten the acting bee out of her bonnet. "Looking back on my acting days now, I'm sorry I didn't stay with it," says Peterson, now living on the California coast (with ocean view). "I did a lot of work in those couple years [in Hollywood] but I kinda wish that I had stuck with it. Because that was really my true love."

Peterson was born in Minneapolis, Minnesota; the family relocated shortly thereafter to Mitchell, South Dakota, where they resided until her senior year of high school. At that time, they returned to Minneapolis. "All throughout while I was living in Mitchell, I would give readings around the state," she recalls. "I started when I was about six. 'Declam' readings and humorous readings, readings for Kiwanis Club and things like that. My mother started me in dramatic classes, and it kind of piqued my interest. Also, I had a cousin who was pretty well-known in the movies, his name was Roman Bohnen. He played the father in *The Song of Bernadette* [1943], and the old man with the dog in *Of Mice and Men* [1939]. We would visit him out in Hollywood, and I was always very impressed, so maybe that's where I got started. He was also in the Actors Lab [and got in trouble with the House UnAmerican Activities Committee]. He always said he was innocent." *Was* he? "Yes, I think so."

For her first two years at the University of Minnesota, Peterson majored in radio speech and minored in journalism. "Then my junior year I attended UCLA and was a theater arts major, and did a bit of little theater work there. Through the social studies department at UCLA, eight or nine of us went to Europe that year. We went to all the countries: I studied with Marcel Marceau briefly, at the Sorbonne ... London, I studied there briefly ... the University of Heidelberg." Along the line she also competed in a number of beauty contests and even the Miss Minnesota pageant.

After graduation, Peterson landed a job with KELO-TV in Sioux Falls, South Dakota, where she directed her own 15-minute show. "It was called *Pay's Art Store*—it was like a china-jewelry store—and I talked about different products. We had one cameraman, we shot it in 16mm (if you can imagine that), and I wrote my own scripts and directed my own shows. Very corny! KELO went into four states, so we had good coverage there." At this same time, Peterson also wrote the society column for the *Sioux Falls Argus Leader*.

Peterson did some of her first professional acting on the stage of the Empress Theater in St. Louis, where she played junior leads opposite stars June Lockhart, Marie Wilson and Joe E. Brown. "We did some touring around the country, and eventually I ended up in Hollywood. At that point I really didn't know if I wanted to act or if I wanted to write. I tried to get a job at *The L.A. Times*, but they didn't have any openings. So I moved into the Studio Club [a rooming house for wannabe movie actresses], right near Warners, and from then on I just fell into the acting. For the first year or so, I did a lot of modeling around town, and had a lot of funny titles like 'Queen of the Firemen's Ball' [*laughs*]. I got a lot of publicity." In addition to modeling, Peterson also did some stage work at Pasadena's Players Ring.

"I lived at the Studio Club with Joan Blackman ... Jo Anne Worley ... Jo Morrow ... we were all in the same 'group,' and all kind of ran around together. Jeanette Taylor was my first roommate, and then Shirley Knight. Shirley and I actually finally got to the status of where we had our own suite. Funny thing about Shirley. After I did *Sun Demon*, after I was in Hollywood for a while, I started working all the time—about every week, I was doing something. And Shirley hadn't gotten into it yet. She used to hold court with all the little girls who would come up to the room, she would be talking about how great she was going to be in show business. They would talk and giggle 'til about two in the morning—and *I* would have to get up at four to get to the studio! We remained friends, but I was really peeved about that. In fact, later on she got a part on Sunset Boulevard in a play called *Five Finger Exercise*, and I went to see her hoping she'd bomb! But she was so good, it made me furious [*laughs*]! She was just terrific! She had quite a rep at Warners for being very temperamental, but she has 'gone on,' hasn't she? She's still playing great parts."

Peterson made her film debut in *The Hideous Sun Demon* (originally titled *The Sun Demon*), actor Robert Clarke's valiant attempt to improve his Hollywood fortunes by branching out into producing-directing; Clarke stars as a scientist who transforms in the sun's rays into a

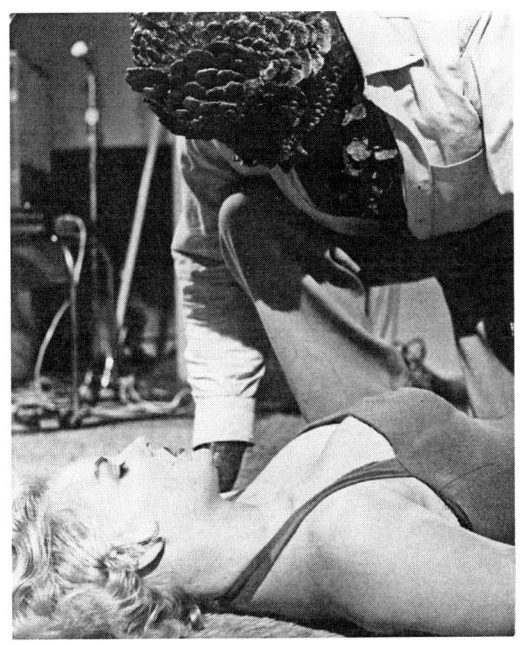

Following TV work, Nan Peterson finally had her time in the sun movie-wise co-starring as the buxom Trudy opposite Robert Clarke in *The Hideous Sun Demon*.

scaly, murderous creature, and third-billed Nan plays a gangster's moll who takes pity on him (without knowing about his horrific "Hyde side"). "I did not have an agent then," she recalls. "That was when I was doing a lot of modeling for Catalina Bathing Suits and touring all over the country as 'Miss Vornado'—Vornado was an air conditioning firm. It was during that time, when I was at the Studio Club, that Bob Clarke came along. Bob came to the Studio Club and interviewed different girls for the role of Trudy. I don't know if I read for him—I probably did—and then he told me I had the role. I had to do my own makeup, use my own clothes—it was a very low-budget film!"

Peterson and Clarke arrive in Texas for the world premiere of *The Hideous Sun Demon*.

Peterson is first seen in a bar, playing the piano and singing the torchy "Strange Pursuit." "I played the piano, but the singing was actually Marilyn King, one of the King Sisters, one of Bob Clarke's sisters-in-law. I could sing; in fact, in 1957 or '58 I sang at the Palladium when I was the 'Queen of the Firemen's Ball.' I'd gone to 26 fire stations and been in parades, and then the culmination was this big ball at the Palladium. Nelson Riddle played and I sang for him. So I don't know why they didn't let me do my own singing in *Sun Demon*, unless Marilyn wanted to sing it herself. She also wrote it.

"Bob and I also did a scene out at Malibu, on the beach, and I had to fall into the water. It was cold out at Malibu; I think we shot some of the scenes early in the day, when it *would* be cold! I don't think I got paid much for *Sun Demon*, but I did get *some*thing, I'm sure. Even if they *didn't* pay, I was so happy to have the part [*laughs*]!"

As for her leading man-director, Peterson enthuses, "Bob was super—*very* nice. We had a lot of fun later with the premiere. We premiered at a drive-in in Amarillo, Texas, where his brother worked at a radio station—that's probably *why* we had the premiere there. At one point we went up on top of the concession stand and we were being interviewed. Then Bob snuck off while I was speaking, changed costume and came back dressed as the monster! Which was fun."

As a director, Peterson says, Clarke was "excellent, very nice to work with. I can't say enough good about him. In my career, I ran up against only three people who were terrible people. Bob was a nice fellow, and most of the people in Hollywood *were*, the people who I worked with. But Lloyd Bridges was really a bad guy. He had been with the Actors Lab that Roman Bohnen was with, and he was the star of the TV series *Sea Hunt*. I was on *Sea Hunt* twice, and I told him that I was Roman Bohnen's third cousin. Well, after the second *Sea Hunt*, he was driving me home. By that time, I'd moved from the Studio Club and I had my own home that I was renting above Sunset Strip, a beautiful home—I rented the whole lower part. And he made a pass at me! He wanted me to go to bed with him. When I refused, he said, 'If you don't, you'll never work [on *Sea Hunt*] again.' I was going to be given a continuing part. And, sure enough, the next day I got a message from the studio *not* to report, that I was off *Sea Hunt*. That *really* made me mad, especially since I had met his whole family; at a big Christmas party, I met his two sons, and his wife, and they were all very nice. He seemed like such a nice family man. So when he put this ultimatum to me—even though he knew my cousin Roman Bohnen—I was just shocked.

"Also for TV, I had done three episodes of *Lawman*, and I was set to do the continuing role as Peter Brown's girlfriend. It was the same thing: I got a phone call from the Warner Brothers casting director, a proposition, right over the phone! If I wanted to continue in the series, I'd have to [go to bed with him]. And that really hurt me, because they all came to watch me at Warners and I would probably have had a contract there. But I refused, and again I was dropped from the part.

"And then the other fellow was Roger Corman. It was the same thing, a proposition in his office and so I never got the part. My agent Herman Bernie sent me over there; I don't think Herman knew that Corman had a reputation that way, and I didn't know that either. Anyway, those were my only three incidents. And, who knows, they may have kept me from going on, I don't know."

Wasn't this an occupational hazard for pretty blondes in Hollywood back then—and something she should have anticipated? "No, it wasn't. The consensus of a lot of people in the Midwest back then was, 'Oh, you go to Hollywood and you're going to go to bed with somebody.' But it really *wasn't* that way, most of the people that I ran into were really super people—Don

The movie was titled *The Sun Demon* when it made its bow in August 1958, double-billed with the year-old creature feature *Attack of the Crab Monsters*. Clarke and Peterson wowed the crowd during the intermission.

McGuire and Rod Serling and Gig Young and so on. Lee Sholem, the director of *The Louisiana Hussy* [1959], was terrific."

In that heavy-breathing melodrama, Peterson plays the title role, mysterious seductress Nina Duprez, who turns up in the bayou backwoods and causes friction between fur-trading brothers Robert Richards and Peter Coe. "The original title was *The Pit*, then they changed it to *The Secret of Nina Duprez*, and from there they changed it to *The Louisiana Hussy*. I think I got that part as a result of an interview: Herman Bernie sent me to [*Hussy* producer] Charles Cassinelli and I interviewed and read for the part. I had worked with Lee Sholem the director in a *Men into Space* TV episode in '59, so maybe I was recommended by him for it. *Louisiana Hussy* was shot in Morgan City, Louisiana, a very small town in the bayou. I don't remember if I did my own makeup but I did furnish my own clothes, and we stayed in a motel, all of us, *and* the crew."

As usual on low-budget action productions, there were the usual surprises and accidents. "I didn't have any doubles for all the dangerous scenes, and I was probably a fool not to. For instance, that scene where I was on the horse galloping away. I *do* ride horses, but this was a cutting horse, the kind of horse that, if you pull on the reins, it doesn't go the way it's supposed to, it goes the opposite way! I didn't know that! I jumped on that horse and they hit the horse's behind to get it going, and we galloped through some low-hanging cypress trees. The horse did not go the way I wanted it to go, and we ended up heading into the branches. I ducked down, but a tree branch scraped my head. I fell off the horse, and they had to put me in the infirmary for several days—I had a gash on my head. *That* was dangerous! And shooting the scenes in the swamp at the end was dangerous too, 'cause there were actually snakes and alligators. But I just went through there, even though I thought that was dangerous! Also, the motel where we were all staying one night caught fire, and we all had to evacuate! Herman Bernie later wrote me a letter saying, 'You poor dear—what you've gone through on this movie!'

"But it was a lot of fun and they were very nice people. There were some nice homes in that area—I remember we were entertained at one big mansion. They had a lot of lovely old homes ... and then, of course, a lot of shacks in the bayou area. The lady who played the old gris gris woman [witch], I think she was a native, and Rosalee Calvert was the wife of Peter Coe. She was a model and she was very nice. They were *all* nice, they were all just terrific."

But the surprises didn't stop when production wrapped: During the making of the movie, Peterson was asked if she'd be willing to skinny dip in a lake scene. That wasn't called for in the script, and she refused, and mistakenly thought it would end there. "Then when I saw the movie, when it played in Long Beach and my husband and I went to see it, I did see a girl getting out of the lake and running away with her derriere showing! But they said right up front in the opening credits that there was a double [Marcia Jordan]. I wasn't a prude, but I just didn't think I needed to do that." Even the packaging of the recent Englewood Entertainment VHS pre-record has Peterson blushing a bit. "I've got a copy but I haven't really shown it to anybody, I was kind of embarrassed with the packaging, with what they wrote [the tag line "Born to take love, and make trouble"]. I only showed it to one girlfriend. She came over and we ordered in some dim sum, and I said, 'I'm gonna show you a movie now—and don't laugh!' But the way they wrote it up, I hesitate to show it to people!"

Peterson was under contract to 20th Century–Fox for a time during this era, although the studio loaned her out more than they used her themselves. "I did a lot of TV things. I was up for a part in *The Diary of Anne Frank* [1959] but I lost out to Diane Baker, and I was supposed to have gotten a part of *Parrish* [1961], a picture that was done at Warners with Troy

Above: Her name on the marquee: A shot of the Tascosa Theatre where Peterson and Clarke made their appearance. *Opposite top*: An invitation to a cocktail party held on the night of *Sun Demon*'s premiere.

Donahue. They would just loan you out to the different studios. Most of my work, it was either at Warners or MGM."

Peterson's other TV credits include *Rawhide, Gunsmoke, Perry Mason, The Loretta Young Show, Black Saddle* and *The Untouchables*; she was also (fleetingly) seen in three episodes of the classic anthology series *The Twilight Zone*. "Rod Serling was just very nice and he did use me a lot. He was very above-board and so forth. In 'From Agnes—with Love' [a comedy episode], Wally Cox was very good and a lot of fun to work with. Gig Young ['Walking Distance'] was a very nice person, and I was saddened to hear when he committed suicide." The third *Twilight Zone* episode, hailing from the series' unfortunate shot-on-video season, was the comic "The Whole Truth" with Jack Carson as a crooked used car salesman who—in the presence of a haunted jalopy—finds that he can tell nothing but the truth. Peterson and Jack Ging play a young married couple, prospective customers. "Jack Ging was pretty well-known as a football player, and he was very nice. But Jack Carson was really full of it [*laughs*], he was very impressed with himself. He was not pleasant, in other words. He kind of ignored us. He was a good actor, and he didn't do anything *wrong*, it's just that he was sort of an egomaniac and thought he was very good. Back in those days, certain actors were very nice to up-and-coming actors—Robert Stack, on *The Untouchables*, was a very gracious person to work with, and Loretta Young was also very nice. But Jack Carson was *not* that nice!"

One of her final film roles was in *Shotgun Wedding* (1963), a Hatfields-and-McCoys-type exploitation item scripted by Ed Wood and shot in Apache Junction, Arizona. "I was hired here by the director, Boris Petroff," Peterson reminisces. "I just re-read the script the other night and I thought it was really cute. William Schallert played a preacher and *he* was very good, and we had a lot of fun in a cute scene where I was milking a cow. I knew how to do

Nan with her husband Dr. James C. Doyle (1923–2008).

that because my grandparents lived on a farm and I *did* know how to milk a cow. It played in a theater on Vine Street in Hollywood and I went with my husband to see it. I remember his remark at the time: He thought it was kinda dumb [*laughs*]!"

Nan's husband is Dr. James C. Doyle, whom she married in 1963. "When we first got married, I kept up [the acting] for a little while, doing commercials. My agent would call—usually at the last minute!—for 'cattle calls' for different things. We were living in Newport Beach then, and I always had to have my hands perfect for the commercials—I couldn't do the dishes or anything [*laughs*]! After a while, although Jim never told me this, I just figured that he did not want me to continue that career. So I began to phase it out. Around that time, one agent called me and had me do a pilot as an Elvira-type character, a spooky character who'd introduce movies, do a spiel in the beginning. We shot the pilot, and it was never sold. Then, as I said, I more or less segued out of it. I continued writing for the *Orange County Sun*, as food editor, but I really didn't get back to the acting. Years later he asked, 'Why didn't you keep it up?' [*laughs*], and I said, 'Well, I didn't think you'd *want* me to do that!'"

Even without the acting, Peterson maintained a busy schedule. Along with Debbie Reynolds, Margaret Whiting, Hugh O'Brian and others, she was an early member of The Thalians, a charity group working on behalf of emotionally disturbed children; and, after learning in the wake of an ectopic pregnancy that she couldn't have children, she and her husband adopted a little girl (now a mother herself, making the Doyles grandparents). "Then in '89 my husband decided that it would be a good idea to get into real estate—he just decided for *me* [*laughs*]! That was not at all my cup of tea, it was not creative, but I took the test and passed it, and then I got into real estate and was successful in that right up until I quit when he had a heart attack about two and a half years ago." In addition to caring for her husband, Peterson would like to return to writing; she ghost-wrote a book (*I Raised Three Daughters*) back in her Midwest days, and recently started two more, one about the real estate industry and the other a children's book.

"Somebody recently asked me if I'd like to go back to acting. I would still *like* to act—I know, of course, that I'd have to go into the 'mature' roles, like Shirley Knight. And I would like that. Looking back, I'm very happy that I *did* [act]—that's what I studied in school, and I'm glad I made use of it. I am sorry I didn't continue when I had the chance. I had some great experiences. For a girl from the Midwest to see all these studios and meet all the stars and work with them ... it was a big thrill for me."

24

Richard Erdman on Face of Fire *(1959)*

"I do not think that American criticism has yet done justice to the unsurpassable beauty of [Stephen] Crane's best writing," H.G. Wells wrote after the untimely turn-of-the-20th-century passing of the New Jersey–born novelist. "And when I write those words, magnificent, unsurpassable, I mean them fully. He was, beyond dispute, the best writer of our generation...."

Crane's best-known work remains The Red Badge of Courage *(1895), the Civil War saga that pigeonholed him as a writer of war stories (and eclipsed most of his other writings). In 1951,* Red Badge *came to the screen with Audie Murphy as the Young Soldier, direction by John Huston and a script co-authored by Albert Band. During that early '50s era, Band also read Crane's novella "The Monster" and, for the next several years, tried to find the financing for a film adaptation. Finally he did, as a U.S.–Swedish co-production, and by casting Richard Erdman in a supporting role, Band came full circle: It was boyhood friend Erdman who had introduced him to the works of Stephen Crane in the first place!*

In Face of Fire, *a tale of social ostracism, James Whitmore stars as a handsome, well-liked handyman who suffers severe chemical burns in the fierce fire which destroys the home of his employer, local doctor Cameron Mitchell. Mitchell dedicates himself to caring for Whitmore, whose face is burned away (and whose mentality has also been affected), but frightened townsfolk now reject the pair. Erdman plays the ne'er-do-well conniver Al Williams, who sees dollar signs when asked to allow Whitmore to move into his (Erdman's) white-trash family's remote home.*

In this interview, Erdman tells the behind-the-scenes story of the making of this unusual combination horror movie–adult drama.

The director of *Face of Fire*, Albert Band, and I were at Hollywood High School together. Albert was an immigrant: His father Max Band was sort of a prominent painter, a Russian who had migrated to Paris. Albert was born in Paris and had grown up and gone to school there until he was 15 or 16, and then he and his father and his mother Bertha came to America, to Hollywood. Albert brought along with him a part of his father's accent, plus a sort of a Continental, semi–British, mid–Atlantic speech. It was very slight, and as he moved along, it became more and more American.

At Hollywood High, Albert helped me learn French and I helped Albert learn English, and part of it was giving him books like *The Red Badge of Courage* and other material by Stephen Crane. *Red Badge* was a book I gave him to begin with, and then several years later Albert showed it to [director] John Huston, and John decided to do it as a movie at MGM. I turned down one of the parts because it wasn't the part I wanted to play. I wanted to play the Loud Soldier, and it got played eventually by Bill Mauldin, the cartoonist. John hired Bill Mauldin because he liked him. I don't blame him, I liked Bill Mauldin too, but he was not an actor!

Albert eventually got the idea that there was a movie in Stephen Crane's short story "The Monster." *I* didn't think there was, but at any rate, Albert went ahead. Looking for co-production deals, he wound up in Stockholm, Sweden, where money was available, and he managed to put together a deal to do the picture there. I was thrilled to be offered a part; I was always eager to go to Europe. I had been there earlier on, doing a movie [*Swiss Tour*, 1950] in Switzerland, but I had not been to Sweden.

The flight was long. After stopping in Copenhagen, we then flew on up to Stockholm, which was all socked in—fog. We had to circle the city until we practically ran out of fuel, but then we finally landed. The studio where we shot was called the Svenskfilmindustri Studio, which was Ingmar Bergman's company. It was a small studio, I think they had three stages. It was on a little hill with a nice dining area and some

Richard Erdman (left) and Albert Band as youngsters. Years after Erdman helped Band learn English by introducing him to the works of Stephen Crane, movie producer-writer-director Band cast Erdman in *Face of Fire*, based on Crane's "The Monster."

offices. We used one soundstage and the rest of *Face of Fire* was shot exteriors. The town exteriors were shot in a little town near Göteborg, in the south part of Sweden.

Shooting a movie in Sweden was surprisingly the same sort of thing as shooting in Hollywood, except they had longer lunches. [Production] would start mid-morning and go 'til about one, and then knock off for a couple of hours, and then come back and shoot 'til like 11 o'clock at night. About half of the Swedish people working on the movie spoke fairly good English; of course, almost none of us [Americans] spoke Swedish. But we didn't have a language problem that I remember. The crew was very professional, and I don't recall any problems of any kind. I learned to speak some Swedish ... enough to try to get laid [*laughs*]. The essentials came first! Ordering food and getting taxis and ... *other* little things.

James Whitmore was one of the best actors we had. Jim liked his solitude, he was a loner, and so he had his own separate place in Stockholm. We got along fine, but I didn't really get to know him until later, back out here [Hollywood], when we did a couple things together, I think some stage projects. He was certainly wonderful to act with, but I didn't really get to know him well. In the Stephen Crane story, the man who gets burned was a black man. I didn't think it was a good idea to change it [to a white man] for the movie, not at all. But I believe that somebody at the distribution end did. This was still early on in the relaxing of racism here. I think Albert thought the change was okay, and ... what are you gonna do? It was his baby.

Royal Dano played one of the townsmen in *Face of Fire*. It was on *The Red Badge of Courage* that Albert had met Royal. The first time *I* ever saw or heard of Royal was one night when I was out at MGM at a screening of *Red Badge*, before it was released. Royal had a scene in *Red Badge* that was just him [as The Tattered Soldier] against the sky, walking down a mountain; I think it was a hundred-yard dolly track that John Huston set up. It was one of the great performances in the history of film. When it was over, I said, "Jesus Christ, he's got himself an Oscar, that's all there is *to* it." Except that when [the executive producer] Mr. Dore Schary showed the film to his wife, she said, "You gotta cut that scene. It makes Audie Murphy look like a coward." Which shows you what kind of an idiot she was; that was the whole point of the picture, of course! She was sick, and I'm sorry about that, but as a result, they cut that scene. It nearly broke Royal's heart; I spoke to him about it years later. Anyhow, I got to know Royal *very* well and liked him a lot. He was a good fellow and a wonderful actor. His Abraham Lincoln on [the TV series] *Omnibus* was just beautiful, it was as good as it gets.

Cam Mitchell [the doctor in *Face of Fire*] was the playboy of all time, and he hooked up with a little Swedish girl the minute he got to Sweden and hardly anybody ever saw him. I don't blame him much, she was gorgeous. Robert Simon [the judge] was a very nice fella but I didn't get terribly close to him ... I think there was another Swedish girl involved there, as I recall [*laughs*] ... I'm a little dim on that one! Albert and Sam Jaffe were close friends, Bettye Ackerman was married to Sam, and I guess Albert hired Bettye [to play the *Face of Fire* female lead] because she was Sam's wife. She was very, very nice and perfectly good in the picture. Lois Maxwell, who later played the secretary in the James Bond series, came over from England to do *Face of Fire* [as Dano's wife]. Howard Smith [the sheriff]—crazy old Howard! I'd known him for years. He was a good ol', rascally fellow, just wonderfully irreverent!

Most of us stayed at the Palace Hotel, a very nice, modern place, but I believe Albert had some sort of little home somewhere, and as I said, Jimmy and Cam Mitchell had their own places. Louis Garfinkle [*Face of Fire*'s screenwriter and co-producer] was over there with us, too. Louis and I were pretty close friends. Frankly, I think it was the best thing Lou wrote, and Lou wrote a lot of stuff through the years. He wrote one wonderful script for Albert, for a movie called *The Young Guns* [a 1956 "juvenile delinquent Western"] and it got screwed. It was a *very* tough script—honest, real, very hard-hitting. They called me over to Albert's home one day and they made me sit there while they read it to me, and I said, "My *God*, guys, you've got a good script. I think it's *damn* good." But I didn't think they'd ever get it made, because in the 1950s we weren't used to Westerns that were ugly, and *The Young Guns* was ugly. It was Albert's first directing, too. What happened to the script was a tragedy; it was castrated. I think it was Allied Artists, one of the Mirisch brothers, who decided it was too rough, and so they cut out almost every really good, strong scene, and *The Young Guns* wound up a silly movie. Then in 1957 Albert and Louis did a picture called *Killer on the Wall*, which came out as *I Bury the Living*; I wasn't nuts about it. Then *Face of Fire*.

For the scene in *Face of Fire* where the doctor's house burned down, the big deal was finding enough cameras, because they wanted five cameras to cover it in case anything went wrong. It was near the studio that they built that house and then burned it down, but I don't remember exactly where. [Whitmore's burn-faced look] ... well, it got by. We did not have the best makeup man in the world on that movie, but it worked. I think it was a mask but I'm not positive about that, I only saw it on the screen.

As you know, I'm not in an *awful* lot of *Face of Fire* so I had quite a lot of time off. A wonderful girl who was a production assistant at Svensk had one of the early little Vespas [motor scooters] which she loaned me from time to time. I went toodling all over the place on that

Vespa, which was a lot of fun. I explored Stockholm and got to know the restaurants and the good times, and I went out to Drottingham Palace, that wonderful little intimate theater they've got there, and saw an opera. I had a fine time.

One day when we were having lunch in the little dining area at Svenskfilmindustri Studio, Ingmar Bergman's cinematographer invited myself and Royal Dano to see Bergman's new movie that evening, in a screening room there at the studio. Well, that night Royal and I sat there and watched it for almost two hours, flabbergasted. "Flabbergasted" because, first off, it was a *very* strange movie, and secondly, because the language barrier knocked us dead; it was in Swedish, of course, and there were no subtitles. Royal and I talked about it over a full bottle of wine that night, tried to figure out what it had been about, but we couldn't arrive at any sensible decision. So the next day we ran into the cameraman and we said, "Thank you very much for letting us see Mr. Bergman's picture.... Could you tell us what it was about?" "Well," he said, "*you* know Ingmar, Ingmar is a very great moviemaker, and ... uh ... he is a very special man, and the picture has ... uh ... uh ... the picture is...." Then, after a pause, he said, "*You* know Ingmar. He fools them all!" [*Laughs*] He was Ingmar's cinematographer, and *he* didn't know what it was about!

In 1958 when *Face of Fire* was made, Erdman had been in the movie biz for almost 15 years, initially under contract to Warner Brothers. Here he is in a (much) more recent shot.

[*What was Band like as a director of actors?*] Well [*sigh*], that's a toughie, because Albert's dead, he just died a couple of years ago [2002], and we were old friends. I think Albert should have been a producer rather than a director, because he got deals together that nobody could believe he made. I think *Face of Fire* was the best job he ever did. I saw it again recently and I was surprised to find that it was better than I remembered it being. I wasn't nuts about it when I first saw it. The first time was at a preview out here somewhere. It was very European, because *Albert* was very European. At that particular time, everybody in Hollywood was looking at European movies, as a contrast to the rather shallow stuff we were then doing here, for the most part. At that time I thought *Face of Fire* was very European and that it was slow. Sam Jaffe came to see it, and he said, "The only good thing in the movie is Erdman!" [*Laughs*] I don't agree with that, incidentally—I thought Cam and some of the other actors were fine. But according to Sam, "The only good thing in the movie is Erdman!"—Sam was a fan of mine!

Anyhow, as I mentioned a moment ago, I just watched the movie again and it holds up better than I thought it would. In fact, I was kind of fascinated by it. And the whole experience of going to Sweden to make it was nice; we were there, I think, six weeks. Stockholm was a beautiful city and we had a fine time. When you're an actor and you get trips and you get treated like a prince and live better than you do at home, it's a good time!

25

The Calvin Beck– "Norman Bates" Connection

Fans of vintage horror films tend not to be drawn to the exploits of real-life serial killers; for *our* "fixes" of macabre mayhem, we turn instead to the silver screen and the (generally bloodless) bloodbaths harmlessly play-acted on Hollywood soundstages. And yet the name Ed Gein is familiar to most *all* horror fans: We know that in the 1950s, the shiftless, middle-aged Wisconsin ne'er-do-well was responsible for a string of grisly backwoods killings and mutilations (not always in that order), and the *reason* we know is because Robert Bloch reportedly used him as the model for the character of Norman Bates in the novel *Psycho*.

But, apart from their respective homicidal streaks, similarities between the two are elusive. Bloch wrote in his 1993 autobiography *Once Around the Bloch* that he "knew very little of the details concerning [the Gein] case and virtually nothing about Gein himself" when he wrote his 1959 page-turner. The author claims to have created Norman "from whole cloth," basing his story on no person, "living or dead, *involved in the Gein affair*" (italics mine). And, true to Bloch's disclaimers, there's precious little resemblance between the grinning, gregarious small-town loafer Gein and the Norman Bates described in Bloch's novel: a plump, bespectacled, 40-year-old motel clerk who relishes his books, basks in gruesome fantasies, and squirms under the ruthless domination of his ever-present, nagging mother.

Noël Carter, ex-wife of renowned fantasy-SF writer Linwood Carter (1930–1988), says that "Norman" can be traced to a far more likely sounding source of inspiration. "I heard about this from Lin," offers Mrs. Carter (an author herself). "Lin and I met at the end of 1962 and were married in '63, and I became very involved with science fiction and fantasy, and with all Lin's cronies. Among his cronies were Chris Steinbrunner from [New York City's] WOR-TV, a wonderful, dear friend, and an awful lot of people who had been around in the '50s. They were all older than I, and among the people in the group that sort of ebbed and flowed with time was Robert Bloch. And Bloch was fascinated by [*Castle of Frankenstein* magazine publisher-editor] Calvin Thomas Beck. Calvin was also in that group, on the fringes of it, with his mother constantly in tow.

"When I met Lin, we saw all the Hitchcock retrospectives and were avid Hitchcock fans. I told him how much I liked *Psycho* [the 1960 Hitchcock movie based on Bloch's novel], and he told me the story that, when Robert Bloch was part of this group, Bloch got the idea for *Psycho* and he based it on three characters. One was the Wisconsin murderer Ed Gein, who killed women and hung up their eviscerated bodies. Ed Gein is the one everybody knows about. But Norman was also based on Calvin Thomas Beck—and his mother.

"Chris Steinbrunner [author of two renowned film books and the Edgar-winning *The Encyclopedia of Mystery and Detection*] later confirmed this, so it wasn't just from Lin. This was common knowledge, but it wasn't discussed a great deal because Calvin was part of the group and it might hurt his feelings. Calvin's mother was a noisy, dominating little Greek woman who followed him most everywhere. She told me herself that she went to his college classes, she monitored classes *with* Calvin. As she told me this, I thought to myself, 'He must want to kill her!'—but he was completely dominated by her."

John Cocchi, one of America's top film researchers, recalls, "Chris Steinbrunner used to invite me to the very elaborate Halloween parties that Noël and Lin gave out in Queens, and I met Calvin there. Calvin and I became friendly, even though the mother was always with him. And, yes, I heard the [*Psycho*] rumor, people were always saying that about Calvin. He and his mother had a very close relationship which he didn't care for, but he just couldn't get rid of her. I guess he was too polite to tell her off, to say, 'I'm a grown man, I'm middle-aged [Beck was born in 1928 or '29]. Don't follow me around!' But she didn't have any kind of a life aside from him, so I guess she had nothing else to do!"

Writer James H. Burns first met Beck in the "Hospitality Suite" of a 1976 Lunacon; Burns walked in and saw a man on the phone with the hotel operator, imitating Orson Welles and asking to be connected with the Diamond Exchange in South Africa ("That was my introduction to Calvin Beck!"). Burns questions the persistent Bates-Beck rumor. "It sort of smacks of something that may have started as a funny joke, and became a rumor, and then was around so long and seemed to have so much going for it that it became accepted as truth," says the *Esquire-American Film-Preview-Starlog* scribe. "There could have been grudges back in the '60s that continued for a long time, or even resentment that Calvin was the only person of that fan group who was publishing a successful magazine. He may have been the only fan ever to publish a national magazine, at least, one that lasted that many years. Maybe secretly people resented that; fandom can be an envious place. And any negative thing you could say about Calvin would stick in people's minds. The [*Psycho* rumor] is the kind of story that has such resonance to it, such bizarre juice, that over 30 years of thinking about it, you could start accepting it as fact without even realizing that you first heard it as a rumor."

Mrs. Carter sticks to her guns. "I was told that Robert Bloch *admitted* it, but he was a little reluctant [because] he was afraid of a lawsuit or something! It was common knowledge, and it was not something that people surmised.

"Lin and I used to give what was quite a celebrated Halloween party every year, starting in 1964 maybe," Carter continues. "For about 12 years, we gave a big, big party. People came from all over, it was well known in fandom and a lot of people from fandom were part of the group, science fiction and fantasy writers and artists. And Calvin always used to angle for an invitation. I had never invited him because of his mother, because his mother went with him everywhere. For instance, she went to all of the cons. Whatever con he went to, she was there too. What happened finally was, Calvin called me up and asked why he was never invited to the party. I said, 'Well, frankly, Calvin, it's because of your mother. I'd love to have you come, but we're all grown-ups here, and we don't invite our parents to parties!' He said he understood, and he would like to come, and he would make sure his mother didn't.

"So he came to the party, and she called up virtually every hour on the hour. She called up to check that he was *there*, she called up *several* times. I'd say, 'Mrs. Beck, he is with a group of friends. They're upstairs, they're in the library, looking at books. No, I'm not gonna call him to the phone. Yes, he will get home safely.' This is the kind of woman she was! I presume she was like that throughout his life, and this is what Robert Bloch observed. The whole Mother business in *Psycho* comes from Calvin's mother. August Derleth wrote about Ed Gein in the book *Wisconsin Murders* [1968]; I read it years ago, and nothing about Gein made me think of Norman and Mother. And the more I thought about it, the more I realized that [what Lin Carter, Steinbrunner and, allegedly, Bloch] said was true. As a writer myself, I know that one thing will stick in your mind, and that will be a jumping-off point. Calvin Thomas Beck's mother was the jumping-off point for *Psycho*."

> His mother was a clinging, demanding woman, and for years the
> two of them lived as if there was no one else in the world.
> —Dr. Richmond (Simon Oakland) in *Psycho*

Beck even *resembled* the fictional Norman. "Calvin was overweight, very greasy-looking, with a full, fat-cheeked face," says Carter. "He had black, wavy hair that was very unattractive, and a mustache. And he did wear glasses. Calvin was always overweight, and unhealthy looking."

"But he was wall-eyed," says Cocchi, adding a detail not found in the Bloch book. "One eye was straight, and the other one looked over to the side. So he never looked directly at you. I think that was a defect he was born with; he told me once that he had like 30 percent impaired vision. He didn't explain why he never tried to have it fixed; maybe it couldn't have been."

"I was with Calvin and a friend at a convention in New York," reminisces Ted Bohus, New Jersey–based filmmaker and editor-publisher of *SPFX* magazine. "Calvin was saying something and I was totally ignoring him. My friend said, 'Ted! Calvin's talking to you.' I said, 'Oh! I'm sorry! I didn't know—'cause he was *lookin'* at *you*!' One eye went one direction and one eye went the other direction [*laughs*]! We were hysterical. Fortunately, Calvin had a pretty good sense of humor about those things."

Bohus first met Beck in the late 1960s; introduced by a mutual friend, they discovered they not only shared an interest in movies and magazines but that they lived five blocks from one another in North Bergen, New Jersey. Despite their proximity, however, Bohus entered the Beck house (9008 Palisade Avenue) just once. "I had heard that people had a lot of trouble trying to get in to see Calvin," says Bohus. "A lot of times they would go to the door if they were supposed to give him an article or something, and he'd open the door a crack and put his hand out and grab the article and just slam the door in their face. One time he asked me to bring to his house something he needed for the magazine. I went over there and he opened the door a crack, and I said, 'Well, can I come in?' He looked behind him, like he was worried that something was gonna descend on him, but then he said okay. As I walked in this house, out of one of the adjoining rooms I heard this 'voice' [*Bohus makes bird-like shrieking noises*]. A horrible, screeching voice! It would yell his name, and then start ranting and raving. I got in for a little while (the place, of course, was all stacked up with crazy shit), but with her ranting and raving so much, I felt embarrassed. I didn't know if she was gonna come out and stick a knife in my back or not! *It was that scary*. I said, 'Look, Calvin, maybe we'll get together some other time.' And it was a shame, because he seemed to like certain people, like myself, who [shared his interests]. He really seemed like he wanted to get out and do stuff. Boy, it was very strange."

> I think that we're all in our private traps—clamped in them—
> and none of us can ever get out.—Norman Bates (Anthony Perkins)

CoF writer-artist Richard Bojarski recalls the one time Beck complained to him about the mother: "He said, 'You have to understand my mother. I'm the only son she has, and I have to live with it.' It was kind of an emotional outburst; he was unhappy about something his mother did, and he said to me, 'She never allows me to have any friends.' That's the only time I ever saw him become emotional. One time his mother got so emotional that [*CoF* associate editor] Bhob Stewart, who was working there at Beck's house, got so upset he couldn't work any longer. He just dropped everything and walked out of the house and took the bus back home. Beck had to call him and reassure him it wasn't gonna happen again." Stewart quit the magazine after a subsequent North Bergen visit ended with Helen Beck raising a shoe over her head and physically threatening him.

> My mother—what is the phrase?—she isn't quite herself today.
> —Norman Bates (Anthony Perkins)

Noël Carter remembers one of *her* stranger encounters: "When I was very new in Lin's group, I did not know that you were supposed to avoid the mother like the plague. We were all at dinner, at a steak house in New York, and Calvin and his mother were there. Everybody rudely just jumped for seats, and I ended up at the end of this long table with Calvin's mother, because everybody else was smart enough to avoid her. She said to me [*in a heavy Greek accent*], 'So, tell me, dahling, vot you theenk Greek men?' (That's the way she spoke.) I did not want to talk with her [*laughs*], and I figured, 'If I'm rude, she will ignore me, and I can continue with the conversation at the other end of the table.' So I said, 'Well, frankly, from my experience in college, I think Greek men are dreadful.' She looked at me and she said, 'You're absolutely right!'—and to her, this made us *soulmates* [*laughs*]! She then told me about her relationship with her husband, including some of the intimate details, such as the fact that they never slept together after Calvin was born. (You can see what a burden that put on Calvin.) She made her entire life around Calvin. She hated the father; the father was hated and reviled. They lived together but they had no relationship. Her whole life went into Calvin, and Calvin's education: 'I even went to college with Calvin,' she told me.

"Then she went on to say that her husband (who was no longer living) had been ill for many years. Well, I later found out that the story was that the father had evidently had a stroke or something, and he had been

Psycho producer-director Alfred Hitchcock poses with the silver screen Norman Bates, attractive young leading man Anthony Perkins.

upstairs in the bedroom for years. *And no one ever saw him.* So, you see, this was another aspect of Calvin's story that Robert Bloch picked up on. The father disappeared up there to the bedroom, and nobody was quite sure when he died. All of a sudden, he just wasn't around any more. I mean [*laughs*], they could have kept him a prisoner, for all anyone knew! One could really embroider this—I'm just giving you the bare bones, which is that he was up there, a stroke or heart attack victim, cared for, *but never seen* by anyone after a certain point. Ironically, many, many years later, Calvin's mother became ill and bedridden, and *she* retired to the upstairs, where she was taken care of *but never seen*. Then, ironically, *he* became ill, and was bedridden for a long period of time. It's sort of like a generational thing—goodness knows what was going on in that house. I would not particularly like to think about the psychodynamics of it, *Psycho* being the operative word!"

> But she's harmless. She's as harmless as one of these stuffed birds.
> —Norman Bates (Anthony Perkins)

John Cocchi also got the impression that Helen Beck hated her husband Thomas, Calvin's dad. "Well, I think she didn't like too many people. When Calvin and his mother were with us, and one of us had to speak to her (we always avoided her, we always thought she was odd), she would always tell us about her life. But never about her relationship with Calvin, that was never spoken of. She was always saying, 'I was a great concert pianist, but when I married my husband, he forced me to give it up.' She said she had been living almost on the dole since then. We didn't know whether or not to believe her, I *didn't* really believe her, but I never contradicted her. We always took her with a grain of salt."

"She would always have stories to tell," laughs *CoF* contributor Charles Collins, who first met the Becks (again through Steinbrunner) back in the '50s when father, mother and son lived in Elmhurst, Queens. "Oh, she said she had worked for the FBI and J. Edgar Hoover had gotten down on his *hands and knees* to thank her for the work she did. She was very anti–Communist at the time, and she always felt there were Communists pursuing her [*laughs*]! Then we'd hear about all the other great things that she did, and what an artist she was in the old country."

Collins continues, "After *Psycho* came out, the [Calvin-Norman] rumor was very prevalent among the science fiction crowd. I met Robert Bloch on a couple occasions, like when he was guest of honor at the first World Fantasy Convention, but I did not feel that I knew him well enough to ask. But the rumor was always there, and I always wondered about it myself."

Author Bill Warren (*Keep Watching the Skies!*) got the scoop from Bloch first-hand. "I met Bob Bloch in 1966 and a few years later, at a party or a convention, we talked about *Psycho* and Norman Bates. He said that while Norman's activities were based on those of Ed Gein, his personality and his physical description and his relationship to his mother were based on Calvin T. Beck. He said this in so many words, identifying Beck as the editor of *Castle of Frankenstein*. He also asked me never to mention this in print and, until now, I've followed his request."

While preparing his 1975 book *Heroes of the Horrors*, Beck contacted New York–based movie producer Richard Gordon and asked to speak with him about his experiences with Bela Lugosi. "This must have been in the early 1970s. I was at my old office at 120 West 57th Street," says the veteran filmmaker. "He called me and asked me if he could come interview me. It was, I think, the first interview I ever did for a genre magazine. He came up, and his mother, whom I had heard about from [Gordon's film historian friend] Bill Everson and other people, came along with him. He came into my office and sat down, and she stood in the corner behind his chair. Didn't say a word throughout the entire interview, just kept her eye on him. He was dressed very informally, but she was dressed completely in black, rather like Mrs. Danvers always was in *Rebecca* [1940]. He must have been in my office for about a half-hour or so. And when he finished, he got up and thanked me and he and she walked out. She was silent throughout the entire session. I was reminded of Norman Bates and his mother in *Psycho*; the whole ambience of having him and his mother in my office was very reminiscent of *Psycho*. That's the thought that's crossed my mind any time I've thought of him, down through the years." (Gordon made this observation *without knowing* the Calvin–Norman connection.)

"Calvin's mother was extremely possessive and controlling—and quite mad," Charles Collins charges. "She had the classic delusions of grandeur and delusions of persecution. So our relationship with Calvin ran in cycles. We would go over there and visit him, we'd go out with him, but every time we went out, his mother always came with us. Always, right up until she got so elderly that she couldn't. But whenever she felt that we were getting close to Calvin, she would break up the relationship in very bizarre ways. We'd be friendly with Calvin for a while, and then the mother would intervene and we wouldn't see him any more. Then a few years would pass and everything would be all right again."

In *Psycho*, Mother's most annoying trait—apart from wholesale murder—is the way she berates and belittles her mama's boy son. "Probably [Calvin's mother] did that, too, but I can't be certain of that," says Noël Carter. "But her behavior toward him was extremely aggressive. We were in a hotel in New York and there was a big convention going on, and everybody went downstairs to the restaurants. Lin was in the men's room and so was Calvin, and I guess they were in there, talking with people. Lin came out, and Mrs. Beck was standing outside the men's room. She finally knocked on the door of the men's room and shrieked out, 'Calvin! Calvin! Come out of there! You've been in there long enough!' That gave me an idea what it must have been like to be a teenage Calvin, hanging out in the bathroom!"

> It's not as if she were a maniac, a raving thing. She just goes ...
> a little mad sometimes.—Norman Bates (Anthony Perkins)

Carter continues, "To me she said that the sun rose and set on Calvin. But I believe Mrs. Beck hated men, and I think it must have been very easy, once the husband wasn't around, for her to sometimes take out her aggressions on Calvin. So it would not surprise me to learn that someone had heard her reviling him in some way."

"Only once or twice he got mad," says Bojarski. "One day in the living room of their home she was picking on me, and he turned on her and chewed her out. That was the only time I ever saw him do that. He bawled her out, and she left the room. I kind of admired Calvin for doing that—I'd never seen it happen before."

> Huh, boy? You have the guts, boy?—Mother

"His mother, I think, was just overly possessive," says John Cocchi. "I don't know how much she loved Calvin; she never demonstrated any affection around us. But he could never get rid of her unless he said, for instance, 'The Carters don't want you to come, I *can't* take you'—and he had to force her to stay home. Which I'm sure she didn't appreciate! I don't know how much she loved him, but she did seem to have pride in his accomplishments. And she tolerated all his weird friends—who *were* pretty weird!

"Calvin was a very knowledgeable buff. He was interested in all the old movies, as we were, and he kept up with the new films, especially the genre-type films that he liked. And I thought his magazine was the best of its kind. Occasionally I'd loan Calvin some material—

stills, and maybe some press material on the films he was writing about. And occasionally I even got it back [*laughs*]!"

"A lot of the writers who worked for Calvin had a hard time getting any money from him," says Charles Collins, who handled *CoF*'s book review column. "Mrs. Beck would tell them, 'Calvin is giving you a break. *You* should be paying *him* for contributing to his magazine!' I got to know some of the other writers, who were all more or less people with talent who were just kind of starting out. Calvin was great at exploiting people like that. He pulled a couple of things on me that were not nice, but he was a very likable person and I couldn't really get mad at this fella. Despite the underhanded things that he did, the next time you'd get together it was like nothing had happened!"

Beck may not have been crooked but he certainly was suspected of beginning to curl, at least by folks who sent their hard-earned bucks for merchandise advertised in *CoF* (an act equivalent to tossing it down the nearest manhole). According to Dick Bojarski, Beck's mother was in charge of the mail order end, so perhaps the sticky fingers were hers and not Calvin's. Calvin, however, took the heat when he'd be confronted at cons by *CoF* customers. "That happened on several occasions," says Bojarski. "I also used to bring it Calvin's attention, but he'd sort of pooh-pooh it. He'd say, 'We send that stuff out. They've got nothing to complain about.'

"Beck claimed that *Castle of Frankenstein* was a small magazine and he couldn't pay much," he adds. "But from time to time, whenever I visited his office-home, I would see a new TV set there, or some kind of expensive-looking hi-fi equipment. I'd ask him, 'I see things are picking up, Calvin. Do you think you'll be able to pay me a little more money?' And he'd say, 'I'm getting these things on installments'—he always had some kind of excuse."

Did Beck know that he and his everpresent mom-tourage had provided the basis for the combined Norman-Mother character? "He had to have heard about it," says Noël Carter, "but he never said anything. But, you see, people realized that it would be [a sore subject]. When the book came out is probably when it was discussed and when he was aware of it. No one would have dreamed when the book came out that eventually it was going to be blown up into a major film by a major director. It was after the movie was made that people became more reticent, because they didn't want to hurt Calvin's feelings. But when the book came out, it was a topic of conversation among writers that one of their ilk [Bloch] had a book published, and they all knew who the book was based on."

"Oh, yeah, Calvin was aware of it," says Cocchi. "He always made a joke of it." Bojarski got the same reaction: "I mentioned it to Calvin one time, and he just gave a hearty laugh and sort of sloughed it off and changed the subject. But his mother could be ... difficult."

The *Castle of Frankenstein* was razed in the

Calvin Beck knew how to strike a Sven-goofy, "You are in my *power*!" pose, but reportedly it was *he* who was held in thrall for his entire life.

mid–1970s, after issue #25 (June 1975), although Beck kept busy with book projects. Then, in the early 1980s, Beck did something that his friends admit they never thought he would ever do: "He *married*," Noël Carter marvels. "And she [Sharon Kayser] was just as dominating and forceful as his mother. He was led around by a ring in his nose, just as he had been by his mother."

"They married pretty shortly after he first met her," adds Cocchi, "and they were all three living together in the house. There was always animosity between the mother and Sharon—obviously—because the mother was so possessive. I don't really think that Sharon encouraged it, because she had nothing against the mother that I know of. Although I'm sure Sharon would have been happy if the mother lived somewhere else!"

"His wife was as crazy as his mother," Charles Collins chimes in. "Oh, she was insane! Very domineering, very paranoid. Sort of spiritual, but in a very bizarre way."

Cocchi: "Sharon was very much into religion, and about once a year she'd change her religion. I think she was raised as a Catholic, but she tried a lot of other religions. As I remember it, Calvin's mother got sick and was in the hospital, and then Calvin was ill, too. At one point, they were in the *same* hospital! Calvin had a stroke a little bit before his mother died, and he was paralyzed through the last few years of his life. Through virtually all his married life, he was paralyzed, and Sharon took care of him." And the strange behavior continued: When Cocchi told *Fangoria*'s newly minted editor Tony Timpone that Beck was down to his last nickel, Timpone offered Beck a job as one of *Fango*'s freelance reviewers and sent him some new books. Like the money that *CoF* readers remitted for merchandise in decades past, the

Perkins outside the Bates house in *Psycho*. Of the real-life Beck residence, Noël Carter says with a shiver, "Goodness knows what was going on in that house. I would not particularly like to think about the psycho-dynamics of it, *Psycho* being the operative word!"

Fangoria package vanished into the Black Hole at 9008 Palisade Avenue; despite his poverty, Beck never took Timpone up on his offer of employment.

On May 14, 1989, Calvin Beck, age 60 (or thereabouts), went to that big Editorial Office in the Sky. Sharon Kayser Beck told an obit writer that her husband was a political visionary who (back in the 1950s) predicted the impeachment of Richard Nixon; a civil rights activist who marched with Martin Luther King and was shot and jailed in Alabama; and a movie-TV "ghost writer" whose credits included episodes of *Star Trek* and *Mork and Mindy*. Some of it might even be true. Who knows.

"After Calvin passed away, I told Sharon that I would be interested in buying part of Calvin's collection," says Collins. "She kept me dangling for a long, long time, at least a year. Then she called one day and said she was interested in selling the collection. (She said, 'I got a sign from Calvin. It's okay to sell it.') So we made a deal and I went over there one afternoon; I brought a friend to help box it up and take it out to the car. By this time, the house was a real rat trap, and you could barely get into the room the books were in. You had to excavate to get into an area, you'd go through the books you could get at and then excavate a little bit *more* to get into the *next* area. And she only gave us a certain amount of time, because at four o'clock she had to meditate, and we couldn't be in the house when she was meditating!

"All the time that we were there, in the next room was this enormous Doberman on a leash attached to a doorknob. The Doberman was barking and howling, and I was thinking that if she had a mood swing and released that Doberman, we were in trouble [*laughs*]! And all the time she kept talking to the Doberman, saying, 'What's the matter, baby? You miss Calvin? You miss Calvin?' My friend was terrified, he thought that at any moment she would unleash the beast [*laughs*]!"

Sharon Beck later moved to an Arizona trailer park. She was 56 years old when she died in Arizona on October 11, 1997.

Ted Bohus: "I liked him. I *liked* Calvin Beck. And a lot of times, I'd say, 'Hey, Calvin, let's go out. Let's do something.' 'Oh, no, no, I can't, I can't.' And he would never come out. So we'd meet at conventions. Once he was there at the show, we'd sit down and talk, and he was fine. But it was a weird thing: He would go out and go to a show, and then get sucked back into that little world of his with the mother."

> Well, a boy's best friend *is* his mother.
> —Norman Bates (Anthony Perkins)

26

Roger Corman on House of Usher *(1960)*

Imagine our surprise and delight, perusing the new [December 20, 2005] list of movies added by the Library of Congress to the prestigious National Film Registry, to find that one of the 25 titles being honored and permanently preserved is Roger Corman's *House of Usher*, the low-budget, high-quality "candlelight thriller" that kicked off AIP's celebrated Edgar Allan Poe series. Then imagine our surprise—shock!—to phone Corman several days later to ask for his reaction, and to discover that no one had yet told him about it!

"I'm finding out from *you!*" says the once, current and future king of maverick moviemakers. "I had seen the articles about [additional National Film Registry titles] in *Variety* and *The Hollywood Reporter*, but I just looked at the new list quickly and saw movies like *Giant* [1956] and *Cool Hand Luke* [1967] and so forth, and never bothered to look over the whole thing." So that's the kind of list he just doesn't look for himself on? "Right!" Corman laughs. "I feel very happy about it, because *House of Usher*, the first of the Poe pictures with Vincent Price, was something of a transition for American International Pictures, and an important transition for me also.

"In the late '50s, I was making pictures for AIP and for Allied Artists," he continues, "and [both distributors] had a style of doing two black-and-white pictures together as a double bill, sending 'em out together. For instance, two horror pictures, two science fiction pictures, two gangster pictures, each budgeted at anywhere from, say, $70,000 to $100,000, and shot in ten days. AIP asked me to make two ten-day black-and-white horror films, and I was a little bit tired of that. Also, I felt that the sales gimmick of putting two low-budget pictures together was wearing thin at the box office. I had always liked the Edgar Allan Poe story 'The Fall of the House of Usher'; I'd read it as a child, in school, and asked my parents to give me for Christmas the complete works of Poe, which they were happy to do. And I always wanted to make the picture.

"So I told AIP—Jim Nicholson being the producing end of the company and Sam Arkoff the business end—that instead of making two $100,000 pictures, I'd make *one* $200,000 picture, in color. Jim agreed. Sam was very dubious, because they'd never spent that much money, and he also complained that there was no monster in it. I thought for a moment, and then I said, 'Sam, the *house* is the monster.' He thought about that a little bit, and then he said [*in a grudging tone of voice*], 'All right....'"

In his 1992 autobiography *Flying Through Hollywood by the Seat of My Pants*, Arkoff recalls the initial *House of Usher* discussion, and slips in the zinger that he "was probably more of a Poe fan than either [Corman or Nicholson]." Corman's reaction—after the laughter—is exceedingly diplomatic. "Sam was remembering incorrectly. Again, Sam opposed *House of Usher* because it didn't have a monster. Jim Nicholson, after a *very* brief discussion, agreed with me. Sam was the holdout who didn't want to do it, because he was more conservative financially. Jim Nicholson was president of AIP and head of production, Sam was vice-president and head of business affairs, and as head of business affairs, he opposed the making of the film. He never had *any*thing to do with the production of the pictures. In fact, I don't think he was ever even on the *set*."

Working from a Richard Matheson screenplay that greatly expanded Poe's 1839 short story, Corman came to this directorial assignment with a definite approach in mind. "I had a theory that Poe was working creatively as Freud would work, a little bit later, in medicine: with the concept of the unconscious mind. I felt that the unconscious mind was not aware of the outside world, only the *conscious* mind was. So I felt I should shoot everything inside a studio. And everything *was* shot inside, except for the opening sequence, where Philip [the younger male lead, played by Mark Damon] rides up to the house on horseback. I didn't want anything to look realistic in that scene. There had recently been a fire in the Hollywood Hills, so I took [cinematographer] Floyd Crosby, a camera operator, Mark and a horse to one burned-

By the late 1950s, making back-to-back cheapies for double-bill release was old hat for Roger Corman, who wanted to take a step-up in class with *House of Usher*. (Above: Corman, at left, in 1955 on the set of one of his Western shoestringers, *The Oklahoma Woman*, with actor Bob Burns.)

out area, and had Mark ride through. That gave almost a surreal look to the opening of the picture."

Corman admits that at the time when he directed *House of Usher*, he had seen very few classic fright features. "I'd seen, of course, the original *Dracula* and *Frankenstein* [both 1931]—but I don't remember *what* other horror films I might have seen." He *had* caught the period chiller *Dragonwyck* (1946) and now recalls that Price's portrayal of the sullen, aristocratic master of a spooky mansion in that production made him think of the actor for the role of the white-haired, hyper-sensitive recluse Roderick Usher. "It was interesting: Jim Nicholson and I both wanted Vincent Price," Corman says. "Often, the studio has an idea [who should star in a picture] and the producer-director has a different idea, but this was one of those times when we both had the *same* notion: Jim and I both wanted Vincent. I remember that I put a line of dialogue in, 'The house lives, the house breathes,' some such thing, for Vincent to say, because I had promised Sam Arkoff that the house would be the monster. When it came time to shoot that scene, Vincent came to me and said, 'I don't understand this line'—he didn't get it, maybe wasn't quite sure how to play it. I told him what had happened with Sam and said, 'Vincent, that's the line that let us *make* this picture.' *Now* he understood, and said, 'Okay, I can play that!'" [*Laughs*]

As for behind-the-scenes *House*-mates who also deserve a nod for the movie's quality,

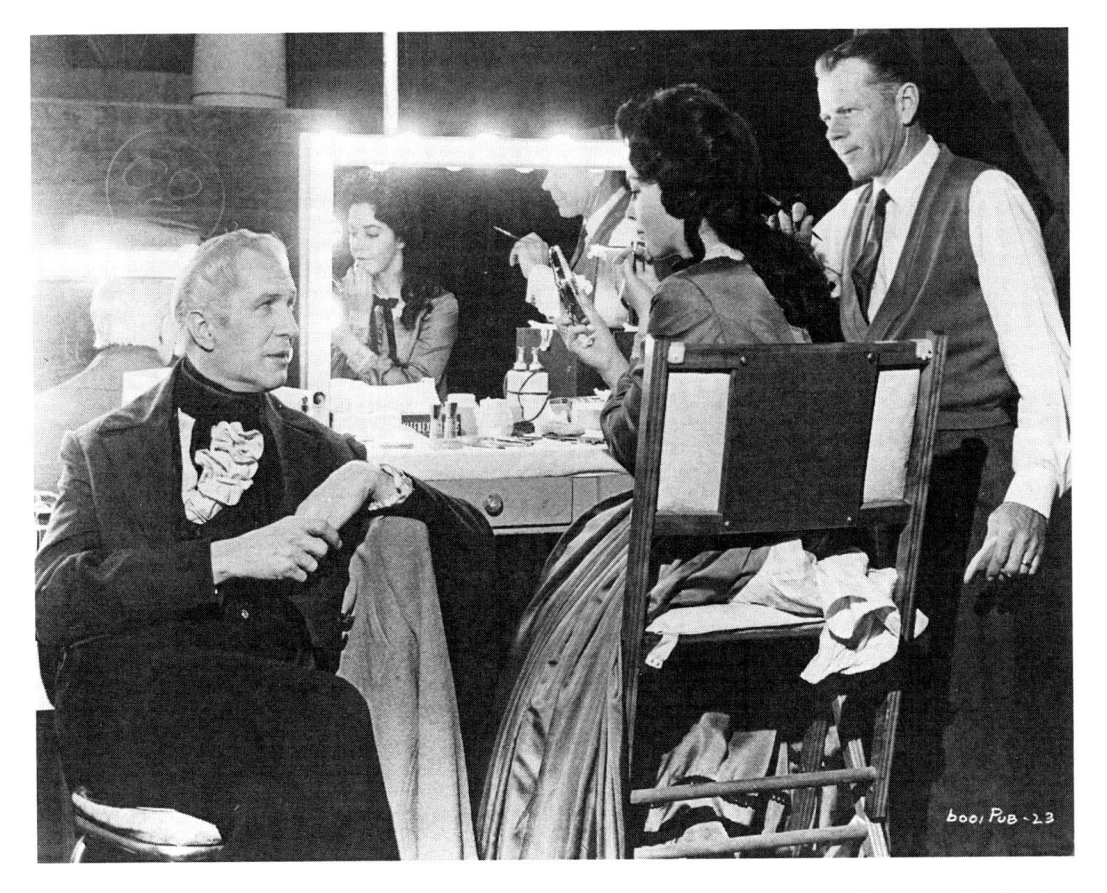

Seeing Vincent Price in the Gothic melodrama *Dragonwyck* (1946) made Corman think Price might be right for the starring role of Roderick Usher. In this behind-the-scenes shot, Price hangs with co-star Myrna Fahey and makeup man Fred Phillips.

Corman singles out three. "Number one, I would say Floyd Crosby. Floyd was unique in that he was very good and very fast. Hollywood is filled with good cameramen who work very slowly to get their effects, and with cameramen who can work rapidly—and who are not very good [*laughs*]. Floyd was the best cameraman I worked with, and I've worked with a *number* of them. He understood what I wanted, he could *give* me what I wanted and we collaborated quite well. And he also could do it rapidly. Another one who probably doesn't get enough credit would be Dan Haller, the art director. We had not much money to work with, and yet he created excellent sets. He could redo an interior—for instance, one bedroom would become another bedroom and so forth—without a great deal of money. And Les Baxter did an *exceptionally* good job on the music score."

AIP's first-ever class act, *House of Usher* had what the company called a "gala charity premiere," a June 18, 1960, Palm Springs shindig with co-stars Damon and Myrna Fahey (the death-obsessed Madeline Usher) in attendance, along with a who's who of rising stars, among them Michael Landon, Tuesday Weld, Doug McClure, Cliff Robertson, John Saxon, Dyan

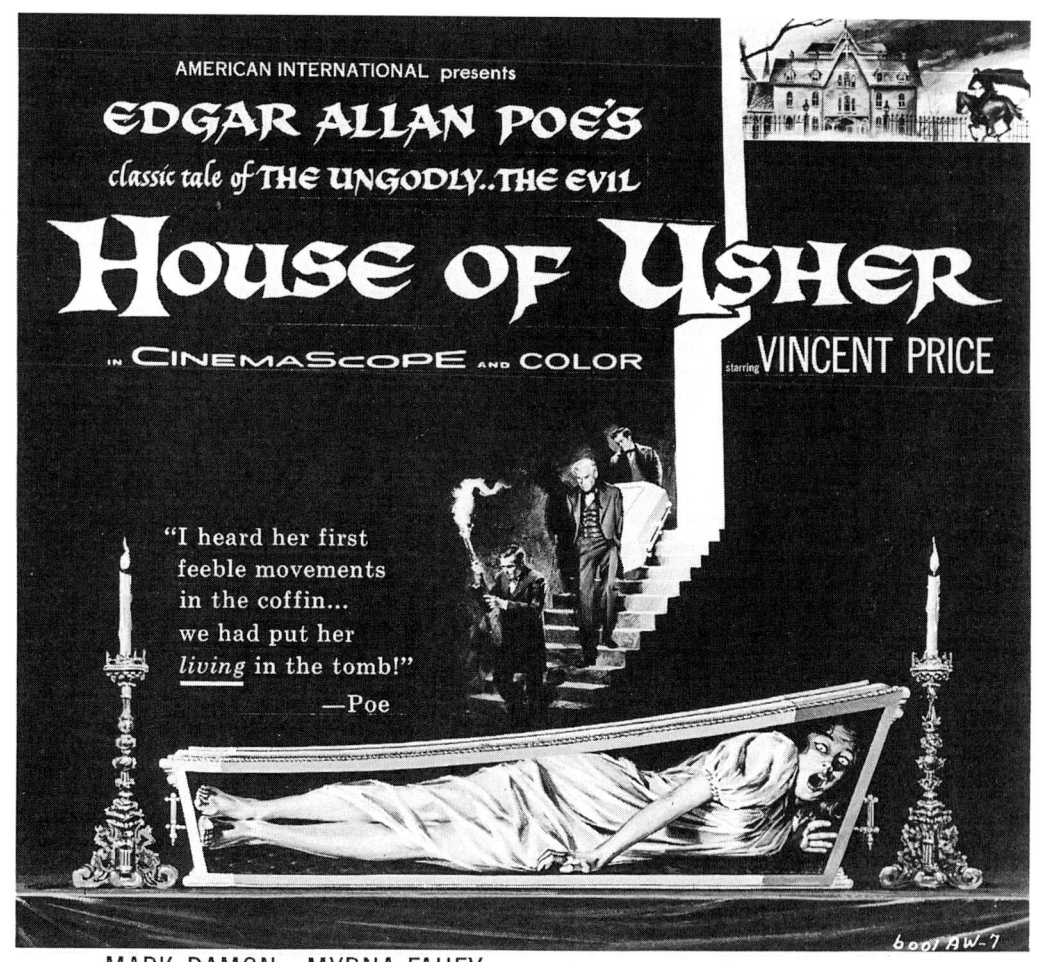

Corman calls *House of Usher* "something of a transition for American International Pictures, and an important transition for me also."

Cannon and Burt Reynolds. Reviews, both here and abroad, were peppered with adjectives ("superb," "first-rate," "fascinating," "flawless") making their debut appearance in critiques of an AIP movie. "At the time, it was the biggest-grossing picture AIP had released," Corman says of the movie that "ushered" in a new era for the company.

"When it was successful," he continues, "AIP asked me to make another film based on a Poe story, and my first thought was 'The Masque of the Red Death.' But Ingmar Bergman had made a picture just a few years earlier, *The Seventh Seal* [1957], and there were a few elements of 'Masque,' *just* a little bit, in that. I felt that if I did 'Masque of the Red Death,' I'd be accused of copying Bergman, so for the second picture I chose 'Pit and the Pendulum.' I finally *did* 'Masque of the Red Death' later on [in 1963], because I'd run out of all of the better Poe stories. I thought to myself, 'The best of the ones left is "Masque," it's now a few years later, and if somebody says I copied Bergman, I don't care, I'm gonna make it!' [*Laughs*] And, as it turned out, nobody even mentioned *The Seventh Seal.*"

It would be ungracious to ask Corman to second-guess the Library of Congress, but we do anyway: If it ends up that only one of his Poe pictures is honored and preserved by the National Film Registry, should *House of Usher* be the one? "My choice, if I had to pick just one, would have been probably one of three: *House of Usher, Pit and the Pendulum* or *The Masque of the Red Death.* Maybe *Masque.* I think they chose *House of Usher* because it was the first one, the one that started the series."

It's now (gulp) close to 50 years since the historic Corman-Nicholson-Arkoff meeting that spawned *House of Usher* and helped Corman take a big career step—and the workaholic moviemaker, whose eightieth birthday looms (April 5, 2006), may finally be finding time to smell the roses. Or rose. But probably just on the run. "I will *never* stop," he says, "but ... I *am* slowing down. I'm making fewer pictures now. We [Concorde–New Horizons] *were* making 10, 12 or more pictures a year, and we had our own DVD company. I recently made a deal with Buena Vista, which is now distributing all of my library, and is also going to distribute my new films on DVD. They've already released *Big Bad Mama* [1974], *Rock 'n' Roll High School* [1979], *Death Race 2000* [1975] and *Dinocroc* [2004], and they did well, so they're releasing four more immediately. So I've closed my DVD operation and I will make fewer films. Instead of 10–12, I'll probably make five or six films a year now."

After 50-plus hyperactive years in one of the world's most overpaid professions, and with business savvy which has insured that he "never lost a dime" (as per the title of his 1990 autobiography)—what *is* Roger Corman worth these days? "Well, I *haven't* made enough money to finance major-studio-type pictures," he says, the soon-to-be-octogenarian filmmaker still flashing that boyish grin, "'cause I don't want to blow, on any one picture, my life's savings! So let's just say I've made enough to live comfortably and to finance my own pictures—providing I don't spend too much money on them!"

Roger Corman spend too much on a picture? Nevermore!

27

Alan Young on Jack P. Pierce

A succession of mad scientists (Colin Clive, Basil Rathbone, Boris Karloff, more) brought life to the Frankenstein Monster on-screen ... but his creator in real life, off-camera, was Jack P. Pierce. Head of the makeup department at Universal, birthplace of the movie horror genre, Pierce was also the artist who devised the never-to-be-forgotten look of the Mummy, the Wolf Man and most of the rest of the studio's ghoul gallery.

In Pierce's post–Universal career, monsters remained his specialty, and even his final credit was in the fantasy category: CBS-TV's Mister Ed, *the 1960s sitcom in which the day-to-day life of architect Wilbur Post is complicated by his talking (but only to Wilbur!) horse. The actor who played Wilbur, English-born, Canadian-raised comedian Alan Young, remembers the final professional days of Jack Pierce, Hollywood's Master Monster Maker:*

I have to admit that I'd never heard of Jack Pierce before I worked with him on *Mister Ed*. It was probably Arthur Lubin, the producer-director of *Mister Ed*, who hired Jack for the show, because Arthur had worked for years at Universal, and Jack had been there too. What I liked about the little guy was that he was so devoted to his craft, so conscientious. The cute thing was that he kept all his old equipment. He had toothbrushes that he put makeup on with, that were wooden—wooden toothbrushes to apply makeup! He just liked those wooden toothbrushes!

Jack used to reminisce about the old Hollywood and what it was like, he was very willing to share his experiences. Young people on the set, some of them wouldn't listen to him. And that *hurts* a guy like Jack. But I would listen, because I was very interested in the motion picture business. And he was a great talker! He did *every*thing at the beginning [of his movie career]—that's the way it was in the teens and '20s. People did everything, stunts and ... well, you name it. Jack was very athletic, I guess, because early on he did stunts, and then he became an assistant director. When I knew him on *Mister Ed*, he didn't have much patience with assistant directors any more. They *can* be a nuisance sometimes!

Jack was a great sports fan. He loved basketball, and when he was a young man, he said, he used to coach a basketball team here in Hollywood. That was his *big* pride and joy. He was too short [to play] basketball, but he loved it and he coached it.

When I first started doing *Mister Ed*, there was a problem: I was very blond, and when I walked by the horse, my head "disappeared"! My hair and the horse were same color, almost! So they decided that Jack had to color my hair a little darker than the horse. But instead of using dye, Jack would take some brown pencils, tear them apart and melt the core down—and then he'd take this old toothbrush and work it into my hair. The only trouble was, I'd go home and go to bed, and my pillow was black in the morning! Jack was hurt when they decided they'd better just dye my hair dark—he was *very* hurt about that. But he "took" it. And when

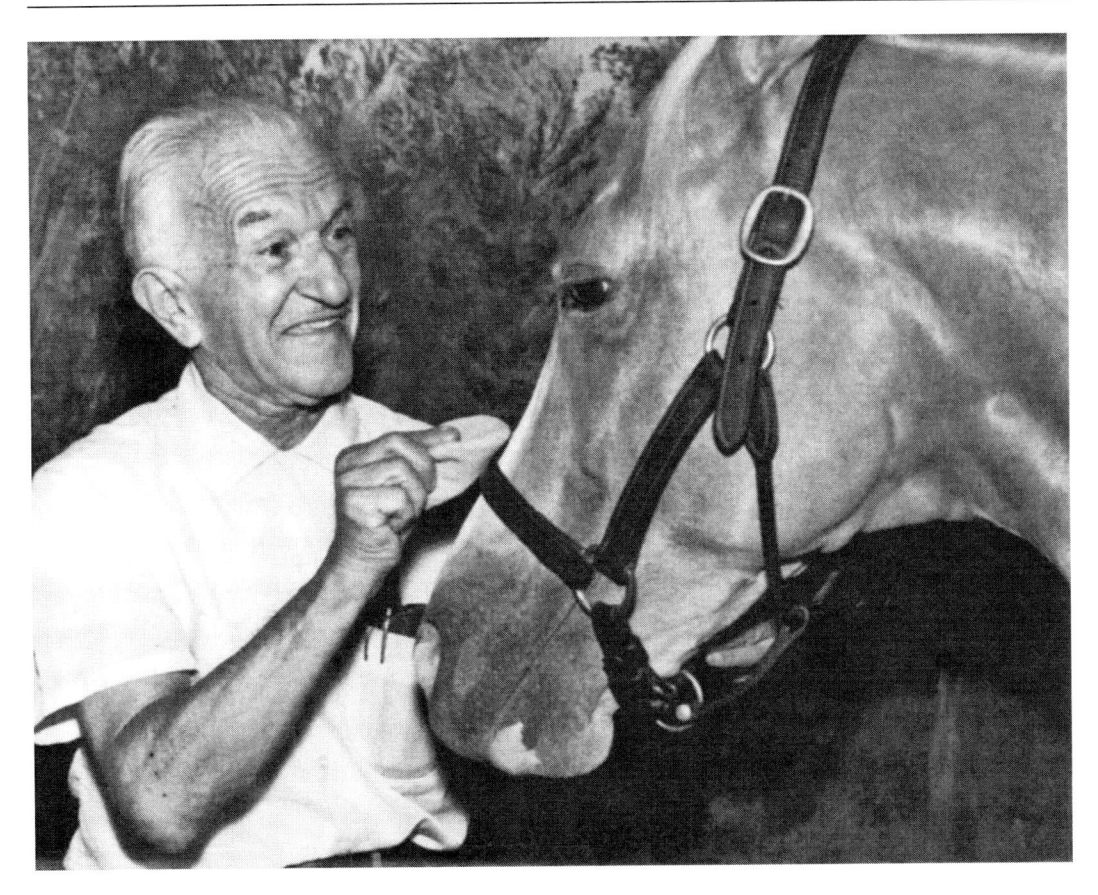

Actors, actresses, kids, talking horses—it was all in a day's work for makeup artist Jack P. Pierce, seen here powdering the nose of TV's Mister Ed.

he made me up as my own father for one episode ["Wilbur's Father"], again he used all his old equipment. The day I played my own father, I got there at six in the morning for an eight o'clock shoot. He wouldn't use gutta-percha or anything like that, he used makeup of his own making. He was fast—but meticulous, though. Some might say he took a long time.

Jack liked me and I liked him. He invited me out to his house once, *why* I don't remember ... maybe I told him I'd like to see the old stuff he had, I don't know. He had a nice little house in the Valley and he took me in and I met his wife. And when I went in the garage, it was just *full* of all his equipment. He showed me all the makeup stuff he'd used for Frankenstein and Dracula and all the different characters, all the wigs and things. The fact that monsters [were his claim to fame]—he was *proud* of that. Later, in London, I met Boris Karloff's wife, and she said, "My husband would *love* to meet you." So I went to his lovely little apartment and we had tea ... and we talked about Jack. [*Young imitates Karloff:*] "Oh, Jack, yes! Jack did lovely, creative stuff, you know...." So Karloff was very fond of Jack, too.

We shot at General Service Studios, a very lovely studio. *Ozzie and Harriet* were our neighbors. Jack would be on the set to watch things, to watch how things were going, sitting at the back. It was so cute: Near the end, he used to doze in the chair, fall asleep. *Not* all the time, but now and again. We worked long days, getting there at six in the morning and working 'til five, six at night. And Jack wasn't any kid, he was gettin' on. So if, after he fell asleep, somebody told us that our makeup needed checking, we'd just go right past him, go to the

Now "ready for his closeup," Ed joins Alan Young in a cute publicity pose.

makeup table and do our own [*laughs*]—we didn't want to wake him up! He was so independent, he'd get very annoyed when we did our own makeup without him. But he also loved us for not disturbing him, I think!

Arthur Lubin treated Jack nicely, but Lubin could get very impatient with things. But Jack understood Arthur, and would just smile at him. Jack was the only person I ever heard argue with Arthur. It made Arthur furious, the fact that Pierce would talk back [*laughs*]! But Pierce was at the age where he didn't *give* a shit, you know!

Mister Ed may have been the last thing Jack ever did; in fact, he *didn't* do the last year. They had to let him go, very gently. I forget the excuse. We all loved him, but you could tell that it was very hard on him. I was very fond of Jack—well, you *had* to be fond of him, he was a dear little man. And quite a worker, *very* serious about his business. I loved him and he talked and I listened…

28

David Whorf on Thriller's *"Pigeons from Hell" (1961)*

Thriller *has been called one of TV's top horror series and, among aficionados, the consensus seems to be that the installment "Pigeons from Hell" is the scariest of its 67 episodes. Based on the posthumously published* Weird Tales *story by Robert E. Howard, it stars Brandon deWilde and David Whorf as brothers Tim and John, whose car breaks down one gloomy midnight in a Southern swamp, forcing them to seek shelter inside an abandoned plantation house swarming with ... guarded by? ... a flight of pigeons. And "no ordinary pigeons," according to host Boris Karloff; "They were the pigeons from Hell!" That right there ought to be enough to get Blassenville Manor bumped from Triple A's "Points of Interest" list, but the night holds yet more terrors, including the death of John (his head split by a hatchet), his resurrection as a zombie, and the appearance of an undead hag (Ottola Nesmith) called a zuvembie! In his 1996 book* This Is a Thriller, *Alan Warren called the episode "television's most memorable excursion into the macabre."*

The son of actor-director Richard Whorf, "Pigeons" co-star Whorf began acting as a child, appearing in movies and TV and on the stage. He later moved behind the camera, working as a production manager and assistant director, and eventually TV director. Now "Pigeons"'s sole cast survivor, Whorf retains a few recollections of making the classic chiller...

I cannot recall exactly how I got the part in "Pigeons from Hell." I'm sure there was an interview and I did a reading, the way *every* actor does at that point. I don't have a lot of memories of "Pigeons from Hell"; in fact, re-watching it again the other day, I was surprised how little I remembered of it. For instance, I don't remember the car sequence at the beginning at all. But, gosh, that was over 45 years ago [*laughs*]—my Lord! I do, however, remember more about it than I remember about the other *Thriller* I did ["Flowers of

John (David Whorf) nervously explores Blassenville Manor in the June 6, 1961, *Thriller* "Pigeons from Hell." Whorf later began assistant-directing and production-managing, and even doing some TV directing (*Cannon, The Streets of San Francisco, Spenser: For Hire*).

243

Evil," 1962]; my memories of that are *none*! When you're starting, you get parts like, for example, an elevator boy who says "Going up?" and that's the sum total of it! I had a number of those parts and I just don't remember them.

Brandon deWilde was a nice lad and we got along fine. We weren't social friends; I was born in '34, I guess I was 27 when I did "Pigeons from Hell," so he was my junior by about

Above and following two pages: A montage of fun photos of "Pigeons from Hell"'s unforgettable zuvembie (Ottola Nesmith): striking a coquettish pose, socializing with a skeleton, and behind-the-scenes with co-stars Crahan Denton (page 246 at left) and Brandon deWilde.

eight years. As it happened, when the two of us were together I carried most of the scenes, although [in the big picture] my part was smaller. We didn't have a *lot* of shooting together, and what there *was* was pretty much walk-and-talk stuff. But I enjoyed working with him and he seemed like a nice young man, he didn't seem to have any affectations, he wasn't at all difficult in any way. It was just a very nice experience. I never worked with him again before or after.

Interiors and exteriors were all shot on the Universal lot, which is the way they did a lot of that stuff then. They had the old mansion out there and they dirtied it up a bit and "down-dressed" it with some simulated Spanish moss, trying to make it look old. It was effective, it worked. To have all those pigeons on the lawn of the mansion, they must have had a pigeon wrangler come in. How you do a scene like that is, somebody brings them in and lays the feed out and they start eating. Then I would just go out there and stand in the middle of them as quiet as I could until they settled down. To make them take off, they'd shoot a blank or something off-stage to startle 'em. I wasn't doubled in that scene, because there was no particular danger, I didn't feel I had to be doubled in a thing like that.

The mansion interiors, all the scenes set inside that place were shot on a regular soundstage. We'd go up the stairs to that second-floor landing and walk until they said *cut*, and then we'd come down the stairs and walk over to another set representing an upstairs hallway and an upstairs room.

The outstanding memory I have of the entire show is of the makeup I wore when I came back from the dead. It wasn't "stage blood," it was chocolate—Hershey chocolate. I was a little surprised! And every fly on the stage wanted to sit on my head [*laughs*]! I had to wear this stuff for at least a couple, three hours and, oh, God, I couldn't wait to wash my face and get that stuff off of me!

I worked with ["Pigeons" director] John Newland a couple of times. He was a very effete and rather *elite* kind of man, but very bright and knowledgeable about his business. He was a good director from my point of view, but he had likes and dislikes. I wasn't really aware of this so much in "Pigeons from Hell," but on some other show, he and the leading actress got into it. He couldn't *stand* her—and he wasted no time telling her so [*laughs*]! If you tried to do something [acting-wise] that you didn't talk to him about ahead of time, or if you threw in an extra word, there could be trouble. I forget what this lady had done—and I can't even recall *her* name—but I sure remember him blowing up at her. With John it was just "Stick to the script" and "Do as I *tell* you."

[*"Pigeons from Hell" has been called* Thriller's *scariest episode. Do you often have people ask you about it?*] No, this is the first time, Tom! But I'll tell you what happened when I got the part. At that time, many of the parts that I was securing were characters who *died* as a second act or even a first act climax. On a *Have Gun Will Travel* ["The Manhunter," 1958], I was shot before the first commercial! And I did a *Climax!* ["Time of the Hanging," 1958] where I played the youngest of three brothers—my brothers were William Shatner and Lee Marvin. (Think of that, Lee Marvin, William Shatner and me as brothers!) And I was hanged in that show. So after I got the part in "Pigeons from Hell" and I read the script, I went to my parents' house and told them I was going to be in a *Thriller* and I said, "Guess what? I die again—but *I come back!*" [*Laughs*] I told 'em, "My career is changing, I can *feel* it!"

29

Alex Gordon on The Underwater City *(1962)*

The road to scientific progress is fraught with unexpected perils—particularly when it leads offshore and to the floor of the ocean, as in The Underwater City. *This SF entry depicts the building of a futuristic manned complex 30 fathoms under the sea, with William Lundigan as the head construction engineer, Julie Adams as a female physician and Carl Benton Reid as the head of the project. A forward-looking subsea adventure, it was made in color and "FantaScope" and features an array of impressive low-budget effects, miniatures and ingenious dry-for-wet sets.*

Unfortunately for producer Alex Gordon, the road from script to screen to distribution was also fraught with a number of perils and pitfalls, from casting disputes to ongoing set battles with the film's alcoholic star—the whole frustrating experience eventually culminating in a lawsuit by Gordon's "Neptune Productions" against Hollywood giant Columbia Pictures! Gordon dredges up the dramatic story...

The idea for *The Underwater City* started with my wife Ruth Gordon, or "Ruth Alexander" as she called herself professionally. In an issue of *American Weekly*, she saw an article about scientists looking into the possibility of a farm type of community on the floor of the ocean. The idea was to build structures on land, tow them out to sea and lower them to the bottom, where the inhabitants would harvest the sea (fish, plant life and other edibles) to provide food for the ever-increasing number of hungry people in the world. Ruth said it might make a good movie—she was *always* finding things in the papers and coming up with ideas. We had already done *The Atomic Submarine* [1959], which dealt with bottom-of-the-ocean activity, so we thought, "Well, maybe this might be a good one to follow up with, if we can get a deal somewhere."

I went to my then-partner Orville H. Hampton, who had already written *Jet Attack* and *Submarine Seahawk* [both 1958] for me at American International, and had written *The Atomic Submarine*. He thought it was an *excellent* idea, and agreed to do an outline on speculation. At the time, my agent was Lester Salkow—he handled Vincent Price and other well-known names. When Hampton's outline was written, I gave it to Salkow and he said he'd take it to Columbia, to Irving Briskin, head of second-level productions. Salkow had an "in" with Columbia, because of Vincent Price—Salkow had made the deal for Price to be in Columbia's *The Tingler* [1959] and other films.

An appointment was made and Orville Hampton, Salkow, Salkow's "second in command" Maury Calder and I had what I thought was a very nice meeting. Briskin called himself the King of the Bs because he was in charge of the second level unit there—the Westerns and the second features. Making some small talk, I threw out all kinds of things that I knew about the early days of Columbia Pictures, because I knew that Briskin had been there since the early '30s. Later on in life, I realized that those things don't really *mean* anything to these people. They don't care about the past, just their position within the company and what they're doing *now*.

Once we got down to business, we talked budget and schedule and so on. Briskin was sounding us out and trying to figure, very roughly, what kind of budget category the picture would fall into. Finally Briskin offered two options. If I would let Columbia producer Charles Schneer produce *The Underwater City* under his banner (I would be associate producer), they would give it a budget of $650,000. If I insisted on producing it myself, then we would get a much smaller budget, 350,000. I said, "I have made about 18 pictures, American International and Allied Artists and so on, and so I certainly would like to be the producer on this." Briskin said okay. When the question of black-and-white or color came up, there was an immediate mutual agreement that it *had* to be in color, especially as there was going to be bottom-of-the-ocean activity in it.

Hampton and I formed a company called Neptune Productions to make this picture with Columbia. My salary as producer was $5000. Initially Hampton wanted to be co-producer, but I had to say, "Look, I've got solo producer credits on all my pictures. I don't mind if you're associate producer, as you were on *The Atomic Submarine*, but I don't feel I should split co-producer credit with you." He went along with that (although, ultimately, he didn't take a producer credit at all, and in fact put his pen name "Owen Harris" on the picture). He began writing the script, and when he was done, which didn't take very long, Columbia did budget the picture at $350,000. A budget of $350,000 meant that we had six days of principal photography, and then a few weeks of special effects. When they asked who I would get to do the special effects, the miniatures of the underwater city and so on, I suggested Howard Anderson and his company, because Howard had a very good reputation for such work. And, to lay it out and oversee it, Howard Lydecker, one of the top special effects men in the business. Columbia approved that.

For director, I suggested Edward L. Cahn, who had directed several of my films at AIP. Columbia agreed to Eddie, so Hampton and I went to see him at Edward Small Productions, located on the Sam Goldwyn lot. Eddie said he'd *love* to do it with us, but he had an exclusive deal for about a dozen B pictures at Edward Small and he really didn't have the time to do an outside picture. I next pitched Spencer Bennet to Columbia and they nixed him. Bennet had done many Westerns and serials, and they felt he was too identified with B product. At that point, I suggested Frank McDonald. I knew McDonald personally, he'd directed a lot of Gene Autry's Westerns—not only features but also TV episodes. He was a very nice guy and very efficient, and I knew we would have no problem with him. (And I knew he would give me no trouble on casting [*laughs*]!) We met with him and he said he'd be very pleased to do it, and Columbia approved him.

When it came to the casting session, I had to go through Max Arnow, who had been the casting director at Columbia for many years. I suggested Richard Denning, whom I had worked with on *Day the World Ended*, *Girls in Prison* and *The Oklahoma Woman* [all 1956] and who I knew would be very reliable. But Arnow rejected the idea, even though Denning had worked for Columbia not only in leads but then later in second leads, supporting people like George Montgomery and so on. By that time, they'd figured he'd done too many cheapies, and Arnow wanted somebody a little "stronger" for the lead. He soon began sending actors 'round to see me, and one of them was Glenn Corbett. Columbia had Corbett under contract and they were willing to go with him in the lead because they were trying to "build" him. I thought he was

Already the producer of the subsea action movies *Submarine Seahawk* and *The Atomic Submarine*, Alex Gordon "threepeated" with *The Underwater City*. Dry-for-wet sets were used in scenes set in Davy Jones' Locker, including the "aquaculturalists" leaving their mini-sub (*top*) and pilfering potables from a sunken ship (*above*).

capable of doing a good job, but I had to tell him, "This is my first picture for Columbia and I really *do* need a more identifiable 'name.' I'm not trying to insult you, and I'm sure that you'll go far." He said he understood perfectly.

After I turned down Corbett, and a couple of others who Arnow suggested, Arnow started throwing around crazy names like Joel McCrea and George Hamilton and a few others in that bracket. It made absolutely no sense—I even said to him, "We can't *possibly* afford these kind of names on a budget of $350,000. We've got to get somebody who's $10,000 *tops*." (Actually, I'm sure Arnow had no intention of actually trying to get those people—I think he was just grandstanding a little bit.) Finally, at a meeting, Irving Briskin said, "Well, how 'bout William Lundigan? Lundigan did that TV series *Men into Space* and he's identified with science fiction." I didn't know Lundigan personally, but I'd always thought he was all right on the screen—nothing special, but "all right"—and certainly a "medium" type of name. I said, "Okay, why don't Hampton and I have lunch with Lundigan and his agent, and see if he would be interested?" So we did, we met for lunch at the Nickodell, a hangout for the movie crowd on Melrose, just around the corner from Paramount. And, yes, Lundigan was interested and said that he would do it. I'm pretty sure his salary was less than 10,000, but then, it *was* a six-day picture.

Next it came to casting the girl. I don't know if Nancy Kovack was Max Arnow's girlfriend or not, but it seemed she was around all the time, and he had her come in. She was very nice, but I said, "She's not a *name*. Yes, she's played supporting roles in a couple of Columbia pictures, but I really think that, even though this is a low-budget picture, we need *some* sort of a name that is recognizable." *I* wanted Audrey Dalton, but she was at this time too expensive. Finally somebody mentioned Julie Adams, and as soon as they did, I said, "Oh, *yes*! If we can get her for the price, I would be *delighted* with Julie Adams." They had her come in, and she was *very*, very nice. I remember discussing with her the six pictures she did simultaneously for Ron Ormond [in 1949], six Westerns with James Ellison and Russell Hayden in which, acting under the name Betty Adams, she was the leading lady. They shot six pictures all at the same time with the identical cast! Anyway, Julie Adams agreed to do *The Underwater City*.

Now it came to casting the older scientist, and I offered it to Basil Rathbone. I didn't know him personally but I thought he would be a good choice for that role. And I got a *very, very* nice letter from Basil Rathbone, which I still have, in which he thanked me profusely for thinking of him, and said he would love to do it, but then went on to say that he was just leaving on a one-man lecture tour of colleges that would take him out of the area for three months or longer. We now began kicking other names around, and one agent said, "How 'bout Raymond Massey?" I said [*with disbelief*], "Why, you don't think Raymond Massey is going to do a *six-day picture*?" The agent said, "He's back East right now and he isn't doing *any*thing. As long as you stop for half an hour at four o'clock every afternoon and serve him tea—he's an English gentleman and likes to have his tea—he'll do it. $7500 a week." I said, "My *God*, just $7500 for *Raymond Massey*? Certainly!"—*I jumped* at it!

As for the rest of the cast, Roy Roberts [as businessman Tim Graham] was sort of a mutual agreement—I didn't care too much one way or the other. Chet Douglas [as frogman Marlow] was a young guy who used to come around *constantly* to audition. Paul Dubov [geophysical engineer Burnett], of course, was one of my "regulars." Karen Norris [Phyllis the dietitian] I didn't really know but I didn't object when they suggested her. Edward Mallory [Lt. Wally Steele] was unfamiliar to me, but he looked all right. Kathie Browne [as Steele's newlywed wife] was very sweet. She later married Darren McGavin. And, of course, I also wanted my "regular oldtimers" Edmund Cobb and Frank Lackteen in the picture, and there was no problem from Columbia about that.

Now I had my interview with the man who used to say, "You have nothing to fear but Fier himself!": Jack Fier, the production manager at Columbia. He was a tough-talking oldtimer, a John Ford type, loud and intimidating. I'd heard horror stories about him, so in order to perhaps mollify him a little bit, perhaps ingratiate myself with him, the first time I met him, I brought in a bunch of pressbooks from Mascot serials (I knew that he had in the early '30s worked on the Mascot serials). I wanted him to know that I knew his background, that I knew he had worked on those serials and he had produced the Tim McCoy films at Columbia and I said I knew Tim McCoy and so on. That sort of softened him—but only temporarily! He didn't really fall for all that, but at least he *acknowledged* it! A short time later, just a couple of days before shooting was scheduled to start, Fier had the whole crew in to give them a pep talk—like Gen. Patton would do before the Battle of the Bulge! It was right at Columbia, in one of the meeting rooms, and I would say there were about 30 of us there altogether, crew members and so on. He told everybody that they'd better shape up if they ever wanted to work at Columbia again; "If you think that the Army was rough, you haven't seen *anything* yet!"; he said that what *he* says *goes*, never mind about listening to anybody else; and, of course, "You have nothing to fear but Fier himself!"—which he said sort of jokingly. He was a tough hombre, but I guess he knew his stuff. I felt like I was back in the Army with my sergeant major!

A day or two before the picture was due to start, we had our first problem: Raymond Massey was on his way out to Hollywood from New York when there were weather problems and the plane had to be diverted to Boston. All of a sudden, it was going to take an extra day for him to get out here. Irving Briskin announced that he certainly wasn't going to shoot around Massey or change anything, and so we would have to get somebody else to play the part. And then he pushed in Carl Benton Reid. Reid was a very good actor, certainly nothing wrong with him, very nice guy—but there's a vast difference between having Raymond Massey in a picture, and Carl Benton Reid!

The second problem came on the first day of shooting. I got there a couple of hours ahead of time, and as the morning progressed, we realized we couldn't find William Lundigan—that he wasn't there! An hour later I finally found him in his dressing room, just sitting there, completely unprepared, and he had the most tremendous hangover. He hadn't read the script, he didn't know any lines, he didn't know *anything*. He said, "I'm not feeling well this morning ... I don't know whether I can do this...." I said, "Listen, you *gotta* come out...." I was absolutely *frantic*, because this was the first day of shooting—what was I going to *do*? I don't remember if I called Frank McDonald in or not, I *may* have; I know I wasn't alone in pushing him out there onto the set. Of course he still didn't know his lines, and McDonald had to feed him his lines.

And so it went throughout the picture: Lundigan was always late coming on set and always, when he stepped into the scene, he wasn't ready with his lines. He blamed it all on, "I don't know what's wrong with me ... I must have the flu..." but it was obvious he'd been drinking. We lost hour after hour when he couldn't do his stuff. It was an absolute disaster.

For scenes of the actors walking on the ocean floor, we shot on Columbia's Stage 33. It was a large soundstage, perfectly dry of course, but "dressed" to look like the bottom of the ocean. The set was impressive-looking in person, because it covered most of the stage. The camera shot through a large fish tank in which we had some very small fish swimming. To heighten the effect, there was a continuously revolving paddle in the tank, stirring the water in order to create a bit of a ripple effect. Lights were reflected off huge tinfoil flats, suspended from the stage ceiling and rolled slightly. This bathed the entire set in what looked like reflected rays of the sun, so familiar underwater. To complete the illusion, we also had the actors walking in slow motion. Between the set dressing and the tank and the fish and the reflected light and the slow-motion actors, we actually did achieve the effect that they were on the bottom of the ocean. Incidentally, some of the diving equipment that the actors wore, and a few other things on the underwater set, were supplied by Jon Hall, who by this time had retired from acting. He was now developing underwater camera equipment and renting out stock footage and so forth.

Again, however, there was trouble. I believe we began shooting these ocean floor scenes on the third day—and Lundigan refused to get into his diving outfit. As usual, he said he just wasn't up to it, he kept saying he wasn't feeling well. He even refused to come out of his dressing room. So I called for a double. And then Lundigan had the effrontery to call the Screen Actors Guild and have a representative come out to Columbia and threaten to *fine* us, because there was another actor there in his part when he, Lundigan, could and should be doing it! It was ridiculous! I told the Guild guy, "*You* get him out there. *We* can't get him out of his dressing room, he doesn't know his lines—how the hell can we shoot with him in this condition?"

"He'll be all right, he'll be all right," the Guild guy said. "You've got to use the actor if he's able to play the part...." So on the other days of shooting on the ocean floor set, we had to use Lundigan, even though it took forever to get that outfit on him. (At least when he was in that diving outfit, he didn't have any dialogue.) I don't know if the Screen Actors Guild actually did make Columbia pay a fine, but they *said* they would. I'm sure Columbia was probably very well "in" with SAG and probably worked it out some way, and it wouldn't have been a large fine in any case. But it caused a problem on the set.

There was an additional problem on the ocean floor set. The actors' air tanks produced helium-filled bubbles that rose up into the air, and the effect was marvelous. The problem, the thing that nobody anticipated was that they would then come back *down* again! We had bubbles coming out of these tanks, and it looked very realistic, but then as the scene continued, suddenly you saw the bubbles dropping down again, and everybody was saying, "What the hell is *that*?" We had to put men up in the rafters of the soundstage with fans to blow the bubbles away before they could come back down into the scene. That took us a little while to solve, but it turned out all right.

We shot some exteriors at the Columbia Ranch—that was where Eddie Cobb and Frank Lackteen were going to shoot their scenes. But that morning, when I went to pick up Frank Lackteen at his little one-room place in Hollywood and drive him to the Columbia Ranch, he was in bed, shivering, and he said he was sick and that he couldn't do it. I realized that there wasn't really anything wrong with him, that it was stage fright—he just felt he couldn't do it. He said, "I'm really ill, I'm in such a bad way. I don't even have my rent...," which was $125. I said, "Frank, let me take care of that," and I wrote him a check for $125. Then I said, "Obviously you *need* the 250 that we can pay you, so get in the car. I'll drive you there, you don't have to work, you certainly don't have any lines, you don't have to even step in front of the *camera* if you don't want to. I can 'cover' that. But you've got to come to the lot, you've got to sign in. Then I can pay you the 250 bucks for a day's work. If you don't come out there at *all*, then you can't get paid." That was the way I persuaded him, and he came along with me. And once he was out there, he was okay. But at first he wasn't going to do it, he was suffering from such stage fright. It was a strange situation!

But even stranger was the fact that we had a second assistant director who, all he did was report to the front office. Jack Fier never came on the set but he had this second assistant director reporting to him every hour whether we were behind schedule or if there was a problem and this and that and so on. That was very, very awkward, a tough situation to *be* in. It was like a police state, everybody was watching us all the time! But before everything started going downhill, with Lundigan and with this second assistant director and all, I *loved* being at Columbia. Every day I looked out of the window of my office, overlooking the Columbia lot, and it was amazing to me: "Here I am in an office at Columbia, producing a picture!" And, another nice experience: The Three Stooges were shooting on the set next to us, so it gave me an opportunity to meet Moe Howard. Larry Fine I just sort of said hello to; he was always off to Vegas, gambling and so on. But Moe I talked to almost every day. Actually, *he* came on *our* set and he wanted to know what we were doing. I was absolutely dumbfounded: Here I'm standing, talking to somebody who *looks* like Moe, and yet he *talks* like the most creative kind of producer-writer-all-around-filmmaker. Obviously I knew that he wasn't going to be like he was in his movies, but I also didn't expect *this*. If you closed your eyes, you'd think you were talking to any one of the Hollywood big shots. It was very, very impressive, the way he knew the business inside out. He was a remarkable person.

Instead of going six days, *Underwater City* went seven, a day over schedule, which everybody was very unhappy about. It was Lundigan who caused the delay—nobody else held us up in any way. Well, we *did* have that little problem with the bubbles, but we solved that very quickly. So that alone would not have caused it, it was strictly Lundigan. With him refusing to come out of his dressing room and never knowing his lines, we just kept getting behind and behind and behind; I remember Frank McDonald going out of his mind. Lundigan was responsible, completely responsible, for the delay and the extra day. It was nothing but a hassle with him.

Now it was time for the special effects guys to start shooting the effects footage. We'd made a deal with Howard Anderson and Co. to do the special effects *under* Howard Lydecker's supervision. Lydecker was absolutely great. He did the special effects on most Republic pictures, everything from *S.O.S. Tidal Wave* [1939] to serials and Westerns, he and his brother Theodore. Howard had the whole layout, every shot storyboarded—there was a completely detailed storyboard, down to the tiniest thing, in his office at Columbia, which was next to mine. He knew exactly what he was going to do all along the way.

Actor Frank Lackteen was busy in films right from silent days, so Gordon (pictured here with Lackteen on the set of 1957's *Flesh and the Spur*) was surprised when the actor got heap-big nervous about taking the *Underwater City* plunge.

I don't remember how long the post-production special effects took—maybe about six weeks. Not awfully long, but certainly longer than the principal photography on the picture! The destruction of the underwater city and the scenes of the octopus and the giant eel, those were shot by Howard Anderson in a tank in Santa Monica. The octopus and the eel, they didn't hurt each other in their fight scene, they just sort of swam against each other and so on, but neither one was hurt. (The octopus stuff was not all that exciting, but at least it was *there*!) I wasn't there for the shooting of any of that, but I *was* on the set every minute at the studio and at the Columbia Ranch.

Ronald Stein did the music score for *The Underwater City*. I remember I had to put up a little bit of a fight for him, but I'm glad I did. Briskin said, "Look, we've got George Duning here at Columbia, he's our music director. Why not use *him*?" I said, "It would be very expensive to do it the way Duning would do it, with a big orchestra and 'scoring to picture'* and so on. Ronnie Stein does it with*out* 'scoring to picture.' He looks at the movie on a Moviola and he times every sequence where he will write music, and then he goes away and he does it all. He doesn't have to 'score to picture.'" I won Briskin over that way, I said, "We just don't have the budget," and he gave in. Briskin insisted, though, that we use a studio orchestra; Ronnie couldn't go down to Mexico or anywhere else on *The Underwater City*, Columbia being a signatory to the guilds and all that. So Ronnie Stein conducted the studio orchestra.

When we finally got to the end of the picture, I thought it wasn't bad. Briskin looked at the rough cut and made some comments, I forget now what they were, but nothing disparag-

Mission accomplished: The establishment of Amphibia City is celebrated on the sea floor— which will soon open up and swallow it!

"Scoring to picture": The orchestra performs while the scene for which that piece of music was written is projected on a screen behind them.

ing. He thought it was all right for a co-feature. Columbia was going to put it out with *The Three Stooges Meet Hercules* [1962]—*Hercules* was supposed to be the companion picture, because it was in black-and-white, and *Underwater City* was supposed to be the top of the bill. Or at least equal-billed. Anyway, we had *Underwater City* all done and Irving Briskin approved it, and now it was supposed to be shown to Sam Briskin, Irving's brother, who was head of production on a higher level there.

The screening for Sam Briskin was an absolute disaster. Irving was not present, it was just Sam and me in the Columbia executive screening room. He blew his top: "We can't release the picture this way! It doesn't have enough action, it doesn't have *this*, it doesn't have *that*. It needs all *kinds* of things." And he told me, "Put together about ten minutes of stock shots from other pictures, real disaster footage and creatures and all that sort of thing, and we'll put that on at the front of the picture, or work it in *some*where with some narration over it. Maybe *then* we can release the picture." When I came away from that encounter, of course, I could hardly *walk*! Here Irving had *approved* it, and Sam said it was unreleasable!

It took me about a week to scour every stock shot library in town. I borrowed everything from Cecil B. DeMille's *Reap the Wild Wind* [1942] on down, and I got a *terrific* ten-minute reel of action and ships being crushed and just *everything*—it was absolutely great. And Sam Briskin told me, "Well, we'll let you know about this...."

That was on a Friday. And the following Monday, I found out that *The Underwater City* was already *playing*, I forget where, *some*where on the West Coast—and *in black-and-white*! Here I'd been working on this reel of action for a week or longer, of course getting all color footage, and then I come to find out it's already playing and it's playing in black-and-white! (And I had a *contract* that specified that it would be in color.) It had opened somewhere solo, and then went out as the second feature to *The Three Stooges Meet Hercules* instead of the other way around!

I went to see it in a theater and sure enough it was in black-and-white. It looked completely washed-out in black-and-white because (naturally) the underwater stuff had been shot as though for color, and timed for color. When you see *that* in black-and-white, it's just like running off a black-and-white print of a color picture. In the bottom-of-the-ocean scenes, you couldn't see the bubbles, you couldn't see *any*thing distinctly—there was no real contrast. Hampton went by himself and saw it too. That's when we decided we would sue. The picture's box office potential had obviously been damaged, you could tell that from the bookings that it got. The bookings it *didn't* get, I should say!

I got in touch with my lawyer Irwin Spiegel, and we tried to get Columbia to give us an explanation. Well, they said, they didn't want to spend the money on color prints, this and that, so on and so forth. Anyway, the end result was that we had to sue them—I wasn't going to stand for *this*. So Neptune Productions sued Columbia, and the thing dragged on for about five years. Then Spiegel lost interest because he was working on spec, and eventually the statute of limitations simply ran out. By then, of course, I'd started getting reports on the picture, and we were deeper in the hole every time a report came in. Finally Columbia just stopped sending reports altogether, they told us it really wasn't worth it because no money was coming in on it. So that's how that situation ended.

Needless to say, Columbia didn't pick up my option. I had a six-picture deal, but they cancelled that. So I was *out* of Columbia, and that was the end of the saga of *The Underwater City*. I was glad that eventually it began playing on TV in color, and if it ever comes out on home video, I hope it will be in color. Naturally I want my stuff to be seen in the best possible light.

Gordon poses with posters for his aquatic action-adventures *The Underwater City* and *The Atomic Submarine*. He died in 2003, his screenwriter wife Ruth in 2006.

It's not one of my favorites amongst my movies, it's way down on the list. Hampton, Salkow and I hoped for much more, and we hoped we might get a multiple picture deal out of it. We thought this might help us get into a slightly higher bracket. With all the problems that we had, and the end results, it was a very disappointing experience. But we had embarked on it with the best of intentions. I still remember how *very* excited my wife Ruth was when she saw the article about the underwater farm community. Which is a notion that keeps popping up, it's never a dead issue for long. In fact, just last week [May 2002] it was on the radio—somebody in the House or Senate brought it up, they were talking about trying to figure out how they could farm the ocean floor, to alleviate world hunger. It's definitely an ongoing thing in the various think tanks, but I guess they haven't yet figured out how to do it properly, and "at a price." We've always thought that this is one idea that should certainly be followed up and investigated.

30

Arch Hall, Jr., on Ray Dennis Steckler

(The following reminiscence appeared on Fangoria *magazine's website on Friday, January 9, 2009, two days after the passing of Steckler.)*

Ray Dennis Steckler, the maverick producer-director-writer-actor-cinematographer(-and-and-and) who created such cult flicks as The Incredibly Strange Creatures Who Stopped Living and Became Mixed-Up Zombies!!? *(1964) and* The Thrill Killers *(1964), died Wednesday night at age 70.*

At the beginning of his nearly half-century career, the rebel moviemaker was a fixture at Fairway International, the Burbank-based indie film company established by Arch Hall, Sr.; Steckler began as a camera assistant on Fairway's caveman-loose-in-Palm Springs campfest Eegah *(1962) and then directed their next feature* Wild Guitar *that same year. Using his frequent nom de screen Cash Flagg, he also co-starred in the latter as the thuggish henchman of a record company executive (Hall, Sr.).*

The star of Eegah *and* Wild Guitar, *Arch Hall, Jr., knew Steckler from Fairway days until his final (November 14, 2008) public appearance at a special Los Angeles County Museum of Art screening of* No Subtitles Necessary: Laszlo & Vilmos, *a documentary about Fairway cameramen-turned-world-class cinematographers Vilmos Zsigmond and the late Laszlo Kovacs.*

I first met Ray at Fairway Studio in Burbank, when he was associated with some of the films that I was involved with. Ray was capable of doing almost *anything*—coming up with story ideas, working as a director, working as a camera operator, a cinematographer—and he had the respect of people who were good at each one of those skills. So I would say he was a genius. In the late '50s when he was in the Army Pictorial Corps, he had gotten into movie cameras, and I think that's where he got the spark of "I'm gonna be in the movies."

I met him through Fairway International Films and got to know him slowly, working with him first on *Eegah*. I didn't know him too much then and didn't really see his talents; on *Eegah* he was more or less backing-up Vilmos Zsigmond as an assistant cameraman as well as other capacities. He was well-liked by everyone. But he was the director of the next film after that, *Wild Guitar*—that was his first time directing a film. He was probably 23, 24, and as a director he was intense! He definitely had a style of his own. When he and I did the fight scene, it was like two or three in the morning (when working on a Fairway film, it *always* was two or three in the morning, it seemed like!), and we were tired. We kind of choreographed the fight, blocked it out several times and figured out how we were going to do it. Then when they actually rolled the film and we did it, I misjudged distance and I actually hit Ray. I mean, I hit him *hard*—I knocked his teeth out. Some were broken back out of position and some came out of his mouth. Well, Ray got Vilmos to paint a piece of Styrofoam white like teeth and he used duct tape to keep it in place in his mouth, and we kept on shooting, in order not to lose time and to stay on schedule. *That's* how hardcore Ray Dennis Steckler could be. He was not a candy ass at all, he was *tough*. Ray was somethin' else.

My dad and Ray may have not always seen eye to eye. They were different generations and of course my dad was always looking at the clock and thinking practically while Ray would get off on these creative tangents. Ray had such a colorful imagination—look at the titles of some of the things he came up with! You just read the list of titles and you can see what a vivid imagination he had. And he would coin things like "Shot in Hallucinogenic Hypno-Vision" [*laughs*]—just crazy stuff! My dad had a vivid imagination too, but when you've got two real Type-A Alpha dogs in the same area, there are going to be sparks once in a while. It was never anything of any magnitude, it was just differences of opinion on the details, because my dad had great respect for Ray and knew he was a talented guy. My dad called upon Ray's genius imagination often on a variety of issues across the board. Ray was such a "Swiss army knife–type person" to have around because he could pick up *any*thing and figure out a way to fix it and make it work, especially when it came to cameras.

Of course, one of the films that he's most famous for is *The Incredibly Strange Creatures Who Stopped Living and Became Mixed-Up Zombies!!?* and that's one that kind of "describes" Ray Dennis Steckler's ability to come at you from all points of the compass! Whatever genre you could name, horror, crime, comedy, he could do it. He even got into the subterranean-budget "adult movie" thing in the '80s which he didn't really brag too much about but he wasn't ashamed of it either. He could do *any*thing, and worked with some of the best people in the business. Early on, he did a lot of music videos too: He worked with Jimi Hendrix, he worked with Janis Joplin, worked with Frank Zappa ... Alan O'Day ... even with Arch Hall, Jr. [*laughs*]!

I'm so glad I was able to see Ray in November. Ray called me and said, "Hey, you gotta come out to L.A. this month. On the 14th, they're screening *No Subtitles Necessary* at the L.A. County Art Museum." I said, "I *think* I'd like to do it but I dunno, Ray, let me think about it a couple days." So I thought about it and, to be perfectly honest, it was gonna be tough to get away from home, it was an expense to go out there, and I made up my mind that I was going to say no and apologize and tell him to enjoy it without me. But then I had a dream about my father, and in the dream he told me I *must* go to Los Angeles. No kidding! So I took off for L.A. and met Ray and his wife Katherine and daughter Laura, who had driven down from Las Vegas where they live. When we met in the lobby of the hotel where we were all staying, I told Ray about the dream, and he put his arms around me and gave me a hug.

When we went to the screening, it was a big shindig, a lot of A-list people; we saw Vilmos outside and we all started talking, me and Vilmos and Ray and [Fairway acting veteran] Burr Middleton. Ray got sidetracked, several people got him talking, and while this was going on, Vilmos told me, "After the screening, there's going to be a panel discussion and Ray is going to be up there participating." I thought that was great. They screened the documentary, and excerpts from *Wild Guitar* and *Incredibly Strange Creatures* were featured in it. When it was over, there was the panel—the director of the documentary James Chressanthis and Vilmos and the producer and Peter Fonda. And there was a chair for Ray—I'm *sure* it was for Ray, after what Vilmos told me—but no one told Ray! *Now* it kind of pisses me off to think about it, because after a while the panel began to drag on and got not-so-interesting. Fonda went on and on and on and the audience was chuckling courteously but ... I think it was kind of boring them! Finally towards the very end of it, Vilmos asked if Ray was in the audience and

In one of his early flicks, the kooky *Lemon Grove Kids Meet the Monsters* (1965), "Cash Flagg" (Steckler's *nom de screen*) runs afoul of the Mad Mummy (Bob Burns).

would he please stand up and identify himself, which he did. Of course people applauded, and that made me feel really good. And Ray began to participate in the panel from the aisle, with a wireless hand mike.

You have to understand how ill the man was. Cardiac-related things ... he was very weak. He probably should have not come to Los Angeles, but he did. But Ray got up and in a booming voice—they didn't even give him a microphone at first!—he was talking to the audience with a terrific volume and was *very* entertaining, and told a couple of anecdotes. He said, "Do you remember, Vilmos, the night we were in Hollywood about 3:30 in the morning shooting *Wild Guitar*, and some union goons came down?" Vilmos was outside changing film magazines in the Arriflex when these goons showed up and said, "Give us the film." Vilmos kept on working, fidgeting inside the black bag changing film, showing no sign of being intimidated. The union guys made some bodily threats, "We're gonna bust somebody up tonight, and why don't we start with *you* guys?," and they started pushing and shoving, roughing Ray and Vilmos up a little bit. So Ray turned to Vilmos and said, "Hey, Willie, just give 'em the damn film. It's not worth getting knifed over!" So Vilmos said, "Well ... okay..." and he pulled 200 feet of film out of the bag and gave it to 'em, and these guys snickered and spat on the ground and turned around and walked away. And after they walked away, Vilmos winked at

In his later years, low- and *no*-budget moviemaker Steckler (1938–2009), at right, ran a Las Vegas video store. At his last public appearance (a November 2008 screening of *No Subtitles Necessary: Laszlo & Vilmos* at the Los Angeles County Museum of Art), he posed for a picture with old pal Arch Hall, Jr.

Ray: Vilmos had given 'em the brand-new, unused film that he was about to *load* into the camera, not the film that they had just shot [*laughs*]! You don't survive the hell of the 1956 Hungarian revolution the way Vilmos did, by being easily intimidated! Of course Vilmos remembered that incident and he was laughing about it, this man who is at the top of his game, an Academy Award recipient whose career is not slowing down. After Ray shared that story with Vilmos and the audience, he carried on in great style and got many laughs and applause. [*TW: Sounds like he "saved" that part of the evening!*] This was a *very* savvy audience and, yes, it was a very good night. Vilmos and Ray had a great love and respect for one another and it was very evident to everyone who saw them together that night.

After the screening, a group of us went to Canters Delicatessen on Fairfax and we spent a couple hours visiting and reminiscing. It was such a wonderful experience. Even in his failing health, Ray still had dreams of going on to do other things. But—I didn't know this 'til later—but at five or six A.M. the next morning while I was already on my way to the airport to go home, Ray took a turn for the worse and he was taken to a hospital in Torrance where he spent about four days. When he got well enough to travel, they drove back to Las Vegas, and he was home no more than a day or so before he was back in a hospital again. I happened to call not knowing this and his wife answered his cell, and she was in the emergency room or the intensive care area as they were booking him in there. I heard Ray in the background, "Who is it, honey?" and when she said, "It's Arch," he said, "Oh, let me talk to him." She handed the phone to Ray and he asked me how it was going, and I said, "I don't want you to get tired talking. Is it okay with the doctors if you talk?" He said, "Don't worry about that. Oh, and I apologize, I wanted to send you a poster, remember I talked about that?" "*Ray!*" I said, "Relax! Take it easy!" But that was Ray: He was super-intense and focused all the time!

Ray loved the business, he loved films, and the fact that excerpts from *Incredibly Strange Creatures* actually played at the Cannes Film Festival [as part of *No Subtitles Necessary*] pleased him to no end. He may have never achieved the mainstream status of a very famous producer or director or anything like that, other than his high cult status, but as far as his intellect and his wit and his understanding of the business, be it in front of or behind the camera, he really *knew it all*. His career spans so many different genres, so many different periods, and at so many different levels, and he made a living at it, and had fun being part of the industry no matter *how* crazy and obscure things would be. As far as cult films and everything, I don't think it's *possible* to get much more far-out than Ray's imagination. And don't forget, above it all, he was a devoted family man, husband, father, and a man of great character. That's why I feel so privileged to have worked with him and to have known Ray Dennis Steckler.

31

Arnold Drake on 50,000 B.C. (Before Clothing) *(1963)*

After 20 years of writing about veteran science fiction filmmakers (and living my entire life with these cockamamie movies), it occurred to me about halfway through watching Image Entertainment's recently released DVD of the "nudie cutie"–comedy 50,000 B.C. (Before Clothing) *that I was perhaps seeing one of the most bizarre old movies I was ever* likely *to see. The scene which caused this thought to cross my mind: A feeble-minded twentieth-century schnook (played by an seedy-looking older actor obviously at death's door) staggers around a prehistoric land of topless cave girls, doing burlesque comedy routines, wearing a tuxedo and a stovepipe hat which just happens to explode any time he whistles "Dixie." And* this *is the movie at one of its more lucid moments!*

The man with the, shall we say unique *imagination who dreamt up this underdressed exercise in Stone Age sci-fi-comedy delirium was Arnold Drake, the New York–born comic book legend behind the classic titles* Challengers of the Unknown, Deadman *and* The Doom Patrol *(and the writer and co-producer of the no-holds-barred SF shocker* The Flesh Eaters *[1964] with Martin Kosleck). In this interview, Drake looks back 50,000 years-plus and explains his involvement with what he maintains is "one of the worst 'comedies' ever filmed."*

I met Herbert Lannard, the producer of *50,000 B.C.*, through Jack Curtis, the director of *The Flesh Eaters*. Jack began his career as an actor and he had a great voice, and he had done some voiceovers for Herb. Herb lived in New York, on the West Side, and he was in the "vanity production" business. What he did was, he would go to some self-made character and tell him, "I want to make a documentary about you and your marvelous company and how you climbed the ladder of success. The only thing that prevents me from doing it is ... I don't have enough money." [*Laughs*] This schmuck of a businessman would then say, "Well ... okay ... yeah ... we could use that for promotion. But—how do I know that anybody'll ever *see* it?" But Lennard would guarantee it. And the reason he could guarantee it was, this was in a time, the early '60s, when television stations didn't have enough material and couldn't afford to buy much material. Whatever they got, they got as cheaply as they could *get* it. Well, Lannard could give his vanity productions to them for *nothing*, 'cause he was paid in front by the guys whose egos were bankrolling the whole scheme. The productions were less than shoestring, but some of them actually appeared on TV because the stations were hungry for cheap product to fill their schedules. And Lannard's was the cheapest: zero. The guys at the TV stations knew he needed their air time as much as they needed his product, rotten as it was. One hand washed the other, but neither one got very clean.

Anyway, Herb was doing that kind of junk, and along the way convinced himself that he could make movies. "What the hell ... I've done it, and I even got it to market." He didn't get *paid* for it [by the TV stations], but he *did* get it to market! He convinced himself, therefore, that he was a moviemaker. And what was the easiest film market to get into? Softcore porn! So he decided he wanted to make a softcore flick. He even had a piece of a story idea: A burlesque comic is forced, by his termagant of a wife, to leave the biz for a job with the Department of Sanitation. Somehow or other he escapes from his miserable life into the far past. Herb also came up with the title, which at first was *20,000 B.C.* It took him so long to put the whole thing together that it went from being *20,000 B.C.* to *50,000 B.C.* [*laughs*]!

Herb told me he had this idea, but he said, "I don't know how we're gonna get [the burlesque comic] *back* there, back in time." I said, "Let me worry about that, Herb. I'm a science fiction specialist, I've written a couple of thousand science fiction stories." So I created the character of a taxi driver who's really a crazy inventor. He uses the taxi as a front for his activities, but the taxi is actually a time machine. It's in this guy's time machine that the burlesque comic goes back to 50,000 B.C.

Herb went to see [stripper] Ann Corio, who was then doing one of her final tours. Like Sarah Bernhardt, who I believe did "final tours" for about 15 years, Ann Corio I think did that for a couple of years as well. In the show, which was at a theater on Second Avenue between 13th and 14th Streets, Ann Corio's top banana was a burlesque comedian named Charlie Robinson. My guess is that Herb initially went to that theater to try and find some women he could use in his flick; if a woman's going to do a burlesque show, then it's probably not too hard to convince her to do a topless flick! But while he was there, he saw doddering Charlie Robinson and he must have said to himself, "How much can a guy like that *cost* me these days? There aren't too many people knockin' on his door, I'm sure." So he decided he was gonna buy the old guy cheap.

When Herb told me *that*, and I realized that Charlie *was* getting on in years, I came up with the notion that [in the twentieth century scenes] Charlie does all of these famous burlesque routines. And when he goes back to prehistoric times, he lands in a place where the people *live* like they are in a burlesque sketch. It's their *reality*—their reality is like a burlesque sketch. So my idea was to do three burlesque sketches up front [in the twentieth century scenes] just as they *were* done in the old days, and *then* go back in time and treat them as reality—"caveman reality." The principal reason for this was to take advantage of the fact that Charlie had been doing these for 30 or 40 years, and therefore he could wing them. I thought that was important, considering Charlie's age. So that's probably the most significant contribution I made to the storyline, my idea of the parallel worlds, the "make-believe" of burlesque and the reality of the caveman. The trouble was, I don't think Herb ever understood that I wanted to do [the modern-day burlesque routine scenes] *as* Charlie would have done them right on the stage. If I had my way, we'd have gone into that 14th Theater and shot them right there, *on* the stage, with Charlie doing the old routines. Herb instead kind of integrated them into Charlie's life, which means there was no contrast between the burlesque sketch and the "reality" of the caveman life. I don't think Herb "got" that. I don't want to watch the film closely enough to figure out exactly where he fell off the trolley [*laughs*], but somewhere along the way he forgot what the hell I was trying to do.

[*How did you know these burlesque routines? Did you grow up seeing burlesque shows?*] Not really, because by the time I was old enough to legitimately attend one of those, Fiorello LaGuardia had banned them from New York City. So the only way I was able to see them was by crossing the Hudson over to Newark, and lots of people did; the Newark burlesque theaters were full of boys from Manhattan, Brooklyn and the Bronx. I did that twice. But I was very *aware* of burlesque comedy. Remember that Red Skelton came from burlesque. Abbott and Costello came from there. "Rags" Ragland came from there. So from seeing *them* [in movies and on TV], I knew the standard routines from their movies and TV shows. By censoring them a little bit here and there, these comedians had been able to get them into the movies and TV shows.

The "director" of *50,000 B.C.* was a guy named Werner Rose, a guy who could not direct traffic on a one-way street at midnight. Rose had built his own studio in New Jersey. He did *every*thing in his studio, and I use the word "studio" very loosely; it was a phone booth with delusions of grandeur. He cut the lumber, he painted the sets, he applied cosmetics, he did everything. I suppose it was the only way that he could make a living, because he was not a very good filmmaker. At the time, he was making very low-cost TV commercials. I would assume that Herb learned about him in the process of making those vanity films of his, and decided this was the right guy to do the job [direct *50,000 B.C.*]. This guy would do it reeeally cheaply.

They started to work out in New Jersey. I was busy on something else at the time, so I could only make one trip to the set. I think I probably would have gone a number of times *if* what I had seen had engaged me in any way. But what I saw turned my stomach. It was at this point that I said, "The script can't be *that* bad." I'd written it in a week—maybe a bit *less* than a week—but, nevertheless, I felt that it just couldn't be that bad. So I asked Herb to let me direct one of the scenes. I don't remember exactly what I did, I think I did a scene in the cave, when the king of the cave people is talking to Charlie. It took me about two hours. Of course, Rose would have shot *four* scenes in two hours. But at the end of the two hours, I was satisfied that that particular scene was pretty funny, and that therefore the entire script *might* have worked if somebody had taken the time and the talent to make it work. That was the point at which I left the New Jersey studio and decided I didn't want to work with Herb any more— despite the fact that I was already *into* writing a second film for him. I had begun a straight thriller-kind of film about three women convicts who escape jail, one of them pregnant. It seemed like it might make an interesting story. I stopped in the middle of it and told Herb I didn't want to do business any longer. I said something like, "You paid me very poorly [for the *50,000 B.C.* screenplay] but I did it because I thought that it would be a worthwhile experience. Having seen what you're doing with my work, I don't consider it to be a worthwhile experience. So I'm being underpaid for a bad experience!" I don't think he was too happy about it. He *had*, incidentally, paid me a small advance on the second film, which I never returned because my final payment for the *50,000 B.C.* script never arrived. So that sort of made us even.

Herb appears in the film briefly, in a scene based on the burlesque sketch "Niagara Falls." The basic "Niagara Falls" plot is, a guy has just gotten married, he's dying to get into bed with his wife, but there's always *some*body knocking on his door, interrupting him. Every time he tries to take his pants off, there's another knock on the door. That's the basic "tension" of that sketch. In the movie, three or four guys knock on the door, interrupting Charlie when he's about to get into bed on his honeymoon, and Herb is one of them, the one selling insurance. He's of medium height, he's overweight, and with an almost cherubic face—which really *is* demeaning angels [*laughs*]!

Charlie Robinson was all right in the film. I wish we could have caught Charlie ten years earlier, but he was okay. Between takes, he was pretty quiet. I think he was saving his energy. He didn't have a hell of a lot of it, and I think he was saving himself for the production. To me he appeared to be a man who was dying—literally. I don't know anything more about Charlie. I don't think he lasted much longer, he was not in good shape. The guy who played the king was okay, he was kind of amusing. On the set, I could see that there *was* potential with the guy, and that was the reason I wanted to do *that* scene. Nobody else sticks in my head. Most of the women were ... one shade this side of ugly [*laughs*]! It'd take a *lot* of Viagra to go with one of *those*!

They did a lot of stuff *ex tempore*. A *lot*. There are chunks in there that I don't recognize at all. Of course, time will *do* that; there are an awful lot of comic book stories I've written that I forgot I wrote. I get fans calling me and mentioning a story, and I'll say, "I have to be frank with you, I don't remember it." So I may have forgotten large chunks of the script. I may have *wanted* to forget large chunks of the script! The stuff they did extemporaneously in *50,000 B.C.*, I didn't mind it in the case of Charlie 'cause Charlie had been doing that all his life. But there's a scene where the mad inventor is introduced, and he goes on and on and on. It's dreadful. I think part of the reason for that was that Herb was concerned about having enough footage; he wanted to be sure he had at least 65 or 70 minutes or whatever. So I think he *let* the actor go on that way, in part because he was filling up the footage that he needed. [*If I were to walk onto the set or the location at any given moment, how many people would I be likely to see working behind the camera?*] Two. Maybe.

Seeing this new DVD of the film was, I think, the first time I ever saw it. It's about as bad as I thought it would be. I knew the core plot was wild, so I threw [into the script] as many crazy sight gags as I could. Portions of what I wrote were surreal. But there has to be some kind of consistency even to surreal comedy. There is none in this film. Yes, I had things popping in from out of nowhere for comic effect. But Herb had them doing that for *no* effect. When that begins to happen, you've lost your audience completely.

I have no idea if the film was successful or not. I think Herb may have been "late"; I think, when he did it, the big change in softcore porn was taking place, and it was beginning to be not just topless but bottomless as well. I think, therefore, he may have missed the boat. If he'd done it a year or two earlier, he might have made a pretty good dollar.

I've since lost track of Herb Lannard. He's still around; within the last year, I saw him in the street one day here in New York, so I know that Herb is still around. And chances are he is still making very low-budget *some*things, God knows what. For the script of *50,000 B.C.*, he paid me 500 bucks. But that probably was the equivalent of five *thousand* today, and since it took me a week or less to do it, I would gladly do an assignment for 5000 a week *today*. [*Just not for Herb Lannard!*] That's right!

32

Tony Randall on 7 Faces of Dr. Lao *(1964)*

There were many sides to Tony Randall, whom TV audiences will always remember best and most fondly as the fussy, neatnik half of The Odd Couple. *But many movie fans recall, with equal fondness, his* tour de force *performances as five of the* 7 Faces of Dr. Lao *in the George Pal fantasy adventure: the wizened, doddering Merlin the Magician; the fortune-telling seer Apollonius, cursed always to tell the truth; the flute-playing satyr Pan; the snake-haired Medusa; and, of course, the pidgin-English-speaking Chinese Dr. Lao, proprietor of the mysterious traveling circus ("The Greatest Show on This or Any Other Planet") that appears in the troubled Old West town of Abalone.*

An Oklahoma native and the son of an art dealer, Randall made his stage debut in 1941 just prior to World War II service with the Army Signal Corps, then branched out into radio and early television after his discharge. Many of his greatest successes were on TV—none greater than his Emmy-winning Felix Unger—but there were also many movies, among them some of the hugely popular Doris Day–Rock Hudson sex comedies of the late '50s and '60s. He went completely against type in Dr. Lao, *emoting (under Oscar-winning William Tuttle makeup) in the aforementioned quintet of roles—the remaining two "faces," the Abominable Snowman and the Giant Serpent, being (respectively) played by producer-director Pal's son Peter and provided by the SFX department.*

In more recent years, he realized one of his dreams by founding New York's National Actors' Theater, partly maintained at his own expense (and also realized, at age 75, most every *man's dream, marrying a beautiful ingenue 50 years his junior, in a ceremony presided over by New York Mayor Rudy Giuliani). He died on May 17, 2004, leaving behind his wife and their two children, seven and five.*

[*Do you know how George Pal came to select you to play Dr. Lao?*] Not really. I emceed some show in Los Angeles, a Golden Globes Awards or something like that—I just stood up and did the jokes. George Pal saw me on it and said I would be good as Dr. Lao. That's as much as I know. Of course, in preparation for my role in the picture, I read the Charles G. Finney novel *The Circus of Dr. Lao*, and then since, for pleasure. It's a marvelous novel, it's an oddity. It's really unlike any other novel that I know of.

[*Did you find Pal to be a good director?*] Yes and no. He was all right. He was at his best with technical things, he was a wizard at that. [*Pal seems too affable a person to do a director's job. He didn't seem to have been a "take charge" kind of guy.*] You're partially right, but he was able to exert sufficient authority at all times. There was never a problem with that. [On a personal level,] oh, he was a doll. A charming, lovely man. He and his wife Zsoka were just the most charming people, warm, very friendly. We had good times together; we went to his house for dinner, went out together. Lovely man. [*Did you stay in touch with him after* Dr. Lao *wrapped?*]

32. Tony Randall on 7 Faces of Dr. Lao (1964)

Tony Randall amid six of the 7 Faces of Dr. Lao. In George Pal's "fairy tale of the Old West," the *real* purpose of Lao's circus is to hold a proverbial mirror up to inhabitants of a frontier desert town.

Yes, more or less, as you do and don't. It's a peculiar thing: [Show business] is a very small world, where everybody knows everybody else, but you don't really see each other unless you're working together!

In his field, William Tuttle was a person of the greatest distinction. If you can use the word "genius," he was a genius at makeup. And he cared, and he was interested. He and I got together on our own and worked out those makeups. There was no money for it. That's the terrible problem about working, always. Either you have a wonderful budget, or you don't. And we *didn't* on this particular picture. So he and I just got together. He had his own method: He was a very talented watercolorist, and he conceived of the characters and the makeups in watercolors, and then proceeded to turn my face into the hue that he had created. And if it didn't work—if I said, "No, let's add this, let's add that"—he was amenable. Each makeup took approximately two hours, and some days I was in three different makeups. So that meant six hours in the makeup chair. So it was more tedious and uncomfortable for the makeup man than for me!

As I said before, the makeups were designed by Bill Tuttle, and sometimes he worked on them. But more often Charlie Schram, who was a technical wizard, applied them. (Bill had a wonderful staff; any person on it could have executed them.) But as head of the makeup department, Bill didn't necessarily come to the set; someone else has to be on the set with you [the star] at all times, taking care of all the makeups during shooting. Between takes, your makeup runs, it has to be repaired, sometimes it has to be completely redone and so forth. That's the man on the set.

I shaved my head and eyebrows. A bald wig shows, it wrinkles up in the back of the neck and all that, and it just doesn't look right. It didn't take long for my hair to grow back. You'd be amazed how fast it grows back. [*Did you have a favorite character in the movie?*] I think Merlin. He was a sweet, dear fellow, and I thought it was my best.

I don't know how much faith MGM had in the picture. They didn't *show* much faith, and once it was ready to be released, they didn't promote it. It was perceived to be, at least by the promotion department, a horror film. And so they promoted it as a horror film! A film with *Run for Your Lives! Dr. Lao Is Coming!* ads, and things

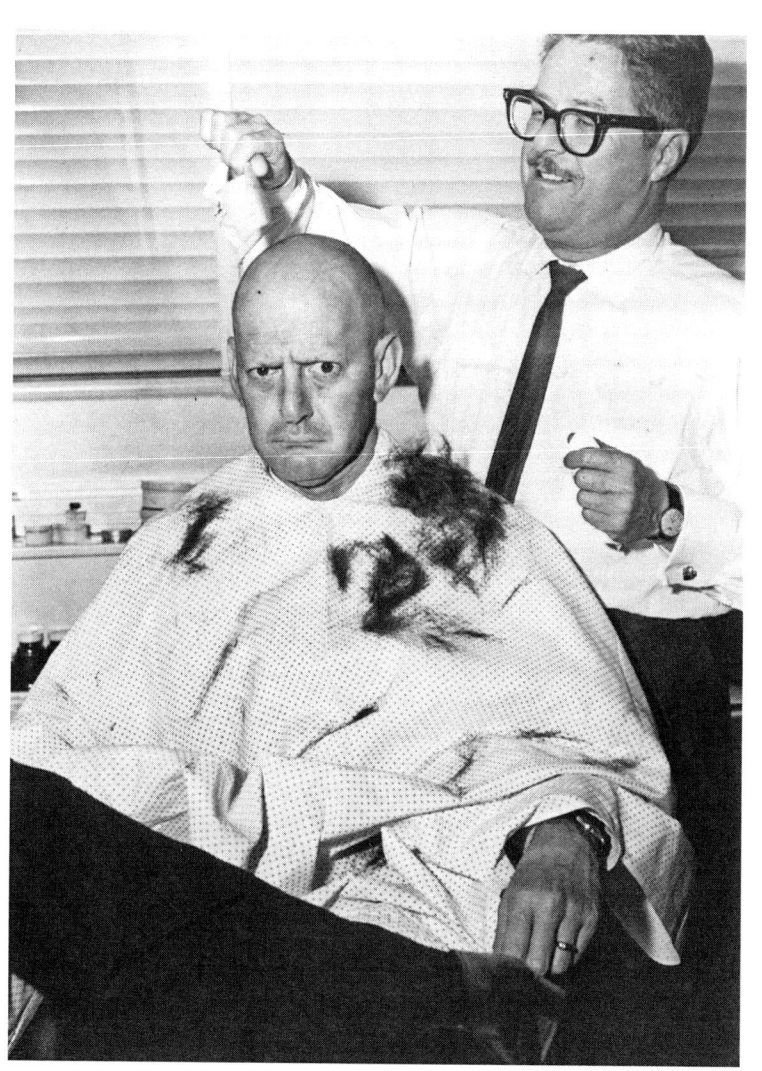

By sacrificing his hair and eyebrows to makeup creator William Tuttle, Randall was more easily transformed into some of his characters.

like that! They completely missed the point. When I objected, they sympathized ... and did nothing about it.

Arthur O'Connell and Barbara Eden were very pleasant people. I still see Barbara Eden from time to time, and whenever I bump into her, it's always fun. We made several movies together, as a matter of fact. I don't own a tape of *Dr. Lao*; I don't own any of my movies. None. I know what they look like [*laughs*]—I can't *abide* sitting there and looking at myself.

[*What do you tell people who say that your performance in* Dr. Lao *is the best of your career?*] That's very nice, except that ... I don't think it's true. I think it's *good*. But every time *7 Faces of Dr. Lao* is on television here in New York, *The New York Times* repeats its capsule criticism, which brings me down to earth: "All seven are Tony, and all are terrible." They print that every time it comes on TV!

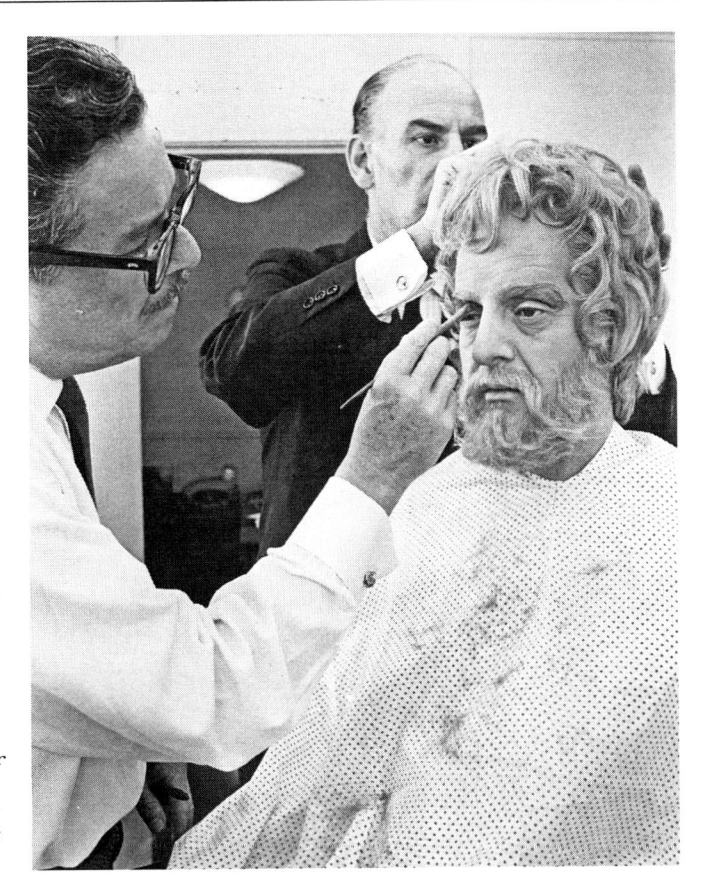

Tuttle's Lao creations, like Apollonius, earned him (left) an Honorary Oscar. Decades later, *Makeup Artist* magazine called his *Lao* work one of the 50 greatest makeup jobs of all time. Randall at right, other fellow unidentified.

33

Frederick E. Smith on Devil Doll *(1964)*

Frederick E. Smith, author of the short story which provided the basis for the Bryant Haliday-starring chiller Devil Doll, *is an award-winning English novelist who believes that new experiences, new faces and extensive travel are vital to him in his writing career.*

After serving in England's Royal Air Force during World War II, Smith (1923–) and his wife relocated to South Africa, where he worked at a variety of jobs. It was then that his lifelong desire to write became irresistible, and for four years he dedicated five evenings a week to learning the craft. His earliest stories, including "The Devil Doll," were horror tales for the English-based publication London Mystery Magazine.

The idea for "The Devil Doll" grew from my seeing a ventriloquist on the stage in my home town Hull in Yorkshire, England, when I was a child. Perhaps it was also influenced by the two years I spent in India during World War II when, in unusual circumstances, I met an Indian yogi who took me under his wing and helped to cure me of a serious illness I had contracted out there. I met my yogi near the town of Quetta, which was then in British India but now is in Pakistan. It is situated less than 20 miles from Afghanistan, which is so much in the news these days. [Author's note: This interview took place days after 9/11.] Oddly enough, he did talk about soul transference although, being a very young man in those days, I did not take too much notice of this aspect of his conversation. I feel it almost certain those were the influences that later led me to write "The Devil Doll."

I went out to South Africa shortly after the end of World War II and, while working in my brother-in-law's business, got the bug to write. My first ventures were supernatural stories, and an English magazine called *London Mystery Magazine* began to publish them. In all, they took 12 or more over a period of four years and one of them, entitled "Twelve Peaks to the Sky," was chosen for an anthology called *Mystery*. Another one was "The Devil Doll."

I've been asked if the 1945 movie *Dead of Night*—a marvelous movie—was an inspiration for "The Devil Doll" because I used the same name, Hugo, for the dummy as was used in that film. I don't remember copying this name (although one can never be sure that one's subconscious didn't do so). It was just that Hugo seemed a good, creepy name for the dummy.

"The Devil Doll" appeared in issue #23 of *London Mystery Magazine*. I don't recall any immediate reaction to it after publication but as there were approximately 15 stories in each magazine, one seldom got individual reactions. *London Mystery Magazine* paid me £10—roughly $14—for the rights to publish. Moreover, the magazine's checks were so designed that when they were cashed, one lost all rights in everything else, which was the reason why I lost the film rights in the story and never found out the magazine had *sold* those rights because they

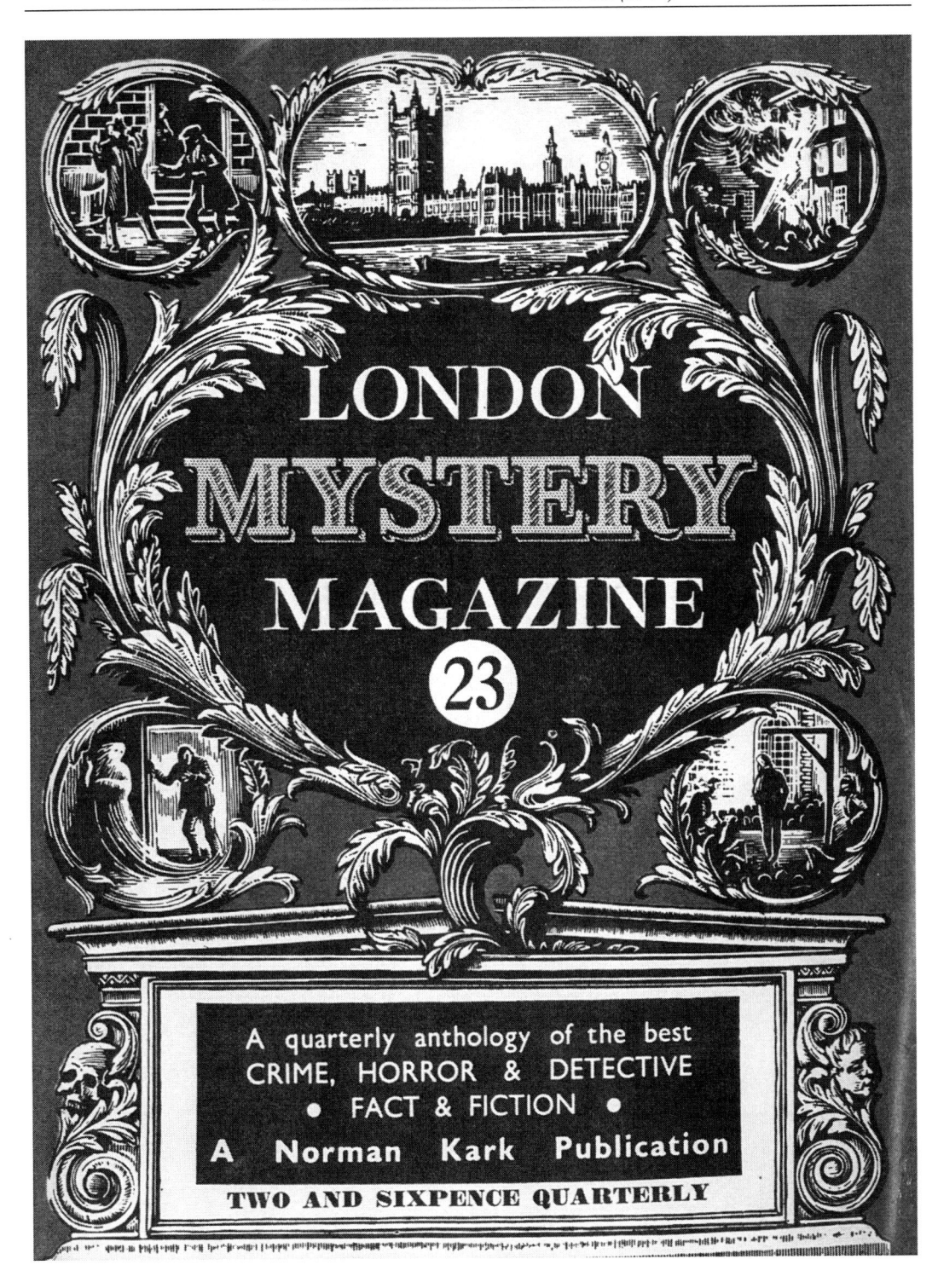

The cover of the issue of *London Mystery Magazine* that featured Frederick E. Smith's "The Devil Doll." The 14-page story earned him approximately $14.

never told me. (They didn't have a bad deal going at that time, did they?) I've no doubt that the producers of *Devil Doll* had to pay *London Mystery Magazine* much more for the story than my single $14. It was only later, when I heard the rumor they had sold the film rights to other stories, that I got wise and kept those rights for myself.

I wrote over 80 short stories on all kinds of subjects before I had the urge to write a novel and decided to make it an anti-apartheid novel. My wife Shelagh and I detested apartheid. I wrote the novel, which I called *Laws Be Their Enemy*, in South Africa but, because it was an offense in those days to attack apartheid, Shelagh and my small son Peter had to return with me to England before we could offer it for publication. It was eventually published in 1954 and I received death threats from certain fanatics in South Africa.

Regarding "The Devil Doll," I didn't know it had been filmed until one afternoon years later, when my son Peter came back from school and asked me, "Dad, didn't you once write a short story called 'The Devil Doll'?" When I told him I had, he said there was a film showing in Bournemouth (where we now lived) but it was the last evening showing of the week. So Peter and I dashed into town and found it *was* a film based on my story. As can be imagined, I wasn't pleased at the time at being kept ignorant about it although I now realize it wasn't the fault of the film's producers, who would naturally think that the news had been passed on to me.

Since then I have published 40 novels on a variety of subjects because I am not a genre novelist. Generally I try whenever possible to travel to the country where the novel is based. I have been in over 40 countries now, and try to experience as much as possible the conditions experienced by my characters. For example, for *Laws Be Their Enemy* I disguised myself as a

Devil Doll ventriloquist Vorelli (Bryant Haliday) torments his dummy Hugo … or is it vice versa?

black for seven days, which was a dangerous thing to do in South Africa during the days of apartheid! I don't know if you have heard of the film *633 Squadron* but it broke box office records here in England in 1964. It was from my 1956 novel of the same name, which to date has been published in 32 countries, including the U.S. and Japan. I've sold three other novels outright to film companies and options on a few more. I wrote the novel of the Rod Steiger film *Waterloo* [1970], and my novel *A Killing for the Hawks* [1966] won the American Mark Twain Literary Award. This book was going to be filmed by Arthur P. Jacobs, with Gregory Peck and Sophia Loren in his cast, but after Terence Rattigan's screenplay was rejected by Jacobs and another script writer engaged, poor Arthur dropped dead of a heart attack and so the film was never made. This was a blow to me as it is one of my favorite novels. However, I consider my best to be *The Tormented* [1973], a novel of modern revolution and dealing with the problem a pacifist has to face when the things he loves are being violated. Does he turn the other cheek or does he fight? My character does fight and so in a sense sacrifices his conscience for the things he holds dear. (Come to think of it, it could hardly be more topical today.) Certainly I'm hoping that one day someone will pick it up for a film.

I haven't seen *Devil Doll* since that day many years ago in Bournemouth but I do remember thinking at the time how creepy it was and how well it was handled. In fact, I thought it one of the best things of its genre that I had ever seen.

34

Memories of Tickle Me *(1965)*

Edward Bernds

We movie fans have certain expectations when we sit down to watch an Elvis Presley movie: The King with his crown of perfectly sculpted hair, lots of pretty girls, singing and dancing. Not on the list of likely elements: a ghost town setting, thunder-lightning-howling wind, a hand reaching through a sliding panel, an invisible ghost, a werewolf, a gaggle of ghouls, and "scare gags" and slapstick taken right out of the Three Stooges–Bowery Boys playbooks! But that's what we get in the closing reels of Tickle Me *because it was written by two veterans of the Stooges–Bowery Boys laugh factories, Edward Bernds and Elwood Ullman.*

Tickle Me is a comedy-musical with Presley as a rodeo rider spending the off-season working at the Circle Z Ranch, a fat farm where wealthy glamour girls spend $500 a week to shed unwanted pounds. But it builds to that extended climax in which Presley and Circle Z co-workers Jocelyn Lane and Jack Mullaney are trapped by rain in the abandoned Old West town of Silverado—where, local legend has it, the ghosts of the oldtimers come down from Boot Hill on stormy nights...

The president of Allied Artists wanted to make a picture with Elvis Presley because Allied was in rough shape. A deal was made with [Presley's manager] Col. Tom Parker, but the picture had to be made at Paramount—Presley wouldn't design to work at shabby, small little Allied Artists studio. Allied Artists also had to hire a Paramount cameraman [Loyal Griggs].

[Producer] Ben Schwalb set Elwood Ullman and me to writing it, but I guess that was no gamble on Col. Parker's part, because if he didn't like the script, he could reject it. Ben wanted me to direct it, too, but Col. Parker [nixed that]. Perhaps Parker conferred with Elvis, but it's more likely that Parker, who acted kind of like a stern father, wanted a director that Elvis had worked with before and liked. So the man who directed *Tickle Me* was Norman Taurog* and I didn't get the job of directing.

Apparently the Allied Artists studio was considered slums [by Presley's people], because we had to move the production office and *every*thing to Paramount. Elwood and I were given offices on the Paramount lot to write the script. We were like big-time people there: We had separate offices with our names on the doors, we had assigned parking spaces [*laughs*]—everything we *didn't* have at Allied Artists! We wrote *Tickle Me* and it was accepted. We liked the device of having Elvis play a rodeo rider because this kind of gave him a macho, masculine background. He was just an ordinary rodeo rider, looking for a job, and mistook a fat farm for a dude ranch. That device was what triggered the whole thing.

Elvis was quite shy. Now, he was on the Paramount lot, and the Paramount brass got a

---

**Presley's most frequent director, Taurog had already helmed four Elvis vehicles—*G.I. Blues *(1960),* Blue Hawaii *(1961),* Girls! Girls! Girls! *(1962) and* It Happened at the World's Fair *(1963)—by 1964 when* Tickle Me *was shot.*

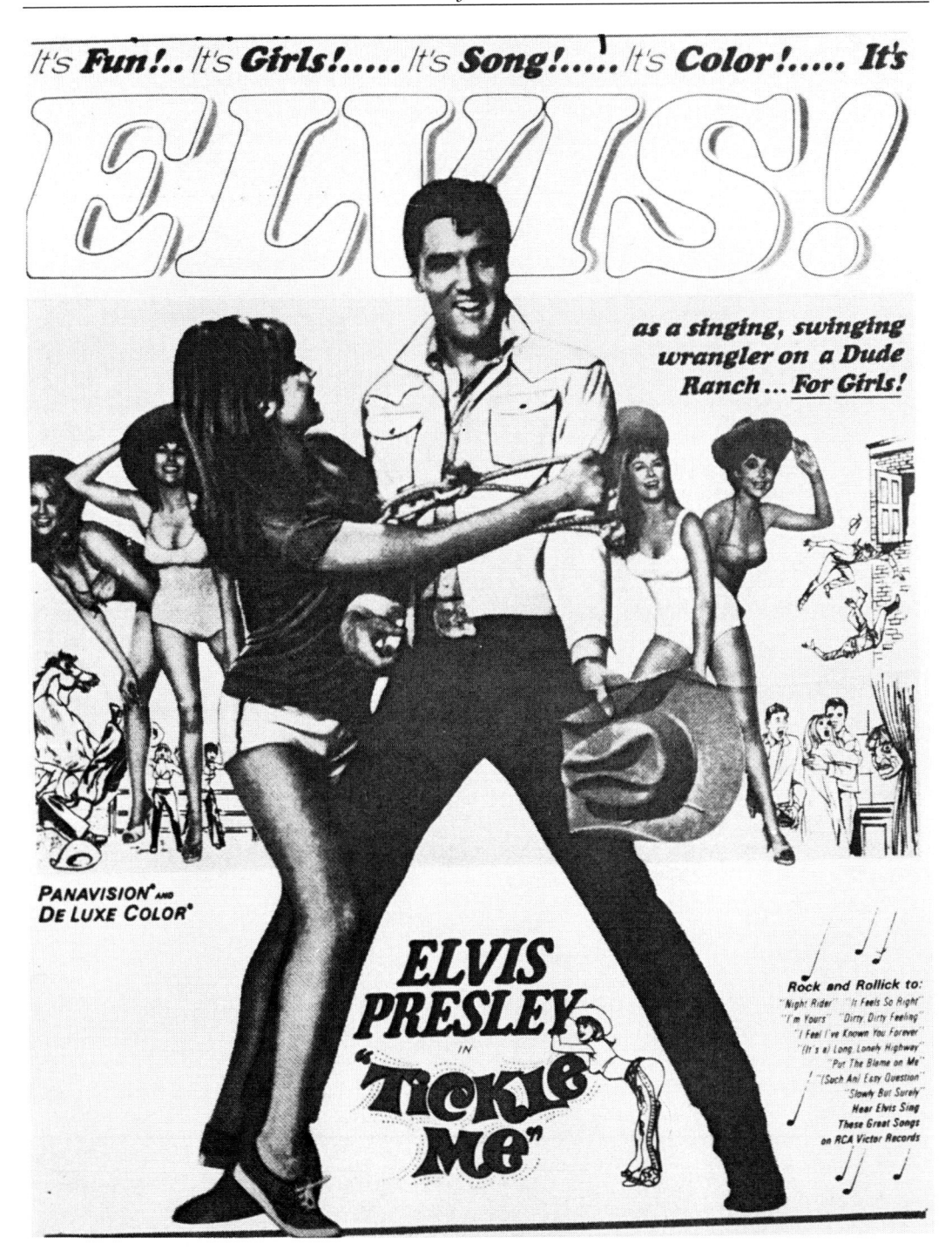

Edward Bernds (1905–2000) and Elwood Ullman watched an Elvis flick or two, to get an idea what was needed, before writing their script for *Tickle Me* (perhaps *the* most meaningless Elvis movie title!). Exhibitor demand for *Tickle Me* resulted in the biggest print order in the then-history of Allied Artists.

visit—not an official visit, just kind of sightseeing—from some FBI guys. High-up guys. Paramount, kind of anxious to show 'em a good time, took 'em on the Presley set, with*out* asking permission. After all, it was their studio, and they were accustomed to doing what they wanted there. This upset Presley a *great* deal. *Maybe* the fact that they were FBI had a *little* to do with it—although he probably didn't have a guilty conscience. But he was so shy that it affected him. They couldn't ask the FBI guys to leave, but Elvis was so upset that he couldn't work right. So he didn't work the rest of the day and they made some excuses [to the Paramount brass and the FBI men] and they had to fill in with "knickknacks"—closeups of other people, scenes not involving Elvis, inserts and so on. [*Was Elvis surrounded by his friends from Memphis?*] Yes, and they were *in* the picture. For instance, the band that he worked with were his old buddies [The Jordanaires]. Again, the remarkable thing is how shy he was. One would think that he'd be brassy and assertive, but he was *not*.

He didn't object to my being on the set, or Elwood. We didn't spend an awful lot of time there. We really enjoyed working at Paramount, and we roamed the lot. They were making the John Wayne picture *In Harm's Way* [1965] at that time, and the wonderful miniature fleets of Japanese and American warships were being built and made ready. There was a great big stage set aside for painting them and outfitting them with guns and things like that. Most of the miniatures were big enough for a man to be inside and operate the guns and the explosions and the propulsion.

Taurog shot our script pretty much the way we wrote it, with *some* changes, some of 'em actually improvements. *Tickle Me* has been criticized in reviews for the fact that we shot everything indoors. The ranch scenes were shot on Paramount soundstages with Western scenery on painted backdrops. I don't think it really bothered the moviegoing public much. We previewed it at (I think) Huntington Beach, and we had an absolutely *riotous* preview. The audience was a bunch of kids; the "book" picture there was something that attracted kids, and when they saw *Tickle Me* they really tore the place down. There was a lot of Stooge stuff in *Tickle Me* and it paid off like crazy. (The fact that *Elvis* was doing it, I think, *added* to it—the "scare gags" and the "indignity gags.") The preview cards were collected after the preview, and apparently with the young punks, male and female, "bitchin'" was then the big word; if something was really good, it was bitchin'! The kids stood in line to get preview cards, and the word "bitchin'" appeared time after time! So the preview was very successful.

We hoped to do another [Presley picture]. Allied Artists was kind of disintegrating at the time, but *Tickle Me* was quite successful; I think it damn near rescued Allied Artists from oblivion. It made a lot of money because it had been made relatively cheaply. Col. Parker wasn't as particular as he should have been about material; what he was particular about was that Elvis got his fee, which was a *fat* one! On *Tickle Me*, about one-half of the budget was Elvis' salary. Ben Schwalb would be in even worse shape than Elwood and I [if Allied Artists folded]; Elwood and I could get other jobs, but getting another job as producer would be difficult. Ben desperately wanted to have another project at Allied Artists, so we tried to cook up another Elvis story and present it. We had a story that we thought was pretty good. Well, we had *several* ideas, but I think this one involved Elvis in the Navy. We had a pretty good outline set, we could have made a good script and a good picture out of it, but it just never came off.

Merry Anders

As Elvis Presley movies go, Tickle Me *has one of the more "Monster Kid–friendly" displays of feminine pulchritude: In addition to stars Jocelyn (*The Gamma People*) Lane and Julie (*Creature from the Black Lagoon*) Adams, the luscious lineup also includes cult favorite Allison Hayes (the 50 Foot Woman herself), Francine (*Space Monster*) York, Angela (*Night of the Blood Beast*) Greene and Merry Anders of* The Hypnotic Eye, House of the Damned, The Time Travelers *et al. Anders, fifth-billed, is prominently featured in a comic role as the forever-famished Miss Penfield, a fat farm guest whose attempts to get more food run the gamut from flirting with male employees, to donning a disguise, to hatching a kooky plan to steal other diners' meals at a luau (which results in slapstick and chaos).*

I count myself lucky to have been in *The Hypnotic Eye* [1960] because the producer was Ben Schwalb, and he later called me in for the Elvis Presley movie *Tickle Me*. If I hadn't worked with Ben in *The Hypnotic Eye*, I don't think I would have ever had the opportunity to work with Elvis Presley. Ben was just a wonderful man to work for, he was very tasteful and a terrific gentleman—which you didn't run into too often in the industry [*laughs*]. He treated his people extremely well.

I got my part in *Tickle Me* through quite a bizarre set of circumstances. I hadn't worked in several months and I had picked up *quite* a bit of weight. I was called for the interview for *Tickle Me* and they wanted me to play a Joan Blondell type, a compulsive eater. I was perfect for the part at the time I interviewed ... but unfortunately, I was then called and asked to do a Bob Lippert movie [*Raiders from Beneath the Sea*, 1964], and in it I had about an eight-page scene in a bikini. So, needless to say, I dropped the weight. I finished *Raiders* on a Friday morning, and I was scheduled to start the Presley movie on Tuesday. Well, I started eating Friday morning and I had a Henry the Eighth weekend. Chocolate malted milks and and peanut butter and banana sandwiches ... it was just fabulous, I never *had* so much fun! Unfortunately, I was only able to gain 12 pounds, but in four days that's not bad. They [the *Tickle Me* moviemakers] *were* a little disappointed, and so I didn't watch my dietary habits while I was working on the picture so that, if I gained a bit more for some scenes, that was fine.

Working with Elvis was a little bit overwhelming. When I met him and we did one of our first scenes together, he was *so* kind and *so* helpful. We were doing a barbecue scene where Estelle [Anders' character] is trying to go through the chow line twice, the second time disguised with a cowboy hat down over her brow and a jacket. I had the first tray of food behind my back and I was holding the other tray out in front. As I went through, something struck Elvis and me funny and we both got the giggles, and it took us about seven takes to try and get past the first two or three lines. The director [Norman Taurog] was not pleased, but *we* were having a whale of a good time! Elvis was just very charming to work with. I got to talk to a few of the fellas who were part of his group, and they were all just very flattering about what a terrific person he was.

I knew that on the last day we only had about a half-a-day of scenes to do, and so I asked if I could bring my mother and my daughter down on the set. Elvis came over and sat down in the director's chair next to my mom and talked to her for about 45 minutes. Mother told me later that she thought he was the most well-mannered, charming young man that she had met in a long time. Unlike the usual, run-of-the-mill, trying-to-impress-everybody [actor], he was just a down-to-earth good kid. And then he took Tina [Anders' eight-year-old daughter] by the hand and lifted her up in his arms and walked her all around and showed her the various portions of the set. He was just darling with her. Tina said, "I can't believe it ... I can't believe it...."

They were really good to the people who worked on *Tickle Me*. I had a star dressing room on the Paramount lot where I could go every day. It had a shower and tub, it was really class A. And Col. Parker came down on the last day and he brought some packets that had record albums and photographs, and he handed those out to each of the cast members, which was a really nice gesture.

I really enjoyed my time on the set, and Elvis was very pleasant whenever we had scenes

Merry Anders put the "gorge" in "gorgeous": In the few days after playing a stunner opposite Ken Scott in *Raiders from Beneath the Sea*... (*continued next page*)

34. Memories of Tickle Me (1965)

...the actress pigged out and put on enough pounds to play the paunchy Miss Penfield in Presley's *Tickle Me*.

to do. He tried to give everybody a certain amount of attention—and, you know, that's very tiring, it's very draining to try to think of something nice to say to everybody. But he was very interested in making sure that it turned out right. And because I was fortunate enough to have the same hairdresser that did *his* hair, I learned on that movie that he dyed his hair. I didn't know he was a blond before that [*laughs*]!

35

Ib Melchior on Lost in Space *(1965–1968) and* Lost in Space *(1998)*

If you're one of the fans of the *Lost in Space* TV series who felt that New Line's 1998 movie version was a crime ... well, according to veteran writer-producer Ib Melchior, you don't know the half of it. "The miscarriage of creativity perpetuated by New Line is *nothing* compared to the miscarriage of decent behavior and common ethics perpetrated by this apparently unscrupulous multi-million dollar company," declares Melchior, creator of the original *Lost in Space* series.

Not that you'll find his name in that TV show's credits.

Right from the start, it's been a tale that would bring a tear to a glass eye. It begins in 1960 when the Danish-born Melchior, then new to Hollywood, had the idea of taking classics of literature and retelling them in motion pictures as they might happen in the future. He wrote five screen treatments: *Robinson Crusoe on Mars*, based on Daniel Defoe's *Robinson Crusoe*; *The Time Travelers*, from H.G. Wells' *The Time Machine*; *Treasure Asteroid*, a futuristic version of Robert Louis Stevenson's *Treasure Island*; *Gulliver's Space Travels*, based on Jonathan Swift's *Gulliver's Travels*; and, most pertinently here, an SF re-imagining of Johann Wyss' *Swiss Family Robinson*. Melchior's space-age update was titled *Space Family Robinson*.

In late 1963, two of these, *Robinson Crusoe on Mars* and *The Time Travelers*, were being made as films almost simultaneously, the former at Paramount under the direction of Byron Haskin, the latter at Carthay Studios with Melchior himself directing. *Time Travelers* producer William Redlin and Melchior were set to next co-produce *Space Family Robinson*; the package was submitted to several independent producers and one major production organization, CBS-TV. That last submission yielded no results. When Redlin tried to contact CBS executive Hunt Stromberg, Jr., to whom he had sent the script, he was stonewalled.

Melchior was in negotiations to write and produce *Space Family Robinson* for AIP when the script for the pilot episode of a TV series to be titled *Space Family Robinson* was registered with the Writers Guild on August 10, 1964—over five months after Melchior registered *his* script. According to Melchior, his script and the TV pilot script were almost identical. "And we are not talking about the obvious similarities that would occur, but specific scenes, descriptions, dialogue, dates and general story material unique to my script. In fact, industry people who saw the TV pilot script [credited to Irwin Allen and Shimon Wincelberg], and were familiar with *my* work, congratulated me on having sold my property!"

The inevitable happened: Now that CBS was proceeding with an exactly alike TV series (soon retitled *Lost in Space*), AIP bowed out; the company's Samuel Z. Arkoff wrote Melchior that *Lost in Space* "would seem to destroy the possibility of our proceeding with your project." Melchior consulted three lawyers, and got the same feedback from each: "They all agreed that of *course* Allen had stolen my material ... and they all advised me to let it go. I was still relatively new in Hollywood, and I was told that if I made waves I would never again work in town. I would be blackballed."

Interestingly, there had been a brief period of time when it didn't appear as though the *Lost in Space* pilot was going to lead to a series, but then the title suddenly showed up on the CBS schedule for the upcoming (1965-66) season. According to *Variety* (March 4, 1965), *Lost in Space* looked to be a goner until an executive personally intervened and pushed for it to go to series. The executive: "coast program veepee Hunt Stromberg, Jr."—the man to whom Redlin had sent Melchior's script!

Needless to say, the success of the ensuing series, in three years of first-run and decades of syndicated reruns, was a source of aggravation for Melchior. "How could it *not* be?" the writer says with a sigh. "I was watching someone else, someone who had stolen my stuff, making millions which rightfully should have been mine. But ... I did not let it destroy me." Heeding the counsel of his lawyers, Melchior remained silent as the statute of limitations expired, and never saw a dime.

In 1994, Melchior got a call from Mark Koch, CEO of a production company called Prelude Pictures. Koch said that Prelude was in the process of buying the rights to *Lost in Space* from the estate of the late Irwin Allen for a feature film, and he was phoning because he'd learned that Melchior had been involved in a similar project for Disney. That was wrong, but the call gave Melchior the opportunity to tell Koch that *he* had created *Space Family Robinson/Lost in Space* and would be glad to furnish proof. "Once this was done, Mr. Koch and his legal advisors were convinced that *Lost in Space* had indeed been created by me and not by Irwin Allen. This presented them with a dilemma: With a *new* production of the property, I was now free to sue, and could possibly derail the project. So Koch made me part of the production company. They contracted to buy my *Space Family Robinson* property to form the basis of the feature motion picture and made me their special advisor.

"My remuneration for this transfer of rights was generous. I was to get a lump sum up front, and two percent of the producers' gross receipts from the picture. The contract contained two specific clauses to protect my interests. The first clause reads as follows: 'No amendment or modification of this letter, nor waiver of any obligation or provision herein, shall be valid unless written and signed by both parties hereto.' And: 'This agreement may be assigned or otherwise disposed of or transferred by the Prelude Parties and such assignee, disposee or other transferee shall be bound by the terms of this agreement.' I felt that I was secure."

For financial reasons, Prelude later aligned itself with another production company (New Line) for the making of the movie—a more or less normal procedure in the filmmaking business. After a proposed shooting script was approved by New Line, Melchior was asked to go over it. "I was appalled by some of its inane and ridiculous aspects," he recalls. "I prepared a list of 12 areas which had to be fixed, with suggestions as to how to fix them. Only *one* of the 12 was followed: The script had a man hanging from his Army dog tag chain. That was changed when I pointed out to New Line that the dog tag chain was designed to break with a pull of a few pounds, and that millions of men who had been in the Army *knew* it. It was a struggle, but that scene was finally changed. Interestingly enough, *all* of the remaining 11 story points that they would *not* change were picked up on by the newspaper critics and cited as being particularly ridiculous!"

The reviews were scathing—but when *Lost in Space* opened in 3,306 theaters over the April 3-5, 1998, weekend, it racked up a North American box office take of $20 million-plus, enough to cause James Cameron's *Titanic* to sink from the number one position it had held for a record-breaking 15 weeks. The SF adventure managed, in fact, to have the largest April opening on record. Its critical savaging meant nothing to Melchior, who felt that his financial future was assured. "When the dollar amounts were announced and were really big, I was of course pleased. It would mean a greater share for me the more the film took in. I was a little surprised at its success, although I have gotten used to some very questionable movies making it big. But my feeling was one of satisfaction at looking to greater revenue.

"My up-front money had been paid to me by New Line, and I had no reason to believe that my percentage payments would not also be given to me by that company. In due time I requested an accounting of what was my share. That was when I was told by New Line that I had *no* money coming to me at all, because there was no contract between me and New Line!"

In 2000, Melchior filed suit in the Superior Court of the State of California, and in the course of pursuing this legal action came to the conclusion that Prelude and New Line had conspired to deprive him of the money he was owed. "This was accomplished by an agreement [between Prelude and New Line] made unilaterally and in willful violation of Paragraph 9 of my contract, an agreement by which Prelude sold the rights obtained from me to New Line for a lump sum, and a participation designed in such a way that it would preclude Prelude from ever getting any gross receipts from the picture. In this unilateral agreement, New Line asserted that it had read all contracts and would abide by all obligations *except* the obligation toward me, which New Line stipulated must be borne by Prelude. Since Prelude would never see any gross receipts, then neither would I. It was designed as a perfect way of depriving me of my percentage, and it had been deliberately kept secret from me to keep me from acting against this illegal modification of my contract. To keep me quiet during the making of the film, when action by me might have interfered with the production, my up-front money was paid to me by New Line. It is interesting to note that New Line kept all the obligations to companies with some clout of their own, while singling out me to deprive me of my rights, I being only a single individual, an old man, and easy prey."

To Melchior's chagrin, the judge who heard the case, James R. Dunne, wrote that he did not understand the wording of the contract, ending by "summarily dismissing the case and depriving me of my day in court. In his opinion he indicated that he did not understand all the show business terminology which of necessity appears in a show business contract, and being unable or unwilling to differentiate between the picture's gross receipts at the box office level and the picture's gross receipts at the producer's level although it is abundantly clear which is which in the contract. He ruled that since there was no signed contract

Oh, the pain, the pain! First the concept for the TV series *Lost in Space* was stolen from writer Ib Melchior; then he was wooed and screwed by the makers of the 1998 feature film version.

35. Ib Melchior on Lost in Space (1965–1968) and Lost in Space (1998)

Melchior watched some episodes of *Lost in Space* and thought the early ones were "okay." But as the series continued, "it became too camp and inane for me." (Above: The Robot and Jonathan Harris.)

between me and New Line, that company had no obligations toward me, deliberately ignoring the special clauses in my contract. He also failed to acknowledge that it was impossible for any signed agreement *to* exist between me and New Line, since I was deliberately kept in the dark as to the *total* takeover by New Line until I found out in the course of our suit. Before then, I was under the impression that, although Prelude shared the responsibilities with New

At a Hollywood party thrown by Prelude Pictures, Melchior poses with Crystal Bernard of the TV series *Wings*, a contender for the role of Judy in the *Lost in Space* movie.

Line, Prelude was still very much the producer. And I was never aware that a new contract between Prelude and New Line had been drawn up clandestinely and anti-contractually. I did not anticipate that two supposedly reputable organizations would deliberately and maliciously change my agreement, necessitating a new contract to be signed. Quite obviously I would never have agreed to a contract which would rob me of the payments due me!"

When Melchior appealed to the Appellate Court in the County of Los Angeles, they took his original contract into consideration and reversed Judge Dunne's ruling. The Appellate Court stated, "We agree that, by law, New Line assumed the obligations of the Release Agreement," and held that New Line "stood in the stead of Prelude."

"That ruling was published in the Court of Appeal, State of California," Melchior continues. "Then the case was returned to Superior Court—and to Judge Dunne! Incredibly, he once again denied me my day in court and dismissed the case. He composed a new reason for his ruling, depending heavily on the unilateral, clandestine agreement which was designed to negate my valid and legal contract. Once again we were forced to approach the Appellate Court. But *this* time, to my consternation and disbelief, the Appellate Court refused to reverse Judge Dunne! Guided, apparently exclusively, by the unilateral [Prelude–New Line] agreement, even quoting it, and disregarding the clauses in my original contract that were violated, they let the judgment by Judge Dunne stand, thus ignoring their own published prior ruling!"

Melchior was now faced with the bewildering problem of one court (the Appellate Court) judging the same case and the same contract twice, and arriving at two totally different judgments. "At this point, there was only one way to settle this dilemma and that was to try the case in court. Consequently we petitioned the California Supreme Court to review the case and allow me to be heard in court. But we did not make the two percent of cases submitted to the court and accepted, so the unjust judgment was let stand. I had effectively been robbed of my money—conservatively to date about $2,000,000—by deviously manipulative lawyers aided by the judicial system of our state. I took the liberty of writing a personal letter to the California Supreme Court chief justice, but was not afforded the favor of a response of any kind."

Unfortunately, situations like these frequently bubble up in the Hollywood shark tank. "Oh, I was told by a friend of mine, a prominent lawyer, that this situation was not unusual at *all*," Melchior says sadly. "There is little justice, little truth to be found in our courts. It is all a matter of *law*—and law and justice are seldom synonymous. Perhaps that is why it is called a court of law—not of justice. Disingenuous lawyers and some judges will go to all lengths to find anything that can be twisted to mean something else and fit into some law, from the meaning of words to misplaced commas. They'll do *any*thing to find a loophole, however small, which can be misinterpreted and maneuvered into whatever meaning is desired. Anything to get away from the intention of what was written. In my case, the court questioned what was meant by 'Prelude'! Did 'Prelude' mean 'Prelude,' or something *else*? That question meant that the contract was invalid! After all the legalese maneuvering was done, the fact remains that when I sold the rights to my property and entered into my contract, I was assured a lifelong and deserved income to take care of my waning years; but after the legal system got through with me, I have nothing. *That* is justice ... California style."

Lawyers for New Line had also played up the fact that *Lost in Space* lost money; they cited *Variety*'s report that the movie made only $75 million. "But that was the *domestic* gross," Melchior points out. "Traditionally, foreign distribution surpasses domestic. And it also does not include television, DVDs and tapes, etc., all part of the contract. It is in any case a moot question since my percentage is of the *gross*, not the *net*. New Line claims there were no gross receipts. If so, one must wonder why they spent years in court trying to prevent me from collecting a percentage of nothing!

"Granted I am not a lawyer and not at home in all the legal shenanigans possible. I can only go by what was obviously intended. In the words of my favorite character, the real Hamlet, the ninth-century Danish prince who became the prototype for Shakespeare's *Hamlet*: 'I wish to be held stranger to untruth.' I had a bona fide contract. Through legal maneuvering, it was negated. If this can be done to my contract, no contract is safe. If this can be done to me, then a contract is not worth the time it takes to sign it. I would rather believe that there has been a miscarriage of justice in my case."

Melchior wrote to California Senator Diane Feinstein asking if an inquiry might be made. "Perhaps the court might reconsider and allow me to be heard in court. That is all I ask. As it is, I am effectively prevented even from being allowed to present my case to a jury of my peers. I also sent letters to the presiding judge of the Los Angeles County Superior Court, to Governor Arnold Schwarzenegger and to President Bush. I am now 87 and my earning days are all but over. Granted I am not a native-born American, I was a Danish subject and *chose* to make the United States my home and was naturalized in 1943. I have always been a law-abiding citizen, I pay taxes, vote, contribute to charities, and I spent four years of my life fighting for my country, being decorated by three governments—including the U.S.A. I was honorably discharged with a 50 percent service-connected physical disability. But I am being treated by the courts of my chosen country with deep injustice. My hard-earned funds are allowed to be usurped by a multi-million dollar company to add to their millions, while I now must scrounge to retain enough money to sustain my health. It was not an easy time fighting New Line for my rightful dues, and watching my chances for justice become increasingly questionable. In 2001 I had open heart surgery and bypass surgery and wear a pacemaker, and I am able only to do the most rudimentary walking. Even with Medicare, my medicinal expenses are considerable, which is why I set up my [*Lost in Space*] payment to last over a period of many years. A feature film such as *Lost in Space* has a life of at least 30 years, during which time it earns money. I am still collecting residuals for *Robinson Crusoe on Mars*, which was

The cast of the *Lost in Space* movie, including the Robot—with Melchior's face superimposed on it. New Line gave this photograph to Melchior at the after-premiere party as a souvenir of the occasion.

released 41 years ago! *Lost in Space* was supposed to provide me with such funds. But I have been robbed of that luxury. The funds were also supposed to help defray some of the costs incurred by the condition of our son, who for five years has been in a nursing home, unable to walk. He will *never* walk, but he looks at television and can have the pleasure of seeing the shows produced by a firm who deprived him of some of the niceties of life.

"Some while ago, Senator Feinstein was most courteous and helpful to me in establishing contact with the State Department regarding getting the Melchior family estate in Germany restored to the family, inasmuch as the Bundesrepublik insisted it belonged to the state. During the course of that suit, we learned of a document which irrefutably proved my claim, a document signed by the German government. However, the government went to court and insisted that no such document was in their possession; they insisted, in fact, that no such document *existed*. We were successful in obtaining a copy of the document from another source and went to the court to rectify the situation. However, the court refused to rule against the state. We approached the German Supreme Court, proving that the government had lied in court and concealed documentation of imperative importance to the case. But the German Supreme Court would not even listen to us. The state had spoken. The Melchior property had effectively been stolen by the German government. The case is now at the European Court, but the wait is almost punitive.

"This was in Germany, and to be expected. So imagine my shock, my disbelief, my disillusionment ... when I found out that our own judicial system in California is no better."

36

Memories of The Wild Wild West *(1965–1969)*

Whitey Hughes

Yes, The Wild Wild West *had unique spy-fi plots and Bond-like gadgets and Ross Martin's marvelous disguises—but for many fans, the secret of the far-out Western TV series' success was the team of stunt performers putting their necks on the line (literally) throughout its four-year run. No less fearless, according to* Wild West *stunt coordinator Whitey Hughes, was star Robert Conrad, who was almost always right in the thick of action with the corps of stuntmen and brawlers the two of them had handpicked.*

Robert "Whitey" Hughes learned to ride horses, break horses and drive horse teams on the Arkoma, Oklahoma, farm where he was raised. In 1936, when he was 16, the family moved to California where Whitey finished school and, in 1947, began working in the movie business. Because of his farm upbringing, Hughes specialized in Western stunts and, because of his height (5'6"), he could also stunt-double women and even children (Bobby Diamond on Fury, *Johnny Crawford on* The Rifleman, *more). In 1965 he stunted on his first* Wild West *and soon became the show's head honcho in the action department, happily working out elaborate fistfights and "ungodly" stunts with the equally gung-ho Conrad. Now living in retirement in Arizona with his wife Dotti, and still a "good ol' boy" in his late eighties, Whitey reminisces here about* Wild Wild West; *describes his ups and downs with Conrad; and salutes other members of the greatest stunt team in TV history.*

Bill Catching was the stunt coordinator the first season of *The Wild Wild West*. He was a stuntman who had done the pilot, which was partly shot up north in Sonora, and then started working on the show. One day Jerry Summers, one of the stunt kids, was supposed to work for Bill on a *Wild West* ["The Night of the Steel Assassin"], but Jerry called in, said he wasn't gonna make it. So Bill called me to replace Jerry. That was my first *Wild West* episode.

Bill and Bob Conrad didn't get along worth a hoot. They was fussin' and fightin' all the time—Bob didn't like Bill and I guess Bill didn't much care for Bob. CBS didn't want Bob to do any action that might result in injuries, so Bill didn't let Bob do a lot of things that Bob wanted to do. This resulted in Bob being very unhappy with Bill's stunt coordinating. Bill didn't want Bob to do aaaanything. Also, Bill used to make the remark that he'd saw the furniture off so Bob would look taller [*laughs*]. That made Bob mad, and he didn't get along with Bill after that! And once Bob and Bill weren't getting along, Bill was just mean about things he said about Bob.

I went in to do that ["Steel Assassin"] show, a fight scene in a wine cellar, and I saw that we were gonna have kind of a free hand at doing what we had to do. It was gonna be Bob takin' on me and [stuntman] Chuck O'Brien and Mike Masters, an actor-friend of Bob's. I hadn't even met Bob formally yet but we were talking about what we were gonna do, and I said, "Mr. Conrad," I said, "you knock Chuck down over here, and you knock Mike down over here, and then I'll dive at ya from up on top of that big wine barrel." Bob said, "You mean you're gonna *jump* at me," and I said, "No, I'm gonna *dive* at ya." He said, "You're gonna *dive*? How will I know when?" I said, "When you hit Mike and knock him down, I'll say 'Bob!' and you'll know I'm on my way. Just put your hands up and catch my body, and turn my body a half-turn, and use it to knock Mike down again." I'd already set it up with Mike that I was gonna use him as a catcher. Bob said fine. We done the shot, and it worked out perfect. It impressed Bob so much 'cause it was a wild gag.

As I was getting ready to go home, I was going past the makeup man Don Schoenfeld. I was talking to Don when Bob walked up and I said, "Mr. Conrad, it sure was nice workin' with ya." Don said, "Whitey, have you *met* Bob?" and I said, "I didn't meet him formally, I've just talked with him." So Don introduced me, he said, "Bob," he said, "this is one of the best stuntmen in the business"—he gave me that credit. Bob said, "Well, I like your work. You'll be back." And I *was* asked back and worked in other episodes that first season.

After the end of the season, when the show was on hiatus, Bob asked my wife Dotti and me to go to dinner with him. It was Dotti and me and Bob and *his* girlfriend Andi Garrett, an actress, and we went out to a place called Du-par's on Ventura Blvd., just a short distance from the studio [CBS Studio Center, formerly Republic Studios]. Bob asked me, "How would you like to coordinate the action on the show?," and I said, "Bob," I said, "I don't have a chance to get the stunt coordinating job. There are so many guys ahead of me on that thing." Bob said, "I asked you how you'd like to run the show." I said, "I would be honored and I'd love to do it." He said, "Go in and see Eddie Denault."

I went in to see Eddie, who was runnin' production at CBS, and Eddie said, "Bob wants you to come on the show as stunt coordinator. You want it?" And again I said, "I'd be honored. I'd love to do it." Eddie said, "Well, you *got* it." Bill Catching was going off to do the TV series *Branded* with Chuck Connors, 'cause Bill knew he was done on *Wild Wild West*; one way or the other, Bob was gonna get rid of him. So Bill was jumpin' off the wagon and going with Chuck Connors. That's the way I wound up with *Wild Wild West*.

Incidentally, there was another reason why maybe Bob wanted me on the show: I think Bob had heard the story of something that had happened when I was in Mexico on *Major Dundee* [1965]. We had a bunch of stunt guys, about 21 of us, down there, and every night they'd play this dice game. My brother Billy was always lucky, always winnin' at this game; he couldn't do anything *but* win. Finally one of the guys, Herbie, a big ol' horse wrangler, told Billy, he said, "You can't

Hollywood's wildest stuntman, Whitey Hughes.

play no more," and he wouldn't let Billy play. Well, that turned into a situation where I had to stand up to Herbie. Word got around about my run-in with this big wrangler, and I guess Bob heard about it. I think Bob was kinda impressed with the little guys who didn't always get shoved aside. So when he asked me what happened down there in Mexico, I told him the story. And Bob was always tellin' *me* about him and Nick Adams and Little John [John Ash-

In his debut *Wild Wild West* stunt, Hughes (top of picture) dives from atop a wine vat at series star Robert Conrad in "The Night of the Steel Assassin." Also pictured: Chuck O'Brien (lying on stairs) and Sara Taft.

ley], the little actor out of Tulsa. They was always runnin' together because they was little guys, and always tryin' to talk tough; Bob would tell me stories about how they was pretty tough little guys.

Bob had an inferiority complex about being small, and he didn't like big guys around on *Wild West* when it first started. I told him one day, I said, "Bob, you're a good actor, a good little man, you're handy—*you* don't have to have any complex that way." I think he liked me because of that attitude. I never seen the guy that I was afraid of. I wasn't no bully-bully fighter but I wasn't *afraid* of nobody, and I let Bob know that up front: "I don't turn my back on any man that's tryin' to get *on* me for anything." My dad always told me, "Take the difference [a difference-maker] if you need it," whatever it [the difference-maker] has to *be*—a club, a ball bat, or whatever.

As stunt coordinator on *Wild West*, I would come up with the stunts that we would do. I'd read the scripts and devise different gags to fit different places, and I'd present 'em to Bob. Bob, if he liked something, would check it, and if he *didn't* like it, we'd scrap that one and go for somethin' else. Bob and I had a rapport about checking our stunts and okaying 'em and doing the things we thought was exciting. When I went on the show, Bob was into that karate thing; somebody had told him he was a great karate man. I told him, I said, "Bob, if we go to the old 'knockdown drag-out,' the old barroom fight [instead of karate], it'll give us more area, more room to *do* things that's gonna be exciting." He said, "Okay. I like that. We'll do that."

Years before *Wild West*, Hughes was already a specialist in Western stunts, including horse falls and (pictured) saddle falls.

I didn't have a say all the time about what other stuntmen we called. Some of the times, Bob would let me select, but he liked to pick the people *he* wanted to see come in. It got us in trouble, 'cause the group that he put together didn't include any Western boys. Bob Herron, who was Ross Martin's stunt double, was the only horseman on the show outside of me. When Western gags would come along, wagon stuff for instance, some of these [Conrad-selected] stunt guys didn't know how to *do* 'em. We ran into a few problems there! My job was to set up the gags and help the other stunt guys. Bob's favorite expression was, "Get 'em up, Whitey, get 'em up! Put the needle in 'em!"—meaning, "Get their adrenalin goin'." I was so "high" all the time in my thinkin', always thinkin' wild crazy stuff, and Bob was so [enthusiastic about] me and about my work, that he wanted me to get the other stunt guys up even with *me*: "Put the needle in 'em, Whitey! Get 'em up, get 'em up!" Bob just *lived* action and he *loved* it. He liked exciting things, and stunts that had a lot of hazard involved. He thought that the simple stuff was stuff that most anybody could do, and both he and I wanted to do things *bigger* than that.

When I first went to work for Bob, I liked him very much, and he liked me. He gave me a break that I hadn't got in Hollywood, a break I'd waited a long time for. He gave me that break and I just loved Bob like a brother, and I *told* him that one time.

Bob will tell you he done all of his own stunts, but you know that's not true, and you can quote me if you want to. He was doubled quite a bit. We had Louie Elias double him, we had Chuck O'Brien double him, we had our wardrobe man Jimmy George double him—it was three or four guys we had to double him. If it was a hazardous gag, we most generally tried to cover him. Bob didn't like that. He didn't like it when his stunt doubles were walking around in the double Jim West clothes, he wanted 'em to stay out of sight. He had an ego thing about action.

But don't get me wrong, Bob was handy. As far as actors are concerned, Bob was as handy a little man as I ever seen in the action department, and he proved it whenever he went through a routine. For the fight scenes we used three cameras a lot of times. We'd go through a routine where he handled a *lot* of guys and it'd come out really good, 'cause he remembered the routines really well. And I don't think he ever asked anybody to do anything [any stunt] that he wouldn't do. But when he'd come to a hazardous thing where he might get hurt, CBS told me, "We don't want him doin' things that he shouldn't be doin'." I promised 'em that I wouldn't let that happen. But Bob went ahead and got hurt [on "The Night of the Fugitives"] by not minding what I told him. It was on a crazy gag that he shouldn't have been doing, but I was gone that day. We'll get into that later.

I loved Ross Martin. Ross was just a sweetheart of a guy, and he was soooo cooperative in so many ways. We got along great. When I was planning a fight routine where Bob and Ross would take on a gang, I'd always find some place where Ross would encounter me and get into it with me, and I'd dream up a fun thing for him to do. For instance, [in "The Night of the Burning Diamond"] I was playin' a one-eyed butler and Ross was in disguise, a wig and everything, as he was coming up a long staircase. I said, "Ross, as you're comin' up, I'll dive at you from higher up on the staircase, and you do the bullfighter thing. Just kinda step aside and let me go by." He *loved* that. Then later in the fight, he let me pull his wig off of him—that was a funny little "bit." I don't think Bob wanted Ross doing too much action [*laughs*], but Ross liked to do the funny action, like bumping me with skillets [also in "The Night of the Burning Diamond"]. I liked Ross and I loved to give him things to do because he loved to work.

The day Ross broke his leg [on "The Night of the Avaricious Actuary"], he did it by tripping over a rifle on the floor of the set. A very simple, simple thing, he tripped over a rifle that had been used in the scene and was now lying on the floor, and he broke his leg. So for a short time we lost him. Then later he had a heart attack and we had to do a number of episodes without him, with guys like Charlie Aidman [and Alan Hale, Jr., and Pat Paulsen] now playin' Jim West's partner. I liked ol' Charlie Aidman, but none of 'em was a Ross Martin. As far as I'm concerned, Ross Martin carried 75 percent of the show—I think he was *that* strong. People loved the makeups he wore and the characters he dreamed up. There was a lot of Ross in all those characters and their dialogue. I loved his part of the show, Ross was a *big*, big part of it, and I think Bob knew, too, that Ross was a big part of the show.

People often ask how Bob and Ross got along. Not too good. I think Bob was just a *little* bit jealous of Ross' popularity [*laughs*]—honestly, I think he was. Bob was always trying to put Ross down to a certain extent, and not wanting to recognize too much what Ross' input was. Ross spent a lot of his own time on the characters that he did, many, many hours working on them and figuring them out. I don't think Bob appreciated Ross' efforts that much. If Ross ever resented that, he didn't show it. He might have, *inside*, had a little feeling that he was not being treated right by Bob, but he didn't show it. Ross was a real trouper, a real showman, and I think that's why he was such a success. I had made a show called *Geronimo* [1962] with Chuck Connors and I think I first ran into Ross at that time. I learned to like him then, because it was funny to see him doin' an Indian on that show [*laughs*]. He did a good job, but I just couldn't see Ross bein' an Indian!

As I said before, I didn't get to use any really good Western people on the show; in the stunt group Bob put together, there weren't a lot of guys who could do Western gags. For Western gags, we had a kid named Jack Lilley who was pretty handy. Little Billy Shannon, a tumbler, I got to use quite a bit. And Chuck O'Brien, one of the men Bill Catching brought on. I liked Chuck and I used him as much as I could, because he was a good stuntman and a good close double for Bob. But after Bill left, Chuck didn't get to work too much on the show because Bob would put the [stuntmen] names in to me. We used Bear Hudkins—I liked Bear, Bear was a Western guy. And when I got into trouble with things, like with saddle falls, that's where I needed guys like Bear Hudkins and his brother Dickie Hudkins. Their parents had

According to Hughes (heavily made up as a villainous butler in this shot from "The Night of the Burning Diamond"), Ross Martin (right) "carried 75% of the show."

the Hudkins Stables and they furnished livestock and the wagons and so on [for use in movies and TV shows]. The Hudkins always had first chance to ride horses on any show that the Hudkins Stables provided horses for. In other words, any time you ordered horses, Clyde "Ace" Hudkins would say, "Our guys [his family members] go with the horses." That meant that none of *my* stunt guys would get horses until after all these Hudkins guys was on horses. For any other stuntmen or extra cowboy to be able to work on that show, there had to be more horses than there were Hudkins [*laughs*]!

The stuntmen that Bob brought in were good in their own way, especially in fight stuff. And we had a *lot* of fight stuff! The only place they ever got in trouble, really, was on horse and wagon stuff. I liked "Bob's guys," and they were qualified guys ... *most* of 'em. But when you're doing precision work, stunts that have to be really nailed on the head, you have to have people that know how to *do* it. That's where we got in trouble: I had to double people that were supposed to be doin' the job. In other words, I'd have to have a stuntman doubling a stuntman [*laughs*]! We done one show ["The Night of the Tartar"] where Bob was tied to a pole, and we [stuntmen] all had sabers, and we'd ride by this pole one at a time on our horses, takin' a whack at it and takin' a piece off the top. The pole was behind Bob's back and the top of it was above his head. And Bob said, "Whitey gets the last cut at this pole!" [*Laughs*] Bob didn't want one of them other guys takin' the last, and lowest, slash at it!

[Stuntman] Red West was pretty much all-around. I liked Red, he was a very nice man, and he was really a great karate man. He was a tough, rough dude but he got along with Bob good. I had seen Red around a few times and I'd heard that he was Elvis Presley's bodyguard at one point, and one day when we were doing an episode, Bob walked Red up to me and introduced him, Bob said, "Red West, Whitey Hughes. Whitey, what do you think about bringin' Red on as one of the regulars on our group?" I said, "Well," I said, "I know Red for his karate work. He's supposed to be good. *You're* the boss, Bob. I like the fact that Red's handy with the fight stuff." And it turned out Red could ride. He was not an accomplished horseman but when it came to ridin', he could get it done.

In fact, when it came to horse work, Red helped me out a lot with [stuntman] Dick Cangey. Now, Dick ... well, he was somethin' else! I *loved* Dick, so I hate to talk about Dick's abilities, but he didn't want to get more than 12 inches off the floor—he wasn't a high man. When you put him on horseback to do a saddle fall, he just couldn't hit a spot [he couldn't fall where he was supposed to]. He'd be told to get "shot" and drop off the running horse right in front of the camera. Well, he'd pass the camera on the horse and go another 15, 20 feet before he would fall off! One day we were shooting a shot where Dick [on a running horse] was supposed to fire a rifle a couple of shots and get rid of the rifle and do a saddle fall. I thought, "Ohhhh, boy ... why did I let them get this far along with the thing?," 'cause I knew Dick couldn't do it and I should have gotten a double for him. That's what I was talking about before, gettin' a double for a *stuntman*! Dick did it twice and missed the spot both times, and finally I told Bob, I said, "Bob," I said, "you're *killin'* this guy. Let me do the saddle fall." "Okay, Whitey, you do the saddle fall." So I put the clothes on and I done the saddle fall for him.

Dick *was* good at fight stuff: He could throw guys around, he liked to go through windows, he could do whatever you told him to do, as long as you kept him on the floor! Don't get Dick up high, because he won't perform [*laughs*]! I loved him. But he was also a go-fer for Bob. I don't want to defame anybody, but Bob would send Dick to do errands for the wife and pick up the kids and go to the drug store and do all that stuff. I didn't like Bob using a guy like Dick for that kind of purpose. And I don't mind tellin' *him* that, so you can say that in print, if you want to, that I didn't like the way he used Dick Cangey.

Also, Bob would *hurt* Dick, Bob crippled him up pretty bad. Bob took Dick on personal appearance tours with him, like to rodeos, and did fight stuff with him. Bob would dive at Dick and do things that Dick really didn't [know how to safely withstand]. Dick should have had the power to set up stunts like that, he should have told Bob, "Let's do it *this* way." But Dick would always let Bob set it up and do it, and Bob would mash him! Dick didn't *belong* there.

At first, it was *me* and Bob doing the weekend things [the personal appearances]. There was a booking man, Andrew King, who would book actors for weekend tours, or whatever. I knew this guy 'cause he'd set it up for me to make a couple of tours with different people, like me and Chief Thundercloud, and me and [stuntman] Tom Sweet. Anyway, King wanted to

According to Hughes, Conrad didn't much like acknowledging the value of Martin's contribution to the series. Conrad must have loved this cartoon ad (Conrad prominent and in action, Martin a smaller, distant onlooker).

book Bob for some one- or two-day dates, and he asked me if I'd put a word in for him. So I told Bob, I said, "I don't particularly *like* this guy, but he can book you in an outdoor shithouse for more money than most of these agents can get you in the big halls!" Bob laughed like hell and said okay, and we made some appearances here and there. King paid Bob like $1500 to come for one day, and naturally I was just on my regular pay [a stunt double's daily pay], which I think was around $250–300 per day. Bob made those tours, and then when he kinda got tired of *me*, he started using Dick, who wanted to go on these things. I wasn't really big enough for Bob to be jumpin' at, so Bob thought, "Well, Dick is big and heavy, and he can catch me." But it wound up where he *hurt* Dick real bad.

Dick would get hurt on the show, too. I took Dick home one night after he had missed a saddle fall thing [in "The Night of the Winged Terror"]. A medicine show wagon was going down a street and Dick and Red West, on their horses, were riding alongside; Jimmy George, doublin' Bob, was gonna dive out of the wagon and take Dick and Red off their horses. It's called a double saddle fall. Well, Dick just wouldn't go [wouldn't fall off the horse when hit].

Or he'd miss the spot where he was supposed to fall. It wasn't funny but it *was* funny in a way, 'cause he wouldn't go off the horse. Finally I said, "I don't know what we're gonna do here," and Red walked over to me and said, "Dick'll go *this* time." [*Laughs*] Red was handy that way—he was tough! Red said, "Let's go again. *He'll* go." Sure enough, Jimmy George dove out of the wagon at them, and as ol' Red went down, *he* [Red] took Dick off of his horse! Red took Dick down and, boy, banged him up so bad.

Well, I had to drive ol' Dick home that night; he lived somewhere out in the South Gate area. I got him home and his wife Mary opened the door, but by this time that poor boy was so sore, he couldn't pick his feet up. To get from the ground up the four stairs into the house, he was havin' to pick his legs up and set 'em up on the steps. He had hit the ground so many times that his back was just killin' him. That's the thing that I disliked about Bob insisting on these guys, like poor Dick, doing these kinds of stunts. That's where I should have been able to bring in a guy who knew how to *do* that gag. Red could do it because Red was tough; I think he could do saddle falls on his head! But poor Dick just wasn't "into" that, and that's the way he got crippled up and hurt. I didn't like Bob using Dick like that. 'Cause Dick was a good guy, he didn't mean any bad toward *any*body.

Tom Huff came to us as a carpenter. He was carrying lumber on the lot when I first seen him; I'd spoken to him a couple times, but I didn't get acquainted with him. Well, he was carrying lumber one minute, and then the *next* minute, I guess Bob found out that Tommy had been a boxer, Tommy had fought a few fights, so [*laughs*] Bob brought *this* one to me! Again, "Whitey, meet Tommy Huff. I wanna bring him onto the team," and again I said, "You're the boss!" Well, ol' Tom was all right. He was willing and had a lot of heart. The first job he had was down by the Duchess House [a house seen in the Republic Red Ryder movies]. There were a couple, three little chicken coops sittin' there and we were trying to figure out something for Tommy to do rather than just (what we call) an MGM slump.* We wanted him to fall over something or make a little noise or *some*thing. I said, "Tom," I said, "when Bob lets you have a right hand, just fall back over these chicken coops here." Well, he drove his head right into the damn chicken coop, the wire and all, and cut his head open [*laughs*]! That was his introduction to *The Wild Wild West*.

Tommy Huff went on to work a *lot* on the *Wild West* shows, you see him all the time in it. He was a good fight man. But he didn't fight [in the style] I liked. I liked them old Western brawls where the guys would lock up and knock each other through things, and pick up things and knock each other down with 'em. Those were the things I liked to do. But when you came to the guys like Tommy who were used to boxing, they'd take that boxing stance. Bob Herron was bad, too, about doin' the boxing stance; he'd put the dukes up and do the feinting and all that stuff. In all of the guys, I wanted to instill how to throw Western punches and how to take punches. They learned how to do it.

Another stuntman on the show was Calvin Brown, the black boy; him and I played them two butlers [in "Burning Diamond"]. We had to take on a black man at that time because in that era, they was makin' people give a little more work here and there to the black people, and we were told, "You gotta put one in your group." That's how we come to wind up with Calvin Brown and another black guy or two. Calvin was a good man, and made a good stuntman.

At MGM, says Hughes, stuntmen who were about to get hit or shot in a scene would be told not to do any sort of wild fall, just a slump, "because MGM didn't want to pay for any big stunt. To save money, they'd tell ya to just slump down. So we named it 'the MGM slump.'"

Terry Leonard was a sad case. I just got through seein' him at [stuntman] Jackie Williams' funeral [April 2007]; he's been busted up so bad over the years, he's got two false hips. On one *Wild West* ["The Night of the Underground Terror"], we were about to do a fight, and we didn't have no breakaway chairs that day. All of a sudden I saw this guy Terry Leonard, and I didn't know who he was, but I thought, "Well, I guess Bob brung him in." As I was "routine-ing" the fight, I told Terry, "You pick this chair up over your head like you're gonna bust Bob, and he'll give you a punch in the belly. You react to the punch, and drop the chair behind you." Well, "Action!," the fight started, the first part of the fight went according to plan, and then Terry picked the chair up over his head and Bob hit him, and Terry came down with that chair and hit Bob right on top of the head [*laughs*]! A big ol', oak captain's chair, and just knocked the shit out of him! I could tell Bob was about half knocked-out, but he was able to shake the cobwebs out and continue. After the scene was over with, ol' Bob said, "Who was that son of a bitch who hit me? How'd he get on the show?" I said, "*I* didn't bring him on the show, I thought *you* did!" [*Laughs*] I still don't know how Terry got on the show, but it was probably through one of our assistant directors, either Charlie Scott or Mike Moder—Mike was guilty once in a while of tryin' to sneak a stuntman in. Well, little Terry Leonard went on and made himself a top name in the business, and even stunt-coordinated the *Wild Wild West* movie [1999]. But he got busted every time he *done* somethin'! [*How often did you get hurt in a* Wild West*?*] I got hit a lot, and [*laughs*] *damaged* here'n'there, but it wasn't nothin' bad. The worst

Cackling madly and sporting (dyed) red hair, Hughes (left) played his most prominent henchman role in *Wild Wild West*'s "The Night of the Vicious Valentine." Robert Conrad is being held by an unidentified actor.

thing I got was getting clipped by a hoof as I was doing a back flip off a running horse ["The Night of the Golden Cobra"].

We had one man, Jerry Laveroni, who couldn't even take a punch and go back against a wall and dribble down the wall [*laughs*]—it took him all day to register that he got "hit"! Laveroni was just *big*. Laveroni was kind of a smart, college-educated–type man. Bob brought him on the show. Now, Bob never *was* one for big guys, he didn't want big men around on the show for the first season or even the *second* season, he didn't want nobody over five-foot-nine on the show. So here comes Laveroni, six-foot-two or -three, weighs probably 220, 230, and he *dwarfs* Bob and me and *most* of the guys that was on the show. But Bob wanted to put Laveroni in there and use him. And the day Bob got hurt [on "The Night of the Fugitives"], they blamed Laveroni, but I don't think Laveroni was really the cause of Bob getting hurt that day.

Well, lemme start at the beginning. The stunt called for Bob to dive from the top of a staircase on a two-story saloon set, grab a chandelier and swing and kick a guy [Laveroni] down on the *first* floor. The same day that saloon fight was going to be shot, I was offered a job playin' a jockey with a loaf of bread under his arm in a bread commercial, and I said, "No, I can't take it, I'm workin' [on *Wild Wild West*]." Bob came to me and said, "Whiiiitey ... *take* that commercial. We can do without you that day."

I said, "Bob, you got an important shot [the chandelier stunt] coming up here that has to be worked out."

"Everything'll be all right," Bob said, "don't you worry about it. You take the commercial," and I did. Well, we *had* discussed that chandelier stunt, how he was gonna *do* it, and I had looked at it realistically and I thought, "Here's a chandelier hanging straight down, and Bob's gonna be up there on the top of the stairs, maybe a little bit *higher* than the chandelier. So he's gonna have to dive *down* at it." Now, you can't dive down at an object that's hangin' straight down, and get a swing out of it. So I knew something would have to be worked out, in order for Bob to do it safely. But at Bob's insistence, I took the bread commercial and I wasn't there to work it out with him.

I got home after doing that commercial and I found out Bob was in the hospital. I was told that he dove down at the chandelier and grabbed it, but Laveroni, instead of waiting to be kicked, left [backed away] too early. In other words, I was told that Laveroni wasn't there to stop Bob's swing. When Laveroni wasn't there to stop Bob's momentum, Bob's hands came off the chandelier and he fell to the floor. I'd taken off to do that commercial, a commercial that I don't think was ever even shown, and so I was gone when Bob got hurt bad that day. That night I went over to see Bob at the little hospital on Riverside Drive [North Hollywood Medical Center, now used as the set for the TV sitcom *Scrubs*]. He was still kind of "out of it," but I told him, I said, "Bob ... I *knew* I shouldn't have gone." He said, "Awww, don't worry about it...." By the way, I looked at the [diving-for-the-chandelier] footage afterwards, looked at it again and again and again. There'd been all this talk about Laveroni leavin' early on the thing, but Bob never even got *to* him. The problem was that Bob dove off that balcony at a chandelier that was a-hangin' straight down. But Laveroni didn't work on the show too much afterwards. Laveroni didn't belong on the show anyway, he was just there because maybe Bob was indebted to him, or because Bob didn't want Laveroni poundin' on him, or *some*thing [*laughs*]!

Right across the street from CBS Studio Center was a bar called the Back Stage where Bob got into a fight with a guy one night. I was standing at the bar when it started, and all of a sudden somebody was pinnin' my arms behind me. I never did see who it was! He grabbed

36. Memories of The Wild Wild West (1965–1969)

This author's brother Jon (left) arranged a 1986 reunion of *Wild Wild West* stuntmen, among them (continuing from left) Hughes, Red West, Dick Cangey and Tom Huff.

me and pinned both arms behind me, and I couldn't move, as Bob was wielding a chair and fighting out there in the middle of the floor. I thought, "What the *hell* is goin' *on*?" as whoever was behind me, the guy who had my arms locked, said, "Don't get into it, Whitey, don't get into it!" Come to find out later that Bob was fightin' [stuntman] Tony Epper's brother-in-law, a studio driver. This boy and Bob got into it, and I don't know what the hell even *started* the fight, unless this guy said something derogatory about Bob—about his size or something [*laughs*]! Bob talked to me later and he said, "I want you to go out and see Tony Epper." That's the only time he ever sent me on an errand. I didn't *want* to go, I couldn't see any reason for going. "What do you want me to say to Tony?"

Bob said, "Tell him that I'm sorry that this happened" and blah blah blah.

I said, "Well, what the hell has Tony got to do with it? This is his brother-in-law."

"Yeah, I know," Bob said, "but Tony might take it different." Tony was a big ol', tough kid who liked to fight, and I think Bob was afraid Tony was gonna pound on him. So he wanted me to go out and reconcile Tony over this thing.

I don't like that kind of tactics, that's kind of racky-tacky to me, sending somebody to ward off a problem you're goin' to have later. Handle your problem yourself! I was a little guy, but I never did have somebody handle my problems. But that was one of Bob's bad habits. And yet, when it came to stunts, he had a lot of guts. I'll never forget the *Wild West* ["The Night of the Tycoons"] where Red West and Dick Cangey were gonna chase Bob up a 14-, 15-step flight of stairs on the side of a building, and fight with him on the landing at the top. There was a door into the building there at the top of the stairs, that door was gonna get knocked open, and the three of them would disappear inside for a moment. *That* was the point at which Jimmy George was gonna take over for Bob. Then Red, Dick and *Jimmy* was supposed to come back out the door and the three of 'em was gonna bust through the rail and fall to the ground below. In the spot where they was gonna land, I'd dug a pit and put a mattress in it, wide enough for all three of 'em to go into, and then covered it up with dirt.

I was standing there watchin' the action: Bob, Red and Dick run up the stairway, they fight at the top, they go through the door—and Red and Dick come back out with *Bob* between 'em. And they go off of that landing into the mattress, and I almost had a heart attack! I told Bob, I said, "You're tryin' to get me fired, boy!" [*Laughs*] But I gotta say, Bob did it just perfect. Bob had planned to do it, he'd told Jimmy George, "*I'm* gonna do this," and off that landing with Red and Dick he went. Yeah, he was one gutsy little bastard!

Every so often, somebody asks me to name a few favorite stunts from *Wild West* and I think to myself, "Oh, mercy!" They were *all* my favorites. I was the kind of guy who always wanted to top the *last* one I did. I did some Western stuff that I liked very much, transferring from a running horse to a stagecoach. Remember that one ["The Night of the Amnesiac"] where Bob was ridin' in a coach, and I was a Mexican heavy? I rode and overtook the coach and transferred to the team of horses. Incidentally, that stagecoach almost turned over. Jack Lilley was driving the four-up and he pretended to get shot and he slumped over in the seat, and then I transferred to the team and I pulled up the team. After it wasn't Jack Lilley drivin' no more, 'cause he supposedly got shot; the team was handled by what they call "a blind driver," a guy inside the coach where the camera couldn't see him, with a little hole he peeped through. Which is a tough thing to do, drive a four-up lying on your belly inside of a blind place. The coach went slightly uphill and the dang thing almost turned over—with Bob hangin' out the side of it [*laughs*]! It was so close!

Next the scene called for Bob to stand up in the driver's seat and point a gun down at me and then get shot [by a sniper in the nearby trees]. I told him, I said, "Bob, when you get shot, just do a fall out over the left wheel horse and then go to the ground." Well, he missed the damn horse and went head-first down to the ground! It wasn't funny but it *was* funny! I said, "How in the hell did you miss that horse?" [*Laughs*] So that's some of my favorite stuff, the Western stuff that I did. And I liked the fight stuff that we routined.

Oh, and Jimmy George and I did some "high work." For instance, [in "The Night of the Fugitives"], Jimmy was doubling Bob in a scene where he comes out a high church steeple window and slides down a zip line from the steeple to a building across the street. With *me* on his shoulder! We was up pretty high, we wasn't safety-ed in any way. I was just kinda draped over Jimmy's shoulder and I said, "Think you can carry my weight across the street?" "Oh, yeah!" Jimmy said, and we got it done. We done some good, good stuff together.

At the end of ["The Night of the Vipers"], which I think was the last show Nick Adams ever did, I doubled Nick falling out of a church bell tower. He was playin' a little crooked sheriff, he was up in the tower with a rifle, and Bob took a shot at him from the street and got him. And then I came out of the tower and landed, supposedly, in the street. Of course, in the street they had a catcher [mattress] for me. And it was a smaaall catcher, nine feet long by maybe six feet wide, and it wasn't over 36 inches high. Well, I saw that I'd have to come out over a roof [in a lower part of the church], and to clear that roof, I'd have to push off from the tower. I knew that if I hung my foot on the edge of that roof, I'd land down in the street and I'd be hurt bad or killed or whatever. And of course I had to land on the catcher just right; you have to get into it flat on your back or else you're liable to get hurt pretty good.

As I was gettin' ready to do the stunt, Bob said, "Whitey, hold it just a minute. Before you go up there [to the tower] ... where are you gonna land on this catcher?" Well, that *reeeeally* put me on the spot. But I took some black tape and made an X on the catcher and I said, "The middle of my back will be *there*," and I made another X on the edge of the catcher, "and my right foot should be about *here*." And I went up to the tower and got ready to do the fall. From the tower, I couldn't even *see* my catcher, but I knew where it was at. Then we done the shot. When you watch that show, you can see the little push-off that I did coming out of the tower, in order to clear that roof. (I never did like to do a push on a high fall, 'cause it kinda gives away what you're doin'.) To make a long story short, after the director [Marvin Chomsky] said, "Cut," Bob said, "Hold it, Whitey, hold it. Don't move." He came over

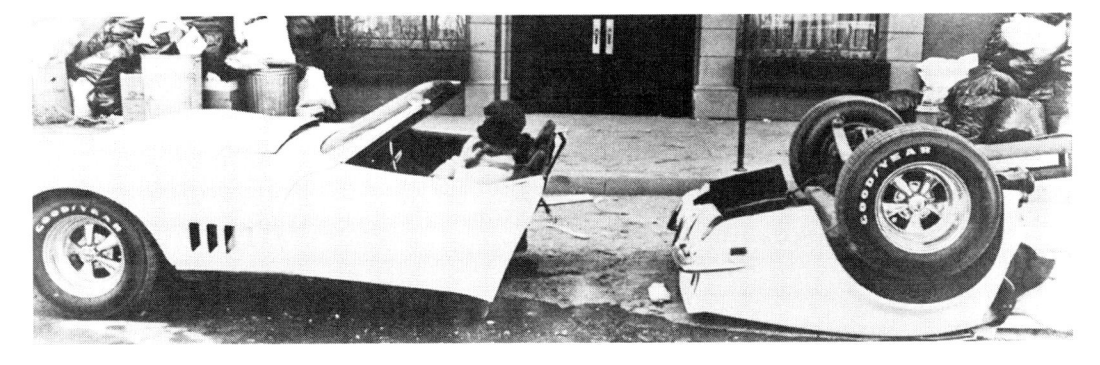

In the years after *Wild West*, Hughes performed hair-raising stunts in more motion pictures: taking a loooong fall between two "mothball fleet" ships into Suisun Bay in 1975's *The Killer Elite* and crashing a Corvette through a street construction site (slicing the car in half) in 1976's *The Gumball Rally*.

to me, I was still lying on the catcher, and he said, "Get up." Well [*laughs*], my back was lying right on the one X, and my heel was on the *other* X. I had *so* much fun doin' stuff with Bob.

Then there was one episode ["The Night of the Sedgewick Curse"] where I was a doubling a girl [Sharon Acker] in a runaway buggy, and I had Jimmy George doubling Bob, catching the horse and doing a Pony Express up onto the horse and stopping it. It was a great shot, it worked so good. That's the kind of stuff that I enjoyed doing so much. [*Were there any stuntwomen on the show?*] No, they didn't use any women stunt doubles. If there were women to double on *Wild West*, I'd double 'em—I was the right size. Like, we had a girl [Melinda Plowman in "The Night of the Doomsday Formula"] who was supposed to be in the middle of a ring of fire, and Jimmy George, doubling for Bob Conrad, slides past her on a zip line and picks her up. I doubled her. I doubled women in movies too. In *Love Has Many Faces* [1965] I doubled Lana Turner in a horse fall. The horse in that scene was my falling horse Poco a Poco—I gave him that name because I trained him "little by little." The stunt girls hadn't yet started their association [The Stunt Women's Association, founded in 1967]. Polly Burson was the top woman double at that time, but she didn't raise as much hell about men stunt-doubling women as some of the younger stunt girls did. They said, "Whitey, you gotta stop doublin' these women. That's *our* job."

Another fun memory was the time Bob made an appearance on [the talk show] *The Joey Bishop Show*. Bob was out on the stage awhile talking to Bishop, like talk show guests do, and then Bob mentioned me and had me come out, and he said I was the greatest stuntman in the business. Boy, that's quite a coast-to-coast compliment! Then, just like Bob and I had planned, he and I started fighting. In fact, I knocked Bobby back over Joey Bishop's desk, right onto ol' Bishop's lap [*laughs*]. This just shocked the hell out of him, he didn't know *what* was going on! The fight went on, and finally Bob throwed *me* out into the audience. We had Red West and Tommy Huff sitting out in the audience to catch me when Bob knocked me off the stage. And my wife Dotti and Red's wife Patty and Andi Garrett were all sitting behind Red and Tommy, so that if anything went wrong, they would be an *extra* buffer between the audience and the action. They were all catchers, so we didn't get lawsuits! We had a hell of a wild time, and it went over good. *So* good, in fact, that later on, when Don Rickles was a guest host on *Joey Bishop*, he wanted to have us do it again, so we re-did it for Rickles!

Bob always carried a couple of ex-boxers on the set as stand-ins and extras. Well, Dick Cangey had been a boxer himself, and he really started touting the boxing idea to Bob. Once Bob got interested in boxing, and Dick started teachin' him to box, we used to go over to Stage 9, to the old set where the *Joe Palooka*s had been shot, and during our spare time we'd spar around in the boxing ring used in the *Palooka*s. We'd also go over to Inglewood, a suburb of L.A., to the boxing matches, and also to the Olympic Auditorium for the matches there. Then Bob found out there was a boxer named Frankie Crawford whose promoter-manager wanted to sell his [Crawford's] contract. Bob wanted all of us guys to go in $1000 each. I told Bob that Frankie had already had his best fights and that Frankie was now on the downhill slide, and that we should buy some young boy who had a lot of potential and train him ourselves. That didn't set good with Bob. We were going on hiatus for the summer so I had a chance to go to Mexico on Sam Peckinpah's *The Wild Bunch* [1969] and then be back for the start in the fall of *Wild Wild West*. I was still telling Bob that it was a bad deal to buy Frankie. Anyway, I told Dotti not to give any money for Frankie and I would take care of the matter myself when I returned. Well, when I returned, Bob started treating me differently and I knew I had fallen out of favor with him.

An actor named Ramon Novarro was killed [in October 1968], murdered by a young man from back east somewhere. This young guy had made some phone calls from Novarro's house to his girlfriend, so the police later followed up on the calls and picked the girl up and had her extradited to Burbank. The police had her in their custody one night at the Back Stage, police from Chicago who were working on the Novarro case. It just so happened that I was there that night too. Me and Dotti and my brother Billy and his wife Alicia had been to the Imperial Garden over on the Sunset Strip for dinner, and now we were sitting in a booth at the Back Stage. There in a booth in the corner were them two or three cops from Chicago, *and* the girl, *and* Bob Conrad, *and* a couple friends of ours, Norm and Bob from the North Hollywood police. Naturally, my wife being with me, we didn't drink heavy, we were just having a drink or two.

My brother Billy had on what they called a Nehru jacket, and this Chicago cop came by, drunk, and started picking on Billy's Nehru jacket. And he reached over to Billy and flipped his tie and said, "Buy your tie a drink." My brother, who was about as fast as a guy could be, jumped up, and I said, "Sit down, sit down, sit down...." The cop was just more or less jokin', but it irritated Billy. I sat Billy down, and this cop went on to the men's room, or wherever he went. When he came back by, he again reached over and touched Billy's tie and again: "Give your tie a drink." Again I sat my brother back down and I said, "Now, listen. Shut up about these cops. Don't worry about these cops, just sit down and let's have a drink." Well, Bob overheard me saying "cops." I don't know why he took it out on me, but he jumped up and ran over and stuck his finger across the table at my nose: "You say 'cops' one more time and you're off the show!" And I knocked the *shit* out of him! I just reached over and stuck one on him, and I went over the table after him. The only thing that saved him was Norm and Bob, the North Hollywood policemen; one of 'em had me around the throat and one of 'em had a hammerlock on me. They were tryin' to keep me off of Bob, and they were talkin' to me: "Whitey! Whitey! Whitey! Settle down now, settle down!" I was gonna *work* on Bob that night, and he knew it—he kept back-pedalin' away from me.

Bob said, "I'll see ya at work in the morning," and I said, "No, you won't see me at work. You don't want me back to work." He kept after me to forget about it, but I said, "No. *you'll* never forget about it, Bob, so ... let's just don't worry about it. I won't be in." Well, he talked to me a little bit, kept telling me, "Come on in," and I said okay.

I didn't feel good about it, but the next morning I took my script and walked on in, walked over to the outdoor set where we were gonna work that day. Everybody was there, the associate producer Leonard Katzman and everybody, and when I walked on the set, Bob approached me, chest out, and said, "When you get time, I want to see you in that ring" [the Joe Palooka boxing ring]. He was challenging me in front of all the gang, because he was embarrassed over what happened. Well, that just upset me so bad. Red was standin' there, and Dick Cangey, and Tom Huff, and Jimmy George, and the producer and actors. It embarrassed the hell out of me. I said, "*You're* in the ring right now, Bob. Let's get your ass out the gate, let's get out there on the street, and you and I will have it out. *We'll* straighten this thing out. There won't be nobody responsible but me and you." Well, he couldn't take me up on it, because of his contract with CBS. I threw my script and said, "Now, stick that up your ass," and I turned to Leonard Katzman and I said, "*Thank* you, Mr. Katzman, and everybody, for all these wonderful times," and I started walking off the set. And Red and Dick, as God is my witness, were walkin' along with me: "Whitey, don't go, don't go, don't quit!" I said, "Hey. Guys. You saw what happened. How can I *stay?* I can't stay under these conditions." My guys loved me so much that they didn't want me to go off the show. But Bob pulled that on me. With Bob, it came down to "I forgive you but I don't forgive you."

And later on, down the road, I got paid. Bruce Lansbury was the producer of the show, and the brother of Angela Lansbury incidentally, and he went ahead and paid me for two episodes that they had yet to do, that I didn't work on. But I had kinda prepared 'em, and so he paid me. Bruce Lansbury was a super-great guy, a *terrific* guy to have in your corner. In 2002, he came to the Golden Boot Award show [at Merv Griffin's Beverly Hilton in Beverly Hills] when I got the Boot, and I was greatly honored by his presence.

On Balboa Boulevard in Encino, about a mile from my house, and about a mile from Bob's house, there was a golf course with a jogging trail around it, and it was great to go jogging there. During the run of *Wild West*, Bob and I would always go there; we could do an Air Force 11-minute mile at that time. Later, after *Wild Wild West* was cancelled, but the falling-out between me and him was still fresh in our minds, I was out jogging the trail and I saw ol' Bob comin' toward me. I just kept joggin' toward him and about 100 feet before he got to me, he stuck out his hand and said, "Friends?"

I said, "Bob, I was always your friend. I was never anything *but* your friend, Bob. You're the one that wanted to tear it up." I told him the truth that day, standin' there on that jogging trail. I said, "*You're* the one who tore up our friendship, Bob. I loved you like a brother and I worked for you hard, I gave my all for you, Bob, just because you gave me a break in the business." And he and I became talkin' friends again. Then one night I was in my car and I heard this horn a-honkin' alongside of me and I said, "What the hell *is* that?" and Dotti said, "It's Bob Conrad, in the next lane." He was a-wavin' at me and a-wavin' at me. We stopped, and he said, "Let's go have a drink," and I said okay. So me and Dotti and him drove up on Ventura Boulevard and we sat there in some bar 'til two in the morning talkin' about the good ol' days. Our fight didn't even come up at all, we just talked about the fun we'd had [on *Wild Wild West*]. But I nnnever got to work with Bob again ... not one more day did I ever get to work for him. He had several TV series after *Wild West*, and he never called me to work for him. I never worked on anything Bob ever did after that.

For me, *The Wild Wild West* was party time. It was not a job. I just loved workin' that show, and I think most of the other guys did too. I especially loved the Western action stuff,

Whitey poses with the woman he calls "the sweetest gal in the world," his wife of 70 years Dotti.

where we used horses and wagons—I thought they were the best episodes. Well, no, I shouldn't say that, 'cause I liked all the rest of 'em too. It just wasn't like any other work. I'd go to work and felt free to do whatever Bob and I wanted to do, and we'd dream up stuff—and some of the stuff we'd dream up was ungodly stuff [*laughs*]. On that *Wild West* set they used to say, "Roll the cameras and call the ambulances!"—all of us were so damn wild, they thought it was just a matter of time before somebody got hurt! We did a lot of things that was waaay out of reason, like my fall out of that church tower. It was a fun show, and I enjoyed it so very much. And I want to make it clear to you that I have no regrets about *anything* about *Wild Wild West*. I enjoyed every minute of *The Wild Wild West* and every show was interesting.

And I want to express the fact that I enjoyed working with Bob Conrad *so* much. To this day I love Bob, even though he was not loyal, as far as friendship was concerned. I never worked with Bob after *Wild West*, and neither did Dick Cangey. Dick had served Bob faithfully, but in all his series after *Wild Wild West* Bob never gave Dick a day of work, and I didn't think that was fair. Bob wasn't always loyal to the people that were loyal to *him*, and he doesn't appreciate what we did [on *The Wild Wild West*] to make him look good. But I see Bob occasionally, and I talk to him once in a while.

It was the spring of 2002 when I was told that I was getting the Golden Boot for my stunt work in pictures. They wanted Bob to present it to me in August. I called him and asked if he would be my presenter but at that time he wasn't sure if he would be able to. I was really pleased when he called the Golden Boot Awards Committee and said he would, and he paid me the compliment of saying I was the greatest stuntman ... ever.

I loved Bob like I loved my own brothers and to this day I still have that feeling in my heart.

Author's note: When I learned on July 9, 2009, that Whitey Hughes had died, I immediately phoned Robert Conrad, got his answering machine and said that I'd like some comments about Hughes and his passing for publication in *Western Clippings* magazine. Two days later, Conrad called back to comply with my request: "If he wasn't the best, he was one of 'em. [*Silence*] That's *it. That's* the quote."

Richard Kiel

One of The Wild Wild West's *great casting coups was getting 3'10" Michael Dunn, the accomplished actor of* Ship of Fools *(1965) fame, to sign on to play the series' popular recurring villain Miguelito Loveless—and it was also a brilliant stroke to hire the 7'2" Richard Kiel to play his mute henchman Voltaire. Childlike but frighteningly imposing, the towering, black-clad Voltaire devotedly bodyguarded his diminutive master in three of the ten Loveless episodes, including the first and best, "The Night the Wizard Shook the Earth." Playing the showy role was a highpoint in Kiel's early career, leading to other good TV parts and eventually international fame when the actor played another* oversized underling, *the steel-toothed Jaws, in Roger Moore James Bond movies of the '70s.*

Why did the loyal, lethal Voltaire leave Loveless' side after three episodes? Richard Kiel here tells the tangled real-life story of Voltaire's reel-life vanishing act.

When I was offered the role of Voltaire in *The Wild Wild West*'s first Dr. Loveless episode, "The Night the Wizard Shook the Earth," the show was not yet on the air. It was sort of surprising to be asked to be in a series starring Bob Conrad, because he was on the short side, and I'd heard that you couldn't work in his shows if you were over six feet. Well, I was 7'2"! But since I was a giant and always played giants, since I towered over everybody in *all* the shows I did, I guess Bob knew it wouldn't reflect on him. Also, he was gonna beat me up [*laughs*], so that would make him look even better! I was in good shape in those days, and I was able to take the punches and make it look good. It helped me to be successful at playing villains.

Apart from the fact that Bob Conrad did his own stunts, one of the things that I remember most vividly about him was that, as we were sitting chatting one day, he said, "It's very important to me that this show be a success. If it can stay on for three years, I'll be a millionaire." As we kept chatting, he mentioned that when he did the TV series *Hawaiian Eye* for Warner Brothers, he really got screwed, and ended up doing those for like 500 bucks an episode.

Like two other memorable Richard Kiel characters, Eegah (in *Eegah*) and Jaws (in *The Spy Who Loved Me* and *Moonraker*), Voltaire was a mute. "Window-dressing" in scenes featuring his minuscule master Dr. Loveless (Michael Dunn, left), he could convey emotion only via facial expressions.

At the time, I think the Screen Actors Guild minimum for a TV show on a weekly basis was $315 an episode, and Warners paid Bob 500 an episode—but that also bought him out on all his residuals. The Screen Actors Guild has made it illegal to do that, but they hadn't yet at that time. Bob told me that he got a total of 500 and that was *it*, and no residuals even if those episodes were run over and over. He said, "By the time you pay your agent and your p.r. guy their percentages, and they take out the income tax, the $500 was eroded to about 275. *Then,* I got all this fan mail, and when I took it to Warners to discuss how the costs of answering it were going to be paid, they said, 'That's *your* problem!'" So he was ... I won't say bitter, but let's say he'd gotten very *savvy*. I remember hearing, too, that at one point the network wanted to change the day or the time that *Wild Wild West* aired. The show was doing well, Bob was concerned that the ratings might drop, so he personally went to the network and got them to let it be. Bob was a real hands-on, involved guy who was out there to make sure that the thing was a success. Then, years later, when Bob played "Pappy" Boyington in the series *Baa Baa Black Sheep*, he got $600,000 an episode, which is a far cry from the 500 an episode with the buyout included for all residuals, and you pay your own fan mail! So I gotta hand it to the guy, he did a good job as a businessman. As for Ross Martin, he was a nice guy and a good actor. I remembered seeing him in a thriller called *Experiment in Terror* [1962], where he played an asthmatic psycho who terrorizes Lee Remick and Stefanie Powers, and he was very, very good in that.

Doing "The Night the Wizard Shook the Earth" was almost like doing a pilot, because the director was Bernie Kowalski, an absolute perfectionist. Kowalski was *very*, very good, he gave you a lot of good direction. We did scenes over and over again, like we were making a movie. I was used to working on episodic television and B-movies ... or C-minus movies [*laughs*]—where they didn't take the time to shoot things over and over and over. But apparently Bernie Kowalski had permission to do this. As a result, it took something like eight or nine shooting days to do the episode, which for a weekly TV show was a long time; they were normally done in four or five days, six or seven at the very most. "Wizard" was *extremely* well-done. I think it was because they had Michael Dunn, who had just done the movie *Ship of Fools*, for which he received an Oscar nomination. As we were doing "Night the Wizard Shook the Earth," he was handled like a big star, and they wanted to make sure that they utilized him to the utmost.

I got along with Michael Dunn fine, except for the fact that he was an egomaniac. He was a brilliant guy and he had an absolutely perfect memory. From shot to shot, he could remember what his foot was doing in the shot before, what his finger was doing, every time. On "Wizard" we did maybe six or seven takes of each shot on the average and, again, I think it was because they had Michael in it. He was highly respected, treated like he was Elizabeth Taylor or Paul Newman, and catered to.

Michael Dunn was in a lot of pain. Either somebody told me that, or *he* mentioned it. But even without being told, you could tell by looking at him when he walked and when he sat down. His upper body was bigger than his legs, he was not proportionate, and people with that condition have problems with joints and things. I was careful in the scenes where I carried him around. But Michael drove his own car, he had special stuff to enable him to do that, he was a guy who still managed to get around. I respected him for that, and for being very intelligent.

I was once asked whether I thought it would be tougher to be a giant or a dwarf. I think it must be much tougher to be a dwarf. Just the fact of having people looking down at you, and having to look up at everybody from down there ... it's gotta be tough. Michael Dunn compensated for all that, and grew beyond that, and that's what made him so brilliant. He was a talented guy and, considering his limitations, he did really well. Michael made [being a dwarf] work as an advantage, as I have with being a giant; he did it with Dr. Loveless, me with Jaws. Another thing I remember about Michael is how he would really study his script. In the beginning of my career, I was much the same way. I remember doing an episode of *Thriller* ["Well of Doom"] where I had 27 lines of English dialect. Well, by the time I finished studying, I knew *every*body's part in the script. People considered me a pain in the ass when they couldn't remember their lines and I'd start 'em out [*laughs*]!

Also in "Night the Wizard Shook the Earth" was Phoebe Dorin [as Dr. Loveless' accomplice and singing partner Antoinette], a nice lady. I thought she was Michael's girlfriend but in your recent interview with her, she said that they were just good friends. Boyfriend-girlfriend was the impression *I* got, but she denies that. They'd had a successful nightclub act, singing and so on, and so he was able to get her on the show and do a song with her ["Bring Me Little Water, Sylvie"]. Which was a little odd in an episode of *The Wild Wild West*, it really seemed like it would be out of place, but they made it work.

As we were doing "Wizard," I was doing my best to try to be interesting in the scenes. For instance, I was in the background as Michael and Phoebe were singing, and as I enjoyed the song I opened up a little leather bag and started popping licorice pieces into my mouth and tapping my feet. Robert Conrad being a very sharp guy, he noticed that and he made a big joke about it to me. He knew what I was up to, scene-stealing. The next day they shot a closeup of my tapping feet.

Another thing I liked about that show: Leslie Parrish [playing Loveless' partner in crime]. Oh, God, what a crush I had on her. On one of my first half-dozen dates as a young man, I took a girl to see *Li'l Abner* [1959] and came away with crushes on Leslie Parrish, who played Daisy Mae, *and* on Julie Newmar, who was also pretty exciting in that—and then I later had the opportunity to work with both of them. Leslie Parrish was an absolute sweetheart, unpretentious and down-to-earth. She was very, very, very nice and sweet to me and talked with me a great deal. I was recently married at that time, and wasn't the kind of guy who steps out on his wife—because if I *was*, I would *definitely* have been asking her out! I remember she found some kittens on the soundstage there at CBS Studio Center, wild ones, and she rescued them and took them home with her. I was a little jealous of those kittens [*laughs*]!

The combination of Dr. Loveless and Voltaire was very successful, and they kept wanting me to come back. The second Loveless episode was "The Night That Terror Stalked the Town," directed by Alvin Ganzer, someone I worked with many times. Then, two things happened more or less simultaneously, which affected my future on *Wild Wild West*: One was that I decided that I didn't want to keep doing shows where I didn't talk, because I was starting to realize that a lot of people thought that I *couldn't* talk. I told my agent Herman Zimmerman, "I really don't want to do any more of these *Wild Wild West*s where I don't talk," and so when he was contacted about me doing another one, he said, "Richard doesn't want to do any more unless he gets to talk." The casting people got real outraged and uptight and angry and said, "He'll find himself *not* working for CBS again if he takes that attitude." *My* reaction to that was, "Well ... so *be* it," because I'd been in other situations that were similar. For instance, I did a *Lassie* episode and worked on Thanksgiving Day, we worked into what they call Golden Time, and so I was supposed to be paid about four times my usual daily rate. When there wasn't any overtime on my check, I questioned it, and I was told, "Just forget about it, kid, and we'll use you again." I figured it out, and ... with the four-times payment ... who *cares* whether they use me again [*laughs*]? So that's what I told 'em [that he wanted the overtime payment]; they said they weren't gonna pay me; and I ended up having to go to Screen Actors Guild, who pursued it. The Screen Actors Guild ruled against the *Lassie* show and the producers were told to pay up—and if they didn't, if they were found in non-compliance, they would get fined a percentage each *day*. It's really cost-prohibitive *not* to pay, and so I ended up getting a check for like twelve, fourteen hundred bucks. And the *Lassie* producers did use me again! I learned a great lesson from that: When people shaft you, they never want to see you again, but if they end up having to pay you what you deserve, then they're more likely to hire you again. It's really weird! So I wasn't really worried about the idea that I would never work for CBS again, because I was kinda threatened on *Lassie* and I came out all right.

The other thing that happened around that same time was that my writer-friend Robert V. Barron, who'd written a number of *Bonanza* episodes, including one called "Hoss and the Leprechauns" which was very popular, wrote and submitted a *Bonanza* story that I could be *in*, playing one of the main guest stars. As I was looking forward to doing that, I got a bad-guy role in an episode of *Honey West* ["King of the Mountain"] with Anne Francis. My uncle was in town from Michigan, and he and my grandfather wanted to come out to CBS Studio Center and visit me while I was working. Anne Francis is a dear lady: That particular *Honey West* was being shot on a house set with a big staircase, and she sat on the stairs chatting with my grandfather and my uncle. My grandfather knew she was a movie star, and he was quite enchanted with the whole thing.

Just before we went to lunch, I said, "Why don't we drop by the *Wild Wild West* show, and I'll introduce you to Robert Conrad." My grandfather and uncle were all excited about that. I had already done two *Wild West*s so I had no problem getting in there with them, and I introduced 'em to Bob. He was very nice to them, and he said to me, "In a couple of weeks we'll be doing another show that you'll be in, so we'll see you then." I said, "Bob ... I don't think I'm gonna be *doing* it. I really hate to get caught in this rut of never talking, doing show after show without talking. The casting people said, 'Take it or leave it, Voltaire's not gonna talk,' so I decided not to do it." Bob said, "*Don't leave the lot* until you come back and see me. We'll get that worked out."

My uncle and grandfather and I went to lunch in the commissary, I remember it very well because Gene Barry was having lunch in there and my uncle and grandfather were excited about seeing him. But he just shined 'em on, he was really rude—just the opposite of Anne Francis! They asked him for his autograph and he just sort of [*Kiel lets out an angry-sounding roar*] and scribbled it out! Anyway, when I got back to the *Honey West* set there was a message for me to call my agent. When I did, he said, "I just got called by the casting people for *The Wild Wild West*. They're rewriting the script and you're going to talk."

Well, [the "down side"] of this is that I'd been looking forward to doing that *Bonanza* because it was a really good part with all kinds of dialogue and I wanted to do it. In fact, Robert V. Barron had gotten me a copy of the teleplay and I'd taken it to an acting coach and had him work with me on it. When I found out that I'd be returning as Voltaire to *Wild Wild West*, I checked and, sure enough, the two shows were going to film at the same time! And we couldn't get the *Bonanza* people to change that shooting date. I'd already agreed to do the *Wild West*, and the script had been rewritten at my request, so I felt that I was obligated to do the *Wild West*. Dick Peabody, a tall, skinny guy, six foot eight or something, got the *Bonanza* part that had been written for me and which I wanted so badly.

That third *Wild West* episode ["The Night of the Whirring Death"] had a director who went on to do some big-time movies, Mark Rydell [*The Cowboys, The Rose, On Golden Pond*, etc.]. At that time, he wasn't as serious as a director as he probably became later, and it was sort of a lark. He was havin' fun, a nice guy who did a good job. In the beginning of that episode, Artie [Ross Martin] asks James West [Robert Conrad], "Who's the biggest man that you know?" and West answers, "Voltaire." Artie says, "Well, he's back. And, what's more, he *talks.*" That's all they had to do to explain it!

As I mentioned before, Michael Dunn was also an egomaniac. I don't think he liked what I was doing to steal scenes, and I'm sure he didn't like the idea that suddenly Voltaire was *talking*. And all of a sudden, after this third one, I wasn't asked back as Voltaire. I can't help but think that the producers of *Wild Wild West* had respect for me as an actor, because they came up with another episode that I did [the non–Loveless "The Night of the Simian Terror"]. It's always been my feeling that the reason that "Night of the Whirring Death" was the last show I did with Michael was that he didn't like the fact that I was trying to hold my own and talking. I wasn't out as far as the *show* was concerned, but I was out as far as working with Michael. In your interview with Phoebe Dorin she said that, after a while, Michael had *her* replaced—he wanted to have his own wife play Antoinette. Well, the way they were treating Michael, it couldn't help but give *any*body a big head. That's the movie business.

My fourth and last *Wild Wild West* was "The Night of the Simian Terror," a more dramatic show for me, and one where I got to talk quite a bit. Dabbs Greer played a Senator who had four sons, three of normal size and a fourth who was too big and was rejected, and was given away to a scientist and grew up with gorillas! I of course played the rejected, discontented son who finally comes back to take revenge. I was allowed to talk in the third Loveless episode, which was good even though I was sort of like Lennie from *Of Mice and Men*; and now I was talking again in "Simian Terror," where they let me do more than that. The problem I ran into at that time was that actors of my size were pigeonholed into either monsters or dummies. They used to have a guy at Universal Studio Tours all made-up like Frankenstein, and I was offered that job. I turned it down. I was struggling to try to be a tall actor, rather than Frankenstein or Lennie. But those types of roles [Frankenstein and Lennie] *can* lead to better things, like it did with Boris Karloff, and with Lon Chaney, Jr. And with me.

I think doing those four *Wild Wild West*s was good for my career, especially the two where I talked. That gave me the opportunity to do shows like *I Spy*, where I got to be dramatic and talk. I also did an episode of a Western series called *The Monroes*, a well-done show with Barbara Hershey and Michael Anderson, Jr., who had gone to a special voice coach-dialect coach to get rid of his English accent and make him sound more like an American Western guy. It was an episode called "Ghosts of Paradox"—and also in it was Michael Dunn! In that show, I had as big a role as he did, and he was ... like ... *furious* when he found out that I was on it. I was a little disappointed by [his attitude]. This *Monroes* was done while he was still regularly appearing as Loveless on *Wild Wild West* but I didn't feel too bad that I wasn't continuing to be used as Voltaire because you can wear something like that out. In "Ghosts of Paradox," I wasn't carrying him around quite as much, I was helping him out, and I was equal to him in terms of the characters' strength and the dialogue. And I could tell that he was furious. Actors are usually pretty intuitive, and I knew he was not happy to be doing a show with me.

The Wild Wild West was a huge success as a TV series because Bob Conrad and Ross Martin worked really well together. Bob knew what he was doing as an actor. He wasn't very tall—in fact, he was a pretty short guy—but, like another short actor, Alan Ladd, he didn't come off that way. I liked Bob because he was a good actor who had developed a strong voice and great techniques, and a presence, and carved out a marvelous career for himself. To me he was like a mentor, somebody to learn from, because I was trying to get ahead except, instead of being short, I was too tall. He knew that I was trying to be a scene-stealer and trying to be

36. Memories of The Wild Wild West (1965–1969)

noticed in that "Night the Wizard Shook the Earth" scene and he thought that was *good*. If everybody in a show is doing that, if everybody's interesting, you end up with a better product. I thought he had a lot on the ball, he was a very competitive, macho guy in real life, and it came through in his role on *The Wild Wild West*. In the fight scenes he was very good, very athletic. He was pretty confident in his own abilities. I *liked* him. He was a very determined guy, and I think I understood where he was comin' from: He wanted that show to be a success, and it did what he wanted. I think James West was the best role he ever played.

And Michael Dunn did really well as Dr. Loveless. He was well-received by the public, they loved him and they appreciated his talent. Of course, it didn't work out for Phoebe Dorin or for myself, but ... I still liked him. And understood him, and felt sorry for him. I understood his pain, and his ego, and so I didn't have any problem with Michael. I didn't want to

After years of oxymoronically playing "small parts," the sky-high Kiel shot to semi-stardom with prominent roles in two James Bond adventures (one of them, *Moonraker* with Blanche Ravalec, pictured). Visit his fan club website (www.RichardKiel.com).

have a whole career of carrying this dwarf around [*laughs*], but I understood what they were doing and I tried to help make it work.

Kenneth Chase

In every episode of The Wild Wild West, *Secret Service agent Artemus Gordon would don an elaborate, usually outlandish disguise in order to work undercover and/or to infiltrate the gang of the Villain of the Week. As at least one critic pointed out, all this subterfuge was pointless since no one ever recognized Gordon as a government man when he was* un*disguised. But it provided the series with its weekly dose of comic relief and kept Ross Martin happy; he accepted the role only after being told that he would be able to enjoy the character actor's dream of a strong new role in each segment. In* reel *life it was master-of-disguise Gordon who changed his own features but in* real *life the magic was worked, in the series' fourth season, by a young, new-to-the-business makeup man named Kenneth Chase.*

My wife Marylyn's father was a makeup artist; before she and I got together, I wasn't aware such a job existed. His name was Bob Mark and he had been the head makeup guy at Republic Pictures for twenty years. When I met him, Republic was no longer in business and he was working freelance. My getting into the makeup profession was his idea, because Marylyn and I were both 19 when we got married and my prospects weren't very good. At first my wife's mother and father *weren't* interested in trying to get me into that business, for all the obvious reasons: because of all the temptations, and the lifestyle. But I guess they thought it would still be a better alternative than where I was at that time.

I was "on permit" when I first started, meaning that I wasn't a regular member of Makeup Artists and Hairstylists Local 706. But things were so busy in those days that they went outside of the regular membership to people who were related to members and had received training. The very first assignment I had was a TV series called *The Long, Hot Summer* [1965-66]; I worked for Tony Lloyd, the head guy on that, for a while. Then I bounced around doing different things, including the TV series *The Time Tunnel*, and the first big break I had was *Planet of the Apes* [1968] on which I did the makeup for Dr. Zaius [played by Maurice Evans], who was one of the main characters. To get to work on that movie was a big deal for *anybody* who was starting out in makeup. John Chambers was the mentor of all of us [the *Apes* makeup artists] and there were training sessions at 20th Century–Fox and I guess he felt I was doing really well in the training sessions because he encouraged me and actually assigned me that plum character, which was unusual 'cause I wasn't even a journeyman makeup artist at that time. And it didn't go unnoticed by a lot of the older guys, who sort of resented that. There were little pitfalls here and there on *Planet of the Apes* but it worked out just fine. Once that movie was over, I started building some false noses and things, teaching myself how to do that, with John Chambers' help.

Prior to the start of *Wild Wild West* Season 4, I got a couple of jobs working on that series as an extra helper, when Don Schoenfeld was the head makeup guy. I kind of established myself there as being pretty handy, and when Don decided to leave the show and I heard about it, I showed up at George Lane's office door at CBS Studio Center where *Wild West* was shot. George was the head of the makeup department, and I came in with a jar full of false noses and things that I had made at home. I guess that worked, because he gave me the show. For a young guy, which I was at the time, it was a great opportunity to get to do all those *Wild West* make-ups, it was just fantastic. I wanted that job in a big way.

Ross Martin was a little reluctant about me at first because I was so young, only 26, which was really young in those days. In fact, he didn't know that I knew this, but he actually went to George Lane and tried to get George to hire somebody else. But that was before I actually did any of those nice makeups on Ross. He was great after that.

Robert Conrad was kind of an odd character.

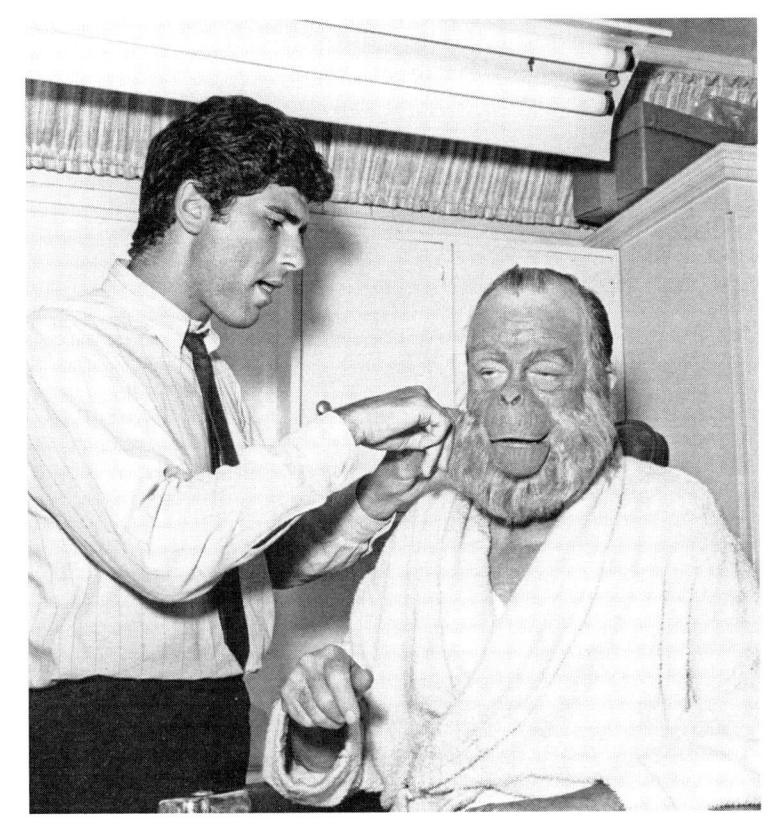

Kenneth Chase applying Maurice Evans' orangutan makeup on *Planet of the Apes.*

He was pretty close to Don Schoenfeld so I don't think he particularly liked me, and he didn't have much to do with me. Conrad didn't wear makeup, incidentally. He was a pretty good-looking guy and had a nice skin tone, and didn't really require any. He was a little bit full of himself, but the nice thing about him was that whatever you saw was *real*. If he didn't like you, at least he wasn't somebody who went behind your back. Conversely, at least in that one instance, Ross Martin was just wonderful to *me* and then went behind my back to try to get me fired, so ... you can take that for what it's worth! I'm speaking ill of the dead so let me quickly add that I really liked Ross and we became very cordial and had a very nice relationship once I proved myself to him. Ross' makeups usually involved false noses—there was always a false nose—and a beard. Ross' makeup as a Russian priest [in "The Night of the Cossacks"] was a favorite of mine because I hand-laid a long beard, which was a skill I worked very long and hard to develop. I used to really love doing beards. John Chambers was the one who had the molds of Ross' face and supplied the noses and the different things that we put on him.

It was just a great job for a young guy. We worked 13, 14, sometimes 15 hours a day, and there was a lot of action and activity on the set, a lot of bravado. There was a lot of testosterone goin' on there [*laughs*]. If memory serves, we had to be there by six in the morning, and we'd still be there at seven, eight o'clock at night. I think I was there pretty much all the time. The hairdresser was a woman named Esperanza Corona, who was Tyrone Power's hairdresser. She was a very elegant Mexican woman and a real pleasure. The hairdressers did men *and* women, and they did wigs and haircuts and all that stuff.

Early on in that fourth season, Ross Martin broke his leg on the set [while shooting the episode "The Night of the Avaricious Actuary"]. While he was being moved to an ambulance on a gurney, I followed along, peeling off his makeup from his face [*laughs*]. Then later in the season, he had a heart attack, so for several episodes he was replaced in the role of Jim West's partner by a couple of pretty well-known character actors, Charlie Aidman and William Schallert. They were really, really nice guys, and cooperative. That's all you have to do to have the makeup man like you, just be cooperative [*laughs*]! For one episode ["The Night of the Pelican"] I did Aidman as a Chinaman with a bald cap—a pretty elegant makeup. Bald caps were difficult and I loved the challenge of doing them.

I'll tell you one thing that was very funny, but Ross Martin sure didn't think it was funny: He was a little bit of a prima donna, and one of the things that irritated him more than aaanything else, was sitting in the makeup chair for two hours and then, once he was made-up and ready, being kept waiting to do his scenes. There was one regular director, and I don't remember who it was, who didn't really like Ross very much and, I swear, kept him waiting on purpose [*laughs*]. This director would keep Ross sitting around for *hours*. Actors don't necessarily like having to be *in* that makeup to begin with, and then to have it go on needlessly used to drive Ross crazy! He didn't mind getting made-up, but he didn't like wasting *his* time waiting. He thought he was a little above that.

Ross was a real old-school actor and he definitely wasn't "one of the boys" [Conrad's crew of regular stuntmen]. *That* was a real collection of characters! They were a terrific bunch of stunt guys who would do *anything*, because they had this false sense of indestructibility. They were like Conrad's stooges. [*What was the atmosphere on the set when a fight or action scene was about to be shot?*] Usually there'd be a little excitement in the air, because they weren't the "normal" bunch of people that you'd find on a set; they had that "bravado" thing, and it usually led to some pretty good results.

There was a guy who was Conrad's wardrobe man, Jimmy George, who became Conrad's stunt double because there really *was* a physical likeness. Jimmy got banged-up on a lot of the stunts he did. In one episode ["The Night of the Diva"] he was supposed to fall from the landing at the top of a staircase and land on his back on a balsa wood table. It was a 15-, 18-foot fall. On his first attempt, he missed the table. He turned white, and it looked like he was gonna die, but ten minutes later he got up and did it a second time. If he had landed on the table as planned, he would have been all right but this time he clipped the edge of it and hit the floor again. Not one of these guys would ever admit if he was in pain!

Then there was one incident [also on "The Night of the Diva"] where Jimmy had to dive through a breakaway wall that had been made out of stucco. Well, when they had him do it, the stucco hadn't yet dried, so instead of smashing through, he hit this wet stucco with a thud and just barely got through, and fell short of the mark on the other side where he was supposed to land [atop stuntmen waiting to catch him]. *That* knocked him silly too. So Jimmy's stunt career wasn't that long-lived! He was a really nice guy and he was trying so hard. He went back to being a wardrobe man, which is not a terrible job, and finished out his career that way. He was a great guy and everybody liked him.

Well, the stuntmen were *all* the nicest guys. Red West was Elvis Presley's pal; Red had a career working with Elvis, and played parts in lots of Elvis' movies. Then finally he actually became a character actor and got some pretty decent roles. *Very* nice guy. Whitey Hughes was a terrific little guy, Dick Cangey was also a good guy, and Tommy Huff was great too.

[*You had to come up with different makeups for the stuntmen every week, so that viewers wouldn't realize that they were every villain's henchmen in every episode!*] I had to make-up the stuntmen

36. Memories of The Wild Wild West (1965–1969)

Ross Martin as Artemus Gordon in three Chase makeups. It was while playing the gas inspector in "The Night of the Avaricious Actuary" (right) that the actor tripped and broke a leg.

every day; it became a joke! Those stunt guys had to wear every style of mustache and beard. It was just ... wild. On that show, there was no stopping: You'd be doing makeup literally all day long. Then after work, there was a cantina across the street called the Back Stage which was the scene of a brawl or two. I never got into one there; I came awfully close, but never actually landed a punch. Those kinds of things [after-hours brawls] were not uncommon. When [makeup artist] Frank Griffin and I were doing *The Time Tunnel*, one night at a bar near 20th Century–Fox I saw Frank, a real big, strong, muscular guy, get into a fight with another makeup man, Harry Maret, and they were so drunk they fought for about 20 minutes and neither one of them ever landed a punch [*laughs*]!

Wild Wild West was a great show to work on. I wouldn't want to do it when I was 50, but when I was *that* age, it was fantastic, a wonderful opportunity for a young guy simply because of what I got to do. I went from that onto the *Gunsmoke* series, which was shot on the same lot. That was another real interesting job for a young guy—a lot of sunburns, bruises, beards and scars—but not quite as exciting as *Wild West*. After *Gunsmoke*, I started doing movies. Prosthetic aging and character makeup was really my specialty. For *The Golden Child* [1986] with Eddie Murphy, I created some really bizarre characters. Also memorable for me were *Back to the Future* [1985], *The Stunt Man* [1980] and *The Color Purple* [1985, for which Chase received an Oscar nomination]. My absolute favorite was *Midnight Train to Moscow* [1989] with Billy Crystal, an HBO special filmed in Russia. I did Billy as several characters including a black musician. an old Jewish woman and director Martin Scorsese. [Chase received an Emmy for *Midnight Train to Moscow*.]

In the '60s when I worked on *Wild Wild West*, the movie business and TV was different than it is now. It wasn't so much business, it was a lot of fun. People were light-hearted and knew how to have a good time. Today, working on a TV series is drudgery, it's just not the same. On a given day on *Wild Wild West*, we would do 14, 15 hours worth of work, and yet a group of us on the set intermittently would play Liar's Poker all day long. There were poker games at lunchtime, there were brawls at the Back Stage across the street, a lot of kidding-around and a lot of just having a really good time.

37

Burt Topper on Space Monster *(1965)*

In the mid–1960s, years before the concept of made-for-TV movies became a small-screen institution, American International Pictures ventured down that unexplored avenue, commissioning a number of low-cost flicks that could be used to "sweeten" the packages of older AIP titles they were preparing to offer to local TV stations. Producing a movie on a shoestring budget presented no major challenge for Burt Topper, already an old pro at making pictures for a price: With his partner Leonard Katzman, he signed on to produce for AIP-TV the science fiction adventure The First Woman in Space *(ultimately released as* Space Monster*). Shot in March 1965 and set in the year 2000, the film featured Francine York, Jim Brown, Baynes Barron and Russ Bender as Earth astronauts streaking through space aboard the rocketship* Hope 1 *seeking a planet suitable for colonization—and instead encountering monsters and more monsters.*

Topper gave the following interview during the final phase of his battle with cancer. On April 3, 2007, just days after sharing these reminiscences about Space Monster *and the beginnings of his motion picture career, the World War II Navy veteran turned filmmaker died at the age of 78. He was survived by his wife Jennifer.*

In 1957 I made a picture called *The Ground They Walk*, a war story. In order to make it on a low budget, we sewed all our own uniforms, I built my own power units to power my camera, I built my own reflectors and, oh God, I built even a camera dolly. I used a crew from SC [the University of Southern California], and we'd go out on the weekends and shoot. Meal-wise, what I did was go to the Central Market and, for about 40 bucks, get enough to feed the whole cast and crew. For two days! I did a lot of my own effects at that time, 'cause I had worked with explosives a little bit. At that time, you didn't even need permits, you could just go in and buy what you needed. I bought some bullet hits from [grip] Chuck Hanawalt, who was a friend of mine, and I used dynamite for explosions. I also bought a little surplus machine-gun, had it de-wadded, and I bored it out so I could fire blanks. We shot out in Indio, where [real-life soldiers] trained for desert warfare, and where they had all these trenches dug. I was in the Navy reserve, so when I needed a shot of a landing craft with my people in it, we went to the base up at Oxnard where I knew they had, in front of a museum, an old LCVP landing craft. I told them we were doing a training film and, by God, they saluted me and we got to go in. I had all my actors in the landing craft [in front of the museum], we got some sailors to get a hose for us, the hose squirted water into the landing craft like it was moving, and that's how we got that shot of the guys in the landing craft goin' into the beach [*laughs*]! You remember Bob Clarke, the actor? When I was doing *The Ground They Walk*, he was makin' a monster picture [*The Hideous Sun Demon*, 1959] the same kind of way, with a crew from SC.

They thought that science fiction was the thing that was selling and, yeah, actually, they were right, but I didn't know anything about science fiction. Anyway, that's how Bob and I became friends, when he did his science fiction picture and I did the war story.

Sam Arkoff, who with Jim Nicholson was running American International, bought *Ground They Walk*, which AIP put out in 1958 as *Hell Squad*. For years and years I never did tell Sam what the picture cost, because I didn't want him to get angry that it was so little. It cost so little, it was ridiculous. Well, I can tell you if you want: The whole damn picture cost me $11,500 [*laughs*]. Just for the *television* rights, I got more than that! Anyway, Sam also put me under contract to AIP as a producer-writer-director at that time. For AIP I made a couple of pictures, one called *Tank Commandos* and one called *Diary of a High School Bride* [both 1959], and then I went out on my own for a couple of years.

After making two pictures for Allied Artists [*War Is Hell*, 1963, and *The Strangler*, 1964], I came back to AIP and made a deal with Sam to make some pictures, because AIP needed some product for television. Leonard Katzman and I became partners and we made *Space Monster* for them. Leonard's uncle was Sam Katzman, and for years Leonard had worked for his uncle as an assistant director and so on. Leonard and I were friends from the time we were in Fairfax High School. I produced *Space Monster*, and Leonard directed and wrote it. [*Did research of any kind have to be done?*] Naaaah! We really didn't know anything about space in those days anyway. Nobody really knew what the hell the inside of a [multi-passenger Earth rocketship] would eventually look like. All there were at that time, were things like the John Glenn capsule. The picture was originally going to be called *The First Woman in Space*, but later it was changed it to *Space Monster*.

I built all the interiors of the Earth rocketship set at Producers Studio. I could do it myself [without union interference] because I was the producer. It took me about a month. I had a plot table and all the lights and all that stuff. You remember how the exterior door of the rocketship slid open? *All* that stuff I did. I got electric motors which were drives from aircraft, B-25s and so on, and that's how I made the doors. I put these motors in and I had a console and I operated everything. As a matter of fact, a couple of years later, when Bert Leonard, a producer at Columbia, was doing a show where he

The girl we'd most like to be marooned in a capsule with: Francine York starred in *Space Monster*. Co-producer Burt Topper also played a small part.

needed a space capsule, I rented that to him, and went over there and worked the console myself. We used our imagination in those days [building sets like these] because we really didn't have anything to go on. I built the Earth ship myself; Al Kanter, a grip, came in and helped build the alien spaceship.

A friend of mine owned Rueco Electric, a little electric shop business, and he had a lathe. So I went down there, and he and his dad and I made the Earth rocketship [miniature], and then I put the lights in it and all that stuff. I bought an old lathe from them, and that was the lathe I used up in the studio, in one of the offices, to make all the miniatures. You'll see in the credits of the movie, "Miniatures: B T Industries." Well, B T Industries was *me* [*laughs*]!

Francine York was my girlfriend at the time, so it was a no-brainer putting *her* in it. And she was pretty good in it. In recent years her boyfriend was that famous director Vincent Sherman, who died last year [2006] at 100; he saw *Space Monster* and he also thought that she was very good in it. And Vincent Sherman certainly knew women actresses [having directed great stars, including Bette Davis and Joan Crawford, in his heyday]. Francine's really a fighter, and a good person. She was very much *into* her career, and actually gave up a lot of her life for it. Maybe she should have eventually got married and had children, but she was into the career and she wanted to be a star, and she was like an Auntie Mame. I've always liked Francine.

Leonard was the one who brought in James Brown to play one of the leads. Brown went on to do [the TV series] *Dallas*, which Leonard produced. Brown was a nice man—a *very* nice guy. He was a good sport, he'd do *any*thing. For instance, for the scene where he's floating in space, going from the Earth rocketship to the alien ship, he had to lie on top of a clothes rack! There was a black background [representing outer space] and I got a clothes rack and painted it black, so that you couldn't see it against the black background. And right there on the soundstage, a couple, three guys hoisted James Brown up and set him down on the top of this clothes rack. On the top of it, instead of the bars from which you'd hang the clothes, I had two or three bars bent in a U so he could lie down in there. It was on wheels, and we hauled it slowly across the stage, and that's how we got the shots of him floating in space. In the movie, it cuts back and forth between shots of him and shots of the miniatures [two spaceships and an astronaut with backpack] that I'd worked on the lathe.

Baynes Barron was in Europe for a few years during the war. He was a hell

Like she needs *it! The most beautiful woman in space (York) gets a backstage touch-up from makeup man Harry Thomas.*

of a nice guy and a good friend of mine, and I had him in a number of my pictures, *The Strangler* and *The Devil's 8* [1969] and of course *War Is Hell*—he had the lead in that. Well, *I* was the lead in *War Is Hell* for the first 20 minutes, and then he took over in the picture. Russ Bender had worked for AIP for years, and so he was a good friend too. In those days, we worked not only with the crews that we knew, we also worked with any of the actors that we knew. Like Wally Campo, who was in *Hell Squad*, I went on to use a few more times, and Tony Russel was a friend of mine so I'd use him.

Al Kanter, the grip who built the alien spaceship, was also in the monster suit *playing* the alien. He was a good friend of Leonard's, and I knew Al too. I think that monster suit had already been in some movie [*The Wizard of Mars*, 1964], and that we got it from AIP.

My folks had a big house above Sunset, and that's where we—Leonard and I, and a second unit cameraman named Lippy—did the shots of the giant crabs attacking the spaceship. On a big tabletop there at my folks' place, we set up a fish tank, full of water, and we put in it the miniature Earth rocketship and some little Japanese crabs. Then I took a couple of metal clothes hangers and put them into the tank, and hooked the wires on the hangers up to a plug,

The Space Monster, downright inhospitable in the movie, gets along better with a pair of young set visitors.

so now I could run current into the tank. In the movie, when the crabs are attacking the rocketship, the guys inside talk about turning on "the force field" to stop them. Well, to get that footage of the crabs hitting the force field, I hit the plug in the 110 [the wall socket], and it would shock these little crabs. At the same instant, they'd all stop moving [*laughs*]. Then I'd pull it out very quickly and they'd be all right—I had to take 'em back to the pet shop where I got 'em! But the current would stun 'em and they'd freeze, or float down off of the side of the rocketship. That was really somethin' else.

The rest of the underwater stuff was shot at Catalina off my boat, the *El Perrito* ["little puppy"]. It was built in 1919, it was 62 feet, it was an old classic. That boat was also in *Operation Bikini* [1963], another AIP picture. Shooting the underwater stuff for *Space Monster* was a funny situation. The first guy I hired to photograph underwater was Fouad Said, the guy who later developed the Cinemobile [equipment trucks for location motion picture production] and got an Academy Award for that. He was just a kid when I hired him to do the underwater camerawork for *Space Monster*, and one of the first things he did, when we were testing a camera, was shoot him*self*! He had this underwater camera turned around and photographed himself; when we looked at the dailies, there he was [*laughs*]! When he [screwed up], I hired Mike Dugan as my second unit photographer. Mike knew a lot of guys over at Catalina and, for the underwater scenes in *Space Monster*, he had a friend who was a diver dress up in the sea monster suit [salvaged from AIP's *War-Gods of the Deep*, 1965], and he had another diver double Baynes. Or maybe *I* doubled Baynes. *Space Monster* was my first time working with Mike Dugan, and we became *very* close friends: Mike later did all the racing pictures with me, *Thunder Alley* [1967] and *Fireball 500* [1966] and so on, at Darlington and ... well, *all* over. Mike is now gone.

If you look at the monsters in *Space Monster* now, they look corny as hell. I can't believe some of the pictures we actually put out, that went to the big screen, the drive-ins and all that. But the kids just were crazy about 'em. Well, that's the audience you made 'em for. It was mostly teenagers sittin' in drive-ins, and they loved *any*thing. If they even saw half the picture when they were in a drive-in, beside neckin', you were lucky [*laughs*]! Today science fiction is the most expensive kind of movie to make, but in the old days it had to be the *cheapest* kind. Because it was "anything that we can do." Nobody knew what the hell they were doing anyway, so whatever we did was okay, and we did it for ten cents [*laughs*]! It is amazing what they're spending on these today.

[*Francine York told me that, even though Leonard Katzman gets credit as director, you directed the movie.*] Well, Leonard was behind the first three days—and it was only a five-day schedule [*laughs*]. I tried to help him as we were doing it, 'cause we didn't have a lot of money. But *he* directed the actors, there's no question about that. I never got in there with the actors. Francine likes to say that, because she's a fan of mine [*laughs*], but I didn't direct her in that. Even when I was head of production at AIP, I never interfered with a director, except I had one incident with Richard Rush [on *Thunder Alley*]. Richard was directing a scene with Fabian and Annette Funicello in a car, and there was a process scene going in back of 'em. I walked in and I was watching, and all of a sudden the process screen went off—it went white. And he never cut the scene, he just kept directing it and directing it. Finally I said, "Cut!" Well, I wanna tell you somethin', boy: He got *so* pissed! "*Nobody* cuts my scene!," and this and that. Then, later, after it was over, he came into my office on the lot and he started up, and I was ready to knock him on his ass! Dick was a good guy, a talented guy. But he had to sow his oats a little, you know ... the *nerve* of me, that *I* would come in and cut *his* scene. As head of production, I'm thinking about the money he's spending, and *he's* thinking about making artistic postage stamps [*laughs*]!

This "seasoned citizen" seldom slowed down: Topper enjoyed many late-in-life vacations and activities like driving an amphibious car and skydiving.

On top of everything else, in the *Space Monster* scenes set on Earth, I was a general or something. And I did the narrating. I also used to narrate a lot of the trailers for AIP. Casey Kasem was always trying to get me into doing voiceovers. But I just did it for AIP. Of course, I was a little naïve in those days, 'cause I did [voiceovers for AIP] and I didn't even charge anybody for it; to me, it just was part of the job. Actually, AIP *was* like a family. Sam Arkoff and I were the closest of friends, we were *best* friends. When I used to deal with Sam over there, I used to say to myself, "For Christ's sake, I'd be better off a stranger than his best friend!" But that's business and I can't hold it against him, the fact that he was a *tough* businessman. I loved him dearly. Jim Nicholson was a sweet man, too, and we became good friends. Jim also had a big boat, and we used to go out on it. And we'd double-date—I doubled with Francine and Jim and Jim's [girlfriend, later wife] Susan Hart. We were like a family, truthfully.

We did *Space Monster* in 35mm, with a $50,000 budget, in five days. And it was made all IA; if you notice, it has the seal on it. We made that IA in five days, except for the stuff I shot at Catalina and the miniatures, and we didn't have crews for that. [*What did Nicholson and Arkoff think of* Space Monster?] Well, hell, for *that* price ... I mean, what the hell [*laughs*]? It was for a television package. AIP made a lot of money on those TV packages. What AIP did was, they had a lot of good pictures ... well, not *good*, but good for "our market" ... and a couple years after they played theatrically, AIP would put them in packages for television, and in the packages they would mix in a few of these little [made-for-TV] cheapos and get money for the whole package. That's the way they got away with these pictures that were very cheaply made. There was a man named Larry Buchanan in Texas who did a lot of pictures for AIP to put into these TV packages. We paid him like $35,000 for each movie, and he made 'em in 16mm in Texas. I was head of production there at AIP at the time. Larry made these pictures with locals, non-union, and we'd send the star down. Francine did a picture down there [*Curse of the Swamp Creature*, 1968], and so did John Ashley [*The Eye Creatures*, 1967], and John Agar was in several of 'em [*Curse of the Swamp Creature, Zontar the Thing from Venus*, 1967, *Hell Raiders*, 1969]. When Larry made a war story, *Hell Raiders*, I had a lot of equipment and uniforms and other stuff of my own, and I sent my whole "armory" down to him. When you're makin' pictures for that money, you call in all your friends, all the people you know! You did whatever you had to do.

[*Susan Hart tells me you were great at getting footage with no permit.*] That's right, that's what we *did* in those days! When we did the racing pictures, *Fireball 500* and all of those, we used to "steal" a lot of that footage. Mike Dugan and I would go to the tracks and we'd hire one of the drivers, a guy was actually racing, and set up a camera in the front and the back of his car. He had a button for the camera, like an aircraft armament button, when you're firin' your guns. Well, he "fired" his camera when he saw an opportunity—for instance, when he was passing cars. That's how we got a lot of the footage of actual races. And on his pit stops we would change out the cameras. We had like four or five cameras with us and we'd load one up as he was racing, get it ready. As soon as he'd make a pit stop, while the pit crew was changing the tires or whatever, *we'd* plug in another camera. Well, hell, I used to carry a camera in the back of my car and try to pick up shots. One time they had a forest fire in Topanga, or somewhere around there, and I took one of my friends, Jack Sowards, an actor in *Hell Squad*, up there. I had passes from AIP as "press," all different cards to get into different places, and we got past the fire units [*laughs*]! Oh yeah! I took him up there, and I took my Arriflex, and we were gonna do a picture about a pyromaniac. I had him on the hillside, and he was goin' nuts up there, runnin' back and forth and raisin' his arms. We had that footage for years, but never got to making the movie.

Those days were really interesting...

38

Peter Marshall on Edgar G. Ulmer

The life and times of the "Miracle Man of Poverty Row" were recently celebrated in Kino International's Edgar G. Ulmer—The Man Off-Screen *(2004), a direct-to-DVD documentary in which a number of Ulmer's Hollywood co-workers reminisce about their work with the Austrian-born wunderkind director. Among the group is Peter Marshall, one of the stars of Ulmer's final film, 1965's* The Cavern. *An international co-production, European-made, the offbeat World War II story is set in Italy and begins with an aerial bombardment trapping a polyglot crew in a mountainside "supply dump" cave: a British general (Brian Aherne), an American captain and private (John Saxon, Larry Hagman), an Italian soldier (Nino Castelnuovo) and his girl (Rosanna Schiaffino), a German lieutenant (Hans von Borsody) and a Canadian officer (Marshall). The group works as a unit to search for an escape route out of the labyrinth of tunnels, but as months pass and their efforts prove futile, emotional tension builds—not to mention the many-men, one-woman angle.*

The road from script to screen was every bit as twisty as the cave passages, says Marshall...

I remember vividly how I got my part in *The Cavern*. I did a film called *Ensign Pulver* [1964] and a lot of people who weren't yet known were in it: Jack Nicholson and Jimmy Coco and Larry Hagman ... take a look at the castlist, it's amazing. We shot in Acapulco, and Larry Hagman and I became friends. One day he said, "I'm going to be doing a picture in Yugoslavia, it's really a good script, and there's a wonderful part in it for an English guy. Why don't I set an interview up for you?" The interview was with Edgar Ulmer.

I went over to some office in Beverly Hills and I met Edgar, and we talked about the part in *The Cavern*. I said, "My English accent isn't the greatest, to be frank with you, Edgar. Why don't you make the character Canadian?" He said, "Terrific." So I read for him and I got the part. The producer was Marty Melcher, who was married to Doris Day. The money was lousy but, as Hagman said, it *was* a good part.

To get to Yugoslavia, first we flew to Rome, then we took a train from there up to Trieste, Italy, and then a train from Trieste into Yugoslavia. I loved the hotel we stayed at, which was in the Italian section of Yugoslavia. I felt like a monk, because the rooms were like monks' quarters. There was a bed, a pot for water and a little place to poop. So Spartan! However, there was a restaurant in the hotel that was terrific. But we all had spies. *Why* we were being spied on, I have no idea, but in those days, Yugoslavia was Communist-run and each one of us had somebody watching him. I had my own spy, who was not very good. He was so obvious, I used to wave at him and things like that.

In the beginning, Joachim Hansen was going to play one of the leads in the film, the German lieutenant. He was Austrian, a handsome guy, and I think very well-to-do. I used to kid him a lot, I would say to him, "Tell me, Joachim, vuzz you effer a Nazi?" And Joachim would say [*agitated*]: "I vuzzn't a Nazi!" "Come on, Joachim, you can leffel with meee. I mean, I sympathize in many vays...." "I vuzz never a Nazi!" I did that the entire time, and Joachim just didn't understand [that he was being kidded]. Still to this day, when John Saxon sees me, he says, "Vuzz you effer a Nazi?" [*Laughs*] Joachim was a lovely man and he even came and visited me many years later, here in L.A.

We were in Yugoslavia when for the first time we sat down together and had a read-through. And we got to go down into the caves in which we were going to shoot, which were near a little town called Postojna. The caves were very cold and dripping wet and quite ominous—they were just magnificent. It would have been a wonderful place to shoot. But it was not to be.

The way it turned out, we shot very little in Yugoslavia, just some exteriors for the opening of the film. The first thing we did was shoot those opening scenes for a day or two in the mountains of Yugoslavia, and I sprained my ankle badly. Up in these hills, where we were freezing our butts off, I had a misstep as I stepped on a rock and, boy, I limped for days. Around that same time, Joachim Hansen got really banged up. I can't remember now if it was because he fell, or if it had something to do with a car, but Joachim was injured very badly and they had to bring in Hans von Borsody to replace him. Joachim is still in the film, however; a little of the footage he *was* in was used at the beginning. Joachim was then a huge star in Germany, he was like their Montgomery Clift, but in *The Cavern* he only has this bit part as a German soldier! Hans von Borsody plays the rest of what *would* have been Joachim's part.

Then, all of a sudden, we had to get out of Yugoslavia quickly. It had to do with Marty Melcher not paying for something, or not *getting* paid for something, and it had to do with Yugoslavian boats at Long Beach—I don't know *what* all the trouble was, but we got a notice that we had to sneak out of Yugoslavia. Literally! Like thieves in the night! Then on the train, Edgar became ill. I thought he was gonna die, to be frank with you. I just kind of consoled him and talked to him, and tried to keep him calm.

What we did was, we went to Italy—to Trieste—and they *built* caves there. I wouldn't bet the house on this but I believe it was some public place with an indoor swimming pool where they put up cave sets, and that's where we were going to do all the cave scenes involving the water. Then before we even started shooting in Trieste, something happened where we were going to have like four or five days off, and Brian Aherne said [*Marshall affects an English accent*], "Why don't we go to Venice?" And of course I said, "Fine!" Brian had a big ol' Jaguar sedan and the four of us, Brian and his wonderful wife Eleanor and Larry Hagman and myself, we all headed to Venice and stayed at the Danieli [a luxury hotel]. For some reason, they gave Hagman and me the honeymoon suite [*laughs*]! I don't remember how he and I afforded it, three days or so at the Danieli, because we weren't making very much money on *The Cavern*, but we had a marvelous time. Brian and Eleanor were wonderful to us, they were so gracious.

One day Edgar said to me, "I understand you're a writer," and I said, "Well ... yes." He said, "Could you help me in certain areas?" and I said sure. He started asking me what I thought of *this* and what I thought of *that*, and I made a few script changes here and there. It's been so long, I can't tell you what changes, certainly no major changes—the script was pretty solid. Maybe just a scene or two dialogue-wise, it wasn't anything that important I'm sure.

Edgar was *very* European, and such an emotional man. Breakfast was a scene! With him, everything was very dramatic and he would be screaming and carrying on. I guess he was doing *The Cavern* on a budget and Marty Melcher wasn't sending him the money, and the poor guy was scrambling—he scrambled through the whole film. I must blame Melcher. I don't

Cult director Edgar G. Ulmer's final feature was *The Cavern*, an international co-production about a disparate group trapped in an Italian cave during World War II.

remember what I got paid, but it was barely enough to send home to my wife and four kids. And I felt like we were lucky when we *got* paid!

As for Edgar as a director, I loved working with Edgar, he was just a wonderful director. He let you do what you did, he gave you your head, and he was really interesting to watch and work with. I enjoyed him very much. I had no idea that he was a legend when I worked with the man, but he'd done some terrific things. His biggest fan, of course, was his wife Shirley, who was also his script supervisor. She just thought he was the greatest thing that ever came down the pike. I don't know how she put up with him at times, I really don't! Was he Hungarian? No, Austrian! I had a grandmother like that, real Bavarian—everything was a scene. And that was Edgar. Nothing was easy with Edgar.

I remember vividly that Edgar and Larry Hagman just did not get along. I can't remember why, but they fought through the whole film. I thought Larry was gonna throw him out a window one day [*laughs*]! I have no idea what the argument was about, but it was about *something*, lemme tell ya! They had a big brouhaha.

One night, four of us went out for dinner, Larry, Johnny Saxon, the Italian kid Nino Castelnuovo and myself. John spoke Italian, and Nino of course *is* Italian, and so they knew all the great Italian joints. (By the way, from that film *The Cavern*, Nino got the lead in *Umbrellas of Cherbourg* [1964].) When we came back to the hotel, some people were on a porch, like a veranda, and crying. I said, "My God, what happened?" Well, John F. Kennedy had been assassinated. Everybody remembers where they were when they found out John Kennedy had been assassinated; well, that's where I was, at that small hotel in Trieste. Then later, watching the news coverage on a big TV in the hotel lobby, we saw the killing of Lee Harvey Oswald and I saw the gunman and I said, "Hey—that's Jack Rubinstein! That guy's a *friend* of mine!" And he *was*! Jack Rubinstein [a.k.a. Jack Ruby] used to own a private club down in Dallas at the time when I was doing nightclubs with Tommy Noonan, and that's how I met him: He took us to his club before it opened and he cooked dinner for Tommy, myself and the heavyweight champion of Texas at the time, Buddy Turman. So when he was on TV shooting Oswald, I said, "That's Jack Rubinstein—*I* know him! That's a guy I know from Dallas!"

After Trieste, we went to Italy, where we finally shot in some real caves. They were outside of Rome, near Cinecitta Studio, and quite famous; that's where they did Hercules pictures and all those kinds of things. Brian Aherne wrote in his book [*A Dreadful Man: The Story of Hollywood's Most Orig-*

Offered the role of an English officer in *The Cavern*, Marshall felt his attempts at an English accent weren't up to snuff and got Ulmer to make his character a Canadian instead.

inal Cad, *George Sanders*] that we worked in ankle-deep mud, but I don't remember ankle-deep mud. I just remember being *cold*. So you'd go to the trailer, and *it* was cold. I was in Italy during the War, and I was never that cold in my life. Working in Italy on *The Cavern* reminded me of when I was in the War.

I can remember Brian Aherne saying to me one day, referring to John Saxon, "He's really a terrible actor, isn't he?" But then we would go watch the dailies and *we* would be really lousy and John would be terrific! I said, "Brian, this man *knows film*. He knows exactly what he's doing"—and he *did*. Go see a picture called *The Appaloosa* [1966] with Brando and John Saxon and you'll see what I mean. Johnny makes Brando look like shit! John is a *really* good film actor. But Brian, when he would do scenes with him, would say, "I don't believe that chap's a very good actor...!"

But the guy that I felt was the best actor in the film was Hans von Borsody. Watch his stuff. Wonderful, wonderful actor. And a great guy. I taught him how to play gin—and he was a terrible gin player! We would play for those exorbitant amounts of money, which I knew we would never pay. At the end he owed me $800. I said, "Now, listen: You're a terrible gin player and this was all for fun. You don't owe me a penny." He said, "No, I—" I said, "Really, Hans. I've taken advantage of you." Well, later on, after he had checked out of the hotel in Rome, in my box at the desk was $800 in cash. I felt so badly about it. I didn't really want that money but I couldn't find him, and I never heard from him again.

In Rome, I eventually wound up in a beautiful apartment. Do you remember a very big actress in Germany by the name of Heidi Bruhl? Well, her future husband, the actor Brett Halsey, was a friend of mine. [The *Cavern* troupe] was staying at some hotel in Rome, and one day Brett said to me, "How long you gonna be here?" I said, "I dunno, maybe three months." He said, "Heidi and I are going to Germany, so why don't you take over our place? You can live up there." So that's where I lived, at Brett and Heidi's *gorgeous* apartment! In Rome, I palled around with Hans and Larry. John Saxon had his own thing—John knew so many people in Rome, and he kinda ran a different game than we did. He and Nino were good friends, and they did "the Italian thing."

It just took forever to shoot *The Cavern* but we finally finished, and what broke my heart is that they then looped it [the actors re-recorded their dialogue]. If you'd seen *The Cavern* before they put us in a studio to loop it, you'd have loved it. It was just great, and lit beautifully—I loved the cinematographer Gabor Pogany, who was very famous. And because we had actually shot in caves, it had the ominous sound of the caves, which was just terrific.

Marshall still does big band concerts around the country and a radio show that can be heard in 233 cities (and on your computer at www.musicofyourlife.com).

But Marty Melcher didn't like the sound and he insisted that it be looped. So I never again enjoyed the picture like when I first saw it. We looped it in Rome, and I had to do *my* part of it quickly. I only had two days to do it because I had to get to the Thunderbird in Vegas because I was scheduled to open in a show there, *Anything Goes*. In Rome, I got a call from the *Anything Goes* producer, Monte Proser, like on a Tuesday and he said, "You're opening in Vegas next Monday." I finished looping on Friday and caught a plane home, had one day of rehearsal and opened on a Monday. I'd learned the script in Rome as we were looping *The Cavern*.

Before they looped it, it was a brilliant movie; after they looped it, I wasn't that thrilled with it. But you know where *The Cavern* did great? In Germany. It did reeeally big in Germany, it was a big, big classic there. People have told me, "You know, that's a huge picture in Germany." I had no idea!

I loved [the experience of making] *The Cavern* because I had a lovely part in it, and I loved Edgar's wife, Shirley Ulmer. I became very close to Shirley, and remained so. Several years later [1972], I went to Edgar Ulmer's funeral; I think I was the only one from the cast of *The Cavern* who was there. One of the worst things that ever happened to me was, when Shirley passed away [in 2000], her daughter Arianne called and asked me to do the eulogy and I said absolutely I would. But I came down with the flu, *very* bad, and couldn't attend, and I had no way to get in touch with Arianne, I found that I didn't have her number. So I never showed up for Shirley's funeral, I always regretted that so much, and I feel like I've never been able to properly apologize to Arianne.

I got along with Edgar very well, even though he was a gruff guy. I enjoyed him, and we became good friends. I believe he was frustrated with life, because he was a very talented guy and he should have been bigger and much more well-known than he was. He was very kind to me, I was very fond of Edgar, and of course Shirley was an angel. I don't know how John Saxon reacts to the movie, or Hagman, but it was a wonderful experience for me. I saw it again a few years back at the Egyptian Theater, when they had an Edgar Ulmer week. I took my wife, who's quite young. Watching it up there on the big screen ... I never looked that good in my life [*laughs*]! Everybody in the film looked gorgeous. And the thing was lit so beautifully—Pogany was just a *great* cinematographer.

Hagman wasn't that crazy about Edgar, Saxon wasn't that crazy about Edgar, but I liked him very much and I think Brian Aherne liked him too. For some reason, difficult people—if they're talented—I get along with. But he was never difficult with me. I *never* found him difficult. I liked Edgar Ulmer.

39

Tom Reese on Murderers' Row *(1966)*

In the four-film Matt Helm series of the 1960s, the hard-drinking, soft-singing secret agent (Dean Martin) ran a gauntlet of super-villains and deadly dames. In Murderers' Row *he had one of his most formidable foes in Ironhead (Tom Reese), a physically imposing baddie with a shiny black steel pate topping his egg-bald head. Henchman of a megalomaniac (Karl Malden) plotting to menace the world with his "Super Helio Beam," Ironhead regularly battles Helm on land, sea and discotheque throughout the garish, funny spy spoof.*

Reese (real name: Tom Allen) was born in Chattanooga, Tennessee, on August 8, 1928; his father Austin Allen and uncle Lee Allen, the country–Western singers "The Chattanooga Boys," traveled around performing their bluegrass music with their families in tow. Around 1940, Austin's family relocated to New York, where Austin was an ironworker in the daytime and a singing waiter in an Irish pub at night.

Tom later held an assortment of odd jobs (Automat busboy, usher, etc.) in New York and, starting at 17, served two tours of duty in the Marine Corps. He later studied dramatics at the American Theater Wing under the G.I. Bill and spent 15 years on the road working nightclubs (emceeing, doing stand-up, etc.). He studied with Lee Strasberg, did some work Off Broadway and in local TV shows and made his film bow in John Cassavetes' New York–lensed Shadows *(1960). Cassavetes also had him fly out to California to star as a mentally unbalanced Korean War veteran in "The Return," an episode of his detective series* Johnny Staccato, *Reese's Hollywood debut. Reese was ready to return to New York after doing the show but an agent signed him "and I've been here ever since." His first major film was* Flaming Star *(1960), an Elvis Presley Western and the start of Reese's long career in big- and small-screen oaters (*Gunsmoke, Bonanza, The Virginian, Rawhide, Branded, *many more).*

My agent called me to go to Columbia on an interview about playing Ironhead, a big guy with a bald head, in *Murderers' Row*. There was an ex-prizefighter there for *his* interview, and when I saw him I said to myself, "Well, I've got no chance...." But he had no acting experience, and so after I had my interview with the casting director and Irving Allen the producer, *I* got the part. I had a 12-week guarantee, but minimum salary. But to work with Dean Martin and Karl Malden...! I had met Dean 20 years earlier in New York; one New Year's Eve after I'd hocked my overcoat, I met him in his agent's office, and he gave me an overcoat. I remembered that, of course, and he vaguely remembered me. I spent 12 weeks with him on *Murderers' Row*.

Ironhead was a takeoff on Oddjob from the James Bond movie *Goldfinger* [1964]—I *think* that was the idea. (Incidentally, in the book *Murderers' Row*, Ironhead is black.) I'm 6'3" and they gave me elevator shoes and that terrible green suit, two sizes too large, to help make me look bigger on screen. And, for the first three days, a skullcap to make me look bald, and the steel plate attached to the skullcap with double-sided tape. Having that skullcap thing put on in the morning is a miserable process. It took about two hours for them to plaster my hair down and put it on me, then they had to take it off me at night and I'd get in the shower and scrub out all the spirit gum ... it was miserable. Then when Irving Allen and the director Henry Levin watched the dailies, they could tell that I was wearing a skullcap—for instance, in the closeups I had, like in the scene at the disco, they could see the wrinkle in the back. They didn't like that, and so they had the casting director come over to my dressing room to ask if he could make some kind of a deal with me and get me to agree to shave my head. I said, "I can't shave my head. It would take a couple of months to grow back, and I do a lot of Westerns." But then I went over to talk to Karl Malden, I asked him what I should do, and he said, "Ask 'em for [an extra six weeks salary] to shave your head." I thanked him, I went back to the producers and asked 'em for six and we settled for three. So somebody in the makeup department shaved my head and they gave me three weeks extra salary. And, actually, it was a lot better than wearing the skullcap. I wore hats and caps [outside the studio] for those 12 weeks, and they gave me a wig to wear if I wanted to. It was worth it, because when it was all over, my hair grew back thicker and stronger.

Dean Martin was a lot of fun, very funny, a nice guy, very friendly. Hanging around Dean all the time was his manager Mack Gray, who had been George Raft's manager before that. He was kind of a Mafia-looking guy with the slicked-back hair and the suit and tie and everything. Dean always had a glass in his hand but it wasn't booze, it was ginger ale or apple juice. He would come in one morning on his Harley motorcycle, and then the next day he would come in some Italian sports car that was given to him. He was always there early, seven o'clock, eight o'clock, and ready to go. And, again, always so funny. God, it was tough to stay straight with him because he would kid around. He'd call me "The Jolly Green Giant"! There was a scene where I had a bear hug on him, I was supposed to lift him up and bounce him and squeeze him, and Henry Levin the director said, "Tommy, you don't look like you're really squeezing him hard enough." Dean turned to me and he said, "Yeah, squeeze me 'til my *eyes* clear up!" [*Laughs*] He broke me up with a lot of funny lines like that. I had a very nice time on that film, working with Dean.

I talked to Karl Malden about his career and he gave me some advice. He also was very friendly. I was a little in awe of working with Dean Martin and Karl Malden but I got over it and just played the part as menacing as I could possibly be. Ann-Margret, who would *also* come in on a Harley, was at that time kind of ... giggly. This was before she really turned into the fine actress she is today. Camilla Sparv was kind of quiet—the "star-," "leading lady"-type attitude.

We shot at Columbia Studios in Hollywood, and every morning when I came in, the makeup man would run the electric razor over my head. Especially on Mondays, because the fuzz would grow in over the weekend. The makeup man was bald, and he said, "I'm doing the same thing to you that I do for my *self* every morning!" [*Laughs*]

I did most of my own stunts—the fight scenes where Dean kicks me, the punches, I did all that. Dean did a good job in the fight scenes, because in the past he *had* been a fighter. We'd have a routine worked out—left, right, left, right, hook, uppercut, stomach punch—and he was very handy. For my stunt double, I had a guy who'd doubled me before. Prior to *Murderers' Row*, he had doubled me in a TV series called *The Iron Horse* with Dale Robertson, and he had doubled me in a *Gunsmoke* or something. Every time I had stunts, I'd always ask for him, because he was a great stuntman, and you could put a hat on him and from a distance he looked like me. He was an ex-fighter and great stuntman, and his name was Chuck Hicks.

He wasn't asked to shave his head for *Murderers' Row*, they just put a bald cap on him, because from a distance you couldn't see it. He made more in one day than I made in a *week*, because producers pay good for stunts. Chuck doubled me in the fight scene that Dean and I did near the docks at San Pedro; for instance, Chuck took the tumble down that hill. That was him, I wasn't gonna do *that*. One *day* when he doubled me at San Pedro, I think he made $1700. Then he doubled me in many films after that.

I met a guy on that show, a stuntman named Sol Gorss. He was an older man [58 years old], very friendly; he was doing a couple stunts in the film, and I think he was also doing a little of the choreographing of some of the stunts. One day when we were having some coffee and

Six-foot-three ex–Marine Tom Reese wore elevator shoes and a too-big suit—not to mention the steel plate on his bald pate—to make him an even *more* intimidating bruiser of a baddie in the Matt Helm spy spoof *Murderers' Row*.

talking about stunts, he told me that he had been Errol Flynn's double—he had done all the fencing for Flynn. It was quite interesting to listen to him. And then he died a few days later! We finished work one Friday and he died over that weekend, and when we came back, somebody said, "Sol Gorss *died*." Jeez, I couldn't believe it...!

There was a car chase they shot in Monte Carlo, where Ironhead is in a convertible chasing Matt Helm's car. For that scene, they filmed the closeups of me on a stage, but they had to have doubles for me and Dean and Ann-Margret in Monte Carlo. I talked to my agent about that, and to Screen Actors Guild, and for every day the stuntman doubled me over there, they had to pay *me* [*laughs*]. I got seven days extra pay out of that, which was a *great* bonus. Minimum [weekly salary for an actor] at that time was $650 a week, I think, and that's what I got on *Murderers' Row*. But for 12 weeks, that's fine—plus the bonus I got for shaving my head, and seven days' extra pay because of the stuntman in France, and overtime ... I did very well on *Murderers' Row*! That amazing hovercraft stuff was also shot in France. They had a mock-up of part of the hovercraft on an interior set at Columbia, a mock-up that we'd get in and out of, with a process screen of the water behind us. The fight scene that Dean and I had aboard that hovercraft was, again, shot on a set—*very* tight quarters. There was *very* limited space on the set where I had the fight scene with him.

I saw *Murderers' Row* when it came out and I thought it was funny and fun. It was playing on Broadway in New York, one of the theaters around Duffy Square. I was back there for six weeks on vacation, and I walked down Broadway and there was *Murderers' Row* playing on Broadway. I went in to see it, and that was fun—*really* fun. In fact, I went in to see it a *coupla* times [*laughs*]. I'd walk in, watch my scenes and walk out! And of course this was the first time I had seen myself bald on a screen! As I mentioned, while the picture was in production, I had a wig that they'd given me, to wear [in my off-hours]. I would also wear golf caps and fishing caps to cover my head in public; people were always asking me, "What did you shoot today?" and "What did you catch today?" One night my mother came over to my place for dinner, and she knew I would be bald because I was working on the picture. But at one point I went into the bedroom and came back out with this wig on, and she did a great double-take [*laughs*]—I'll never forget that! And another time I had to go downtown L.A. to pay a parking ticket that went into a warrant. I said to myself, "If I go in there bald, the judge is gonna think I'm a real mean s.o.b. I gotta wear a tie and a suit, and I'll wear the wig, so I look presentable." I wore the wig, I paid the ticket, and then I went back over to Hollywood and Vine, to this bar called The Office—I needed a drink. I went in there to have a drink, I still had the wig on, and next to me was some drunk—*really* drunk. He looked at me and he said, "Boy, if I had a head of hair like you, kid..." I said, "Here! You *want* it?" and I took it off and handed it to him. He, too, was taken aback! I had a lot of fun with that wig!

Looking back on it, doing *Murderers' Row* with Dean was a big feather in my cap.

40

Richard Gordon on Protelco Productions

The mid–1960s were the heyday of Hammer and Amicus Films as England's top suppliers of horror movies—but suddenly a new company, Protelco Productions, burst upon the scream scene with two 1966 films that put them in the same class overnight. Island of Terror *starred Peter Cushing and Edward Judd as scientists battling bone-eating creatures (inadvertently created by cancer researchers) on a small island off the Irish coast;* The Projected Man *featured Bryant Haliday as a professor hideously burned in a teleportation experiment and now, hate-maddened and filled with lethal electricity that gives him the touch of death, seeking revenge on the unscrupulous men responsible.*

The fright flicks were distributed separately in England but in 1967 they were paired as a pulse-pounding Protelco double-bill in the U.S., the home (since 1947) of their London-born co-producer Richard Gordon. Gordon began as a moviemaker with made-in-England crime melodramas in the 1950s, but then hit the horror trail in a big way with the 1958 twin-bill of Fiend Without a Face *and* The Haunted Strangler *and never looked back; he specialized in macabre moviemaking for the next quarter-century. In this interview he recalls his producing partner Gerald A. Fernback and the rise and fall of Protelco Productions.*

During the 1950s, when I was making a series of B-movie co-productions in England for which I also negotiated the American distribution deals, Gerry Fernback was the head of Republic Pictures there. When I screened him a print of my film *The Fighting Wildcats* [1957] which Keefe Brasselle starred in and also directed, Gerry liked it and, on behalf of Republic, bought it for distribution in America. We became friends and shortly thereafter he left Republic to go into business on his own. He bought a travel agency called Embassy Travel and was very successful in that field. I was not involved but we remained in contact, and in 1961 he suggested to me that we form a company to supply American films to British television which, at that time, consisted only of the BBC and one commercial channel [Granada Television]. The Hollywood major studios had all agreed *not* to release their films to television in England, and British films were also restricted. We formed a company which we called Protelco Productions. Gerry came up with the name; I don't remember from where it derived. Protelco became the leading supplier of independent product to the networks.

When I was getting ready to make *Devil Doll* [1964] in association with the U.K. distributor Gala Films, Gerry offered to participate in the financing and become a partner in my production plans. *Devil Doll* was very successful, both in England and in the United States

A photograph from the press party for Richard Gordon's 1958 film *The Secret Man* shows the producer (center) and Gerry Fernback (with mustache) together years before their fright flick collaborations. Also pictured: Gordon's 1950s production partner Charles Vetter, Jr. (left), and husband-and-wife actors Kim Parker and Paul Carpenter (right).

where I released it through Joe Solomon's Fanfare Films, so we followed it quickly with a film based on a screenplay which had been submitted to me under the title *Lion Man*. Gala Films released it in the U.K. as *Curse of Simba* and I renamed it *Curse of the Voodoo* in the United States where Allied Artists released it [in 1965]. Meanwhile we continued our television business in the U.K. and Gerry expanded his travel agency into the freight business, where he specialized in providing the facilities for film companies that were going overseas on location.

Around this time, there was an independent British production-distribution company called Planet Films which was owned by Tom Blakeley and Bill Chalmers, whom I knew well. Blakeley had been producing low-budget movies in Manchester for several years and Chalmers was running a distribution company called Butcher's Films. I was selling their films in America and finding product for them to distribute in the U.K. Planet had just finished a vampire movie, *Devils of Darkness* [1965], which I sold on their behalf to 20th Century–Fox for distribution in America. Blakeley had a script called *The Night the Silicates Came* [later retitled *Island of Terror*] which was sent to him by its two writers who were then living in Spain, Edward Andrew Mann and Allan Ramsen. Ramsen was an American expatriate who had tried to become an actor at Universal in Hollywood with no success. Blakeley wanted to film *The Night the Silicates Came* as his next production but it was a much more expensive project than his usual films and he needed a partner. He brought the script to Gerry and me and asked if we would like to participate in it. The idea was that Planet would distribute the film in England and we could have the rest of the world rights.

When I read the screenplay, I thought it was exactly the kind of thing that we were looking for, and as close to being "ready to go" as any script I had ever read. However, I was hesitant to say yes because, as I explained to Gerry, programming in the U.K. and America, and most of the rest of the world, was still double feature and if we did not have a second film to go with it, we would end up as someone *else's* second feature and get the short end of the deal. We would have to have another film to make up our own double program, especially for the American market where I had done a deal like that with MGM a few years earlier for *The Haunted Strangler* and *Fiend Without a Face*. Gerry agreed.

My brother Alex was then working in Hollywood and very much involved with Jim Nicholson and Sam Arkoff at American International. He used to send me scripts and story ideas that Nicholson and Arkoff had turned down for one reason or another, in case I could use them in England. One such script was already in my possession, called *The Projected Man*, by a Hollywood writer named Frank Quattrocchi. Of course it had an American setting, I believe it was Los Angeles, and Gerry and I decided that it could just as well take place in London or anywhere else. I asked John Croydon [Gordon's collaborator on *Fiend*, *Haunted Strangler* et al.] to take a look at it and he agreed and said that he could easily supervise a quick rewrite to change the location and have it ready in time to shoot simultaneously with *The Night the Silicates Came* (the title of which I wanted to change to *The Night the Creatures Came* as I felt that no one would know what the word "silicates" meant and therefore it was meaningless). With Alex's help I acquired the *Projected Man* film rights directly from Quattrocchi, who agreed to accept a story credit. John Croydon, who was also a professional writer for which he used the *nom de plume* John C. Cooper, then rewrote the script in collaboration with Peter Bryan to give it an English setting.

It would not have been possible for Tom Blakeley to produce two pictures at the same time, and I would not have been keen on that anyway. So I talked about *The Projected Man* with several other people in London, including Michael Klinger and Tony Tenser of Compton Films, with whom I was on friendly terms. They showed an immediate interest and said yes, provided we kept to a minimum budget, and I made a deal with them very quickly.

The two films were scheduled to go into production more or less at the same time. Gerry and I agreed to supervise both projects, *The Night the Silicates Came* [hereafter called *Island of Terror*] at Pinewood Studios and *The Projected Man* at Merton Park Studios. Pinewood, which was about 30 miles outside London, belonged to the Rank Organisation and was England's largest studio. Merton Park, much smaller and less expensive than Pinewood, was in a suburb of London. I knew it well because several of my co-productions were shot there.

At that time, I was also friendly with Jimmy Carreras, the head of Hammer Films, and he had always been very helpful to me. The industry wasn't as big then as it is now, especially in London, and most of the independents knew each other well and always helped one another. We met socially and all belonged to organizations like the Variety Club, frequented the same restaurants and shared information. The idea was that we had to work together in order to compete with the major Hollywood studios and their London subsidiaries as well as the British studios like Rank, Associated British and British Lion.

When I told Jimmy Carreras that Gerry and I were about to start on two new productions on our own and that we had a great script [*Island of Terror*] that I particularly liked, he told me that if we were ready to go, he could make available to us on loan two people whom

Hammer had under contract but who were at that moment not working on any projects: Terence Fisher and Peter Cushing. Gerry and I jumped at the chance. Tom Blakeley was delighted; he would never have dreamed of going after them on his own, and probably would not have spent that kind of money anyway without our partnership. On our own, we also got Edward Judd for *Island of Terror*. As far as I was concerned, he was a very good leading man who had already been in some successful pictures like Val Guest's *The Day the Earth Caught Fire* [1961] and Ray Harryhausen's *First Men in the Moon* [1964]. I was happy to have him. In later years one heard stories that he had been difficult on other movies but we did not have *any* problems with him on our picture. I already knew Carole Gray from *Devils of Darkness* and I was aware that she had some other good credits including *Curse of the Fly* [1965] and I thought she would be very good as Judd's girlfriend in our film.

Eddie Byrne [as the island's doctor] and Niall MacGinnis [as its leading citizen] were good value for money and could be kept within the limitations of our budget by scheduling their scenes to be shot together on fixed days so that we did not have to employ them for the entire shooting schedule. The same applied to several other supporting players. The film went ahead under the expert guidance of Terence Fisher, who insured that it would come in on budget and on schedule.

Production on *Island of Terror* was scheduled to commence on November 22, 1965, for five weeks of principal photography. It was shot in its entirety at Pinewood, using their very large back lot that stood in for most of the film's outdoor settings and also their "lake" which appears in the pre-credits sequence. Exteriors like the cancer research team's building, described in the film by Peter Cushing's character as resembling Wuthering Heights, were shot around the studio's permanent buildings.

I had met Terence Fisher casually in 1957 when he directed one of my co-productions called *Kill Me Tomorrow* for which I had brought Pat O'Brien to England. It had been a difficult picture to make because Pat O'Brien had a drinking problem but Fisher handled it very well. He was directing all kinds of independent pictures and was in great demand when Hammer signed him to an exclusive contract. I found him great to work with but he was reclusive. He didn't like to mix socially with anyone when he was working, and during the filming of *Island of Terror*, at midday when most of us went to lunch, he would lock himself in his office with a sandwich and work on the afternoon's and next day's shooting. I never had much opportunity to spend time with him alone—no opportunity at all, really—and I was also preoccupied with *The Projected Man*. I simply saw him whenever I visited Pinewood during the production to see how it was going.

I first met Peter Cushing when I went to Pinewood to see what was going on with *Island of Terror*. He was very pleasant, very low-key. The character he played had a sense of humor about him, but I honestly can't recall whether or not the character was written that way in the original script. My guess would be that the humor was added after it was decided that Cushing was going to play the role, because that's not the kind of thing that just *any* actor could do. For instance, it wouldn't have worked if we'd hired Christopher Lee [*laughs*]!

After *Island of Terror*, I never met with Cushing again, but some years later, a newcomer named Ken Wiederhorn was trying to put together his first movie *Shock Waves* [1977] and was looking for some actor he could get at a reasonable price to come to Florida and play in it. I suggested Cushing as a possibility, but Ken never could get through to him because Cushing's agent in London, John Redway, wasn't interested in having some independent young American who'd never made a movie, come along and try to get one of his actors on the cheap. I told Ken that I could probably put him in touch with Cushing personally, and I did get hold of

Regarding *Island of Terror* star Peter Cushing (lower left), Gordon says he was "very much in the Boris Karloff class"—the ultimate compliment!

Cushing on the telephone and he said he'd be happy to talk to Ken. Ken then contacted him directly, and the outcome of it was that, despite the agent's unwillingness to cooperate and the fact that there was very little money involved, Cushing thought it would be a nice idea because he could have a holiday in Florida at the same time. Ken very much enjoyed working with him—as did I on *Island of Terror*. When I think back on Peter today, he was very much in the Boris Karloff class: very quiet, very conservative, great sense of humor, not pushing himself into the limelight, and quite content to be there and do what he had to do without making a big fuss about it. And, acting-wise, impeccable. Whatever he was asked to do on *Island of Terror*, he either did it *or*, if he thought it wasn't reasonable or if he felt that he had a better idea, he discussed it. Of course, he *was* working with his old friend Terence Fisher.

    The Silicates were made by the special effects department at Pinewood and I was quite satisfied with what I saw when their scenes were shot. They were moved around by wires that were so carefully placed that you could not see them on the screen. It was my idea for them to make a slurping sound very much like that of the Fiends in *Fiend Without a Face*; I thought that sound was effective in *Fiend* and that it would give the Silicates more menace. The props representing the corpses of their victims were, in my opinion, well done. Although Hammer was pushing the envelope all the time with censorship in that era, you must remember that it was a very different time then than now and *Island of Terror* was considered quite gruesome in its day. Likewise, there was a topless girl [Norma West] on a morgue table in *The Projected Man*; this was done at Compton's insistence because it would help sales overseas. Then there was the scene in *Island of Terror* where Edward Judd has to cut Peter Cushing's hand off with an axe to save him from a Silicate that has him by the wrist.

The first time I saw the insert shot of the [prop] hand coming off and the arm spurting blood was when we screened a finished print at Pinewood Studios. Gerry, Fisher and I all agreed that it didn't work and was badly done. It was an obvious fake, it looked amateurish. Tom Blakeley was the only one who disagreed because he didn't want to spend the money to re-shoot it. I had to get up and say that I didn't want that shot in the film, especially when we screened it for the major distributors in America because it would spoil the mood and make it look like a low-budget movie. I felt an audience would start laughing.

Meanwhile, *The Projected Man*, based at Merton Park Studios, was under the supervision of John Croydon as I could not go tearing back and forth all the time between Pinewood and Merton Park. Croydon had introduced Gerry and me to a young writer who was new in the business and was enjoying considerable success in television. His name was Ian Curteis and he was obviously going to go places although he had not yet attempted a feature film. Croydon was so confident of his success that he persuaded Gerry and me to sign Curteis to direct *The Projected Man*. It turned out to be an unfortunate choice.

To play the title role, I did not want a British actor and frankly we didn't have the money to import a Hollywood star because of our limited budget. It was not a situation like *Witchfinder General* [aka *Conqueror Worm*, 1968] which Compton made with AIP who furnished the services of Vincent Price and paid his salary and expenses. The logical conclusion for me was to sign Bryant Haliday, whom I had already used in *Devil Doll* and *Curse of the Voodoo*. He had achieved a certain success in America because *Devil Doll* did so well there. Bryant, [an American] living in Europe, was a big fan of horror movies. He had two great ambitions, which unfortunately he was never able to realize: to star in a remake of *The Most Dangerous Game*, and to play Svengali. He loved doing *Projected Man*. I thought he was particularly good in it once he became the "monster on the loose" with the heavy burn makeup.

Compton got Mary Peach for the female lead. She was a stage actress who had also been in some successful British films and they regarded her as good value for England and insisted that she must have top billing. Norman Wooland, the villain, was a well-known character actor, and also a Shakespearean actor on the stage. Wooland, Derek Farr, Derrick de Marney—as I mentioned earlier, these were the kind of people that we could get for pictures, and even though their names may not have meant anything in the United States or elsewhere, they gave the pictures a lot of extra weight in the U.K.

Unfortunately, *Projected Man* got into trouble early in the filming. Because of his lack of feature film experience, combined with the tight schedule and limited financing, our young director Ian Curteis wasn't able to handle it, it all became too much for him. The picture started falling behind schedule and going over budget, and I found myself spending most days at Merton Park with John Croydon by my side while *Island of Terror* was running smoothly at Pinewood. There came a moment when Michael Klinger and Tony Tenser, who were looking over our shoulders, threatened to step in to take over the production as they were not prepared to increase their financing. Croydon and I decided that there was really only one thing to do: fire Ian Curteis and replace him for the completion of the film. As Croydon had hired him for us, it fell on him to fire Curteis and step in personally as a replacement to finish the last week's shooting. I don't remember any big drama at the studio [when Curteis was notified] and I think Curteis was relieved to step out because he simply didn't know any longer what to do. Croydon, one of England's most experienced production supervisors, was capable of doing *any*thing: He could write, he could produce, he could direct, and it became his responsibility

For *The Projected Man*, Ian Curteis received director credit on-screen (and on the movie's posters) even though he was fired in the homestretch. Writer-producer John Croydon brought the picture across the finish line.

to direct the balance of the picture. I would say that Ian Curteis directed 90 percent of *The Projected Man* and Croydon finished it. Croydon's work as director was not reflected in the on-screen credits which list only Curteis as director. One tries not to publicize such incidents.

Now the time was coming for me to take over the responsibility of selling both films in America. In those days, all the major companies had distribution headquarters in New York. I had a pretty good relationship with most of them, having sold them films that I represented over the years. Universal, which occupied a building on the corner of 57th Street and Park Avenue, was my first choice because I was on very good terms with "Hi" Martin, their executive in charge. He had bought several films from me previously which had been quite successful for them and he seemed to like me. *The Projected Man* was not yet ready because they were still finishing the special effects in London so I ran *Island of Terror* for him in Universal's screening room. He liked it and expressed an interest in acquiring the rights for Universal. I decided to stall for time because, as I mentioned earlier, if it went out alone, it would end up as a second feature with one of Universal's own productions and we would end up being the bottom half of the bill which would be no good for us financially. I told Hi about *The Projected Man* and that it was nearly ready to be shown and I wanted to withhold from making a decision until I could show him the first print of *The Projected Man* for a possible two-picture deal. He went along with that. To speed up matters, I brought over a work print of *The Projected Man* and ran it for him so that he would know what was happening (and I did not want him to go cold on us!). I don't remember now which scenes were unfinished but the end of this story is that he liked it well enough to say yes and we made a deal for Universal to release the double bill. The price that Universal paid us for the Western Hemisphere rights covered our production costs for the two films; *Island of Terror* was budgeted at £70,000 which would not have included the fees of Protelco, Gerry Fernback and myself. I don't exactly remember the budget of *Projected Man* but it was substantially less.

Now, a funny thing happened involving the hand-chopping scene in *Island of Terror* which was not in the film when I screened it for Hi Martin. I had previously given Universal a copy of the shooting script to keep their interest high and because they wanted to be sure they would have no censorship problems. At the end of the screening, Martin asked me what happened to that shot. I wasn't going to lie about it, I said, "Frankly, I wasn't happy with it. I didn't think it would matter if we left it out; in fact, I thought it would look more horrific if you don't actually see it." He asked, "If we *want* it, can we get it?" I said, "Well, you're certainly entitled to it if you buy the picture for the United States and you want that shot included." He said, "Have it sent over from England, and let the people at the studio in California look at it." Well, they looked at it and they said, "Yes, we want it"! At that time, it was actually surprising that Universal got that shot past the MPAA, that Universal was not forced to cut it. So that's how it came to be in the film. I still think it spoils the mood. When I see the film today with an audience, somebody usually lets out a laugh when they see that shot, because it's so obviously phony. In horror films, sometimes if something's happening off-screen, and you know it's happening but you don't see it, it's actually more horrifying than if it's put on the screen in front of you. Especially if what's put on the screen in front of you looks amateurish and doesn't work properly!

I saw both movies again recently, in preparation for this interview. The pre-credits sequence in *Island of Terror* was, I thought, a little bit too long and slow, but *everybody* was doing pictures with pre-credits sequences at that time. I thought the first killing, the Silicate attacking the farmer [Liam Gaffney] off-camera in the cave, was very effective; Terence Fisher handled that particularly well. Also the first visit to the cancer researchers' laboratory, where more bodies are found. The "worst" thing about the movie was the day-for-night shots, particularly the lift-off of the helicopter; one minute it looked like day and the next minute it was dark. But that was a matter of budget.

The Projected Man started off a bit slow, and in fact Universal cut it because they felt that it took too long to get going. Uncut, the picture opens with the scientists teleporting a guinea pig, and then after the arrival of Mary Peach there's *another* experiment with the teleportation machine; Universal cut the guinea pig experiment. Also, I could have done with less of the scantily clad secretary [Tracey Crisp] and the so-called nudity, but that was a necessary ingredient at the time. I thought Bryant was very effective and handled his role extremely well. Towards the end, he was actually able to arouse the sympathy of the audience and did not come across as just a monster on a killing spree. It reminded me of so many films in which Boris Karloff had played a scientist who becomes a monster through no fault of his own, as opposed to Bela Lugosi who was usually an outright villain. In fact, you might say that Bryant paid tribute to the memory of Bela in *Devil Doll* and Karloff in *The Projected Man*! As for the female lead Mary Peach, she later became Mrs. Jimmy Sangster, and the last time I saw her was with Sangster at one of the FANEX conventions in Baltimore [July 1997]. When I mentioned *The Projected Man*, she said, "Oh, I don't want to talk about that film!"—I think she didn't want to appear to have been a horror film leading lady and become a part of that "clan" alongside actresses like Ingrid Pitt [*laughs*]. So I stayed away from saying anything more about it!

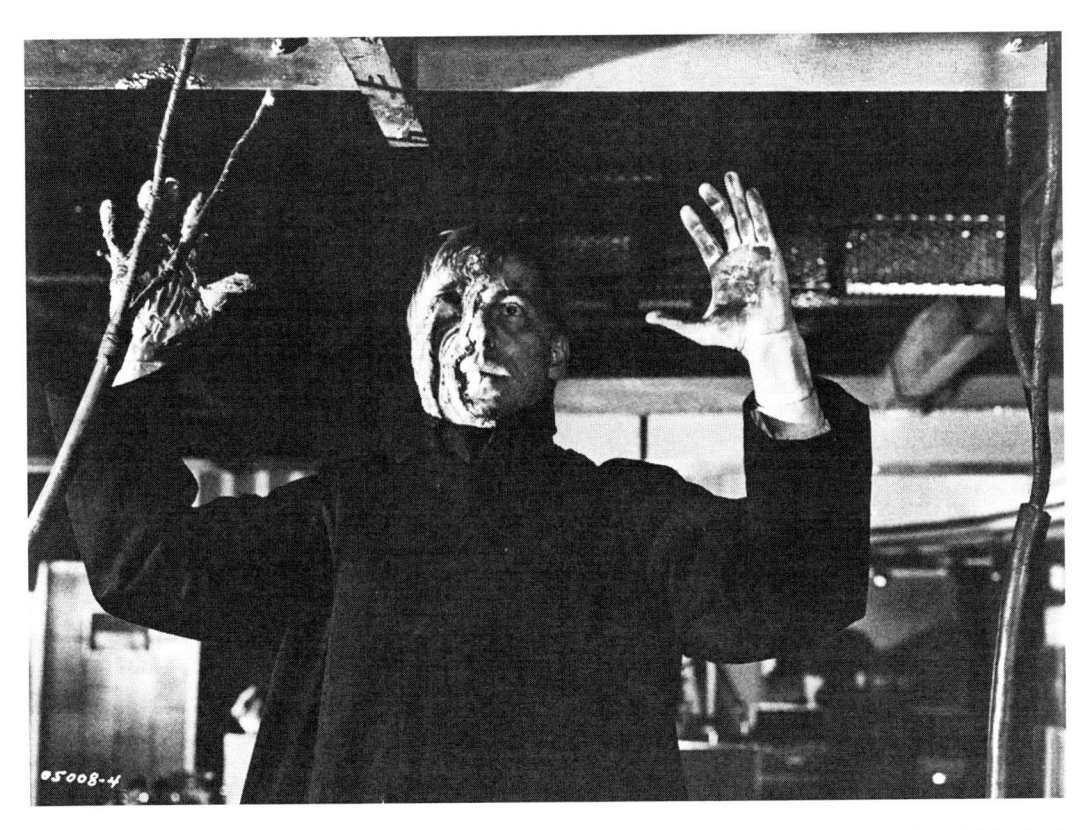

Another actor who made Gordon think of Karloff: Bryant Haliday, who in *The Projected Man* had the Boris-like ability "to arouse the sympathy of the audience and did not come across as just a monster on a killing spree."

Tom Blakeley was so struck by the success of *Island of Terror* and the deal with Universal that he wanted to rush immediately into a follow-up project, using Terence Fisher and Peter Cushing again while they were still available, and adding Christopher Lee. He hurriedly bought the film rights to a novel called *Night of the Big Heat* which he felt he could make on a very low budget and he thought would interest Gerry Fernback and me. Neither Gerry nor I liked the script. It was too long, too talky, with not enough action, and the budget was much too low to allow for really good special effects. Protelco withdrew from the production and Planet went ahead on its own. No one liked the finished film. I tried to help Planet make an American sale but every studio where I screened it, including Universal, turned it down. Eventually [1971] I sold it off to an American independent distributor who retitled it *Island of the Burning Damned* and paired it with a Japanese Godzilla picture [*Godzilla's Revenge*]. The program was a total failure and helped to lead Planet into bankruptcy.

Gerry and I wanted to get another picture going quickly with Protelco but we didn't have anything of our own that was ready. Allan Ramsen [co-writer of *Island of Terror*] continued to write genre screenplays on spec and submit them to us but neither Gerry nor I liked any of them. At that point, we were approached by Steven Pallos, a producer of some importance in England. He originally came from Hungary along with Alexander Korda to form London Film Productions, and for many years he was Korda's partner. When they split up amicably, Steve formed his own company, Britannia Film Distributors, and also a production company called Gibraltar Films. I sold a number of their films in the U.S. including two titles to Hi Martin for Universal distribution in the Western Hemisphere, *Nearly a Nasty Accident* [1961] and *Mystery Submarine* [1963].

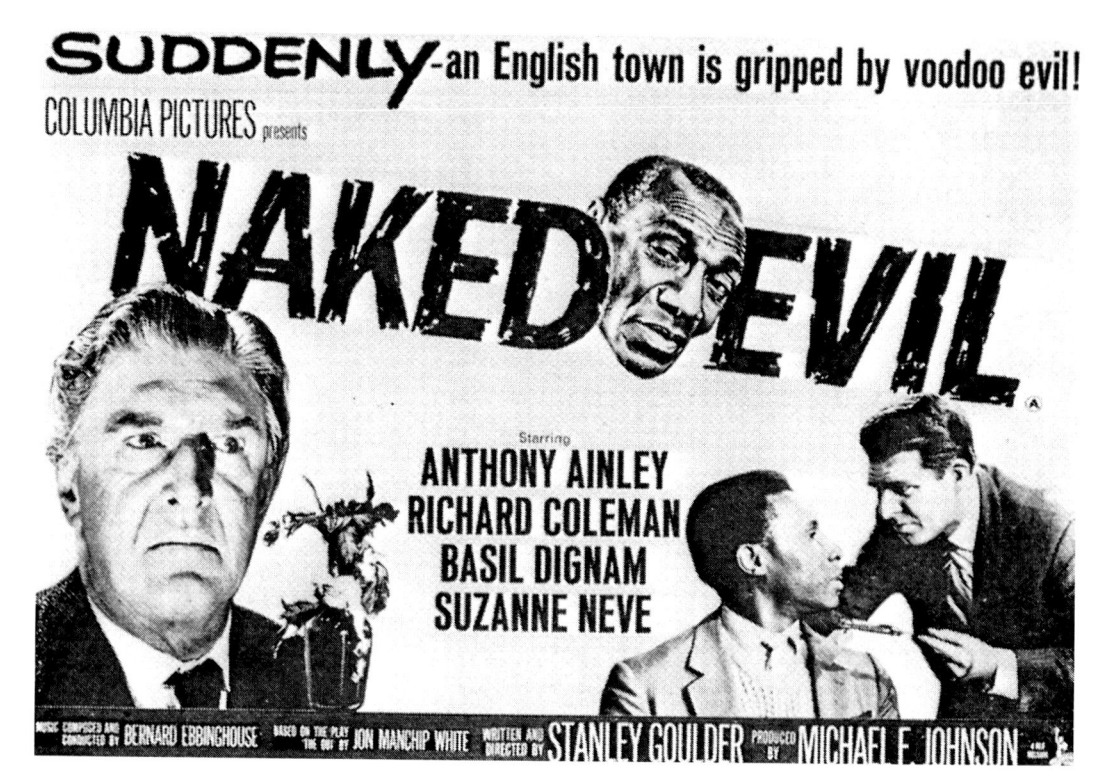

What Gordon learned from the *Naked Evil* experience was "never to become involved in a production unless I was able to *be* there and be in charge during the making."

Steve approached Gerry and me because he had been offered a property called *The Obi*, a play about voodoo witchcraft that Jon Manchip White had written for the BBC. Steve thought [a movie version] would make a very good second feature for distribution both in England and overseas. He talked to Gerry about the possibility of Protelco helping to finance it, and Gerry referred him to me. Steve and I discussed it, and I thought it was quite a good idea. Even though I had done a previous picture of that type [*Curse of the Voodoo*] which hadn't been too successful, I thought that *this* had a chance to be something better and that it was worth doing.

Steve already had a deal in place with Columbia Pictures, which was prepared to participate in the financing and to distribute the film in the United Kingdom and some European countries. However, Columbia envisaged the film [released as *Naked Evil*, 1966] as a low-budget second feature that would be useful for them for British quota purposes and wanted it to be made in black-and-white on a budget not exceeding £60,000. Since the industry was switching almost entirely to color except for second features, we tried to persuade Columbia to let us do the film on a higher budget, in color, to increase its potential internationally but Columbia refused to consider it. Color was then still much more expensive than black-and-white, particularly the cost of release prints, and Columbia saw this proposed picture as nothing more than a second feature for their quota.

In order to keep Protelco active, Gerry and I agreed to do it the way Columbia wanted. However, Gerry was very busy with his other business activities at that time, and I could not see myself going to England to supervise the production since Pallos, an experienced filmmaker with a very good reputation, was already on board. Actually, this is the only film in my career as a producer in which I took no part in the physical activities and was not even in England during any phase of the production. We left it all up to Steve, which in retrospect was a

Fernback and Gordon celebrate something—possibly the success of *Island of Terror* and *The Projected Man*—in a Soho restaurant in this mid–1960s shot. In a 1966 *Variety* ad, Protelco announced the properties they had available for production, among them *Creatures from Under the Sea*, *The Brainsnatchers*, *Invasion of the Apes* and the Algys Budrys sci-fi novel *Who?*, but none eventuated.

mistake. He assembled the unit, did the casting, supervised the script and generally took charge of the whole production.

Stanley Goulder was Steve's choice to finalize the screenplay with Jon Manchip White and to direct the film. Goulder had just made a picture for Steve called *Silent Playground* [1963] that had been very well received by critics although it was not a great commercial success because of its subject matter. Goulder had worked on several films of mine in earlier years [as assistant director and location manager]. Shooting took place at various locations in greater London and at Rayant Studios in Bushey, Herts. *Naked Evil* was a considerable improvement over *Curse of the Voodoo* but not enough to create any excitement in the U.S.

When Gerry decided to give up his film activities and concentrate on his other business interests, that was the end of Protelco as far as we were concerned and I produced my subsequent pictures under other auspices. Steven Pallos continued his own production and distribution interests for a number of years and then decided to retire when Raymond Rohauer agreed to buy his film library. He moved to Spain and, as far as I know, withdrew from the business altogether. He was a very fine gentleman whom I greatly respected and I would have welcomed a closer partnership in production under other circumstances.

As well as *Island of Terror* and *The Projected Man* did in American distribution, even getting a review in *Variety* that described us as joining the Hammer and Amicus league, Universal has never released either film on DVD; in fact, they've never released *The Projected Man* on home video at *all*. I have no say in the matter so there is nothing I can do about it although I've suggested it several times when talking with their studio executives. Both films have been released independently on DVD overseas. Protelco closed its doors on film production after only the three films *Island of Terror*, *The Projected Man* and *Naked Evil*, and when I resumed production myself, including *Tower of Evil* [1971], *Horror Hospital* [1973], *The Cat and the Canary* [1978] and *Inseminoid* [1981], it was on my own. But that's another story!

42

Nick Webster on Mission Mars *(1968)*

It must have seemed like a good idea in 1967, with the U.S.–U.S.S.R. "space race" still anybody's game: a movie about a manned space flight to Mars. Its opening act would be devoted to dramatic scenes of astronauts Darren McGavin and Nick Adams bidding adieus to their better halves (Heather Hewitt and Shirley Parker, respectively), and then it would segue into the saga of the three-man (McGavin, Adams, George DeVries) mission's trip through space to the Red Planet. Unfortunately, science, logic—and audiences—all took a beating from the resultant movie, which was filled with bad acting, stock footage, boring cliches, more *stock footage, a fourth-rate pop score, kiddie show–level Martian surface sets, and skinny, crooked stalks representing one-eyed monsters who operate out of an appearing-disappearing sphere (one reviewer likened it to "a rolled-up ball of aluminum foil"!). Instead of debuting on TV as originally intended, this interstellar trashterpiece instead received theatrical release from Allied Artists several months following the February 1968 suicide of Adams.*

*The movie's director Nick Webster may have been an award-winning television documentarian and a proficient helmer of episodic TV (*The Big Valley, Get Smart, The F.B.I., Mannix, Bonanza, *many more) but he had less success with features and* no *success with tales of Mars, as witness this movie* and *his best-remembered credit, the notorious* Santa Claus Conquers the Martians *(1964).*

This interview is extremely short because, actually, it never "officially" happened: I phoned and asked Mr. Webster if he'd allow me to do a Mission Mars *phone interview some time in the near-future, and during that initial call he invited me to turn on my tape recorder and began giving me some background that he said would be helpful as I formulated my list of questions. He passed away at age 94 in August 2006, before I had a chance to get back to him. Film-TV historian Mark Phillips was kind enough to provide me with a few quotes from his August 1991 interview with Webster to stretch it out a bit for publication here:*

I was a prominent documentarian with ABC-TV when I was contacted in New York by a New York company to do *Mission Mars*. The script was rather good, with a mysterious alien power as the foe instead of guys running around in monster suits. It was also very timely since we were in the middle of the space age and Mars has always fascinated people.

I knew it was going to be very low-budget. One way to [get around] that was to shoot on location, which was one of my specialties. I suggested to the producers that we film all of the Mars scenes in the Badlands of South Dakota; this way we would be able to shoot in any direction among the strange land formations, which really did look like another planet. It would be cheap and great once we got up there. We could also tint all of the outdoor scenes slightly red. Since the actors would be wearing space helmets, we could shoot these exterior scenes silent and dub in the sound later. Everyone agreed that this was a very good, logical plan and it would give the film an authentic eeriness.

I then went off to Greece to direct a show for ABC and when I came back, the *Mission Mars* people had gotten a good financial offer to shoot the film in a studio in Miami [the then-new "Studio City" complex] and they decided to go that way. They built some outdoor Mars sets, sort of a screwy imitation of Mars landscape; a hurricane came alone and blew the sets down. And so we had to go *in*side the studio to shoot the Martian landscape. You can imagine what that looked like! We had to get a great big cyc to be the background for Mars, and when the cyc came, it had a seam across the middle of it [*laughs*]. I was very disappointed. We could have done magnificent filming in South Dakota and instead we ended up with a very claustrophobic, low-budget–looking film. It was a lost opportunity but I did the best I could within those limitations.

The next thing that happened is, Darren McGavin and Nick Adams arrived, and their elaborate space helmets had been made for them [based] on their hat size. Darren tried to get the helmet on and he couldn't get it on and it hurt and it didn't fit him, and he got furious and he slammed it down. And it broke into a hundred pieces. There was a dead silence, at which point I said, "Okay. Lunch." *That* was a little odd, because it was 10:30 in the morning. Then we went down to a motorcycle shop and bought motorcycle helmets and had the art department dress them up.

Another thing was that the rocket [interior] set wasn't ready. We were starting out shooting the blast-off and the set wasn't painted yet. So I said, "Okay, put the camera up in the air and we'll shoot straight down at them." And so while we were shooting them lying down in the

Spacesuits with stable internal pressure, oxygen, temperature regulation—*pfffft*! For *sissies*! On the Red Planet surface, men's men Nick Adams, George DeVries and Darren McGavin "make do" with motorcycle helmets in the *lowwwwww*-budget *Mission Mars*.

blast-off scene, the painters were madly finishing painting the set, just outside of camera range!

Nick Adams was a very sincere, thoughtful and hard-working actor. Very likable, always prepared, very easy to work with. There was no pretense with Nick. He used to work out every day outside the studio; every time we were in between scenes, he'd run outside and he'd be out there with barbells and weightlifting and that sort of thing, keeping himself in trim. When I heard about his death, I thought, "My God, why would a guy who's working out commit suicide?" I don't see anybody [*that* serious about] getting himself in trim killing himself.

We did *Mission Mars* in three weeks, and I got a big kick out of doing a science fiction film.

42

Gary Conway on Land of the Giants (1968–1970)

In the golden age of SF-TV for Baby Boomer Monster Kids, 20th Century–Fox producer Irwin Allen dished up a triple-play of weekly wonder with his series Voyage to the Bottom of the Sea, Lost in Space *and* The Time Tunnel, *and then hit a towering homerun special effects-wise with his fourth and perhaps most visually impressive series,* Land of the Giants. *Debuting on ABC in the fall 1968 season, the Sunday-night adventure show was set in futuristic 1983 as suborbital passenger flight 612, London-bound, encounters an area of solar disturbance and passes through a space warp. Landing on the planet on the far side, the seven aboard (pilots Gary Conway and Don Marshall, stewardess Heather Young, passengers Don Matheson, Deanna Lund, Stefan Arngrim and Kurt Kasznar) soon find that they are (space)shipwrecked on a "mirror Earth," one whose most notable feature is that its denizens are 12 times the space travelers' size!*

For the Little People, the challenges of living in this nightmare world include being hunted by the Giants (who consider them invaders) and menaced by dogs, cats, gophers, insects ad absurdum near their forest crash site. For the actors, some of the challenges were working with giant props, running and climbing on an almost-daily basis—and giving realistic performances despite the always far-out storylines.

Longtime fans and newbies alike can rate the results now that Fox Home Entertainment's appropriately outsized, extras-packed DVD box set Land of the Giants: The Full Series *has hit store shelves. But before you judge, first get the long and the short (mostly short!) of it from series star Gary Conway: Today a winery owner and artist, he describes some of the David & Goliath battles he and his castmates had to fight in hopes of bringing their best work to the screen.*

Although Irwin Allen never told me directly, I'm pretty sure I know how I got my part on *Land of the Giants*. I had done the lead in a pilot for ABC called *Attack*, the "Japanese version" of the very, very successful, very popular, long-running TV series *Combat! Attack* had James Whitmore in it, Dan O'Herlihy, and a guy who became quite a successful actor afterwards, Warren Oates—an incredible cast. Whereas *Combat!* took place in Europe, *Attack*—which had the same producer, Selig Seligman—was to take place on the Pacific front. It was the most expensive pilot ABC had ever done, they got the best director [Arthur Hiller], the best of everything. We went to Hawaii to shoot it, we were there two or three weeks, and it turned out sensational. The only reason it didn't [make it to series] was because the Vietnam War was heating up, and when people saw *Attack*, although they loved it, it started becoming reminiscent of what was going on in real life at the time.

Irwin Allen saw that pilot, I have to *assume*, and from that they asked me to play the lead in *Land of the Giants*. At that time, I only knew that Irwin Allen was one of *the* major producers. I was familiar with some of his shows; at that time, you could not be *un*familiar with them. That was an era when, essentially, there were three networks and, unlike today, everybody was aware of *every*thing on television. I have friends who are now doing TV series and, I swear to God, I don't know when they're on and I don't see them. It's embarrassing! There are 300 or more channels and who knows *how* many series on the air, so you can be on a series and most people will not even be aware of it. But in *those* days, when you were on a series, a *lot* of people saw you. Back then when a network ran an episode of a show I was in, let's say *Land of the Giants*, the following day if I went to the market, I bet two-thirds of the people I'd encounter had seen it, because there were only three networks. Our show ran on Sunday nights, which I think was probably the single largest night for viewing, at seven o'clock, and we pretty well dominated, and therefore a tremendous number of people would have seen it. So I was *definitely* aware of Irwin Allen through the series that he had done. I had no idea, though, that he was the character he was.

Gary Conway—serious on TV as *Land of the Giants'* Capt. Steve Burton, serious on-set about giving performances that would not make a mockery of the way-out series: "Believe me, making a mockery of it would have been very easy to do."

I had no hesitation about getting involved with *Land of the Giants*, and I'll tell you why. When I was a young boy, I didn't realize that some motion pictures kept coming back to the theaters [kept being re-released]. Today you see a movie, it's around for two weeks, and if you miss it, that's the end of it, it's on television. But back then, you as a child could go to the movies and see a movie that you thought was current, but it was actually a re-release. I'll give you an example, [the animated] *Gulliver's Travels*, the great great classic. It first came out in 1939 and I must have seen it ten years later, but I thought that it was just out. When I, as a young boy, saw that, it was probably the most effective film experience I'd ever had. To this day I remember how wonderful it was seeing those little tiny people tying up, putting the little ropes around Gulliver, who was a giant to them. It was of course based on the novel by Jonathan Swift, a great writer, it had a lot of political and social commentary in it, and it was one of the great classics of literature of all time. That's not a bad model to have, going into a TV series, is it? When I got the offer to do *Land of the Giants*, which to me was a modern version of that motion picture, I thought that it could become an interesting and rather exciting series.

On *Land of the Giants*, the forest set for the Little People was huge. We were essentially on two stages at Fox, the first two stages you come to after you come through the gate. That very large forest set took over one whole complete stage. Also, within that stage they could readjust [the plants, bushes, etc.] so things looked different, and make it work for various episodes. Create a new clearing, have another spaceship land there, and so on. I'm not sure that the other forest set [the conventional forest set used in scenes showing the actors playing giants] was on the same soundstage as "our" forest, I have the feeling it was on the other soundstage. We did everything on the Fox lot, we were almost always on a stage, we weren't often outside ... and after a while, that got old. I wish we could have gone out [on location] occasionally, but because of the way they had to shoot, and because of technical aspects, it couldn't happen. So for those *Land of the Giants* years, our *life* became that soundstage. I had already done a series called *Burke's Law* [the mid-1960s police-detective drama] and we were always out in wonderful places all over town, in mansions and in nightclubs and so on, and it was fun to get *out* all the time. In the case of *Land of the Giants*, we were there on the Fox lot for over two years.

As I say, the forest was on one soundstage; on the second stage there would be, say, the giant table that we would climb up onto, and things like that. And all the big props. That stage had the big doors, and they'd bring the huge props in. Which, by the way, was always quite an event. Each episode had "a weekly prop," a "focus prop." One week it might be a giant camera, the next week a giant gun and so on, and they'd be very impressive. Let's say, for example, the camera: It would open, it had all the features of a regular camera, it was *exactly* like the small version. As we [actors] saw each new "focus prop," it would take us a while to get through with the oohs and aahs of how well it was done. Even the giant hand seen in so many episodes, even *that* was impressive up-close, actually. If you squinted, it did look kind of real. In the show, it was borderline: If the shot was quick, if you only saw the hand for a moment, it would work.

Those were still "the studio days," which we don't really have any more. What comprised a studio in that era were all the various departments—large wardrobe departments, prop departments, special effects departments and so on. Special effects-wise, we had the best in the world there at Fox; for instance, the guys who invented the blue screen, [L.B.] Abbott and [Art] Cruickshank. And the department people were there *all* the time; the prop guys, for instance, would be there day to day, making giant props that, considering the time constraints, were amazing. As I say, when they'd move these props onto our stage, it would take us a half-hour sometimes just to examine them and play with them. It was like we were back in our childhood, all us so-called adults, because these were the greatest toys you could ever imagine.

[*In shots where we see the Little People from a high angle, like from a giant's point of view, how was your dialogue recorded with no booms anywhere near you?*] They would hide them. And then we would always have little mikes on our person, in our clothes. The cameras were on cranes. They had so many different cranes there.

It was very difficult to have a stuntman. There are countless stories of what happens when actors *don't* use a stuntman, like in my case getting my ribs, both sides, cracked. But only on *rare*, rare occasions did we have stuntmen [on *Giants*]. If we were doing, for instance, a big fight scene, then there would be stuntmen. But the climbing and all *that* stuff was something we [the actors] had to do. And, frankly, we didn't mind doing it, because with the exception of Kurt Kasznar, we were all at an age when we could *do* that pretty easily. It was almost as if it were a recreation, and in a way it was kinda fun doing these odd things like climbing up onto big tables. I mean [*laughs*], who wouldn't enjoy doing that? It was Disneyland. There was a lot of energy in that show: We were always on the run, always running into a scene, running *out* of a scene, we were being chased, we were hiding ... there was a lot of physicality to the whole thing. When I could, to keep in shape I would go to the gym, and I would run, and I was a

42. *Gary Conway on* Land of the Giants *(1968–1970)*

For *Giants* cast members, oohing and aahing over each episode's "focus props" (the show's *other* "stars") became part of the ritual. (Above: Conway, Kurt Kasznar and Stefan Arngrim with, kneeling, Deanna Lund.)

little conscious of what I ate. But my weakness is ice cream, and ... unfortunately ... near Fox, there was a Will Wright's. Will Wright's was the consummate ice cream parlor, they had the greatest ice cream sundaes, and there was one within a mile of the studio. When I'd have an hour, on occasion, I would ... "find myself" there. I don't know *how* I got there ... I would lose my mind [*laughs*]. And then I had to do extra table-climbings, to burn up a little bit of that. *Fortunately*, Will Wright's is no longer around, so I don't have that fight on my hands any more!

Anyway, as I said, all of us [the younger cast members] did our own climbing and so on. And it becomes a macho thing after a while. The two Dons [Matheson and Marshall] weren't about to see Gary climb up onto the table and not climb up—and vice versa! We'd always make it a little bit of a game: If we were going to climb, we all really scampered up those ropes. It's very easy for that to happen when you're all a little competitive.

There was a lot of physical stuff to do, and I was hurt, several times. You know the actor Zalman King, who now does a lot of soft porn? (Actually, terrific filmmaking.) I'll tell you the kind of character *he* was: There was an episode ["The Lost Ones"] where he and I had a fight in a box cage, and they had a stuntman for him. They may have had a stuntman for me, too, because it was close-quarters fighting. In those cases, a stuntman is valuable because you really *don't* want to get hurt; if you do, it's expensive for the company, and in many of the shots, it's irrelevant *who's* doing it. But Zalman was the sorta "Actors Studio" actor, the Brando thing, the Method—he was Method all over the place [*laughs*]. And so he thought that he should be doing the fight, to add a certain insanity to it. I went along with it and, man, at one point he miscalculated and *plowed* his fist into my ribs and cracked them. And that's why you have to have stuntmen: It stopped the shooting. He was very sympathetic and all that, he was very sorry, and I had to go to the emergency hospital and get taped up. That may have been on a Thursday or Friday, and then when we came back on Monday, we had to resume doing the fight. We went at it again, things were going along pretty well, he was more controlled ... and all of a sudden, his Method acting took over, and he let me have it with his fist again, and this time he cracked the ribs on the *other* side! That was Zalman King. So, don't ever do a stunt with Zalman King. Maybe a sex scene *for* him [*laughs*]! [*Was he sorry the second time too?*] I guess he was. By that time, it had become ... pretty pathetic. And I think Irwin Allen was ready to work on *Zalman's* ribs [*laughs*]!

I seldom got to meet the guest stars who played giants. Which was quite a change from *Burke's Law*, where without a question we had, and I got to meet, the greatest array of guest stars any show had, then and since. Think about it: Gloria Swanson's not bad to have as a guest star for a day! It seemed like every day, we had a different film idol. The amount of people that I personally met on that show was really quite amazing. On *Land of the Giants* the only guest stars you'd work with were ones who played other Little People. That's when we worked with Bruce Dern and people like that. Bruce Dern ["Wild Journey"] was a very good actor ... a very *interesting* actor, let me put it that way. And when he did *Land of the Giants*—talk about working out!—to get to Fox, he would run from Malibu, every day. I was doing *some* running to keep in shape, but I thought, "My God...!" What an ordeal *that* must have been. It was miles and miles from Malibu to Fox—can you imagine? He'd have to leave hours ahead of time, to do that.

Because of the series' unusual sets, there were always a certain number of visitors, and they would ooh and aah; they got a big kick out of it, as they should. They also would act as an audience for us, and that's not all bad, because we were then performing as if we were in the theater. We would not only perform for ourselves, but also for these people who happened to be our temporary audience. That brought a little theatricality to it. Irwin Allen would come in on occasion and check things out. Most of the time he was quiet. Once in a blue moon, he'd put in his two cents. But he was usually not usurping the director's authority. When he did, he was pretty well nipped in the bud by us. Especially by me. [*When he came on the set, was it "Oh, good, here's Irwin!" or "Oh-oh, here's Irwin"?*] I think it was more like "Oh-oh, here's Irwin." That's not necessarily to reflect badly on Irwin. Irwin was definitely the authority figure. Pleasing Irwin was not something that was written that we had to do, but it was inherent; the guy hired us, he was the producer. But when he came on the set, you wondered whether it was because there were some bad dailies, or something like that. Aaron Spelling [producer of *Burke's Law*] had a lot more style to him, and he'd always make a big point to be very complimentary. When *he* came on the set, it was quite a pleasure, because you knew you were going to get a nice compliment ... whereas you weren't sure with Irwin.

When Irwin would start usurping the director's responsibilities, I really stopped that, because, boy, I couldn't let that happen. When you're acting, there are lights all over, you [the actors] are just in your world, and the rest of the soundstage is something that's just "out there" in the fuzzy outer world. We were in the middle of a scene, and dealing with it, and probably trying to take our time with it a little bit ... and from way out in that fuzzy outer world, I heard this huge, booming voice: "Get *on* with the scene!" or "Finish it!" or whatever the command was. Well, a scene has to have its own life in order to jell, in order to make sense, in order for the people to be real, so when I heard that voice saying, "Get *on* with it," I instinctively thought to myself, "You can't allow that to happen," because that kind of thing compromises the work. A lot of people think, when you're doing something like a *Land of the Giants*, that work can't be taken seriously, the actors can just wing it, or throw it out there, or do it in a tongue-in-cheek manner. But it's quite the contrary. So when I heard that booming voice, I responded in an *equally* booming voice, "We will take our *time*, thank you!," or what*ever* it was I said, I don't remember. I do remember that everybody suddenly was stunned, because it was Irwin who was saying that. But he didn't pursue it. He realized maybe that he had overstepped his bounds.

That's another difference I notice between "those days" and "*this* day": Back then, TV actors had a certain amount of power. Not that you'd take advantage of it and become a jackass, but it wasn't real easy to fire you then, because if you were the lead in a series, what were they gonna do? In those days, how could they fire, say, David Janssen [star of TV's *The Fugitive*]? Many series back then had maybe two leads, or even *one* lead, and then some sub-leads. They could probably get rid of a sub-lead, but they couldn't get rid of the lead—because the lead was the lead [*laughs*]! And I notice that the current producers must have all been trained in that era, and their main lesson coming out of it was, "Don't ever make anyone *the* lead in a series." I notice all the series today have *endless* people attached to them, so if somebody gets out of line, he or she is gone. But [in the old days] we could exercise our authority at some points.

[*Here's the funny thing about you saying that Irwin Allen would come on the set and start usurping the director's job: In the chapter on* Land of the Giants *in the book* Science Fiction Television, *a lighting guy named Bill Neff says that* you *would try to get a-hold of the directing reins, and that* Irwin Allen *would have to nip it in the bud. The exact opposite of what you just told me!*] Well, sometimes the scenes could be quite complicated. We shot eight, nine, ten, eleven pages a day, and some of the scenes had *all* the regulars in them. So there'd be challenges in the coverage, in the blocking. A scene with that many people, it's not easy to make it look natural, so that the actors don't look like lined-up wooden Indians up there. Our directors were not directors in the sense one thinks: They didn't really deal with performances, they dealt more with, "Is the lighting okay?," "Is his key light okay?," "Is her makeup right?"—that's where they were coming from. And sometimes the scene would just not be working because, for example, we were all lined up in a silly way. *That's* usually what happened, because for lighting purposes, it was easier to shoot it if we *were* all in a line! Well, if six, seven people are standing together talking, they don't line up [*laughs*], they're in a circle, and they have a certain flow. And often—and maybe Bill Neff was referring to *this*—we being actors, we would take a little bit of the scene in our own hands and say, "May I move?," "Can I stand over here so we don't look as if we're in an Army formation?," things like that. Now, the crew didn't mind if we were all lined up; they were just lighting, and they'd just as soon get home early. They would have very little patience with performers trying to do their best. And that [desire to have a say in the blocking] not only came from myself, it would come from both Dons, and others, when they felt uncomfortable in a scene. So there were two worlds going on, there was *our* world, trying to keep a believability, and then the world of, "Let's hurry up and get this over with and get on to the next shot. We don't want to be here again tonight 'til 7:30 or 8." Which was often what we did: start at 6:30, 7 in the morning and work a 12-hour day. That was commonplace.

Irwin Allen himself ... somebody could make a good series right now about Irwin [*laughs*]. There's endless material to draw from, believe me! [*For instance?*] Everything about him! His

The *Land of the Giants* directors' penchant for shots featuring lined-up cast members rankled Conway, but it sure makes a caption writer's job easier: left to right, Don Matheson, Heather Young, Kurt Kasznar, Deanna Lund, Conway and Don Marshall.

hair, the way he dressed, where he lived, who he lived with, how he conducted his shows. For instance, when he summoned you—and it *was* a summons, to come up to see him. Other producers, if they wanted to talk to you about something, you'd come quietly into their nice little office and usually it would be just the two of you, there would never be anybody else. With Irwin, if he wanted to discuss something with you, even something that might have a privacy component to it, he'd always conduct it in the biggest room that he had, with a big table, and there were always at least eight other people there [*laughs*]! So with Irwin, there was no intimacy, there was never a one-on-one; it was one on ten!

During this period of time, I was building a house on a street called Stradella, up in Bel-Air, and I would leave the Fox lot during lunch and go up there to meet with the builders. One of the times that Irwin called me in to have a little conversation (in front of eight people), he mentioned that one of the reasons was because I'd been late coming back from lunch a couple times—which I had *not*. But I thought to myself, "How the hell does he know I'm getting away during lunch?" I hadn't told a soul, and I just couldn't figure out how he knew. Well, lo and behold, right below *my* new house, he had *his* house, and I was passing his house every damn day. So he would know where I was going, all my comings and goings, all the time! His house, incidentally, was an odd little house perched out like a little eagle's nest, it was one of those hillside deals that looked like it had no ground underneath it. And it was the only house in L.A. that was a flamingo pink [*laughs*]. Or was it coral? Anyway, whatever it was, it was one of Irwin's favorite colors. He had favorite colors that I had never seen anywhere else in the world!

He never even once invited me, or any other cast member, or anybody I knew, to his house. Unlike, let's say, Aaron Spelling, whose house I went to many, many times—he always had beautiful homes. Producers would *always* end up having a party or two at their house, but never once with Irwin. I often wondered what went on at his house! [*Did he have a sense of humor?*] I'm not sure. I think he did, but if so, it was one that I never could quite connect to. Incidentally, Groucho Marx was a friend of Irwin's; as a matter of fact, he was I believe an investor in one of Irwin's shows, it could have been *Land of the Giants*. (Too bad Groucho was never on one of our shows—even though, again, we probably wouldn't have worked with him directly.) Anyway, Irwin was a buddy to Groucho Marx, and I guess you couldn't have a friend like Groucho Marx and not have a sense of humor. But Irwin's was a humor that escaped me in many ways. I could not say that I was laughing out loud every time I was with Irwin. In fact, quite the contrary!

As director of the first episode ["The Crash"], Irwin was very detail-oriented, needless to say. And a lot of his directing, I felt, was from [the old school]. You remember seeing pictures of directors from the old days standing with the bullhorn? He was that kind of director. I think Irwin lacked intimacy. They say that of certain people; I hear that of Ronald Reagan and others who you'd think must be very friendly, but actually they were never able to be intimate to their children or to those around them. I think this [inability] was part of Irwin's personality. He would never find that moment to connect with you, just you-and-him together.

Sobey Martin and Harry Harris directed most of the episodes. I think Irwin liked them, they seemed to be able to deliver on time, and that was the criterion. And also, it came to a point where directors were almost not needed. On the show, we were only doing certain things, and I don't ever remember a director giving us anything to help our performances. Because what in the hell was a director going to say, really, at that point? Everything was pretty much pre-set, the lighting and camera people knew what to do, and so on. So they could fall asleep in their chair as a director—and they *did*—and no one would notice.* Anyway, Irwin just probably liked those guys a lot, they didn't create any havoc, they were competent, they were able to get the job done efficiently. And, really, that's all Irwin cared about.

As I mentioned before, amazingly, we all got along very well, and genuinely liked each other. It would have been hell if we didn't. I think we allowed each person to have some idiosyncrasies, some areas to be an individual, and even to be perhaps ... maybe offbeat. Deanna Lund was always very sweet and very accommodating, and essentially gentle, and never ever demanding in any way.

Don Matheson was a terrific guy, very even-tempered ... a real gentle man. And an underrated actor, but *not* by those who worked with him. The best actors have always been the underrated ones, because they make it look easy. Don and I never had one tense word between us, which is pretty remarkable for actors thrown together in a very challenging, no-escape environment where tempers could have really frayed.

Don Marshall, at times, perhaps was like myself, maybe would take things a little seriously—which is to the good in the long run. We did not allow ourselves to make this [acting in *Land of the Giants*] just a big joke, which could very easily happen. Perhaps I was the one who was the most adamant about that. And today when I look at the work in the show, even though it *is* in a cartoon context, I'm not embarrassed with my performances, I feel they maintain a certain realism, a certain honesty. Whether you're doing Shakespeare or Irwin Allen, you have to play the notes well. Like a musician: All the conductor asks is that you play the notes in tune, and you play them well. That *is*, really, what an actor should be doing, playing the notes and playing them in tune, and not making a mockery out of it—and, believe me, making a mockery of it would have been very easy to do. After a while on some series, and with *Land of the Giants* this was certainly the case, the lines begin to seem redundant, you feel like you just did this scene the week before [*laughs*], and so on. But we would stop ourselves from giving in to the temptation to *not* take it seriously. [The actors] on some other shows were unable to do that, and the shows don't stand up, time has not been kind to them.

[*Having a black actor, Marshall, play one of the heroic leads was unusual back then—and there reportedly* was *concern that that might get the show in trouble in certain parts of the South, where TV stations might not want to run it.*] It's almost astonishing today to think about that, but [his hiring] *was* somewhat controversial. But Irwin Allen wanted one of the leads to be a black guy. If you go back to that time, you can't remember too many other shows that had that situation. Especially a show that was going to be on Sunday nights, seven o'clock; *Land of the Giants* was for families, a "South" or "Midwest" kind of show, not a ten o'clock, edgy show. So, yes, it was kind of a breakthrough, and that really goes to Irwin Allen's credit.

To me, there are two Steven Arngrims: There was the Steve of *Land of the Giants*, this little, cute boy who was *very* professional and who had two good parents who made sure that he did what he had to do. And there's the Steve Arngrim of today, very different, a tall kid, a musician. Honest to God, I can't put the two together [*laughs*]. If you were to meet any of the rest of us today, we're kind of like we were *then*. Obviously younger/older, but we were more or less fully formed human beings when we did *Giants*. Stefan was the exception; I see Stefan today and I see him as a different guy, I can't put the two together, and it's ... strange!

Heather Young was a very, very sweet girl, never anything but cooperative, and extremely professional. Well, they *all* were. No prima donna attitudes, not in the slightest, with *any* of

---

*Interviewed on-camera for the Land of the Giants *DVD, Stefan Armgrim talks about Sobey Martin often falling asleep while directing.*

42. Gary Conway on Land of the Giants (1968–1970)

Left to right: Don Matheson, Heather Young and Conway. Playing their Lilliputian roles straight and "keeping things real" was the key to making *Giants* scenes jell, according to Conway.

these people. And they still have the same attributes. All of us would kid each other—well, I certainly would—about politics, about religion, there was nothing sacred when it came to that cast, and to this day we're the same way. When I get together with them, we have great fun, we laugh, we kid each other in a nice way. In some respects, we may even like each other more now than we did *then*.

Kurt Kasznar was a delightful guy. The rest of us were all very young people at the time, and Kurt ... although he wasn't *all* that old [his mid–50s] ... was "the older guy," obviously, to us. He had a tremendous reputation as a stage actor and film actor, I mean, *beyond* Jonathan Harris [the actor playing the equivalent "scoundrel" role on Allen's *Lost in Space*]. Kurt had a great background as an actor, a real high-quality career. We all respected that, and we thought that that brought something to the show, the fact that Irwin didn't just get *any* ol' guy, but he got a guy like Kurt Kasznar. Kurt was great to work with. He also had his idiosyncrasies, but (as I said earlier) we gave people some room to be who they were. Even if it was not something that we were entirely okay with, we worked *with* it. Kurt, again, was a consummate professional, as *every*body was.... As an example of Kurt's idiosyncrasies, I remember he wanted us, on occasion, to speak up in the scenes. At the time, I let him go with that, because I figured he was from the stage, where speaking-up is very important. But in film, sometimes speaking-up can make the scene seem corny, it can be *too* big, and the intimacy is lost. He would say, "Speak up that line," and you didn't *want* to speak up that line because it was perhaps a more intimate line! It wouldn't create a conflict, but you'd have to ... *pretend* you were speaking up. Then later on I realized, he was hard of hearing [*laughs*]. And so, if we'd [followed his instructions], we would have been giving entirely different performances, really over-reaching performances, just because he was a little hard of hearing!

[*Interviewed in* Starlog *magazine, Deanna Lund mentioned your "idiosyncrasies": She said you drove her crazy with your perfectionism!*] When she refers to my perfectionism, I think she's referring to my [attitude of] "Let's get the scene right, let's not succumb to the temptation to [take the easy way out]." In television, you're under the gun time-wise and there are occasions when a simple scene, even scenes as simple as some of the ones in *Land of the Giants*, could become most difficult. From the simplest to the more complicated scenes, you had to spend a certain amount of time on them before they would jell, before everybody was comfortable in it, before we were in command of what we were saying. I think that Deanna may have been referring to the fact that I would insist that we keep going with a rehearsal, I would insist that we *not* shoot quite yet, or we would re-do something if it fell short. All that, of course, today, is a very vague memory, but what does *stay*, and will exist forever, is the *work*; there it still is, on the screen.

It was amazing that the cast didn't get on each other's nerves. Considering the circumstances, we probably got along as well as *any* group of people, let alone actors, could have gotten along! For some reason, our personalities jelled. There was nobody who wanted to become a prima donna, there was nobody who had problems. All we needed was one person who was kind of "off," and it would have been hell. So we were very lucky. To this day, they're all very sweet people, and I always enjoy seeing them.

Right from the beginning, one of the things that I always felt was that, in many ways, *Land of the Giants* would be most challenging for an actor because we didn't have the great dialogue to rely upon. And a lot of the things that we were acting *opposite* were not there; we'd just be looking up high and talking, but of course there was no Giant there. And after a while there was often a sense of "We've done this before," "We're repeating ourselves." *All* of those aspects were really stacked against us actors when you think of doing the kind of work that would stand out critically. But take the greatest actor in the world and put him in our situation, and let's see what he would do. How great would Marlon Brando have been had he, early in his career, gotten a series instead of being on Broadway? And if that series happened to be *Land of the Giants*, how would he have dealt with it? It *was* a challenge, and to this day I don't look at it, or anybody else doing anything similar, in a demeaning way. Great acting, like great painting, is not necessarily about the subject, it's about how well it was executed. You can look at a painting as simple as a jar of sunflowers and it might be as great a painting as "Guernica," that huge, very complex mural that Picasso did in 1937. That's the important point: Was the [actor] kind of true to himself? Did you get a certain reality from him? Did you get caught up? Did you feel he was faking it? Those are the important things. And when you're doing these episodes back to back to back to back to back to back ... to be able to survive that, I think, is a certain kind of accomplishment.

Spooning on a spool: Conway and *Giants* glamourpuss Deanna Lund in a fun promotional photograph.

[*Deanna Lund and Don Matheson had a romance that later led to marriage.*] Early on, I worried about that getting in the way of things. It seems to me they each had ... or at least Don had ... a spouse at that point. It was no really *big* deal, but somehow when you bring romance into the work, it can become an issue. In their case, it didn't. They really kept everything pretty well under control, and so I have to give 'em credit for that.

Wearing the same clothes in every episode was both convenient *and* a drag. When you have to deal with a lot of different wardrobe, and suits and ties and shirts, you go into your trailer and there's all your wardrobe lined up. Well, in my case, on *Land of the Giants*, there would always be just *one* thing I'd find, that red suit! And the only variation on it was when I would take off the jacket and just have the gray shirt. I just accepted that, and never thought much about it once we got going. The fabric allowed me to move, and it was not a pain. It was better than being in a regular suit. By the way, I was informed that, about 15, 20 years ago, somebody who had gotten a-hold of that suit sold it at an auction, and my memory is that it went for *many* thousands of dollars. I don't remember the amount, just that at that point it was an unbelievable figure to me. So somebody still has that suit!

[*Recently watching a bunch of episodes, I remembered all the things that made me scratch my head even as a 10-, 12-year-old, watching the show originally. Like the fact that the Giants could never find your ship, even though it was as big as a kid's wagon, and sitting right out in the open in the forest with lights flashing!*] Actually, in an episode or two, the *Spindrift* was found by the Giants. But, yeah, that was a cheat. [*Every room in every house and every building had an opening for a drainpipe that led right out to the street—very convenient for you guys!*] That's right, that was a world where plumbing and drainpipes were very important [*laughs*].

The series was expensive, and I think that was one of the reasons that it was taken off the air probably before its time. In those days, the producers and the studios didn't have a sense of how huge the foreign sales would be. *Especially Land of the Giants*, which as I understand— and I was told by somebody who would know—*was* one of the most "played" shows around the world. That's easily understandable, in that it was a show where the dialogue didn't matter all that much.

A couple years after the show ended, maybe '73, '74, my mother and father happened to see an episode in Poland. While on a trip in Europe, they went to Poland and went to a friend-of-a-friend's house. As they were sitting there, suddenly the whole family went to the TV set and turned it on, and there was *Land of the Giants*. They all started watching the show very carefully; my mother didn't want to say, "That's my son there," because it would be too weird. When the show ended, they turned it off and went back [to socializing]. The point is, that was an incredibly important show for them to see. That was a time when Poland was still part of the Soviet empire, and Poland has a history of wanting to be free of its giant oppressors whoever they may be, the Germans or the Soviets. And this show represented that to them. They saw the world of the Giants as a totalitarian state and they saw them*selves* as the Little People. They were seeing it completely symbolically. So, yeah, around the world, it was popular. I once had the privilege of seeing a report from Fox on the sales in various countries, and it was astonishing how many times it had run, and on how many stations; for Australia and England, there were pages and pages. *Star Trek* didn't even get *close* to that, because *Star Trek* was very verbal, was very much dependent on dialogue. And all the comedies [on American TV] were completely dialogue-dependent and culturally dependent. But *Land of the Giants* was very visual, it had wonderful color, and so you could see how it could become very popular overseas. If Fox had had any idea that they were going to make so much money from this show, they would probably have kept it alive a while longer, no matter *what*.

[*Making the Giants' world a totalitarian society was a nice touch. Even for some of the Giants, it was a grotesque, awful place to live, which added to the mood of the thing.*] Watching the show, you had a sense that this was kind of a *1984* world. There was definitely a police state feel. And the way some of the Giants looked, and even the way they walked, gave them a soulless aspect. The show really was symbolically interesting. That aspect of it was not picked up so much in the United States. I think the show was vastly more appreciated foreign than in the United States. [*I especially liked the ones with Kevin Hagen as the inspector, because he was like Javert in* Les Miserables, *he was going to catch the Little People or die trying.*] I had very little contact with Kevin while we were shooting but subsequently, a couple times, I went to conventions that were featuring *Land of the Giants* and Kevin would be there, and it was kind of fun to see him again. It was funny the way that series worked; there were two sides [actors playing Little People and actors playing Giants] and they never met.

[*Did plots ever get so silly—Jonathan Harris as the Pied Piper, let's say—that you thought to yourself, "This is not what I signed up for"?*] Yeah, there were times when it seemed that they were stretching. But, honest to God, at those times I felt that it was even more important not to "give in" to that. As a performer, it was important to be even more truthful, more realistic. When things got silly, I still think we pretty well stayed true to ourselves, and didn't become silly ourselves.

We did a bit of traveling around to promote the show, especially in the beginning. Irwin sent me out to various cities all over the United States. One time, believe it or not, I was in Tennessee on one of these junkets, and it was late when I was picked up by a p.r. person. I didn't know quite where I was, but I remember driving to some place, I think it was at night, and the guy telling me, "Walk out there on the stage and talk about the show." I walked out on the stage—and it was the Grand Ole Opry [*laughs*]! Somebody introduced me ("This is Gary Conway and he's going to be starring in a new series," blah blah blah), and then I said whatever the heck you say in those situations. Of course it got a big cheer. So Irwin was sending me to all kinds of places, and *that* was probably as good a place to go as any! The other day I came across a picture which must have been taken during *Giants'* second year: I was visiting some city, in the back of a big convertible waving to people, and, my God, there was a huge crowd out there. It looked like I was a presidential candidate! That shows the power of television in those days: There were three networks, ours was a popular show, it was on at a popular time, a very big *family* time, and so if you were in a car, waving, the whole crowd had *seen* you. That wouldn't be the case for most of today's [TV actors].

We now have a tasting room here at our winery, and my daughter Kathleen thought it would be fun to play a lot of the episodes on the TV in there. And people really enjoy seeing it. Again, that goes back to its visual qualities: You can play it and not have the sound turned up, and the show still works incredibly well. People can tell what's going on because the characters are rarely sitting around talking to each other, there's a lot of action. So they're great to show when you want to turn off the dialogue and just play it in the background [*laughs*]!

To be honest with you, I don't remember how I felt when I heard that the series was cancelled. By that point, it was probably close to three years of our lives that we'd spent on *Land of the Giants*; some actors like series that last years and years and years, but I really wasn't one of 'em. I always felt there were other things to do. Really, after two years and 50-something episodes, everything we could ever do on the show, we'd already done, and at that point it really *was* just a job. So I don't think I was overly disappointed. Also, we were not quite in the era of the great residuals, so it wasn't as if we felt we were leaving millions of dollars behind.

These days we have a winery, Carmody McKnight, where we make wine, which is a wonderful thing. Carmody is the name I was born with, and McKnight is my wife Marian's maiden name, and we decided to go back to our roots when we named our winery. And one of the ways I'm able to please the segment of [movie-TV] fandom that seeks out autographs and other special things, is sign wine bottles for them [*laughs*]!

I planted this vineyard 20 years ago, and the other day when somebody asked me for my bio, I gave them my regular spiel—"I did *Burke's Law* and *Land of the Giants*" and so on and so forth—and suddenly at the end of it, for the first time *ever*, I said, "...And I'm a *farmer*." Because I figured, 20 years in a vineyard qualifies me! So suddenly I'm this actor-writer-*farmer* guy [*laughs*]! It's a lot of fun, it allows me a fantastic opportunity to live in one of the most beautiful places on Earth [Paso Robles, California], I have a lake right in front of my front door and we make wine. What's more pleasurable than making wine? And if you can't sell your wine, at least you can drink it!

We have five, six more-or-less permanent employees. But then, when we have to do var-

Conway and his wife Marian McKnight (1957's Miss America) at their winery; visit their website www.carmodymcknight.com.

ious chores in the vineyard like pruning and thinning and, later on, of course, harvest, you hire those crews for several weeks, and they can be up to 50 or 100.

    I started out to be a painter—which is something I do now more than anything else. Being an actor was a marvelous way to make a very good living and raise a family, but I never saw it as a primary creative art. It was never *in* me to be elated or disappointed [about the ups and downs of his acting career]. I was earning a great living; I didn't know it at the time, but the Screen Actors Guild has a good medical plan and I never had to worry about not having medical insurance; we always lived in a nice neighborhood and our children were able to go to good schools; I met incredible people—you couldn't *ask* for anything more. And acting, even if it's *not* a primary creative enterprise, is a *hell* of a lot of fun. It is basically being an adult and yet being able to continue as a kid, and play make-believe throughout your life. When you're a kid, playing make-believe is more fun than anything else; and then, for everybody else, it *ends* at some point, and you have to get serious and become a lawyer or a doctor or go into insurance. But when you're an actor, it never ends, and when you're 40 years old and 60 years old and sometimes even 80 years old, you're playing make-believe. And *that's* a good thing!

43

Memories of Nightmare in Wax *(1969)*

A throwback to *Mystery of the Wax Museum* (1933) and *House of Wax* (1953), the low-budget indie *Nightmare in Wax* was unique in its own small way, adding to the time-tested horror formula a motion picture industry background and a number of surreal flourishes. Many of the latter came courtesy of Cameron Mitchell, who starred as Paragon Studios makeup department head Vincent Rinard, horribly burned by his vindictive boss (Berry Kroeger at his ickiest); fire-scarred and wearing an eyepatch, Rinard goes from makeup man to operator of a Hollywood wax museum where, "coincidentally," the main attractions are astonishing lifelike figures of all the Paragon Studios stars who have recently started disappearing without a trace. Without credit, Mitchell also overhauled the script, deleting scenes, writing others (including a head-scratcher of an "It was all a dream ... or *was* it?" ending) and suggesting additional weirdness which, *he* felt, "saved the picture."

Fans can decide whether Mitchell helped or harmed the picture now that it's new on DVD from Navarre Corporation, half of an "Exploitation Cinema Double Feature" with the same-year *Blood of Dracula's Castle*. In the following two interviews, the making of the movie is recalled by John "Bud" Cardos, who played the part of a police sergeant, worked behind the scenes, and stunt-doubled Mitchell in his fire scene; and Martin Varno, the movie's makeup man.

John "Bud" Cardos

The executive producer on *Nightmare in Wax* was Rex Carlton, who also wrote that picture. I knew Rex very well and I did a number of pictures with him. He was a quiet, nice guy, very gentle, easy to get along with. I do believe he was gay. But that didn't make any difference—he never made any passes [*laughs*]! He committed suicide later on. Another producer was a guy named Marty Cohen, who was involved in a picture called *The Rebel Rousers* [1970] which I also worked. In other words, how I got the *Nightmare in Wax* job was because I'd worked with all these guys before. I did a whole bunch of pictures [on that level] as production manager, first assistant director, I'd do parts in 'em, I did all the stuntwork ... back in those days, that's what you did, you wore three or four hats. The job of the production manager (which was *one* of the jobs I did on *Nightmare in Wax*) is, you put everything together: You go out and you find the locations with the location guy, you hire all the crew, you work out a budget and a schedule with the director and the producer, you make sure that things are paid for, and you try to hold it *on* budget and *on* schedule all the time you're going through the show.

Cameron Mitchell, who played the madman with the eyepatch, was a great guy, he really was. Look back over his career, he did a lot of big pictures. Cameron always treated me great, so we got along fine. Over the years until he passed away, we kept in contact a little bit; in

43. Memories of Nightmare in Wax (1969)

"Bud" Cardos (left), playing a police sergeant with the soundalike character name Bud *Carver*, and Scott Brady inspect a wax(?) head in *Nightmare in Wax*.

fact, when I directed *Act of Piracy* [1988] in South Africa, I ran across Cameron a couple of times over there. He was great to work with.

Scott Brady [who played a police detective] and I also "went way back," we did four or five pictures together, Westerns and other stuff. Scott was another great guy. We not only worked together, we were also social buddies, he and I and Jim Davis and so on. Scott and I used to go out and have a few drinks now and then, but he was never like his brother [notorious Hollywood "wild man" Lawrence Tierney]. Scott and I were friends for a lot of years. Here again, Scott was, like Cameron, a pretty big actor [in his prime]. I can't say enough good about him, he was just an all-around good guy.

It was interesting, shooting *Nightmare in Wax* in the Movieland Wax Museum out near Buena Park. Part of it was shot there, but the wax museum workroom with the big tank was actually a soundstage. That's the only thing that I can remember we shot on a soundstage, the interior of the workroom; the rest of it was the real wax museum and then we shot in people's houses. In those days, just like now, you can go to a company that [arranges for] location shooting and they'll open a book and show you 500 houses.

I do believe that that particular house with the pool that we used in *Nightmare in Wax* belonged to a friend of Rex Carlton. At that house, by the pool, was where I doubled Cameron Mitchell after Berry Kroeger threw the alcohol in his face and set him on fire. Back in those days, we didn't have all the protections that you got now. In those days, we [fire stunt guys] used to put on long underwear; and then we would wrap aluminum foil around; then we would

Cardos (left) and his longtime stuntman-actor pal Gary Kent at a 2008 film festival in Bicknell, Utah.

put on a wetsuit or a running suit or a jogging suit *over* all that. Then we'd put on the wardrobe, and smear some rubber cement on the wardrobe, and give it a couple of squirts of lighter fluid. As soon as a spark hits it, it *goes* [*laughs*]! When it started getting too hot, you had to have a safety man there to put it out for you.

In the case of *Nightmare in Wax*, I controlled the heat by how long it took me to get to the pool. 'Cause I knew, once I got to the pool, the fire would be out [*laughs*]! It was primitive in those days compared to now; today they've got all kinds of liquid gels you put on yourself to stop the heat from getting to you, they've got all kinds of fire suits and so on. We didn't *have* that back then. Back then, the fire suits we had were the ones like, if your airplane crashed, the fire department guys would come wearing them. But, my God, if you wore one of those [in a movie], you'd look like some kind of monster!

The fire stunt in *Nightmare in Wax* was not that elaborate; just my head was on fire. Well, actually, my head was not on fire, the fire was on the back of my shoulders, but the way they shot it [from the back], it *looks* like my head was on fire. [*How did you protect your hair and your ears?*] Just by tuckin' my head down [*laughs*]. I tucked my head down and let the flames go up the back. I think I got a little singed, the back of my hair, but nothing that burned *me*.

Back then, on those little shows, if you wanted to work, you'd *better* know how to do more than one job; otherwise, your chances were few and far in between. I was pretty cocky back in those days as far as my talent. When I went to get a job as a production manager, I used to tell 'em, "Look, here's what I can do, this and this," and I told 'em, "If I don't save you money each week, you don't have to pay me." I could promote ice cubes to Eskimos, you know what I mean [*laughs*]?

43. Memories of Nightmare in Wax (1969)

Martin Varno

How I got the job on *Nightmare in Wax* was, I went out to an office off the Sunset Strip and interviewed for a fellow, one of the producers of the thing. He was a very nice little man, and he killed himself a few years later. Rex Carlton. He seemed to be fairly sharp, and he was very nice to me. I did several pictures for [*Nightmare in Wax* director] Bud Townsend, another nice guy. He was in that particular strata that was making that particular type of picture, and he made a lot of them, 'cause he was good at it.

The only real sour note on the thing was Cameron Mitchell. I will go on record as saying, I think that man was *so* mentally ill, *so* disturbed at the time, that he should have been committed. He was a complete jerk. I'm sure you've heard that before. He was probably real pissed-off that he wasn't doing big pictures at Fox any more. I had one incident where *I* really got pissed off: We were on location in somebody's private home up in the hills above the Valley side of the canyon, real nice place, and it was night and so we had it all lit and so on. It was the scene where Cameron's supposed to be at a Hollywood party and as he's lighting a cigarette, Berry Kroeger throws a glass of cognac (which was actually tea) in his face and it ignites and he goes crashing out of the house through a glass door and jumps into the pool. Of course, a stuntman [Bud Cardos] doubled for Cameron when he was burning and crashing through the sugar glass door and diving into the pool.

For the shot where Cameron was going to pop out of the water directly into camera and we see his burned and cut face for the first time, I spent a half-hour in the dining room of that house making his face up. I specialized in special effects makeup, and I did a real nice job. Well, the son of a bitch, I got him all made-up and he was standing next to me right next to the swimming pool and *just* before he went in, I mean, literally seconds before, he said, "Oh, no, no, no, this [makeup] won't do...." And he reached over, grabbed my bottle of Technicolor blood and splashed it all over his face. He poured about a pint of this stuff all over himself— it was a quart bottle, and he almost emptied it. Obliterating all the burns and bloody gashes and everything I'd done. When he came up out of the water, he looked like a great big red seal! That was the most overt of several incidents I had with him on that picture. He had the idea that he was like "the master," that he knew about everything, that he'd been in such wonderful pictures. He was very much in love with his work, and an incredible ham.

Incidentally, in the backyard of the house next door, another very low-budget picture was being shot. The house where we were shooting *Nightmare in Wax* belonged to *some*body connected with our picture, and I assume that the house next door belonged to somebody who was connected with *that* picture. Between our shots, we'd be looking over the fence watching them shoot, and in the picture was a kid, maybe 17 years old, playing a psychopathic killer. Nobody knew who he was, he was an unknown, but everybody said, "Gee, that kid's pretty good!" because he could lay out a page and a half of dialogue in one take, and do it very nicely. Then, a few years later, somebody tapped him on the shoulder and asked, "How would you like to be 'John Boy' on *The Waltons*?" I'd see Richard Thomas every once in a while in our local market and I got to talking with him several times. He was a hell of a good actor, even [in 1966] when we saw him playing the insane teenager in whatever movie that was; I don't know that it ever got released.

For the burns on Cameron's face in *Nightmare in Wax*, I used mortician's wax. I also used mortician's wax on *The Las Vegas Hillbillys* [1966], a picture that starred a very nice guy by the name of Ferlin Husky. Ferlin had in his younger years gotten into a bar fight, because these Western singers *do* that a lot, it seems. It was a horrible bar fight where the other guy broke a bottle on the edge of the bar and went after Ferlin's face with it, and connected. Ferlin's nose ... [*pauses, groans*] ... his nose was all kinds of scar tissue and cuts and pits. So we had to fill in all those holes with mortician's wax. And once we did, I would say that he looked pretty good; you can't really tell that his nose was pretty well chopped up.

Anyway, back to *Nightmare in Wax* and that psychotic man Cameron Mitchell. There was a scene where Cameron, who was supposed to be this great makeup man turned wax sculptor, was sitting at a table making up what was supposed to be a wax head. Carlton said to me, "Hey, can we use your makeup case in the scene?" My makeup case was a wooden fishing kit that I had bought and fixed up into a makeup case. I said, "Look, this is how I'm making my living now. Be careful with it, don't let him throw Technicolor blood all over it or something." So they started shooting the scene and there on the table was my makeup case, as if it were *his*, and on another part of the table were my different bottles of stuff and my brushes and sponges and things. When they started shooting, he began being "dramatic," he began being The Actor, and within the scene he got angry about something—and he decided to extemporize a little bit and surprise us all, and he slapped all the bottles off the table and also pushed my whole makeup case off the table onto the floor. Smashed God knows how much. Because he was "act-ing," and of course he didn't think, "Hey, this is somebody else's property." The prick. The moment they cut the camera, I yelled at Carlton, "God damn it, you're gonna pay for this!" and he said, "Yes we will! Oh, yes, everything! Just make a list of everything"—but I forgot to ask him to pay for everything. It wasn't a great deal, it was about 250 bucks, but at the time, that was a lot of money to me. I remember saying to somebody, "I'm gonna *walk*. Right now. I'm either gonna walk or I'm gonna kill this cocksucker." And somebody said, "Don't kill him, he hasn't finished the picture yet!" [*Laughs*] But after that, I never said a word to Cameron, and I didn't make him up any more after that. Let him make his *own* fucking self up! I rebuilt the makeup case and I've still got it, but it's still loose, some sections of it, and one corner of it is still banged up.

A good look at the Martin Varno burn makeup on Cameron Mitchell is provided by this *Nightmare in Wax* shot. Victoria Carroll is the gal being menaced by Mitchell's mad wax sculptor.

And, oh, yeah, he pulled another thing

too. The scenes in the wax museum workroom were actually shot on a stage at what is now KCET, which used to be the old Allied Artists studios over in East Hollywood. A small studio. There's a sequence where, in his mind, all his victims are coming to get him. Well, he didn't like the way I had made them up, so when I wasn't looking, he got a-hold of some greasepaint, different colors, and on the actors' faces he put big stripes of yellow, and blue, and red, and green. They now looked like clowns or something. I was really angry and I told Carlton, "Fuck it. That's it. I'm goin'. You wanna sue me?, go 'head and sue me. I'm judgment-proof!" I *all* but walked out on the last couple of days of the picture, 'cause I was really very unhappy. But he was the only person there that I disliked. Really, I didn't like him from the beginning, because he was such a fucking ham.

Berry Kroeger [as Max Black, head of Paragon Studios] was a pretty well-known actor at one point, he was the bad guy in a lot of major-studio pictures. He was always very nice, he was never rude or nasty, or threw my makeup case around or anything like that. Victoria Carroll [a go-go dancer–victim] was probably the dumbest woman I have ever met in my life. She was *so* incredibly dumb! Oh my God! The poor little thing, she didn't *mean* to be dumb, she was just *born* that way [*laughs*]! I think that they assigned a special woman to stick with her in case she had to go to the toilet, to remind her how to do it.

Then there was the guy who I reeeally liked—this man was Old Hollywood, or he was *trying* to be Old Hollywood, he was trying to recapture the days of glory, and he was a sweetheart. That was Scott Brady. Near the museum in Buena Park, there was a nice steak restaurant with a bar—a quality place. One night as we were wrapping up, four or five of us decided to go out for a drink, and somebody suggested, "Let's go down to so-and-so's," the steak restaurant. We did, and we walked in, and there was Scott, and half the crew guys were sitting there with him. And Scott was a little tight. Well, *more* than a little tight. A *lot* tight [*laughs*]! He was buying drinks for ev-er-y-bod-y in the bar, *and* their dinners—steaks, filet mignons. "Hey, come on over here, you guys, sit down, have dinner!" "But we just *had* dinner, Scott—thank you anyway!" "No, you gotta have dinner! Come on, sit down!" We finally talked him out of that, then we went to the bar and we each had a drink and so on. And the bartender said, "Oh, no, no, keep your money, Mr. Brady says it's going on *his* bill." Years later I went out with a girl who was a nurse at a special respiration hospital in Echo Park, a place for patients with heavy emphysema. It was her job to operate a machine which essentially vacuums out your lungs—it's better than drowning in your own juices. And Scott Brady, who'd been like a 40-pack-a-day smoker in his time, was a patient there in his final days, and that's what he died of, emphysema. That's a bad way to go. He was an awfully nice man. He was stoned most of the time when I knew him, but then again, so were *many* actors that I knew. Lon Chaney, Jr., I did a couple of pictures with him, and, man, I have seen him so drunk, he couldn't stand up. We had to practically poke a gobo stand up his ass to keep him perpendicular!

Nightmare in Wax was partly shot on location at the Movieland Wax Museum in Buena Park, a very nice place. We'd get there at, like, three in the afternoon and do some shooting of establishing shots while there were still tourists milling around. (That, by the way, is *tremendously* illegal, shooting real tourists walking around looking at things, not even knowing that they were *being* shot.) I think the place normally closed around eight o'clock, and then we'd have the place to ourselves and shoot till about midnight or so, without the tourists underfoot. Actually, the crowds were very, very nice, and delighted to see a real movie being shot. The tall fellow who played the wax museum tour guide in the movie [Hollis Morrison], dressed in an old Keystone Cop uniform, decided to pull the old gag—*some*body had to pull it—of just standing there amidst the wax figures, perfectly still and perfectly silent. Tourists would walk up to him and say [*whispering*], "Boy, they really look real, don't they?," and then of course he'd jump and roar, and the people would practically pee all over themselves. In fact, one poor woman *did*. A tourist. It was very funny, but she was so embarrassed. I hope she didn't sue them!

So we did have some fun moments on that picture. It wasn't the worst that I ever did. They even gave me a screen credit ... but they spelled my name wrong [*laughs*]!

44

Jan Merlin on The Twilight People *(1973)*

"Movies based on The Island of Doctor Moreau *have been popular, and movies based on 'The Most Dangerous Game' have been popular—so shouldn't an exploitation movie based on* both *be even* more *popular?" In 1971, a train of thought probably very much like this one led to the production of* The Twilight People, *a horror-action adventure revolving around a mad scientist (Charles Macaulay) whose mix-and-match surgical experiments result in Panther and Wolf Women, a Bat Man and other "humanimal" abominations. That right there provides about as many monsters as any B-movie leading man (in this case, John Ashley, a prisoner of the doctor) ought to be expected to handle, but* Twilight People *stacks the deck against Ashley even higher: The "security officer" of the mad doctor's jungle island compound, a Germanic sadist named Steinman (Jan Merlin), wants and encourages Ashley to attempt an escape—so that he (Steinman) and his henchmen can then enjoy the thrill of the hunt.*

A novelist and Emmy-winning TV writer in more recent years, Merlin devotes part of his newest book Crackpots *to a fictional story based on his* Twilight People *experiences—but here in this interview, he describes the actual adventure, and some of the "dangerous games" that filmmakers in the Philippines must play.*

The St. Valentine's Day Massacre [1967] was the first of six or seven films where I worked for Roger Corman—I played one of the thugs in it. I remember they used real flowers in a funeral scene and I thought how wasteful it was [*laughs*], they could have used phony flowers. For days, these poor things wilted more and more but we kept on shooting anyway! I think Roger, being our director, felt it needed the reality and smell of the flowers for those people playing the scene. I admire Roger, I find him an interesting, happy, dedicated man who built himself an empire out of what many people dismissed as crappy pictures. But, by *God*, even if they *weren't* getting him Oscars, they made him money!

Roger's office contacted me again in 1971—the end of August—and asked if I'd come in and see them about *The Twilight People*. At the time, I wasn't working in any film, I was concentrating on writing a book, *Brocade* [a.k.a. *Ainoko*], which was about a mixed-blood boy in postwar Japan. Roger's casting head saw me and I was told the film was to be done in the Philippines, and I jumped at the chance because I dearly *love* going on foreign locations. I had one stipulation: I was to be provided with a typewriter overseas, because I was nearing the closing chapters of my book, and I wanted to be able to finish it while there. They didn't find that an odd request at all, and guaranteed I'd have a typewriter. As it turned out, when I got to the Philippines, it seems the little company there had *one* typewriter [*laughs*], and they were hesitant about letting me have it because I was going to keep it in my hotel room. We had a few terse words, but ended up friendly, and I wound up with their typewriter and *they* wound up getting themselves another one.

That was sort of the only bump in the road I had at the beginning. Going to the Philippines was really odd and peculiar and wonderful, and also nostalgic-in-a-*bad*-way for me, because during World War II, I was with the forces that went in and retook those islands from the Japanese. As it turned out, I was to run into one of the Filipinos that I knew from the time when we invaded the islands, and he couldn't *wait* to rush me off to his house so that I could have dinner with his family. I was so impressed by the Filipino people, who are very devout and behave as if in a long-past era. Even though the children and young adults dressed in garish American styles, their families maintained old-fashioned manners. At dinner, for instance, the fellow I knew from the war sat at the head of a long table and his children came in politely and every one of them, no matter what age, approached their father first to kiss his cheek before taking a seat at the table. It was a grand meal ... and I learned to like meat-filled lumpia, which are similar to egg rolls. I was hugely impressed by this man's family and the people of his nation in general. They're a curious people, the Filipinos. I found much to like about them and much to feel sad about them. There's an enormous amount of poverty in their country. And an enormous amount of enthusiasm and hope. It was fascinating to be there in peacetime.

The novel *The Island of Doctor Moreau* and the short story "The Most Dangerous Game" were stories I'd read before, and liked. I felt the picture would be a lark. My wife at the time, Patricia Merlin, had to remain at home with my son, who was seven years old. My mother, who normally would have looked after him, had died in August, so I had to leave my wife behind. On the flight, [co-stars] Pat Woodell, Charles Macaulay, Pam Grier and I got along rather well and we looked forward to having a good shoot. We arrived there rather worn—it's hard to sleep well on a plane, no matter how long the flight. After arrival at Manila Airport, we were put up at the Manila Hilton, a modern hotel which overlooks Lunetta Park, a national memorial park. There are huge fountains in the park with geysers of water that "dance" [rise and fall] to the sound of music being piped out over loudspeakers. Very entertaining! Little stands all around the fountains sell foodstuffs and soft drinks, and there's an outdoor theater area where folks can perform—it looks almost like *Amateur Hour*! Entertainers sing and dance before an appreciative seated audience. There's also an extensive Oriental garden, with a wide pond full of Koi to feed breadcrumbs.

By the 1970s, playing psychos like Steinman was second nature to Jan Merlin, a veteran of scores of villainous TV and film roles.

Lovely, lively place. I used to walk in that part when I had the chance. Youngsters and old folk often recognized me from my oater films and the kids would challenge me to draw. I also remember that the billboards atop most of the buildings surrounding the park's perimeters advertised Japanese company products. One might wonder who won the Pacific after all!

It was October and the climate was tropical, very hot, very sunny. The magnificent azure East China sky is something you have to see to believe—it's not the kind of "civilized" sky we look at here. I used to look from my hotel window at the sea of black heads above vivid clothing all through the park, and it suddenly struck me, "I don't see a single blond head *any*where." And there I was with *platinum* hair—I'd had my hair cut into a crewcut, a real Nazi type, and had it bleached very blond. John Ashley wanted me to be blond since he was brunette. He was the hero and I was gonna be the heavy. It was like changing hats for a Western.

I think we went the first day to the studio, which was a very small, barn-like structure in downtown Manila. They were preparing a set, the interior of the doctor's house. It was to be an entry hall, and they were gluing newspapers to the wooden floor throughout. At one end, where they had already glued the newspapers down and it had dried, men painted what looked like a marble floor on the papers. They did the same thing with the walls: If they didn't have the wood to create a fancy-looking wall, they'd put up newspapers and they'd *paint* a fancy wall on it. It was remarkable, the way they did so well with so little. And it held up, it lasted while we shot the scenes—it was really extraordinary to me. The studio may at one time have been a large warehouse or something of the sort. It had a great door that would slide open and let the heat and the sun in. And there'd always be a little ice cream vendor outside, waiting to make some pesos from us. We received 20 Filipino pesos to the dollar in those days.

Going out on location was a little bit hairy, unsettling for the queasy. You got into cars and trucks, this whole company, and took off in a long caravan, because nobody travels out into the hinterlands *unless* they are in a caravan, with everybody fully armed. They do this because it was frequent that travelers on the roads would be stopped by the tulisans—the bandits. They'd stop your car and order you out and take everything you had. If you were lucky, maybe you got to keep your car, and you could drive back to Manila. But certainly you returned without any of your money and jewelry and stuff. Even caravans have been halted by these ever-present gangs of tulisans. We practiced the same method of travel 17 years later when I went back to the Philippines to do another Corman feature, *Silk 2* [1989]. The situation for that one was still much the same, we still traveled to locations with armed guards. The women don't wear jewelry in public. They wear it at home but they won't wear jewelry outside because of the amount of crime.

We went to a place called Teresa, which is north of Manila. We stayed in a small, neatly kept hotel, from which we'd drive to the outdoor locations, like the cave where the scenes of the animal people in their cages were shot. It was an enormous cave which opened into a mountain and led into smaller and smaller caves. You could see where Japanese troops had established living quarters, but it was emptied out by the time we were in it. Our film crew had built cages in there so that we could stroll through and look at the animal creatures. The cave was one of many caves in that mountain—not a very big mountain, encircled by a high wire fence and owned by a cement company slowly cutting it down to make cement and gravel out of it. Except for those working within that fence-enclosed compound, we had the place pretty much to ourselves. Every day, at noontime, a siren sounded and we'd stop filming—*every*one would stop whatever they were doing. Women who'd come to wash clothing in a nearby stream would stop immediately and pick up their things, and all headed away to get to safety. Our film company piled into the cave in order to be out of danger. After a brief period, two police whistles blew shrilly, and then a vast explosion occurred at the mountain's top. All this debris would rain down, gravel and earth and foliage. It was exciting [*laughs*]! Once they had done that, trucks would rumble in, and they'd go winding up the mountain to collect what was needed to take to wherever cement was made. I think all we American actors were fearful of cave-ins when the explosions took place, but it didn't appear to worry the Filipino film crew. They had used this location on other films.

There was just one explosion a day. The otherwise peaceful setting had the stream in it, and also a very large old bomb crater. During the war, when the Japanese used to hide out in those caves, they'd been bombed by Allied aircraft. It was spooky to think of the violent deaths which had taken place in that beautiful area, but after a while I got accustomed to it. The location had an exquisite loveliness to it, a look of Eden, very lush, very green. The water of the little stream was clear as could be. And there were golden dragonflies floating by constantly in the air. The only things we were cautioned about were green snakes that might be lying on overhead tree branches. They were deadly vipers. We got so we didn't pay attention to those. The crew was good about checking the area before we worked, to make certain there was nothing lurking in the trees. Yet every once in a while they'd miss one, and we'd stop until they killed it with their broad machetes.

The opening scene on the boat was shot off Bataan Peninsula, of dreadful historic fame. There we were out on the boat, floating around all day, and of course at midday we broke for lunch. And to my great surprise, our Filipino boat crew dove overboard to harvest oysters from the bottom! Then they fried 'em up for us on the deck of this little scow. While they cooked, I talked about it with the Filipino sailors, who replied that they often brought up relics from the bottom ... leather and belt buckles and cloth remains of the fellows who tried to swim from Corregidor to Bataan when the Japanese were attacking Corregidor. Some made it ... many *didn't* make it. And those who *did* make it wound up captured. I couldn't eat the oysters. [*Those who didn't make it were still on the bottom?*] Oh, yeah, but these sailors who would dive for relics respected the dead and didn't touch any bones. I was disturbed by it, because my destroyer sailed closely past that place during the war, in late fall of 1944. But I didn't brood over it; now I just had a film to do.

The jungle scenes were on the perimeters of the nearby mountains. Those are true jungles, but they seemed to have only insect, snake and bird life present. If there was anything else, I didn't see it, although I was told there *was* plenty of wildlife there. Almost everywhere in the Philippines are beds of low, spreading plants—tiny, delicate leaves and tiny pink and purple flowers. They called them "shy flowers." I asked *why* they were called shy, and they said, "You'll find out." And I did find out later. We had no john up in those mountains, and when you went off to a side to pee, why, if you peed on that little plot of flowers, the leaves would fold up, like little shy plants [*laughs*]! I was charmed by them. I pressed one of the flowers in the script and brought it home with me.

When I first read the script, Steinman was evidently much the old-time German heavy that one always saw in pictures. I made him pretty much what you'd expect, *except* ... John Ashley and I were quite evenly matched and I figured, "Let's make it even hairier." I decided that, in the scenes, I'd "lean" on him a little further by acting as if I was *more* than a little bit interested in him [attracted to him]. I meant it to look mostly like a desire to hunt him down, but there was a scene in which Pat Woodell accused me of being gay, which colored the interest. That got the attention of reviewers, who I think were either intrigued or offended, I don't know which [*laughs*]. But *I* thought it was amusing. I don't think John Ashley thought the same, but he didn't object to my characterization. We got along very well. I used to kid him

The "humanimal" hordes of *Twilight People* included Pam Grier as the Panther Woman and Tony Gosalvez as the Bat Man.

about having homemade food brought to him in jars by a well-known Filipina "Bomba" star. She and he were a couple while there and she loved to visit the set, always with food she'd prepared for him. They'd go off to sit under a tree and have lunch while the rest of us looked on with envy. [*What the heck is a "Bomba" star?*] It refers to risqué movies produced weekly in Manila. She drove a crimson T-Bird and was always waved at by passersby with warmest affection.

I later did a prison picture, *The Slams* [1973], where I pulled the same routine [acting gay], surprising our leading man, Jim Brown. Jim didn't know what I was gonna do. I was supposed to have a scene talking to him in the prison exercise yard, and he didn't rehearse with me. I thought, "Well, okay, then you're in for a surprise." They set up the camera and, when we shot the scene, to his great disturbance and amazement, he discovered that I was playing a *very*, very campy character, and it was quite obvious the swishy prisoner and Jim Brown's character were lovers in the film [*laughs*]. Which wasn't in the script at all! The extras were appalled. They were accustomed to seeing me perform as a macho heavy in other films. The scene wasn't re-shot, so I got away with it. Every once in a while, I'd alter what I did with a role, because it's hard to keep playing heavies all the time and make them differ from one another. After a while, you run out of ways to *die*! I've always tried to find *some*thing, *some* way I could change the way my character did things. Ninety percent of the time, the directors always wanted the kind of grinning, evil character that they *got*, but sometimes I could vary it by dumping quirky bits in, just for the hell of it. Sometimes it worked, sometimes it didn't, but nobody ever complained [*laughs*].

The director, Eddie Romero, thought up the idea to have me drinking milk throughout the picture. Because of the way I'd been playing Steinman, he suddenly decided, instead of Steinman sitting there having a shot of booze, why, let him drink some milk. To add to the character. I agreed at once. Eddie Romero, by the way, is a clever and pleasant little guy. He knew what he wanted, knew how he wanted it done, he had total rapport with all of his crew. He was generous with all the actors, he'd say, "*This* is how I'd like the scene" and, bingo, you were left to do it. I can't remember any time that he'd come up and say, "No, would you try it another way?"

[*What did you and the other Americans do with your free time?*] There were discos that we could attend. They were too noisy for *me*, and anyway, I wanted to stay in my room and finish my book. There was a jai alai stadium that people enjoyed going to. And there was one lovely restaurant in Makati, one of the better districts of Manila, a restaurant called Sulo, where they had the Fiesta Filipino Dance Company, who would perform after you'd had your dinner. They'd appear on the dance floor and execute folk dances from different regions of the Philippines. It was a marvelous show I never would have seen otherwise. And the food they served there was equally as good.

The American producers were *not* there at any time. Since John Ashley was also one of the producers, I guess he represented their interests. John had done quite a number of films there, and they all knew him and loved him. He was very efficient: He knew what he wanted, and he got them to work for him very well. Pat Woodell, the leading lady, was married at the time to the actor Gary Clarke. She was rather quiet and made friends easily. I think she had a good time on the shoot. There was a very noted Filipino actor who worked with us, playing another one of the mad doctor's captives—Eddie Garcia. Being quite a big star in the Philippines, he was kind of ambivalent about what he was doing, I think, because it wasn't generally the kind of role he got [*laughs*]. He has a scene with Ashley on the balconies of the doctor's estate, in which he warns Ashley about the place, his hair covered with a plastic sheath to make him look bald. Garcia and Woodell became good friends while he worked with us.

Charles Macaulay [playing the Moreau-like Dr. Gordon] was somewhat aloof and pretty much kept to himself. I don't know *what* he did with himself in Manila; the only time I saw him other than on the set was when a lad related to one of the wardrobe people died of some sudden illness, and we all attended the wake. The coffin had a window so that you could see the child's face, and you left a little donation for the family. It was ... disturbing to me. Just the Sunday before, when the wardrobe crew was getting me fitted for the uniform I wore throughout the show and sewing it up for me, this ten-year-old boy had been sitting in the room reading the funny papers. [*Pause*] You never know what's gonna happen in the tropics...

Pam Grier, who played the Panther Woman, was a delight. I thought she was wonderful, an uncomplaining actress, despite the disfiguring makeups. And she did a damn good job. When she was not working, and was seen at the hotel or strolling through Manila, this stately black woman *towered* over everybody, because almost all Filipinos are quite short. They'd turn to *stare* at her, she was like a rare black pearl amongst them, and they were agog to see her! She never mentions *Twilight People* in any of her bios, and you might say to yourself, "Well, I understand *that*" [*laughs*]!

But the actor who really did the best as one of those animal creatures was an American living in Manila, Ken Metcalfe, who played the Antelope Man. I rarely got to speak to him because he was not involved in most of the scenes I did. I suspected he must have had training as an actor because he really worked out that character. He developed a peculiar little stomping kind of walk that almost had you imagining, "Jeez, he *is* growing hoofs!" I thought he did an excellent job. I've since learned he's done many films over there.

The makeups on the animal people were really extraordinary, for what they worked with, very unlike the mask disguises I wore in *The List of Adrian Messenger* [1963]. They assembled them with bits of hair and globs of *this* and globs of *that*, forming each and every day directly on the actors' faces. Their bodies were left pretty much as they were, but from the head up, they actually got the actors to look as though they *were* animal people. I had a lot of sympathy for the guys playing the animal men, because I knew how awful it was to take that sort of makeup off. The Bat Man [Tony Gosalvez] who kept trying to fly through the entire picture, and finally *did*—I was wondering how they were going to accomplish that. For that effect, a crane was used. Tony was tied to one end of a cable from the crane. He was on a branch of a tree and when he leaped off, the cable swung him above the line of everyone below him in the scene, while he shrieked with joy.

[*At the end of the picture, when we see Steinman's dead body, what is that on your forehead? A bee?*] No, a spider. They put a spider on my head but, unfortunately, without a closeup it's not clear, you can't tell that they had this spider up there, because the damn thing decided to just stay still, instead of moving around as it *had* been doing in rehearsal! So there we were, with me staring and the spider deciding, "Well, if *you're* gonna pose, *I'm* gonna pose!" [*Laughs*]

We shot all through October and well into November. Once we got into November, I started getting very itchy—I was anxious to complete that turkey so I could get home for the Thanksgiving Day bird I'd share with my wife and son. I started to grumble about it, and began to get questioned by the Filipinos: "What's the matter? Don't you like us? Why do you want to *go*?" Sometimes they have a kind of a childlike reaction to things you say or do, and so you've got to be careful not to be critical. Because if you criticize them or anger them, they can get quite ... violent. But otherwise, they are the most charming, helpful, eager and *dangerous* children you ever saw [*laughs*]!

It took 14 hours to get to the Philippines by plane, and the same amount to return to the States. On *The Twilight People*, the flight to the Philippines and back was uneventful but for seeing pods of whales making their way through the ocean below. The second time I flew home from the Philippines, after doing *Silk 2*, I was trying to doze but kept staring out over the head of the woman asleep in the seat ahead of mine. My new wife, Barbara, was sound asleep next to me. I became aware of what looked like a small hand creeping along the top of the woman's seat ... it paused, and I realized it was a large, hairy spider. Before I could knock it off, it fell over upon her, and I expected a scream or wild movement of some sort. The plane remained silent for quite a while, and then a Filipino stewardess walked down the aisle, stopped suddenly to look at the deck and promptly did a very quiet dance in place. I realized she had killed the monster! Which is what my wife almost did to *me* when I told her about it after she awakened. We didn't tell anyone else on the plane about it, but were uneasy in our seats all the way back to Los Angeles. I mentioned it to the stewardess, as I left the plane, and she merely shrugged and smiled me out.

I first saw *The Twilight People* perhaps four months later, back here in the States. John arranged for the American cast to see a sneak run of the picture in a small movie theater. I don't remember if Pam Grier was with us; Ashley, Macaulay, Woodell and I watched the picture, and afterwards, when we were out on the street, John unfortunately asked me what I

A 2005 shot of Merlin (left) and actor Frankie Thomas, in Thomas' Sherman Oaks living room. The two were friends for 56 years, from the start of their *Tom Corbett, Space Cadet* TV co-starring days until Thomas' 2006 death.

thought of it. I'm terrible that way; you ask me a question, I'm gonna give you what I think! I said I thought it was a bomb, a terrible picture. John didn't reply to me about my remark then, but I kind of had an inkling about how he felt when I later saw a press sheet for the movie. On it were stills from the movie, and representations of its posters, plus little biographies of John and Pat Woodell. I am in *none* of the pictures. The only mention of me is in billing on the posters, because by contract that *had* to be there. It didn't bother me. I never again had anything to do with John, I never saw him again. He was a producer of one of the TV series shows I worked in briefly, *The A-Team* [the 1985 episode "Mind Games"]; I didn't know that at the time. He may not even have known I was cast in it, because all that casting was done by the casting office.

Incidentally, when *The Island of Dr. Moreau* [1996] with Marlon Brando came out, I saw some stills [of the man-animal makeups] and I sort of broke up because I thought, "My God, their makeups aren't any better than what we had on *Twilight People*!" I decided I'd better not go see it, because I'd destroy the audience by sitting there laughing like crazy.

[*When everything was said and done and* Twilight People, *turkey though it may be, was out, were you glad you had done the picture?*] Sure. I even got a book titled *Crackpots* out of it. Some time ago, I wrote a couple of short novellas which I wasn't going to publish, and then thought, "Well, what if I put them together into a single book?," because they both dealt with Hollywood types. One story, "The Bakla's Cross," is about a film company in the Philippines—I based it upon my stay in Manila for *The Twilight People*. The other was about the cuckoos who live in Laurel Canyon, up on Wonderland Avenue. I put the two stories together into *Crackpots* and it's coming out next month [February 2004]. In "The Bakla's Cross," the descriptions of the Filipino people are *very* accurate, and I hope I've depicted 'em as amusing as they can be. And as likable as they can be. And as trigger-happy as they can be [*laughs*]!

45

Robert Pine on Empire of the Ants *(1977)*

In the 1970s, the "nature amok" B-movie genre again became an exploitation staple and producer-director-SFX maven Bert I. Gordon, veteran of such '50s favorites as Beginning of the End *(giant grasshoppers),* The Cyclops *(lots of plus-sized critters) and* Earth vs the Spider *(nufsed), went right back to the old stand. Gordon had better names in the casts of his* The Food of the Gods *(1976) and* Empire of the Ants—*and H.G. Wells "source novels" in the writing credits!—but otherwise they were the same sort of popcorn terror, more fun than frightening, and with "effects" that were anything but "special."*

Empire, Florida-set and -shot, was the tale of hapless humans (Joan Collins, Robert Lansing, Albert Salmi, more) slogging through middle-of-nowhere swamp mud, on the run from ants that have mutated into giants after munching on radioactive waste. Supporting player Robert Pine, best known by Baby Boomers as Sgt. Getraer on TV's long-running ChiPs, *happily describes the unhappy experience:*

My agent told me, "I've got a film for you. It's called *Empire of the Ants*." I thought about it for a moment or two and I said, "You know ... I think I'll pass." He said, "Bob, do the film. No one will *ever* see it." Well, it's been, what?, 25 years now, and that sucker is *still* followin' me around [*laughs*]!

Bert I. Gordon, who was the director, was this funny little man. He'd just finished doing a picture called *The Food of the Gods*, which was a similar thing—human beings being overcome by giant rats. Our movie was human beings being overcome by giant ants. I remember this one scene in which we were being confronted by the ants: Bert says, "When I yell 'Ants!' you all react." He gets all ready and then he says, "Okay, roll 'em ... action..." and then he yells, "*Rats!*" [*Pause*] "No, no, no, no, no! *Ants!*" [*Laughs*] He couldn't even keep his pictures straight, 'cause it was the same b.s. he had just *done!*

Of course, we never *saw* our foes [the ants]. To show you the importance of the human beings in this picture, there was an 11-week shooting schedule for this picture ... five weeks for the human beings, and *six* weeks for the ants [*laughs*]. I couldn't believe this: They actually went down to South America and photographed these really dangerous ants. You had to count them, count each ant [that was used] and make sure they got 'em all *back*, 'cause these ants were actually poisonous. Why [the moviemakers] didn't just go in my backyard, I don't know. I've got ants, and if you blew *them* up, *they'd* look terrible too.

We all said to ourselves, "I hope the six-week schedule of the ants goes well, or we're gonna reeeally look stupid." And unfortunately, I *don't* think it went that well, because the ants that they [photographically] blew up ... guess what? ... they looked like ants that had been

45. Robert Pine on Empire of the Ants (1977)

Robert Pine says that cold Florida weather and primitive working conditions made him happy that his *Empire of the Ants* character was an early casualty: It allowed him to go home ahead of other cast members!

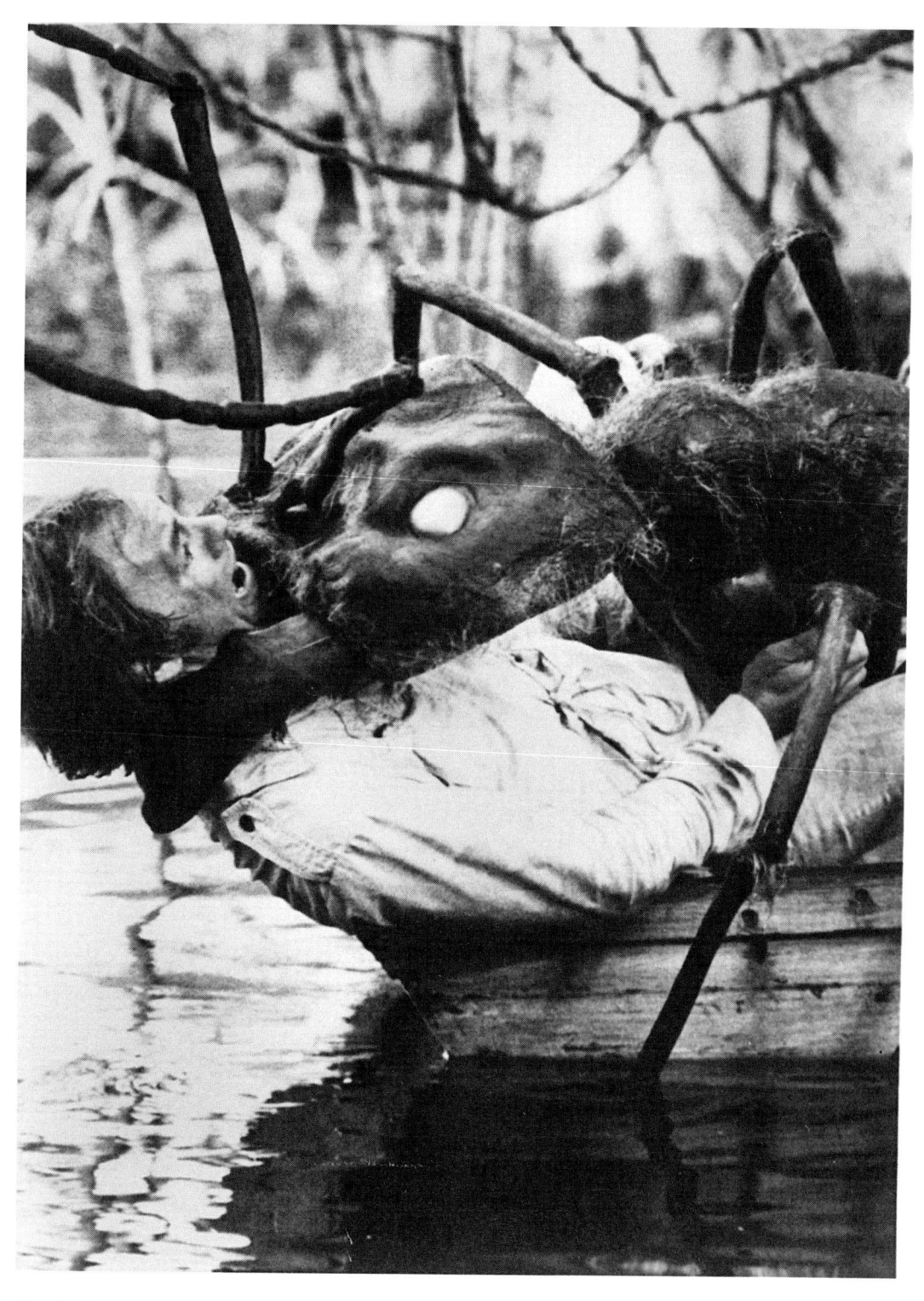

Pine's death-by-ant was no unusual acting job for his family: His mother-in-law was horror film heroine Anne Gwynne; Pine's wife is Gwynne Gilford of *Beware! The Blob* and *Fade to Black*; and *their* son Chris Pine played James T. Kirk in 2009's *Star Trek*.

blown up! Then for the closeups, they had these giant rubber ants that were cut off at the waist. A prop guy would hold this big rubber ant around himself like this [*Pine puts his hands on his hips and starts swiveling around like a hula dancer*] and then wiggle 'em at you. It was *so* ridiculous!

We shot the film in Florida, in the fall. I worked right through Thanksgiving and then was able to get out of there, 'cause my character got killed. But *some* "lucky" people were there almost up to Christmas. It was cold down there—*very* cold. If I'm remembering right, it might have even *snowed* at one point! And I'm thinking, "This is *Florida*??" We were *cold*!

At one point, we were way off in the boonies and we all had to fall out of a rowboat into the water. And there were crocodiles down there! Bert said, "Don't worry. There'll be a cage [underwater] and they won't be able to get ya." Well, I don't know what happened to the cage but it never arrived, and so we did the scene without it. And the poor girls! *Guys*, you gotta go to the bathroom, you go behind a swamp bush and let 'er rip. But the poor women...! You had to travel for I think an hour and 15 minutes to get to a commode.

I gotta tell you, the people on this shoot were great. Joan Collins was a peach. We played Scrabble all the time, and if anybody out there gets a chance to play Scrabble with Joan for money, don't *do* it. You heard it here first. I'm not bad, but *this* woman is a killer. And she's a good broad. I had a great time with her, *every*body did. This was before [her hit TV series] *Dynasty*, of course. I hear she doesn't even include *Empire of the Ants* on her résumé any more. It was sort of the pits of her career, she was on her way down, and then *Dynasty* came along and things went right back *up*. Jacqueline Scott is a dear, a very sweet woman; all I can say is nice things about her. And Pamela Shoop is a family friend of ours and a lovely lady also. *All* the actors on it were great, it was really a game bunch. It was good people and we all had a lot of laughs 'cause that was all that was *left*! But remember, I was only there for two and a half or three weeks of the five-week shoot for the humans, and after I left, they took off from the coast of Florida and went to the interior. I think the interior of Florida is a lot more sinister than where *I* was, so it could have rapidly gone downhill. I may be telling you about the "honeymoon" of this shoot!

Empire of the Ants was, if I may say so, *not* a "career move" [*laughs*]. It was a lot of fun, but a *terrible* movie. It was one of those pictures that, while you're shooting it, you're wondering, "Why the hell am I doing this? *Is* there enough money to make this worthwhile?" But afterwards, I've had more fun telling stories about it, and that's made it worthwhile. It's good cocktail conversation.

46

Ken Kolb on Sinbad Goes to Mars

Ray Harryhausen says that, still today, any time he mentions the title of his proposed fourth Sinbad film, Sinbad Goes to Mars, *it brings polite smiles to the faces of his listeners. This unmade movie's campy title, and the ridiculous images it can conjure up, have certainly made many fantasy film fans smile (or laugh out loud!) in the decades since it was first announced in the late 1970s. It may, in fact, have become a bit of an industry in-joke: In "Pros and Cons," a 1983 episode of the action-adventure series* The A-Team, *there is a comic interlude in which Hannibal (George Peppard), leader of the commando unit and (in his "civilian life" identity) a star of low-grade monster movies, confers with Hollywood's top schlock producer, passionately pushing for a role in his upcoming production* Sinbad Goes to Mars!

Does any of this upset the man who wrote the script of this non-existent but nevertheless notorious movie mix of Arabian Nights and outer space flights? "No," laughs Ken Kolb, "because the premise was repugnant, even to me!"

Sinbad Goes to Mars (synopsis based on Kolb's Revised Treatment of April 7, 1978):

Sinbad Goes to Mars begins in the bedchamber of the sultan as the beautiful Sheherezade, who has already told him 1001 wondrous tales, prepares to tell the one she has saved for last because she felt it might strain his powers of belief. In the story that she relates (and we see), a multi-colored, laser-like beam of light emanates from the golden cone atop Gizeh's Great Pyramid and up into the night sky. The caliph orders the valiant Capt. Sinbad to investigate.

From the deck of his ship, Sinbad and his men watch as two spaceships engage in battle, the smaller sustaining a hit and plunging into the Mediterranean. After the other spaceship has soared off, an escape capsule bobs to the water's surface, its one occupant Princess Tanila, daughter of the king of Mars. For years that planet has been embroiled in civil war, its benevolent king battling the evil sorcerer Zangor and his mutant race of Skalers. The reptile-like Zangor, master of scientific and occult powers, has come to Earth (in the other spaceship) to steal the Ion Crystal, a power source installed in the Great Pyramid centuries before by its Martian architects. (The Pyramid is a Martian "listening station," keeping track of the state of Earth civilization.) With the Ion Crystal, Zangor can construct a doomsday weapon and rule the solar system.

In Tanila's escape capsule, she and Sinbad descend to the ocean floor and board her rapidly flooding spaceship. They locate a map of the Pyramid and leave the spaceship just before it explodes. The resultant upheaval of water destroys Sinbad's ship and crew.

Sinbad and Tanila enter the Pyramid through the cone at its peak and, with the help of the Genie of the Pyramid, find the Ion Crystal chamber. Zangor and his second-in-command Radek, who entered through a subterranean tunnel, strike: Zangor ensnares our hero and heroine in coils of magical wire and takes them and the Ion Crystal to his spaceship, where their friend Filcher, a comic-relief merchant–con man, is already imprisoned. Just outside the atmosphere of Mars, the spaceship encounters magnetic mines. In the commotion, Sinbad, Tanila and Filcher use "emergency evacuation" plastic bubbles to escape from the ship to the surface of Mars.

Zangor learns that one of his generals, Rudoro, has surrendered and ended the war in his (Zangor's) absence. Infuriated, Zangor destroys a squadron of interceptors and heads the spaceship toward his emergency base in the Marsh of Eternal Fog.

On foot and tracked by Skalers, Sinbad, Tanila and Filcher make their way to a deserted, war-ravaged city where, in an ancient temple, a section of floor gives way, revealing murky water and the tentacles of a monstrous anemone creature. Through Sinbad's cleverness, their Skalers pursuers soon find themselves in the grip of the beast. Sinbad, Tanila and Filcher board a rescue craft sent by the king; Sinbad takes the gunnery position and destroys an enemy air cruiser.

In his underground fortress, Zangor uses the Ion Crystal to complete a heat ray device. Despite the Genie's admonition that misuse of the Crystal will unleash occult powers beyond control, Zangor destroys the yacht of Gen. Rudoro—and the entire lake in which it was sailing. He next uses the ray to destroy Mars' capital city and then one of its three moons, which turns into blazing meteors which spread fire over the entire planet. True to the Genie's warning, the heat ray can no longer be deactivated. As the Ion Crystal approaches critical mass, Sinbad and Zangor battle throughout the laboratory. Zangor kills onlooker Filcher with a knife before a blow from Sinbad sends him reeling into the white-hot framework of the Ion Crystal chamber; Zangor vanishes in a flash of fire. As Sinbad and Tanila escape in a spaceship, the Ion Crystal explodes like a hydrogen bomb and lethal clouds spread over the entire planet.

Ending her story, Sheherezade tells the sultan that the Martian holocaust destroyed all life there, and that when men look upon its surface in perhaps 1000 years, they will still find it desolate, with but two moons remaining in its sky.

* * *

Kolb's initial association with Ray Harryhausen and his producer-partner Charles H. Schneer was in the 1950s, when the 30-ish writer was still new to Hollywood: A Phi Beta Kappa out of Berkeley with a master's degree in English literature, he crafted the screenplay of their first mythological movie, Columbia's *The 7th Voyage of Sinbad*. It was "a lunch pail job that I didn't want," but the resultant Technicolor production became one of the top grossers of 1958–1959, prompting Schneer to offer Kolb additional writing gigs. He toiled on a screenplay based on one of Antarctic explorer Richard E. Byrd's expeditions (the film was not made) and wrote a first draft of 1961's *Mysterious Island*. "I did that right after *7th Voyage*, and I was still young in Hollywood and was not used to raping nuns. But I couldn't bring myself to screw up Jules Verne's novel *Mysterious Island* enough to suit Charles [*laughs*]—I had too much respect for Verne, because *Mysterious Island* was one of my favorite books of boyhood. I wrote an entire first draft trying to give Ray plenty of opportunities, but Charles and I finally came to disagree when I realized what Charles wanted to *do* with it; he wanted a monster behind every corner. I wasn't used to destroying the classics yet, so I did not want a credit on that."

For the next two decades, the paths of Kolb and Schneer-Harryhausen did not cross, the former becoming one of TV's busier scribes (*Have Gun Will Travel, Dr. Kildare, Dragnet, Hawaii Five-O*, scores more) and the latter continuing to produce their effects-laden fantasy films for Columbia and Warners. "During that time, Ray made several other [mythological monster] pictures with Charlie and none of them were as good or as popular as *7th Voyage*," says Kolb. "Then in 1977, my agents came to me and said, 'Hey, Charlie Schneer is about to make another Sinbad picture, and he'd like to talk to you.' As I say, he'd made more money with my Sinbad picture than with anybody else's, so I was willing to try it again. So, no, *Sinbad Goes to Mars* was *not* my idea. Writing *7th Voyage* wasn't such a delightful experience for me that I would look up Charlie and say, 'Hey, now let's do *this*!'"

It was in a long-distance telephone conversation with Schneer that Kolb, a resident of Northern California, learned that the new movie Schneer wanted written was to be titled *Sinbad Goes to Mars*. "I thought to myself, 'Hey ... *bizarre*. You're mixing genres here, Charlie.' But Charles doesn't think in those terms at *all*, he thinks in terms of marketability, and Sinbad and space were both highly marketable products. So combining Sinbad and Mars was their idea, absolutely. I could *never* take credit for an idea like that, *I* would not have sent Sinbad to Mars! Incidentally, when Charles said to me, 'How 'bout *Sinbad on Mars*?' I wise-assed-ly said, 'How 'bout *Sinbad on Venus*?'" [*Laughs*]

"Charles asked, 'You wanna come down and talk about it?,' so I flew down and talked about it with him, at his office at Columbia. The same building down on Gower where he'd had his office, and *I* had an office in which I did my writing, when we did *7th Voyage*. On *7th Voyage*, I had had input from Ray Harryhausen in the form of pictures: He showed me 8 × 10 glossy blow-ups of his black-and-white charcoal drawings of the skeleton, the Cyclops, the dragon and the two-headed bird. *This* time around, I had two words: 'Sinbad. Mars. *Go!*'" Writing a story partly set in space and on another planet was something new for Kolb. "Yeah, *I'll* say!" he laughs. "In 1957, *Sinbad* was something new for me. I never considered myself a fantasy writer. My novels are all strictly realism. Given my own choice, I write short stories for men's magazines, and short, crisp, insightful novels; it doesn't really thrill me to be writing in the Arabian Nights genre, *or* in the future. The present seems difficult enough for *me*, I don't need to invent stuff.

"But apparently I have a facility. Over my 25 years of television, it seemed to me not to matter whether I was writing *Honey West* or *Court of Last Resort* or *Wild Wild West*. I understood what each series *was*, I understood that it was going to be made very

SINBAD GOES TO MARS
PRINCESS TANIA'S SPACESHIP
BY CHRIS FOSS FOR ANDOR FILMS

For *Sinbad Goes to Mars*, illustrator Chris Foss was hired to draw Martian weaponry, landscapes and spacecraft—like the ship which brings Princess Tanila to Earth.

SINBAD GOES TO MARS
ZANGOR'S SPACE SHIP
BY CHRIS FOSS FOR ANDOR FILMS

Zangor may derive his powers from the realm of the occult, but his spaceship looks more like something from a galaxy far, far away.

quickly, it was going to be made on a soundstage, and so on. I had a good grasp of the limitations of the medium. I was raising a wife and three children, and I was pretty much unbothered by the ethics of writing trash [*laughs*]. I never saw the innate universal usefulness in loading boxcars in a cannery [one of Kolb's earliest jobs], and I felt that what I was doing was no worse than the manual labor most of us have to do. So I could enjoy it."

In preparation for this interview, Kolb reread parts of his *Sinbad Goes to Mars* treatment and first-draft screenplay, many of the details of which he had forgotten. "This is all like it was done by someone whose shell I inhabit now!" he admits. "I enjoyed creating the character of Filcher. I *like* Filcher, I think Filcher was the best characterization that came out of all this. I would have loved to see *Sinbad Goes to Mars* made, because I think Filcher had genuine comic possibilities. I think Filcher shows the influence of my work with [cartoon producer] Joe Barbera. There was a time when he wanted to make pictures with live people and he hired me to write a bunch of things, most of which never got made. I've got a finished script that Joe Barbera paid for, about the Thief of Bagdad. And the Thief's not named Cheney either [*laughs*]!

"As for the character of Sinbad, well, you can't mess with Sinbad. Your villain [the reptile-like Zangor] also has always got to be a certain kind of guy. And you *have* to have a princess, Jeez, what *else* you gonna do? You can't have Sinbad rescue a chorus girl from Mars, right? Or a reformed crackhead prostitute! Sure it's gotta be a princess!"

One assumes that any 1978 script featuring a swashbuckling hero, villains bent on galactic domination, battling spaceships, a princess and outlandish aliens *had* to have been commissioned as a result of the success of *Star Wars* (1977); although at that time Kolb had not yet seen *Star Wars*, he agrees that it was probably the motivating factor. "Yeah, very likely. I mean, every week *Variety* publishes the box office receipts, and Charles would be watching that, and always wondering whether he can make a cheap picture of the kind that had the

SINBAD GOES TO MARS
THE ESCAPE BUBBLES
BY CHRIS FOSS FOR ANDOR FILMS

As Zangor's ship contends with magnetic mines, Sinbad, Tanila and Filcher make their getaway in plastic bubbles.

biggest take that week." As for similarities in plot and characters, of course, both *Sinbad Goes to Mars* and *Star Wars* hearken back to comic book tales of space adventure and 1930s serials, which Kolb unhesitatingly admits he *had* seen. "Oh, yeah! I'd seen the old *Flash Gordon*s and even *Buck Rogers*. Every page of *Sinbad Goes to Mars* is a deep bow to the clichés of the Arabian Nights, *and* to the clichés of *Flash Gordon*.

"In the treatment, I established that if Zangor gets a-hold of the Ion Crystal and gets his heat ray weapon in place and becomes ruler of Mars, he'll then invade the Earth. [*Sarcastically*:] It's like George [Bush] says, 'If we don't fight 'em in Iraq, we'll have to fight 'em here.' I felt that that was 'sound plot thinking,' to get Earth involved." There's also a subplot in which Zangor plans to drain the blood of Sinbad and Filcher, for he has learned that the blood of Earthlings, when transfused into Martians, enables them to live 1000 years. "The notion that Sinbad's blood carries the secret of eternal life up there on Mars, and that the guy is going to be slowly drained in order to give permanent life to the heavy—I thought that was a decent touch. And I enjoyed creating some of the 'surprising' things that happen. I think there are a few special effects that would have been new in '78. For instance, I suggested that the Genie of the Pyramid be a three-armed genie and that it wrap the Ion Crystal in a three-cornered silken cloak with a mystical knot that only it [the Genie] can unravel. I also mention that Zangor and the other Skalers don't look anything at all like humans; Ray might have given them extra limbs or whatever. And I thought there was plenty of room for Ray in the fact that Zangor is also a magician, and when necessary can go into trance and create anything he wants. Once we're in a magician's trance, there's plenty of opportunity for Ray to operate. So, yeah, there's a lot of juicy stuff in the treatment that could have been stretched out. It would have made a good movie. Not that I would have been *proud* of it, necessarily!"

Kolb says that his main problem was "tying all of Ray's abilities together. No wonder people worship Ray Harryhausen: He creates monsters who know where to go and what to do [*laughs*]! It has always interested me that no one has ever shown any interest in whoever plans when these creatures ought to appear and what they ought to *do*. I do think the story is what makes *7th Voyage* the best of Ray's [mythological] pictures: It holds together, there's a reason for the things that happen, and there's a rooting interest as you go along. Which, *for me*, some of his movies did *not* have." Three-dimensional viewing screens and holograms are called for in Kolb's treatment; interesting notations and "asides" include references to NASA's Mars-bound Viking I and II (comparing them to the Martian listening station inside the Great Pyramid), suggestions that the Genie of the Pyramid be neither he nor she ("A genie should actually be robotic—that would make it seem less controllable") and that its metallic voice be provided by a Moog synthesizer; and that some of Zangor's spaceship's engine sounds be taken from the 1968 album "Switched-On Bach" by Walter Carlos ("He later had the operation and became a woman, surprising all of his music fans!").

Throughout the writing process, Kolb received letters from Schneer telling him that Columbia was happy with the treatment, and learned that Harryhausen was also pleased with it. Correspondence from Schneer also mentioned that space illustrator Chris Foss and production designer Seamus Flannery had been engaged, the former to design the spacecraft, weaponry, Martians landscapes, etc., the latter to commence work on the actual sets. So it came as a surprise to Kolb when, after all this positive news, he was told that Columbia had decided not to proceed. He and his wife Emma were preparing to leave on a trip when he got the word. "The money I'd been paid for first draft was taking my wife and me on some trip, I

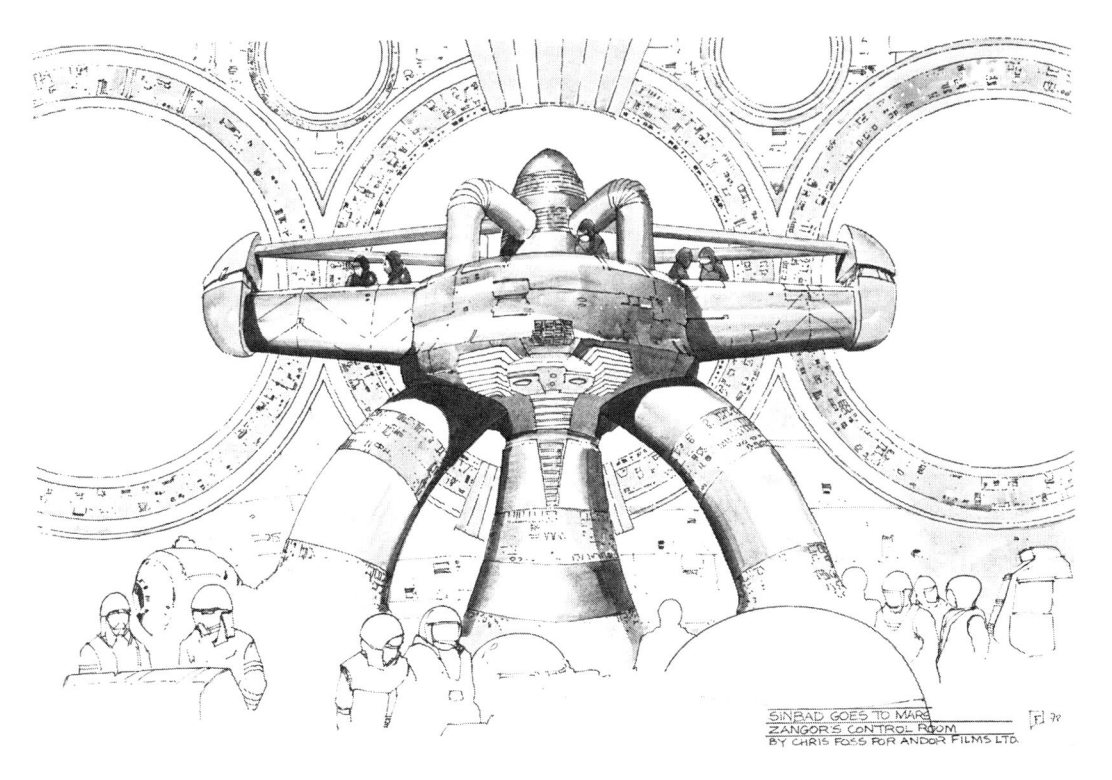

Here's a look at the control room in which Zangor carries out his megalomaniac plan to conquer the solar system.

don't now remember where—it might have been to the great falls of Iguazu in Brazil. I phoned Charlie from a Chinese restaurant in the big San Francisco development called The Cannery, and the news was not good. The news was, 'Columbia is not interested.' It was a total turnaround between their great approval of the treatment; I was told *in writing* they were very pleased with it, but now, suddenly, the script was 'unsatisfactory.' And the script was not that different from the treatment; it was, if *anything*, an *improvement* on the treatment. As I returned to the table, I was trying to figure out whether I was glad or sorry. Emmy and I went on our trip, and when I got back, I was still 'hot,' my agents had other work for me, and I really never gave *Sinbad Goes to Mars* another thought. That's the way it all ended for me, as I went on a trip between first and second draft, and it turned out there never *was* a second draft.

"I do believe *Sinbad Goes to Mars* failed on a personality basis, that Charles probably got into some kind of argument with whoever was running Columbia at that time, that there was one of those clashes where everybody was trying to flex their muscles, and the guy at Columbia said, 'Hey, [bleep] off, we're not gonna fund it.' (Charles knew how to irritate people. Without hardly *trying* [*laughs*]!) I can't see what possibly could have gone wrong, *except* that. Whoever [pulled the plug] must have been one dumb-ass executive, because if you have the opportunity to fund a picture for Charles and take half the profits, it's always a wonderful idea to do so. I'm sure that on most or all of Charles' pictures, there was a big return on the investment, right back to his first one with Ray, the black-and-white *It Came from Beneath the Sea* [1955]. So turning down *Sinbad Goes to Mars* was not a good business decision by any means."

For Kolb, one fond *Mars* memory is that he was much better paid for his work than he was for *7th Voyage* in the early days of his Hollywood career. "Charlie decided to pay me a lit-

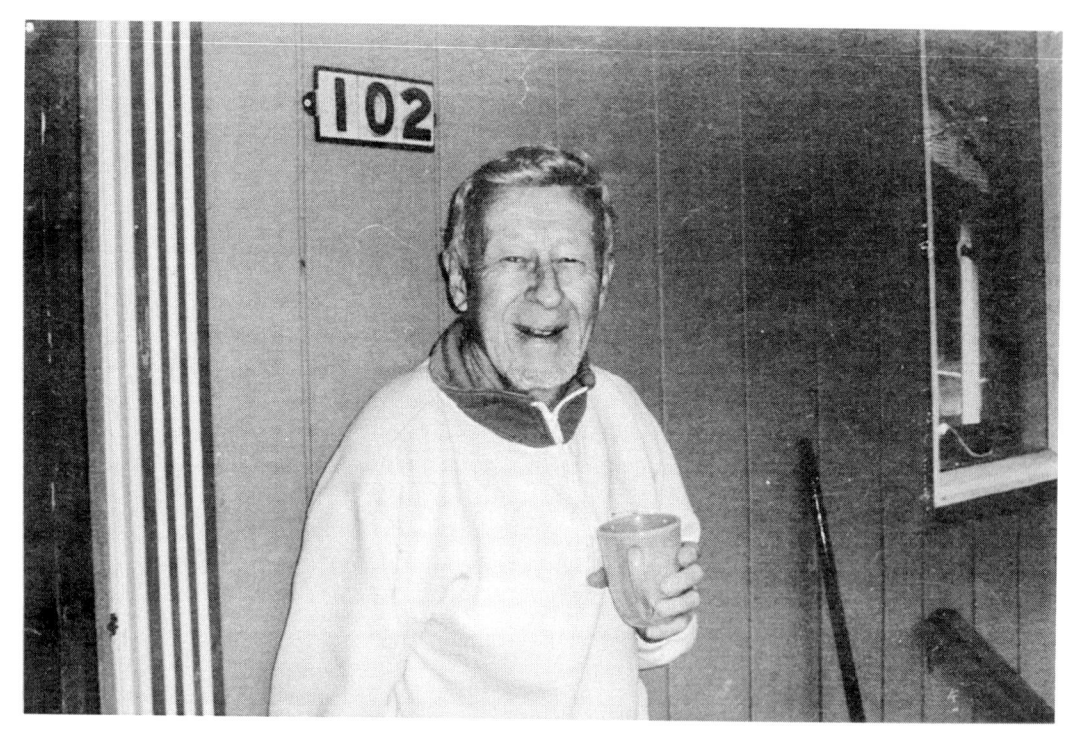

His rep as the sultan of Sinbad screenplays is no source of pride for Kolb, who would rather write about our trying present days than Arabian Nights.

tle better if I'd like another go-round, and as I recall, I got six times as much for *Sinbad Goes to Mars* as I got for *7th Sinbad*. There would have been *more* [money] coming after I did a second-draft screenplay, but they cut us off at first draft." Kolb has learned now (2007), for the first time, that in 1979, Beverly Cross, screenwriter of the Schneer-Harryhausen *Jason and the Argonauts, Sinbad and the Eye of the Tiger* and *Clash of the Titans* (and husband of actress Maggie Smith), was hired to write a *Sinbad Goes to Mars* script; "I had no idea," says Kolb, "and I have no qualms with that. And apparently he had the same kind of luck *I* did. Which would tend to support my theory that there was a clash of personalities going on. Beverly Cross was a competent writer, and if neither of the two of us could churn out a script that Columbia would accept, then I think probably there was some other problem." A synopsis of Cross' script appears on page 293 of *Ray Harryhausen: An Animated Life* (Billboard Books, 2004).

August 11 of this year (2007) was the 50th anniversary of the Kolbs taking possession of their country-style home in California's Plumas National Forest, where they still live, and where Kolb, at 81, still chops wood. ("I've got a pretty good tennis serve for an octogenarian, and it comes from splittin' wood with an eight-pound maul!") Although he retired from the business more than 25 years ago, "I'm a writer, I can't stop," and the project on which he now occasionally works is called *The Lord of Look Behind*, a tale of skullduggery in the dangerous wilds of Jamaica's interior. Nevertheless, "Buy real estate!" is his advice to young writers, "because that's what has kept me afloat since Hollywood tired of me. I bought real estate while I was hot, and it has been wonderfully kind to us, and I don't think I'll ever really need to go to the agency again. Because at 81, my children are grown and my *grand*children are doing wonderfully, and I don't have a great need—and I certainly don't have any great ambition [*laughs*]!"

And, as for *Sinbad Goes to Mars*, the unmade movie which next year (2008) marks its 30th un-anniversary, "I think I did a pretty good job. Considering the fact that the premise was, as I told you, repugnant to me, I've had some fun re-reading it today. I think it would have been a tremendous hit with Ray's fans, and I still don't know why it never got made. But I wouldn't put it past Charles to get it made *yet*."*

---

*Schneer died in January 2009, 14 months after this interview first appeared in print.

Index

Numbers in *bold italics* indicate pages with photographs.

The A-Team (TV) 381, 386
Abbott, Bud 265
Abbott, L.B. 352
Abbott and Costello Go to Mars (1953) 196
The Accused (1949) 100
Acker, Sharon 304
Ackerman, Bettye 224
Act of Piracy (1988) 367
Adams, Betty *see* Adams, Julie
Adams, Ernie *51*
Adams, Julie 248, 251, 278–79
Adams, Nick 292, 302, 347, 348, *348*, 349
Adams, Ron 2
Adrian 152, 153
The Adventures of Ellery Queen (radio) 74
The Adventures of Frank Merriwell (1936) 33
The Adventures of Hajji Baba (1954) 158
Adventures of Superman (TV) 162
The Adventures of Tom Sawyer (1938) 45, 47
Agar, John 152, 155, 156, 324
Aherne, Brian 118, 325, 326, 328–29, 330
Aidman, Charles 295, 316
Airmail (1932) *17*
Alberni, Luis 11–12
Albuquerque (1948) 98–100, *99*
Alexander, Ruth 248, 258
Allen, Austin 331
Allen, Irving 331, 332
Allen, Irwin 282, 283, 350, 354, 355, 356–57, 358, 360, 363
Allen, Lee 331
Anders, Merry 278–81, *280*, *281*
Anderson, Bronco Billy *91*
Anderson, Gene 111
Anderson, Howard 249, 255
Anderson, James 123, 128, 129, 130
Anderson, Judith 57–58, 192
Anderson, Michael, Jr. 312
The Andromeda Strain (1971) 108
The Andy Griffith Show (TV) 86
Ann-Margret 332, 333
Anna and the King of Siam (1946) 76, 78, 81, *82*
Antosiewicz, John 2
The Ape Man (1943) 89
The Appaloosa (1966) 329
Arkoff, Samuel Z. 88, 92, 235–36, 237, 239, 282, 319, 324, 337
Arlen, Richard *91*
Armstrong, Paul 8

Armstrong, Robert 5–14, *6*, *7*, *8*, *9*, *11*, *13*
Armstrong, Rolf 8
Arnaz, Desi 96
Arness, James 149, *149*
Arngrim, Stefan 350, *353*, 358
Arnold, Jack 209, 210
Arnow, Max 50, 249, 251
Arsenic and Old Lace (stage) 86–87
Ashcroft, Dame Peggy 73
Ashley, John 292–93, 324, 373, 375, 376–78, 380–81
Askins, Monroe P. 189, 190
Astaire, Fred 137
The Atomic Monster see Man Made Monster
The Atomic Submarine (1959) 248, 249
Attack (TV pilot) 350
Attack of the Crab Monsters (1957) 178, 180–82, *182*
Attack of the 50 Foot Woman (1958) 180
Atterbury, Malcolm 190
"August Heat" (short story) 81
Autry, Gene 116, 249
Avalon, Frankie 63
Ayres, Lew 52

Baa Baa Black Sheep (TV) 309
Bachelor Father (TV) 205
Back from the Dead (1957) 184–88, *185*, *186*
Back to the Future (1985) 317
Backus, Jim 170
Baker, Charlie 23, 26
Baker, Diane 217
Ball, Lucille 96, 116
Band, Albert 222, 223, *223*, 224, 225
Band, Max 222
The Band Wagon (1953) 76
Bannon, Jim 138, *138*
Barbera, Joseph 389
Barker, Lex 160
Baroud (1933) 72, 73
Barron, Baynes 318, 320–21, 322
Barron, Robert V. 311
Barry, Donald 119
Barry, Gene 147, 311
Barry, Joan 136
Barry, Philip 75
Barrymore, John 12
Barrymore, Lionel 52
Barty, Billy 180
The Basketball Fix (1951) 93
Baxter, Les 238
Bau, George *163*, *176*

Baumann, Marty 2
Bautzer, Greg 152–53
Beach Red (1967) 81
Beaudine, William 89, 90, 92, 95
Beaumont, Hugh 120, *120*
Beck, Calvin Thomas 226–34, *232*
Beck, Helen 226–34
Beck, Sharon 233, 234
Beck, Thomas 229–30
Beebe, Ford 42, 43
The Beggar's Opera (stage) 74
Beginning of the End (1957) 382
Behlmer, Rudy 2
Bela Lugosi Meets a Brooklyn Gorilla (1952) 88–92, *90*, 93–97, *94*, *95*
Bellamy, Earl 2, 86–87, 88
Bender, Russ 318, 321
Bendix, William 102
Bennet, Spencer Gordon 249
Bennett, Bruce *51*
Benny, Jack 61
Bergman, Ingmar 223, 225, 239
Berman, Harry 118
Bernard, Crystal *286*
Bernds, Edward 2, 199, 200, 202, 276–78
Berserk (1967) *97*
The Best Years of Our Lives (1946) 22
Beyond the Fog see Tower of Evil
Beyond the Time Barrier (1960) 1
Biberman, Abner 155, 156–57
Big Bad Mama (1974) 239
Big House, U.S.A. (1955) 172
Bikini Beach (1964) 63
Birch, Paul 200, 202, 205–6
The Birth of a Nation (1915) 108
Bishop, Joey 304
The Bishop's Wife (1947) 22
Bissell, Whit 120, *120*
The Black Castle (1952) 63–64
The Black Cat (1934) 102
Black Fox: The True Story of Adolf Hitler (1962) 133
Black Saddle (TV) 219
The Black Sleep (1956) 159, 160–62, *161*, *162*, *163*, 164, 172
Blackman, Joan 213
Blaine, Jerry 190
Blair, George 9–10
Blair, Patricia *see* Blake, Patricia
Blake, Michael F. 2
Blake, Patricia 164–66
Blake, Robert 82
Blakeley, Tom 336, 337, 338, 340, 344
Blanchard, Mari *169*
Bloch, Robert 125, 226, 227, 228, 230

395

Block, Irving 136, 137–38
Blood of Dracula (1957) 189–90, *189*
Blood of Dracula's Castle (1969) 366
Blue Hawaii (1961) 276
The Bob Cummings Show (TV) 205
Body Heat (1981) 108
Bogart, Humphrey 121
Bohnen, Roman 212, 215
Bohus, Ted 2, 228, 234
Bojarski, Richard 228–29, 231, 232
Bomber's Moon (1943) 76, 77
Bonanza (TV) 311, 331, 347
Bondi, Beulah 56, *56*, 60, 61, *61*
The Boogie Man Will Get You (1942) 50
Boone, Richard 191, 194
Booth, Shirley 54
Born Yesterday (1950) 106
Born Yesterday (stage) 103–7, *104*, 107
The Boston Strangler (1968) 108
The Bounty Killer (1965) *91*
Bowe, Rosemarie 152–58, *153*, *155*, *156*, *157*
Bowers, Hoyt 148
Boyington, Pappy 309
The Boys from Syracuse (1940) 21
Brady, Scott 367, *367*, 371
Brahm, John 67
Brand, Harry 159
Branded (TV) 291, 331
Brando, Marlon 114, 329, 381
Brasselle, Keefe 335
Brecher, Egon 102
Brecher, Irving 2, 102
Brewster, Diane 173–74
Bride of the Gorilla (1951) 93, 96
Bride of the Monster (1956) 88
Bridges, Lloyd 215
The Bridges at Toko-Ri (1954) 24, 26, 28
Briskin, Irving 108, 248–49, 251, 252, 255–56
Briskin, Sam 256
Britton, Layne "Shotgun" 46
Broder, Jack 88, 92–93, 94, 95, 96–97
Broder, Robert 93–94
Bromfield, John 164
Bronson, Charles 172
Brown, Calvin 298
Brown, James 318, 320
Brown, Jim 378
Brown, Joe E. 213
Brown, Peter 215
Browne, Fayte M. 110–11
Browne, Kathie 251
Bruce, Nigel 70, 76, 78, 79, *79*, 80
Bruhl, Heidi 329
Brunas, John 2
Brunas, Michael 2
Bruns, Mona 38
Bryan, Peter 337
Bryant, Nana *9*
Buchanan, Larry 324
Buferd, Marilyn 200
Burke's Law (TV) 352, 354, 355, 364
Burns, Bob (living legend) 2, *261*

Burns, Bob (Western actor) *236*
Burns, James H. 227
Burson, Polly 304
Burton, Richard 82
Bush, George H.W. 126
Bush, George W. 287, 390
Bye Bye Birdie (1963) 102
Byrd, Richard E. 387
Byrne, Eddie 338

Cabot, Bruce *11*
Cady, Frank 56
Cagney, James 8, 9, 64
Cahn, Edward L. 249
Calhern, Louis 186
Calvert, Rosalee 217
Calvert, Steve 96
Camelot (1967) 108
Cameron, James 283
Campo, Wally 321
Cangey, Dick 296–98, 301–2, *301*, 304, 305, 307, 316
Cannibal Attack (1954) *114*
Cannon, Dyan 238–39
Captain from Castile (1947) 55
Captain Video (TV) 179
Cardos, John "Bud" 366–68, *367*, *368*, 369
Career (1959) 183
Caribbean (1952) 83
Carlos, Walter 391
Carlton, Rex 366, 367, 369, 370, 371
Carnival in Costa Rica (1947) 59
Carpenter, Paul *336*
Carradine, John 159, 161
Carreras, James 337–38
Carroll, Sydney W. 71
Carroll, Victoria *370*, 371
Carson, Jack 219
Carter, Linwood 226, 227, 229, 231
Carter, Noël 226, 227, 228, 229–30, 231, 232, 233
Cartwright, Lynn 202
Caruso, Anthony 126
Casablanca (1942) 116
The Cases of Eddie Drake (TV) 132
Cassavetes, John 331
Cassinelli, Charles 217
Castelnuovo, Nino 325, 328, 329
Castle, Peggie 184, 186, *186*
Castle, William 113, 114–15, 170, *171*
Castle of Frankenstein (magazine) 226, 227, 228, 229, 230, 231–34
The Cat and the Canary (1978) 346
Cat Women of the Moon (1953) 196
Catching, Bill 290, 291, 295
The Cavern (1965) 325–30, *327*, *328*
Cell 2455, Death Row (1955) 114
Challengers of the Unknown (comic book) 264
Chalmers, Bill 336
Chambers, John 314, 315
Champion, Gower 68, 152
Champion, Marge 152
Chandler, Chick 120, *120*
Chandler, Jeff 211

Chaney, Lon 102, 140, 172
Chaney, Lon, Jr. 86, 88, 98–107, *99*, *107*, 159, 161, *162*, 172, 312, 371
Chaplin, Charles 118, 136–37, 138
Chaplin, Oona 137
Charlita *90*
Chase, Kenneth 314–17, *315*
The Chattanooga Boys 331
Chatterton, Ruth 76
Chauvel, Charles 74
Chekhov, Anton 123, 124, 130
Cherry Orchard (stage) 123, 124, 126, 129, 130
Chief Thundercloud 297
ChiPs (TV) 382
Chodorov, Edward 83
Chodorov, Jerome 54
Chomsky, Marvin 303
Chressanthis, James 260
Chu-Chin-Chow (1934) 72
The Circus of Dr. Lao (novel) 268
Clark, Edward 56
Clarke, Gary 378
Clarke, Robert 2, 212, 213–14, 215, 318–19
Clash of the Titans (1981) 393
Clatterbaugh, Jim 2
Clift, Montgomery 76
Climax! (TV) 247
Clive, Colin 66
Cobb, Edmund 252, 253
Cocchi, John 2, 227, 228, 230, 231–32, 233
Coco, James 325
Coe, Peter 217
Coghlan, Frank, Jr. 43
Cohen, Herman 2, 88–89, 91–97, *97*, 189, *189*, 190
Cohen, Martin B. 366
Cohn, Harry 113, 154
Collingwood, Charles 83
Collins, Charles 230, 231, 232, 233, 234
Collins, Joan 382, 385
Colman, Ronald 81, 137
The Color Purple (1985) 317
Combat! (TV) 350
The Comedy of Errors (stage) 74
Conne, Edward 172
Connolly, Marc 53
Connors, Chuck 291, 295
Conover, Dave 2
Conqueror Worm (1968) 340
Conrad, Robert 290, 291–94, *292*, 295, 296–97, *297*, 298, 299, *299*, 300, 301–6, 307, 308–9, 310, 311, 312–13, 315, 316
Conway, Gary 350–65, *351*, *353*, *356*, *359*, *361*, *364*
Coodley, Ted 168
Cook, Elisha, Jr. 167–68, 169
Cool Hand Luke (1967) 235
Cooper, John C. *see* Croydon, John
Cooper, Marilyn 183
Cooper, Melville 83
Corbett, Glenn 249–51
Corden, Henry 2, 63–66, *64*, *65*
Corio, Ann 265

Corman, Roger 178, 179, 180, 182, 215, 235–39, *236*, 373, 375
Corona, Esperanza 315
Cossart, Valerie *9*, 83
Costello, Lou 266
Coulouris, George 56
Court of Last Resort (TV) 388
Cow Town (1950) 116
Coward, Noël 76
Cox, Wally 219
Crabbe, Buster 33, 34, 36, 37, 39, 43, *91*
Crane, Stephen 222, 223
Crawford, Broderick 36, 106, 162, 172
Crawford, Johnny 290
Creature from the Black Lagoon (1954) 140, 278–79
Crime Against Joe (1956) 164–66
Cripe, Arden 168, 169
Crisp, Tracey 343
Cromwell, John 76
Crosby, Floyd 191, 192, 193, 195, 236, 238
Cross, Beverly 393
The Crowded Sky (1960) 85, 210
Crowther, Bosley 134
Croydon, John 337, 340, 342
Cruickshank, Art 352
Cry Danger (1951) 47
Crystal, Billy 122, 317
Cukor, George 183
Cummings, Bob 203, 205
Curse of Simba see *Curse of the Voodoo*
Curse of the Fly (1965) 338
Curse of the Swamp Creature (1968) 324
Curse of the Voodoo (1964) 336, 340, 345, 346
Curteis, Ian 340, 342
Curtis, Billy 116
Curtis, Jack 264
Curtis, Tony 211
Cushing, Peter 335, 338–39, 340, 344
The Cyclops (1957) 382

Dahl, Arlene 83
Dallas (TV) 70, 320
Dalton, Audrey 251
The Dalton Girls (1957) *203*
Damon, Mark 236–37, 238
Dana, Mark 173
Daniel Boone (TV) 148
Daniell, Henry 66
Dano, Royal 224, 225
Dante, Joe 2
Darios, George 154, 157, 158
Darkroom (TV) 125
Darrow, Barbara *199*, 200
da Silva, Howard 82
Davis, Ann B. 203
Davis, Beryl 197, 204
Davis, Bette *134*
Davis, Jim 367
Davis, Joan 96
Davis, Lisa 196–208, *197*, *199*, *201*, *203*, *205*, *207*
Davis, Owen 76

Day, Doris 268, 325
Day for Night (1973) 72
The Day the Earth Caught Fire (1961) 338
Day the World Ended (1956) 249
Dead of Night (1945) 272
Deadman (comic book) 264
Dean, James 96
Dear Phoebe (TV) 160
Death Race 2000 (1975) 239
Dee, Sandra 209
Defoe, Daniel 282
DeHaven, Gloria 125
de Marney, Derrick 340
DeMarney, Terence 173
DeMille, Cecil B. 15, 26, 27, 256
Dempsey, Jack *6*
Denault, Edward 291
Denning, Richard 249
Denton, Crahan *246*
Derleth, August 227
Dern, Bruce 354
Desert Sands (1955) 174
The Desert Song (stage) 70–71
The Desperate Hours (stage) 55–56
Destination Moon (1950) 136
Devil Doll (1964) 272–74, *274*, 275, 335–36, 340, 343
"The Devil Doll" (short story) 272–74
The Devil's 8 (1969) 321
Devils of Darkness (1965) 336, 338
Devon, Richard 180
DeVries, George 347, *348*
DeWilde, Brandon 243, 244–45, *246*
Diamond, Bobby 290
Diary of a High School Bride (1959) 319
The Diary of Anne Frank (1959) 217
Dinocroc (2004) 239
Disney, Walt 149, 204, 206, 207, 208
Disneyland (TV) 148, 149
Dmytryk, Edward 44, 48
A Dog of Flanders (1935) 38
Donahue, Troy 2, 209–11, *210*, *211*, 217–19
Donlevy, Brian 89
The Donna Reed Show (TV) 62
Don't Give Up the Ship (1959) 183
The Doom Patrol (comic book) 264
Dorin, Phoebe 310, 312
Douglas, Chet 251
Douglas, Earl 42, 43
Douglas, Gordon 148–49
Douglas, Kirk 100
Douglas, Melvyn 162
Douglas, Paul 103
Douglas, Susan 123, 125–26, 130, 131, 133
Dracula (1931) 237
Dragnet (radio) 191
Dragonwyck (1946) 237
Drake, Arnold 2, 264–67
Drake, Coleen *199*
Dream Girl (stage) 103
Dreifuss, Arthur 44
Dressed to Kill (1946) 78
Driscoll, Bobby 59

"Drop Dead!" (album) 129
Drury, James 82
Dubov, Paul 251
Dufour, Val 180
Dugan, Michael 322, 324
Duke, Maurice 92, 93, 94, 96, 97
Duncan, Pamela 2, 178–83, *179*, *181*, *182*
Duning, George 255
Dunn, Michael 307, *308*, 309–10, 312, 313–14
Dunne, Irene 81
Dunne, Philip 77
Durant, Marjorie 200, 202
Durbin, Deanna *19*, 42
Duryea, Dan *91*

Earhart, Amelia 17–19
Earl Carroll Vanities (1945) 58–59
The Earth Sings (1951) 131–32
Earth vs. the Spider (1958) 382
Eden, Barbara 271
Edgar G. Ulmer—The Man Off-Screen (2004) 325
Eegah (1962) 259
Elias, Louis 294
Ellison, James 251
Elsom, Isobel 76
The Emperor Waltz (1948) *141*
Empire of the Ants (1977) 382–85, *383*, *384*
Ensign Pulver (1964) 325
Epper, Tony 301
Erdman, Richard 222–25, *223*, *225*
Escape from San Quentin (1957) 110
Evans, Maurice 57–58, 314, *315*
Everitt, Dave 1
Everson, William K. 230
Exodus (1960) 191
Exorcism at Midnight see *Naked Evil*
Experiment in Terror (1962) 309
The Eye Creatures (1967) 324

Fabian 322
Face of Fire (1959) 222, 223–25
Facing the Music (1933) 73
Fahey, Myrna *237*, 238
"The Fall of the House of Usher" (short story) 235, 236
Fame (TV) 70
Fanchon 44, 45
The Far Horizons (1955) 128
Farr, Derek 340
Feinstein, Diane 287, 289
Feldman, Charles K. 153–54
Fernback, Gerald A. 335–36, *336*, 337, 338, 340, 342, 344, 345, *345*, 346
Ferrer, Mel 83, 113
Fess, Simeon 148
Field, Margaret 123
Fields, Joseph 54
Fiend Without a Face (1958) 335, 337, 339
Fier, Jack 252, 254
50,000 B.C. (Before Clothing) (1963) 264–67
The Fighting Wildcats (1957) 335

Fine, Larry 254
Finney, Charles G. 268
Fireball 500 (1966) 322, 324
Fireside Theatre (TV) 160
The First Hundred Years (TV) 9, 10, 12
First Men in the Moon (1964) 338
Fisher, Terence 338, 339, 340, 342, 344
Fitzgerald, Barry 77
Fitzgerald, Michael 2
Five (1951) 123–35, *129*, *134*, 136
Five Finger Exercise (stage) 213
Flagg, Cash *see* Steckler, Ray Dennis
Flaming Star (1960) 331
Flannery, Seamus 391
Flash Gordon (1936) 33, 34–37, *35*, 39
Fleming, Eric 200
Flesh and the Spur (1957) *254*
The Flesh Eaters (1964) 264
Flynn, Errol 74, 333
Fonda, Henry 8
Fonda, Peter 260
Fontaine, Joan 192
The Food of the Gods (1976) 382
Forbidden Planet (1956) 27, 196, 199
Ford, Glenn 118
Ford, John 77
Ford, Mary *199*
Forsythe, John 205
Foss, Chris 391
The Four Horsemen of the Apocalypse (1921) 72
Fox, William 160
Foy, Bryan 151
Francis, Anne 196, 311
Francis, Connie 212
Frankenstein (1931) 24, 66, 237
Frankenstein Meets the Wolf Man (1943) 80, 86
Frankenstein 1970 (1958) 172
Franz, Arthur 184, 186, 209, 210, *210*, *211*
Frawley, William 10
Freud, Sigmund 236
Freulich, Henry 111
Freund, Karl 116
From Here to Eternity (1953) 154
Fulton, Fitch 23
Fulton, Joanne 15–32, *28*, *31*
Fulton, John P. 15–32, *16*, *18*, *19*, *20*, *21*, *25*, *28*, *29*
Funicello, Annette 63, 322
Furie, Sidney 119
Fury (TV) 290

Gabor, Jolie 202
Gabor, Zsa Zsa 196–99, *199*, 200, 202, 203–4, 206, 208
Gaffney, Liam 342
Gallagher, Ed 41
Gallipoli (1981) 73
The Gamma People (1956) 278
Ganley, Gail 190
Ganzer, Alvin 310
Garcia, Eddie 378–79
Garfinkle, Louis 224

Garland, Beverly 180
Garland, Judy 55
Garland, Richard 180, *182*
Garrett, Andi 291, 304
Gay, John 74
Geeson, Judy *97*
Gein, Ed 226
Gemora, Charles 140–47, *141*, *145*
Gemora, Diana 140–47, *147*
George, Jimmy 294, 297, 298, 302, 304, 305, 316
German, Edward 74
Geronimo (1962) 295
Gertsman, Maury 190
Get Smart (TV) 86, 347
The Ghost in the Invisible Bikini (1966) 79–80
Ghosts on the Loose (1943) 89
G.I. Blues (1960) 276
Giant (1956) 235
Gibson, Mary Whitlock 190
Gibson, Mel 73
Gielgud, John 73
Gilbert, Anthony 83
Ging, Jack 219
Girls! Girls! Girls! (1962) 276
Girls in Prison (1956) 249
Gish, Dorothy 71
Gittens, Wyndham 42–43
Giuliani, Rudy 268
Gleason, Jackie 102
Gleason, Jimmy 6, *6*, 8, *8*, 9
Glenn, John 319
Godzilla's Revenge (1971) 344
Gold, Ernest 191
Golden Boy (1939) 118
The Golden Child (1986) 317
The Golden Mistress (1954) 152, *153*, 154–58, *155*
Goldfinger (1964) 331
Goldwyn, Samuel 21, 25
Gone with the Wind (1939) 50
The Good Companions (1933) 73
Gorcey, Leo 95
Gordon, Alex 2, 88–92, *91*, 248–58, *254*, *257*, 337
Gordon, Bert I. 382, 385
Gordon, Max 53, 54
Gordon, Richard *91*, 230–31, 335–46, *336*, *345*
Gordon, Robert 113, 114
Gordon, Ruth *see* Alexander, Ruth
Gorss, Sol 333
Gosalvez, Tony *377*, 379
Gosnell, Ray 112
Goulder, Stanley 346
Grady, Billy 53
Gray, Billy 59
Gray, Carole 338
Gray, Gary 59
Gray, Mack 332
Green Acres (TV) 118
Green Waters (stage) 74
Greene, Angela 279
Greer, Dabbs 312
Gregory, Paul 126, 127
Grey, Nan 42
Grey, Shirley *73*
Grier, Pam 374, *377*, 379
Griffin, Frank 2, 317

Griffith, D.W. 15, 16, 44, 47
Griggs, Loyal 276
Grimes, Karolyn 98–100
Grinde, Nick 53
Guest, Val 338
Guillot, Alvaro *164*, 173, *176*
Gulliver's Travels (1939) 350
Gulliver's Travels (novel) 282
The Gumball Rally (1976) *303*
Gunsmoke (TV) 149, 219, 317, 331
Gwenn, Edmund 73

Hagen, Kevin 363
Haggerty, Don 186
Hagman, Larry 325, 326, 328, 329, 330
Hale, Alan, Jr. 295
Haliday, Bryant 272, *274*, 335, 340, 343
Hall, Arch, Jr. 259–63, *262*
Hall, Arch, Sr. 259, 260
Hall, Huntz 95, 128
Hall, Jon 253
Haller, Daniel 238
Halls of Montezuma (1950) 191
Halsey, Brett 2, 329
Hamer, Rusty 63
Hamilton, George 251
Hamilton, Margaret 56, *56*, 60, 61
Hamlet (stage) 71
Hampton, Orville H. 248, 249, 251, 256, 258
Hanawalt, Chuck 318
Hansen, Joachim 325–26
Harbord, Carl 78
Hardwicke, Cedric 73, 83
Harris, Harry 357
Harris, Jonathan 285, 360, 363
Harris, Owen *see* Hampton, Orville H.
Harrison, Rex 48, 81
Harrison, Sandra 189, *189*, 190
Harryhausen, Ray 338, 386, 387, 388, 390, 391, 392, 393
Hart, Susan 324
Hartford, Huntington 192
Harvey, W.F. 81
Haskin, Byron 282
Hassan (stage) 71
The Haunted Strangler (1958) 335, 337
Have Gun Will Travel (TV) 247, 387
The Haven (stage) 83
Hawaii Five-O (TV) 5, 387
Hawaiian Eye (TV) 308–9
Hawkins, Jack 73
Hay Fever (stage) 76
Hay Fever (TV) 76
Hayden, Russell 251
Hayes, Allison 180, 279
Hayes, George "Gabby" 98
Hayworth, Rita 44, 118
Heart of a City (stage) 78
Hecht, Ben 187
Heft, Richard 2
Hell Raiders (1969) 324
Hell Squad (1958) 318–19
Hellzapoppin' (1941) 49

Hendrix, Jimi 260
Henreid, Paul 116
Henry, Thomas B. 190
Henry, William 103–4, 105, 106, *107*
Hepburn, Katharine 74, 75–76
Herron, Bob 294, 298
Hershey, Barbara 312
Heston, Charlton 27
Hewitt, Heather 347
Hickman, Dwayne 203
Hicks, Chuck 332
The Hideous Sun Demon (1959) 212, 213–15, *213, 214, 216, 218, 219,* 318–19
The High and the Mighty (1954) 158
High Noon (1952) 192
Highway Patrol (TV) 36, 162
Hiller, Arthur 350
Hilliard, Harriet 96
Hilton, Conrad 198
Hilton, Paris 198
Hitchcock, Alfred 226, *229*
Hoey, Dennis 70–85, *71, 72, 73, 75, 77, 79, 80, 82*
Hoey, Iris 71, 74
Hoey, Michael A. 70–85, *75, 84*
Hoffman, Howard *171*
Hoffman, John 134
Hogan, Paul 74
Holiday for Lovers (stage) 203
Holliday, Judy 103
Holloway, Stanley 73
Honey West (TV) 311, 388
Hope, Bob 121, 152
Hopper, Hedda 158
Horror Hospital (1973) 346
Hoskins, Bob 78
House of the Damned (1963) 279
House of Usher (1960) 235–39, *237, 238*
House of Wax (1953) 366
How Green Was My Valley (1941) 76–77, 81
How the West Was Won (TV) 175
How to Make a Monster (1958) 189, 190
Howard, Leslie 55, 67
Howard, Moe 254
Howard, Robert E. 243
Howard, Ronald 66, 67, 68
Howard, William K. 6
Hoyt, John *120*
Hubbard, John 47
Hudkins, Bear 295–96
Hudkins, Clyde "Ace" 296
Hudkins, Dickie 295–96
Hudson, John 191, 192, 193–94
Hudson, Rock 211, 268
Huff, Tom 298, *301,* 304, 305, 316
Hughes, Billy 291–92, 305
Hughes, Dotti 2, *306*
Hughes, Howard 74, 205
Hughes, Whitey 2, 290–307, *291, 292, 293, 295, 299, 301, 303, 306,* 316
The Hunchback of Notre Dame (1923) 144
Hunt, Helen 178

Hunt, Marsha 184–88, *186, 187*
Hurok, Sol 71
Husky, Ferlin 369–70
Huston, John 222–23, 224
Hutton, Barbara 170
Hyams, Nessa 71
Hyams, Peter 71
Hyman, Eliot 172
The Hypnotic Eye (1960) 279

I Bury the Living (1958) 224
I Love Lucy (TV) 10, 93, 116
I Married Joan (TV) 96
I Remember Mama (1948) 62
I Spy (TV) 312
I Walk Alone (1948) 100
I Was a Teenage Frankenstein (1957) 189, 190
I Was a Teenage Werewolf (1957) 92
In Harm's Way (1965) 278
In the Wake of the Bounty (1933) 74
The Incredibly Strange Creatures Who Stopped Living and Became Mixed-Up Zombies!!? (1964) 259, 260, 263
Indusi, Joe 2
Inescort, Frieda 86
Ingram, Rex (actor) 81
Ingram, Rex (director) 72
Inherit the Wind (1960) 191
Inseminoid (1981) 346
An Inspector Calls (stage) 83
Invisible Agent (1942) 21
The Invisible Man (1933) 16
The Invisible Man Returns (1940) 21
The Invisible Woman (1940) 21
The Iron Horse (TV) 332
Irving, Richard 56
Is Zat So? (stage) 6, *6*
The Island of Dr. Moreau (1996) 381
The Island of Doctor Moreau (novel) 373, 374
Island of Terror (1966) 335, 336–40, *339, 341,* 342–43, 344, 346
Island of the Burning Damned see *Night of the Big Heat*
It Came from Beneath the Sea (1955) 108, 110, *111,* 392
It Came from Outer Space (1953) 140
It Had to Be You (1947) *109*
It Happened at the World's Fair (1963) 276
It's a Mad Mad Mad Mad World (1963) 191
It's a Wonderful Life (1946) 98
Ivo, Tommy 56, *56,* 58–63, *61, 62*

Jacobs, Arthur P. 275
Jaffe, Sam 224, 225
Jane Eyre (stage) 74–76
Jason (stage) 101
Jason, Neville 77, 78–79
Jason and the Argonauts (1963) 393
Jeans, Isabel 74
Jenkins, Allen 8
Jennings, Gordon 15, 26
Jensen, Paul 2
Jet Attack (1958) 248

Jezebel (stage) 76
The Joey Bishop Show (TV) 304
Johnny Staccato (TV) 331
Johnson, Chic 49
Johnson, Lamont 67, 194
Johnson, Tony 194
Johnson, Tor 161–62
Jones, Carolyn 174
Joplin, Janis 260
Jordan, Marcia 217
The Jordanaires 278
Judd, Edward 335, 338, 340
Juke Box Jury (TV) 197–98
Jungle Goddess (1948) 172
Jungle Heat (1957) 160, 168
Jungle Patrol (1948) 100

Kane, Joe 2
Kanin, Garson 103
Karloff, Boris 50, *51,* 52, *53,* 55, 56, *56,* 57, 58, 59, 60, 61–62, *61, 63*–66, *64,* 67, 102, 159, 161, 167, *168,* 172, 241, 243, 312, 339, 343
Karloff, Evelyn 241
Kasem, Casey 324
Kasznar, Kurt 350, 352, *353, 356,* 360
Katinka (stage) 70
Katja (stage) 71
Katzman, Leonard 305, 318, 319, 320, 321, 322
Katzman, Sam 38, 89, 108–117, *110,* 319
Kaufman, George 54
Kaufman, Millard 138
Kaye, Danny 21, *21,* 63
Kayser, Sharon *see* Beck, Sharon
Kazan, Elia 170
Kellogg, Bruce 138, *138, 139*
Kelly, Paul 44
Kennedy, John F. 328
Kent, Gary *368*
Kent, Robert E. 109–10
Kesler, Sue 7
Keyes, Evelyn 81
The Keys of the Kingdom (1944) 78
The Kid from Texas (1950) 83
Kiel, Richard 66, 67, *68,* 307–14, *308, 313*
Kilian, Victor 138, *139*
Kill Me Tomorrow (1957) 338
The Killer Elite (1975) *303*
Kind Lady (stage) 83
King, Bob 2
King, Dennis 83
King, Henry 76
King, Marilyn 215
King, Zalman 354
King Kong (1933) 5, 7, 10–11
King Kong (1976) 108
Kitt, Eartha 67
Kitty (1945) 85
Klancke, Geraldine 123, 126, 127, 129, 130, 132
Kline, Benjamin H. 108, 111
Kline, Richard 87–88, 108–117, *109, 117*
Klinger, Michael 337, 340
Klondike Kate (1943) 114
Kneubuhl, John 192, 195

Knight, Fuzzy 91
Knight, Shirley 213, 221
Knock on Any Door (1949) 100, 121
Knox, Mickey 100–2, *101*
Knudson, Barbara 103–7, *103*, *107*
Knusch, Jim 2
Koch, Hawk 171
Koch, Howard W. 159–60, 161, 162, 166, 167, 168, 169, *169*, 170–71, 172, 173, 174, 175
Koch, Howard W., Jr. *see* Koch, Hawk
Koch, Mark 283
Kolb, Ken 386–93, *392*
Korda, Alexander 344
Kosleck, Martin 264
Kovack, Nancy 251
Kovacs, Laszlo 259
Kowalski, Bernard L. 309
Kroeger, Berry 366, 367, 369, 371

Lackteen, Frank 252, 253, *254*
Ladd, Alan 82
The Lady from Shanghai (1948) 114
The Lady in Question (1940) 118
Lady L (1965) 183
Lady Sings the Blues (1972) 119, 121
Laemmle, Carl 16, 20
LaGuardia, Fiorello 265
Lampkin, Charles 123, 130–31
Lancaster, Burt 100
Land of the Giants (TV) 350–65, *351*, *353*, *356*, *359*, *361*
Landers, Lew 86, 113
Landers, Muriel 96
Landis, Carole 44, 46, 47–48, 49
Landon, Michael 238
Lane, George 314–15
Lane, Jocelyn 276, 278
Lane, Lupino 73
Lannard, Herbert 264–65, 266, 267
Lansbury, Angela 204, 306
Lansbury, Bruce 306
Lansing, Robert 382
The Las Vegas Hillbillys (1966) 369–70
Lassie (TV) 310–11
Laughton, Charles 123, 126–27, 130
Laveroni, Jerry 300
Lawford, Peter 160
Lawless Cowboys (1951) 178
The Lawless Rider (1954) 88
Lawman (TV) 215
Leave It to Beaver (TV) 86
LeBorg, Reginald 160–61, 166, 168, 169, 170
Lee, Christopher 344
Lee, Earl 123, 130
The Left Hand of God (1955) 44
Legend of the Lost (1957) 187
The Lemon Drop Kid (1951) 121
Lemon Grove Kids Meet the Monsters (1965) 261
Leonard, Herbert 319–20
Leonard, Queenie 83
Leonard, Terry 299
Leontovich, Eugenie 123
Lerner, Murray 119

LeRoy, Mervyn 52, 82, 152, 153
Levin, Henry 113, 332
Lewis, Jerry 88, 89, 90, 92, 93, 94, 198
The Life of Riley (1948) 102
The Life of Riley (radio) 102
The Life of Riley (TV) 102
The Light of Western Stars (1940) 53
Lights Out (radio) 135
Li'l Abner (1959) 310
Lilley, Jack 295, 302
Lippert, Robert L. 118–19, 121, 279
The List of Adrian Messenger (1963) 379
Lloyd, Tony 314
Lockhart, June 213
Locy, William Jenkins 132
Lollobrigida, Gina 183
Lombard, Carole 6, 7, 46
London Mystery Magazine (magazine) 272–74
The Long Gray Line (1955) 204
The Long, Hot Summer (TV) 314
Looking for Love (1964) 212
Loren, Sophia 183, 187, 275
The Loretta Young Show (TV) 219
Lorre, Peter 161
Lost Continent (1951) 118, 119–22, *120*
Lost in Space (1998) 282, 283–89, *288*
Lost in Space (TV) 282–83, *285*, 350, 360
The Lost World (1925) 44
The Louisiana Hussy (1959) 217
Love Has Many Faces (1965) 304
Love Lies (1931) 73
Lovely to Look At (1952) 152–53
Lowry, Morton 77
Loy, Myrna 118
Lubin, Arthur 240, 242
Lubow, Sidney 131, 133
Lucas, Donna 2
Lucas, Tim 2
Ludwig, Edward 83
Lugosi, Bela 73, 86–89, *87*, 90–91, *90*, 92, 93, *94*, 95–96, 97, 159, 161–62, *162*, 230, 343
Lugosi, Lillian 89
Lund, Deanna 350, *353*, *356*, 358, 360, *361*, 362
Lundigan, William 248, 251, 252, 253, 254
Lupino, Ida 73, 160
Lupino, Stanley 73
Lydecker, Howard 249, 254
Lydecker, Theodore 254
Lydon, Jimmy 5–14, *9*

Macabre (1958) 170, *171*
Macaulay, Charles 373, 374, 379, 380
Macbeth (stage) 57–58
MacGinnis, Niall 338
MacQueen, Scott 2
MacRae, Henry 33, 34, 39, 41–42, 43
Madonna 200
Magers, Boyd 2

The Magic Carpet (1951) 116
The Magic Touch (stage) 119
The Maid of the Mountains (1932) 73
The Main Event (1927) 6
Major Dundee (1965) 291–92
Make Room for Daddy (TV) 118
Malden, Karl 331, 332
Mallory, Edward 251
Maltin, Leonard 70
Man Afraid (1957) 209
Man Made Monster (1941) 88
Man of a Thousand Faces (1957) 209
The Man They Could Not Hang (1939) 50
The Man with Nine Lives (1940) 50, *51*, 52–53, *53*
Mander, Miles 78
Mann, Edward Andrew 336
Mannix, Eddie 205
Mantz, Paul 17, 22
Marceau, Marcel 212
Marco 44
Maret, Harry 317
Margie (TV) 62
Margulies, William 166
Mark, Bob 314
Marshall, Don 350, 354, 356, *356*, 358
Marshall, Laurie 2
Marshall, Peter 325–30, *328*, *329*
Martin, Dean 88, 89, 92, 93, 94, 198, 331, 332, 333, 334
Martin, "Hi" 342, 344
Martin, Mary 46
Martin, Quinn 170
Martin, Ross 290, 294–95, *295*, 297, 309, 312, 314, 315, 316, *317*
Martin, Sobey 357, 358
Martin Kane, Private Eye (TV) 178–79
Martucci, Mark 2–3
Marvin, Lee 247
Marx, Groucho 357
Mason, Jackie 183
The Masque of the Red Death (1964) 239
"The Masque of the Red Death" (short story) 239
Massey, Raymond 251, 252
Masters, Mike 290, 291
Maté, Rudolph 128
Matheson, Don 350, 354, 356, *356*, 358, *359*, 362
Matheson, Richard 236
Matinee Theater (TV) 67
Matlock (TV) 38
Matthews, Jessie 73
Mature, Victor 44, 47, 48
Mauldin, Bill 222–23
Maverick (TV) 174
Maxwell, Lois 224
Maxwell, Paul 190
Mayer, Louis B. 52
Mayeski, Darryl 3
Mayo, Frank 41
Mayo, Virginia *64*
McCallister, Lon 45–46
McCloud (TV) 70

McClure, Doug 238
McCoy, Tim 252
McCrea, Joel 251
McDonald, Frank 249, 252, 254
McDonnell, Dave 1, 3
McDowall, Roddy 67, 77
McGavin, Darren 251, 347, 348, *348*
McGuire, Don 215–17
McGuire, Dorothy 83
McHugh, Frank 8, 9, 11–12
McKnight, Marian 364, *364*, 365
McNally, Stephen 64
Meadow, Herb 82, 84
Meeker, Ralph 172
Meet Me in St. Louis (1944) 102
Melcher, Marty 325, 326, 330
Melchior, Ib 282–89, *284*, *286*, *288*
Melton, Sid 118–22, *120*, *121*
Meltzer, Lewis 118, 120
Men into Space (TV) 217, 251
Meredith, Lee 183
Merlin, Jan 373–81, *374*
Merlin, Patricia 374
Merrie England (stage) 74
Merrill, Gary *134*
Metcalfe, Ken 379
Meyler, Fintan 2, 66–69, *68*
Middleton, Burr 260
Middleton, Charles 34
Midnight Train to Moscow (1989) 317
Mighty Joe Young (1949) 23
Mike Hammer (TV) 62
Miller, Ann 152
Miller, Ivan *51*
Minardos, Nico 67
Minevitch, Borrah 96
Minnelli, Vincente 152
Missile to the Moon (1958) 196
Mission Mars (1968) 347–49, *348*
Mister Ed (TV) 240–42, *241*, *242*
Mister Roberts (stage) 148
Mr. Saturday Night (1992) 122
Mitchell, Cameron 222, 224, 225, 366–67, 369, 370–71, *370*
Mitchell, Carlyle 190
Mitchell, Duke 88, 89, 90, 91, 92, 93, 94–95, *94*, *95*, 96, 97
Mitchell, Laurie 196, 200
Mitchum, Robert 126
Moder, Mike 299
Mohr, Hal 156, 157
Moise, Nina 137
Molant, Jacques 155
The Monolith Monsters (1957) 209
The Monroes (TV) 312
Monsieur Verdoux (1947) 136, 137
"The Monster" (short story) 222, 223
The Monster and the Girl (1941) 140
Monster on the Campus (1958) 209, 210–11, *210*, *211*
Montgomery, George 187, 249
Moonraker (1979) *313*
Moore, Constance 58–59
Moore, Roger 307
Morgan, Ira 110

Morgan, Ralph 56, *56*, 60, 61, *61*, 64
Mork and Mindy (TV) 234
Morrison, Hollis 371–72
Morrow, Jeff 82
Morrow, Jo 213
Morse, Terry 138
The Most Dangerous Game (1932) 340
"The Most Dangerous Game" (short story) 373, 374
Mrs. Henderson Presents (2005) 78
Mulhall, Jack 41, 42
Mullaney, Jack 276
The Mummy (1932) 172
Munster, Go Home! (1966) 86
The Munsters (TV) 86
The Murder in the Red Barn (1935) 73
Murder She Wrote (TV) 70
Murderers' Row (1966) 331–34, *333*
Murderers' Row (novel) 332
Murders in the Rue Morgue (1932) 140
Murphy, Audie 83, 222, 224
Murphy, Barry 3
Murphy, Eddie 317
Murphy, Tim C. 3
My Old Duchess (1933) 73
My Sister Eileen (stage) 54
My Three Sons (TV) 86
Mysterious Island (1961) 387
Mysterious Island (novel) 387
The Mystery of the Mary Celeste (1935) 73, *73*
Mystery of the Wax Museum (1933) 366
Mystery Science Theater 3000 (TV) 195
Mystery Submarine (1963) 344

Nader, George 209
Naked Evil (1966) *344*, 345–46
Nash, Marilyn 136–39, *137*, *138*, *139*
Nearly a Nasty Accident (1961) 344
Neff, Bill 355, 356
Neill, Roy William 78
Neise, George *164*, 173
Nelson, David 96
Nelson, Ozzie 96
Nelson, Ricky 96
Nesmith, Ottola 243, *244*, *245*, *246*
Neufeld, Sigmund 119
Neumann, Dorothy 180
Never Trouble Trouble (1931) 73
The New Adventures of Sherlock Holmes (radio) 80
New Orleans Uncensored (1955) 110
Newfield, Sam 119, 121
Newland, John 247
Newman, Paul 174
Newmar, Julie 310
Newton, Richard 38
Nicholson, Jack 325
Nicholson, James H. 235, 237, 239, 319, 324, 337
Nicol, Alex 191, 192, 193, 194, 195
Nielsen, Ray 3

Night of the Big Heat (1967) 344
Night of the Big Heat (novel) 344
Night of the Blood Beast (1958) 279
Nightmare in Wax (1969) 366–72, *367*, *370*
No Questions Asked (1951) *125*
No Subtitles Necessary: Laszlo & Vilmos (2008) 259, 260–63
Noonan, Tommy 328
Norris, Karen 251
Not Wanted (1949) 160
Novarro, Ramon 304–5

Oates, Warren 350
The Obi (TV) 345
Oboler, Arch 123–24, 125, 126, 127–29, 130, 131–32, 133–34, *134*, 135
O'Brian, Hugh 220
O'Brien, Chuck 290, 291, *292*, 294, 295
O'Brien, Edmond 172
O'Brien, Pat 8, 338
O'Connell, Arthur 271
O'Connor, Donald 198
O'Day, Alan 260
The Odd Couple (TV) 268
Odets, Clifford 118
Of Mice and Men (1939) 100, 102, 103, 172, 212
Of Mice and Men (novel) 103
Of Mice and Men (stage) 100–2, 103
O'Herlihy, Dan 350
O'Keefe, Dennis 58
The Oklahoma Woman (1956) *236*, 249
Olsen, Ole 49
Omnibus (TV) 84, 224
On Borrowed Time (1939) 62
On Borrowed Time (stage) 55, 56–57, *56*, *57*, 58, 59–62, *61*, 63
Once Upon a Time in the West (1968) 100
One Hundred and One Dalmatians (1961) 196, 206, 207, 208
One Million B.C. (1940) 44, *45*, 46–49, *46*
One Million Years B.C. (1966) 49
O'Neill, Eugene 137
Open 24 Hours (stage) 183
Operation Bikini (1963) 322
Ormond, Ron 251
Oswald, Lee Harvey 328
The Other One (novel) 184
Outside the Wall (1950) *101*

Pal, George 141, 268–69
Pal, Peter 268
Pal, Zsoka 268
Pal Joey (1957) 117
Palance, Jack 178–79
Pallos, Steven 344, 345–46
Palmer, Max 116
Parker, Fess 148–51, *149*, *150*
Parker, Jean 103
Parker, Kim *336*
Parker, Shirley 347
Parker, Col. Tom 276, 278, 280
Parrish (1961) 217–19

Parrish, Leslie 310
Parrish, Robert 47
Parsons, Louella 158
Patrick, Milicent 140
Paulsen, Pat 295
Payne, John 83
Peabody, Dick 311
Peach, Mary 340, 343
The Pearl of Death (1944) 78–79, *79*, 80
Peck, Gregory 78, 83, 275
Peckinpah, Sam 304
Penn, Leo 123, 124
Penn, Sean 123
Peppard, George 386
Perkins, Anthony *229*, *233*
Perrin, Vic 123, 126
Perry Mason (TV) 219
Peter Potter's Platter Parade (TV) 197
Peters, House 33, 37
Peters, House, Jr. 2, 33–38, *36*, *37*
Petersen, Paul 63
Peterson, Nan 212–21, *213*, *214*, *220*
Petra, Hortense 112
The Petrified Forest (1936) 55
The Petrified Forest (stage) 55
Petrillo, Sammy 88, 89–90, *90*, 91, 92, 93, 94, *94*, 95, *95*, 96, 97
Petroff, Boris 219
The Phantom of the Opera (1925) 144
Phantom Ship see *The Mystery of the Mary Celeste*
Pharaoh's Curse (1957) 159, 162–66, *164*, *165*, 172, 173–77, *174*, *176*
The Philadelphia Story (stage) 75–76
Phillips, Fred *237*
Phillips, Mark 3, 347
Phipps, William 123–31, *124*, *125*, *129*, *131*
Picerni, Paul 3
Pickford, Mary 89
Picnic (1955) 172
Picnic (stage) 172
Pierce, Jack P. 240–42, *241*
Pine, Robert 382–85, *384*
Pine, William H. 83
Pit and the Pendulum (1961) 239
"Pit and the Pendulum" (short story) 239
Pitt, Ingrid 343
Planet of the Apes (1968) 314, *315*
Playhouse 90 (TV) 67
Plowman, Melinda 304
Plymouth Adventure (1952) 83
Poe, Edgar Allan 235, 236, 239
Pogany, Gabor 329, 330
Pomeroy, Jack 33, 38
Porter, Jean 44–49, *46*, *48*
Potter, Peter 197–98
Powell, Dick 47
Powell, William 62, 118
Power, Tyrone 33, 55, 76, 315
Powers, Stefanie 309
Preminger, Otto 25–26
Prescott, Guy *164*

Presley, Elvis 276–78, 279, 280–81, *281*, 296, 316, 331
Presnell, Robert 187, 188
Pretty Kitty Kelly (radio) 74
Price, Vincent 235, 237, *237*, 248, 340
Priestley, J.B. 83
Prince, William *171*
The Projected Man (1966) 335, 337, 338, 339, 340–42, *341*, 343, *343*, 346
Proser, Monte 330
Provost, Jeanne 3
Provost, Oconee 3
Pryor, Roger *51*, 52, *53*
Psycho (1960) 226–34, *229*, *233*
Psycho (novel) 226–34
Putnam, George P. 19
Pygmalion (stage) 76

Quattrocchi, Frank 337
Queen of Outer Space (1958) 196–204, *197*, *199*, *201*, 205–6, *207*, 208

Rabin, Jack 136, 137–38
The Racketeer (1929) 7
Raft, George 332
Ragland, "Rags" 266
Raiders from Beneath the Sea (1964) 279
Ramona the Chimp *95*, 96
Ramsen, Allan 336, 344
Randall, Tony 2, 268–71, *269*, *270*, *271*
Rappaport, Fred 3
Rathbone, Basil 70, 78, 79–80, *79*, *80*, 159, 161, *161*, 167, 251
Rattigan, Terence 275
Ravalec, Blanche *313*
Rawhide (TV) 219, 331
Read, Barbara 42
Reagan, Ronald 151, 357
Reap the Wild Wind (1942) 256
Rebecca (1940) 191–92
The Rebel Rousers (1970) 366
The Red Badge of Courage (1951) 222–23, *224*
The Red Badge of Courage (novel) 222
The Red Skelton Show (TV) 90
Redlin, William 282, 283
Reed, Donna 154
Reese, Tom 331–34, *333*
Reeves, Richard *56*
Reid, Carl Benton 248, 252
Remick, Lee 309
The Return of the Vampire (1943) 86–88, *87*
Reventlow, Lance 170
Reynolds, Burt 239
Reynolds, Debbie 220
Rice, Milt 166
Richards, Robert 217
Rickles, Don 304
Riddle, Nelson 215
The Rifleman (TV) 290
Rio Grande (1950) 100
Roach, Hal 44, 47, 49
Roach, Hal, Jr. 44, 47, 49

The Robe (1953) 82
Roberta (stage) 152
Roberts, Roy 251
Roberts, Tony 96
Robertson, Cliff 238
Robertson, Dale 332
Robinson, Ann 147
Robinson, Charlie 265, 266, 267
Robinson, Frances 41, 42, 43
Robinson Crusoe (novel) 282
Robinson Crusoe on Mars (1964) 282
Rock Around the Clock (1956) 108, 111
Rock 'n' Roll High School (1979) 239
Rocketship X-M (1950) 136
Rocky Jones, Space Ranger (TV) 5, 179
Rodann, Ziva 173, *174*
Rode, Alan 3
Rogers, Budd 93
Rogers, Ginger *8*
Rogers, Jean 34
Rogers, Will 71, 148
Rohauer, Raymond 346
Romeo and Juliet (stage) 74
Romero, Cesar 59, 120, *120*
Romero, Eddie 378
Rooney, Mickey 198
Rooney, Pat *91*
Rose, Ruth 7
Rose, Werner 266
Rosenstein, Sophie 209
Ross, Diana 121
Ross, Frank 82
Rotter, Robert 3
Royle, Selena 82
Rubirosa, Porfirio 198, 203–4
Ruby, Jack 328
Rudley, Herbert 2, 54–58, *55*
Runser, Mary 3
Rush, Richard 322
Russel, Tony 321
Russell, Bayka 83, 84, 85
Rydell, Mark 311–12

Said, Fouad 322
The St. Valentine's Day Massacre (1967) 373
Salkow, Lester 248, 258
Salmi, Albert 382
Sandrich, Jay 82
Sangster, Jimmy 343
Santa Claus Conquers the Martians (1964) 347
Saville, Victor 73
Saxon, John 238, 325, 326, 328, 329, 330
Sayers, Jo Ann 50–54, *51*, *53*
Scapperotti, Dan 3
Scarface (1932) 64
Schaeffer, Chester W. 132
Schallert, William 219, 316
Schary, Dore 84–85, 205, 224
Schenck, Aubrey 159, 160, 161, 163, 170–71, 172, 173, 174–75, 176
Schenck, George 171
Schiaffino, Rosanna 325

Schneer, Charles H. 249, 387, 388, 389–90, 391, 392–93
Schoedsack, Ernest B. 7, 10, 11
Schoenfeld, Don 291, 314, 315
Schram, Charles 270
Schwalb, Ben 200, 202, 276, 278, 279
Schwartz, Arthur 76
Schwarzenegger, Arnold 287
Scott, Charles, Jr. 299
Scott, Evelyn 186
Scott, Jacqueline *171*, 385
Scott, Randolph 98, *99*, 159
The Screaming Skull (1958) 191–95, *192, 193, 194*
Scrivani, Rich 3
Scrubs (TV) 300
Sea Hunt (TV) 215
Sears, Fred F. 113–14
The Secret Life of Walter Mitty (1947) 22, 63, 64–65, *64*
The Secret Man (1958) *336*
See My Lawyer (stage) 118
Seinfeld, Jerry 160
Seligman, Selig 350
Selznick, David O. 6, 7
Sergeant Dead Head (1965) 79
Sergeant Rutledge (1960) 77
Serling, Rod 217, 219
7 Faces of Dr. Lao (1964) 268–71, *269, 270, 271*
The Seventh Seal (1957) 239
The 7th Voyage of Sinbad (1958) 387, 388, 391, 392–93
77 Sunset Strip (TV) 205
Shadow of the Thin Man (1941) 118
Shadows (1960) 331
Shanghai (stage) 70
Shannon, Billy 295
Shapir Ziva *see* Rodann, Ziva
Shapiro, Mel 132, 133
Shatner, William 247
Shaw, George Bernard 76
Shaw, Peter 204
Shawn, Philip *see* Waltz, Patrick
She-Wolf of London (1946) 80
Shean, Al 41–42
Sherlock Holmes and the Secret Weapon (1942) 78
Sherman, Harry 199
Sherman, Vincent 320
Shield for Murder (1954) 172, 173, 174
Shiffrin, Bill 157–58
Ship of Fools (1965) 307, 309
Shock Waves (1977) 338–39
Sholem, Lee 164–66, 173, 217
Shoop, Pamela 385
Shore, Dinah 187
Shotgun Wedding (1963) 219–20
Sidney, Sylvia 83
Silent Playground (1963) 346
Silk 2 (1989) 375, 380
The Silver Chalice (1954) 174
Silvers, Phil 81
Simmons, Jean 204
Simon, Robert F. 224
Simon and Simon (TV) 5
Simpson, Mickey *94*
Sinatra, Frank 10

Sinatra, Frank, Jr. 119
Sinbad and the Eye of the Tiger (1977) 393
Sinbad Goes to Mars (unmade movie) 386–93, *388, 389, 390, 391*
633 Squadron (1964) 275
The Six Million Dollar Man (TV) 5
Skelton, Red 90, 152, 265
The Slams (1973) 378
Slaughter, Tod 73
Smith, Frederick E. 272–75
Smith, Howard 224
Smith, Maggie 393
Solomon, Joe 336
Son of Fury (1942) 76
Song and Dance Man (1936) 44–45
The Song of Bernadette (1943) 212
S.O.S. Tidal Wave (1939) 254
Sowards, Jack 324
Space Monster (1965) 279, 318, 319–24, *319, 320, 321*
Sparrows (1926) 89
Sparv, Camilla 332
Spelling, Aaron 355, 357
Spiegel, Ed 131, 134
Stacey, Olive *9*
Stack, Robert 154, 157–58, *157*, 219
Stage Door (stage) 55
Stallings, Laurence 76
Stander, Lionel 102
Star Trek (TV) 234
Star Trek: The Motion Picture (1979) 108
Star Wars (1977) 389, 390
Steckler, Ray Dennis 259–63, *261, 262*
The Steel Helmet (1951) 121
Steele, Marjorie 119, 192
Steiger, Rod 275
Stein, Ronald 255
Steinbeck, John 103
Steinbrunner, Chris 226, 227, 230
Stephani, Frederick 34
Stephens, John G. 172–77, *173*
Stephens, William 172
Stevens, Marya 200
Stevenson, Robert Louis 282
Stewart, Bhob 228–29
Stewart, James 98
Stewart, Marianne 186–87
Stoumen, Louis Clyde 123, 124, 128, 131, 133
The Strangler (1964) 319, 321
Strasberg, Lee 331
A Streetcar Named Desire (1951) 153
Strock, Herbert L. 2, 189–90, *190*
Stromberg, Hunt, Jr. 282, 283
The Stunt Man (1980) 317
Sturgess, Olive 203
Submarine Seahawk (1958) 248
Suicide Fleet (1931) *8*
Sullivan, Francis L. 73
Summer and Smoke (1961) 183
A Summer Place (1959) 209, 210
Summers, Jerry 290
The Sun Sets at Dawn (1950) 206–7
Sunny (1941) 53, 54

Sunrise at Campobello (1960) 84–85
Suspense (radio) 81
Swanson, Gloria 354
Sweet, Tom 297
Swenson, Inga 67
Swerdloff, Arthur L. 2, 130, 131–35
Swift, Jonathan 282, 350
Swiss Family Robinson (novel) 282
Swiss Tour (1950) 223

Tabakin, Bernard 172
Tabu (1931) 192
Taft, Sara *292*
Talbot, Lyle 203
Talman, William 172
Tamiroff, Akim 161
Tank Commandos (1959) 319
Taurog, Norman 45, 276, 278, 279
Taylor, Jeanette 213
Tearle, Godfrey 71
A Teaspoon Every Four Hours (stage) 183
Tell England (1931) 73
The Ten Commandments (1956) 24, 26–27, 28, 31
Tenser, Tony 337, 340
Terror by Night (1946) 80
Terry, Alice 72
Thatcher, Torin 67
The Theater Guild on the Air (radio) 74
Them! (1954) 148–49, *149*, 151
They Came to Blow Up America (1943) 76
The Thief of Bagdad (1940) 81
This Above All (1942) 76
Thomas, Frank M. 38, 39
Thomas, Frankie 2, 38–43, *40*
Thomas, Harry *320*
Thomas, Richard 369
Thomas, William C. 83
Thompson, William C. 157
Thomson, Barry 76
A Thousand and One Nights (1945) 81, 85
Three Smart Girls (1936) 42
The Three Stooges Meet Hercules (1962) 256
The Thrill Killers (1964) 259
Thriller (TV) 66, 67–68, *68*, 69, 243–47, *243, 244, 245, 246*, 310
Thunder Alley (1967) 322
Thunder in the Pines (1948) 172
Thundercloud, Chief *see* Chief Thundercloud
Tickle Me (1965) 276–81, *277, 281*
Tierney, Lawrence 367
Tigger 3
Tighe, Virginia 184
Tim Tyler's Luck (1937) 38–43, *40*
The Time Machine (novel) 282
The Time Travelers (1964) 279, 282
The Time Tunnel (TV) 314, 317, 350
Timpone, Tony 1, 3, 233–34
The Tingler (1959) 170, 248
Tiptoes (1927) 71
Titanic (1997) 283
Tobin, Ann *56*, 60, *61*

Tobin, Dan *9*
Tom Brown's School Days (1940) 5
Tom Corbett, Space Cadet (TV) 38, 43
Tompkins, Darlene 1
Topper, Burt 2, 318–24, *319*, *323*
Topper, Jennifer 3
Tough Assignment (1949) 119
Tower of Evil (1971) 346
Townsend, Bud 369
Tracy, Spencer 8, 9
Treasure Island (novel) 282
Treasure Island (stage) 71, *71*
The Treasure of Lost Canyon (1951) 62
Treasure of Monte Cristo (1949) 118
Treasures of Literature (TV) 191
Treasury Men in Action (TV) 162
The True Story of the Civil War (1956) 133
Truffaut, François 72
Tulsa (1949) 22–23, 31
Turman, Buddy 328
Turner, Lana 304
Turney, Catherine 184
Tuttle, William 268, 269–70, *270*, *271*
TV Reader's Digest (TV) 162
Twelve O'Clock High (TV) 170
Twentieth Century (stage) 56
20,000 Men a Year (1939) 159
The Twilight People (1973) 373–81, *377*
The Twilight Zone (TV) 219
Two Dollar Bettor (1951) 93
Two Years Before the Mast (1946) 82
Tyler, Beverly *168*

Ullman, Elwood 276, 278
Ulmer, Arianne 330
Ulmer, Edgar G. 325, 326, 328, 330
Ulmer, Shirley 328, 330
Umbrellas of Cherbourg (1964) 328
Uncivilised (1936) 74
The Undead (1957) 178, 179–80, *179*, *181*, 182
The Underwater City (1962) 248–58, *250*, *255*
The Unholy Three (1930) 140
The Uninvited (1944) 175
Unknown World (1951) 136, 137–39, *138*, *139*
The Untouchables (TV) 219
Ustinov, Peter 183

Valentino, Rudolph 72
Van Damm, Vivian 78
Van Enger, Charles 95
Varno, Martin 366, 369–72
Veidt, Conrad 73
Velia, Tania 200
Vera-Ellen 59
Verne, Jules 387
Vetter, Charles, Jr. *336*
The Violent Men (1955) 128
The Virgin Queen (1955) 204
Virginia (stage) 76
The Virginian (TV) 82, 331
Viva Zapata! (1952) 170

Voice in the Mirror (1958) 210
von Borsody, Hans 325, 326, 329
Voodoo Island (1957) 159, 160, 161, 166–69, *168*, 172
Vorkapich, Slavko 126, 128, 132, 134
Voyage to the Bottom of the Sea (TV) 350
Vye, Murvyn 167

Wagner, Laura 3
Wake of the Red Witch (1948) 83, 85
Waldis, Otto *139*
Wallis, Hal B. 94, 96–97, 100
Walters, Nancy 209, 210
Waltz, Patrick 200, *201*, 202, 206–7
The Wandering Jew (1933) 72–73
War-Gods of the Deep (1965) 322
War Is Hell (1963) *319*, 321
The War of the Worlds (1953) 140, 140–47, *143*, *145*
Warde, Anthony 41
Warner, Jack L. 85, 149
Warren, Alan 243
Warren, Bill 230
Warren, Charles Marquis 188
Waterloo (1970) 275
Watson, Bobs 62
Wayne, John 83, 100, 144, 187, 278
Weaver, Edric 3
Weaver, Jon 3, *301*
Webb, Jack 191
Webber, Peggy 191–95, *192*, *193*, *195*
Webster, Nick 2, 347–49
Wednesday's Child (1934) 38, 39
Weiler, A.H. 149
Weird Tales (magazine) 243
Weisbart, David 148–49
Weissmuller, Johnny *114*, 115–16, *115*
Welch, Raquel 49
Weld, Tuesday 238
Weldon, Joan *149*
Wells, H.G. 222, 282, 382
Werner, Mort *56*
West, Norma 339
West, Red 296, 301–2, *301*, 304, 305, 316
Westmoreland, Josh 110
What Price Glory? (stage) 76
Whelan, Tim *56*
The Whistler (radio) 80–81
White, Christine 170
White, Jon Manchip 345, 346
White, Sam 86
Whiting, Margaret 220
Whitley, William 111
Whitlock, Albert 84
Whitmore, James 222, 223, 224, 350
Whorf, David 243–47, *243*
Whorf, Richard 243, 247
Wiederhorn, Ken 338–39
Wilcox, Herbert 71
The Wild Bunch (1969) 304
Wild Guitar (1962) 259–60, 262–63
Wild Wild West (1999) 299

The Wild Wild West (TV) 290–317, *292*, *295*, *297*, *299*, *308*, *317*, 388
Wilde, Cornel 81, *109*
Wiley, John 150
Williams, Jackie 299
Williams, Lucy Chase 3
Williams, Rhys 77
Willis, Matt 86, *87*
Willis, Norman 41
Willock, Dave 200
Wilson, Marie 213
Wilson, Whip 178
Wincelberg, Shimon 282
Wing and a Prayer (1944) 77
Wingfield, Mark 3
The Winning Team (1952) 151
Wisbar, Frank 160, 179
Wisberg, Aubrey 118
Witchfinder General see *Conqueror Worm*
The Wizard of Mars (1964) 321
The Wizard of Oz (1939) 61
The Wolf Man (1941) 98
The Woman in the Hall (1947) 204
Wonder Man (1945) 21–22, *21*, 28
Wong, Anna May 72
Wood, Edward D., Jr. 88, 91, 219
Woodell, Pat 374, 376, 378, 379, 380, 381
Wooland, Norman 340
Worley, Jo Anne 213
Wray, Fay *11*
Wright, Ben 173
Wright, Frank Lloyd 123, 132
Written on the Wind (1956) 158
Wurtzel, Paul 159–71, *169*
Wurtzel, Sol M. 159, 160, 161, 166
Wynn, Keenan 54, 55, 56, *56*, 59, 60
Wyss, Johann 282

Yaconelli, Frank 42
A Yank in the R.A.F. (1941) 76
Yeager, Robert 116
Yellowstone (1936) 33
Yordan, Philip 137, 138
York, Duke 33, 34
York, Francine 3, 279, 318, 320, *320*, 322, 324
Young, Alan 240–42, *242*
Young, Gig 217, 219
Young, Heather 350, *356*, 358–59, *359*
Young, Loretta 22, 219
Young Dr. Kildare (1938) 52
The Young Guns (1956) 224

Zabel, Edwin F. 174
Zanuck, Darryl F. 159
Zappa, Frank 260
Zimbalist, Efrem, Jr. 205
Zinnemann, Fred 154
Zontar the Thing from Venus (1967) 324
Zsigmond, Vilmos 259, 260–63